South Asians
in East Africa

■

South Asians in East Africa

An Economic and Social History, 1890–1980

Robert G. Gregory

Westview Press

BOULDER • SAN FRANCISCO • OXFORD

For
Bachulal Gathani
Amritlal Raishi
& Lakhamshi Shah

101124602

Copyright © 1993 by Westview Press, Inc.

Published in 1993 in the United States of America by Westview Press, Inc., 5500 Central Avenue, Boulder, Colorado 80301-2877, and in the United Kingdom by Westview Press, 36 Lonsdale Road, Summertown, Oxford OX2 7EW

Library of Congress Cataloging-in-Publication Data
Gregory, Robert G.
    South Asians in East Africa : an economic and social history,
1890–1980 / by Robert G. Gregory.
        p.   cm.
    Includes bibliographical references and index.
    ISBN 0-8133-1403-8
    1. South Asians—Africa, East—Economic conditions.   2. South
Asians—Africa, East—Social conditions.   3. Occupations—Africa,
East.   4. Immigrants—Africa, East—Economic conditions.   I. Title.
DT429.5.S68G74   1993
304.8'540676—dc20   92-3854
                                                                                            CIP

Printed and bound in the United States of America

The paper used in this publication meets the requirements
of the American National Standard for Permanence of Paper
for Printed Library Materials Z39.48-1984.

10   9   8   7   6   5   4   3   2   1

Contents

Tables and Maps

Tables

Maps

Preface

After completing *India and East Africa: A History of Race Relations Within the British Empire, 1890–1939,* which was mainly a political study of the policies of Britain and India toward the settlement of South Asians in East Africa, I decided to undertake a further study specifically on the Asians. What seemed to be most needed was an economic and social history. The Asians appeared to have been far more involved with commerce, road transport, crafts and construction, clerical service, and professional work—even with agriculture and industry—than with political careers. Their contribution to the economic development of East Africa seemed far more important than the changes wrought by their political agitation. Yet because this agitation, supported by influential organizations and individuals in India and Britain, posed a serious problem for the British administration and the European community, it naturally had attracted most of the scholarly attention. The economic and social history had received only cursory description.

As I explain in the following chapters, the study proved rewarding in that the Asians' economic and social contributions appeared far more important than I had imagined. It also indicated that there were serious misconceptions of the Asians' role and that a number of the scholarly interpretations of the economic and social history of East Africa needed revision.

When the study was begun, Syracuse University had undertaken with the Kenya National Archives a seven-year co-operative project for the microfilming of historical records. Most of the records of the British colonial administration, from the files in the Kenya district offices to the correspondence in the British Colonial Office, and many newspapers and private records were being collected and filmed. In directing the microfilming, which eventually produced nearly 3,000 reels, I was able to include nearly all the extant Asian records: those of the community's political and economic organizations as well as newspapers and private papers.

The research in the British and Asian sources—and the Asians appear in almost all of them—consumed a number of years. Fortunately, during one year in East Africa I had the help of three senior graduate students—Charles Bennett, Martha Honey, and Dana Seidenberg—who were writing Ph.D. dissertations on the Asians. They assisted not only in the examination of written sources in Kenya and Tanzania, including Zanzibar, but also in the interviewing of Asians from these areas and Uganda. Subsequently I was able to undertake further interviewing and the examination of written sources in India and Britain. In all, approximately 200 Asians, most of whom had reached positions of economic and social leadership, were interviewed. The records of these interviews, together with the written sources, constitute an invaluable collection of information on the Asians and East Africa.

A number of organizations facilitated the research and writing that resulted in this book. The National Science Foundation and the National Endowment for the Humanities joined Syracuse University in support of the microfilming and compilation of indexes. Bachulal Gathani, Amritlal Raishi, R. P. Chandaria, Hansa Pandya, Robert M. Maxon, Dana Seidenberg, William Stinchcombe, and my wife, Pat, who assisted in almost all the research and interviewing, read all or much of the manuscript. My colleague in African history, Alan K. Smith, offered valuable insights into the nature of merchant capitalism and world trade. To all these, including the three assistants, and to the many others who cheerfully provided information, I wish to express my gratitude.

Robert G. Gregory

A Note on Currency

Four currencies are cited in the following chapters: those of India, East Africa, Britain, and the United States. The Indian currency between 1890 and 1980 was the rupee (R), which was divided into annas and pice (R 1 = 16 annas = 64 pice) until 1957 and then, following a decimal system, into 100 pice. British East Africa was served by the Indian currency until 1905 when the annas and pice were replaced by cents (R 1 = 100 cents). After a brief experiment with a florin at the end of World War I, East Africa adopted a shilling divided into 100 cents (Sh 1 = 100 c), and this remained the currency until the late 1960s when each of the East African countries set up its own currency. Until 1971 Britain divided the pound into 20 shillings and each shilling into 12 pence (£ = 20 shs = 240 d), but it then converted to a decimal form of 100 pence (£1 = 100 d).

During the years when the British shilling was divided into 12 pence, monetary values were expressed in two forms: either, for instance, as '4s 6d' or as 'Shs 4/6'. Early rupee values appeared as R6 4a 10p.

Because there were many fluctuations in the relative values of the currencies, sometimes from month to month, any brief depiction of the values will lack precision. However, the following summary, showing the exchange rates at five-year intervals, probably provides adequate information for purpose of comparison in this study. Decimal equivalents of the British pound are expressed in the Indian, East African, and U.S. currencies.

Years	India	East Africa	United States
1890–1920	Rs 15	Rs 15	$ 4.88
1925	10	Shs 20	4.87
1930–50	13.33	20	4.87
1950	13.33	20	4.04
1955	8.63	20	2.80
1960	13.33	20	2.79
1965	13.33	20	2.78
1970	10.91	Kshs 17.17	2.38
1975	18.75	16.59	2.33
1980	17.64	15.78	2.15

Introduction

If a comprehensive history of Africa is to be written 'from below', it must tell the story of small businessmen and artisans as well as of 'peasants' and wage earners, and it must do so with a similar degree of empirical care and historical empathy.

—A. G. Hopkins, 1987[1]

Although they had had a long association with the Zanzibar islands and the East African coast, it was in the decade of the 1890s that immigrants from South Asia began to exert an exceptional influence on the history of East Africa. For many centuries and perhaps, as some authors have claimed, as far back as the first millennium B.C., immigrants from the area of present-day India and Pakistan had settled on Zanzibar and the East African coast and engaged in an extensive trade throughout the Indian Ocean. After 1840 when Sultan Seyyid Said transferred his capital from Oman to Zanzibar, the Asians assisted in the development of the Omani empire and furthered its exportation of ivory and slaves from the African interior.[2] It was in the last decade of the nineteenth century, however, that Britain and Germany established their protectorates over Zanzibar and the mainland territories, inaugurated the colonial era, and laid the basis for an extensive settlement by Asians as well as Europeans. In the 1890s the first indentured servants from South Asia entered East Africa to begin construction of the Uganda Railway. In succeeding years as new Asian immigrants followed the railway and spread throughout the interior, such profound changes were to occur in the lives of all the peoples—Asian, European, African, and Arab—that a new era of history may be said to have opened.

The history of the Asians in these decades is, like that of the other peoples, a study of economic, political, social, and religious change that, at least in its more positive aspects, may be categorized as development.[3]

1

Certainly, there was a remarkable transformation of East Africa. It was evident not only in the highly visible farms and plantations, railways, harbours, airports, roads, and buildings and the various machines associated with them, but also in the somewhat less visible new lifestyles, habits, wants, and aspirations of the peoples. Not so discernible but equally significant were the systems of law and order, medicine, religion, international trade, class relations, and the power structure associated with colonialism. Much of all this could be described as modernization in the sense that East Africa underwent many of the changes that have occurred in the Western world during the modern age.

Apart from the Africans, whose initiatives are now recognized as having been very important, the principal agents of this transformation were the Asians and the Europeans. Most Asians thrived in circumstances in which there was a maximum of free enterprise. The British colonial governments, in contrast, pursued policies that involved, at least for the Africans, a strict regulation of the economy. As a result, the Africans throughout the colonial period were subjected to two powerful stimuli of social and economic change. One was the contact with the Asians, which from the outset drew them into a capitalistic form of economic endeavour. The other was their association with the government, which ultimately channelled much of their production and distribution into a socialistic system based on public agencies, parastatal companies, and co-operative societies. The Asians and the governments were thus almost perpetually in conflict. This situation, however, offered many Africans an alternative to the status of wage labourers constrained to spend six or more months of every year away from their *shambas* (farms) under contract to European settlers or the governments. They could associate with the Asians and ultimately compete with them as skilled artisans and merchants, or they could develop as independent farmers through organizations designed to eliminate middlemen.

For most Africans there were thus two streams of development. In the early 1960s both were left as colonial legacies for the new African nations that from the beginnings of their administrations faced critical decisions as to what they would retain of the two systems and which of them they would emphasize.

Among all the historians and social scientists who have examined the colonial records, few seem to have conceived of development within this context. Some early administrators foresaw advantages in the Africans' association with Asians, but during the years of the British administration there emerged a colonialist school that assumed development was mainly a European phenomenon. East Africa, the colonialists believed, was being developed primarily through a combination of government direction, missionary instruction, and settler enterprise. They tended to ignore or deprecate the roles of the other communities, including that of the Asians, and to regard nearly all changes introduced by the Europeans as beneficial to the Africans.[4]

The nationalist school, which became influential after political independence, had for the most part a Marxist orientation and tended to equate colonialism with capitalist exploitation. Scholars such as Walter Rodney, Colin Leys, and E. A. Brett viewed the imperial and local governments as instruments of metropolitan and international capitalism and the missionaries, settlers, and Asians as the governments' agents in a process not of development but under-development. Most desirable changes were ascribed to African initiatives.[5] Because of socialist leanings, writers in this school valued the stream of development for Africans that the colonial governments had stressed. Assuming that African economic progress could best be achieved through government agencies, parastatals, and co-operatives, they were highly critical of the free enterprise stream of development. Like those in the colonialist school but for different reasons, they criticized the Asians' role. Not surprisingly, the new governments of East Africa, which reflected the views of the nationalist school, proclaimed goals of African socialism and regarded the continuation of Asian enterprise as antithetical to these goals.

Some colonialist and most nationalist scholars recognized a socioeconomic class stratification in Africa and a class struggle as important factors of causation in East African history. Some envisaged a three-tiered structure stratified horizontally largely by race. The top layer, it was thought, consisted of a highly privileged planter aristocracy of Europeans—and on Zanzibar, Arabs—who were highly favoured by the governments. The bottom layer, the least privileged and most economically disadvantaged, comprised Africans. In between, occupying the middle-class position, were the Asian businessmen and skilled artisans who jealously guarded their semiprivileged position and somewhat ruthlessly exploited those in the other two classes.[6] Other scholars, mostly representative of the nationalist school, described a two-class system composed of bourgeoisie and proletariat, and they turned from the conception of a racially based structure to one that was somewhat heterogeneous. Thus the bourgeoisie were seen to include African entrepreneurs as well as Asian and European merchant-industrialists, and the proletariat was perceived as a working class of Asians and Arabs and even some Europeans, as well as Africans. According to this view, the Asians themselves were thus stratified horizontally in a way that restricted economic and social mobility and entailed an exploitation of one class of Asians by another.[7]

Although most scholars concerned with East Africa still share many of these interpretations, there has been in recent years evidence of a third school that for want of a more specific name may be regarded as revisionist. Attention has focused on Kenya and culminated in what has been called the 'Kenya debate', an intense controversy over factors of change in the colonial period.[8] In two seminal articles in 1976 the economist-historian A. G. Hopkins, aware of the emerging different interpretations, called for a comprehensive study of imperial business in Africa. Twelve years later in another important article, Hopkins described the essence of the revisionist studies. Scholars such as M. A. Bienefeld, Gavin Kitching, Steven Langdon, Robin Murray, Sharon Stichter, and Nicola Swainson, mostly from a Marxist view, had reassesed the role of capitalism in a focus on three groups of entrepreneurs: transnational corporations, state agencies, and indigenous firms. Although they differed considerably over the nature and influence of these respective groups and the overall effect on development, there was an underlying conclusion in the new studies that capitalism was not so deleterious in its effects on colonial society as most nationalist writers had assumed.[9]

The revisionist scholars have also reexamined the effect of capitalism on agriculture and rural society. Jon M. Lonsdale, David Anderson, and David Throup, relating the political protest of the 1950s to rural unrest, revised the chronology of socioeconomic change in Kenya agriculture. Goran Hayden and Stephen Bunker discounted agricultural transformation by arguing that a precapitalist mode of peasant production continued during the colonial period and successfully resisted forces of change introduced by both the private and government sectors. Differing markedly with this view, Apollo N. Njonjo and some other scholars emphasized the capitalist penetration and asserted that it destroyed the peasants' self-sufficiency. Leys and Michael Cohen recognized the emergence of rural capitalists ('accumulators') but asserted that their development into a class of agrarian capitalists was thwarted by competition from settlers and international capital.[10]

In most of the revisionist writings, despite the emphasis on reassessing the effect of capitalism, the Asians have been accorded little more attention than they had received from colonialist and nationalist scholars. After examining the literature, one of the assistants on this project exclaimed, 'The Asians have been written out of East African history'.[11]

Among the revisionists only a few have recognized that the Asians, Arabs, and some other peoples have not been accorded due recognition. *India and East Africa*; the books by Dharam P. Ghai, J. S. Mangat, Paul Marett, J. M. Nazareth, Kauleshwar Rai, R. R. Ramchandani, and Dana April Seidenberg; and the dissertations by Charles Bennett, Martha Honey, Shirin Waljee, Mary Varghese, and John Zarwan were direct assessments of the Asians' role.[12] Some other revisionist writings have presented a more balanced view of the colonial period than that conveyed by the colonialists or nationalists. Three of the most valuable within this context, illustrating aspects of the Asians' importance in the colonial and post-colonial economies, are Peter Marris and Anthony Somerset's study of African businessmen, Kenneth King's book on the African artisan, and Cyril Ehrlich's writings on the Uganda cotton industry. Three others of note are Hugh Fearn's study of Nyanza Province; Robert L. Tignor's book on the Kamba, Kikuyu, and Maasai; and I.R.G. Spencer's article on the Kenya government's first attempts to restrain Asian traders in the reserves. With a concentration on rural areas, Fearn, Tignor, and Spencer have described the Asians' influence in collecting cash crops, introducing manufactured goods, and fostering the spread of a monetary economy.[13]

These writings reveal aspects of the particular Asian-African stream of development that has been largely overlooked. They indicate a need for a study specifically on the Asians not only to examine the new interpretations as far as they affect the Asians but also to describe more precisely the nature of the Asians' relationship with the other peoples within the context of development. These writings also illustrate the need to assess the Asians within the context of the unfavourable view that has been presented by colonialist and nationalist authors and expounded by the Africans in calling for and justifying discriminatory policies.[14]

In succeeding pages the Asians are examined, not within the confines of their communal religious orientation but in the manifold activities that brought them into association with the other peoples of East Africa. Some of these activities are well known but have never been examined in detail. Commerce, money lending, artisanry, and clerical service are the primary occupations that are most familiar; but road transport, another endeavour within this category, has scarcely been recognized. Also relatively unknown are what might be called the Asians' secondary occupations—their professional work in law, medicine, and teaching and their involvement in agriculture and industry.

Notes

1. A. G. Hopkins, 'Big Business in African Studies', *Journal of African History*, 28 (1987), 136.

2. The most detailed description of the early association between India and East Africa is the chapter by B. G. Vaghela and Dr. J. M. Shukla, 'Indo-African Contact Through the Ages till Today', *East Africa Today (1958–1959): Comprehensive Directory of British East Africa with Who's Who*, ed. Vaghela and J. M. Patel (Bombay: Overseas Information, 1959), pp. 327–482. See also Abdul Sheriff, *Slaves, Spices and Ivory in Zanzibar: Integration of an East African Commercial*

Empire into the World Economy, 1770–1873 (London: J. Currey, 1987), chap. 1; and Dharam P. Ghai and Yash P. Ghai, eds., *Portrait of a Minority* (Nairobi: Oxford University Press, 1970), chap. 1.

3. The following definition conforms generally to that of Anthony Rweyamamu, ed., *Nation-Building in Tanzania: Problems and Issues* (Nairobi: East African Publishing House, 1970), pp. 5–8.

4. A foremost example is Elspeth Huxley, *White Man's Country: Lord Delamere and the Making of Kenya*, 2 vols. (London: Macmillan, 1935). There were, of course, some exceptions. Outstanding among the authors who recognized the Asians' contribution was S. Herbert Frankel, *Capital Investment in Africa: Its Course and Effects* (London: Oxford University Press, 1938). For a description of favourable views of some early administrators, including Frederick D. Lugard and Winston Churchill, see Robert G. Gregory, *India and East Africa: A History of Race Relations Within the British Empire, 1890–1939* (Oxford: Clarendon, 1971), pp. 47–50, 83–84.

5. Walter Rodney, *How Europe Underdeveloped Africa* (Dar es Salaam: Tanzania Publishing House, 1972). E. A. Brett, *Colonialism and Underdevelopment in East Africa: The Politics of Economic Change, 1919–39* (New York: NOK, 1973). Colin Leys, *Underdevelopment in Kenya: The Political Economy of Neo-colonialism, 1964–71* (London: Heinemann, 1975).

6. I presented this interpretation in my first book: *Sidney Webb and East Africa: Labour's Experiment with a Doctrine of Native Paramountcy, 1924–31* (Berkeley: University of California Press, 1962).

7. See, for example, Mahmoud Mamdani, *Politics and Class Formation in Uganda* (London: Heinemann, 1976).

8. Bill Freund, 'Modes of Production Debate in African Studies', *Canadian Journal of African Studies*, 29/1 (1985), 23–29. Gavin Kitching, 'Suggestions for a Fresh Start on an Exhausted Debate', ibid., pp. 116–26.

9. Hopkins, 'Big Business', p. 136. Hopkins's earlier articles were 'Imperial Business in Africa', part 1: 'Sources', and part 2: 'Interpretations', *Journal of African History*, 18 (1976), 2–48, 267–90. For the works by Bienefeld et al., see the Bibliography. For a survey of the pertinent literature, see Colin Kirkpatrick and Frederick Nixson, 'Transnational Corporations and Economic Development', *Journal of Modern African Studies*, 11 (1981), 367–99.

10. John Lonsdale, 'The Depression and the Second World War in the Transformation of Kenya', *Africa and the Second World War*, ed. David Killingray and Richard Rathbone (New York: St. Martin's, 1986), chap. 4. David Anderson and David Throup, 'Africans and Agricultural Production in Colonial Kenya: The Myth of the War as a Watershed', *Journal of African History*, 26 (1985), 327–45. Goran Hyden, *Beyond Ujamaa in Tanzania: Underdevelopment and an Uncaptured Peasantry* (Berkeley: University of California Press, 1980). Stephen Bunker, *Peasants against the State: The Politics of Market Control in Bugisu, Uganda, 1900–83* (Urbana: University of Illinois Press, 1987). Apollo L. Njonjo, 'Kenya Peasantry: A Re-assessment', *Review of African Political Economy*, 20 (1981), 27–40. Colin Leys, 'Accumulation, Class Formation and Dependency: Kenya', chap. 8, *Industry and Accumulation in Africa*, ed. Martin Fransman (London:

Heinemann, 1982). Michael Cohen, 'Commodity Production in Kenya's Central Province', *Rural Development in Tropical Africa*, ed. Judith Heyer, Pepe Roberts, and Gavin Williams (New York: Oxford University Press, 1981).

11. First expressed by Dana Seidenberg in 1973.

12. Ghai and Ghai, *Portrait*. J. S. Mangat, *History of the Asians in East Africa, c. 1886 to 1945* (Oxford: Clarendon, 1969). Paul Marett, *Meghji Pethraj Shah: His Life and Achievements* (Bombay: Bharatiya Vidya, 1988). J. M. Nazareth, *Brown Man, Black Country: A Peep into Kenya's Freedom Struggle* (New Delhi: Tidings, 1981). Kauleshwar Rai, *Indians and British Colonialism in East Africa, 1883–1939* (Patna, India: Associated Book Agency, 1979). R. R. Ramchandani, *Uganda Asians: The End of an Enterprise* (Bombay: United Asia, 1976). Dana April Seidenberg, *Uhuru and the Kenya Asians: The Role of a Minority Community in Kenya Politics, 1939–63* (New Delhi: Vikas, 1983). For the dissertations and other writings on the Asians, see the Bibliography.

13. Peter Marris and Anthony Somerset, *African Businessmen: A Study of Entrepreneurship and Development in Kenya* (London: Routledge and Kegan Paul, 1971). Kenneth King, *African Artisan: Education and the Informal Sector in Kenya* (London: Heinemann, 1977). Hugh Fearn, *An African Economy: A Study of the Economic Development of the Nyanza Province of Kenya, 1903–53* (London: Oxford University Press, 1961). Cyril Ehrlich, 'Building and Caretaking: Economic Policy in British Tropical Africa, 1890–1960', *African Historical Review*, 26 (1973), 649–67; 'Marketing of Cotton in Uganda, 1900–50', Ph.D. diss., University of London, 1958. Robert L. Tignor, *Colonial Transformation of Kenya: The Kamba, Kikuyu, and Maasai from 1900 to 1939* (Princeton: Princeton University Press, 1976). I.R.G. Spencer, 'First Assault on Indian Ascendancy: Indian Traders in the Kenya Reserves, 1895–1929', *African Affairs*, 80/320 (July 1981), 327–43.

14. For instances of adverse opinion by administrators, settlers, and scholars, see Spencer, 'First Assault', pp. 327–29; and M. Tamarkin, 'The Changing Social and Economic Role of Nakuru Africans, 1929–52', *Kenya Historical Review*, 6/1–2 (1978), 109, 114.

CHAPTER ONE

■

The Pattern of Settlement

All Indian immigrants to East Africa are born with private enterprise in their blood.

—Yash Tandon, 1973[1]

When they sold gray sheeting ('merekani'), the outer cover of the bale was their profit. When they sold matches, the match boxes were their profit.

—K. P. Chandaria, 1973[2]

What the Asians were like before they left India or Pakistan, why they emigrated, where they settled, and what they became in East Africa are questions that have not been adequately answered. Some differences among the Asians are readily apparent, but they have often been regarded as essentially a single community with common ties of race and culture and with common interests, goals, and behaviour. Their economic and social exclusiveness has been attributed to feelings of superiority and racial prejudice. They have also been viewed as representative of what they were in South Asia except for a certain degree of Westernization. The Shah, Patel, or Ismaili businessman has been perceived as the latest in a line of businessmen extending back through many centuries who have been specially endowed with remarkable commercial skills, and the Sikh or Hindu artisan is thought to have inherited his facility in craftsmanship from many generations of skilled forebears in the Punjab. Within another context the Asians have been described as immigrating to East Africa solely for economic gain, and in extreme opinion, they came specifically to exploit the disadvantaged Africans. From another view they have been regarded as instruments of European imperialism, that is, they were brought to East Africa to fill a position as middlemen in a scheme of exploitation by British industrial and commercial interests. As the pattern of Asian settlement reveals, however, these conceptions deserve considerable modification.

9

The Migration from South Asia

Asian migration to East Africa can be divided into four chronological periods. The first, beginning at a remote time perhaps several centuries B.C., extended almost to the end of the nineteenth century. Like the Arabs, the Asians for millennia plied the Indian Ocean in small sailing ships. Through the Persian Gulf they traded with ancient Babylon and through the Red Sea with Egypt, Greece, Rome, Axum, and Kush. Near the end of the first century A.D. when the *Periplus* was written, they apparently were trading with Rhapta in the area of East Africa. The Asians left commercial agents in the places of barter, and from these initial trading posts sizeable settlements emerged. In 1497 when Vasco da Gama explored the area, there were many Asians on Zanzibar and Pemba and along the coast in towns such as Kilwa Kivinje, Bagamoyo, Mombasa, and Malindi. During the eighteenth century after the Portuguese decline and the end of Dutch rivalry, both Asians and Arabs expanded their trade and settlement. After 1840 when Seyyid Said moved from Oman to Zanzibar, many Asians resident in Oman followed; and during the latter half of the nineteenth century, Zanzibar flourished as the focal point of an extensive trade between the African mainland and the outside world.

By 1890 when East Africa had been partitioned among European powers and the old period of Arab ascendency was at an end, the Asians were the dominant economic community on Zanzibar and along the East African coast. An economic and social pattern had already been established in which the Asians constituted the vital middle class. Through the centuries they had proved that under conditions of relatively free competition, such as those provided by the Zanzibar sultanate, they could compete successfully with Arabs, Europeans, and Africans and attain a controlling interest, often a monopoly, in finance and commerce. The decline of the slave trade and slavery, which had been a source of profit to them as well as to Arabs, had not seriously affected their commercial interests. Sensing opportunity on the mainland, they began to migrate from Zanzibar and Pemba in increasing numbers.[3] In 1887 when the detailed census summarized in Table 1.1 was taken, approximately half the Asians were already on the coast.

A second wave of Asian migration, much larger than the first, occurred between 1890 and 1914. Within this period the British, employing Indian troops, established a firm control over the new East Africa (later Kenya) and Uganda Protectorates, and the Germans, using their own forces against a similar opposition, founded German East Africa.[4] Both European powers built railways to the great lakes, encouraged European settlement, and imported indentured labour from India. Between 1895 and 1914 the British imported 37,747 Asians, mainly from the Punjab, on

11

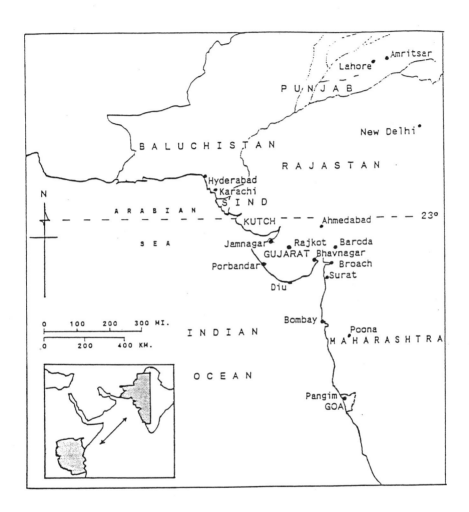

MAP 1: NORTH-WEST INDIA, 1890-47

Areas of Asian Emigration to East Africa

Source: reprinted from Robert G. Gregory, *The Rise and Fall of Philanthropy in East Africa* (New Brunswick, N.J.: Transaction, 1992) with permission of the publisher.

TABLE 1.1 Asian Population of East Africa, 1887*

Town	Residents	Town	Residents
Zanzibar	3,086	Mandani (Pemba)	133
Mombasa	533	Tanga	127
Bagamoyo	493	Pangani	123
Jumba	373	Dar es Salaam	107
Kilwa	252	Malindi	82
Lamu	230	Other places (24)	622
Kwale	184		
		Total	6,345

*The census did not include Goans and Baluchis and was thought to have been conservative in its survey.

Source: 'Census of British Indian subjects in dominions of Sultan of Zanzibar', in Major J.R.L. Macdonald to Foreign Office, 19 Dec. 1887, F.O. 84/1854.

three-year contracts to provide the labour essential for construction of the Uganda Railway and other public works. The Germans, utilizing more African labour, imported less than 200 Asians. Of the total indentured labourers, about 18 per cent (some 7,000) elected to remain in East Africa on expiration of their contracts.[5] Although some continued to work on the railway or took other employment in government service, most became artisans or merchants in the many towns that sprang up behind the advancing railhead. These towns had been swelled by a far more numerous free-immigrant population from western India.

Between 1890 and 1921 the expanding sphere of government protection, the provision of rail transportation, and the opportunity to supply the wants of European settlers and to begin a trade with the Africans attracted between 10,000 and 20,000 Asian free immigrants. Judging from immigration statistics, the Asians throughout East Africa numbered about 34,000 in 1914. By the time of the census of 1921, shown in Table 1.2,the Asian population of East Africa had risen spectacularly to more than 54,000. The East Africa Protectorate attracted by far the greatest number, but Zanzibar, which was at the height of its prosperity, had a fourfold increase.

A third wave of migration is coterminous with the interwar period. The great influx to the British East Africa and Uganda Protectorates that was interrupted by World War I resumed with the armistice in 1918 and was extended to Tanganyika with the establishment of the British ad-

TABLE 1.2   Asian Population of East Africa, 1921--62*

Dependency	1921	1931	1939	1962
Kenya	25,253	43,623	46,897	176,613
Tanganyika	10,209	25,144	25,000	92,000
Uganda	5,200	14,150	17,300	77,400
Zanzibar	13,772	15,247	15,500	20,000
Totals	54,434	98,164	104,697	366,013

*Figures for 1939 are estimates as the next detailed census after 1931 was in 1948. The 20,000 for Zanzibar was estimated by Lofchie. The 1958 Zanzibar census listed a total of 15,892 Asians.

Sources: Annual Reports of each territory; Robert R. Kuczynski, Demographic Survey of the British Colonial Empire, vol. 2 (London: Oxford University Press, 1948), pp. 144-45, 239, 326, 653-54; and Michael F. Lofchie, Zanzibar: Background to Revolution (Princeton: Princeton University Press, 1965), p. 80.

ministration in 1920. Unlike the situation before 1914, the Asian population after the war grew almost entirely because of free immigration and natural increase. Although 2,024 indentured Asians entered after 1914, a total of 2,905 returned to India on expiration of their contracts. As shown in Table 1.2, the Asians of East Africa numbered 98,000 in 1931 and nearly 105,000 in 1939.[6]

These figures, when compared with those for 1921, indicate that nearly all the growth occurred during the first decade after the war. Between 1921 and 1931 the total Asian population nearly doubled; and during the second decade immigration almost ceased, and the population apparently grew only by natural increase. That the economic depression of the 1930s had so profound an effect on Asian immigration illustrates the continuing importance of economic opportunity as a motivation. Probably the relative lack of economic reward also explains the minimal increase on Zanzibar. New immigrants from South Asia went directly to the mainland where, at least during the 1920s, the opportunities for employment in government service, crafts and construction, and commerce and banking, especially in the wholesale-retail trade catering to European and African needs, seemed boundless.

The end of World War II in 1945 and the conferral of independence on the East African territories during 1961–63 mark the final period of extensive Asian migration. A comparison of the statistics for 1939 and 1962 reveals that the Asian population increased after the war by approximately 260,000. Again Kenya, offering the greatest economic opportunity, was the most attractive territory. After 1939 the Asians in Kenya grew by approximately 130,000 in comparison with 67,000 for Tanganyika, 60,000 for Uganda, and less than 5,000 for Zanzibar.[7]

Unlike in the preceding periods, about half the increase in the Asian population was due to natural causes. In Kenya during the decade ending in 1960, for example, the natural increase and that from immigration were generally the same, at 2.5 per cent per annum. A continuing high birth-rate of at least 30 per 1,000 and a declining death-rate were partly responsible, but independence in India and prospects for independence in East Africa made immigration less attractive. Although the number coming to East Africa grew almost every year, and the Asians continued to outnumber Europeans more than three to one, the proportion of Asian arrivals to residents steadily diminished.[8]

Migration to East Africa began from the coastal trading centres of western India and subsequently drew people from the interior. It was from seaports such as Broach, Cambay, and Surat, as well as Karachi and Bombay, that the early immigrants came to Zanzibar. Engaged in the dhow trade with the Persian Gulf, Oman, and Hadramaut, and the Red Sea and the Benadir and Azanian coasts, these traders naturally were attracted to Zanzibar as commerce developed. Almost all retained ties to their original villages, and as their businesses expanded it was from these villages that they drew their employees. They wrote to relatives and friends or on visits home went to the villages and with tales of adventure and profit recruited the young. So the news spread. Brother attracted brother and cousin. One went, then another, then two or three, and within a generation the entire male line of a family could move to Zanzibar. For a long time only the men and boys hazarded the voyage. They returned frequently to India to marry, to visit their families, and eventually, with savings in hand, to retire. Meanwhile the women remained in the safety of the village to raise the children and till the fields. Not until well into the nineteenth century were many women brought to Zanzibar, and these women, as will be seen, were mainly Muslim rather than Hindu.

The pattern established for Zanzibar was followed as Asians moved to the mainland coastal towns and the interior. First came the young men, then the wives and children, and infrequently some of the older people. Most Asians continued to come from the villages of the Gujarat, Kathiawar, and Kutch where they were mainly occupied in tilling the fields. In India, however, the line between farming and business was often thin. Many peasants supplemented their incomes by running small shops in their villages. In time some switched entirely to business or other occupations and moved to nearby towns or big cities such as Ahmedabad, Poona, Bombay, or Karachi. Most of the immigrants from the urban areas of western India had only recently left the village farms and were facing stiff competition in their new business occupations. Increasingly the peasants and townsmen were accompanied by a professional class. Doctors, lawyers, teachers, accountants, and engineers, after education and qualification in India or Britain, were drawn to East Africa.

It was the potential for financial improvement, particularly in a business capacity, that attracted most of the immigrants. 'My father who came to Dar from the Punjab in 1928', remarked an Asian many years later, 'heard that the streets were paved with gold'.[9] Shah Somchand Keshavji, one of several sons in a well-to-do farming family near Jamnagar, left at age sixteen to join a cousin in a shop in Eldoret. 'It was a family decision', he recalled. 'Each family in my village tried to send one son. When I did well, my brothers followed'.[10] Devra Vrajpal Shah, from another village near Jamnagar, was the eldest of four sons who had no hope for more than subsistence from the family land. At age sixteen he borrowed money from relatives to sail in a dhow with his fifteen-year-old brother Premchand to Mombasa. They hoped to open a shop in Nairobi.[11] The father of Jagannath Bhavanishanker Pandya, one of Kenya's most successful businessmen, sprang from farming stock but was the headmaster of a school in Bhavnagar. Unable to afford more than a secondary education for Jagannath, his eldest son, he sent him with a few friends by dhow to enter business in Mombasa.[12]

The professionals, who came mainly from Bombay, Poona, Goa, and in a few instances from Calcutta, were also attracted by the prospect of financial gain. D. S. Trivedi, raised in a village near Ahmedabad, worked his way through five and one-half years at Bombay University and in 1937 was articled as an accountant. He was then persuaded by a friend from Kenya to open an office in Mombasa. Kuldip Sondhi, though born in East Africa, had intended to settle in India. After receiving an M.S. in aeronautical engineering in the United States, he helped design the engine for India's Gnat fighter. Despite an appeal by Jawaharlal Nehru to help found the country's aircraft industry and an offer for another job by the Tata Industries, Kuldip was disappointed in the monthly salary prospects of Rs 2,000 (rupees). He left India and aeronautical engineering to join his father and brother in Mombasa in a more lucrative vocation of construction and hotel keeping. Ganesh Bagchi was a frustrated teacher in Calcutta. Because of family responsibilities, he had been forced out of teaching, which paid only Rs 125 per month, to take a much better paying position as a customs agent. In 1952 when he heard that the Uganda government was offering a teaching salary of Shs 850 per month, about the same as he was then making, he immediately resigned and left for Kampala to become a teacher of English in the Government Secondary School.[13]

Higher salaries were the principal attraction for clerical workers. In 1920 Bhanubhai Acharya was a telegraphist on a meagre salary with the Indian Railways in Limbdi, Saurashtra. He was only sixteen, had no more than a first-standard Gujarati education, and knew no English. When he heard of the higher pay offered by the Kenya postal service, however, he left and from a position in the Rumuruti Post Office soon persuaded his younger brother to do the same. In 1927 Francis Anthony de Souza, age eighteen with a Cambridge school certificate in hand and poor job prospects in Jansi, his home town, was persuaded by his brother-in-law to join him in the Kenya government. As an accountant he thus began a distinguished thirty-one years in the Kenya civil service. Krishan Lal Vohora, from Bhaun in the Punjab, was like many others from a family of civil servants. His father was an agricultural officer in the Punjab, and two of his uncles were employed on the Uganda Railway. In 1926 the uncles retired to India with 'a lot of money', and impressed by this, Vohora left that same year for Kenya at age eighteen. Within a year he was a clerk in Nairobi's Barclays Bank.[14]

Many Asians were recruited before leaving India by the East African governments or private firms. In 1870 Aziz R. Kassim Lakha's grandfather, seconded by the British governor from Jamnagar, was brought to Zanzibar on a three-year contract to be the customs agent for the sultan. In 1952 when earning Rs 200 per month as a reporter in Bombay, Madhusudn Jethalal Thakkar noticed an ad in the *Times of India* for a position as accountant with the Mehta sugar industries in Uganda. After a successful application, he was in Lugazi, age twenty-four, with a salary of Shs 500. In 1897 Augustino de Figueiredo was recruited as a young man by the Imperial British East Africa Company for work in Uganda. He had been a clerk with the Army and Navy Stores in Bombay. Ramanbhai Muljibhai Patel, from a village near Baroda, lost his father soon after birth but was able to go through Bombay University on scholarships. After receiving a B.S. in agriculture, he hoped to continue towards a Ph.D. in the United States. Lacking financial resources, however, he accepted a position in 1924 with the Madhvani Group in Uganda as a farm overseer. In 1955 Hariprasad Poonamchandra Joshi, who had M.A. and Bachelor of Teaching (B.T.) degrees from Bombay University, was earning Rs 250 per month as a headmaster near Baroda. In dire poverty, he could not even afford shoes. Interviewed there by two agents from Uganda, he was hired as a teacher in Jinja at Shs 900.[15]

As these narrations indicate, the statement so frequently heard that 'Asians came to make money' is essentially true, but as they also reveal, there is need for qualification. Most of the immigrants were drawn to East Africa by a hope of rising above the poverty level. During the century before 1850 the population of India had remained fairly constant at approximately 130 million. During the latter half of the nineteenth century, coincidental with the opening of East Africa, a dramatic growth began. Because of modern medicine, sanitation, and transportation, the death rate from disease and famine declined markedly, as shown in Table 1.3, and the population began to grow at an annual rate of more than 2 per cent. As a result, India's population leaped from 133 million in 1847 to 236 million in 1901, to 251 million in 1921, to 317 million in 1941, and to 439 million in 1961. The later figures would have been far higher if millions of Indians had not emigrated. Much of India's surplus population, usually at a young, productive age, poured into Burma, Ceylon, South Africa, Fiji, British Guiana, and the West Indies as well as East Africa.

Northwest India, which contributed to much of this emigration, was, because of its proximity and its age-old trade ties, the main source for East Africa. The Punjab, land of five rivers whence came most of the indentured labourers, was fertile and well watered but overpopulated, and many small farmers had not sufficient land to sustain their families. Sind, another area of recruitment, was a desert in which any livelihood was difficult to earn. The Gujarat, Kathiawar (Saurashtra), Kutch, and Maharashtra, the homelands of most of the free immigrants, were fairly fertile but dependent on the summer monsoons for rainfall. In time of plentiful rain these lands could be green and luxurious. When the monsoons failed, they were dust bowls. Drought and famine, recurring every two or three years, kept the population density to half that of the Punjab. For the Gujarat and Kathiawar the natural increase—over 16 per 1,000 for 1941–50—was the highest in all India.[16] Portuguese Goa, another source of free emigration, was a verdant, tropical paradise in all but employment opportunity. The Portuguese monopolized the higher positions in the civil service, and there were too many qualified Goans for the remainder.

Although it was usually the desire for a better life than that offered by these inhospitable lands that drove the sons of the small farmers to the big cities of India or the towns of East Africa, the cause in many instances was a mere search for adventure or even curiosity.[17] In some instances it was a severe misfortune. Jashbhai Motibhai Desai left the Gujarat for Uganda in 1925, age seventeen, after his father and brother died of plague. The early death of a father also prompted the migration of Lakhamshi R. Shah at age eleven and Jayantilal Keshavji Chande at age twenty-two. Shah, with no one to care for him in India, joined relatives in Fort Hall, and Chande, considering his prospects as eldest son for supporting a large family better abroad, moved to Mombasa. Adamjee Putwa, who came to Zanzibar about 1850, was driven from Kutch by severe famine. The same is true of Waljee Hirjee, who moved to Zanzibar in

TABLE 1.3   Estimated Birth and Death Rates (per 1,000) in India,
1901-50*

Years	Natural Births	Deaths	Increase
1901-10	52.4	46.8	5.6
1921-30	46.4	36.3	10.5
1941-50	43.0	30.0	13.0

*The figures are adjusted to India's present area.

Sources: S. Chandrasekhar, *Infant Mortality, Population Growth,
and Family Planning in India* (Chapel Hill: University of North
Carolina Press, 1972), p. 248. S. Chandrasekhar, *India's
Population: Facts, Problems and Policy* (Meerut: Meenakshi
Prakashan, 1967), p. 16.

1867. Vaghjibhai Shankerbhai Patel moved from a Gujarat village to
Mombasa in 1920 because his father and mother had died and his two
elder brothers had been sent to prison for supporting Mohandas K. Gandhi. Shantibhai D. Kothari had to leave school at age eighteen and decided to move to Kenya in 1923 when his father, an oil merchant in
Bombay, forsook his business and family to become a wandering Jain
monk.[18]

Some Asians have related even more curious stories of motivation. In
1890 Rhemtulla G. Manji's grandfather abandoned a profitable life as a
bandit in Sind to take up a legitimate business in Machakos because of a
hex placed on his son. He was advised by a holy man that the hex could
be removed only by leaving Indian soil. According to the family history,
the son regained consciousness as soon as they touched East Africa.[19]
Dr. Shankar Dhondo Karve, reminiscing years after his arrival in Kenya,
remarked, 'I am a doctor and could have got on very well in India, but I
wanted butter on my bread, and I wanted whiskey'.[20] Ramanlal Trimbaklal Thakore left India in 1939 partly because life there was intolerable for
his wife. His marriage as a Brahmkshatriya to a Shah was the second outside his own community and the first outside his wife's. Although his
family eventually accepted the marriage, his wife's family never forgave
her.[21]

A few came to East Africa with no intention of staying. Suleiman Verjee in 1878 and Haji Abu in 1896 were en route to Portuguese East Africa
when their dhows dropped anchor respectively at Mombasa and Zanzibar, and Dinshaw Byramjee in 1888 was on his way to South Africa when
his dhow stopped at Mombasa. Each was so attracted to East Africa that
he never rejoined his shipmates. Nauharia Ram Maini was travelling

from the Punjab to South Africa when he left the steamer at Mombasa to buy fruit and vegetables for the crew and passengers. Tarrying, fascinated by the market, he returned to see his ship sailing away. U. K. Oza, principal of the National College in Bombay, intended merely to accompany his friend, the editor of the *Bombay Chronicle,* in 1924 when the latter was asked by Gandhi to investigate Asian political grievances in East Africa. Bhailal Patel, overworked as an advocate, came to Nairobi in 1954 for a short rest. Dr. Sarab Bhatia Singh, who arrived in 1962, is another who came to Kenya only for a holiday.[22]

The sparkling sunshine and temperate climate of Nairobi, the beautiful white-coral sand and gentle surf of Mombasa and Dar es Salaam, the spectacle of the hinterland, the fresh new look of the cities and towns, the excitement of the unknown, and the prosperous, happy look of their late countrymen captivated these Asians.

Motivation varied not only with individuals but also with communities. As shown in subsequent pages, the hope of economic gain was primary with all groups, whether Hindu, Muslim, Sikh, Christian, or Jain, but within this context there was considerable variation. For the Ismailis and Ithnasheris, religious motivation was also very important.

The early immigrants endured many hardships, not the least of which was the voyage to East Africa. Before 1914 and during the two world wars when steamer traffic was interrupted, almost all the Asians came by dhow. Life on these small ships of 80 to 350 tons, 40 to 60 feet long, with wooden hulls and lateen sails, was difficult. The passengers slept on deck and, clustered in groups representative of different religious communities, cooked their own food. They had no privacy and lacked any competent medical service. The ships bobbed and rolled in the monsoon seas even in calm weather, and seasickness was common. A storm—and rarely could one escape one or two during the voyage—was a frightening experience. To allay fears and while away the time, the passengers and sailors would recite religious verses or tales from folk literature. Under the most favourable conditions, the voyage of 2,400 miles to Zanzibar could be made in twenty-six days, but a storm or a calm could extend it by several weeks or even months. Nasser Virjee's passage from Kutch in 1875 took nine months. The price of the fare was as little as Rs 10, but some paid as much as Rs 205. The cost by steamer was considerably more, Rs 35 and up for third-class or steerage in 1900. Although a steamer offered more security and faster travel—usually seven to fourteen days—life aboard was rarely pleasant. Most Asians, at least before World War I, slept on deck and cooked their own meals. Usually they were unable to converse with the foreign crews, and on arrival in East Africa they often faced a week of quarantine.[23]

Adjustments to Africa

Once in East Africa these early immigrants often went through several weeks or months of uncertainty and privation while determining their initial location and employment. Although some had a smattering of English, very few knew any German, Arabic, or Swahili. Even among Asians they were strangers outside their own communities. In most cases, with a life of poverty behind them, they had borrowed the money for the voyage or spent nearly all their savings, and rarely did one arrive with more than a few rupees in his pocket. The Goans and the Patels, fairly versed in English, could hope for some government position. The peasant farmers, such as the Shahs or Punjabis, lacked an adequate knowledge of English and had no skill in crafts or first-hand experience in business. With neither opportunity nor inducement to continue as farmers, they could seek only some menial employment with someone from their own community who was already established. Even food posed a formidable problem. It was not only that most of the Hindus and Jains were vegetarians accustomed to the grains, legumes, garden vegetables, spices, curds, and ghee of their homeland. Nearly all the non-Muslims, because of religious prohibitions, could not eat food prepared by anyone outside their own communities or even their own castes.

Solutions to these problems were difficult in that many of the early immigrants were very young and had few, if any, contacts in Africa. In 1890 after a journey alone by dhow, Mohamedali Pirbhai, age sixteen, stayed in a community rest house in Dar es Salaam until he found work with a German provision store. As a clerk he earned Rs 12 per month and had to provide his own food and lodging. In 1898 Gulamhusein Rajpar Ladak, only twelve years old, arrived in Bagamoyo alone after a similar voyage. After a few days during which a stranger helped him, he began a four hundred mile walk to Tukuyu where eventually he found work escorting caravans at Rs 7 per month. In 1910 Rashid M. Fazal, fifteen years old, landed at Mombasa, where he had no relatives or friends. He was helped by his Ithnasheri community and soon had a clerical job paying Rs 200–300 per year. Like most clerks, he ate with the proprietor's family, slept in the shop, and served the family by shopping and caring for the children. In 1912 Mepabhai Vershi Shah, after a voyage alone on a German steamer, joined the 300 to 400 Asians in Nairobi. He was thirteen, and his first employment was in a stone quarry at Rs 50 per month.[24] In 1920 Girdhar Purshottam Mehta, leaving his wife and two children in his home village, left by dhow for Mombasa. There he was offered a job at Shs 10 per month but was told by a friend that he could get twice as much in Uganda. 'If I came 4,000 miles', he told himself, 'I might as well go another thousand'. Soon he was in Musaka employed as a caravan leader. Not until almost four years later, however, could he send for his wife and children.[25]

For those who joined established relatives or were recruited while still in India, the transition was easier. During and after the 1920s most immigrants were in this category. For those, however, who had to learn a business or trade, become fluent in new languages, and make the many social adjustments, the initial years were trying. In 1929 when he came to Kenya, L. R. Shah was fourteen. He was accompanied only by a twelve-year-old brother, and he had left a bride of one month. Although relatives in Nairobi helped him with employment, he began as a menial clerk, and five years elapsed before he could bring his wife.[26] Kantilal Punamchand Shah, who arrived at age nineteen in 1941, a generation later when the transition was apparently much easier, moved to Nairobi after a month of job hunting in Mombasa. He then found employment as a salesman with a foodstuffs store. He had to spend Shs 85 of his salary of Shs 100 on bed and room, however. To learn English he enrolled in night school but soon had to drop out because he could not afford the Shs 15 monthly fee. Nor was he able to send home each month a promised Shs 15. While learning in his employment to keep accounts in Gujarati and converse in Hindi and Swahili, he bought an old typewriter in partnership with a friend. Then he began to write letters in poor English to the *East African Standard*. 'I wrote about five letters a week, a few of which were accepted', Shah later explained. 'The editor corrected my grammar, and I saw my mistakes'.[27]

Industry, ingenuity, thrift, and education were bound eventually to bring wealth. Though lacking important mineral resources, the country was rich in timber, stone, big game, and in many areas fertile, well-watered land. Africans, introduced to a monied economy, a great variety of commodities from abroad, and radically new concepts and values, were beginning a cultural revolution, and they offered a vast market for consumption of foreign goods and services. They also could be viewed as an unfathomable reservoir for labour. The Europeans, establishing the government, managing the railway, and settling the highlands, constituted another consumer market. Moreover, both they and the Africans could be expected to produce cash crops for export. Then there were the Asians themselves who needed the spices, piece goods, tools, and cooking utensils that they had known in India. They were additional consumers. The combination of opportunities was therefore immense, and the Asians had the unique potential for providing a vital service to all three communities as middlemen—as intermediaries not only among the three communities in East Africa, but also between the three and the world outside.

Business in all its varieties—retail and wholesale shopkeeping, distribution and transport, money-lending and insurance, property rental, construction, and artisanry—posed the foremost opportunity. This is principally why the Shahs, Patels, and Ismailis so easily broke with the tradition of generations by transferring their interests from farming to business when they arrived in East Africa. It explains why so many indentured labourers forfeited their return passages to stay in the country, and why Asian clerks seldom remained in government service sufficiently long to retire with pensions. In fact, it was common for the relatively few who did retire in government service to invest their savings in founding new businesses. Even the professional people were attracted. Doctors and lawyers frequently carried on one or more businesses in addition to their practices. Such activity is found to some degree in every capitalist economy, but it was extreme in East Africa not because the Asians were uniquely business-minded, as is so often assumed, but because the opportunities there were so extraordinary.

The emphasis on business in the mainland territories is evident in Table 1.4, which is drawn from the last censuses before independence. Although comparable statistics are not available for Zanzibar, a similar emphasis prevailed there.

According to a 1966–67 survey of 281 Asian businessmen in and around Nairobi, there was an overwhelming preoccupation with retail and wholesale trade. As many as 36 per cent of the businessmen were primarily in retailing and 31 per cent in wholesaling. In contrast, 13 per cent were in manufacturing, 9 per cent in service industries, 5 per cent in building contracting, 4 per cent in restaurant or barkeeping, 1 per cent in transporting, and the remaining 1 per cent in other types of business.[28] This distribution was probably fairly representative of all the Asian businessmen in East Africa.

The lure of business determined the Asian settlement in East Africa. It was the reason for the initial settlement on Zanzibar and for the subsequent migration to the coastal towns of the mainland. Following the caravan routes from Bagamoyo to the great lakes, the Asians established themselves in Tabora, Ujiji, and Mengo and long before the advent of the Europeans traded as far as the Ruwenzori, the fabulous Mountains of the Moon.[29] As the British and the Germans built their railways, the Asians followed the railheads and set up their shops at each successive stop. They also congregated around the government outposts. The resulting shantytowns with rows of little corrugated-iron buildings—soon tinged red with rust and ochre dust—were in effect bazaars that catered to the growing needs of the Asian railway crews and the neighbouring African cultivators and European planters. From these incipient towns the Asian businessmen, first by portage and later by bullock cart and donkey, car-

TABLE 1.4   Occupations of Economically Active Asians, 1957-62

	Kenya 1962		Tanganyika 1957		Uganda 1959	
	Number	%	Number	%	Number	%
Commerce, banking	16,325	44.5	9,247	50.0	9,426	56.7
Public services	11,474	31.3	1,953	10.5	1,542	9.3
Manufacturing	5,001	13.6	1,999	10.8	1,879	11.3
Construction	1,584	4.3	809	4.4	690	4.1
Private transport, communication	1,085	3.0	1,852	10.0	250	1.5
Agriculture, forestry, fishing	667	1.8	898	4.9	1,737	10.4
Electricity, water	124	.3	113	.6	95	.6
Mining, quarrying	73	.2	149	.8	76	.5
Other	320	.9	1,485	8.0	932	5.6
Totals	36,653	100.0	18,505	100.0	16,627	100.0

Sources: Kenya, Population Census, 1962, vol. 4, p. 28. United Kingdom, Tanganyika Report for the Year 1960: part 2 Statistics (London: HMSO, 1961), Colonial no. 349, p. 9; Uganda, Uganda Census, 1959: Non-African Population (Nairobi/Entebbe: East African Statistical Department, 1960), p. 52.

ried their goods into the hinterlands to trade in the African traditional markets. As they prospered, they were joined by others, and so in scarcely more than one generation towns and trading centres sprang up throughout East Africa. Europeans, Africans, and Arabs contributed to these trading settlements, but the Asians in the early years were the primary participants.

On the eve of independence, the Asians were situated mainly in the cities and sizeable towns, as shown in Table 1.5. By then their activities in rural areas had been curtailed, but far more than their brethren in India, these Asians, because of their focus on business, were an urban people. In Kenya 90 per cent were concentrated in the sixteen largest urban centres. In Tanganyika 71 per cent were in the twelve main centres, and in Uganda 62 per cent were in sixteen. A large proportion of the Asians resided in the principal city in each territory. Nairobi held 49 per cent of Kenya's Asians, Dar es Salaam 36 per cent of those in Tanganyika, and Kampala 27 per cent of those in Uganda. These statistics also reveal

TABLE 1.5   Asian Urban Population, 1957--62

Kenya (1962 census)

Nairobi	86,453	Kericho	1,462	Gilgil	593
Mombasa	43,713	Nyeri	1,147	Fort Hall	556
Kisumu	8,355	Nanyuki	982	Malindi	438
Nakuru	6,203	Machakos	719	Embu	404
Eldoret	3,758	Kisii	673	Lamu	233
Thika	2,336	Meru	662	Elsewhere	15,260
Kitale	2,065	Kakamega	601		
				Total	176,613

Tanganyika (1957 census)

Dar S'm	27,441	Dodoma	2,269	Mtwara	593
Tanga	7,412	Lindi	1,804	Mikindani	370
Mwanga	3,956	Morogoro	1,525		
Arusha	3,496	Iringa	1,238	Elsewhere	22,388
Moshi	3,148	Mbeya	896		
				Total	767,536

Uganda (1959 census)

Kampala	19,268	Iganga	1,005	Gulu	571
Jinja	8,883	Mbarara	919	Fort Portal	519
Mbale	4,575	Entebbe	904	Arua	516
Masaka	2,139	Kamuli	817		
Soroti	1,833	Lira	671	Elsewhere	27,482
Tororo	1,220	Kabale	611		
				Total	71,933

Sources: Kenya, *Population Census, 1962: Tables: Advance Report of Vols. 1 and 2* (Nairobi: Government Printer, 1964), pp. 37-44; United Kingdom, *Tanganyika Report for the Year 1960*: part 2, p. 5; Uganda, *Uganda Census, 1959: Non-African Population*, p. 10.

some major differences among the Asian settlements in the three territo- ries. In Kenya almost all the Asians were in the urban centres, with a heavy concentration in Nairobi and Mombasa. In Tanganyika relatively fewer Asians lived in urban centres, and they were scattered more evenly among the towns. In Uganda where the rural residence was the highest, these characteristics were even more pronounced.

The differences in urban-rural settlement among the three territories are explained largely by the fact that the major cities offered the most at- tractive economic and social opportunities. Kenya had the two most im- portant cities, Nairobi and Mombasa. Nairobi was at the base of the highlands to serve the comparatively wealthy European settlers. It was also the capital, with a large number of government officials, and it was in a central position for trade with the Africans. Mombasa, a port and railway terminus, was the import-export depot for both Kenya and Uganda. In Tanganyika Dar es Salaam had the unique combination of capital, railway, and port. In Uganda Kampala developed more rapidly than the capital, Entebbe, because it was in the heart of the rich Ganda kingdom and had the railway. Attractive initially only because of the op- portunities for business, these cities later afforded the additional advan- tages of the most desirable educational, recreational, social, and cultural amenities, as well as security.

Communal Organization

Despite this rapid and remarkable change from rural peasants to ur- ban businessmen, the Asians in their entirety clung to their communal religions throughout their long residence in East Africa. Their religious orientation not only fragmented the community, but also affected their economic, political, and social activity and determined their attitudes. It was the cause of some misconceptions on the part of the Africans and Europeans. Near the end of the colonial period, the Asians were de- scribed as belonging to four major religions, as shown in Table 1.6.

The predominance of the Hindus and Jains, who are usually com- bined in East African statistics under the label Hindu, did not obtain in the early years. The Asians who first emigrated to Zanzibar and the mainland coast tended to share the Muslim faith of the Arab rulers. Ac- cording to the census of 1887, the British Asians alone in this area in- cluded 4,866 Muslims and only 1,022 Hindu/Jains.[30] Not until the British assumed control did a change begin towards a proportion more repre- sentative of the population in India. In 1911, however, the Muslims of the East Africa Protectorate still outnumbered the Hindu/Jains by 5,939 to 3,205, and in Uganda by 1,102 to 674.[31] At the end of World War I the Hin- du/Jains began to equal the Muslims in these two territories and after-

TABLE 1.6   Asian Religious Affiliation, 1958-62*

	Hindu/Jain	Muslim	Sikh	Christian	Other
Numbers					
Kenya 1962	97,841	40,057	21,169	16,524	1,022
Tanganyika 1957	29,048	36,361	4,234	4,732	2,161
Uganda 1959	47,689	17,818	3,058	3,145	85
Zanzibar 1958	4,243	10,618	30	714	286
East Africa	178,821	104,854	28,491	25,115	3,554
Percentages					
Kenya 1962	55.4%	22.7%	12.0%	9.3%	0.6%
Tanganyika 1957	38.0	47.5	5.5	6.2	2.8
Uganda 1959	66.4	24.8	4.3	4.4	0.1
Zanzibar 1958	26.7	66.8	0.2	4.5	1.8
East Africa	52.5%	30.8%	8.4%	7.4%	1.0%

*Jains were apparently classified as Hindu in Kenya and Uganda but perhaps not in Tanganyika. Zanzibar, which provided the most complete analysis, enumerated Hindus as 4,095, Jains 148, Parsees 241, and Buddhists 19. 'Other' includes Parsees, Buddhists, 'none', and 'not stated'.

Sources: Kenya, *Kenya Population Census, 1962*, vol. 4, p. 28; United Kingdom, *Tanganyika Report for the Year 1960*, part 2, p. 9; Uganda, *Uganda Census, 1959: Non-African Population*, p. 52; Zanzibar, *Report on the Census of the Population of Zanzibar Protectorate . . . 1958* (Zanzibar: Government Printer, 1960), p. 109.

wards increased far more rapidly. By 1948 the Hindu/Jains totalled 45,238 in Kenya as contrasted with 27,583 Muslims, and 20,441 in Uganda compared to 11,172 Muslims.[32] Tanganyika and Zanzibar retained a larger proportion of Muslims because they attracted comparatively few new immigrants from India. Tanganyika's Asian population, even during the period of British administration, grew largely through natural increase and immigration from Zanzibar.

The Hindus, as distinct from the Jains, totalled on the eve of independence approximately 135,000—about 40 per cent of all the Asians in East Africa—and were themselves fragmented.[33] The largest Hindu group, numbering well over 50,000 by 1970, was the Patels, who included not only the Asians of the surname Patel but also some of the Desais and

Amins. Mostly Gujarati speaking and coming mainly from the area of Ahmedabad and Baroda as small farmers, they were also known as Patidars, or landowning peasants.[34] By tradition, however, they were Kshatriyas, and many in India had become landlords, held political office, and received an above-average education; but nearly all who emigrated in the early years were poor. Because of their knowledge of English, they readily found employment in East Africa as clerks with the railway and other branches of government. Most, however, soon found business more rewarding than clerical service. The Patels were especially prominent in Uganda. A survey in the early 1950s showed that 1,446 of the 5,819 Uganda Asians holding trading licenses—25 per cent—were Patels and that they were the most numerous—41 per cent—among the Hindus. Because of their emphasis on education, the Patels became in the second and third generations the main professional people as lawyers, doctors, dentists, pharmacists, and teachers. Perhaps as a consequence, they assumed positions of political leadership.[35]

Next to the Patels, the most numerous Hindu group was the Lohanas. By 1970 there were an estimated 40,000 Lohana adults in East Africa, with 14,000 in Uganda, slightly more in Kenya, and about 7,000 in Tanzania. Although they had been with the Bhatias the first Asians to settle on Zanzibar, they had emigrated from there to the mainland, and only a few remained on Zanzibar after the 1964 revolution. They came to East Africa mostly from Kutch and from several areas of Saurashtra. Like the Patels, the Lohanas in Africa quickly became associated with the *banya* merchant group. Not so well educated or urbane as the Patels when they left India—they had come from more rural areas—they moved directly into business on arrival in East Africa. Collectively they became perhaps the wealthiest of all the Asians. The two most affluent families, the Madhvanis and the Mehtas, were Lohanas.[36]

Though far less numerous than the Patels and Lohanas, other Hindu groups were influential in East Africa. Unfortunately, no co-ordinated survey was ever taken of them in the four British territories. There were at least a dozen others, the most prominent of whom were the Vanias and Brahmins. The Vanias, from whom the name *banya* is perhaps derived, were a large trading caste in northwest India. Like the Vanias, the Brahmins were more influential than their numbers indicate. In India they were priests by tradition but largely soldiers, lawyers, teachers, and other professionals in practice. In East Africa, retaining this professional interest, comparatively few of the Brahmin immigrants concentrated on business. J. B. Pandya, for instance, entered the import-export trade shortly after arrival in Mombasa, but as soon as his resources permitted he turned to politics and rose to a position of eminent leadership. His son, Anant, though inheriting and maintaining the family business, began a political career almost immediately after qualifying for law.[37]

As a whole, the East African Hindus absorbed far more of western culture than did their countrymen in India, but in many ways the appearances were deceiving. Though adopting English and a modified Hindustani, or in some instances Swahili, as a lingua franca, most still spoke within their homes and often in their community their traditional Gujarati, Kutchi, or Marathi. Most of the men by the end of the colonial period had long since abandoned the dhoti, *chappals* (sandals), cap or turban, and hair style still common in India in favour of a smart business suit, polished shoes, and hair trim of western style; but some still clung to a single article—perhaps a Nehru jacket or a Gandhi cap—as a token of Indian identity, and the women nearly all still wore the sari, sandals, long hair, gold bangles and necklaces, and distinguishing red mark on their foreheads. Outwardly nearly all the Hindus appeared the same. They dressed alike, drove Peugeot and Mercedes cars, and lived, at least in the cities, in residential areas where all Asians were intermixed in separate homes and flats. Hindus of all types sat next to one another at the weekly Indian movie, mingled together in Lions and Rotary clubs, and joined in various Asian chambers of commerce and political associations. Each remained, however, acutely aware of his or her origins in India and the pertinent religion, caste, and family traditions.

The Muslims, who at the end of the colonial period totalled approximately 110,000 in East Africa, were overall only three-fifths as numerous as the Hindus but comprised nearly a third of the total Asian population. Like the Hindus, they came mainly from the Gujarat and Kutch rather than the more northern area that became Pakistan. They were attracted to Zanzibar and the African coast long before the European presence mainly because of the Arabs' hegemony, and many Muslim Asians accompanied Seyyid Said in the move from Oman. A census of the sultan's domain in 1887 revealed that Muslims were by far the largest Asian community—4,866 as compared to 1,340 Hindus.[38] Not until after World War I, as explained, did they become the minority. The greater proportion of the Muslims who emigrated to East Africa were Shias rather than the orthodox Sunnis. They traced their spiritual descent to Ali, the Prophet's son-in-law, claimed that the caliphate was inherited rather than elected, and emphasized the importance of living spiritual leaders, the imams. In East Africa they shared a common religion with the Arabs and a large proportion of the Africans, and they associated with these other communities in Muslim councils or associations in most of the cities and towns. The Shia Asians, however, were sharply divided into three main sects: the Ismailis, Ithnasheris, and Bohras.[39]

The Ismailis became the most numerous and most prominent of the Shia Muslims in East Africa. From their origin in Persia the Ismailis had been led by their imam, the Aga Khan, into western India where they converted many of the Lohanas in Kutch and spread into Bombay and a number of Gujarat towns. Accepted by neither the more numerous Sunni Muslims nor the Hindus, these Ismaili khojas (honorable converts) were unable to rise in society, politics, or government and remained mostly petty traders. Early in the nineteenth century they began a migration to Zanzibar and the adjacent coastal towns and became the most numerous Asian community in East Africa. After 1926 when the Aga Khan directed his followers to settle the East African interior, they began an extensive movement into Uganda and western Tanganyika.[40]

Under the Aga Khan's leadership the Ismailis evolved a complex organization and a dedication to mutual service. The two Aga Khans important to the Asians' history in East Africa were Sultan Mohamed Shah, the third Aga Khan who reigned from 1885 to 1957, and his successor, Shah Karim. Both were devoted to fostering their community's interests. In 1945 Sultan Mohamed Shah established a Diamond Jubilee Investment Trust to provide low-interest loans for business and housing, and in 1963 an Industrial Promotion Services for assistance in industry and agriculture. He also organized the Jubilee Insurance Co., a finance company, a building society, and schools, hospitals, clinics, orphanages, hostels, and hotels all for the benefit of the community. The gift of 10 per cent of their income that he received annually from his followers was in large part returned in the form of these services. By the end of the colonial period the Ismailis rivalled the Lohanas in prosperity, and many had become outstanding lawyers, doctors, and teachers. Often viewed as the most liberal, progressive, and accomplished of the Asians, the Ismailis spoke English and wore western dress. They had been the first to put their daughters to work and encourage them in professional attainment.[41]

The Ithnasheris (Ithna Ashariya), the second major Muslim group, had a common origin with the Ismailis and like them represented a diverse background of merchants, farmers, and menial labourers, mostly poor and illiterate when they crossed the Indian Ocean. In the mid-nineteenth century, rejecting the Aga Khan and claiming that the imam was still in concealment, the Ithnasheris split from the Ismailis, and the resulting bitter conflict was a principal reason for their migration to East Africa. The Ithnasheris went initially to Zanzibar and then to the coastal towns in southern Tanganyika where most of them remained through the colonial period. As the Ismailis spread into the interior, achieving a virtual monopoly of business in the Tanganyika highlands, the Ithnasheris became predominant along the southern coast. By 1960 they numbered about 12,000 in Tanganyika, 3,000 on Zanzibar and Pemba, 3,000 in Uganda, and 2,500 in Kenya, nearly 21,000 in all. In 1972 they were estimated at 30,000.[42]

Though sharing with the Ismailis a common cultural background, the Ithnasheris developed differently in East Africa. They were not so tightly organized nor so intent on westernization, education, and communal assistance. A large proportion dropped Kutchi as the language in the home and adopted Swahili. They mingled more freely with Africans and sought earnestly to convert them. Like the Ismailis, however, the Ithnasheris were very successful in business. They specialized in the ivory trade, cotton ginning, coffee buying, sisal production, and other basic industries, and many became wealthy. Jaffer Samji was recognized, at least by his own community, as the 'uncrowned King of Kilwa', Nasser Virjee as the 'King of business in Tanganyika', and Abdulla Fazal as the 'King of Coffee'.[43]

The Daudi Bohras (Bohoras), the third Shia people in East Africa, traced their origin to a much more remote split with the Ismailis but also regarded their imam as living in concealment. Pending his revelation, they entrusted supervision of the sect to a *Dai al mutlaq* who from a headquarters in Surat exercised many of the powers of an imam but unlike the Aga Khan held office by election and lacked a vital ownership of communal property. The Dai differed from the Aga Khan by opposing a rapid modernization, and the Bohras became renowned for their conservatism. They were cautioned by the Dai to avoid higher education and the professions. The focus was on the family directed by the father, and the women clung to saris and remained in the home.[44]

Like the Ismailis and Ithnasheris, the Bohras were attracted to East Africa by economic opportunity. From Kutch and some areas of the Gujarat they followed the usual pattern of migration to Zanzibar and the coastal towns. Residing mainly on Zanzibar and the Kenya coast from Mombasa to Lamu, they numbered about 20,000 in East Africa at the time of independence. The Bohras remained almost exclusively businessmen and became a wealthy community. Most continued in the family traditions as tinsmiths, locksmiths, or dealers in hardware, furniture, and cutlery. 'A Bohra', as a prominent Dar es Salaam businessman noted, 'is a born hardware merchant. It's in the blood'.[45] Two of the most outstanding trading families in East Africa were the Jeevanjees and Karimjees of the early colonial years, and at the time of independence a descendant of one of these Bohra families, Abdulkarim Y.A. Karimjee, was the foremost leader of the Asian community in Tanganyika. At the lower levels of business on the coast, where petty traders and craftsmen were in daily competition with Africans and Arabs, there tended to be a free association between communities. Unlike other Shias, some Bohras took African or Arab wives.[46]

In addition to the three Shia groups—the Ismailis, Ithnasheris, and Bohras—there were Muslims of Sunni and other beliefs mostly from the Punjab. The most influential of the Punjabi Muslims were the Ahmadiyas, followers of Mirza Ghulam Ahmad, who in 1890 had declared himself the Mahdi. From Quadian, a village in the Punjab, Mirza and his successors, the 'caliphs', had directed a missionary movement that quickly spread beyond India. Those who came to East Africa left a peasant background and became traders and artisans with a concentration in Nairobi. In 1924 the Ahmadiyas of East Africa began a campaign to convert Africans. They translated the Koran into Kiswahili, Luganda, Kikuyu, and other languages and built mosques, schools, and colleges. They moved into remote settlements and shared hardship with prospective converts. More than any other Asian Muslims, they lived in equality with Africans and readily accepted them into their organization and society. Not surprisingly, the only woman member of Parliament in Tanganyika, Sophia Mustafa, was an Ahmadiya.[47]

Among the Sunni Asians were several other communities that contributed to the economic growth of East Africa despite their relatively small populations. The Memons (Memans), originally from Sind, had migrated into Kutch and the Gujarat to escape religious persecution, but they came to East Africa primarily as textile dealers seeking an expanded trade. They were among the first Asians on Zanzibar, and from there they moved to the Tanganyika coast to sell *merecani* (American cottons). Exhibiting a common Sunni conservatism, they built their own schools and mosques, rarely married beyond the extended family, and were in effect a closed community. The Bhadias, reputedly the oldest immigrants of the coast, were seafarers who helped develop the coastal dhow trade. Khumbars, farmers from Kutch, established profitable little dairies around Mombasa and other coastal towns. Koknis carried on their traditional vocations as skilled mechanics, engineers, and captains or mates of coastal vessels. Baluchis, once the sultan's guards, turned to trade and, intermarrying with Arabs, gradually lost their separate identity. Another Sunni community, the Bhadalas, were exceptional in retaining their Indian status as labourers.[48]

Next to the Muslims the most numerous and perhaps most influential, certainly the most conspicuous, Asians in East Africa were the Sikhs. Emerging in the fifteenth century as a separate religious community, the Sikhs were followers of Nanak, who defined their religious principles and urged them to resist with force any oppression from the Great Mogul. They were thus a martial people—every man was to carry a sword—and in the nineteenth century they forged an independent dominion in the Punjab. The 'golden temple', which they erected in the middle of a lake in Amritsar, became their sanctuary, and the *Granth Sahib* (master book), their sacred text. Nearly all retained the name Singh (lion). Large of frame, robust, strong, proud, and aggressive, yet beset with poverty in the harsh conditions of their homeland, these independent farmers were logical recruits for work on the Uganda Railway. They were also suited to a career with the army or police.[49]

In East Africa the Sikhs who joined the railway acquired skills as artisans and after indenture, joined by other immigrants, took up construction at first as carpenters, masons, excavators, and iron mongers and later as electricians, plumbers, auto mechanics, building contractors, and merchants selling the tools and materials of their crafts. Their only noteworthy experiment with agriculture was in Kibos, near Kisumu, where beginning in 1903 the government settled and nurtured a small colony of Sikh farmers to raise sugar cane. Though concentrated in Kenya, the Sikhs spread into Tanganyika and Uganda to fill the void between the Hindu and Muslim merchants and the African unskilled labourers. Their disregard of caste and willingness to work side by side with Africans were strong levelling influences. Although the men clung to their traditional beards and turbans through most of the colonial period and the women to their long braids, chemises, pantaloons, and *dupitas* (long scarves), the Sikhs adapted more readily than most Asians to the new way of life. Among them were Makhan Singh, East Africa's foremost trade unionist, Indra Singh Gill, a leading industrialist, Chanan Singh, Kenya high court judge and scholar, J. S. Mangat, the Asian community's chief historian, and Joginder Singh, the East African Safari driver.[50]

Like the Sikhs, the Christian Asians were more influential than their numbers indicate. Although a few Protestant Asians came from various areas of western India, the great majority of the Christian immigrants were Roman Catholics from Portuguese Goa. In Kenya where they were concentrated, the Goans in 1962 comprised 97 per cent of the Christian Asians. Of Hindu antecedent in the Konkani-speaking area of western India, they had embraced Roman Catholicism, adopted many aspects of western culture, and learned to speak and write Portuguese and some English for employment in the Portuguese colonial system. Comparatively well educated but suffering from lack of opportunity as the Portuguese Empire declined, they were attracted to the British East Africa Protectorate for clerical service in the rapidly expanding government, especially the railway. Goans of varied training, however, even professionals, arrived in considerable number from Mozambique as well as Goa during the initial years of British rule.[51]

Though adhering to many traditions, the Goans were a progressive, outgoing people within the Asian community. Far more than Hindus and Muslims, they adopted a western lifestyle and intermarried with Europeans. Their social and political organizations were models of their British counterparts. As competition developed with other Asians, the Goans did not remain prominent as merchants, but they became outstanding in government service and in education, law, medicine, and politics. Dr. Rozendo Ayres Ribeiro, the Nairobi doctor; John Maximian Nazareth, Q.C., legislative councillor and president of the East Africa Indian National Congress; Pio Gama Pinto, trade unionist, journalist, and champion of African nationalism; and Fitzval R.S. de Souza, lawyer, journalist, founder of the Kenya Freedom Party, and speaker of the house—all deserve prominence in East African history.

Quite distinct from Christian, Muslim, and Hindu, the Visa Oshwal immigrants, commonly known as the Shahs, form another vital Asian community. The Shahs are a small segment of the world's Jains, a people dedicated to nonviolence whose antecedents in India are at least as old as the Buddhists'. Their religion was critical of landed wealth but condoned monetary accumulation, and it thus appealed to the commercial classes. The Shahs who came to East Africa differed from most Jains in that they were relatively poor, illiterate farmers. Clustered in fifty-two small villages around Jamnagar where the suffering from drought and famine compounded by overpopulation was most severe, they tilled small plots of land. To send a son to East Africa required a considerable sacrifice from the typical Shah family, which had to save, borrow, and pool resources to pay the cost of the voyage. The first two to leave, Hirji Kara Shah and Popat Vershi Shah, reached Mombasa in 1899 and encouraged others to follow. The word spread from village to village, and a mass movement to the East Africa Protectorate began. 'Within thirty to forty years', as one remarked, 'we emptied our part of Jamnagar'.[52] Their focus of settlement was Nairobi, which by 1972 had 7,430 Shahs out of a total in East Africa of about 15,000, nearly all of whom were in Kenya.[53]

The Shahs' progress in the new environment was remarkable. Conforming to the usual Asian pattern of shopkeeping and regarded in the early years as banyas, they became to Kenya, it is often said, what the Patels were to Uganda. They dealt mainly in textiles, but also in hardware, crockery, and a variety of other goods—in nearly everything except provisions, which normally included meat, fish, and liquor—the particular items that conflicted with their Jain ideals of nonviolence and temperance. The Shahs also avoided the tourist industry with its emphasis on hunting safaris. Like most Asians, they worked hard, saved, and invested. Although retaining close communal ties and preserving their religion, the Shahs emphasized modernization, organized for mutual service, and stressed education and professional attainment for women as well as men. After independence they perhaps surpassed the Ismailis as the best-educated Asian community. Some among them, notably Lakhamshi R. Shah, Meghji Pethraj Shah, and the Chandarias, expanded into manufacturing after successful commercial careers and, like the Mehtas and Madhvanis, contributed significantly to East Africa's industrial development.[54]

Though far less numerous than the Shahs and the other major communities, the Parsees became important to the economic and social life of East Africa. Driven from Persia where in the sixth century they had embraced the teachings of the prophet Zoroaster, the Parsees had settled in Bombay and other centres of western India. As highly successful traders and bankers, they had gained a recognition as 'the Jews of India'. In the East African environment they became involved in many activities including clerical and artisan work, engineering, and contracting. It was a Parsee who built the first customs house in Mombasa. At the end of the colonial period the Parsees numbered about 500 in Kenya and somewhat fewer in Tanganyika and Uganda. They were regarded, however, as an enlightened and progressive community that accorded women the same education, status, and freedom as that of men. More than any other Asians they were accepted socially by Europeans.[55]

The Asians' religious orientation and communal separateness, which determined many of their attitudes and much of their behaviour, were not appreciated by members of the other racial communities. To the tourist, who gained only a superficial impression, but also to the African and Arab and to the local European, whether settler, official, or missionary with long residence in East Africa—all conscious of their own separate identity—the Asians have appeared as an entity. The British administrators at first distinguished between Goans and Asiatics and later between Goans, on the one hand, and on the other, Hindus (including Jains), Muslims, and Sikhs, all of whom received a new designation as Indians. After the separation of India and Pakistan, these peoples in their entirety, including the Goans, were termed Asians. Throughout the colonial period, however, the East African governments adhered to a political, economic, and social system of segregation in which all the Asians were treated as a single unit. The new African administrations, though abolishing the racial segregation, applied new discriminatory measures that were also directed at the Asians as a whole.

The Asians' religious and communal orientation was an essential determinant of their way of life in East Africa. It explains why the Asians have been among the world's leading philanthropists. The welfare of the community was as important as that of the individual, and it was not only the earning of wealth but the sharing of wealth that was valued. The

Asians' religious and communal organization also indicates, at least partially, why they refrained from intermarrying with Europeans and Africans, why they were reluctant to admit individuals of other races to their economic and social institutions, and why they so assiduously sought to preserve their separate traditions.

This observation does not mean that the Asians on the whole lacked a colour prejudice. South Asia, inhabited originally by Dravidian peoples characterized by dark skins, black hair, and brown eyes, had been invaded by waves of Aryans. These fair-complexioned peoples, pressing through the Himalayas, successively conquered and dominated preceding invaders who had begun to merge with the Dravidians. One result through centuries of evolution was a geographic gradation of colour ranging north to south from light to dark. Another was a social stratification, exemplified primarily by the caste system, in which higher status was characterized by lighter skin. All the Asian immigrants to East Africa—Muslim, Sikh, Jain, and Christian, as well as Hindu—carried with them this traditional concept that fair skin denoted superiority. This tradition in the African setting presumably combined with the other factors to promote exclusiveness, and it may explain why many Africans, apparently justifiably, have accused Asians of exhibiting a prejudice.

The Asians' communal organization combined with their traditional struggle for economic security to determine their attitudes towards government. For centuries in India they had struggled to preserve their property and conduct business against usurping officials representative of the Mogul emperor and succeeding local rajas and sultans. The substitution of the British raj for that of a local Hindu or Muslim prince brought no appreciable change, as a comprehensive system of taxation in the form of currency was substituted for the annual tribute in kind. The Asians left India imbued with the concept that the best government is that which governs least. In East Africa they became on the whole even more communally oriented and more communally self-sufficient than they had been in India. In the comparative absence of government that prevailed in the early years of the colonial administrations, the Asians were forced to provide their own schools, clinics, hospitals, and libraries, as well as their own institutions for credit, insurance, sports, recreation, and welfare. They were moved further in this direction by the racial segregation that soon permeated colonial society. The Asians felt slight need for any service from a colonial government except protection, and they tended to regard every law and regulation that impeded their opportunities for economic and social gain in the new environment as not only unnecessary and oppressive but virtually immoral. To evade such laws and regulations imposed by a foreign government that accorded them an unfair representation was almost a virtue.

It seems clear in retrospect that the pattern of Asian settlement in East Africa was not appreciably different from any of the great migrations from Europe and Asia. These people left a hard and impoverished life in a familiar environment to seek a more rewarding future in an unknown land. They did not come consciously to exploit nor were they willing or unwitting participants in any British imperial design. It is true that the indentured servants and some others were recruited by agents of the British government and that Indian soldiers were employed by the British to establish their control over much of East Africa and to win additional territory from the Germans. These immigrants were exceptions, however, to the general trend. Most of the Asians were free immigrants who came with no prompting from the British. As other studies have shown, the former indentured Asians were permitted to settle in the East Africa and Uganda Protectorates only because the government of India and the India Office, mindful of Indian welfare, insisted on it as part of the agreement for recruitment. Later when the swelling Asian population drew protest from the European settlers, the doors of immigration were kept open to Asians only because of pressure from Delhi and the India Office. On the whole the Asians were wanted in East Africa neither by the British officials, settlers, traders, and missionaries there nor by the Colonial Office in the metropolis.[56]

It is also evident that most Asians concentrated on business in East Africa not because of a business background in India—nor because business was 'in their blood'—but because of the unique potential for enterprise in East Africa. The great majority of the immigrants were peasant farmers who for generations had struggled for survival and prosperity with no marked success in a harsh environment. In East Africa where the European settlers were engaged in the establishment of large agricultural estates and had laid claim to the most suitable land and where European commercial interests were devoted to large-scale development, the Asians were able to serve the interests of all the major communities by turning to the neglected areas of petty trade and artisanry. For those with some formal education and knowledge of English, the lower ranks of the rapidly expanding government service also offered an opportunity. Entrance into these new occupations of commerce, artisanry, and clerical work required no capital investment. For all the Asian immigrants in the early years it was easy to find employment either with the government or the relatives and village acquaintances who had preceded them. Only after this pattern of settlement was firmly established did the Asians turn seriously to road transport, agriculture, industry, and the professions.

Notes

1. Yash Tandon, 'Pragmatic Industrialist', chap. 5, *Jayant Madhvani*, ed. Robert Becker and Nitin Jayant Madhvani (London: W. and J. Mackay, 1973), p. 11.

2. K. P. Chandaria, interviewed by Gregory, 9 May 1973, Addis Ababa.

3. Robert G. Gregory, *India and East Africa: A History of Race Relations Within the British Empire, 1890–1939* (Oxford: Clarendon, 1971), p. 45.

4. Ibid., pp. 118–20, 146ff.

5. Ibid., p. 61.

6. Robert R. Kuczynski, *Demographic Survey of the British Colonial Empire*, vol. 2 (London: Oxford University Press), pp. 653–54.

7. Agehananda Bharati, *Asians in East Africa: Jaihind and Uhuru* (Chicago: Nelson-Hall, 1972), pp. 19–20.

8. Kenya, *Sessional Paper no. 4 of 1959–60* (Nairobi: Government Printer, 1960), p. 5. *Kenya Population Census, 1962:* vol. 4, *Non-African Population* (Nairobi: Government Printer, 1966), pp. 31, 54, 60, 68.

9. J. R. Sondhi, interviewed by Gregory, 3 Mar. 1973, Mombasa.

10. S. S. Keshavji, interviewed by Gregory, 22 July 1973, Jamnagar.

11. G. D. Shah (son), interviewed by Gregory, 12 July 1973, Jamnagar. Dhiru P. Shah (nephew), interviewed by Gregory, 10 Mar. 1973, Nairobi.

12. A. J. Pandya (J. B.'s son), interviewed by Gregory, 2 Dec. 1972, 27 Feb. 1973, 1, 4 Mar. 1973, Mombasa; 17 Nov., 16 Dec. 1972, Nairobi.

13. Dr. S. D. Karve, interviewed by Gregory, 26 Feb. 1973, Mombasa. D. S. Trivedi, interviewed by Gregory, 27 Feb. 1973, Mombasa. J. R. Sondhi (brother) interview. G. Bagchi, interviewed by Gregory, 22 July 1973, New Delhi.

14. M. B. Acharya (son), interviewed by Gregory, 5 July 1973, Baroda. F. A. de Souza, interviewed by Gregory, 28 June 1973, Porvorim, Goa. K. L. Vohora, interviewed by Martha Honey, 23 Dec. 1973, Arusha.

15. A. R. Kassim Lakha, interviewed by Charles Bennett, 9 May 1973, Mombasa. M. J. Thakkar, interviewed by Gregory, 29 May 1973, Addis Ababa. H. S. Figueiredo (grandson), interviewed by Gregory, 27 June 1973, Saligao, Bardez Goa. R. M. Patel, interviewed by Gregory, 6 July 1973, Baroda. H. P. Joshi, interviewed by Gregory, 6 July 1973, Baroda.

16. Saurashtra and Kathiawar are names for the peninsula. The Gujarat, a name often loosely applied to the whole of the peninsula, properly includes as a geographical term only the northeast part of the peninsula and extends inland. It is the flat land north of the Narbada River. Politically, Gujarat is now a state including Kutch, the peninsula, some of the coast to the south, and considerable inland territory. S. Chandrasekhar, *India's Population: Facts, Problems and Policy* (Meerut: Meenakshi Prakashan, 1967), p. 16. Even in the more favourable circumstances some of these areas could not grow wheat and rice. F. Kapadia, interviewed by Gregory, 23 July 1973, New Delhi.

17. Adventure was the main motive of C. K. Patel, interviewed by Honey, 10 Sept. 1973, Dar es Salaam; and D. S. Dass, interviewed by Seidenberg, 5 May 1973, Nairobi.

18. J. M. Desai, interviewed by Gregory, 31 Jan. 1973, Nairobi. L. R. Shah, interviewed by Gregory, 27 Nov. 1972, 8, 9 Mar. 1973, Nairobi; 30 June 1973, Bombay; 9

July 1973, Ahmedabad. 'The Late Keshivji Jethabhai Chande', essay submitted by Jayantilal Keshavji Chande (son) during interview by Honey, 7 Aug. 1973, Dar es Salaam. Nuriddin Hassanali Putwa (great grandson), interviewed by Honey, 8 Feb. 1974, Dar es Salaam. Abdulla Rahimtulla Waljee Hirjee (grandson), interviewed by Bennett, 18 Apr. 1973, Nairobi. V. S. Patel, interviewed by Honey, 8 Jan. 1974, Dar es Salaam. S. D. Kothari, interviewed by Gregory, 10 July 1973, Rajkot.

19. R. G. Manji, interviewed by Gregory, 6 Feb. 1973, Nairobi.

20. Quoted, Zafrud-Deen, interviewed by Gregory, 6 Jan. 1973, Nairobi.

21. R. T. Thakore, interviewed by Gregory, 7 Feb. 1973, Nairobi.

22. Badrudeen Rajabali Sukman (Jimmy), Suleiman's great grandson, interviewed by Seidenberg, 10 Apr. 1973, Nairobi. Haroon Ahmed (Haji Abu's grandson), interviewed by Seidenberg, 3, 4, 5 July 1973, Nairobi. J. D. Byramjee (Dinshaw's son), interviewed by Gregory, 24 Jan. 1973, Nairobi. Sir Amar N. Maini (son), interviewed by Gregory, 22 Nov. 1984, London. Pushkar U. Oza (son), interviewed by Gregory, 2 July 1973, Bombay. Bhailal Patel, interviewed by Bennett, 2 May 1973, Nairobi. Dr. S. B. Singh, interviewed by Gregory, 26 Jan. 1973, Nairobi.

23. A dhow wreck with loss of twenty-four of sixty-four passengers was described in *East African Standard* (Nairobi), 19 Sept. 1908, p. 9. For a detailed account of a voyage by dhow, see Nanji Kalidas Mehta, *Dream Half Expressed: An Autobiography* (Bombay: Vakils, Feffer and Simons, 1966), pp. 34–47. N.M.H. Virjee (grandson), interviewed by Honey, 5 Jan. 1974, Dar es Salaam. Others consulted: Y. Pirbhai, interviewed by Honey, 25 Feb. 1974, Dar es Salaam; D. C. Patel, interviewed by Bennett, 28 Apr. 1973, Nairobi; K. R. Paroo, interviewed by Gregory, 1 Mar. 1973, Mombasa; M. V. Shah, interviewed by Gregory, 11 July 1973, Jamnagar; and V. R. Boal, interviewed by Gregory, 2 July 1973, Bombay.

24. Yusufali Pirbhai (son) interview. G. R. Ladak, interviewed by Honey, 24, 18 Jan. 1974, Dar es Salaam. Abdulla Fazal (brother), interviewed by Honey, 22 Nov. 1973, Upanga. M. V. Shah interview.

25. G. P. Mehta, interviewed by Gregory, 10 July 1973, Rajkot.

26. L. R. Shah interview.

27. K. P. Shah, interviewed by Gregory, 7 Feb. 1973, Nairobi.

28. Peter Marris and Anthony Somerset, *African Businessmen: A Study of Entrepreneurship and Development in Kenya* (London: Routledge and Kegan Paul, 1971), p. 244.

29. Charles Bennett, 'Persistence amid Adversity: The Growth and Spatial Distribution of the Asian Population of Kenya, 1903–63', Ph.D. diss., Syracuse University, 1976. Gregory, *India and East Africa*, pp. 7ff.

30. 'Census of British Indian Subjects in Dominions of Sultan of Zanzibar', in Major J. R. MacDonald to Foreign Office, 19 Dec. 1887, F.O. 84/1854. The census did not include Goans and Baluchis and was considered very conservative in its survey.

31. Gregory, *India and East Africa*, p. 80 n. 5; p. 113 n. 4.

32. J. S. Mangat, *History of the Asians in East Africa: c. 1886 to 1945* (Oxford: Clarendon, 1969), p. 142.

33. Jains in East Africa were estimated as approximately 45,000 at independence by Amritlal Raishi, interviewed by Gregory, 25 Jan. 1973, Nairobi. This figure is subtracted from that for Hindu/Jain in Table 1.6.

34. Bharati, *Asians in East Africa*, pp. 34, 44–49. Donald Rothchild, *Racial Bargaining in Independent Kenya* (New York: Oxford University Press, 1973), p. 43. In a strict sense, Patidars came from Charotar in the Gujarat, Kadva Patels from Saurashtra, and Kutchi Patels from Kutch. Hansa Pandya, interviewed by Gregory, 7 July 1977, Syracuse, N.Y.

35. Zarina Patel, interviewed by Gregory, 22 Jan. 1973, Nairobi. Surendra Mehta and G. M. Wilson, 'Asian Communities of Mombasa', chap. 6 in typescript, 'Mombasa Social Survey, Part 1', ed. Gordon Wilson (no publishing information), pp. 180–81, Syracuse University microfilm 2081, reel 12.

36. Bharati, *Asians in East Africa*, pp. 53, 57, 59. R. B. Kara, interviewed by Gregory, 23 Feb. 1973, Tanga. L. R. Shah interview.

37. Bharati, *Asians in East Africa*, p. 42. A. J. Pandya interview.

38. 'Census of British Indian subjects . . . Zanzibar'.

39. H. S. Morris, *Indians in Uganda* (Chicago: University of Chicago Press, 1968), p. 183.

40. F. Kurji, interviewed by Honey, 28 Feb. 1974, Dar es Salaam. At the University of Nairobi in 1970–71 Kurji, an Ismaili, researched the geographical distribution of Ismailis in Kenya. Vazier Jimmy Verjee, 'Ismailism and the Challenge of the Seventies', address to Vancouver Jamat, 11 Dec. 1972, nineteen-page typescript, presented to Seidenberg during interview, 10 Apr. 1973. Kassamali Rajabali Paroo, 'Ismailia Settlement in East Africa', six-page typescript presented to Gregory during interview, 1 Mar. 1973. Mehta and Wilson, 'Asian Communities of Mombasa', pp. 160–61. The most detailed study of the Ismailis in East Africa is Shirin Remtulla Walji, 'Ismailis on Mainland Tanzania, 1850–1948', Ph.D. diss., University of Wisconsin, 1969. For a penetrating study of the Aga Khan, see H. Stephen Morris, 'Divine Kingship of the Aga Khan', *Southwestern Journal of Anthropology*, 14/4 (1958), 454–72.

41. Morris, *Indians in Uganda*, pp. 80–81.

42. S.S.A. Rizvi, interviewed by Honey, 18 Feb. 1974, Dar es Salaam. A. Fazal interview. Morris, *Indians in Uganda*, pp. 68–75 passim. Emigration to escape religious persecution and physical harm was stressed by Y. Sheriff, interviewed by Honey, 4 Jan. 1974, Malindi.

43. S. Abdulrasul, interviewed by Honey, 19 Oct. 1973, Dar es Salaam. S.S.A. Rizvi interview, 18 Feb. 1974. Ali Mohamedjaffer, interviewed by Honey, 22 Oct. 1973, Arusha.

44. R. G. Datoo knew several instances of Bohra-African intermarriage in Mombasa: interviewed by Gregory, 22 Nov. 1972, Nairobi. Pirbhai interview. Bharati, *Asians in East Africa*, pp. 85–87. L. W. Hollingsworth, *Asians of East Africa* (London: Macmillan, 1960), pp. 144–48. Morris, *Indians in Uganda*, pp. 66, 77, 87–88.

45. Pirbhai interview. Major F. B. Pearce, *Zanzibar: The Island Metropolis of Eastern Africa* (New York: Dutton, 1920), pp. 255–56.

46. Mehta and Wilson, 'Asian Communities of Mombasa', p. 163. Morris, *Indians in Uganda*, pp. 87, 184–85.

47. Morris, *Indians in Uganda*, pp. 87–88. Hazrat Mirza Bashir-ud-Din Mahmud Ahmad, *Admadiya Movement* (Rabwah, W. Pakistan: Ahmadiya Muslim Foreign Missions, 1967). Sophia Mustafa wrote one of the few Asian

autobiographies, *Tanganyika Way: A Personal Story of Tanganyika's Growth to Independence* (London: Oxford University Press, 1962).

48. Mehta and Wilson, 'Asian Communities of Mombasa', p. 166–67, 187–88. Zahid H. Adamjee, 'History and Life of the Memon People', research paper, History Department, Syracuse University, May 1974, based largely on Hashim Zakariya, *Memon kom ni itehas* (Karachi: Arafat Printing Press, 1971). H. Pandya interview.

49. Mehta and Wilson, 'Asian Communities of Mombasa', pp. 175–77. Rothchild, *Racial Bargaining*, p. 131.

50. Gregory, *India and East Africa*, pp. 69–70. There was also a small settlement of Jats, a subcaste who, as relatives of Indra Singh Gill, were placed by him on farms near Eldoret to grow wheat. Bharati, *Asians in East Africa*, pp. 101–2.

51. Rothchild, *Racial Bargaining*, p. 46. Dr. A. Ribeiro, interviewed by Gregory, 12 Nov. 1972, Nairobi.

52. A. Raishi and L. R. Shah interviews. Gulabchand Bhalibhai Shah, 'History of the Birth of the Oshwal Society', three-page typescript presented to Gregory by G. D. Shah during interview. Mehta and Wilson, 'Asian Communities of Mombasa', pp. 178–79.

53. L. R. Shah interview.

54. Ibid. K. P. Shah interview.

55. Mehta and Wilson, 'Asian Communities of Mombasa', pp. 187–88.

56. See especially the sections on immigration in Gregory, *India and East Africa*, and Mangat, *History of the Asians*.

PART ONE

The Primary Occupations

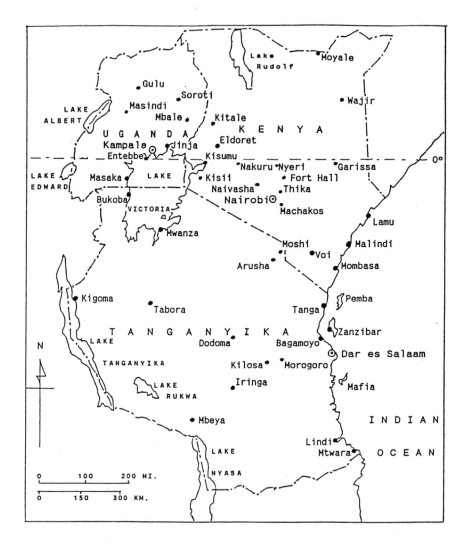

MAP 2: BRITISH EAST AFRICA, 1960

Main Commercial Centres

Source: reprinted from Robert G. Gregory, *The Rise and Fall of
Philanthropy in East Africa* (New Brunswick, N.J.: Transaction,
1992) with permission of the publisher.

CHAPTER TWO

— ■ —

Commerce

When East Africa becomes a real Indian colony, Indian commerce and enterprise will have outlet for a great trans-African development, with the Congo, Egypt, North and West Africa, and the South. The East Coast will be for India a shop window open to the West.

—The Aga Khan, 1918[1]

Indeed, the remarkable tenacity and courage of the Indian trader has been mainly responsible for stimulating the wants of the indigenous peoples, even in the remotest areas, by opening to them a shop-window on the modern world.

—East Africa Royal Commission, 1955[2]

Commerce—consisting of importing manufactured products, wholesaling, retailing, purchase of produce, and exporting—remained through nearly all the years of their residence in East Africa the Asians' primary vocation. To them it was far more important than any other occupation, and it dominated their lives and their interests. The pattern was established, as explained in Chapter 1, in the initial years of settlement. Later when many of the second- and third-generation immigrants qualified in the professions, commerce still held a peculiar fascination. Most of the doctors, advocates, engineers, architects, and other professionals invested their income in some form of commercial enterprise. Many sought early retirement to devote the remainder of their lives to running an established family business or beginning a new venture. In all the Asian schools, in 1960 as in 1910, 'accounts' was the foundation of the curriculum and by far the most popular subject of study. To further their commercial interests, the Asians formed numerous economic and political organizations, and they campaigned strenuously to oppose the restrictions on their commercial activity imposed by the colonial and post-colonial governments. Because it was the foundation of their very

43

existence, commerce forms the central thread of Asian history in East Africa, and its eventual demise clearly marks the end of the Asian era.

Initial Asian Enterprise and the Trade with India

How the trade between India and East Africa began is, in the absence of historical records, still a matter of speculation. Perhaps as far back as the time of Mohenjo Daro and Harappa in the second and first millennia B.C. South Asian seaborne traders had contact through the monsoon winds with the coast from the Horn to approximately the Zambezi River where the winds abated. It is known that a trade existed between these two centres and ancient Babylon in Mesopotamia. If not then, the Asians became involved in a direct trade with East Africa later through contact with the Persians and the Arabs. By the end of the first century A.D., when the *Periplus of the Erythraean Sea* was written, they had an extensive trade with the Zanzibar islands and the opposite Mrima coast, named by the Greeks Azania, and with the principal town, Rhapta, which was probably the later Kilwa Kivinje. They were well established along the coast in 1498 when Vasco da Gama anchored at Malindi and employed an Asian navigator to guide him to India. After 1840 when the Omani Sultan Seyyid Said moved his court to Zanzibar, the Asian activity greatly increased and began to receive detailed description in written records.[3]

On Zanzibar, where they dominated the trade, the Asians were valued by the sultan and appointed to important administrative posts in the government. In 1835, five years before Said's move to Zanzibar, one of the leading Zanzibar merchants, the Hindu Bhatia, Jairam Sewji (Jeram Shivji), was honoured with three offices: collector of customs for the sultan's realm, chief officer of the Port of Zanzibar, and the state banker. The position of collector was farmed to the highest bidder and entailed a complete monopoly of the customs. In organizing the collection of duties associated with the dhow trade, Sewji put other Zanzibar traders in charge of customs at each of the mainland ports from Kilwa to Mogadishu. His agent at Dar es Salaam, Ramji Pragji, another Bhatia, was to become the counsellor and confidant of Said's successor, Sultan Majid, in all imperial matters relating to the mainland. As state banker, Sewji lent large sums of money. He provided financial support for state projects and those of the large, established trading firms, whether European, Arab, or Asian, and he generously assisted the new arrivals from South Asia, many of whom were destitute. In his various capacities, Sewji was regarded as the second most important man in the Omani realm. Except for one brief interval, he and his family were to control the customs and finance of Zanzibar until 1886.[4]

Sewji's position was temporarily occupied during the reign of Sultan Barghash by Tharia Topan, an Ismaili whose community was second to that of the Bhatias in Zanzibar's commerce. Having left Kutch as a twelve-year-old stowaway (as described in Chapter 1), Topan found work as a menial garden sweeper for Sewji's Zanzibar agent, Ladha Damji. A diligent worker, he attracted the notice of his employer, who gave him a place in the firm. Topan quickly advanced to a position of leadership, accumulated a fortune, and on Damji's initiative became assistant collector of customs. For his assistance to the British at a time critical in their association with Zanzibar, Topan was knighted in 1875 and was the first Asian to receive this coveted honour. It was then that he was advanced to the position of collector, or chief of customs, a post he was to hold for the next five years. Sir Tharia's progress from stowaway and sweeper to wealthy trader, then to knighthood, and finally to the sultan's chief administrator and most trusted adviser was for the Asian traders a remarkable accomplishment.[5]

The Asians' importance in the Omani realm was vividly described in 1876 by the sultan's British physician, James Christie:

> The Banyans are the capitalists, and the merchant princes of Zanzibar, and in many respects they are the real ruling power. They farm the customs and draw all the duties levied, paying to the Seyyid a certain sum, annually, according to the contract. They have agents at all the ports of the Zanzibar territories where duties are levied, and, being extensive merchants as well as the capitalists and bankers of the place, they are connected directly with the principal mercantile transactions thereof. Directly, and indirectly, they hold almost unlimited sway over the commerce of the place.[6]

In addition to investing their profits in clove plantations and lending large sums of money to the Arab clove growers and the sultan, the Zanzibar merchants financed most of the caravan trade into the East African interior. The Asians did not initiate this trade in which ivory succeeded slaves as the dominant commodity. Some Africans of the interior, especially the Yao and Nyamwezi to the south and the Mijikenda and Kamba to the north, had developed a long-distance trade with the coast before the Asians became prominent.[7] Nor did the Asians frequently accompany the caravans, which were led mostly by Arabs and Swahili. Very few settled in Tabora and other inland trading centres before the establishment of the European protectorates. During the nineteenth century, however, the Asians apparently provided most of the initiative and stimulus for the very profitable caravan trade with the interior.[8]

At the turn of the century when the new European governments were constructing railways and roads, the Asians began an extensive settlement of the interior. Then, as explained in Chapter 1, they erected their makeshift *dukas* (shops) of corrugated iron at the successive railway stops and from the bazaars that so developed soon spread to the European farming areas, the new government outposts, and, often beyond the area of official authority and protection, to the remote African markets. As an elderly Dorobo later recalled, 'First came Indians, then came Europeans'.[9] In some places the traders were preceded by the government officers who set up stations not only to administer but also to engage in retail trade by offering a variety of imported merchandise for sale to Africans. Later when the Asians opened their dukas, the government closed down its stores.[10]

The lifestyle of the typical Asian trader in these early years was austere. The bazaars that became a prominent feature of the new towns were often situated on swampy ground whereas the higher, better-drained areas were reserved for government offices and European commercial buildings. The bazaars were composed of row on row of shops separated from one another by only a few feet of earth to permit the construction of an open sewer. The adjacent plots, typically 5,000 square feet, were leased from the government for a period usually of twenty-five years, sometimes as long as ninety-nine, at an annual cost of Rs 10–50 (Shs 11–38).[11] When savings permitted, the shopkeepers sent for wives whom they had left abroad or, returning to India briefly for marriage, brought their brides to Africa. For most, a small room hastily constructed at the back of the shop, covered with an iron roof that radiated a sweltering heat under the midday sun, became the new home, and it was in such conditions that the initial Asian trader raised his family. The shopkeeper, his wife, and eventually their children—often aided for a time by new arrivals from the extended family or village friends in India—worked together to build the business.

For the Asians life in the towns was hazardous as well as uncomfortable. The dense population, poor drainage, open sewers, garbage, and inadequate storage of food supplies in the bazaars created an environment attractive to rats, with the result that bubonic plague, which at the time was endemic in Bombay, spread to East Africa. Twice, in 1899 and 1902, the Nairobi bazaar was burnt to the ground by the colonial government, and the displaced Asian families were housed temporarily in tents at the racecourse and protected from looters by a guard of the Uganda Rifles. Fresh outbreaks recurred in the new Nairobi bazaar in 1905, 1906, 1911, 1912, and 1913, and subsequently plague caused temporary abandonment of bazaars in other centres. Not until the 1930s was the problem finally brought under control by regulations governing sanitation. Although the mortality was never high—no more than nineteen in the Nairobi case of 1902—there was always the fear for the shopkeeper that a severe epidemic killing thousands could ensue.[12]

The Asians who left the rail line to move into the remote interior faced even greater hardship. With their trade goods and few personal belongings packed on donkeys or sometimes only on the heads of porters, these daring Asians followed footpaths into unknown areas well before the construction of roads. During the long journeys, lured by dreams of profit and apparently revelling in the adventure, they risked encounters with lions attracted by their donkeys and occasionally with peoples who sought to take their goods by force.[13] Upon reaching their destinations, the Asians had to negotiate—without the benefit of a common language—with chiefs, headmen, or elders for permission to barter. Initially almost all these traders were itinerant, in that they returned to the towns after conducting their exchange. In time a large number settled in the African areas and were accompanied eventually by their wives and children. Then it was often a partner or employee who made the regular trips to and from the towns. For most of these rural traders a hut of wooden poles interwoven with wattle bark, plastered with mud, and roofed with thatch served as the first combined shop and home. If a family took up residence, the hut was soon succeeded by a more permanent building with living quarters. Once the government established a station in the area, dirt roads replaced the paths, and bullock carts, bicycles, and eventually automobiles, lorries, and motor cycles succeeded the donkeys and porters.

For those who moved into the settler areas the establishment of business was much less arduous. There was more security, the railway and towns were nearby, building materials were readily available, and roads to and from the farms alleviated the transportation problem. At least some of the trade could be transacted in English, a language known to most of those who chose such location, and there was the Indian rupee, East Africa's official coinage until 1920, to serve as a medium of exchange.

The items of trade varied considerably depending upon each area's potential customers. In the towns the general store—stocking a wide assortment of imported provisions, clothing, and hardware—was common, and the items varied depending on whether the service was designed primarily for the European, Asian, or as it soon developed, the African community. Although some continued with a general store through successive generations even in the cities and larger towns, most Asians in urban centres soon concentrated on one type of merchandise. Some sold fresh produce obtained from local farmers. Those Asians in the rural settler areas also set up general stores with two types of merchandise, one for local settlers and the other for African labourers. As in the urban areas, goods were sold for rupees to both peoples, but some of the rural Asians became involved in the marketing of settler agricultural products. Goods were usually sold on credit to the settlers, a minimum of currency was exchanged, and the accounts were rarely balanced.

In the African areas the items and form of trade were considerably different. The general store was universal, and it was stocked mainly with blankets and merekani cloth; beads and bangles; pots, pans, and other cooking utensils; wire, rope, and twine; hoes and *pangas* (two-foot, heavy knives used mainly as agricultural tools); umbrellas, looking glasses, cooking oil, sweets, salt, pepper, and other spices. With the growth of African demand for more western goods, items such as bicycles, paraffin (kerosene) lamps and cooking stoves, corrugated iron sheeting, hammers, saws, nails, shoes, and ready-made clothing were added. The typical rural shopkeeper soon acquired a sewing machine to cater to the local demand. He exchanged both goods and services for ivory, rhinoceros horn, wild rubber, hides and skins, and the surplus of subsistence crops such as maize, dried lentils, and sesame seed that could endure the long haul to town.[14] If distance and transportation permitted, the trader would also market more perishable produce, such as yams, cassava, plantain, taro root, bananas, and papaw (papaya). In the coastal areas Asians traded for coconuts, dates, and cashews. As Africans turned to the production of cash crops, commodities such as cotton, tobacco, wattle bark, sesame, wheat, and where permitted, coffee were added to the traditional produce. Ghee (clarified butter) also became a valuable new commodity. When Africans acquired coinage, transactions in rupees and later in shillings replaced much of the trade in kind. There was also, as explained in Chapter 3, a considerable exchange based only on credit.

The initial profits were meagre, and the shopkeepers had to pare their expenses to a minimum. They assigned most of the profits to business expansion, a large amount to the children's education and their daughters' dowries, a sizeable sum to charity, and in some instances a portion to needy relatives in India. Not until the second and, more often, the third generations did their own lifestyles begin to reflect their affluence. By then, however, they had obtained a virtual monopoly not only of shopkeeping but also of the import-export trade associated with it. Few European traders, even though they were immigrants mainly from Europe's 'nation of shopkeepers', were willing to accept a comparable way of life in order to compete.

It was not only thrift but industry and a shrewd business practice that determined the Asians' success. The typical shopkeeper rose before dawn to perform his ablutions and prayers, sweep the floors, and lay out his wares for the shop's opening at 7:00 A.M. For seven days a week he remained at his business until dusk and often until 9:00 or 10:00 P.M.[15] Even after closing, during the middle of the night, the shopkeeper would answer a knock on his door to sell an item to someone in need. As a matter of principle, the customer's needs always received priority, and a sale was all important. When a requested item was not in stock, a shopkeeper would delay his customer in conversation or by serving tea until an employee could run next door to purchase the item from a business rival. Whether the item had to be sold at cost or occasionally even below cost was not so important as retaining a satisfied customer. Unlike the European business community, the Asians usually did not set fixed prices. Transactions were conducted by bargaining. A shopkeeper would ask a price as high as he thought his customer would pay. If he failed to sell at that price, he could be bargained down to the barest profit or even below cost on the asssumption that he would make up the necessary difference in subsequent sales. On the whole, the Asians made their money on rapid turnover and a very low margin of profit.

Another factor favourable to Asian enterprise was the minimum of regulation imposed by the colonial governments during the first four decades of settlement. As the historian M.P.K. Sorrenson has observed, 'Economic development was not at this time regarded as the task of government which was merely expected to provide the conditions which would enable private enterprise to flourish'.[16] The traders enjoyed a policy of laissez faire until the mid-1930s.

The Asians' success in retailing resulted eventually in a network of commerce developed through successive stages of expansion. A new arrival in East Africa, often a youth with little education, few skills, no business background, and more often in debt than having savings, would begin work as a menial employee in the store of some distant relative or acquaintance in a principal African town. After a few years, having learned the rudiments of the business and acquired a spoken knowledge of English or Swahili, he would be sent by his employer to open a similar shop in another urban centre or some rural area. The more enterprising young Asian would leave to start a new venture of his own, and he would purchase his merchandise wholesale either from the firm he left or directly from the importers who had supplied it. As his business expanded, he would send for relatives and friends in India to assist in the establishment of subsidiary stores over a large area. Many eventually took the additional step of bypassing the wholesalers and exporters by setting up their own importing, marketing, and exporting facilities. As the expansion proceeded, usually as family enterprises or as partnerships of families within a single religious community, the Asians tried to retain friendly relations with their associates. Their enterprise was based on mutual service.

Because of their close initial ties to their homeland, the Asians relied heavily on India as their source for imports and market for exports.

Trade was often conducted in the early years through family connections as relatives at one end bought and sold for those at the other. With the expansion of business, the Asians in East Africa entered into importing and exporting contracts with established industrialists and wholesalers in the Indian port cities to facilitate their overseas trade. The relationship was enhanced by the fact that India in 1882 had abolished its import duties and entered a period of free trade. As illustrated in Table 2.1, India was initially East Africa's chief trading partner.[17] In the early twentieth century India happened to be the best source of supply for most of the commodities needed in East Africa, with the result that the Asians had a distinct commercial advantage.

East Africa imported from India a wide variety of re-exports and domestic produce. Most of the goods before World War II were re-exports of foreign manufacture—mainly cotton textiles, followed by provisions, metal products, sugar, hardware and cutlery, silk piece goods, mineral oils, paints and pigments, and processed coffee—essentially the same items in 1938 as in 1900. The items of domestic produce from India were initially, in descending order of value, rice, cabinet wares and furniture, wood, jute manufactures, seeds, wheat, fruits and vegetables, and opium. Unlike the re-exports, the domestic produce varied in time because of India's industrialization. By 1938 the main commodities, in order, were jute and hemp bags and sacking, cotton piece goods, wheat and flour, rice, films, spices, dressed leather, dal (split lentils), ghee, onions, artificial silk piece goods, and boots and shoes.[18] East Africa's two principal imports—machinery and petroleum—came not from India but mainly from the United Kingdom and were imported by large European trading firms. Presumably it was the imports from India, the re-exports as well as the domestic products, that were the main items sold by the Asian importers in East Africa before World War II.

Until World War I India was the leading country for East Africa's exports as well as imports, and after the war it was a very close second to the United Kingdom. The commodities exported to India at the turn of the century were chiefly ivory and cloves but also, in order of importance, fruits and vegetables, jewelry and plate, gums and resins, cowries and other shells, provisions, hides and skins, and wood. By 1938 cotton and cloves were predominant, followed by ivory, sodium carbonate, gum arabic, potatoes, sisal, coconuts, goat- and sheepskins, marine shells, dried fruit, and coffee.[19] Except for sodium carbonate, sisal, and coffee, these items were mainly a product of the Asians' trade with Africans and in the case of cloves, with Arabs.

Though still an agricultural country dependent on Britain for most of its manufacturing needs, India during the interwar period was far ahead of East Africa in the development of industry. Before the turn of the cen-

TABLE 2.1 East Africa's Trade by Country (£1,000), 1900-38*

Imports from	1900-1901	1910-01	1920-21	1931	1938
India	679	994	2,313	1,020	658
United Kingdom	249	526	4,136	3,586	4,745
United States	201	121	614	682	1,145
Germany	224	1,134	46	355	903
France	25	24	111	122	96
Italy	11	18	48	108	100
Japan	negl.	negl.	171	841	1,763
South Africa	30	80	302	196	220

Exports to					
India	136	590	1,652	1,712	3,398
United Kingdom	103	561	3,437	1,908	3,505
United States	77	216	278	395	764
Germany	83	1,910	120	174	384
France	125	322	468	190	290
Italy	negl.	4	46	147	54
Japan	negl.	negl.	10	114	329
South Africa	64	47	99	83	277

* In 1921 the end of the fiscal year for all the territories was changed from 31 March to 31 December.

Sources: *Statistical Abstract for the Several British Colonies, Possessions, and Protectorates in Each Year from 1893 to 1907*, Cd. 4415 (London: HMSO, 1908), and succeeding issues; *Germany, Report for the Years 1909-12 on the Trade, Commerce and General Economic Position of German East Africa*; Diplomatic and Consular Reports, Annual Series no. 5171, Cd. 6665-129 (London: HMSO, 1913); and *Statistics on the Zanzibar Protectorate, 1893-1920* (London: HMSO, 1921).

tury it had begun to organize cotton, jute, iron and steel, paper, and tanning and leather industries on modern lines. Early in the twentieth century it made remarkable progress in the manufacture of cotton textiles and began to offer serious competition to Britain in supplying the textile needs of the non-Western world. By 1930 it was consuming nearly all the exports of Uganda's cotton, which was the long-staple variety far superior to India's short staple. India was also advancing in many new industries and was able to provide, for instance, the iron and steel hardware for much of the construction in East Africa. In its export trade India was more diversified than the African territories and not so severely affected by the world economic depression.

Despite these advantages, India was superseded between the wars by the United Kingdom as East Africa's foremost trading partner. The drop in the imports from India after World War I is explained partly by the increasing competition from Japan and partly by alterations of the trading situation within the empire. The Ottawa agreements of 1932–34 brought India into a system of imperial preference. India, however, enacted a tariff act in 1934 that imposed a 30 per cent ad valorem duty on imports from foreign countries and reduced the duties on imports from British dependencies to only 20 per cent. The United Kingdom, which permitted goods from its empire to enter duty free, thus attracted a considerable portion of East Africa's ivory, sisal, and coffee, which had been prime items in the trade with India.[20]

World War II, though detrimental to East Africa's overall trade, provided a brief stimulus to the exchange with India. During the war the four territories lost a valuable trade with Germany, Italy, and Japan. In 1940 and 1941 when the U-boat menace was at its height, the territories were unable to carry on their extensive trade with Britain, and throughout the war their relations with all the European belligerents were curtailed. Kenya's imports, for example, grew from £4.2 million in 1938 to only £8.4 in 1945 and its exports from £3.6 million to only £5.3.[21] In comparison with the growth in the 1920s and 1950s, these increases appear insignificant. India, perhaps mainly because of its proximity, profited from the disruption of East Africa's trade with other parts of the world. Its imports from Kenya and Uganda increased from £422,000 in 1938 to £6.0 million in 1944, and its exports to these countries expanded from £3.0 million in 1938 to highs of £5.1 million in 1944 and £5.8 in 1945. Even in view of the fact that import prices in less developed countries within this period nearly doubled and export prices trebled, the growth in India's trade was significant.[22] It was, however, only temporary.

The partition of India in 1947 had little effect on the trade with East Africa as the area that became Pakistan had no important role in that trade. Pakistan's total foreign trade in 1950 amounted to only £220,786 as compared with India's £85.8 million. Its trade with East Africa was less than 1 per cent of its total. In 1950 Pakistan's imports from East Africa consisted mainly of cotton, wattle extract, sisal, pulse, mangrove poles, and marine shells. Its exports included carpets and rugs, base metals, surgical and medical instruments, toys, and fancy carvings.[23]

During the two decades following their separation from Britain, both India and Pakistan, as shown in Table 2.2,were relatively unimportant in the overall trade of Kenya, Uganda, and Tanzania. By 1970 India was providing only 6 per cent of East Africa's imports, and less than 3 per cent of its exports.[24]

In supplying East Africa's needs, India by 1970 had been surpassed not only by the United Kingdom, the United States, West Germany, and Japan but also by three countries not shown in the table—Iran, China, and the Netherlands. As a market for East Africa's exports, India had fallen behind the United States and Japan as well as the United Kingdom. Pakistan's role, signifying the historical predominance of Bombay and the Gujarat ports in East Africa's trade, was quite insignificant. In the trade with India, cotton and textiles remained foremost. By far the most important import from India and Pakistan during the two decades was cotton cloth and piece goods, with synthetic fabrics, clothing, motor-vehicle bodies, machinery, and medicine and pharmaceutical products leading the minor imports. India was the second largest importer of Kenya's sodium carbonate, and it received much of East Africa's raw cotton, wattle extract, sisal, and pyrethrum, as well as lesser amounts of oil seeds and prepared meats.[25] Though still sizeable, this trade was far less important to East Africa than it had been earlier in the century.

India's relative decline in East Africa's post-war trade occurred not only because of its diminishing imperial economic ties associated with independence and because of its partition but also because of its comparatively low economic growth and the new economic interests on the part of the Asian trading community. As India, Pakistan, and the East African territories emerged from dependent status, they widened their trading relationships, with the result that the new East African nations became less dependent upon both South Asia and Britain. Kenya, Tanzania, and Uganda increased their trade with the United States, Japan, West Germany, France, and Italy as well as with relatively new trading partners such as Hong Kong, mainland China, the Netherlands, Sweden, and Australia. All these countries, including Britain, far exceeded India in industrial growth during the first three decades following the war.[26]

Another reason for the diminished relationship with India is that the East African Asians, who had dominated the import-export trade before World War I, were assuming a different economic role. In the post-war period, as will be explained, the traders were increasingly displaced by

TABLE 2.2   East Africa's Trade by Country (£1,000), 1950-70*

Imports from	1950	1960	1970
India	7,663	6,888	6,450
Pakistan	18	465	2,314
United Kingdom	42,193	50,466	65,194
United States	3,823	7,187	19,185
West Germany	960	10,662	20,701
France	894	5,075	8,528
Italy	1,961	3,671	11,934
Japan	1,826	15,101	23,478
South Africa	2,821	5,857	--
Exports to			
India	13,944	14,956	14,711
Pakistan	89	185	493
United Kingdom	24,957	33,258	59,837
United States	7,330	15,690	37,953
West Germany	3,993	14,823	12,630
France	358	1,696	1,960
Italy	1,289	4,165	5,597
Japan	1,439	5,640	13,172
South Africa	2,377	2,852	--

*For 1970 East Africa shillings were converted to £ sterling at a rate of Shs 17.1 to £1.

Sources: Statistical Abstracts of each territory; the Annual Trade Report of Kenya, Uganda and Tanganyika by the East African Community; and the annual Report on Zanzibar by the Colonial Office.

government agencies, parastatals, and co-operatives. Some Asians emigrated in search of more favourable economic opportunity, and many of those who remained took up other pursuits such as manufacturing and agriculture. Most of those who, despite the hardships, continued in the import-export trade represented second- and third-generation businessmen who had few ties to India and often had formal training in business administration. It was they who opened many of the new trading relationships with countries other than India.

Leading Traders and Commercial Expansion

Although thousands of Asians participated in the commercial development and many deserve recognition, it is possible here to describe only the few who best illustrate the prevalent economic and social mobility within the commercial community. Jairam Sewji and Tharia Topan of Zanzibar were the forerunners of a number of such men on the mainland.

Among the earliest Asians who concentrated on the coastal trade, the Karimjee Jivanjee family was outstanding. The founding member, Jivanjee Budhabhoy, a Bohra from Kutch-Mandvi, arrived at Zanzibar about 1924 and soon started a small firm to export cloves and copra and import German and American cloth. In the 1860s his second son, Karimjee Jivanjee, began a new business engaged in a similar trade primarily between Zanzibar and Bombay. By the time of his death in 1898 Karimjee had developed a far-flung Indian Ocean trade involving the more southern East African coastal towns, Zanzibar and Pemba, and the seaports of western India. There was also a trade with Europe. Karimjee Jivanjee & Co. had become the foremost Asian firm in East Africa.[27]

During the twentieth century under the able leadership of Karimjee's three grandsons—Hassanali Alibhai Karimjee Jivanjee, Mohammedali A. Karimjee Jivanjee, and Yusufali A. Karimjee Jivanjee—and a nephew, Tayabali H.A. Karimjee, the expansion resumed. While continuing an import-export trade in many commodities and acquiring new shipping agencies, the Karimjees began to supply petroleum to East Africa, and they became the exclusive agents of Caltex for Tanganyika. As explained in Chapter 8, they also invested in sisal and tea estates as well as other forms of agriculture. In 1940 they formed Karimjee Jivanjee Estates Ltd. to manage the new agricultural holdings. Three years later the parent company was incorporated, and two new companies were established: K. J. Properties Ltd. for urban real estate investment, and the International Motor Mart for motor-car sales. In that year Karimjee Jivanjee & Co. Ltd., which had branches in Mombasa, Tanga, Lindi, and Mikindani, moved its headquarters from Zanzibar to Dar es Salaam.[28] There a younger member of the family, Yusufali's son Abdulkarim Y.A. Karimjee, assumed the management of the agricultural and motor-car sales and began an illustrious political career. He was five times mayor of Dar es Salaam, a prominent member of the colonial legislature, and the first speaker of the Parliament after independence. Meanwhile for their many public services and their impressive philanthropic contributions, Yusufali and Tayabali had been awarded knighthoods.[29]

While the Karimjee Jivanjee family concentrated on Zanzibar and ultimately Tanganyika, another pioneer, Allidina Visram, an Ismaili from a small village in Kutch, became the foremost trader in the East Africa and Uganda Protectorates. Arriving by dhow in 1863 at age twelve, Visram found employment with Sewa Haji Paroo, an Ismaili trader in Bagamoyo, the sultan's coastal town opposite Zanzibar. At that time Bagamoyo was the base for most of the caravan trade to the great lakes. When Paroo died without children, Visram took over the business and joined another Ismaili pioneer, Nasser Virjee, in opening a chain of general stores from Bagamoyo to Ujiji.[30] In the 1890s as Germany acquired his trading area, Visram moved to the British sphere where construction of the railway from Mombasa to Kisumu posed an extraordinary opportunity. As the railhead proceeded, Visram kept one stop ahead, building and outfitting his shops; and when the line reached Kisumu, he moved into Uganda to found similar businesses along the caravan routes. Within a few years his Allidina Visram & Co. had over 170 branches.[31]

Like the Karimjee Jivanjees, Visram devoted his profits to many other forms of enterprise. He established a road transport business to serve the railway; and purchasing a number of dhows and a small steamer, he set up a water transport system on Lake Victoria. Meanwhile, concentrating on Uganda, he acquired seven plantations and experimented with numerous crops. He also became involved in the processing of agricultural produce and was one of the first to gin cotton. While developing these many interests, Visram worked in close association with leaders of the British and African communities and won their respect. He was widely known as the friend of kings, kabakas, and chiefs, of ministers, generals, and admirals, and as the 'Un-crowned King of Uganda'. Unfortunately, Visram's vast commercial, agricultural, and industrial empire was weakened by the war and the ensuing depression. Within the decade following his death in 1916, without his resourceful leadership, it all disappeared.[32]

As the Karimjee Jivanjees developed Zanzibar and Tanganyika and Visram established a trading network with a headquarters in Uganda, another Muslim trader, Alibhoy Mulla Jeevanjee, a Bohra of no relation to the other family, assumed a unique role in the British East Africa Protectorate. During the 1880s, aided by his brother Tayabali, Jeevanjee developed a prosperous contracting, shipping, and trading concern, A. M. Jeevanjee & Co., in Bombay and his home city, Karachi. In 1890 while in Adelaide, he was employed by the Imperial British East Africa Company to import artisans and police from India. While recruiting these Asians, he began a business in Mombasa to serve the company further as stevedore and contractor. In 1895 he was hired by the East Africa Protectorate to recruit Asian workers, provide building and railway equipment, prepare earth works, and supply provisions. By the time the railhead reached Nairobi, he was riding in a four-horse carriage and was the government's trusted ally. Performing a valuable service for the new government, Jeevanjee rapidly acquired a fortune.[33]

Like most other successful Asians, Jeevanjee shared his wealth with the public and became a leading politician. He was the first Asian appointed to the Legislative Council and the guiding spirit behind the early Asian political organization. His villa in Nairobi became the home of many of East Africa's British, American, and Indian visitors as well as the centre of Asian political and social activity. Meanwhile, Jeevanjee became a principal landowner and assumed an important role in building and construction. He also founded the country's leading newspaper and established two steamship lines for service from Bombay to Mauritius, Mombasa, and the Red Sea.[34] During the first three decades of the new century, he was in many ways Kenya's leading Asian citizen. For his numerous public services Jeevanjee received the Order of the British Empire (O.B.E.), an exceptional honour in European-oriented Kenya. Like Visram's, his economic empire endured little more than the one generation. His company was dissolved in the great depression.[35]

A trader of a different sort, Nanji Kalidas Mehta, a Lohana Hindu, was the most successful of the Asians who built their fortunes from humble beginnings far in the interior. Born in 1889 in a village near Porbandar, he came alone by dhow to German East Africa at age nine to seek his fortune. After three years of shopkeeping with his brother, who had preceded him, he moved to Uganda. In 1905 he opened a duka in Kamuli, forty miles north of Jinja, to purchase African produce and ivory, and in 1908 he set up a second shop in another location and began to buy the new African cotton. Within six years he had added a shop in Jinja and five more in the 'north country'. Mehta led caravans of porters in transporting his wares to and from Jinja, and for purpose of rapid communication within his trading network he rode a bicycle. Although he never shot anyone, he carried a revolver and had to fire it to frighten away brigands. On one occasion he narrowly escaped with his life. He suffered many trials, not the least of which were malaria and dysentery. Through dogged perseverance, imagination, and resourcefulness, working twenty hours a day for long periods, Mehta prospered and surpassed most of his fellow traders.[36]

For Mehta as well as many other Asians, commerce provided a base for additional forms of enterprise. Sensing the opportunities for industrial and agricultural development, Mehta left trading after World War I to concentrate on ginning cotton and planting sugar-cane and, as explained in Chapters 8 and 9, quickly became Uganda's leading planter-industrialist. Through the last three decades of colonial rule, he was also the most respected and influential Asian not only in Uganda but probably in all East Africa. He appears to have been during those years East Africa's principal donor to libraries, hospitals, schools, temples, civic buildings, and recreational facilities in India as well as Africa. Among the institutions to which he contributed were the Kampala Town Hall, the Kampala Coronation Park, and the Gandhi Memorial Academy that grew into the University of Nairobi.[37]

Though never so wealthy as these others, Jagannath Bhavanishanker Pandya ranks among the early leading traders partly because of his many business activities and partly because of his contribution to commercial organization. When he left Bhavnagar for Mombasa in 1907, Pandya obtained a position with the customs service by placing first in an examination. Though only sixteen years old, he differed from most of the other early immigrants in matriculating from secondary school. He worked for the customs six years, then for a large European firm for three years, and in 1917 he founded his own brokerage and warehousing firm, Pandya & Co. Ten years later, after establishing the Pandya Printing Works, he began publication of the *Kenya Daily Mail,* the Asians' most economically successful newspaper. Subsequently he branched into the hardware business in Mombasa, Nairobi, Kampala, Dar es Salaam, and Bombay. He also formed Pandya Agencies Ltd., a confirming house for manufacturers, and he took over a chemist's business, a contracting-building firm, and a stationery and printing shop. Between the wars Pandya organized the Asian commercial community, particularly in Kenya, and was widely recognized as the community's leader.[38]

While expanding his business interests, Pandya sensed the need for an organization of the Asian business community. Before World War I leading Asian and European businessmen had joined in founding commercial associations in all the major trading centres of East Africa except Nairobi, where settler interests had prompted an exclusive organization, the Nairobi Chamber of Commerce and Agriculture. In Tanganyika the Asians occasionally presided over the chambers in Dar es Salaam, Tanga, and Bukoba. In Uganda they were prominent in the Kampala and Jinja Chambers, and at least one Asian became president of the central Uganda Chamber of Commerce.[39] As racial antagonism increased after

World War I, relations between Asians and Europeans in the chambers were often strained, and Asians were increasingly reduced to a token membership. Moreover, Nairobi became the headquarters of a new co-ordinating organization, the Association of Chambers of Commerce of Eastern Africa, which was exclusively European.[40]

Though honoured with membership in the Mombasa Chamber of Commerce, Pandya fostered the formation of separate Asian commercial associations. In 1925 he organized the Mombasa Indian Merchants' Chamber. Subsequently in all the major urban centres of East Africa except Zanzibar, where Asians were clearly dominant in the Chamber of Commerce, the Asian businessmen, partly at Pandya's instigation, formed either Indian chambers of commerce or merchants' chambers to promote and protect their commercial interests. In 1932 when the governments' proposed marketing legislation threatened Asian traders with exclusion from the African areas, Pandya organized all the new chambers into a Federation of Indian Chambers of Commerce and Industry in Eastern Africa. Based initially in Mombasa and later in Nairobi, the Federation was from its inception the Asians' principal economic organization.[41]

Pandya's leadership led eventually to a political career. In addition to heading Asian political organizations such as the Mombasa Indian Association, he was for several years a member of the Kenya Legislative and Executive Councils. His death in 1942 cut short a life that might have changed the course of Asian politics in the troublesome 1940s and 1950s.[42]

As revealed partly by the careers of the Karimjee-Jivanjees, Visram, Jeevanjee, Mehta, and Pandya, the Asian businessmen engaged in a wide range of activity. Most of those who were successful set up their own general stores shortly after brief experiences as employees, and some remained general merchants through the colonial period. Typical was the firm of Walaiti Ram Khosla & Sons, which had been established in Tororo in 1929. An advertisement in 1963 showed that it was selling 'provisions, wines, spirits, piece-goods, cycle accessories, medicines, sundries, hardware, crockery, toilet goods including soap and elephant soap flakes'.[43] A number of traders were like Karimjee Jivanjee, Visram, and Mehta in extending their businesses far into the interior by the caravan trade. Dewji Jamal of Mombasa and Waljee Bhanjee of Kampala were among the foremost caravan traders.[44]

A first step in expansion was often the addition of wholesaling to what began as a retail business. Many of the established general merchants in urban centres were soon supplying traders who had set up their dukas in rural areas. With some the wholesale trade became their main activity. The Umtali firm of V. Mooljee, for instance, described its business in

1963 as 'wholesale and retail in African consumers' goods, agricultural implements, piece-goods, grocery, clothing and general'.[45] Not many, however, began solely as wholesale firms.

Importing and exporting were also logical additional forms of business for an enterprising general merchant. Only a few started as importers and exporters, and most continued their original businesses as they concentrated on importing and exporting. Hassan Virjee, an Ithnasheri from Jamnagar, was typical. Soon after 1886 when he arrived at Zanzibar at age twelve, he started a small business selling dates and salt. Then he began to import cotton piece-goods and purchase cloves for export. While expanding his retail business in general merchandise, he developed an extensive import-export trade with India and the Middle East. In 1910 he began a political career and helped found the Indian Association. In early commercial and political leadership, Virjee was to Zanzibar what Jeevanjee was to Kenya.[46] The exporters occasionally initiated a new trade of crucial importance. In 1927 the Zanzibar clove exporter Meghji Karsandas Surji was instrumental in beginning the export of cloves to Indonesia, and the clove trade with Indonesia soon far surpassed that with India, Britain, and the United States.[47]

By the end of the colonial period most of the Asian retail-wholesale firms had specialized in one type of commodity. The most prevalent concentrations were hardware, provisions, and textiles. An example of the early commercial companies that turned to hardware is Chhanga Ram & Co., which had been founded in 1919 in Kampala. Among those that emphasized the sale of provisions was Esmail Jetha & Co., a Tanga firm begun in 1910. An early company that concentrated on textiles, Jivraj Bhojani & Sons, opened its business in Dodoma in 1909.[48] There were many other specializations. Among the less numerous commercial categories were chemists, cinemas, cleaners, clothiers, distributors, drapers, cinema managers, and dealers in bicycles, glassware, and insurance. Still others were primarily sellers of jewelry, machinery, motor spares (auto parts), motor vehicles, petrol, sewing machines, stationery, and wines and spirits. Some advertised as brokers and agents of produce. The Goan, J. A. Nazareth, was unique in becoming the official caterer of the Uganda Railway.[49]

Regardless of their specializations, the companies rarely dealt in a single commodity or service and almost always were engaged in a variety of activities. Uganda's Karia & Co. Ltd., which had been established in 1930, described its activities three decades later as agents for sugar, cattle feed, liquors, tea, and mineralized spirits; wholesalers for green, yellow, and black gram, beans, and 'all other produce'; oil milling; and insurance underwriting.[50] The Khanbhai Pharmacy Ltd. of Tanga represented a family interest with roots in buying produce along the coast dating to 1836. By the end of the colonial period the company's business included not only pharmacy but also road transport, dhows, estates, and agencies. It had spawned two other firms concerned with insurance, automobile tyres, brokerage, curios, and auctioneering.[51] Such an assortment of interests was not unusual among the older Asian companies. They started simply and incorporated other forms of business as their capital increased and opportunities arose.

As their names denote, many Asian commercial concerns were family affairs. In fact, nearly all represented a common interest of fathers, sons, brothers, and cousins. By 1963 somewhat less than half the companies had acquired limited liability through incorporation, and very few had become 'public' by augmenting their capital through the sale of shares. They were almost all private companies. Although most had an annual turnover representing thousands, and some even millions of shillings, they operated for the most part on credit without investment of considerable capital. Their records, kept in Gujarati or another Indian language, were not open to public inspection and were usually destroyed at the time of dissolution. Not much is known about the companies apart from what their owners have voluntarily revealed.

The customs of high turnover with low profit, a flexible price structure, and a family and community organization combined with their close ties to the markets and industries of India and their high work ethic to give the Asians a virtual monopoly of commerce at the lower and middle levels through most of the colonial period. Their success was naturally resented by many in the European community.

Settler Opposition and Government Regulation

Like the Asians, the Europeans have had a long history of commercial activity in East Africa. Though concentrating on South Asia and other eastern areas, the British East India Co. was trading along the African coast in the early seventeenth century. From 1888 to 1895 British commerce was centred in the Imperial British East Africa Co., which had a royal charter conveying a monopoly of trade. After its failure, which was an important determinant of Britain's annexation of the East Africa and Uganda Protectorates, a large number of companies, some of which had been trading with Zanzibar, became active in the mainland territories. Among those based in Britain the largest and most influential were Smith Mackenzie & Co., the British East Africa Corp., Mitchell Cotts & Co., A. Baumann & Co., Gibson & Co., and Leslie & Anderson. A number of others, the foremost of which was Gailey & Roberts Ltd., were formed by local Europeans. Except for Gailey & Roberts, which imported agricultural machinery, these companies were engaged primarily in exporting settler produce, at first sisal, wheat, and wattle and later coffee, tea, and pyrethrum. Their one important African export was cotton, and it was only with cotton that they encountered serious competition from the Asians.[52]

By the end of the first decade of independence many other European companies had entered the East African market, and a number of mergers had occurred. Mitchell Cotts and A. Baumann were still prominent, but there were several important newcomers, such as Unilever, Lonrho, James Finlay & Co., and the Twentsche Overseas Trading Co. As in the earlier period the European companies were exporting and importing commodities mainly of concern to the settler community. They still sold a large portion of their imports, however, to Asian middlemen.[53]

The Asian traders were resented through the colonial period not so much by these larger companies as by local Europeans who were engaged variously in commerce and estate farming. The Europeans who opened a variety of stores in the larger towns before World War I met stiff competition from the Asians and few survived the great depression. By the end of the colonial period nearly all their businesses had passed into Asian hands. In Nairobi, for instance, Woolworths, one of the most prominent of the European concerns, was taken over by N. K. Mehta, and R. E. Bentley Ltd., the exclusive men's store on Queensway, was soon to be acquired by Rashmi Amritlal Shah.[54] Almost from the beginning of the European settlement the rapid expansion of Asian business had been a cause of resentment among the townspeople. In 1907 East Africa's leading settler, Lord Delamere, remarked:

> There is no place for the small white man arriving in the country. All the vegetable growing for the towns is done by Indians, all the butchers with one or two exceptions are Indians, all the small country stores are kept by Indians and most of the town shops, all the lower grade clerks are Indians, nearly all the carpentry and building is done by Indians. They thus fill all the occupations and trades.[55]

In 1908 the growing competition in Mombasa between Goan and European bars prompted the following letter to the *East African Standard* from 'A Publican and a Sinner':

> The Goanese bars are practically in every case mere shanties adjoining the shops, anything but cleanly, with the barrest [sic] of fittings and no accommodation bearing perhaps, a table, a bench or maybe a couple of rough stools, a very few rupeys [rupees] sufficing to provide the total outfit. The barman will receive his board and lodging and a trifling wage and here the expenditure side of the account is covered. The majority of these places cannot be labelled by any stretch of the imagination wholesome. Some have been in existence

for years, are dark, damp, noisome and the harbouring place without a doubt for rats with the potentiality of plagues. . . . Here then in these places, drinks are sold at a price that it is impossible for the European hotel keeper, with his heavy expenses, to contend against. . . . Is it any wonder that the sorely tried European hotel-keeper groans and grumbles and asks why he should be penalized in order that the coloured aliens should wax prosperous?[56]

The Asians of Mombasa were attacked in many other letters and editorials before World War I. They were accused of setting a bad example for the Africans by gambling and of spreading East Coast fever by travelling widely in their bullock carts. In an open letter to Winston Churchill during his visit of 1907 the government was severely criticized for hiring Goans rather than Europeans as civil servants. In other letters Asian doctors, cooks, and cab drivers were denounced or ridiculed, and Asian immigrants as a whole were described as parasites living upon the settlers. Asian culture itself began to be impugned: 'It is getting too disgusting for words the way some of the [Banyans] go about the streets of our towns. At the present time it is more noticeable owing to the prevailing high winds. If these people must wear the kind of clothing they adopt for their lower limbs then they should remain home'.[57]

The European estate owners, as distinct from the townspeople, did not initially exhibit the same resentment against the Asians. Because of the difficulty of obtaining food, clothing, and other necessities for their African labourers, the Kenya settlers before World War I invited Asian businessmen to open shops on their farms. By the mid-1920s the highlands, where Asians ironically were prohibited from owning land, were dotted with Asian shops about ten miles apart, one shop on the average for every five farms. The Asians' presence continued until close to World War II, when Africans were beginning to offer a comparable service and prospects for higher profits lured most of the Asians back to the towns.[58]

After World War I a number of social and political changes considerably increased the resentment and brought all sections of the European community into a vigorous opposition. Britain's acquisition of German East Africa prompted a movement in India aimed at transferring the administration to the Indian government and developing the territory as an Indian colony. Vociferous support for the plan by some local Asians and an endorsement by the East Africa Indian National Congress alarmed the European community. The fact that the Asian population of Kenya was growing at three times the rate of the Europeans and was increasingly dominating the commercial sector was another cause for concern. There was also the move by the Kenya Europeans—in Rhodesia as well as Kenya—to follow the example of South Africa by proceeding in Kenya, perhaps in all East Africa, to self-government. The vehement opposition of the local Asians, supported by the government of India and Britain's India Office, augmented the ill feeling. Closely tied to this subject was the question of trusteeship of Africans as illustrated by the League of Nations mandate system. The Europeans called for a share in the trusteeship that until then had been vested in the British government. In response, Asian leaders not only opposed the European request but also claimed that they themselves were better suited to exercise the trusteeship.[59]

For these reasons the European settlers, traders, and missionaries combined at the end of the war in an effort to reduce the Asians' economic, political, and social influence. They agitated essentially for restrictions on Asian immigration, reduction of Asian legislative participation, and constitutional changes related to self-government, trusteeship, and the paramountcy of European interests. In justification they attacked Asian culture. In January 1919, for instance, the European members of the local Economic Commission recommended that Asians be excluded from the East Africa Protectorate because their 'incurable repugnance to sanitation and hygiene', their 'antagonistic' philosophy, and their 'moral depravity' were 'damaging to the African'.[60] At that time Asian traders began to be described as grasping, unscrupulous, and dishonest, especially in their dealings with Africans.[61]

While agitating for changes in official policy, the Kenya Europeans undertook a boycott of Asian traders and artisans. In February 1923 the leading settlers formed a European and African Trades Organization, the basic aim of which was to substitute Europeans and Africans for the Asian businessmen and craftsmen. With the settler leader Lord Delamere as its first chairman, the organization called for an immediate boycott. The Asians were to be dismissed from the farms, expelled from rented premises, and sent out of the African reserves. A fund, guaranteed by Delamere and Sir Northrup McMillan, was set up to assist Europeans and Africans in taking over the Asians' businesses. According to Delamere's biographer Elspeth Huxley, 'the organization met with an immediate success. The Kikuyu chiefs gave their support and several became members'. The organization, she said, was dissolved in 1927 'after achieving much constructive work and finding jobs for numerous Europeans and Africans'. It was terminated only because the White Paper of 1923, in proclaiming a doctrine of native paramountcy, had 'extinguished the Indian controversy'.[62]

The Asians have presented a different interpretation. While admitting that many Asian businessmen were displaced, they claim that the effect was only temporary. In a short time the European farmers and African chiefs realized that they were not getting the necessary services. There simply were not enough willing Europeans to take up business in the rural areas nor were there enough experienced Africans. The few who had agreed to assume the Asians' role soon drifted away—the Europeans to urban centres and the Africans to other employment in the reserves. Before long the desperate farmers had to invite back the Asians, and the organization was terminated because it had failed.[63]

Other measures undertaken by the Europeans were more enduring if not more effective. In 1908 Delamere had formed Unga Ltd. for milling and marketing wheat flour and in 1910 Nyama Ltd. for distributing mutton. In 1916 others organized a Sisal Planters' Association, a Maize Growers' Association, and a Pig Breeders' Association. Subsequently many settlers combined to establish the Kenya Planters' Union and the Kenya Farmers' Association Ltd. for the marketing of a variety of settler produce. Beginning in 1931 with enactment of the first co-operatives ordinance, these organizations, together with others such as the Kenya Co-operative Creameries, were registered as co-operatives.[64] They were, in effect, monopolies that precluded the Asians from a significant role in the marketing of settler produce. Other curtailments on Asian commerce were the clauses in constitutions of public companies expressly forbidding the sale of stock to non-Europeans, clauses in deeds of title to business property reserving use of the premises exclusively to Europeans, and practices excluding Asians from the conduct of business in European-owned hotels and restaurants.[65] Although disturbing to Asians, these measures failed in their general object of curbing Asian commerce. 'Kenya is governed by Great Britain and owned by India', complained a settler in 1943.[66]

The settlers' derogatory conception of the Asian traders continued through the colonial period. Even Karen Blixen, renowned for empathy with the subject peoples, expressed the settlers' view:

> The Indians of Nairobi dominated the big Native business quarter of the Bazaar, and the great Indian merchants had their little villas just outside the town: Jeevanjee, Suleiman Virjee, Allidina Visram. They all had a taste for stonework—stairs, balusters, and vases, rather badly cut out of the soft stone of the country—like the structures that children build of pink ornamental bricks. They gave tea parties in their gardens, with Indian pastry in the style of the Villas, and were clever, travelled, highly polite people. But the Indians in Africa are such grasping tradesmen that with them you would never know if you were face to face with a human individual or with the head of a firm.[67]

The extreme settler opinion was often echoed by European visitors to Kenya. Lady Evelyn Cobbold, writing in 1935, is an example:

> It is unfortunate that many of the Indians who came to Kenya were drawn from the most undesirable class in India. Their style of living is on a a very low

scale, which makes tham unfair competitors. They are prepared to sell at prices that kill competiton, while recouping themselves in other ways not always legitimate. In their squalid surroundings, ignoring sanitary precautions, they are often a danger to the community. Typhoid, smallpox and the plague were unknown in East Africa before the Indian came.[68]

Although the typical settler opinion was hostile, a few among the Europeans expressed gratitude for the Asians' presence. Sir Wilfrid Havelock, who had among his many business ventures a farm in Limuru and who served as Kenya's minister of agriculture in 1961–63, worked in close association with the Asians. Recalling in 1987 the years of the great depression, he remarked:

> What greatly helped many of the European farmers in such hard times was the financing provided by the Asians. Not so much through loans as by allowing them to keep their grocery bills going for periods as long as two or three years. . . .
>
> In a commercial sense, they [Asians] pioneered much more than the Europeans ever did. They were everywhere—in the smallest of the villages. We had good reason to be grateful to them.[69]

In German East Africa the European sentiment was similar to that in Kenya. The German settlers not only resented the Asian traders as commercial competitors but also feared them as potential rebels because of their British ties. In 1906, launching a campaign for restrictions on Asian immigration, the settlers accused the Asians of assisting the Maji Maji rebels and inciting African unrest. They also attacked the Asians' practice of keeping their accounts in Gujarati as creating difficulties in levying the business tax and facilitating fraudulent bankruptcy. Though rebuffed initially by the German Colonial Office, the settlers received considerable support in Germany, particularly from the right-wing, anti-Islamic party, the Zentrum, and the German Colonization Society. The society's branch at Worms, for instance, passed a resolution in 1907 favouring differential legislation against Indians in German colonies.[70]

Before European settler interests became vocal, the German and British governments encouraged Asian settlement and commercial enterprise. Count Leo von Caprivi, who in 1890 succeeded Otto von Bismarck as chancellor, favoured coastal traders like Sewa Haji Paroo. 'We want them', Caprivi explained, because 'they have connections with the interior of Africa and we should not be in a position to replace them'.[71] In 1894 the German government approached the British Foreign Office with a view to promoting Asian immigration to its East African territory. In 1899 and 1900 it also proposed to the Aga Khan and the Indian government a scheme for settlement of Khoja farmers.[72]

Among those who recommended an extensive Asian settlement of the British protectorates were Sir William Mackinnon, Capt. J.R.L. Macdonald, Capt. Frederick D. Lugard, Sir Harry H. Johnston, Sir Arthur Hardinge, F.L.O. O'Callaghan, John Ainsworth, and Winston Churchill. The arguments of these men, who were in the forefront of British opinion on Africa at the turn of the century, have been explained in other writings, but the statements peculiar to the Asian trader deserve emphasis.[73] The Asian commercial body, Macdonald believed, would help solve the problem of obtaining African labour. 'It is anticipated', he reported in 1893, 'that the numbers of Indian traders and *banias*, who would inevitably follow the construction parties, would quickly introduce the system of money payments'.[74] Lugard asserted in his book of 1893 that 'the wants' of 'these more civilized settlers would . . . very greatly add to the imports, and the products of their industry to the exports of the country, thus giving a great impetus to trade'.[75] Ainsworth, extolling in 1905 the traders' impact on the East Africa Protectorate, exclaimed that 'fully 80 per cent of the capital and business energy of the country is Indian'.[76] Johnston, submitting evidence to the immigration committee of 1910, agreed. 'The advent of the Indian', he asserted, 'has conferred an enormous benefit on trade'.[77]

Those who valued the traders' activity promoted their expansion into the interior. In 1897 Ainsworth, as sub-commissioner of Ukamba Province, invited Asians to settle in Machakos. Among those who complied was the Mombasa businessman, Adamjee Alibhoy. Though probably not 'the first Indian trader to venture up-country', as has been said, Alibhoy became through trade with the Kamba and railway employees the first prominent Asian in the interior during the British administration.[78] As new stations were established, Asian traders were encouraged by some other administrators not only to set up dukas at the government centres but also to move into the more remote, rural areas to stimulate commerce among the Africans. In fact, it was not uncommon before World War I for district officers to invite Asian traders to accompany them on safari through the new areas of administration. The Africans were encouraged to buy from the Asians on the assumption that the Africans would begin to invest in imports rather than sheep or cattle and that they would acquire improved agricultural implements.[79]

With the emergence of sizeable European communities in the first two decades of the new century, the governments yielded to the anti-Asian pressures by adopting discriminatory policies and practices. In German East Africa the Asians, unlike Europeans, had no privileged status and were 'treated on the same footing as natives'.[80] They had to pay higher taxes and could be flogged by their employers. In 1908 the German Colonial Office acceded to settler demands by promising to restrict

Asian settlement in European areas and to make literacy in Swahili or a European language a qualification for immigration. After 1910 the application of these restrictions together with the long military campaigns, concentration on a plantation economy, neglect of railway construction, suppression of Islam, and the unfamiliar German language and institutions tended to stifle Asian commercial activity.[81]

The British administrations practised milder but perhaps equally effective forms of discrimination. For the Asians in the British territories the situation was the worst in Kenya because of the emphasis on European settlement and the presence of a large number of settlers. Some administrators were as virulent as the settlers in their criticisms of the Asian traders.[82]

In addition to condoning the various forms of discrimination practised by the settler community, prohibiting Asian settlement in the highlands, and adopting municipal and residential segregation in the towns, the Kenya government pursued an economic policy highly detrimental to Asian commerce. It placed high duties on imports required by the Asian traders while lowering or in some instances even abolishing those on agricultural machinery and other items of value to the European farmers. It levied a similar differential rate for exports. Although refraining until after World War II from imposing an income tax, which the Europeans staunchly opposed, it gained much of its revenue from the Asians through a graduated poll tax and through licensing fees covering every commercial activity.[83] As explained in Chapter 3, the government also discriminated against the Asian traders in transport by levying differential rates for European and Asian goods hauled on the railway and by curtailing the Asians' alternative system of road transport.

In the early 1920s the office of the chief native commissioner issued a series of circulars directing district officers to encourage Africans in opening shops and advise them on methods by which they could obtain goods without recourse to Asian traders. It also gave official sanction to the settlers' European and African Trades Organization. While issuing the circulars, the government secretly negotiated with the European firm Bird & Co. for the sale of wholesale goods to African traders at low price. Later in the 1920s many district officers urged the new local native councils, which had been granted control of trading licences, to withhold licences from Asian applicants.[84]

Though not so oppressive generally to the Asian community, the governments of the other British territories at times discriminated against the Asian traders. The foremost example occurred on Zanzibar. In 1934 the Zanzibar government precipitated a four-year crisis by issuing six decrees aimed at curtailing the Asian trade in cloves and transferring control to the European dominated Clove Growers' Association (CGA).

During preceding decades the Asians had gradually displaced Arabs in the production, marketing, and exportation of cloves. In issuing its new controls, the government claimed to be acting primarily in the interests of the Arabs by alleviating the problem of Arab indebtedness to the Asians. The Asian clove traders were convinced, however, that the true purpose behind the decrees was to transfer the lucrative profits of the clove industry to European business interests. They began an intense opposition and elicited a wide support from sympathetic organizations in India and Britain. Despite the protest, the government retained and applied the decrees, and it was only a concerted ten-month embargo in India, the world's leading market for cloves, that prompted the Colonial Office and the Zanzibar government in 1938 to enter into a compromise agreeable to the local Asians.[85]

In Tanganyika the government in 1922–23 provoked a similar, three-year protest from the Asian trading community by introducing a profits tax, ordering the licensing of all commercial enterprise, regulating the business of hawkers, and requiring merchants to keep all their accounts in English or Swahili. Accusing the government of violating the provisions of the mandate, which guaranteed the equality of all races, the Asians launched a vigorous protest. The country's 6,000 traders, who formed from 90 to 95 per cent of the commercial community, refused to take out licences, sent a deputation to London, and closed their shops for fifty-four days. Not until 1925, after protracted negotiations and a renewal of the boycott, was the legislation withdrawn.[86]

The Uganda government was also unsuccessful in its initial attempts to curtail Asian trading activity. Shortly after 1909 when the government began to distribute seed and encourage Africans in the growing of cotton, the Asians acquired a near monopoly of buying the crop, a large portion of which they sold to ginners in India. The Asians' enterprise was highly detrimental to the European cotton-trading companies, the foremost of which was the British East Africa Corp. (BEAC), a subsidiary of the British Cotton Growing Association (BCGA). Before World War I the BEAC owned most of the ginneries and was itself a cotton buyer. In support of the BEAC the government in 1913 issued the Uganda Cotton Rules, which ordered that none but the ginners could buy cotton. In response the Asian traders formed an Association of Indian Cotton Merchants, engaged a London lawyer, and sent a deputation to the Colonial Office. Because of the protest the government was constrained to amend the rules to permit anyone under licence to purchase cotton.[87]

Although the high licence fee of Rs 100 (£6 13s 4d), forced many of the small traders to become virtual agents of the principal cotton dealers, Asian as well as European, the Asians as a whole continued to corner the market and augmented the European concern. In 1918 the BEAC's

Uganda manager exclaimed, 'A definite crisis has arisen, and we are faced with the prospect of the cotton industry going almost entirely into Indian hands. . . . It appears to be only a question of time and evolution when the whole crop will be bought by Indians'.[88] Confirming the seriousness of the situation, Uganda's Governor Sir Robert Coryndon remarked that 'no responsible man, public or official, seemed to be alive to the hold on the trade of the country which the Indians have already obtained'. It was bad for Lancashire, he said, and 'the influence of this type of commercial morality upon the native African is not good'. Coryndon intimated that controls should be imposed on Asian immigration.[89] Although no steps were taken to curb immigration, the government in 1920 excluded merchants from buying cotton within a five-mile radius of existing or projected ginneries on the assumption that Africans within those areas could sell directly to the ginners.[90] 'By 1921', as the historian Thomas F. Taylor has explained, 'the government was thoroughly involved in every facet of the Uganda cotton industry'.[91]

The new restrictions not only reduced the number of Asian buyers but also created a division within the Asian community. After the war the Asian ginners tended to join with leading Europeans in the Uganda Chamber of Commerce and to ally with the government, whereas the smaller traders formed Indian Associations in the various urban centres and urged political, social, and economic reforms. The division between the two groups became apparent in 1921 when the Uganda Chamber of Commerce and the Uganda Development Commission, both with Asian membership, supported the government in a policy of municipal and residential segregation that the Kampala Indian Association bitterly opposed.[92]

Beginning in 1932 to restrain Asian commercial activity in rural areas throughout East Africa, the governments of Kenya, Tanganyika, and Uganda adopted a common policy of confining trading activity to townships and scheduled markets, fixing prices of produce, and conferring monopolies by licensing only a few select firms for each item of produce. The purpose of the marketing ordinances, according to the governments, was to standardize marketing procedures, increase official supervision, and provide more security for African agriculturists, but the Asians were convinced that the essential aim was to foster European commerce, particularly that of the Kenya Farmers' Association, at the expense of their own. It was to oppose the enactment of the legislation that the traders rallied under Pandya's leadership to found the Federation of Indian Chambers of Commerce and Industry in Eastern Africa. The new federation combined with the East Africa Indian National Congress in a protest movement that extended to Britain and India. The Indian government responded by sending its South African authority, K.P.S.

Menon, on a special mission to East Africa. Although Menon, Pandya, and other Asians sought to have the legislation as a whole withdrawn, they were able to obtain only a few minor amendments during negotiations that continued into 1935.[93]

In subsequent years the Asians' fears were realized. The marketing legislation, which was enacted in all three territories, severely curtailed Asian activities in the rural areas. By 1939, as the historian Cyril Ehrlich has noted, the traders in Uganda were 'operating within a rigidly controlled framework of commerce'.[94] Throughout East Africa the more remote shopkeepers and the itinerant merchants who had previously conducted the bulk of the trade could no longer purchase African produce. In the organized markets the Asian buyers encountered stiff competition from European commercial rivals, such as the Kenya Farmers' Association.[95] In the long run, however, the Asians were displaced not by Europeans but by Africans. The governments delegated the issuance of new licences to the local native councils, which strongly favoured the rising African businessmen. After World War II most Asian traders left the African areas in search of more favourable economic opportunity in the larger urban centres.

The conferral of monopolies implicit in the marketing legislation became a divisive force in the Asian commercial community. Monopolies were set up for a variety of commodities ostensibly for the purpose of promoting the introduction of new crops and new methods of preparing produce. The Asians believed that the essential purpose was to limit their commerce in favour of European. Asians as well as Europeans, however, promptly sought to take advantage of the opportunities for monopoly. In 1932, for instance, Tanganyika Asians petitioned for exclusive rights to set up a rice mill in Ifakara District and another in Mikindani and to buy rice in Rufiji District, groundnuts in the Tabora area, and tung and palm oil near Morogoro.[96] Initially the administrative officers were confused as to how to respond to these requests. They rejected one application on the ground that a trade monopoly was 'contrary to the Mandate', and they favoured a European coffee firm over an Asian because 'Indian buyers are not interested in the quality of coffee at all'. The question of policy eventually involved the chief secretary, governor, and secretary of state who decided finally to require approval of the provincial commissioner in each case and a review by the secretary of state.[97] By June 1935 the territorial government claimed that it had issued only two exclusive licences—one for purchase of cashew nuts in Eastern Province and the other for beeswax in Morogoro District—but the correspondence indicates that there were more.[98]

The system of controlled prices and monopolies produced friction between the government, the licensed Asian buyers, and the African producers. The controls imposed in the Handeni section of Tanganyika's Korogwe District well illustrate this. There in 1947–48 two Asian firms, A. M. Sheriff and the Moshi Trading Co., had received exclusive buying rights for African produce in some twenty-five markets. Their buyers, however, did not always appear at the markets, with the result that the Africans had to go to the neighbouring Morogoro District to sell their produce to other Asians. In this they were exploited by lorry drivers, African as well as Asian, who charged exhorbitant fees for transporting the goods. Moreover, the controlled prices, which in this instance were set by the local administrations, were higher in Korogwe than in Morogoro. The Africans accused both the Asian buyers and the government in Morogoro of trying to cheat them.[99]

In June 1948 the Handeni district commissioner summoned a meeting of the two firms and thirteen other potential Asian buyers and worked out a new arrangement whereby under a very strict supervision the two firms would purchase 60 per cent of the produce and the five other Asian buyers specific portions of the remaining 40 per cent. Shortly after trading resumed, however, the Asian buyers declared the system unworkable and initiated a boycott. The district commissioner temporarily solved the problem by assigning the buying and transporting to the local African Authority. The task soon proved beyond the capability of the authority with the result that the Asian buyers had to be brought in, and a very unsatisfactory relationship was resumed.[100]

In 1934, two years after enacting its marketing ordinance, the government of Tanganyika, purportedly in the interest of the African producers, followed Uganda in regulating the cotton markets by restricting the purchase of raw cotton to a number of select ginneries.[101] Asians as well as Europeans were among the ginners who received the essential licences, but the Asian traders as well as most of the ginners were excluded. Despite vigorous protest from commercial organizations such as the Middlemen Cotton Growers' Association of Morogoro, which charged that the marketing of cotton was being vested in only five Asian firms, the government pursued a policy of favouritism.[102] During the 1940s in Mwanza, the centre of the Tanganyika cotton industry, there were two or three European and eight to ten Asian firms, all enjoying the monopoly. Although the government assured the other Asians that this was in the interest of the country, guaranteeing the production of quality goods, the excluded Asians asserted that it was mainly a scheme to promote European interests and gain revenue.[103]

Tanganyika's system of monopolies and controlled prices proved unsatisfactory not merely because of the general Asian opposition but also because it was very difficult to administer. It greatly increased the opportunities for bribing the licensing officials, and it promoted friction between the government, the licensed Asian buyers, and the African producers. The monopolies were deeply resented by the majority of the Asian traders, who passed resolutions of protest in the Tabora, Dodoma, and Dar es Salaam Chambers of Commerce and put pressure on the favoured few to surrender their licences. Reluctantly Bandali Merali, who held the beeswax monopoly in Morogoro, reported 'his desire under pressure' to give up his licence. This action provoked the Director of Agriculture to exclaim that the 'coercion' exercised by the Asian traders was 'directly antagonistic to public policy, and an example of non-cooperation which is short-sighted and unsoundly based'.[104] Encouraged by the government, Merali decided to retain his licence.[105]

After World War II concepts of state control in Britain, born of wartime conditions and socialist idealism, were increasingly applied to East Africa. The new policy was expressed in the Colonial Development and Welfare Acts of 1940 and 1945, in long-term development plans, and in a number of Colonial Office directives and commission reports.[106] Under the direction of the third Labour government, the local administrations retained wartime price controls as well as the marketing legislation, added new regulations, and increased the taxes and fees. As part of a new development policy, they also encouraged the formation of African co-operatives and through new government agencies began to assume a direct role in the conduct of business. Labour's move to a managed economy was retained and further developed after 1950 by Britain's Conservative governments. The great growth in administrative expenditure—in Tanganyika, for example, from £5.4 million in 1947 to £20 million by 1959—illustrates the governments' increasing involvement.[107]

Although nearly all features of the postwar policy were damaging to the independent businessman, the co-operatives and the government agencies had the most negative impact. The co-operative movement, as previously stated, had been initiated by the European farmers in the early years of settlement to reduce their growing dependence on the Asian traders. Kenya's Co-operative Societies (Registration) Ordinance of 1931 was designed primarily for the new settler organizations. In Tanganyika, where the mandate system imposed an emphasis on African development, the government began to encourage the formation of African co-operatives in the early 1920s. The Chagga coffee farmers were the first to respond by forming the Kilimanjaro Native Producers' Association, a powerful marketing co-operative, and by 1938 Tanganyika had thirty-seven societies with 33,474 members.[108] In Kenya, Uganda, and Zanzibar the governments did not foster the development of African co-operatives until after World War II. In 1946, however, all enacted co-operative societies ordinances and proceeded to establish co-operative departments and appoint registrars and numerous other administrators.[109]

With strong government encouragement, the movement grew rapidly. By 1960 Kenya had 625 registered co-operatives, Tanganyika 691, Uganda 1,638, and Zanzibar 77.[110] Although most were farm producers' societies and a few were devised for credit and consumption, a large number were marketing co-operatives concerned with the purchase, distribution, and sale, even exportation, of African produce.

Government agencies created in conjunction with the co-operatives were also detrimental to the individual trader. Zanzibar as early as 1941 established an Economic Control Board, and the mainland territories followed in the mid-1950s with central agricultural boards and provincial marketing boards. These statutory bodies divided farming into geographic areas on racial lines, served as official buying centres for scheduled produce, adhered to a system of fixed prices, marketed surpluses overseas, and controlled the licensing of traders.[111] The mainland territories also instituted marketing boards for specific commodities. Kenya's Maize Marketing Board, Tanganyika's Bukoba Coffee Board, and Uganda's Lint Marketing Board were typical of the new agencies that became the sole authorities for regulating the purchase and distribution of their respective products. Uganda's Lint Marketing Board, for instance, was empowered to purchase at a fixed price and to sell by auction all the cotton lint and seed produced by the ginneries.[112] In Kenya the new statutory bodies divided farming into geographic areas on racial lines. The growth and magnitude of the central control is illustrated by the fact that by 1963 Kenya alone had twenty separate commodities boards, two development boards, and one related educational board, a total of twenty-three regulating agencies.[113]

The means to support the burgeoning bureaucracies was provided partly by development resources, such as loans and external grants, but mainly by taxation. During the last decade of British rule, for instance, Kenya's revenue from taxation more than doubled, from £13.5 million in 1951 to £30.1 million in 1961–62. Customs duties and excise duties, which were contributed mainly by the commercial sector, provided 50 per cent of the total in 1961/62, income and graduated personal taxes 38 per cent, and licensing fees and other sources 12 per cent.[114] The tax burden, which was borne largely by the commercial sector, fell heavily on the Asians and, as explained in Chapter 9, could be as high as 75 per cent.

Britain's post-war colonial policies, combined with the marketing changes of the 1930s, drastically altered the East African economy much to the detriment of the Asian traders. The marketing restrictions, supported by an official policy that favoured the rise of the African businessman, began the decline of Asian business in the rural areas. Except for a relative few who braved a stiff competition with Africans in the designated trading centres, the Asian businessmen left the African areas to seek more favourable opportunities in the towns. Britain's post-war move to a managed economy, however, precluded a significant development of further Asian commerce even in the larger urban centres. Traders with capital found greater opportunity, as explained in subsequent chapters, in manufacturing and agriculture. Those without capital either retired, left East Africa, or undertook some trading venture that often ended in bankruptcy. In 1960 Kenya recorded a decrease in the incorporation of new Asian companies, Tanganyika reported many examples 'of Asian capital trying to move out of trade into industrial enterprise', and Uganda listed 311 Asian bankruptcies.[115] Although nearly 50 per cent of East Africa's 'economically active Asians', as shown in Table 1.4, were still engaged in commerce, the Asians' commercial role, especially in retail trade, was greatly diminished.

Africanization and Further Curtailment of Trade

Though amicable and mutually rewarding through most of the colonial period, the Asian traders' relations with Africans and their governments eventually became even more deleterious than their relations with the Europeans. The initial harmonious relationship is explained by the fact that the Asian traders formed a much-needed service by offering in exchange for surplus food crops a wide variety of merchandise previously unknown to most Africans. Some instances of conflict between Asians and Africans occurred in rural areas. A few traders were killed in defending their caravans or dukas from pillage. In 1908 a Swahili was sentenced for stealing from an Asian's shop and biting off a piece of the proprietor's ear.[116] In 1911–12 the Doruma in the East Africa Protectorate's Kilifi District undertook a successful boycott of the forty-four Asian shopkeepers to raise the price offered for their maize.[117] Such instances, however, were rare. That nearly all the Asian traders were able to reside and conduct their business in the rural areas for decades, with little or no government protection, attests to the fact that they were appreciated. It is significant that the Maji Maji rebellion, which began in German East Africa in 1905 and, as the historian John Iliffe has said, 'affected almost everyone' and 'was felt on the farthest borders of the country', was aimed only at the German colonialist regime. Asians recount that they were able to remain in the African areas throughout the rebellion. They merely closed their shops and waited.[118]

As the colonial system developed, Africans began to resent the Asians' presence. The changing attitude was noticed by the Asians in Kenya shortly after World War I, in Uganda a little later, and in Tanganyika not until the 1940s. The Africans' position at the bottom of the three-tiered structure of economic reward, political power, and social prestige through the colonial period was humiliating. Denied by government until the last decade the right to raise the more valuable cash crops on their land and forced into employment as labourers, they quickly perceived that their foremost opportunity for improvement was to acquire a manual skill or engage in some entrepreneurial activity as shopkeepers or transporters. Shopkeeping proved the most attractive, but there, as with artisanry and road transport, the Asians were firmly entrenched. Thus the Africans, far more than the Europeans who enjoyed a monopoly of the best land and the most profitable agriculture, were bound to compete with the Asians, and it was easy for the Africans to form a dislike of their rivals, regard them as exploiters, and believe that their displacement was essential.

Africans readily accepted the concept, which the Europeans helped to develop, that the Asians were dishonest and exploitive. Africans believed that most traders deliberately took advantage of the farmers by using false weights and measures, demanding extortionate prices for their wares, and paying less than value for farm produce. Certainly there were instances of this activity in the colonial period. District officers, always on the lookout, were quick to note such practices in their reports, and the European press always gave them attention.[119] Asian corruption was also noted in the post-colonial years.[120] In the long association between trader and farmer involving countless transactions, however, it seems remarkable that more cases of Asian dishonesty were not discovered. From a Marxist view one would expect widespread exploitation in a bourgeois-proletariat relationship, and even outside a Marxist context one would think that the business-wise trader would succumb to temptation by taking advantage of those who were not accustomed to a cash economy. Perhaps the opportunity was not so great as has been imagined. The African was not easily duped, and to regard him as the helpless victim of the wily trader is to impugn his perceptiveness and resourcefulness. Perhaps the Asians' exceptional dedication to religion, whether Hindu, Muslim, Sikh, Jain, or Christian, was a mitigating factor.

The causes of conflict between Africans and Asian traders were more complex than mere dishonesty in manipulating weights, measures, and prices. The Asians in almost all situations were in stiff competition with one another, and their systems of price and credit were severely affected by fluctuations in the international markets. In times of hardship they were constrained for the sake of survival to cut costs and maximize profits by every legal means possible. The forces determining the traders' behaviour were generally not understood or appreciated by either the

European administrator or the African producer and consumer. Both concluded that the Asians were dishonest. In the colonial setting with its disproportions of wealth, racial stratification, and constraints on individual freedom, this conclusion was easily transformed into resentment and resentment into conflict.

In the interwar period a twofold conflict emerged between Africans and Asians. One, involving the African farmer and the Asian trader, developed during the Great Depression. Until then the farmer and the trader had established on the whole a favourable relationship in which the Asians purchased surplus foods, extended a useful credit, and provided aid in time of famine. The depression altered the relationship. Although most Africans were able to continue meeting their essential needs and incurred no great hardship, some cultivators, especially those in Tanganyika who had responded to the government's urging to concentrate on the development of economic crops, suffered from the severe drop in world prices. The new local native councils also found their incomes greatly reduced at a time when they were hoping to expand their activities. Both groups expressed resentment against the Asian middlemen who, because of falling prices abroad, sharply cut their prices for African produce and in many cases substituted payment in trade goods for payment in cash and established a double-tier pricing system. They also resented the fact that in the depression years the Asians' system of credit sometimes led to heavy indebtedness and forced the farmer to sell to his creditor at prices lower than those in the general market.[121] The African protest was subsequently emphasized by the governments as justification for the marketing legislation and the cooperative movement.

The other type of conflict arose between the rising African businessmen and the Asian traders who competed in the purchase of African produce and the sale of commodities, mostly imports, to the African consumers. The conflict was most apparent in the rural areas of Kenya and Uganda where the Africans—mainly Kikuyu in Kenya and Ganda in Uganda—first engaged in retail trade. As is evident in the district records, the African traders were able to win the support of the district commissioners and the local native councils and through the new licensing procedures to gain a distinct advantage. By World War II, though unable to compete successfully in importing and wholesaling, the Africans were able to displace many of the Asian retailers. Before the end of the colonial era, as a Uganda survey of 1952 illustrates, the vast majority of the traders were Africans.[122]

The commercial conflict between Asians and Africans was exacerbated by the British policies of the post-war era. The governments of Kenya, Tanganyika, and Uganda extended their policies of training and assisting individual Africans in entering commerce. Joint boards, which began to be formed in Kenya in 1950 after a grant of £25,000 from the United States and which by 1957 numbered eighteen, became the instruments for providing training and loans to Africans through an International Co-operation Administration. With a balance of members from the African district councils and the central government and with the district commissioners as chairmen, the boards provided financial assistance to African artisans and eventually to industrialists as well as traders. They also subsidized short-term training courses at the Jeanes Schools, the adult-education centres at Kabete and Maseno.[123] Similar provisions for aid and training for Africans were undertaken in Tanganyika and Uganda.

While fostering the rise of the African entrepreneur, the governments introduced the concept of a managed economy and proceeded to establish commercial agencies and encourage the formation of African co-operatives. The contradictions inherent in the two policies do not seem to have been appreciated at the time.[124] As is evident in subsequent chapters, the British administrators, together with the settler community, promoted the concept that the Asians stood in the way of African progress and had to be restrained. With proper training and assistance, it was thought, the Africans could replace them. At the same time the governments inculcated the belief that a system of unrestrained enterprise was exploitive and that socialism was the ideal means to African development. This concept was reinforced by Marxist and neo-Marxist literature on colonialism and liberation.

In the end it was the second concept that shaped the last years of British colonialism. The managed economy retarded economic growth in the last years of colonial rule and effectively thwarted the rise of the African businessman. In one sense it was, to borrow the historian Ralph A. Austen's phrase, a 'paternalistic' idea predicated on the assumption that the Africans could not successfully compete with Asians and Europeans in a free economy. They would continue to need the governments' initiative, direction, assistance, and protection.[125] In another sense the concept was not disparaging of the African but rather of the middle-class entrepreneur. The regulated economy was necessary to prevent a bourgeois exploitation of the working class. Irrespective of the interpretation, the concept augmented the growing estrangement between Africans and Asians in that the Asians were equated with the middle class and exploitation.

It is not surprising that serious conflict between Africans and Asians first occurred near the end of the colonial period when Africans became increasingly frustrated over the lack of opportunity in the stagnating economy. Within the context of prevailing ideology it was inevitable that the Asians rather than the governments would be blamed.

In the post-war years there were three important protest movements in which Africans clashed with Asians. In January 1945 a co-ordinated uprising swept over Uganda. Trains were sabotaged, telegraph lines cut, culverts destroyed, European properties invaded, African hospitals attacked, and Asians set upon with sticks and stones. Before calm was restored, one Asian and eight Africans had been killed. At first the uprising was ascribed to African resentment against Asian middlemen for reaping high rewards on the black market during the period of price controls. A commission of enquiry, however, discovered that there were other causes. The protest began as a political movement aimed at overthrowing Serwano W. Kulubya, a strong man in the Ganda government. Then Ignatius K. Musazi, a Ganda trade unionist, called a general strike, and his supporters sought to paralyze all public services. Eventually the agitation drew in the African elite who were unable to find suitable employment. African resentment against the Asians, the commission concluded, was not a factor.[126]

The same conclusion was reached over what seemed to be an anti-Asian riot in Nairobi in December 1959. Shortly after an Asian motorist hit an African pedestrian, a crowd of 400 to 500 Africans quickly gathered. When a police force led by an Asian inspector arrived, the inspector was struck down. Then the crowd began to loot Asian shops on River Road and to stone both Asians and Europeans. Before the disturbance could be suppressed by a large police force, one Asian had been killed and a European seriously wounded. Although the growing resentment against the affluent Asian businessman was undoubtedly a factor, the main cause seems to have been the lack of rewarding employment for the African urban workers.[127]

In 1959 a much more serious clash between Africans and Asians disrupted the economy of Uganda for almost a year. It began in Katwe, Kampala's African section, in February 1959 when a prominent Asian barrister and businessman, Chandulal Kalidas Patel, was appointed minister of commerce. African leaders, who were dissatisfied with the government's lack of support for African traders in their efforts to displace Asian competitors, held a mass meeting to form the Uganda National Movement (UNM). Under the leadership of a leading Ganda trader, Augustine Kamya, the UNM at once called for a boycott of all Asian shops. It also demanded political independence, abolition of the Legislative Council, and establishment of a National Assembly with an African majority. A populist party, the UNM is said to have spoken the language of the common man and appealed to his pocket. It quickly found support from the Ganda and many peoples of the Eastern and

Western Provinces. Though its leaders preached non-violence, many of its followers turned to violence as Africans clashed with Africans over its issues. They resorted to arson, thrashing of crops, maiming of livestock, and bodily harm. Many Asian shops were bombed, and others went weeks without a customer. Although the movement eventually collapsed because of its violence and stiff suppressive measures by government, it succeeded in driving Asian shopkeepers and transporters from the rural areas. It was in effect the first major expression of the resentment that was to culminate a decade later in the Asians' expulsion.[128]

Concerned over the growing African resentment, the leaders of the Federation of Indian Chambers of Commerce and Industry in Eastern Africa devised a plan to develop a common enterprise with African businessmen. The group included Kishori Lal Bhasin, the Federation's president, and other prominent Nairobi businesssmen, chiefly Bachulal Tribhovan Gathani, Lakhamshi R. Shah, Rajabali Gulamhussein Datoo, and Meghji Karman Malde. In February Bhasin met with Kenya's Minister of Commerce and Industry Masinde Muliro to propose that the government permit Africans and Asians to work side by side in areas that were then denied to Asian traders. The Asians would join with Africans in commercial partnerships, lend them money, and provide training. Bhasin suggested that the government participate by granting loans and guaranteeing the Asians' loans. Muliro's initial response was favourable. The Asians set up three 'watch committees'—in Nairobi, Mombasa, and Kisumu—to explore local possibilities and report to both the ministry and federation. They also encouraged the formation of local 'chambers' of Africans and Asians in Thika, Nyeri, Fort Hall, and Machakos to foster mutual confidence as a prelude to the business partnerships. At Bhasin's request the chambers prepared lists of importers and wholesalers for the use of Africans.[129]

These elaborate preparations proved in vain. Although the potential African traders responded favourably, the government apparently was reluctant to admit Asians into the proscribed areas and was not really interested in undertaking a meaningful development of independent enterprise, especially in co-operation with the Asians. The African government seems to have preferred continuation of the training programs, however ineffective, that had been developed by the British. No African-Asian partnerships were formed.

Independence at first brought no major change in developmental programs. The new African administrations, with considerable guidance and aid from expatriate staff, adhered to the two contradictory policies. They proclaimed African socialism as the goal, reinforced the co-operative movement, added new government agencies, increased the regulations on commerce, and raised taxes and fees. At the same time they endeavoured to foster the rise of the independent African business-man. In 1963 the three mainland governments inaugurated development finance companies—for Kenya, the Development Finance Co. of Kenya Ltd. (DFCK); Tanganyika, the Tanganyika Development Finance Co. Ltd. (TDFL); and Uganda, the Development Finance Co. of Uganda Ltd. (DFCU)—each of which was financed initially at £1.5 million composed of equal donations from the territorial government, the Commonwealth Development Corp., and the West German Development Corp. These companies, unlike some of the agencies, did not operate their own enterprises but lent money for the establishment of individual commercial and manufacturing ventures as well as co-operatives.[130]

Among the East African nations Kenya was the foremost in encouraging African entrepreneurship. In 1964 it formed the Industrial and Commercial Development Corp. (ICDC), which considerably augmented the financial aid to African traders. By 1966 the ICDC had issued nearly £90,000 in loans and £10,000 in credit guarantees to about 170 African wholesalers and retailers. Meanwhile an ICDC subsidiary, the National Trading Corp., forced Asian retailers to purchase their stock from African suppliers and put pressure on breweries and factories to sell only to African distributors.[131] The policy of Africanization evident in the ICDC actions was augmented by measures requiring citizenship for enterprise, the sharing of ownership and management with Africans, and increased participation by government. In 1967 Kenya passed legislation requiring citizenship for employment and the conduct of business. All non-citizens had to apply for re-entry permits and dependents' passes. Greatly increasing the Asians' insecurity, the laws prompted an exodus from Kenya beginning in December 1967. In subsequent years the non-citizens failed to obtain trading licences and work permits, and many who applied for citizenship met delays and obstacles. A large number of those who remained in business were served quit notices, and their premises were assigned to Africans.[132]

The demise of the chambers of commerce was symbolic of the end of Asian commercial enterprise. Early in 1963, several months before Kenya's independence, the European commercial leaders invited Asians to join in a new multi-racial organization, the Kenya Association of Chambers of Commerce (KACC), and they took steps to set up similar organizations in Tanzania and Uganda that were to join in forming an Association of Chambers of Commerce of Eastern Africa. They assumed that all the existing racial chambers—European, Asian, and African—would retain their separate identities as members of the new collective organizations. The three leading Asian organizations—the Nairobi Indian Chamber of Commerce, the Mombasa Indian Merchants' Chamber, and the Thika Indian Merchants' Chamber—agreed, and the new Association was formed in May. Africans, however, had refused to join. A prominent commercial leader, N. P. Gor, insisted that the European and Asian chambers become members of his organization, the Kenya Chamber of Commerce and Industry (KCCI), which was managed by Africans but multi-racial in concept. Gor threatened a boycott of all European and Asian shops.[133] Kenya's new minister for commerce and industry, Dr. Julius G. Kiano, censured Gor publicly for his threat but asserted that 'all essentially racial business associations and social clubs must now open their doors wide for all or else disband'.[134]

The African opposition, which apparently had not been foreseen, prompted both European and Asian leaders to re-evaluate their positions. In July 1964 the Europeans changed the name of the KACC to the Association of Chambers of Commerce, Industry and Trade (ACCIT), but they staunchly refused to join the KCCI or disband their existing chambers.[135] Meanwhile the Asians apparently had ceased to attend the Association's meetings. The Federation of Indian Chambers of Commerce and Industry in Eastern Africa, led by its president, Anant J. Pandya, and its honourary secretary, Madan Mohan Madan, decided to refashion the Asian organizations along multi-racial and national lines. In January 1964 the federation gave up its office and henceforth functioned as a part of the Nairobi Indian Chamber of Commerce (NICC). Shortly afterwards the NICC changed its name to the Nairobi Central Chamber of Commerce and Industry (NCCCI).[136] Other Asian chambers throughout Kenya, in fact throughout East Africa, followed by dropping the word 'Indian' from their titles and proclaiming a multi-racial membership.

Neither of the initiatives, European or Asian, was attractive to the Africans. Francis Nduati Macharia, who replaced Gor as leader of the KCCI, urged the Asians and Europeans to abandon their organizations and join the KCCI. Kiano, however, wanted a multi-racial organization closely associated with the government. At his initiative the KCCI was reorganized and registered in May 1965 as the Kenya National Chamber of Commerce and Industry (KNCCI). Among the officers were Macharia and the European commercial leader, Sir Derek Erskine, but there was no Asian. Two months later Macharia, as president, called a meeting of all the Asian and European chambers to insist on dissolution of the non-African organizations and their replacement with local chapters of the KNCCI.[137] The Europeans, led by Erskine, resisted and had to be threatened into compliance by Kiano, but the Asians, apparently more aware of the full significance of the power change, readily complied. By the end of 1965 nearly all the European and Asian local chambers had been absorbed by new chapters of the KNCCI. The NCCI, the last of the Asian organizations and the vestige of J. B. Pandya's once powerful federation, vacated its office in March 1966 and formally dissolved in November

1968.[138] Commercial organization in Kenya, and indeed in all East Africa, was by then exclusively African.

Although some Kenya Asians doggedly persevered in commerce beyond the 1960s, far fewer were able to continue in Tanzania where the official actions affecting the mercantile sector were much more severe. Until promulgation of President Julius Nyerere's Arusha Declaration in February 1967, Tanzania, like Kenya, continued the British policy of encouraging private business while steadily expanding government control. During its first year, 1962, the government greatly increased the number of co-operatives and established a parastatal company, the Co-operative Supply Association of Tanganyika Ltd. (Cosata), as a wholesaler to the consumer co-operatives. In 1964 it replaced the development agencies inherited from the colonial period with a parastatal National Development Corp. (NDC) that, with far more money (£1 million) than its Kenya counterpart, offered financial assistance to African traders and industrialists and encouraged joint management between Africans and Asians. The NDC formed an investment holding company, the Tanzanian African Finance Co. Ltd. (TAFCO), to promote partnership with the government in commercial and industrial ventures. Although these measures represented, on the whole, further restraints on individual initiatives, Nyerere after five years of experimentation decided that the continuing private enterprise was the root cause of Tanzania's disappointing growth in GDP and the widespread corruption in the co-operatives.[139]

Among the drastic changes announced in the Arusha Declaration was a program of nationalization in which the government assumed either total ownership or a majority interest of the principal instruments of production. The program affected Asians in all sectors of the economy but mainly in commerce. In addition to taking over the key industries, mining, and processing of agricultural produce, the government nationalized banking, insurance, and a large portion of the import-export business. Importing, distribution, and much of the retail trade were assigned to a new State Trading Corp. (STC) which absorbed Cosata and set up a network of retail co-operatives. The STC exported commodities obtained from new parastatal bodies, government agencies, marketing boards, and co-operatives. The aim, attained through a gradual increase of government participation, was a complete socialization of the economy. The result was a rapid decline of private business affecting Asians, Europeans, and Africans alike. Although Nyerere professed adherence to a non-racial policy, his efforts to eliminate the middle class had racial implications. Asian shops all over Tanzania were closed. By 1970 only 3 or 4 per cent of all imports were still handled by private firms.[140]

Uganda, led by Milton Obote, pursued a course very similar to that of
Tanzania by at first retaining the contradictory two-stream development
of the colonial period and eventually moving to a policy of socialism and
Africanization. Initially, while encouraging African businessmen, Obote
emphasized co-operatives much to the detriment of independent business. By 1966, for instance, marketing co-operatives were being allocated 75 per cent of the cotton crop. In 1967, after introducing a new
constitution that vested power in the office of the president, Obote intensified the takeover of commercial and industrial companies and began to regulate the economy through parastatals. As explained in
Chapter 8, however, he failed in his aim to raise farm prices by substituting parastatals for the remaining Asian wholesalers, retailers, and artisans with the result that there was widespread rural unrest culminating
in the assassination attempt of 1969.[141]

Obote reacted with what became known as the 'move to the left'. As a
first step he abolished all political parties except his Uganda People's
Congress. On May Day 1970 he proclaimed a Common Man's Charter
that involved not only nationalization of the banking system but also an
assumption by government of a 60 per cent ownership in all the means
of production.[142] Obote then proceeded to reassert government control
over the co-operatives, which since 1963 had been virtually autono-
mous, and to sponsor a Trade Licensing Act that stipulated an annual fee
of Shs 500 and a minimum capital of Shs 80,000 for the conduct of business. He also appointed a Commission for Africanization of Commerce
and Industry, and the commision introduced an immigration bill requiring all non-citizens to apply for entry permits. The purpose of the bill,
explained by the minister of commerce and industry, was 'to make sure
that Africans go to the top of as many companies as possible'.[143]

Uganda's move to the left was deceiving. Unlike Nyerere, Obote apparently realized in time that the economy was still dependent on the
Asians. He was also concerned with the growing economic and political
influence of the Ganda. To check the Gandas' commercial expansion,
Obote is said to have struck 'an alliance with the Asian commercial and
administrative strata'.[144]

As vacancies occurred in the higher levels of the civil service because
of the departure of Europeans and the continuing growth of the bureaucracy, Obote appointed mostly Asians. Although he nationalized many
of the larger companies, Obote negotiated with the leading traders and
manufacturers with the result that none had to yield a 60 per cent share
to the government. His measures to drive the Asians from the import-
export and wholesaling trade were permitted to remain ineffective, and
the Trade Licensing Act proved as severe a hardship for the aspiring African businessman as for the Asian petty trader. When he perceived that
many Asians were leaving the country, Obote announced that he was

considering granting citizenship, and hence the right to trade, to 30,000 Asians.[145] The contradictions between his policies and actions created widespread unrest, increased African resentment against the Asians, and became a major cause of the military coup of January 1971. It was Obote's successor, Idi Amin, who with his expulsion orders of August 1972, was to terminate all Asian enterprise.

Although the internal policies were primary, the external policies of the East African governments also hastened the decline of Asian commerce. The four countries emerged from the colonial era with the legacy of a common market within the East African Community. The absence of interterritorial tariff barriers was a boon to the commercial interests, particularly in Kenya, through which passed nearly all Uganda's and a large proportion of Tanganyika's imports. In September 1964, to promote industrial development, Tanganyika restricted imports of synthetic fibres, textiles, cycles and spares, skimmed milk, and baby foods. Subsequently it added a long list of other commodities that covered almost all the customary imports from Kenya. Meanwhile it had conferred the authority to import exclusively on its parastal, Cosata. It had also entrusted Cosata with the licensing of individual importers. When Mombasa traders applied and were refused licences, Cosata explained that it was encouraging importation through local merchants. The Tanzanian Asians found, however, that even their applications for licences were ignored. Cosata honoured applications only from Africans and the new semigovernment organizations. The Mombasa Asians alone estimated that as a result of Cosata they were losing an annual Shs 150 million in trade. It dealt, they said, 'a fatal blow to the trade in Kenya'.[146]

Protest from the Kenya government produced a modification of the Tanzanian restrictions, but all the countries were drifting towards a territorial autonomy in trade. In 1965 Uganda imposed restrictions on the entry from Kenya of goods of Japanese and other foreign origin. The Kenya importers who had enjoyed a sizeable trade with Uganda found that their many consignments to Uganda were refused entry and had to be railed back.[147] Beginning in 1973 after Amin's coup the border between Kenya and Uganda was repeatedly closed, and the increasing chaos in Uganda eventually spelled an end to all trade with Tanzania as well as Kenya. In 1977 the countries terminated the East African Community, and subsequently Tanzania shut its border against any communication with Kenya.

The breakdown of interterritorial trade combined with the government's increasing assumption of commercial activity, eradication of private commerce, and Africanization policies to reduce significantly the role of the individual trader. In Kenya and Tanzania there was nothing so extreme affecting Asians as the Zanzibar coup and the Uganda expulsion order, but by the late 1960s and early 1970s everywhere it was evident that the era of free commerce in which the Asian had prospered was at an end. There was no longer a future for the Asian trader in East Africa. During the preceding decades the Asians' impact on the commercial development of East Africa had been extraordinary. In a few instances this was recognized by the colonial administrators. In 1944 at the close of his term as provincial commissioner of Kenya's Southern Province, Arthur M. Champion attributed the following changes largely to the Asians:

> Less than a generation ago money was hardly even heard of, and coins were 'purchased' (to use the natives' own expression) with cattle, goats, and sheep in order to satisfy the tax collectors. Self-sufficiency, with a certain amount of internal trade by barter, was the normal condition, and there was no demand for currency or foreign trade goods. Blankets first began to replace skins, and a man had to work to obtain money to buy them, or exchange the produce of the soil for them. Wire, beads and calico soon followed to widen the breach in the ramparts of self-sufficiency. From assessing his wealth in terms of stock and food, a man began to think in terms of cash with which he could acquire these newfound articles. The cash income became a consideration in the family budget, and could be secured by engaging regular employment, or by the sale of the produce of the land. Luxuries soon became to be regarded as necessaries, and the native began to recognize the coin as a convenient medium of exchange in his extra-tribal trading. . . . The encouragement of cash crops resulted in a great extension of cultivation.[148]

These words describe only a part of the Asians' commercial contribution. As Champion stated, the traders were instrumental in introducing manufactured commodities, mainly imports from overseas, to Africans in both urban and rural areas, and through purchase and sale, chiefly through export, of African surplus foods, they stimulated the development of African cash crops. In encouraging cash crops, as he also noted, the traders provided the Africans a viable alternative to contract labour in obtaining money for payment of taxes. It is evident, however, that the Asians contributed in additional ways. By distributing food through the provinces, they alleviated the periodic famines. By providing many of the commodities needed by the European settlers and their African workers, they supported the development of estate agriculture. They formed a network of trading associations from the retail shops of Africa to the importing and exporting organizations, and they built most of the structures, from dukas to processing factories and warehouses, that were vital to commerce. They were the mainstay of all the urban areas. It is obvious, too, that through employment of Africans in their commercial transactions, they contributed significantly to the rise of African businessmen. It was they whom the Africans chiefly strove to displace and to emulate.

That the Asians formed a middle-class block preventing Africans from rising above the stratum of manual labour needs qualification. Africans encountered manifold difficulties in acquiring a significant place in importing, wholesaling, and exporting primarily because the Asians had developed the necessary commercial relationships with individuals and companies overseas and were well established. The Asians also had the advantage of close association with their Indian homeland, which, as has been seen, was through most of the colonial period one of East Africa's principal trading partners. By the end of the colonial period, however, Africans had displaced most of the Asians both in the purchase of cash crops and the retail trade, and it appeared only a matter of time until they would dominate all the avenues of commerce. Like the Asians they were favoured by an extended-family system, and they had the advantage of conducting business with their own people in their home environment. In the end it was not the Asians, but the British policy of the managed economy carried by the African governments to its logical conclusion as African socialism—with its government agencies, parastatals, co-operatives, monopolies, taxation, and regulation—that dashed the hopes of the African businessmen.

Notes

1. Aga Khan, *India in Transition* (London: P. L. Warner, 1918), p. 129.

2. *East Africa Royal Commission, 1953–55: Report* (London: HMSO, 1955), p. 65.

3. Robert G. Gregory, *India and East Africa: A History of Race Relations Within the British Empire, 1890–1939* (Oxford: Clarendon, 1971), chap. 1. For a general account of the pre-1900 trade, see *Trade and Shipping of Africa*, C. 9223 (London: HMSO, 1899). Also, Abdul Sheriff, *Slaves, Spices and Ivory in Zanzibar: Integration of an East African Commercial Empire into the World Economy, 1770–1873* (London: J. Currey, 1987).

4. Sheriff, *Slaves*, especially pp. 107–9. N. S. Thakur and S. Pandit, 'Brief History of the Asian Settlement of East Africa', chap. 1, *Asians in East and Central Africa*, ed. Shanti Pandit (Nairobi: Panco, 1961), pp. 13–15. J. S. Mangat, *History of the Asians in East Africa, c. 1886 to 1945* (Oxford: Clarendon, 1969), pp. 4, 10, 12, 15–19. For a valuable dissertation on Zanzibar, see Honey, 'History of Indian Merchant Capital and Class Formation in Tanganyika, c. 1840–1940', University of Dar es Salaam, 1982.

5. Sheriff, *Slaves*, pp. 107–9. Thakur and Pandit, 'Brief History', pp. 13–15. Pandit, *Asians*, pp. 97–98. B. G. Vaghela and J. M. Patel, eds., *East Africa Today (1958–59): Comprehensive Directory of British East Africa with Who's Who* (Bombay: Overseas Information, 1959), p. 696.

6. James Christie, *Cholera Epidemics in East Africa: An Account of the Several Epidemics of the Disease in that Country from 1821 till 1872, with an Outline of the Geography, Ethnology, and Trade Connections of the Regions Through Which the Epidemics Passed* (London: Macmillan, 1876), pp. 345–46.

7. For the Yao, see Edward A. Alpers, *Ivory and Slaves in East Central Africa* (London: Heinemann, 1975). For the Nyamwezi, Norman R. Bennett, *Mirambo of Tanzania, c. 1840–84* (New York: Oxford University Press, 1971); and Andrew D. Roberts, ed., *Tanzania before 1900* (Nairobi: East African Publishing House, 1968). For the Mijikenda and Kamba, John Lamphear, 'Kamba and the Northern Mrima Coast', chap. 4, *Pre-Colonial African Trade*, ed. Richard Gray and David Birmingham (London: Oxford University Press, 1970), pp. 75–101.

8. This is a controversial subject, but Sheriff's evidence is persuasive: *Slaves*, chap. 5; see p. 168.

9. Quoted, Thomas Chives Newton Evans, 'Economic Change Among the Dorobo/Okiek of Central Kenya, 1850–1963', Ph.D. diss., Syracuse University, 1985, p. 154.

10. Mervyn F. Hill, *Permanent Way:* vol. 1, *Story of the Uganda Railway* (Nairobi: East Africa Railways and Harbours, 1949), p. 190.

11. From 1890 to 1914 the rupee was equal to 1s 4d in Britain. For lease of business plots, see *East Africa Protectorate: Report for 1910–11*, Colonial Reports—Annual, no. 705, Cd. 6007 (London: HMSO, 1912), pp. 64–87.

12. Gregory, *India and East Africa*, pp. 57, 60, 93. Though often impugned by Europeans for insanitary living conditions, the Asians, especially Hindu traders, avoided many diseases by their personal cleanliness and dietary habits. See Christie, *Cholera Epidemics*, pp. 347–52.

13. See, for example, an account of the slaying of three Goan caravan leaders by the Chinga: John Boyes, *John Boyes, King of the Wa-Kikuyu: A True Story of Travel and Adventure in Africa* (London: Methuen, 1911), pp. 216–20.

14. The preeminence of ivory in the early trade and the extent of the Asian participation are evident in the 'Quarterly Statement of Trade, 1 Aug.–31 Oct. 1893', encl. in Sir William Mackinnon to A. S. Rogers, 5 Dec. 1893, F.O. 2/73. For the nineteenth-century trade, see Sheriff, *Slaves*, pp. 77 ff.

15. For a revealing description of the traders' routine, see Christie, *Cholera*, pp. 351–52.

16. M.P.K. Sorrenson, *Origins of European Settlement in Kenya* (Nairobi: Oxford University Press, 1968), p. 29.

17. Although values changed considerably through the period shown, the statistics in Table 2.1 permit an accurate comparison among the countries in any given year.

18. Compiled from *Statistical Abstract Relating to British India from 1897–98 to 1906–07*, Cd. 4311 (London: HMSO, 1908), and succeeding issues. The rupee appreciated during World War I and reached a high of 2 s 10 d in 1920. It soon settled to 1 s 6 d and retained this value through 1939.

19. Ibid.

20. Ibid., 72d no., Cmd. 6441 (London: HMSO, 1943), pp. 837–94.

21. *Economic Survey of the Colonial Territories, 1951:* vol. 2, *East African Territories: Kenya, Tanganyika, Uganda, Zanzibar and the Somali Protectorate, with Aden, Mauritius and Seychelles* (London: HMSO, 1954), p. 198.

22. East Africa High Commission, *Annual Trade Report of Kenya, Uganda and Tanganyika for the Year Ended 31st Dec. 1950* (Nairobi: Government Printer, 1951), pp. 293, 330. Price increases are from Paul Bairock, *Economic Development of the Third World Since 1900*, trans. Cynthia Postan (Berkeley: University of California Press, 1975), table 38, p. 127.

23. *Foreign Trade Statistics of Pakistan, 1958* (Karachi: Central Statistics Office, n.d.), p. 6. *Annual Trade Report*, pp. 2–290.

24. Despite changing values through time, the statistics in Table 2.2, like those in Table 2.1 permit an accurate comparison among countries in any given year.

25. See, for example, Uganda, *1961 Statistical Abstract* (Entebbe: Government Printer, n.d.), table UD.18, p. 30; Kenya, *Statistical Abstract 1961* (Nairobi: Government Printer, 1961), table 39, p. 31; and Tanganyika, *Statistical Abstract 1961* (Dar es Salaam: Government Printer, 1961), table E.4, pp. 31–32.

26. India's growth rate per capita 1960–74 was 1.1, but for Australia it was 3.2, Belgium 4.5, China 5.2, France 4.4, Hong Kong 6.6, Italy 4.2, Japan 8.8, Netherlands 4.0, South Africa 2.9, Sweden 3.2, United Kingdom 2.3, United States 2.9, and West Germany 3.7.

27. Thakur and Pandit, 'Brief History', p. 16. For the drive for an Indian colony, see Gregory, *India and East Africa*, pp. 156–71.

28. Pandit, *Asians*, pp. 161–62.

29. A.Y.A. Karimjee, interviewed by Gregory, 20 Feb. 1973, Dar es Salaam.

30. For a biography of Virjee, see Vaghela and Patel, *East Africa Today*, p. 154.

31. K. R. Paroo, interviewed by Gregory, 1 Mar. 1973, Mombasa. Paroo's grandfather's brother was Sewa Haji. Paroo's father worked for Visram. See also Pandit, *Asians*, pp. 66–68.

32. Pandit, *Asians*, pp. 66–68.

33. Pandit, *Asians*, pp. 76–78. Jeevanjee was not related to the Jivanjee-Karimjee family.

34. A. Raishi, interviewed by Gregory, 25 Jan. 1973, 7, 10 June 1985, Nairobi; 18 Aug. 1984, 18 June 1989, London. Raishi worked in Jeevanjee's main office during the 1920s and read his personal papers.

35. Pandit, *Asians*, pp. 76–78. Pandit was assembling and indexing these papers when they were suddenly burnt by the Kenya government. Jeevanjee was one of the few Asians who left a large collection of personal papers.

36. N. K. Mehta is the only Asian who wrote a personal account of his business activities: *Dream Half Expressed: An Autobiography* (Bombay: Vakils, Feffer and Simons, 1966).

37. Ibid., and Pandit, *Asians*, pp. 183–84.

38. Anant J. Pandya (son), interviewed by Gregory, 1 Mar. 1973, Mombasa.

39. J. K. Chande (former president, Dar es Salaam Chamber of Commerce), interviewed by Honey 7 Aug. 1973, Dar es Salaam. Gregory, *India and East Africa*, p. 398. K. K. Radia (former president, Kampala Indian Merchants' Chamber), interviewed by Gregory, 12 July 1973, Porbandar.

40. B. T. Gathani (former president, Federation of Indian Chambers of Commerce and Industry in Eastern Africa), interviewed by Gregory, 20 Nov. 1972, Nairobi.

41. Records of the federation and the Mombasa Indian Merchants' Chamber are at Syracuse University as microfilm series 1923 and 1922, each three reels.

42. For some of A. J. Pandya's social and philanthropic activities, see Pandit, *Asians*, p. 203.

43. Ibid., p. 363.

44. Mangat, *History of the Asians*, p. 83.

45. Pandit, *Asians*, p. 328.

46. Ibid., p. 310.

47. Untitled typescript submitted to Gregory by M. K. Lalji during interview, 28 July 1973, Mombasa.

48. Pandit, *Asians*, pp. 295, 303, 315.

49. Mangat, *History of the Asians*, p. 83.

50. Pandit, *Asians*, p. 319.

51. Ibid., pp. 324–25.

52. Nicola Swainson, *Development of Corporate Capitalism in Kenya, 1918–77* (London: Heinemann, 1980), pp. 59–62.

53. M. L. Shah's family, for example, served as wholesale distributors for the Twentsche Overseas Trading Co.: interviewed by Honey, 10 Jan. 1974, Dar es Salaam. Working Party, Department of Christian Education and Training, National Christian Council of Kenya, *Who Controls Industry in Kenya?* (Nairobi: East African Publishing House, 1968), pp. 53–62.

54. *East African Standard*, 28 Oct. 1943, p. 3. Woolworths later passed to Rajani Patel. Zarina Patel, interviewed by Gregory, 22 Jan. 1973, Nairobi. R. A. Shah, interviewed with father by Gregory, 13 Feb. 1973, Nairobi. Rashmi's cousin shared the ownership of Bentley.

55. Quoted, Elspeth Huxley, *White Man's Country: Lord Delamere and the Making of Kenya*, vol. 2 (London: Chatto and Windus, 1956), 206–7.

56. *East African Standard*, 25 July 1908, p. 8.

57. Ibid., 28 Sept. 1907, p. 6; 25 Jan. 1908, p. 9; 1 Feb. 1908, p. 11; 22 Feb. 1908, p. 9; 15 May 1909, p. 9; 22 Jan. 1910, pp. 9, 12, 17.

58. K. R. Shah, interviewed by Bennett, 25 May 1973, Nakuru. V. D. Shah, interviewed by Bennett, 19 Apr. 1973, Nairobi.

59. For detail see Gregory, *India and East Africa*, chaps. 5, 6.

60. The quotations are from the minority report; see Sir Charles Bowring (Acting Governor) to Colonial Office, 25 Mar. 1918, C.O. 533/194.

61. The Hilton Young Commission felt an obligation to reply to these accusations and on the whole defended the Asian traders. *Report of the Commission on Closer Union of the Dependencies in Eastern and Central Africa*, Cmd. 3234 (London: HMSO, 1929), p. 27.

62. Huxley, *White Man's Country*, vol 2., 179–80. I.R.G. Spencer, 'First Assault on Indian Ascendency: Indian Traders in the Kenya Reserves, 1895–1929', *African Affairs*, 80/320 (July 1981), 336.

63. The fullest explanation has been given by A. Raishi, leader of the Shah community: interview.

64. The story of Unga and the European farmer generally is described in Elspeth Huxley, *No Easy Way: A History of the Kenya Farmers' Association and Unga Ltd.* (Nairobi: East African Standard, 1957). See also Swainson, *Development*, p. 53.

65. B. T. Gathani interview. C. V. Madan, interviewed by Gregory, 30 Jan. 1973, Nairobi. It is not surprising that C. B. Anderson, a settler spokesman, blamed free enterprise for the Europeans' problems: Rotary address, *East African Standard*, 1 Feb. 1943, p. 3.

66. Anderson, Rotary address, 29 Sept. 1943, p. 4.

67. Isaak Dinesen, *Out of Africa and Shadows on the Grass* (New York: Random House, 1985, first published 1937), p. 14.

68. Lady Evelyn Cobbold, *Kenya, the Land of Illusion* (London: John Murray, 1935), pp. 73–74.

69. Interview, *Daily Nation* (Nairobi), 12 Dec. 1987.

70. John Iliffe, *Tanganyika under German Rule, 1905–12* (Cambridge: Cambridge University Press, 1969), pp. 95–96.

71. Quoted, L. W. Hollingsworth, *Asians of East Africa* (London: Macmillan, 1960), p. 62.

72. Baron von Waldthausen (German Consul, Calcutta) to T. W. Holderness (Secretary to Government of India, Department of Revenue and Agriculture), 20 Feb. 1900, and encl. 'Memo', Government of India, Department of Revenue and Agriculture, Emigration A, Sept. 1901, no. 12.

73. See, for example, Gregory, *India and East Africa*, pp. 47, 49–50, 65–66, 68.

74. For this and other comments, see *Report on Mombasa–Victoria Lake Railway Survey*, C. 7025 (London: HMSO, 1893), pp. 92–93.

75. Frederick D. Lugard, *Rise of Our East African Empire: Early Efforts in Nyasaland and Uganda*, vol. 1 (London: Frank Cass, 1968, first published 1893), pp. 488–90.

76. Quoted, Hill, *Permanent Way*, vol. 1, p. 286.

77. 'Memo. by Sir Harry H. Johnston', *Report of the Committee on Emigration to the Crown Colonies and Protectorates:* part 3, *Papers Laid before the Committee*, Cd. 5193 (London: HMSO, 1910), pp. 162–63.

78. John Ainsworth, 'Diary', vol. 1, pp. 228, 232, Ainsworth Papers, Rhodes House, Oxford. Sir Frederick J. Jackson, *Early Days in East Africa* (London: Dawsons, 1930), p. 145.

79. See, for example, 'South Kavirondo District Annual Report for the Year Ended 31st March, 1914', p. 11, Syracuse University microfilm 2801, reel 37. Also, Charles Bennett, 'Persistence amid Adversity: The Growth and Spatial Distribution of the Asian Population of Kenya, 1903–63', Ph.D. diss., Syracuse University, 1976, pp. 8–9.

80. *Report on the German Colonies in Africa and the South Pacific*, F.O. Misc. Series no. 346, C. 7582–7 (London: HMSO, 1894), p. 40.

81. Gregory, *India and East Africa*, pp. 100–101.

82. The most eloquent and vigorous was the coastal official and legislator, Shirley V. Cooke, who wrote 'The Indian Question', *East African Standard*, 8 Sept. 1944, p. 10.

83. Asians can be presumed to have provided, for example, most of the £27.4 million in Kenya government revenue in 1958–59 that came from income tax, graduated personal tax, fines and forfeitures, import duties, excise duties, stamp duties, petrol tax, traffic licences, land rent, and land taxes. The total local revenue that year was £41.7 million. *Kenya, Uganda, Tanganyika, and Zanzibar Di-*

rectory: Trade and Commercial Index, 1961–62 Edition (Nairobi: East African Directory, 1962), Kenya section, pp. 107–108. See also E. A. Brett, *Colonialism and Underdevelopment in East Africa: The Politics of Economic Change, 1919–39* (New York: NOK, 1973), chap. 6.

84. Spencer, 'First Assault', pp. 36–38.

85. For a detailed description, see Gregory, *India and East Africa*, pp. 459–75.

86. For detail, see ibid., pp. 381–83.

87. Mehta, *Dream*, pp. 113–14. President, East Africa Indian Association (Kampala) to Colonial Office, 14 Jan. 1914, C.O. 536/74.

88. Henry R. Wallis (Acting Governor, Uganda) to W. C. Bottomley (Colonial Office), 26 Mar. 1917, C.O. 536/88, and subsequent correspondence in C.O. 536. European-Asian rivalry is described in Thomas F. Taylor, 'Role of the British Cotton Industry in the Establishment of a Colonial Economy in Uganda, 1902–1939', Ph.D. diss., Syracuse University, 1981, pp. 147–80.

89. Sir Robert Coryndon to Colonial Office, 10 Nov. 1918, C.O. 536/91.

90. Government Notice no. 73 of 1934, explained by G. F. Sayers (Acting Chief Secretary) to Secretary, Federated Chambers of Commerce Section, Indian Association, Dar es Salaam, 24 June 1935, items 62–65, Tanganyika Secretariat file 20614, 'Applications for Exclusive Licences Under Marketing Ordinances, 1932'.

91. Taylor, 'Role of the British Cotton Industry', p. 176.

92. Edward B. Jarvis (Acting Governor, Uganda) to Secretary of State for Colonies, confidential, 19 Dec. 1921; H.S.L. Polak (Secretary, Indians Overseas Association, London) to Under-Secretary of State for Colonies, 25 Oct. 1921, C.O. 536/115.

93. The introduction of marketing legislation is described in C.O. 533/3102 and Masao Yoshida, *Agricultural Marketing Intervention in East Africa: A Study in the Colonial Origins of Marketing Policies, 1900–65* (Tokyo: Institute of Development Economics, 1984). For the Asians' reaction, see Gregory, *India and East Africa*, pp. 448–50, 477–78, 487–89.

94. Cyril Ehrlich, 'The Uganda Economy, 1903–1945', chap. 8, *History of East Africa*, vol. 2, ed. Vincent Harlow and E. M. Chilver (Oxford: Clarendon, 1965), p. 469.

95. Kenya, *Report of the Economic Development Committee, 1934* (Nairobi: Government Printer, 1935), pp. 124–31. C. C. Wrigley, 'Kenya: The Patterns of Economic Life, 1902–45', chap. 5, *History of East Africa*, vol. 2, ed. Vincent Harlow and E. M. Chilver, pp. 251–52.

96. Tanganyika Secretariat file 20614, 'Applications for Exclusive Licences under Marketing Ordinances, 1932', Tanzania National Archives.

97. Chief Secretary to Director of Agriculture, Morogoro, 30 Nov. 1932, item 44, ibid.

98. G. F. Sayers (Acting Chief Secretary) to Secretary, Federated Chambers of Commerce, Indian Association, Dar es Salaam, 24 June 1935, ibid.

99. 'Handeni, Agriculture, Markets (Tanga Region)', Tanganyika file 6/1/6.

100. See the few letters ibid.

101. Government Notice no. 73 of 1934, explained ibid.

102. Tanganyika Secretariat file 18681, 'Policy for Controlling Competition', includes considerable corrspondence.

103. Akbar Singh (proprietor, H. Samji and Sons, Mwanga) and A. M. Samji, interviewed jointly by Honey, 15 Aug. 1973, Mwanza. Samji named three of the Asians: A. Lalji, Nasser Virjee, and C. K. Patel.

104. Letter, 28 May 1935, item 60, Tanganyika Secretariat file 20614.

105. Director of Agriculture, Morogoro, to Chief Secretary, 24 Sept. 1936. ibid.

106. Pertinent Colonial Office files are: 'Ten Year Development Plan, Kenya, 1951–3', C.O. 822/550; 'Development in East Africa, 1937', C.O. 822/83/2; ibid., '1938', C.O. 822/89/18; ibid., '1940–3', C.O. 822/105/10; 'Revised Development Plan, Tanganyika, 1951–2', C.O. 822/552; 'Development and Welfare Schemes, 1944–8', C.O. 533/536/38557; ibid., '1942–4', C.O. 533/530/9; ibid., '1944–8', C.O. 533/536/1–4.

107. International Bank for Reconstruction and Development, *Economic Development of Tanganyika* (Baltimore: Johns Hopkins University Press, 1961), p. 41.

108. For a brief history of the co-operative movement, see Tanganyika, *Report on Co-operative Development for the Year 1950* (no publication information), pp. 1–3, C.O. 736/30.

109. The British Public Record Office has several large files on the co-operative movement. See especially 'Co-operative Development in Tanganyika, 1951–4', C.O. 822/418; 'Co-operative Movement of Kenya, 1951–3', C.O. 822/416; 'Co-operative Movement, Uganda: Annual Reports', C.O. 533/421; 'Co-operative Societies Legislation, 1944–6', C.O. 533/534/14; ibid., '1943', C.O. 533/528/8.

110. Annual reports on co-operative development, 1960, for Kenya, Tanganyika, Uganda, and Zanzibar, C.O. 544/98, 736/54, 685/52, 688/43.

111. International Bank for Reconstruction and Development, *Economic Development of Kenya* (Baltimore: Johns Hopkins University Press, 1963), pp. 105–9.

112. Uganda, *Annual Report of the Department of Co-operative Development, 1960* (no publication information), p. 12, C.O. 585/52.

113. For a list and description see ibid., pp. 321–30.

114. International Bank for Reconstruction and Development, *Economic Development of Kenya*, pp. 276, 355.

115. Kenya, *Registrar-General Annual Report, 1960* (Nairobi: Government Printer, 1961), p. 30, C.O. 544/98. Tanganyika, *Annual Report of the Department of Commerce and Industry, 1960* (no publication information), p. 6, C.O. 736/67. Uganda, *Annual Report of the Administrator General for the Year ended 31st Dec., 1960* (no publication information), p. 11, C.O. 685/52. Several Asians described the losses of their businesses during the depression: A. Fazal, interviewed by Honey, 22 Nov. 1973, Bukoba; N. S. Patel, interviewed by Honey, 5 Mar., 7 Sept. 1973, Dar es Salaam; Basheer-ud-Deen, interviewed by Bennett, 28 May 1973, Kisumu; V. B. Shah, interviewed by Gregory, 11 July 1973, Jamnagar.

116. *East African Standard,* 5 Dec. 1908, p. 9. For other instances of conflict, see ibid., 16 Jan. 1908, p. 11; 26 Dec. 1908, p. 9; and Pandit, *Asians,* p. 169. Also, Lt.-Col. S. B. Miles (Acting Agent and Consul-General, Zanzibar) to Earl Granville (Secretary of State for Foreign Affairs), 3 Jan. 1883, encl. no. 91, *Correspondence with British Representatives and Agents Abroad and the Treasury Relative to the Slave Trade, 1883–84,* C. 3849 (London: Harrison and Sons, 1884).

117. 'Kilifi Dist. Political Record Book', vol. 2, p. 98, under 'District Economics', Syracuse University microfilm 2802, reel 72.

118. For example, S. Haji, whose father opened a shop in Iringa in 1900: interviewed by Honey, 27 June 1973, Iringa. Iliffe, however, describes one of the first actions of the rebels as the destruction of an Indian trading settlement at Samanga on the coast: *Tanganyika under German Rule*, p. 19.

119. For some records of dishonesty, see Bernard M.N. Broun (Supervisor, Government School, Marsabit) to District Commissioner, Marsabit, 26 Apr. 1960, file T&T.23/1/4, 'Transport: General, Including Contracts', vol. 2, '1955–62', Kenya Northeastern Province records, Syracuse University microfilm 4753, reel 34. 'Rex v. Shah Karamshi Karman', Kenya, *Digest of East African and Kenya Law Reports, 1877–1952* (Nairobi: Government Printer, 1953), 23/2/KLR64. *East African Standard*, 25 May 1951, p. 14. John Stonehouse, *Prohibited Immigrant* (London: Bodley Head, 1960), pp. 39, 90–91.

120. There are many reports in the local press. See, for example, *East African Standard*, 6 Jan. 1973, p. 1. For a visitor's assessment, see J. David Greenstone (University of Chicago), 'Corruption and Self Interest in Kampala and Nairobi: A Comment on Local Politics in East Africa', *Comparative Studies in Society and History*, 8 (1965–66), 204–5.

121. See, for example, 'Tana River District Annual Report, 1935', p. 19, Syracuse University microfilm 2801, reel 51. African resentment against Asian traders became prominent in the Kenya press during World War II. See, for example, letters by Africans, *East African Standard*, 7 Jan. 1943, p. 9; and 22 May 1944, p. 4.

122. H. S. Morris, *Indians in Uganda* (Chicago: University of Chicago Press, 1968), p. 145.

123. Newsletter no. 1, 'International Co-operative Administration Scheme for Assistance to African Industrialists, Artisans and Businessmen', 12 July 1956; no. 2, 10 Nov. 1956; no. 3, 31 May 1957; G. D. Parkin (Minister of Commerce and Industry) to All Provincial Commissioners, 22 Feb. 1961—all in file 'Trade and Commerce: Credit Trade with Natives: Loans to African Traders (not Agricultural) and Traders' Courses, etc., 1951–61', Syracuse University microfilm 4750, reel 348. International Bank for Reconstruction and Development, *Economic Development of Kenya*, p. 168.

124. Joseph Daniel Otiende, who was to become KAU general secretary and a KANU (Kenya African National Union) M.P., typified African leaders' support of co-operatives as early as 1943: letter, *East African Standard*, 6 Sept. 1943, p. 4.

125. Austen applied the term 'paternalistic' to Britain's interwar policy of indirect rule. The term is equally applicable here. Ralph Austen, *Northwest Tanzania under German and British Rule: Colonial Policy and Tribal Politics, 1889–1939* (New Haven: Yale University Press, 1968), pp. 204–8.

126. Uganda, *Report of the Commission of Enquiry into the Disturbances Which Occurred in Uganda during January, 1945* (Entebbe: Government Printer, 1945). Jan Jelmert Jorgensen, *Uganda, a Modern History* (New York: St. Martin's, 1981), pp. 181–82.

127. *East African Standard*, 24 Dec. 1959, p. 7; 13 Jan. 1960, p. 9.

128. Semakula Kiwanuka, 'The Uganda National Movement and the Trade Boycott of 1959/60: A Study of Politics and Economics in Uganda on the Eve of

Independence', typescript, Makerere University Department of History, Kampala, 1973. Jorgensen, *Uganda*, pp. 188–90.

129. 'Minutes' of the 1st, 2d, 3d, and 4th meetings of the Federation's Executive Committee, Nairobi, 10 Dec. 1961, 18 Feb. 1962, 6 May 1962, 5 Aug. 1962, file 7, 'Federation. 3. Minutes, Circulars, etc'., Mombasa Indian Merchants' Chamber records, Syracuse University microfilm 1922, reel 3.

130. International Bank for Reconstruction and Development, *Economic Development of Uganda* (Baltimore: Johns Hopkins University Press, 1962), p. 45. D. S. Pearson, *Industrial Development in East Africa* (Nairobi: Oxford University Press, 1969), pp. 288–89. Kenya, *Development Plan, 1966–70* (Nairobi: Government Printer, 1966), p. 241.

131. Peter Marris and Anthony Somerset, *African Businessmen; a Study of Entrepreneurship and Development in Kenya* (London: Routledge and Kegan Paul, 1971), pp. 10–11.

132. The pertinent legislation was the Immigration Act, no. 25 of 1967, *Kenya Gazette Supplement: Acts, 1967*, no. 68, 25 Aug. 1967, pp. 159–77. It came into operation 1 Dec. 1967 and was augmented by Legal Notices nos. 234, 235, 244, and 253, ibid., nos. 88, 94, and 97. Enforcement continued into the 1970s. In Jan. 1973, for example, 418 traders were served four-month quit notices. *East African Standard*, 11 Jan. 1973, pp. 1, 3. *Sunday Nation* (Nairobi), 14 Jan. 1973, p. 4.

133. The relevant correspondence among the chambers and numerous clippings from the major newspapers are in file 38, 'Kenya Association of Chambers of Commerce', Mombasa Indian Merchants' Chamber records, Syracuse University microfilm 1922, reel 3.

134. Clipping, *East African Standard*, 14 June 1963, ibid.

135. Kenya Association of Chambers of Commerce, 'Minutes of an Extraordinary Meeting . . . 3rd July 1964'; R. J. Hillard (Chairman, Standing Committee, Association of Chambers of Commerce, Industry and Trade) to President, Kenya Chamber of Commerce and Industry, Nairobi, 18 Sept. 1964, ibid.

136. The pertinent minutes of the federation are in file 7, 'Federation. 3. Minutes, Circulars, etc'., ibid.

137. G. M. Motala (Honorary Secretary, Kenya National Chamber of Commerce and Industry) to Chairman, Mombasa Merchants' Chamber, 14 June 1965; 'Kenya National Chamber of Commerce and Industry. Minutes of the Conference Held in Nairobi . . . 7 July, 1965'—file 'Kenya National Chamber of Commerce and Industry', ibid. *East African Standard*, 1 June 1965, pp. 1, 4. *Daily Nation*, 1 June 1965, p. 1.

138. For the correspondence of Kiano and others, see file 38, 'Kenya Association of Chambers of Commerce: 2. Agenda/Minutes/Circulars', Mombasa Indian Merchants' Chamber records; and file 10, 'Other Chambers. 4. Minutes, Circulars', ibid. Also, file 'Minutes of Meeting, Indian Chamber of Commerce, Nairobi', Federation of Indian Chambers of Commerce and Industry of Eastern Africa records, Syracuse University microfilm 1923, reel 3.

139. Issa G. Shivji, *Class Struggles in Tanzania* (New York: Monthly Review Press, 1976), pp. 73–77. For an Asian view of the new organizations, see 'Dar es Salaam Merchants' Chamber: Presidential Address Delivered by the Chamber's President, Mr. M. M. Devani, at the Annual General Meeting . . . 28 March 1964',

file 10, 'Other Chambers. 4. Minutes, Circulars', Mombasa Indian Merchants' Chamber records.

140. Julius K. Nyerere, *Freedom and Development: A Selection from Writings and Speeches, 1968–73* (Dar es Salaam: Oxford University Press, 1973), pp. 312–14. *Tanzanian Second Five-Year Plan for Economic and Social Development, 1st July, 1969–30th June, 1974:* vol. 1, *General Analysis* (Dar es Salaam: Government Printer, 1969), p. 12.

141. Uganda, *Report of the Commission of Enquiry into the Cotton Industry* (Kampala: Government Printer, 1966), pp. 24–25. Mahmood Mamdani, *Politics and Class Formation in Uganda* (London: Monthly Review Press, 1976), pp. 260–62. E. J. Stoutjesdijk, *Uganda's Manufacturing Sector: A Contribution to an Analysis of Industrialization in East Africa* (Nairobi: East African Publishing House, 1967), pp. 34–35.

142. The charter was published as Dr. A. Milton Obote, *Common Man's Charter* (Entebbe: Government Printer, 1949).

143. Uganda, *Parliamentary Debates*, 23 July 1970, pp. 198–201. Yash Tandon, 'Pragmatic Industrialist', chap. 5, *Jayant Madhvani*, ed. Robert Becker and Nitin Jayant Madhvani (London: W. and J. Mackay, 1973), pp. 17–18.

144. Jorgensen, *Uganda*, p. 248.

145. Mamdani, *Politics*, pp. 280–81. S. H. Jaffer, interviewed by Bennett, 9 Apr. 1973, Nairobi.

146. Honorary Secretary (Federation) to Hon'ble Minister for Commerce and Industry, 14 Oct. 1964; T. A. Cooper (Commercial Manager, Cosata) to [name blacked out], 15 Sept. 1964; Chandrakant M. Doshi (Assistant Honorary Secretary, Mombasa Merchants' Chamber) to Permanent Secretary, Ministry of Commerce and Industry, 10 Nov. 1964—file 8, 'Minister for Commerce and Industry: l. Correspondence', Mombasa Indian Merchants' Chamber records.

147. Bhimji B. Shah (Honorary Secretary, Mombasa Merchants' Chamber) to Permanent Secretary, Ministry of Commerce and Industry, 10 June 1965; R. A. Gray (for Permanent Secretary) to B. B. Shah, 16 July 1965, ibid.

148. Memo. by Arthur M. Champion, 19 Sept. 1944, file 'Native Affairs in Kenya', Southern Province daily correspondence, Syracuse University microfilm 2804, reel 105.

CHAPTER THREE

Money-lending, Insurance, and the Extension of Credit

The whole idea of the average petty trader on the Coast is to get the native [cultivator] into his debt.

—S. H. Fazan, 1924[1]

The actual evil appears to be that the cultivator is improvident. . . . If law is brought into being to stop all forms of advances, it would operate against the dealers and the cultivators alike.

—District Commissioner, Lamu, 1921[2]

As retailing led to importing and wholesaling, so the development of business and the accumulation of profit resulted in money-lending, insurance, and the extension of credit. Although carried on informally apart from the formal banking structure and developed not as principal occupations but as sidelines, these activities were very important to the economic development of East Africa and should be regarded as a major Asian contribution.

Money-lending and Insurance

A common practice in the early years of settlement was for a trusted Asian, often the head of a business or a supervisor in construction, to hold money in trust for his employees or fellow workers. Such an arrangement was preferred to dealing with the early banks, which were impersonal, managed by Europeans, fraught with delays, and often remote from the place of business or work. Among the Asians who held money in trust for others was the Parsee boilerman Dinshaw Byramjee, who at the turn of the century directed sixty or seventy men in laying rails and operating a metal lathe on the Uganda Railway. On payday most of the men gave their money to Byramjee to hold for them, and he in turn placed it with Waljee Hadjee & Sons, an Allidina Visram shop that moved every two weeks to keep up with the railhead. One Sunday evening thirty or forty of the Punjabi workers came to Byramjee to ask for their money. They wanted to play cards. That day, however, the shop had moved to the railhead four or five miles distant. Byramjee had not told the men about leaving the money with the shopkeepers, and they were irate. Just that morning the footprints of a lion had been found in Byramjee's tent. The long walk to the shop and back in the dark through a notorious lion country was a fearful prospect. Byramjee barely escaped a serious beating before persuading the men to walk with him by lantern light to the shop. There they found old Allidina Visram himself, and he cheerfully paid out the money.[3] Among other merchants who held money for the railway employees was the Ismaili, Waljee Hirjee. He had come to Zanzibar by dhow in 1867, set up a betel-nut shop, and then moved to Mombasa where eventually he sold provisions to the railway crews.[4]

The practice of entrusting earnings to respected supervisors or merchants was prevalent among the Asians before World War II. Not until after the war did the community begin to deposit much money in the local European- and Indian-owned banks.

Though closely related to the holding of money, money-lending apparently had a separate origin among the clerks and more prosperous merchants. In the early years many of the clerks who worked for the railway or another government agency and in time acquired substantial savings financed other Asians in establishing businesses. Later as merchants accumulated wealth, they too became money-lenders.[5] Madan Behal has described how his grandfather, a Punjabi Hindu, moved to Arusha after the expiration of his indenture as a coolie, opened a small retail shop, expanded into transport, and began to lend money. The Germans would go to him for loans when they were refused by the regular lending institutions. He became a millionaire and was known in German East Africa as 'The Bank'.[6] Behal's counterpart in Kenya was Kanji Naranji Lakhani, a Lohana who emigrated from Porbandar to Nairobi in 1908, worked for his brother, and then founded his own provisions business. By the age of twenty-three he is said to have controlled 50 per cent of Kenya's wholesale trade in groceries and was a shilling millionaire. Among the many he financed as a money-lender were the Mehtas and the Madhvanis.[7]

Money-lending continued through the Asians' residency in East Africa. It was common for the more affluent in any community to help later arrivals finance their businesses. One Shah, for instance, would lend to another Shah.[8] Most such loans were given in a spirit of sharing, and no interest was expected. As the various Asian groups associated in many business ventures, these interest-free loans soon crossed communal lines. In 1972 an interview with the textile merchant Lakhamshi R. Shah in the Nairobi office of Hemraj Bharmal Ltd. was interrupted by a visit of Madatally Mohamed Manji, the Ismaili manufacturer of the Baring brand biscuits. Manji was carrying a briefcase. Fifteen minutes later, after Manji's departure, Shah confided that Manji had just handed him Shs 1,000,000 as repayment of a loan given a few months previously. There was no note and no interest, he said; it was a loan from friend to friend.[9]

Although they did not establish formal banks like Lloyds or Barclays, some Asians developed a merchant banking system that performed essentially the same functions. One of the foremost merchant banks was Keshavji Anandji & Co., which was established at Zanzibar in 1890. As its name denotes, the firm was the creation of Keshav Anand, a Lohana from the Porbandar area who is said to have been the first member of his community to settle in East Africa. During the 1880s Anand learned the banking business while serving as a clerk for a European bank in Zanzibar. His company began with a specialization in international trade, but by 1900 it was primarily a financial concern. At first dealing with Lohanas and then with Hindus generally, it subsidized especially exports of ivory, simsim, beeswax, and hides and skins and imports of textiles, building materials, hardware, and cement. The company worked in close co-operation with European banks and continued through the colonial period.[10]

Two other examples of merchant bankers are Waljee Hirjee and J. B. Pandya. After building a fortune in supplying food to the railway crews, Hirjee branched into banking. He is said to have served the financial interest of the Ismaili community during World War I and to have been instrumental in encouraging the Standard Bank of South Africa to open offices in Kenya.[11] Pandya, who (as mentioned in Chapter 1) came to Mombasa from Bhavnagar in 1907, began as a customs agent and in his spare time was a bookkeeper for various Asian and European trading companies. In 1917 he founded Pandya & Co., a shipping and forwarding agency for importers and exporters. As an advisor to the manager of the Standard Bank, he represented the financial interests of many Asian commercial firms.[12]

As Hirjee and Pandya illustrate, the Asians expanded their commercial activities in close association with the formal banking interests. Though described as the 'best customers' of the European banks, they preferred to deal when possible with the two Indian concerns, the Bank of India and the Bank of Baroda.[13] The Bank of India, which was heavily committed to the financing of Visram's commercial empire, opened its first East African branch in Mombasa in 1923. Two years later when Visram's enterprise collapsed, the bank closed its Mombasa branch and withdrew from East Africa. In 1953 it reopened its Mombasa office and soon after established branches in Kampala, Nairobi, Jinja, Dar es Salaam, and Kisumu. The Bank of India was followed by the Bank of Baroda. Indian enterprise in East Africa, however, suffered with the nationalization of these banks. In 1969 India nationalized its banks and in 1972 withdrew the Bank of India and all but one branch of the Bank of Baroda from Uganda. In 1971, because of President Nyerere's nationalization policy, India had to withdraw all its banking facilities from Tanzania.[14]

The Ismailis were unique in forming their own lending institutions. In 1945, to assist members of the community in building homes and establishing businesses, the Aga Khan created the Diamond Jubilee Investment Trust Inc. Capitalized at £1,000,000, the trust was at that time the largest Asian corporation in East Africa. The Aga Khan contributed 25 per cent of the capital and other investors outside East Africa about 15 per cent, but the rest was subscribed by the Ismailis of East Africa through purchase of £1 shares. With its headquarters in Dar es Salaam, the trust initially opened branches in Mombasa and Kampala. In time the Aga Khan contributed an additional £583,500, more shares were sold, and as many as thirty-five subsidiary corporations and cooperative societies were established. These subsidiaries also lent money at low interest, often on the guarantee of a third party. Offering loans at 6 per cent and on the average matching the amount put up as security by borrowers, the trust fostered a rapid economic development by the enterprising Ismailis. Beginning in 1958 while continuing to finance housing and trade, it subsidized in co-operation with the Tanganyika government a sizeable project for an Ismaili farming settlement. In this instance it issued loans at a low 3.5 to 5 per cent interest rate.[15]

After independence, as a result of consultation with the new African heads of state, the Aga Khan established a second lending institution, the Industrial Promotion Services Ltd. (IPS). With its headquarters in Geneva and branches in the three East African countries, the IPS differed from the trust in that the Aga Khan retained a controlling interest. He donated 51 per cent of the capital of nearly £3,000,000, and his followers in East Africa, through purchase of Shs 200 shares, put up the remaining 49 per cent. In 1964 at the invitation of the Aga Khan, the National Development Corp. of Tanzania purchased 10,000 shares and obtained a 24 per cent interest in the Tanzanian branch. As its name denotes, the IPS was designed to promote an Ismaili move into industry. It financed at low interest in co-operation with government many small-scale industries for the manufacture especially of textiles. It also helped finance several government projects, including the Bahari Beach Hotel near Dar es Salaam and the parastatal textile factory Kiltex in Arusha.[16]

The Asians' financial needs were provided not only by these Ismaili institutions, the Indian banks, and the informal channels of money-lending, but also by insurance companies. During the colonial period, three Asian insurance companies were formed and incorporated in East Africa: the Jubilee Insurance Co. Ltd. and the Pioneer Assurance Society Ltd. in Kenya; and the Pan-African Insurance Co. Ltd. in Uganda. The Jubilee Insurance Co., the first such institution to be 'floated' in East Africa, was established in 1937 by the Aga Khan primarily for the service of the Ismaili community, but it soon served non-Ismaili Asians and other peoples in life, marine, automobile, home, and business insurance. It was very successful and established branches in Bombay and Karachi.[17] Subsequently the Pioneer General Assurance Society was formed by a group of Ismailis on their own initiative. It was the first to sell life insurance to Africans. The Pan-African Insurance Co. was the creation of several Patels.[18]

Many Asians served as agents for Indian or British insurance companies. The ubiquitous Allidina Visram represented the British Dominion's Marine Insurance Company.[19] In Uganda where most of the companies were managed by Asians, the Jaffer family was prominent. In 1923 Habib Kassumali Jaffer left a position with the Standard Bank in Mombasa to open a branch of the South British Insurance Co. in Jinja. Insuring many of the major cotton producers and ginners, including Muljibhai Prabhudas Madhvani, he built up a flourishing business.[20] After 1945 as he began to take a prominent role in Uganda politics, his son Sultan managed the agency. In 1968 Sultan Jaffer became chairman of the Insurance Association of East Africa (Uganda) and also of the Insurance Advisory Board of the Uganda government.[21]

In Kenya the Oza family and in Tanganyika D. G. Patel were typical of the more successful insurance agents. U. K. Oza, who successively edited *Tanganyika Opinion* and the Mombasa *Democrat,* became in 1930 the chief agent in East Africa for the New India Insurance Co. In politics, however, however, Oza became too active in support of Kenya Africans, and when World War I began he was asked by the protectorate government to return to India. In 1961 his son Pushkar, who had entered the insurance business in India, established in Nairobi a branch of the Life Assurance Co. of India, and in three years he was promoted to management of all the company's operations in East Africa.[22] Patel, like many others, began to sell insurance after a successful career in another business. In 1959 while working as an auditor in Kilosa, he became an agent for the Norwich Union Insurance Co. Offering all kinds of insurance, he quickly established five branches and then a central office in Dar es Salaam. He was still expanding in 1967 when the Tanzania government suddenly nationalized all insurance. The consequent termination of commissions caused Patel, in common with other agents in Tanzania, to drop insurance and concentrate on a more profitable business. He had no alternative but to return to auditing.[23]

The Extension of Credit

The advancement of goods on credit, which became a standard practice among Asians in East Africa, is very closely related to the lending of money, but it was so important to the economic development of East Africa that it deserves separate consideration. As conducted within the Asian community in the relations of one Asian to another, it permitted a rapid expansion of business. It enabled Asian enterprise to thrive far beyond the confines of the circulating currency. Moreover, unlike their lending of money, which seldom involved other peoples, the Asians' extension of credit had an appreciable effect on Europeans, Arabs, and Africans.

The credit system in East Africa was derived from India. For centuries the traders of western India had used a system of promissory notes known as *hundi*. It was common among importers and exporters to transact business with DAs, the 'days after bills' which called for payment in thirty, sixty, or ninety days plus three days grace. Traders importing merchandise from Britain on DAs, for example, normally would not have to pay until the goods were sold and thus would need a minimum of capital. In East Africa the Zanzibar Asian merchants with little capital borrowed from the wealthier merchants on DAs or even 'payable when able' agreements. Alibhai Sheriff, manager of Waljee Hirjee & Sons, is said to have invented the promissory note system in East Africa. He took the notes to European banks and the Bank of India, which accepted them at a discount. It was this practice that led the Waljee Hirjee firm into banking.[24]

Credit was apparently a common feature of business enterprise from the beginning of Asian settlement. As the Zanzibar companies expanded their activities to the mainland coastal centres, they served as wholesalers by providing commodities on credit to their coastal agencies. In a very short time the businesses established on the mainland outgrew their parental concerns on Zanzibar and became the central offices for business in East Africa generally. They imported directly from India and in time also from Britain, the United States, Germany, and other countries and acted as wholesalers for the branches they established at the various railway stops and other places in the hinterland.

During this process, a system of rotating credit became the standard mode of exchange not only for the parent companies and their subsidiaries but for all the Asian commercial firms. The retailer would obtain merchandise on credit, sell it, remit payment, and receive more goods on credit. The average Asian shopkeeper in effect owned scarcely any of the merchandise on his shelves, and very little currency changed hands compared to the overall business transacted in the process of importing, wholesaling, and retailing. There is much truth in the remark often heard that the Asians founded their businesses without money.[25]

Credit was extended not only for the purchase of merchandise but also for the performance of services and conduct of business generally. There was often an understanding between the prospective Gujarati shopkeeper and the Punjabi *fundi* (artisan) or contractor that payment for the construction of the former's duka would be deferred until a quantity of merchandise had been sold.[26] Even the banks, European as well as Indian, extended credit freely to their customers through the system of overdrafts. In writing checks or withdrawing money, the Europeans and Asians deemed 'reliable' could write checks or withdraw currency well beyond the amounts of their deposits on the understanding that, when able, they would make up the difference and pay a small interest on the overdrafts. The practice in East Africa was far more prevalent than in Britain. It is not surprising that East Africa as early as 1907 was becoming known as 'the land of the chit'.[27]

The extension of credit carried a high degree of risk. In the highly mobile society of East Africa where both Asians and Europeans made frequent visits to their homelands, the lender had only a tenuous hold on the borrower. This was especially true in the early years. In a letter to the *East African Standard* in 1907, 'an esteemed contributor' pointed out the difficulties of Nairobi retailers in collecting on debts owed by European settlers who were investing all their cash in land. 'Only 50% of the Nairobi outstandings', the author complained, 'can be calculated on'.[28]

In time the European businessmen became much more restrictive than the Asians in their conferral of credit. In 1956 an American graduate student who came to Kenya for research was informed that a reliable used car, which he sorely needed, could not be obtained for much less than £500. He had, however, only £100 to invest in a car. He visited all the European car agencies in Nairobi but found that none would consider selling a serviceable car for a deposit of only £100. In desperation against the advice of European acquaintances, he then approached Jamil Habib, the principal Asian used-car dealer. Habib cheerfully accepted the £100 as down payment on a two-year-old Volkswagen priced at £400 and asked how long the American planned to remain in Kenya. 'Six months', was the reply. 'Then', said Habib, 'you sell the car just before you leave and pay me the remaining £300'. Six months later the American sold the car for approximately the purchase price, repaid Habib, and returned to the United States with a warm regard for the Asians' way of business.[29]

In the extension of credit the Asians made an important contribution to European settlement. In developing their farms the Europeans purchased provisions, clothing, linens, blankets, cooking utensils, and hardware from the Asian shopkeepers in the local towns, often almost entirely from a single store. Usually they received the goods on credit with the assumption, in time of hardship, that payment would be deferred until after the next harvest. Over short terms no interest was asked, and often even for long periods with a view to favourable continuing relationships the Asians requested no interest or kept it to a minimum. Occasionally when hit by some local disaster such as locusts or drought or by a fall of prices in the international market, the farmers would be unable to pay for several years. Such was the case in the late 1920s and early 1930s when a combination of these misfortunes affected Kenya agriculture. As Kenya's foremost colonial minister of finance, Sir Ernest Vasey, averred, the Asians carried the Europeans through the depression on credit.[30]

Despite public denunciation of Asians by European political leaders, many settlers in the postcolonial years expressed privately their indebtedness to the Asian shopkeeper.[31] Some confided that they felt as if they were virtually wards of the Asians. When payment was deferred over long periods, the shopkeepers held the settlers' passports and legal documents for security, and in this way and in the provision of necessities they exercised a subtle but firm control over the settlers and their families.[32]

Like the European settlers, the Arab and Swahili landowners of Zanzibar and the coast borrowed extensively from the Asian merchants.[33] For them, however, the extension of credit often resulted in the loss of their land. Through generations they had developed a plantation economy based on slave labour. In 1873 by treaty between the British government and the sultan, the slave trade was abolished at all the sultan's ports, and the notorious Zanzibar slave market was closed. In 1897 slavery itself was abolished on Zanzibar and Pemba, and in 1907 in all the sultan's mainland dominions.[34] The Arabs and Swahili were unable to make the transition successfully from slave to hired labour. Faced with a shortage of money, they began to receive goods on credit from the Asian shopkeepers with their future crops offered as security. Through the years they fell increasingly in debt. When crops proved insufficient as recompense, they mortgaged their lands, which, unlike the settlers' highland farms, could pass legally to non-Europeans.

Because of the risk of lending to these people who, unlike Europeans, were not favoured by the governments, the Asians frequently charged high interest rates, and some took advantage of the situation. In 1934 an investigating British commission reported that the rates on Zanzibar were frequently more than 100 per cent. It estimated that through fore-closures or purchases the Asians had already acquired more than half the Arabs' clove property.[35] On the East African coast a similar transfer had occurred. A study early in the 1920s indicated that the Swahili and poorer Arabs after selling their lands were drifting into the towns, quickly spending their money, and becoming 'indigent loafers'.[36] By 1929, according to C. W. Hobley, the Swahili had lost all their landed property by mortgaging it to Asian merchants.[37] To the surprise of administrators like Hobley, however, the Arabs and Swahili appreciated the credit system and resisted British efforts to abolish it.[38]

The credit system developed with the coastal Arabs and Swahili was soon extended to the Africans in the interior. In entering the market economy, the African cultivators needed farm implements, seed, fertil-izer, transport, and many items associated with a new way of life. In most instances they purchased these goods and services from or through a lo-cal Asian shopkeeper and sold their produce either to him or an itinerant Asian trader. When short of cash, the Africans very often found that they could obtain the goods and services on credit. In some instances, as in the case of many Europeans, the Africans were not asked to provide any collateral. Their word was sufficient. In 1916 an astonished district offi-cer reported that the Africans of the Bajun Islands off the Kenya coast were borrowing large sums from Asian traders without any security.[39] In most cases, however, the uncertainties involved prompted the Asian lenders to ask for security. The Africans could not offer their lands be-cause Asians, by authority of the Preservation of Property Ordinance of 1916, could legally hold land in the reserves only in specified town-ships.[40]

If Africans had no personal property of value, their only negotiable as-sets were their labour and their future crops. In the early years of associ-ation with Asians, Africans would offer their future labour in return for an immediate grant of money or food. The most common contract of this kind involved woodcutting. Traders would issue money or food to Africans on promises to cut and deliver a specified number of 'korjas of borities' by certain dates.[41] More prevalent in time was the offer to sell future crops at prices at which the Asians thought they could obtain some profit. Often the Africans were also asked to pay interest on the amount of credit. Although most probably benefitted from this arrange-ment, some Africans, as seen in the study of Asian activity in the rural ar-eas, fell increasingly in debt and, over long periods through commitments to the Asians, lost their opportunities to buy and sell at the most favourable prices.[42] Even they, however, were reluctant to report any abuses to the British officials for fear, it seemed, that they would 'never be given credit again'.[43]

African artisans were also affected by the credit system and found it a mixed blessing. As early as 1919 in Seyidie Province, it was customary for a skilled African who had contracted with an Asian for certain work to obtain a substantial amount of his fee in advance. Often by the time he started the work, he had spent the money. In desperation he would then contract with another Asian for a different task and again secure an advance payment. When working under the second contract, he soon would be penniless and would have to undertake a third contract well before he could begin its performance. The improvident artisan would thus subsist through long periods entirely on borrowed money—a circumstance that an observant district officer thought could not 'be otherwise than extremely demoralizing'.[44]

Beginning with the Credit to Natives Ordinance of 1903, credit contracts between Asians and Africans were enforced by the courts. The Malindi district commissioner, the young S. H. Fazan who was beginning an important administrative career, was the first to describe the enforcement of the contracts in the courts. In 1918 in a series of dispatches Fazan explained that if an African defaulted, the trader had redress in the court of the local *liwali* (Arab headman). On notification from the trader, the liwali would issue a summons. The African, not being bound to attend, seldom appeared, and the liwali, after a short formal examination of the plaintiff, almost always pronounced judgment in the plaintiff's favour for the full amount of the contract. The fact that most traders, even the Asians at this time in the coast's history, were Muslims was an additional reason for the liwalis' decisions in their interest.[45]

A judgment against an African, according to Fazan, usually led to a serious indebtedness. The trader sued not for performance of the contract but for the monetary loss that he had suffered as a result of the African's nonperformance. He asked, for instance, not for a sum equivalent to the price that he had contracted to pay for the grain in the reserve but for an amount equivalent to what he would have obtained by selling the grain in Mombasa. The law upheld him in this as a fair compensation.[46]

Largely because of Fazan's criticism the government undertook to revise the law, and this action resulted in the protectorate's first thorough examination of the credit system. In October 1919 on recommendation of Fazan at Malindi, the Mombasa government urged the central government to draft new legislation. Fazan felt so strongly about the issue that he took the highly unusual step of personally approaching the governor and the chief justice.[47] The result was a bill entitled 'An Ordinance to

Regulate the Practice of Advance to Natives on the Security of Crops'. When introduced in the Legislative Council, the bill was referred to a subcommittee composed of three Europeans, an Arab, and the Asian leader Tayabali Mulla Jeevanjee. After sampling opinion from all communities in Seyidie and discovering that Africans and Arabs opposed any changes in the credit system, the committee unanimously agreed not to support the bill. Any restrictive legislation, it decided, would drive the traders from the province.[48] So the bill was abandoned.

The fact that Africans as well as Asians and Arabs opposed any restrictions of the mortgaging system was a revelation to the officials who had so strongly urged its termination. A new senior Coast commissioner adhered to the idea that the system was 'bad and conducive to crime' but confessed that he was unable to suggest any remedy that would be approved by any community, whether European, Asian, or African, 'as the two former are mostly money lenders and the latter are all too willing borrowers'.[49] In reply the acting chief native commissioner confided that he was unwilling to recommend any further legislation.[50] Not until after World War II was the Kenya government, with a new generation of officials perhaps unmindful of the past, seriously to consider again the drafting of legislation to curb the mortgaging of crops and services.[51]

Unlike the African cultivators, the Africans who moved into road transport seem only to have benefitted from the Asians' credit system. After World War II when the Kenya government made available a large number of surplus cars and lorries, many Africans, as will be noted in Chapter 4, borrowed money from Asians to purchase them, whereas others obtained, partially through credit, the older vehicles of Asian transporters. Those Africans who were successful in the ensuing competition repaid their loans and became established transporters. The less successful eventually lost their vehicles, which had been offered as security. Because the licences for transporting goods and passengers, however, could not legally be transferred, the Asians and Africans conspired to conceal the sale, retain the Africans as nominal owners, and carry on the businesses as usual. Although the Asians as the real owners gained the profits, the Africans retained ostensibly prestigious positions, received salaries, and had the opportunity to learn the transporting business and, when possible, to start again on their own.[52]

The rising African retailer, like the transporter, appears to have received only benefit from the Asians' extension of credit. Lending money to Africans to start businesses entirely independent of the Asians' organization entailed considerable risk, but there is evidence that many such loans were made. Very early in their association with traders, some Africans acted as purchasers or sellers for Asians in return for advancements of money. In 1920 'a native of Mtanganyiko' was described by the acting district commissioner of Kilifi as subsisting 'by borrowing money from traders and acting as buyer for them, receiving in payment a proportion of the maize or other crop bought at the average rate of a kibaba for every six pishis brought'. As the African had no shop and did not seem to fit 'the definition of a trader, Hawker or commercial Traveller', the commissioner was perplexed as to how to classify him for tax purposes.[53]

There are records of some instances in which the system of credit was employed decidedly to the Asians' advantage. In 1921, for instance, the district commissioner at Lamu reported that Asian dhow owners were refusing to accept repayment of advances offered to their sailors in order to keep their services. The men, who were paid on a sharecropper system, received no pay during the three months when the boats lay idle. They customarily took advances on their future profits to carry them through this period. On this occasion the Asian owners, needing their help in keeping the boats repaired, were refusing to accept payment.[54]

Most of the Asian credit obtained by African businessmen seems to have been received for the purpose of establishing retail shops in the more remote African areas. The observation of one Asian that Africans were given credit to trade where Asians feared to go may apply to some of the situations, but there were many reasons why the Asians preferred to remain in the towns and cities while expanding their business into rural areas. The usual arrangement was for an Asian retailer and wholesaler to lend money to an African to build a shop in the reserve and then to stock his shelves with goods received on credit. Amritlal Raishi, who in 1933 established a Nairobi crockery firm, Amritlal & Co., and subsequently was involved in many other businesses, has described how, as he said, 'the Asians brought Africans into business'. They used to put goods in a lorry, he explained, then go to the centres of five or six traders in Central Province and sell the goods to them on credit. Several weeks later the Asians went on another round, recovered the money, and let out new goods on credit. Sometimes they covered the lorry and put a lock on the back. Then after counting the goods on the lorry, they sent it out with an African driver. On the lorry's return, they would again count the goods and expect the driver to account for those missing. In this way, Raishi explained, the Asians were giving each trader between Shs 2,000 and 5,000 of credit per month.[55]

There apparently were many such arrangements with Africans who through several years of association had gained the Asians' confidence. In 1972 the amount of such credit outstanding with African businessmen in Kenya was estimated as £10 million.[56] Although the practice was more prevalent after independence, there is considerable evidence that Asians were lending to incipient African merchants in the early years of settlement. Among the Asians the Shahs, who had concentrated on selling consumer goods such as textiles and sundries, took the initiative in lending to Africans. Shah Somchand Keshavji, who in 1926 opened with his uncle a general store in Eldoret, recalled that he had helped from forty to fifty Africans establish affiliated businesses. The Africans, he said, repaid their loans and, while continuing their merchant enterprise, purchased farms with their profits.[57] Vemchand Khimchand Shah stated that after setting up a men's clothing shop in Nairobi, he lent amounts from Shs 500 to 5,000 to Africans entering business. Like Keshavji, he was repaid in all cases and was well satisfied with the ensuing relationships.[58]

Contrary to these statements, the evidence indicates that most Africans did not repay their loans. The Shahs and Bohras of Tanganyika lost considerable money according to Ibrahim Mohamed Jivan, a sisal planter in Arusha whose parents began in East Africa as bead sellers in 1910. They lent sums varying from Shs 20,000 to 50,000, he recalled, and only 10 per cent of the loans were repaid.[59] Lakhamshi R. Shah, the Nairobi textile dealer who from 1955 to 1959 was president of the Indian Chambers of Commerce and Industry, also reported unfavorably on the African repayment. Though noted for his liberality in financial relations with Africans, he confided in 1972 that he personally had lost at least £20,000 by giving Africans credit. Judging from his own experience and from the many cases of which he had knowledge as chamber president, he believed that only 30 per cent of the Africans who borrowed succeeded and repaid their loans.[60]

The risk of lending to Africans was greatly augmented in Kenya by the Credit to Africans (Control) Ordinance of 1948.[61] Entitled in full 'An Ordinance to Provide for Controlling the Granting of Credit by Non-Africans to Africans', the law was designed ostensibly, as the first speaker of Kenya's independent Parliament, Humphrey Slade, said, 'to protect the African from himself'.[62] The Asians who were involved in the extension of credit, however, believed that the ordinance was devised to keep the African in the position of a labourer and diminish the close financial accord that was developing between the Asian and African communities.[63] The ordinance prohibited a non-African from suing an African for more than Shs 200. An exemption clause permitted suits for larger amounts if the contract had been drawn up with the approval of the 'local authority', presumably the district commissioner, but such contracts violated the spirit of the ordinance and very rarely received official sanction. Thus for twelve years, from 1948 until 1960 when the ordinance was repealed, the Asians of Kenya were virtually precluded by law from lending Africans more than £10. That they continued during the twelve years to extend credit for much larger sums attests not only to the Asians' willingness to risk their capital outside the protection of the law but also to the relationship of trust and responsibility that was being established between many Asians and Africans.[64]

Although attempting to restrict the Asians' credit practises, the Kenya government itself assumed the position of a money-lender. From the beginning it prohibited the local native councils from lending money or engaging in finance.[65] In 1954, however, to facilitate industrial, commercial, and other enterprise, it established the Industrial Development Corp. (IDC). During the remaining colonial years, though lending large sums for the development of European industry, the agency provided for Africans only the loan fund of £25,000 donated by the U.S. government, and it seldom extended more than £200 to an African.[66] In 1964 the new African government added a specific commercial function to the IDC, the name of which was changed to the Industrial and Commercial Development Corp. The revised agency began to give loans and credit guarantees to African shopkeepers in amounts of £500 and more. By 1966 it had issued nearly £90,000 in loans and £10,000 in credit guarantees to about 170 African retailers and wholesalers.[67]

Partly because of the alternative avenue for African development but mainly because of the growing restrictions on their business enterprise, the Asians after independence gradually reduced their lending and credit activities. They gave less money and credit not only to Africans, Europeans, and Arabs but even to members of their own community. As it diminished, their lending took somewhat new forms. Whereas most of the credit before independence was given to Africans in rural areas, it went after independence mainly to urban Africans.[68] Some African politicians and civil servants began to take advantage of their positions to obtain in effect forced loans in return for favours. Anant J. Pandya, who represented the Coast Province in the Kenya Parliament from 1956 to 1969, was frequently asked for small loans by the African elected members, including James Gichuru. He gave the money freely, he confided, with the knowledge that he would never be repaid.[69]

Despite the Asians' testimony of considerable financial assistance to individuals in the other racial communities, the initial response of most Africans when questioned in the post-colonial years has been to deny that such financial aid ever occurred. The following, who were interviewed in 1972–73, are typical in expressing the anti-Asian feeling of the time. Samuel Kamau, a restaurant owner in Thika, retorted, 'I have received no help from Indians. When you buy for cash, they give you the goods and like it, but when you need credit, they don't give it to you'.[70] Douglas Karu, owner of a Thika hardware store, stated, 'Europeans help us. They give us credit for ninety days, but the Asians make us pay cash'.[71] Mutisya Kinothya, whose family owned a large textile business in Machakos, hoped that all Asians would leave Kenya. 'They are difficult', he said, 'because they extend no credit, only cash'.[72] Anne Muhoho, owner of a grocery in Thika, asserted, 'An Asian would never extend credit to an African. He would rather see you sinking. He would not even give you a nickel'.[73]

On further questioning many African businessmen admitted that they personally had received some form of aid. Joel M. Mbugua, managing director of a secondhand clothing shop in Nairobi, described the Asian wholesalers as preferring to sell and give discounts to members of their own community, but he admitted that some of his friends were Shahs and that one Shah firm had helped him 'a lot'.[74] John Mwenda, owner of a dry goods shop in Thika, stated that he did not always get credit from Asians when he needed it but that they always treated him fairly.[75] Benson Musau, whose family had a dry goods shop in Machakos, was one of the few who without reservation acknowledged Asian financial help. 'Most Asian firms give us thirty days credit because they know we are an established business', he said. 'Some Africans are new in business and have very little security. You can't give credit to everyone'.[76]

That African opinion has not conveyed an accurate impression of the Asians' financial role is corroborated in a study by Peter Marris and Anthony Somerset who in 1966–67 conducted interviews with 990 African businessmen in Nairobi and rural market centres of Kenya. 'Some who criticized Asians most vehemently', they noted, 'had also been helped by them, and their comments . . . were strikingly discordant with their experience'. The businessmen's resentment, Marris and Somerset believed, was not simply a reaction to ill treatment, but 'a rationalization of hostility towards their principal competitors. . . . In search of a model for their own behaviour, it was natural for African businessmen to identify with the dominant commercial culture against the minority culture which most nearly threatened them'. So they eulogized the Europeans and damned the Asians. 'African businessmen', the authors concluded, 'make Indians the target of all their frustrations and accept Europeans as their ally, unconsciously distorting the qualities of each into simple opposites'.[77] The fact that the Asians were the Africans' chief competitors in business and artisanry was, of course, an underlying reason for the Africans' hostility. In vilifying the Asians, however, the Africans were merely reiterating the view so long expounded by the Europeans.

When all is considered, it appears that the Asians made an important financial contribution to the development of East Africa. The Asians' practice of business through credit and their money-lending in general were to augment a very rapid growth of the economy. Commerce and agriculture obviously expanded at a much faster pace than if the borrowing of money had been restricted to the conservative banking establishment. The Asians not only carried many of the European settlers through the economic crises of the 1920s and 1930s and helped them in other times of need but also provided a great stimulus to the Africans' economic activity. Through extension of credit they helped bring the African cultivators into a cash-crop economy, fostered the business of the African artisans, and promoted the rise of the African businessmen. Unfortunately, the lending of money was very hard on some segments of the population, especially the Arab and Swahili planters who eked out a marginal living in the wake of abolition and the African cultivators who experienced crop failures through several seasons. It is possible, however, that these peoples would have fared far worse in short periods without the Asian financial aid. Certainly, the widespread assumption that the Asians constituted an impenetrable middle-class stratum that prevented the rise of the Africans from peasants to businessmen must be seriously questioned in view of the Asians' extension of credit.

Notes

1. S. H. Fazan (Resident Commissioner, Mombasa) to Senior Commissioner Coast, Mombasa, 22 Dec. 1924, file 1277, MP11/188, 'Credit Trade: Advancing Money to Natives Against Coming Crops, 1918–25', Coast Province daily correspondence, Syracuse University microfilm 1995, reel 89.

2. Letter to Senior Coast Commissioner, Mombasa, 8 Mar. 1921, item 23, ibid.

3. J. D. Byramjee (son), interviewed by Gregory, 24 Jan. 1973, Nairobi.

4. A.R.W. Hirjee (grandson), interviewed by Bennett, 18 Apr. 1973, Nairobi.

5. M. K. Lalji, interviewed by Gregory, 28 Feb., 1, 2 Mar. 1973, Mombasa.

6. M. Behal, interviewed by Honey, 12 Sept. 1973, Dar es Salaam.

7. D.K. Kanji Naranji (son), interviewed by Bennett, 18 May 1973, Nairobi.

8. Mepa Vershi Shah has described how on arrival in East Africa in 1920 he was given loans by other Shahs of Shs 50,000 to start a retail business in Nairobi. Interviewed by Gregory, 11 July 1973, Jamnagar.

9. Lakhamshi R. Shah, interviewed by Gregory, 27 Nov. 1972, 8, 9 Mar. 1973, Nairobi; 30 June 1973, Bombay; 9 July 1973, Ahmedabad.

10. M. M. Devani (grandson), interviewed by Honey, 9 Mar. 1974, Dar es Salaam.

11. Mrs. K. R. Paroo, interviewed by Bennett, 10 May 1973, Mombasa; A.R.W. Hirjee interview.

12. A. J. Pandya (son), interviewed by Gregory, 1 Mar. 1973, Mombasa.

13. M. K. Lalji interview.

14. S. B. Kazi (Deputy General Manager, Bank of India, Bombay) and C. P. Shah (Joint General Manager, Bank of Baroda, Bombay), interviewed by Gregory, 4 July 1973, Bombay.

15. A.A.J. Thawer (Director, Diamond Jubilee Investment Trust), interviewed by Honey, 20 Oct. 1973, Dar es Salaam. K. R. Paroo, interviewed by Gregory, 1 Mar. 1973, Mombasa. Also, 'Ismailia Settlement in East Africa', six-page typescript presented by Paroo to Gregory.

16. K. R. Paroo interview. Another Ismaili, the most informative of all on the Industrial Promotion Services Ltd., requested anonymity.

17. Paroo, 'Ismailia Settlement', pp. 3–4. Shanti Pandit, ed., *Asians in East and Central Africa* (Nairobi: Panco, 1963), p. 316.

18. K. R. Paroo interview. D. S. Trivedi, interviewed by Gregory, 28 Feb. 1973, Mombasa. Pandit, *Asians,* p. 343. *Saben's Commercial Directory and Handbook of Uganda, 1960–61* (Kampala: Saben's Directories, 1961), Uganda Classified Trades section, p. 65.

19. *East African Standard,* 25 Jan. 1908, p. 8.

20. H. K. Jaffer, interviewed by Bennett, 9, 13 May 1973, Mombasa. K. J. Kotecha, interviewed by Gregory, 9 July 1973, Ahmedabad.

21. S. H. Jaffer, interviewed by Bennett, 9 Apr. 1973, Nairobi.

22. Pushkar U. Oza, interviewed by Gregory, 2 July 1973, Bombay.

23. D. G. Patel, interviewed by Honey, 9 and 14 Oct. 1973, Dar es Salaam.

24. A. Raishi, interviewed by Gregory, 10 June 1985, Nairobi.

25. K. R. Paroo interview. Rotating credit has also been described by M. B. Versi, interviewed by Honey, 27 Feb. 1974, Dar es Salaam. A 1966–67 survey of 281 Asian businessmen in Nairobi, Kiambu, and Limuru showed that 73 per cent bought goods on credit of thirty days or more. Peter Marris and Anthony Somerset, *African Businessmen: A Study of Entrepreneurship and Development in Kenya* (London: Routledge and Kegan Paul, 1971), table 34, p. 259.

26. M. K. Lalji interview.

27. See poem with this title, *East African Standard,* 12 Oct. 1907, p. 6.

28. Ibid., 12 Oct. 1907, p. 6.

29. Personal experience of the author, 1956.

30. E. Vasey, interviewed by Gregory, 6 Feb. 1973, Nairobi.

31. Major Patrick Gethin was typical: interviewed by Gregory, 5 Sept. 1981, Syracuse, New York, and previously in Karen, Kenya. Humphrey Slade, Speaker of the House following independence and a prominent settler, has attested to the Asians' service to settlers in Naivasha, his own farming area: interviewed by Gregory, 9 Feb. 1973, Nairobi.

32. Anthony Allinson, a former district officer, knew of many such instances: interviewed by Gregory, 20 Aug. 1972, London.

33. They also borrowed from Arab shopkeepers. Fazan (Acting District Commissioner, Malindi) to Provincial Commissioner, Mombasa, 22 Sept. 1919, item 3, file 1277, 'Credit Trade'.

34. Robert G. Gregory, *India and East Africa: A History of Race Relations Within the British Empire, 1890–1939* (Oxford: Clarendon, 1971), p. 26.

35. C. A. Bartlett and J. S. Last, *Report on the Indebtedness of the Agricultural Classes* (Zanzibar: Government Printer, 1934), pp. 6–7.

36. 'Extract from Mr. Baker's Report on Development on the Coast', file 1277, 'Credit Trade'.

37. C. W. Hobley, *Kenya from Chartered Company to Crown Colony* (London: Witherby, 1929), p. 168.

38. See file 1277, 'Credit Trade'.

39. File DC/KISM/1/2, 'Report on Bajun Islands and Coast', Coast Province daily correspondence, Syracuse University microfilm 4750, reel 370.

40. Acting District Commissioner, Kilifi (H. H. Trafford) to Senior Coast Commissioner, 17 May 1922, no item no., file 1277, 'Credit Trade'.

41. District Commissioner, Voi, to Provincial Commissioner, Mombasa, 6 June 1919, file 1289, MP1/271, 'Native Affairs Reports, 1919–28', ibid., reel 89. Fazan (Acting District Commissioner, Malindi) to Provincial Commissioner, Mombasa, 'Concerning Debts Owed by Nyika Natives to Mohamedans and the Civil Powers of the Liwali Concerning Them', 22 Sept. 1919, item 3, file 1277, 'Credit Trade'.

42. For a detailed description, see file 1277, 'Credit Trade'.

43. 'History of Fort Hall from 1888–1944', file DC/FH6/–, year 1941, p. 4, Central Province daily correspondence, Syracuse University microfilm 4751, reel 24.

44. District Commissioner, Voi, to Provincial Commissioner, Mombasa, 6 June 1919, file 1289, MP1/271, 'Native Affairs Reports, 1919–18', Coast Province daily correspondence, Syracuse University microfilm 1995, reel 89.

45. Fazan to Provincial Commissioner, Mombasa, 'Concerning Debts', 22 Sept. 1919.

46. Ibid.

47. Hobley to Chief Secretary, Nairobi, 31 Aug. 1918, item 1066, file 1260, MP11/111, 'Famine, 1918–19', vol. 6. Fazan (Acting District Commissioner, Malindi) to Provincial Commissioner, Mombasa, 22 Sept. 1919, item 3; and Acting Provincial Commissioner, Mombasa, to Chief Native Commissioner, Nairobi, 8 Oct. 1919, item 5, file 1277, 'Credit Trade'.

48. Acting Provincial Commissioner, Mombasa, to Chief Native Commissioner, Nairobi,'Meeting of Sub-Committee', 4 Mar. 1921, with item 33; and Walter Mayes, 'Notes on Advances to Natives', 3 Mar. 1921, with item 33, file 1277, 'Credit Trade'.

49. J.W.F. McClellan (Senior Coast Commissioner) to Acting Chief Native Commissioner, Nairobi, 20 July 1921, item 36, ibid.

50. Acting Chief Native Commissioner, Nairobi, to Senior Coast Commissioner, Mombasa, 17 Aug. 1921, item 38, ibid.

51. The result was the Credit to Africans (Control) Ordinance of 1948.

52. The best description is T. A. Watts (District Commissioner, Central Nyanza) to Chairman, Transport Licensing Board, Nairobi, 12 June 1951, doc. 407, file ADM.3/3/9(2–823), 'Conferences, Committees, and Commissions: General, Co-ordination of Transport, 1946–50', Nyanza Province daily correspondence, Syracuse University microfilm 1949, reel 3.

53. Fazan (Acting District Commissioner, Kilifi) to Acting Provincial Commissioner, Mombasa, 31 Jan. 1920, item 8, file 1314, 'Trade Licenses and Native Markets, and Trading in Native Reserves' [vol. 1], Coast Province daily correspondence, Syracuse University microfilm 1995, reel 89.

54. Letter to Senior Coast Commissioner, 22 Mar. 1921, item 34, file 1277, 'Credit Trade'.

55. A. Raishi interview. Madhusudn Jethalal Thakkar, interviewed by Gregory, 19 May 1973, Addis Ababa.

56. L. R. Shah (interviewed) was president of the Nairobi Chamber of Commerce and Industry 1955–59 and in 1972 was on the Governing Council of the Kenya National Chamber of Commerce and Industry.

57. S. S. Keshavji, interviewed by Gregory, 22 July 1973, Jamnagar. He named three of the Africans: C. Maini, a farmer near Eldoret; G. G. Kipto, another farmer near Eldoret who became an M.P.; and K. Kibosi, a shopkeeper in Eldoret.

58. V. K. Shah, interviewed by Gregory, 11 July 1973, Jamnagar.

59. I. M. Jivan, interviewed by Gregory, 16 Feb. 1973, Arusha.

60. L. R. Shah interview. Business failures among the first twenty Africans who received loans from the Kenya Industrial and Commercial Development Corporation in 1964, its first year of operation, were 25 per cent. Marris and Somerset, *African Businessmen,* p. 181.

61. Enacted 31 Aug. 1948. See *Laws of Kenya* (1948), CAP. 104, II, 1205–7.

62. H. Slade, interviewed by Gregory, 9 Feb. 1973, Nairobi.

63. L. R. Shah and A. Raishi interviews.

64. L. R. Shah interview.

65. 'Minutes of a Meeting of the South Kavirondo Local Native Council Held in Kisii on 8th Apr., 1942', Local Authority records, Syracuse University microfilm 2246, reel 24.

66. International Bank for Reconstruction and Development, *Economic Development of Kenya* (Baltimore: Johns Hopkins University Press, 1963), pp. 167–68.

67. Marris and Somerset, *African Businessmen,* p. 10.

68. D. S. Trivedi interview.

69. Related by Hansa A. Pandya (Anant's wife) to Gregory, 24 Oct. 1984, London.

70. S. Kamau, interviewed by Seidenberg, 27 Oct. 1973, Thika.

71. D. Karu, interviewed by Seidenberg, 8 Nov. 1973, Thika.

72. M. Kinothya, interviewed by Seidenberg, 13 Nov. 1973, Machakos.

73. A. Muhoho, interviewed by Seidenberg, 7 Nov. 1973, Thika.

74. J. M. Mbugua, interviewed by Seidenberg, 17 June 1973, Nairobi.

75. J. Mwenda, interviewed by Seidenberg, 7 Nov. 1973, Thika.

76. B. Musau, interviewed by Seidenberg, 13 Nov. 1973, Machakos.

77. Marris and Somerset, *African Businessmen,* pp. 96–98.

CHAPTER FOUR

———————— ■ ————————

Road Transport

He [my Asian lorry driver, Karua] drove at breakneck pace over the pot-holes day and night, and appeared never to spare a moment for sleep. It was the busy season, he told me—he took away hides and brought back calico and ghee and other commodities—and every time I saw him there seemed to be a little less of his emaciated frame.

—Vivienne De Watteville, 1935[1]

The development of road transport in East Africa was largely a result of the Asian traders' need for an inexpensive and efficient means for conveyance of commodities. Before World War I when the British and German governments emphasized railway construction mainly to foster European settlement and plantation exports, the Asians trading in most of the non-European areas were forced to rely on bullock carts, donkeys, and human portage. After the war with the appearance of reliable motor-cars and lorries, an attractive alternative was possible. The Asians turned with enthusiasm to the new means of transport. Much to the consternation of the governments, which relied on the railways as a chief source of revenue, road transport rapidly superseded the rails as East Africa's main system of transportation and required a great new expenditure in road building. After World War II when the emerging African businessmen followed the Asians into road transport, Asians and Africans often combined their interests to avoid the increasing attempts at control by the colonial and post-colonial administrations.

European Innovations in Transport Before 1920

Most initiatives in transport before the interwar period were provided by the Europeans. The governments' main contribution was the construction of railways from the coastal ports into the interior. They viewed the railways as important not only for economic development but also for strategic control of the great lakes and the source of the Nile. In the East Africa Protectorate the British purposely routed the rail line through the area with the best agricultural potential, the fertile highlands, and in 1902 began a policy of settling the area as fast as possible with European farmers and developing a plantation economy. Like the British, the Germans emphasized the importance of a rail system but lagged far behind them in speed of construction. The German railways, unlike those in the East Africa Protectorate, were constructed by Africans and passed through important areas of African settlement. In Uganda where European settlement was comparatively insignificant, rails were laid from Jinja to Namasagali to tap African produce in the Busoga area, but Jinja was not connected by rail to Kisumu. Uganda's import and export needs were served by lake steamers plying between the railhead at Kisumu and the centres of Jinja and Kampala.[2]

The Europeans also experimented with a variety of supplementary modes of transport. African portage was the initial means of conveyance in most rural areas, and many travellers were carried in hammocks and palanquins. As settlement developed outside the towns, the mails were carried by African runners. In urban centres rickshaws and bicycles soon appeared, and in Mombasa, Malindi, Lindi, and Nairobi the government built tram lines and in Kampala a monorail. While the governments experimented with steam-powered wagons and tractors, the settlers introduced vehicles powered by internal combustion. By 1913 Nairobi alone had nearly 100 motor-cars. With the cars came lorries, vans, motor cycles, fire engines, graders, tractors, and vehicles of all kinds. During the war Model-T Fords, chugging single file in convoys often of more than 100, provided a vital link between the British coastal ports and the remote military camps.[3]

Despite these developments, the two decades before the war were truly a railway age in that the railways were accorded primary consideration by both the British and German governments and served as the critical channels to the outside world. Road transport was in its infancy and, like human and animal transport, was valued only to the degree to which it served the railway in the collection and distribution of goods. It was in practice as well as theory ancillary rather than competitive. When evaluating road transport, instead of comparing it with the railway, the officials in this period mulled the pros and cons of motor vehicles vis-à-vis portage and other animal transport.[4]

Like the railway, road transport in these early years served mainly the interests of the Europeans, both the officials and the settlers. It was employed initially by government in public works, especially in road construction and maintenance and in sanitation (removal of night soil), and during the war cars and motor cycles began to be used by the provincial and district officers in touring their administrative areas. The loads carried by the new vehicles were mainly European—the exports of agricultural produce from the settlers' farms and the imports of European manufactured goods that the settlers bought. Even the bicycles and rickshaws, which were also European importations, became before the war important modes of European transportation in the urban centres. By 1909 the police in Nairobi had abandoned their horses for bicycles, and the fact that Nairobi was said during that year to have been 'paralysed' by a rickshaw strike illustrates the rickshaw's importance.[5]

Although Europeans before 1920 certainly had the most important role in the new system, Africans and Asians were active participants. Africans provided the unskilled manual labour in any ways mechanical transport required, and even before the war some began to be trained as drivers and mechanics. Apparently Uganda took the lead in this effort. As early as 1909, discouraged by the fact that the 'Asiatic and Eurasian drivers' of its motor vehicles were so frequently ill, the Uganda government began to train Africans. In 1912 after a disappointing initial effort, the government reported 'marked success', and the next year it began to employ Africans as drivers and planned to run them in convoys 'with a European chauffeur in charge'.[6] At the end of 1920 the government reported that 'practically all the driving of motor vehicles, Government and privately-owned, is done by natives, and the large increase in the mileage run points to the high standard of proficiency attained'. It stated, however, that Africans still remained deficient in mechanical knowledge.[7] As for African ownership, there were probably very few Africans even in Uganda before or during the war who combined the essential financial resources and transportation needs to purchase motor vehicles. In the other two territories there does not seem to have been any government-sponsored training or employment of Africans as drivers or mechanics.

The Asians' role in road transport in these early years is more obscure. As their employment in Uganda reveals, they were serving as drivers soon after the introduction of the motor vehicle. In Uganda and elsewhere in East Africa a few of the more enterprising and wealthier businessmen probably purchased cars and lorries and began to use them in their trading outside the towns. The transition in transport is well illustrated by Nanji Kalidas Mehta, the Uganda industrialist who is one of the few Asians to have left a record of his early trading years. In 1901 when he set up his duka in Kamuli, forty-five miles inland from Jinja, he began to transport his goods by African portage in caravan. He himself first walked and later, when weakened by fever, was carried on a palanquin borne by four Africans. By 1914 he was riding a bicycle, and in 1915 he bought a motor-car.[8]

For most traders this was the era of the cart. The first-generation immigrants adopted the bullock cart for their long-distance transportation
because it had been their traditional conveyance in India. Within their
carts the Asians carried the importations essential to their duka trade as
well as the produce they were beginning to buy from Africans. Where the
carts could not reach they travelled on foot with porters or donkeys.
Within the towns the Asians relied on the hand-drawn hamal and gharry
carts. In 1916 the provincial commissioner resident in Mombasa noted,
'At present practically the whole of the imported goods for the use of the
town are distributed in four-wheeled handcarts, which move at about 1
1/2 miles per hour, and take four to six men to propel'.[9] It was apparently
cart transportation that was provided by Ali Khan, a well-known transport contractor serving settlers in the early years of Nairobi.[10]

Although the initial mechanics and the first repair shops for motor vehicles were European, the many Asian artisans must have easily transferred the skills learned in railway construction to those essential for car
repair. After the war the Asian skilled worker, the fundi, was to enjoy a
virtual monopoly in motor vehicle maintenance. The sale of such vehicles before 1920, however, was definitely a European monopoly. The
Asians began to compete only in the sale of bicycles. The Asians' foremost trader before the war, Allidina Visram, is said to have been the largest cycle importer in East Africa.[11]

Asian Domination of Road Transport, 1920–45

After the war while the railway continued as the main form of transport for imports and exports between the various rail stops, the cars, lorries, and motor cycles, as far as roads permitted, rapidly displaced foot
travel, trollies, and gharry and hamal carts in the urban centres, and
bullock carts, mules, donkeys, camels, and human portage in the rural
areas. The use of motor vehicles during the war had portended the
change. In anticipation the East Africa Protectorate in 1919 had incorporated its long-standing Transport Department, which had been concerned only with animal power, into the Public Works Department
(PWD). Henceforth there was to be a Mechanical Transport Branch as
well as an Animal Transport Branch.[12]

Although reliance on draft animals and African porters continued, the
motor vehicle clearly transformed transportation in Kenya (the former
East Africa Protectorate) soon after the war. At the end of hostilities a
large proportion of the military vehicles were converted to civilian use.
These reconditioned cars, lorries, and motor cycles, augmented by importation of new machines, caused the number of vehicles to increase
dramatically. For 1919–20 Kenya's imports of vehicles and parts were val-

ued at £149,024, an increase of $47,072 over those of the previous year, 'the total value being the highest on record'.[13] By 1924 the imports of motor-cars into Kenya and Uganda—995, of which about three-fourths remained in Kenya—were over twice the combined imports of the two previous years. The unusual increase was ascribed to the growth in purchasing power of the community, the extension of roads, the development of road transport for marketing produce, and the lowering of import duties on cars. By 1928 the total imports had increased to 2,298, comprising 1,269 cars, 904 lorries, and 125 motor cycles. The number dropped to a low of 1,187 in 1932, the worst year of the depression, but then gradually increased to a high of 4,507 in 1937 before falling again because of the impending war.[14]

Despite the many evidences in the early post-war years of an impending revolution in transport, the Kenya government was surprisingly slow to appreciate the full potential of the motor vehicle. In April 1922 when faced with a serious deficit in revenue, the central government decided to dispense with all its mechanical transport. All government vehicles—cars, lorries, and motor cycles—were to be returned to the office of the nearest executive engineer by May 31 and there parked to await dispersal and sale by the Central Tender Board. The Mechanical Transport Branch was to be abolished. The decision was a product not merely of the financial crisis but of a deep-seated antagonism between the acerbic director of public works, William McGregor Ross, and other senior officials including the governor and colonial secretary. Because of his virulent criticism of the government's policy of favouring European settlers to the detriment of Asians and Africans, Ross was being forced to resign by drastic cuts in his budget. The decision reflected a surprising lack of appreciation for the new mode of transport.[15]

The order evoked a concerted protest from the provincial and district officers, who by then relied heavily on motor vehicles in performing many of their duties. The compliance date had to be postponed. Finally in June 1924 following a referral of the issue to the secretary of state for the colonies, the order was rescinded. Still the local government continued averse to motor transport. In 1925 it sent out a circular directing all senior commissioners to 'ensure a due proportion of porter travelling being done by officers in the native districts'.[16] Not until 1935 was the government to boast that in the postal service 'the replacement of African runners by mechanical transport is almost completed'.[17]

The Kenya government's main transportation concern in the interwar years was the growing competition between rail and road. Analysts agree that the statistics comparing the haulage of the two systems have been impossible to compile, with the result that no accurate comparison has been possible, but road transport apparently acquired the bulk of the carrying trade between the wars. There is no doubt about the passenger traffic, which was quickly taken over by the private car and motor cycle, the taxi and bus, and even by the lorry. The conveyance of goods by car and lorry, however, also increased immeasurably.[18]

For all areas of the colony, even the most remote wherever roads were suitable, motor vehicles proved far more practical than draft animals and porters for the transport of commodities to and from the railway stops. Motor vehicles served not only the European estates but also the African shambas as the latter were converted to the production of cash crops. In Nyanza Province, for instance, the amount of produce transported by road in 1938 included 50,000 tons of maize, 7,000 of firewood, 6,750 of groundnuts, 4,500 of simsim (sesame), 4,000 of beans, and 2,000 of choroko. In addition, there was a yearly average by then of 4,200 tons of cottonseed. Road transport was also competing effectively with the railway in traffic parallel to the rail line. By 1934 its charges for carrying spirits (liquor), petrol, and cotton piece goods from Mombasa to Nairobi were cheaper than those of the railway. Lorries were loading whiskey and petrol from dhows at Lamu and transporting them to Nyeri at lower rates than the railway could bring them to Nyeri and Mombasa. The administration had inadvertently fostered the competition. Just after World War I as Asians began a motor-car trade within the African reserves, the administration decided that it was within the interest of overall development 'to open up districts', not to close them.[19]

The Kenya government at first tried to alleviate the road-rail competition by revising the railway's rate structure. In 1921 to encourage the haulage of exports by rail, it introduced a system of differential rates whereby the railway classified goods into six categories and charged higher prices for hauling goods with higher value. As imports generally were worth more ton for ton than exports, road transporters seized the opportunity of hauling these imports at lower cost along routes parallel to the railway. Although the government began at the same time a system of tapered rates, whereby rail charges were reduced for longer hauls and even reduced charges on certain routes to ease the competition, the lorry owners were not deterred.[20]

The world economic depression, which began severely to affect East Africa in 1930, prompted Kenya to take more drastic measures. The depression, as one observer remarked, 'plunged the Kenya and Uganda railway into chaos'.[21] In desperation the government enacted two successive Carriage of Goods by Motor ordinances forbidding road haulage on certain scheduled roads where it was severely competitive with the railway. After further study the railway reduced the differential extremes and introduced a policy of levying rates according to 'what the traffic would bear'.[22] When this too proved ineffective, Kenya decided to adopt a policy of restrictive licensing as the best means of diminishing the competition. In 1937 it enacted a Transport Licensing Ordinance that provided for four types of transport licences. Type A (Shs 30/-) was for specialist public carriers who operated only for 'hire or reward'. Type B (Shs 30/-) was for those who carried goods for their own businesses and in addition hauled others' goods for hire or reward. Type C (Shs 10/-) pertained to private carriers who transported only their own goods. A fourth type, for buses and taxis, was the Roads Service Licence (Shs 50/-), which permitted the carrying of passengers and goods over specified routes with regular fares and time schedules. The penalty for infraction was not high—£20 for the first offence and £50 for each subsequent offence—and the control was to be exercised by a five-member Transport Licensing Board (TLB) that was empowered to grant and refuse licences.[23]

To those hoping to limit road transport, the Transport Licensing Ordinance and the previous measures were disappointing. No type A licences were ever issued. Nearly everyone intrested in road transport wanted a type B licence, which offered the maximum utility. A person established in business could transport goods or passengers for hire as a sideline; or if a transporter, he could also carry for his own business. The new board attempted to restrict type B licences by granting more type C licences. It soon became evident, however, that a large proportion of the type C holders were carrying passengers and goods illegally. The board, flooded with applications, delegated the granting of licences to the district commissioners, but the latter proved to be more interested in promoting the economic development of their districts than the finances of the railway.[24]

For these reasons, although the board's policy was 'to look after the Railway interests' whenever an application for a licence was considered, road transport continued to flourish. Through reforms promoting efficiency, the railway preceded the colony in recovering from the depression and in 1937 attained a record peace-time earnings. In succeeding years, however, its profits were steadily eroded by the motor vehicle.

Uganda continued to be much more perceptive than Kenya in recognizing the growing importance of the motor vehicle. In the early 1920s when the Kenya administration was taking measures to dispose of all its motorized transport, the Uganda government entered into an open competition with the private sector. In 1924 the Uganda Railway began a seventy-five mile road service between Butiaba and Masindi to connect two steamer services. The Uganda PWD also began to take contracts for haulage, and the administration even established a special agency, the Uganda Government Transport Service, for the conveyance of private goods and passengers. By 1929 the railway had 34 cars and lorries, the

PWD 82, and the Government Transport Service 62.[25] Despite an auspicious beginning, the administration in the long run was unable to compete with the private transporters. At the end of the colonial period the railway retained a small road service between its lake ports, but apparently the PWD served only the government, and the special Transport Service no longer existed.

Although Europeans remained important and Africans and Arabs increasingly participated, the Asians' ascendency between the wars is clearly evident in the administrative records of Kenya. Shortly after World War I if not before, the Kenya government, like many organizations and individuals in the private sector, began to hire cars and lorries with drivers for specific transport needs. There were no regular fees, so the vehicle owners and those who hired had to negotiate for the price of each rental. Sometimes the charges were exorbitant. In 1922 a district officer complained that a fifty-six mile ride in a taxicab to a hospital had cost £12/10/0, that is, over Shs 4/- per mile at a time when the cost of running a Ford car, including 'native driver', mechanics, and all repairs and petrol, was estimated at 50 cents (half a Kenya shilling) per mile.[26] Apparently the Europeans were at first more prominent in this business than the Asians. Their lead was challenged in the mid-1920s, however, by Asians including F. H. D'Souza and J. M. Santos in Nairobi, R. Pereira in Mombasa, and Jaibali Muhamed Ali, Abdulhussein Adamjee, and Essajee Khadibhoy in Malindi. The two groups collectively offered a wide assortment of drivers—Swahili, Baluchi, Arab, and 'native' as well as European and Asian. During the late 1920s and early 1930s as the settler community acquired its own cars, the European taxi service increasingly served the needs of the tourist trade. Meanwhile Asians assumed the lead in providing taxis for the urban and interurban business of all peoples. They soon found lorries more suitable than cars for transporting large numbers of Africans.[27]

A similar pattern developed in the scheduled bus service. Like the earlier trolley system, this enterprise was designed to accommodate European passengers. The fact that the Mombasa trolley had run from Kilindini Harbour, past the hotel and bank, to the Sports Club well illustrates this. In 1920 after the demise of the trolley, a prominent European, Charles Udall, applied for a licence to construct and run a new passenger service on Mombasa island. He suggested at first a tramway, then an omnibus system driven by electricity, and finally agreed, after a government committee had considered the question, on a petrol-powered bus service. The initial buses were British-manufactured Napier lorries reconditioned, upholstered with coir fiber, and adapted in Kenya to seat thirty-six passengers. Though intended for Europeans, these municipal buses soon attracted non-Europeans in large numbers and eventually were patronized almost exclusively by Africans. Europeans and Asians, both able to buy or hire cars, soon considered it beneath their dignity to use the public transport. As the early bus contracts conveyed monopolies, the Asians were barred from offering effective competition in the municipalities. In the 1930s, however, as bus transport was extended into rural areas and was developed between towns and villages, the government as a matter of policy refrained from conferring monopolies, and in this situation the Asians quickly took the initiative in providing the interurban bus transportation for Africans.[28]

In the conveyance of goods Asians also assumed the lead. During the twenties it was mainly they who seized the opportunity offered by the railways' differential rates to distribute throughout Kenya, often running parallel to the rails, the imported manufactures, including petrol and fuel oil, that had been assigned the higher railway charges. In the 1930s because of their position in the import-export and wholesale-retail trade, as well as their experience in transport, the Asians were primary in responding to the Africans' need to distribute their cash crops, whether to local urban markets or to warehouses and shipping lines. If possible, on their return trips or even together with their loads of manufactures and produce, the Asians carried Africans to and from the reserves and the centres of labour. When barred by legislation from specific roads, they proved adept at devising alternate, parallel routes. When restricted by the licensing system to the carriage of certain goods along designated roads, they ignored the restrictions and cleverly concealed their operations.[29]

Among the owners involved in the new transport only a few have been identified in the documents as specifically operating in the 1930s. On the Kisumu-Nairobi road the active bus owners included H. K. Mirali and Co. and Ladhu Ali Bux. Between Broderick Falls and Bungoma, Mohamed Kanji and Co. was a prominent bus owner. The bus transporters on the road from Kakamega to Busia via Mumias were the four Asians Gulamali Meghji, T. K. Meghji, Noor Mohamed Walji, and Roop Lal, and also the African Nason Ongewe, and an Arab or Somali, Ahmed Ali Arab. Of the forty-three lorry owners in South Kavirondo in 1942, at least thirty-four were Asians, and twenty-two of the forty-six serviceable lorries belonged to Indersingh Bukhan Singh.[30]

The rapid development of the Asian transport industry was distressing not only to the government, including the railway interests, but also to the Asians' European rivals in motorized transport. The British officials between the wars were generally critical of the Asians as well as the Africans in anything concerned with road transport. 'As long as his car gets over the ground somehow', wrote a district officer in 1919, 'the average Asiatic or native Chauffeur is satisfied, he drives his car to death and takes no thought of wear or tear to the mechanism'.[31] Another official complained in 1922 of an 'Indian fundi' who, 'as usual having scamped his work, failed to put a split pin in one of the nuts on the bearing of No. one cylinder with consequent result that when we took it down there was just one thread on the screw between us and another completely smashed car'.[32] A third official reported in 1922 that his car was completely broken down because of his driver Ignasio, presumably a Goan: 'He was grossly incompetent, incredibly lazy and had frequent bouts of drunkenness. Bolts were never tightened unless pointed out by me, the car was never cleaned except by direct order, tools have been lost and broken and no report made. Although minutely instructed how to keep his inner tubes, he destroyed four by failing to obey orders'.[33]

An example of a European company that was bitterly resentful of the Asian competition is Roadways (Kenya) Ltd. Described as the first 're-sponsible European firm in the Nyanza Province to undertake transport on a large scale', Roadways began operations in 1932 with imported, diesel-powered lorries and buses. Though at first successful, the company by 1939 had a very heavy deficit. The managing director blamed the Asian and African competitors:

> Unfair and most unbusinesslike competition, including 'cut' rates, and a reck-less disregard for the safety and comfort of passengers, and reasonable care of vehicles, on the part of the majority of the Indian and Native transport con-tractors. These faults it may fairly be said, are in all human probability due to ignorance, cupidity, and business-jealousy, and result in accidents, mechani-cal breakdowns, bankruptcy, and a general and rapid lowering of efficiency. There is also the grave deterioration of road surfaces, resulting from the ex-cessive pace which a number of the Indian and Native owned lorries are driv-en.[34]

The regular bus service that the company had established between Kisumu and Kakamega was the greatest problem. Roadways began the route in 1932 with a service of three trips per week and soon raised it to six. In 1935 it was joined by another European firm, Goldfields Transport Ltd., with a thrice-weekly service. By 1939 three Asian competitors were running the same route, carrying passengers in lorries, and extending the service on to Kitale. One ran daily, the others on alternate days. There was also an African-owned lorry driving on alternate days. Roadways, to stay in business, had to set a fare of Shs 1/60. Two of the Asians and the African, however, were charging only Shs 1/-, and the third Asian had set a remarkable low of Shs -/50 on the slack, midweek days. In addition to these four, all of which were licensed to carry passengers, there were two lorries licensed only for the carriage of goods that transported passen-gers illegally at Shs -/50.[35]

The Kisumu-Kapsabet-Eldoret-Kitale route posed a similar problem. In 1937 Roadways took over the passenger service that had been established in 1929 by another European firm. Roadways, however, soon faced a competitor, presumably an Asian, who drove the route on the same days at lower rates. This 'undischarged bankrupt', as the managing director described him, operated in another person's name and with such irregularity that he even missed service for one month. He was nevertheless forcing Roadways out of business.[36]

Another competitive situation had occurred on the road from Kisumu to Busia. Roadways had assumed the passenger service in 1938 after the Asian who had it ceased operation. Within a year, however, there were three competing omnibuses that not only charged lower fares—Shs 4 as opposed to Shs 5—but also ran their services on the same days as Roadways and even adhered to the same timetable. Forced to run certain sections of the route 'very nearly empty', Roadways could not continue.[37]

The company was also being displaced in the haulage of goods. Roadways was accustomed to contracting at various centres in Kakamega for transporting all kinds of merchandise, including timber, at a charge per lorry of Shs -/50 per ton-mile. Asians and apparently some Africans, however, had begun a 'price-cutting' competition that made it impossible for Roadways to pay its working expenses. A contractor in Kakamega, for instance, would carry a load of lumber from a sawmill at the Burnt Forest or Elgeyo area to Kisumu. On arrival at Kisumu the driver would 'tout' the township for a load back to Kakamega at any price. By so obtaining a return load, the driver would be able to reduce his regular price of a low Shs -/21.[38]

All these practices in the view of the managing director amounted to a form of 'piracy', and he petitioned the government for 'some form of protection at the earliest possible date'. He suggested in the first instance an exclusive licence for Roadways on the road between Kisumu and Busia.[39]

Though deeply concerned with problems arising from the rapid expansion of road transport, the Kenya government during the 1930s adhered to its policy of open competition among the vehicle owners and surprisingly showed no favouritism among the racial communities. In 1936 the acting provincial commissioner of Nyanza was very critical of Asian-owned buses and lorries. Except for new vehicles, he said, 'it is generally found that brakes are bad, tyres are dangerously worn and steering is loose'. The vehicles were also overloaded, exceeded the speed limits, and frequently had no insurance. Unfortunately, he explained, 'It is very difficult to prosecute because native passengers are generally coached beforehand to say that they are being carried free of charge'.[40] Two years later the new provincial commissioner expressed sympathy with Roadway's managing director. 'I know from my own observation', he confided, 'the truth of what he says about the overloading of lorries, the utter disregard for the speed limit, the safety regulations and regulations prohibiting goods lorries from carrying passengers'.[41] The commissioner recommended, however, only fitting the Asians' buses and lorries with governors, requiring strict adherence to time-tables, and improving police action to enforce control of licences. Roadways's request for a monopoly was denied by the TLB.[42]

What was happening in Kenya between the wars was also occurring, but with considerable modification, in Uganda and Tanganyika. Uganda continued to surpass Kenya in the development of road transport. The facts that the Busoga Railway at Jinja was not joined to the Kenya line until 1927 and that not until the completion of the Jinja bridge over the Nile in 1931 was Kampala linked to Mombasa illustrate the Uganda government's emphasis on road construction. By 1930 it had completed a vast system of roads that through the ensuing decade it steadily improved. Before World War II, according to the principal author of Uganda's transport, A. M. O'Connor, the country's roads were 'much superior to those of most other countries of tropical Africa'.[43] Although it had not the need for as many vehicles as Kenya, Uganda had 1,000 lorries as early as 1930, and by 1938 it had a total of 2,300 as compared with Kenya's 2,700.[44]

Tanganyika made the least progress. Because of the Germans' tactic in World War I of destroying the transportation system as they withdrew, the British had to rebuild the German railways. The railways, however, were not so important to Tanganyika's economy as to Kenya's. The country had a comparatively long coastline, productive areas were widely scattered, and the output of each was relatively small. Also, the two main centres, Dar es Salaam and Tanga, absorbed most of the imports directly from the docks with no overland journey. Ignoring these limitations, the British relied on the railways for the transport needs of their new mandate. In time the railways became a severe financial liability. By 1939 they carried only 32,900 ton-miles of freight as compared with 265,000 in Kenya-Uganda. Nor was the road system a viable alternative. 'The main method of road construction', as O'Connor has observed, 'was to improve tracks laid during the war for the transport of war supplies'. These tracks and the old caravan routes that were to become the trunk roads were 'unduly winding', with the result that their improvement was very costly.[45]

Tanganyika was the exception in that before World War II rivalry between road and rail was not considered a serious problem. Road transport did not become important to Tanganyika's economy until about 1930 when it proved more efficient than the railway in moving sisal, the principal export. Although the road mileage by 1939 was nearly double that of Uganda, Tanganyika's roads as a whole were far inferior and did not reach all productive areas. Its lorries by 1939 numbered only half those of Kenya and considerably less than those of Uganda.[46]

Two of the most successful Asian ventures between the wars occurred in Tanganyika and Uganda. In Iringa where he had developed a business selling piece goods and buying African produce, beeswax, and hides and skins, Asar Sachedina, an Ismaili from Kutch, decided in 1926 to branch into road transport. He bought a lorry and began to carry goods and passengers between Iringa and Kilosa. Three years later he bought a second lorry to serve the new Iringa-Dodoma road, and during the depression, finding transport more rewarding than his retail business, he expanded his lorry fleet to nine. By 1939 Sachedina was the principal transporter serving central Tanganyika. All his drivers and mechanics were Africans whom he had specially trained.[47] The Uganda venture was quite different. In Kampala a group of Asians, including G. A. Kassim, P. Abdulla, and L. K. Ishani, took over a failing European bus firm, the Uganda Transport Co. Ltd., which had been established in 1937. The new owners increased the capital, revised the management, and made the company solvent. By 1955 the company owned one hundred buses, earned a monthly income of £300,000, and had its own depots in Jinja, Fort Portal, Masaka, Mbarara, Kabale, and Mubende as well as Kampala. It carried that year 68,000 passengers in Kampala alone.[48]

As the chief agents in developing road transport, the Asians enjoyed several advantages. The nature of their commercial activity, which required an almost daily movement of commodities, was conducive to integration with an efficient system of transportation. It was more economical for them to purchase and operate motor vehicles than it was for the settlers, whose transportation needs were mostly seasonal. As much of the road transport in these years was devoted to the carriage of goods purchased by Asians, the transporters were serving primarily the commercial interests of their own community. It was natural for an Asian exporter, wholesaler, or produce buyer to turn to a fellow Asian for his transportation needs. As indicated by their behaviour in other forms of enterprise, Asians were generally willing to make their services available more days a week and more hours a day than were Europeans, and for the promotion of their business interests they seem to have been more willing to accept a lower standard of living. The Asians also had an advantage in that those mainly responsible for the maintenance and repair of their vehicles were artisans within the Asian community.

During these interwar years as before, the Africans were generally subordinate in this new form of transportation to both Europeans and Asians. In Kenya and Tanganyika some Africans, as the records indicate, were participating in road transport towards the end of the period as both owners and drivers. By then there were many drivers, and there must have been also a significant number of Africans who, as assistants to European and Asian mechanics, were acquiring the skills of vehicle maintenance. Apparently, however, comparatively few in these countries had accumulated the capital essential for purchasing and operating motor vehicles. The main change for the Africans was that they, like the other communities, were becoming dependent on the new form of transportation. Although bicycles served their local needs, buses or the one-and-a-half-ton or three-ton lorries, filled with standing passengers and their goods, had become the Africans' customary means of long-distance travel. Portage, except for personal use in carrying wood for the home fires or fruits and vegetables for local markets, had all but disappeared.

In Uganda where the government actively promoted their interests, the Africans advanced far more rapidly in road transport and by the eve of World War II had begun to rival the Asians. In 1938 the licensed drivers in Uganda were overwhelmingly African—3,486 as compared with 1,471 Asians and 1,424 Europeans. Of the licensed motor vehicles, one of every five (1,049 of 5,724) belonged to an African. With the omnibuses, 168 were registered to Asians, 16 to Europeans, and 59 (one in every four) to Africans.[49] As these statistics show, however, the Asians still dominated the industry.

This situation was to continue with only one significant change through World War II. Despite curtailment of imports, cessation of vehicle manufacture, scarcity of petroleum products, and changes in personnel resulting from military employment, road transport continued to flourish, and the Asians retained the primary position. During the war years, however, a large number of Africans serving in the armed forces were trained as drivers and mechanics. At the end of the war they returned to civilian life not only with these new skills but also, in most instances, with some savings from military pay. In common with these ex-servicemen were a number of civilian Africans who through the years had acquired driving and mechanical skills in association with Asian and European transporters. At the end of the war both African groups, with support from friends and relatives, were potential new members of the road transport industry. All that was needed was a supply of relatively inexpensive vehicles and a system of hire purchase.

Asian-African Rivalry and Co-operation After World War II

Although an increasing number of Africans began to buy used vehicles during the war, the number burgeoned immediately after as the manufacture of vehicles resumed and Asian and European transporters replaced their much-worn equipment. The records of Kenya's Nyanza Province, where this activity was most intense, reveal that many Africans, mostly ex-servicemen, purchased the discarded vehicles. In 1945 the Africans Nason Ongewe, Omumbo Achola, and Daudi Migot each bought a lorry from the Nyanza Asian transporter Kassam Khamisa. With their lorries Achola and Migot set up a passenger service on the Kisumu-Asembo and Kadimu road, and Ongewe joined two Asians, Gulamali Meghji and T. K. Meghji, in beginning a similar service between Kakamega and Busia. Two other Africans, including Joel Mukoya, bought similar lorries from Khamisa, and four more are known to have acquired lorries from another Nyanza Asian, L. B. Sedani. David Ogega, who entitled his business in Kisii 'Transport Agent, Miller & Posho Supplies', acquired two lorries that in early 1946 were the only African vehicles in South Kavirondo. By the end of 1945 Mruka Zadok Budedu and six other Africans were established transporters in Buhehe Samia Location.[50]

This initial effort by the Africans to enter road transport received an unexpected impetus in July 1946 when the British War Department offered more than 600 Ford, Chevrolet, Dodge, and International lorries to the East African public at a minimal price. The department also made available a large quantity of spare parts, and to facilitate sale, it granted permits for the vehicles. Some of the lorries were acquired by Asians. One of the foremost Asian buyers was Premchand Raichand & Co. Ltd., a Nairobi wholesale-retailing firm, which had many branches in Kenya and twenty lorries already in its possession. In one purchase it obtained sixty-five of the surplus vehicles, of which it sent thirteen to Kisumu to begin a transport business in Nyanza.[51]

How many of the military vehicles were purchased directly by Africans is not clear from the available records, but the number was considerable. Unlike the private lorries that changed hands just after the war, some of which, as one African related, were nine years old and went at 'absurd' (high) prices, these surplus vehicles were relatively inexpensive.[52] Many Africans who had just entered the business sought licences for new, expanded transport ventures, and many others, unable to purchase when the prices were high, now became eager participants. Whether buying from the government or from Asians and Europeans, these Africans had no difficulty in supplementing their savings to meet the cost of purchase. Asian traders or money-lenders, accepting the vehicles as security, readily lent them money.[53]

Unfortunately, a large number of Africans, either through ignorance or misled by the transporters who sold to them, believed that the licence to haul goods or passengers was transferred automatically with the vehicle to the new owner. They thus purchased before applying for licences. When they awoke to the fact that they could not legally engage in transport but still had to make prompt and regular payments on their loans, they were desperate for licences.[54]

Kenya's TLB, which had been constituted in 1937 chiefly to protect railway interests, was thus flooded with new applications. Meeting usually in Nairobi but sometimes in the provinces, the board customarily included an Asian, but no African, among its several members and reviewed applications on recommendation from the district officers. Both the board and the local officers, not only to serve the railway but also to avoid 'wasteful and cut-throat competition' within road transport, followed a very conservative licensing policy. Although appeal to the Supreme Court was possible, few rejected applicants resorted to this expensive procedure.[55]

African applicants, meeting rejection by the district officers and the board, responded with a strenuous protest that soon was argued on racial lines. Local native councils in Nyanza began to demand that Africans receive the greatest proportion of the transport licences. Individual Africans also petitioned. David Ogega of Kisii, for instance, appealed to the district commissioner for help against the Asian transporters. He explained that he and another African, Ismail Owiro, who were already carrying passengers on the Kisii-Kericho route with two vehicles, had encountered stiff opposition from over nine passenger buses owned by Asians 'whose intention is to make me fall'. 'If we could be granted at least three or four passenger buses in South Kavirondo', Ogega wrote, 'I am sure we could fight a good and successful war of the native versus the Kericho Indian passenger transport'.[56]

Another African, Othieno Opondo of Kisii, was even more critical of the Asian competition. 'I do not understand', he asserted to the commissioner, 'why a native of the Nyanza Province should struggle so hard to get a route, while it is so easy for an Indian (the Jews of East Africa) to obtain permission to use roads without difficulty'.[57]

Opondo was allowed to appear in person before the TLB, but Ogega's appeal was denied immediately for reason that he was 'unreliable'. In informing Ogega, the Kisii district commissioner was blunt. 'Practically the first thing you did with your passenger lorry', he said, 'was to go on routes that were not in your licence. . . . Africans of this district will in course of time, perhaps this year, get recommendations from me for lorries, passenger and produce, but I am not prepared to let you have all the routes or all the lorries you want'. As for the Asian competition, the commissioner continued:

> I warned you more than a year ago of the great trouble you would have in combatting Indian transport concerns on the Kisii-Kericho run, but you would not take notice of my warning, and to think that you would be able to

beat them just by having three or four passenger lorries is pure foolishness and would merely lead to a price cutting race which you, having the shorter purse, would be bound to lose.[58]

Although the commissioner's negative response was apparently representative of the government generally in the immediate post-war years, there were some officials who welcomed and fostered the Africans' entrance into road transport. During 1945, for instance, C. F. Atkins, district commissioner of Central Nyanza, let it be known that his policy was to encourage African owners of vehicles to take over progressively the transport in his district. In considering Asian, European, and African applications he would recommend only the Africans.[59] As a district commissioner, however, Atkins was at the bottom of the administrative hierarchy.

Because the ultimate decision in any licensing case lay with the TLB and, beyond that, with the Supreme Court, a policy change in the central government was necessary before there could be any effective change. The Africans soon realized that. Fortunately for them, a major revision of the imperial government's policy towards the indigeneous peoples' status and future in its African dependencies was just beginning. In Kenya that was manifested in 1944 with the admission of the first African, Eliud Mathu, to the Legislative Council. This action was a significant break with the traditional policy of indirect rule. It was the first real recognition of the Africans' potential to participate equally with Europeans in the governance of the country. Henceforth Africans with a realistic hope could support their petitions for reform with a platform of equal rights. Moreover, they could extend the argument logically to the point that the people in a majority deserved a favoured consideration.

Road transport, which offered the enterprising Africans a new and rewarding role in an important sector of the economy, was bound to be drastically affected by this fundamental change in colonial policy. In March 1946 the Nairobi Secretariat, responding to African protest, directed all provincial and district officers to adopt a more liberal policy. 'While every effort must be made', the circular read, 'to keep the number of licences issued within the economics of trade, at the same time it is felt that we should agree on an increase . . . even at the risk of issuing them beyond these limits'.[60] Despite this directive, there was no immediate response evident in the licensing as the provincial and district officers and the board clung to their traditional practices. African protest thus increased. Before the year's end several Africans actually obtained audience with the governor. Others threatened appeal to the Supreme Court.[61]

The new African members of the Legislative Council took up the transporters' cause. Two weeks after the circular councillor F. Walter Odede complained to the Nyanza provincial commissioner about the government's prompt licensing of the sixty-five military vehicles obtained by Premchand Raichand & Co. The commissioner, in a letter to the chief secretary, strongly supported Odede. 'I feel that it is grossly unfair', he remarked, that the African applicants 'should now be denied this business when they have fulfilled our purposes throughout the whole war'.[62] In a confidential reply the chief secretary expressed regret that nothing then could be done about the sixty-five licences and asked the commissioner to explain the position to 'Mr. Walter Odede'.[63] In April Odede and Mathu both supported R. M. Obor and his seven African partners in their application for two bus routes. It was an application that expressly requested a policy of African favouritism. Obor asked that the Asian transporter Kassam Khamisa, who was then serving the routes, be given six months' notice to quit.

> Thereafter the industry will be entirely in our hands. We do hope and expect that there will NOT be lame excuse for this Indian to operate in these areas. . . . We are economically and politically fit to run the business easily without any trouble. [These are Native Land Units] and we are, therefore, entitled by law to have this industry and develop our 'Motherland' with it.[64]

Obor's application required extraordinary consideration as it, unlike all others, was supported by the two African councillors. The government at first explained to Obor that it was not only Khamisa who was operating on the proposed routes but also the European firm of Roadways and that it would be wrong to displace them to grant a monopoly to 'newcomers'.[65] Then the government discovered that in addition to Khamisa and Roadways there were two licensed Africans operating bus services on the two roads. The provincial commissioner apparently persuaded Odede to so inform Obor. In writing to Obor, Odede expressed support for the idea of a monopoly but explained that it would be an injustice to displace the Africans already in business. Pointing out that there was still ample room for more passenger vehicles, he encouraged the partners to retain 'the idea of working in company, because it would be a great lesson to our people if you succeed'.[66] Shortly after receiving Odede's letter, the Obor group reconstituted itself as the Kenya African Industrial Research and Transporting Services and applied for a monopoly on three new bus routes.[67]

Although Obor and his partners do not seem to have been any more successful in their second application, the interest of Odede and Mathu marks a turning point in the government's practice. During the latter part of 1946 as a result of a more liberal attitude towards African applicants, there was a great increase in both licensed vehicles and licensed operators. There was also a new policy of deliberately favouring Africans over Asians and Europeans. Africans received priority, especially in instances where the transport was to serve mainly African areas and people. Table 4.1, showing the results of three meetings of the TLB, well illustrates the new policy of African priority.[68]

Among the Asians refused licences was Harnam Singh, the first man in Kenya to volunteer for military service after the beginning of World War II. His case was taken up by the Asian member of the Legislative Council, A. Pritam.[69]

Reflective of the new policy were the admission of Africans into the decisionmaking of the licensing process and a revision of the appeals procedure. In May 1946 on the advice of the Nyanza provincial commissioner, the TLB appointed councillor Odede as its first African member. From that time the board always included an African. Beginning in 1947 rejected applicants could attain a hearing before an Appeals Tribunal. Because it was no longer necessary to apply to the Supreme Court, there were many more appeals. These changes promoted African transport interests over those of Asians and Europeans. The new District Advisory Committee on Transport Licensing in Kisii, for instance, was composed of two Europeans (the district officer and the inspector of police) and four local Africans. There was no Asian member.[70]

During the years immediately preceding independence, the Kenya government increasingly favoured African interests. This was especially evident in the Northern Province, the former Northern Frontier District. In this vast desert that covered more than two-thirds of Kenya there was no railway, and road transport had gradually succeeded the camel caravans in carrying the food, clothing, and military supplies of the British administrators, the goods of the Asian shopkeepers, and the livestock, hides and skins, building stone, timber, and ivory of the long-distance traders. Road transport had been developed chiefly by the Asians who operated mainly from Nanyuki, the nearest railhead at the base of Mount Kenya, but also from Mombasa, Nyeri, and other centres. As their firm names suggest, many combined transporting with shopkeeping: Ahamed Osman General Merchants of Isiolo, Northern Kenya Auto Stores of Nanyuki, Thika Plumber and Building Contractors, Concrete Block and Ballast Co. of Meru, Embu Trading Co., and Nyeri General Grocers. The same was probably true of others such as Fakirmohamed and G. H. Karim of Isiolo, Bhiku Bros. of Embu, M. S. Noordin of Nanyuki, Yakub-Deen & Co. of Karatina, and B. M. Patel of Karatina.[71] A significant characteristic is that almost all these Asians had their residences and seats of business outside the province.

TABLE 4.1 Applications for Transport Licences in Kenya, 1946-47

	Road Service		B		C	
	Approved	Rejected	Approved	Rejected	Approved	Rejected
20-21 May 1946						
African	17	5	28	4	11	5
Asian	0	10	4	5	12	12
European	–	–	1	1	–	–
15 Jan. 1947						
African	6	29	11	29	7	1
Asian	1	–	–	4	3	1
European	1	–	–	–	–	–
Chinese	–	–	–	–	–	1
14 Jan. 1947						
African	18	34	13	14	7	2
Asian	1	3	4	5	5	3
European	–	–	–	–	–	–

Source: 'Minutes of Meetings of the Transport Licensing Board Held in Kisumu, 20-21 May 1946, 15 Jan. 1947, and 14 Jan. 1947', docs. 68 (encl.), 195A, and 195B, file ADM.3/3/8(2/557)--1934-45, 'Conferences, Committees, and Commissions: General Co-ordination of Transport', Nyanza Province daily correspondence, Syracuse University microfilm 1949, reel 3.

In time the British officials and the Asian traders in the Northern Province developed a symbiotic relationship unlike any in other parts of East Africa. One of the main sources of revenue for the transporters was contracts for haulage with the government. The government also made its lorries available for private use at a charge of 75 cents per mile, and some of the shopkeeping transporters, such as Noormohamed Mangia of Isiolo, carried the government's mail apparently free of charge. Because there was no bus service, the government allowed the Asian lorries to carry passengers illegally. During the disastrous floods of 1961 transporters like Ahamed Osman put all their vehicles at the service of the government.[72]

In the late 1950s the Asians began to be challenged by African transporters, mainly Somalis, who were resident in the northern towns. The government then, for the first time, began to act unfavourably towards the Asians. In 1959 Babu Padamshi of Marsabit was denied a road service licence because he had not yet purchased a lorry. The following year Mangia was reported for falsifying the weight of his load. Meanwhile the government increasingly granted 'B' licences to Somalis and, on further application, permitted them road service licences for carrying passengers as well as cargo.[73]

In 1961 the local Somalis began a vigorous protest against competition from Asians resident outside the Northern Province. In December 1960 after soliciting bids through an advertisement in the *East African Standard*, the Ministry of Works had awarded a Nanyuki Asian, M. S. Noordin, a lucrative contract for hauling cement. Noordin had offered to haul at 40 cents per ton-mile which was well below rates then charged locally. The Somalis, however, had not seen the advertisement. In February the Wajir secretary of a Somali organization, the Northern Province People's Progress Party, complained to the provincial commissioner of the government's decision, and a deputation of Somali traders called on the Isiolo district commissioner. The commissioner then supported the Somalis in a letter to the Ministry of Works: 'I would ask you to bear in mind in the future the great economic importance of giving our traders full opportunity to get those 'plum' jobs, even if you have to pay a bit more. There are not many opportunities like these in the N.F.D. and the Government has always in the past tried to exclude outsiders'.[74]

The next government contract, for the bulk transport of government stores, went to a Wajir Somali, and the central government assured the Northern Province administration that in the future the invitations to tender would not be solicited colonywide.[75]

Despite this assurance, the Ministry of Works in December 1961, after a change in personnel, awarded an alien Asian firm, the N. K. Auto Stores of Nanyuki and Meru, a contract for the transport of government materials on routes between all the urban centres of the Northern Province. Apparently, local Asians as well as Somalis joined in the protest. The provincial commissioner then reminded the ministry of its previous agreement and insisted on a reconsideration of the award. 'In future', he added, 'may we consider such tenders together?'[76] A week later, probably at the provincial commissioner's direction, the Nanyuki district commissioner informed the N. K. Auto Stores that, with the sanction of the TLB, he was withdrawing the firm's short-term licences to operate in the province. 'Kindly arrange to hand the licences back to me immediately', he curtly concluded, 'and I will see if a refund is possible'.[77]

The Asian trader, obviously shocked by this sudden reversal, appealed to the ministry. He declared that he held valid 'B' licences for his six five-ton lorries for the Meru-Nanyuki-Isiolo route and would shortly be opening a branch office in Isiolo. He was, he stated, in the most favourable position to carry out the contract, and 'moreover we are the cheapest of the lot'. In reply the TLB's chairman upheld the withdrawal of the essential short-term licences, and the contract was then reassigned to an Isiolo transporter.[78] Although the local man in this instance happened to be the Asian Ahamed Osman, the change in policy restricting licences and contracts to persons resident in the area of transport was generally much in favour of the Africans. It portended the eventual exclusion of Asian transporters from all the African areas.

The policy of favouring Africans resulted in the rapid appearance on the Kenya roads of hundreds of surplus military vehicles and led to a severe competition. The number of licensed motor vehicles leapt from 15,000 in 1945 to 34,000 in 1950, to 55,000 in 1955, and to 83,000 in 1963. In a typical year, 1955, the TLB refused only 282 of 2,592 new applicants for licences. Established transporters, whether Asian, European, or African, were challenged by the new, eager competitors. The result was not only a cutthroat competition, but also evasion of legal restrictions, a flood of business failures, a rapid turnover in the ownership of vehicles, and a virtual chaos on the roads. As early as March 1947 Roadways complained to the Nyanza provincial commissioner that 'pirate' buses were making it impossible to carry on regular service, and one of the new rivals, the Nyanza African Bus Service of Kisumu, in turn complained of competition from Roadways. The competition, which first appeared in the form of newly licensed Africans contesting with established Asians and Europeans, soon advanced to a state of African transporters' resenting the licensing of more Africans.[79]

The rivalry was fiercest in the passenger service governed by the road service licences. In 1951 a government officer deplored the situation in Central Nyanza: 'At present on certain routes, five or more buses leave the terminus at approximately the same time in the early morning. The drivers and turnboys . . . fight for the passengers; the luggage of a passenger is grabbed perhaps by two separate operators, and then a mad race for the next stage takes place, which is a danger to the bus and the other road users'.[80] Competiveness of this kind was especially trying for passengers in the nonscheduled buses or taxis. As one disgruntled African explained, a driver would tell each prospective passenger that he would take him wherever he wanted to go. After the passenger paid his fare, the driver would keep him waiting while he filled the vehicle far beyond what it should carry—with thirty-six, for instance, instead of the prescribed twenty-seven persons. When ready to leave, the driver would threaten to eliminate those whose destinations conformed least to the route desired by the majority and would agree to take them only if they paid double fare. After a delay of two to four hours the vehicle would at last depart, crammed with disgruntled occupants.[81]

The hazard was increased by the fact that these vehicles were not any better maintained than those before the war. It was not unusual to see a lorry with its suspension so awry that it moved almost sideways down the road. Proper maintenance required money, and many transporters were heavily in debt and operating with a very slim margin of profit. Also, even in urban areas the number of experienced mechanics had probably not kept pace with the ever-increasing number of vehicles, and in rural areas there was often no skilled personnel. In 1949 an African in Butere requested permission to drive his lorry occasionally to Kisumu, off his licensed route, just to keep his vehicle maintained. It is difficult, he explained, 'to get an expert mechanic to repair the lorry or [to know] where to put the grease into the dry parts'.[82]

The poor maintenance together with the competition for loads naturally led to a great increase in the number of accidents. In 1951 Kenya recorded 3,911 motor vehicle accidents with 162 fatalities. Within four years these figures nearly doubled as accidents increased to 7,695 and fatalities to 288. Increasingly through the period the Africans were responsible for the road hazards. In 1963 they accounted for 63 per cent of the accidents, Asians for 18 per cent, and Europeans for 14 per cent.[83]

The competition and the government's new policy of favouring Africans forced the Asians to change the nature of their transport business. When the military vehicles became available, Asians, as noted, lent money to Africans who had insufficient funds to meet the purchase costs. Subsequently as the newly licensed transporters encountered additional expenses of reconditioning their vehicles, converting them to specific transport purposes, and then running and maintaining them, the Asians continued to provide the necessary funds. As a district commissioner of Central Nyanza explained:

> These Africans soon found that they had not the capital to keep these worn-out lorries and taxi-buses on the road. They were faced with heavy garage bills. Their vehicles lay idle outside garages, which refused to repair them until adequate deposits had been made.
> It was at this time that the Indians began to take an interest, and obtain mortgages over these vehicles. The Indians supplied the capital in order to have the vehicles repaired.[84]

Within a short time because of the intense rivalry and inexperience in a business of this kind, a large proportion of the Africans were unable to keep up the payments on their loans. The Asian money-lenders then claimed the vehicles that had been offered as security. The licences, however, were not transferable; and because of the government's attitude, the Asians knew that they had little chance of getting the vehicles relicensed for their own operation.

In this predicament the Asians and Africans conspired in an illegal accommodation. The ownership of the vehicles was transferred to the Asian money-lenders who henceforth managed the businesses under the old names with the former African owners usually as front men. Of course, the government was not informed of the transactions, and the vehicles continued to be registered and licensed in the Africans' names.[85]

The nature of the illicit 'partnership' varied from business to business as each Asian and African worked out a mutually satisfactory arrangement as to how the enterprise would be managed and how the profits would be shared. In the typical situation, as with Kassam Kamisa and Jocobo Orwa, or with Karmala Manji and John Daudi Migot, all of Kisumu, the African declared the Asian his manager, and the employees, when questioned by the government, maintained that the African was still the owner. In a few cases the African openly took the Asian into the business as a partner and then withdrew entirely while the transport company continued to function under its old name. In some others the Asian took out a 'hire agreement' while the African ostensibly remained the owner. Although in all such arrangements the ownership was transferred to the Asians, it would be wrong to assume that there was exploitation of the Africans. In the extensive Kenya files on road transport there is not one complaint from an aggrieved African. The two parties obviously had a mutual interest in this conspiracy against a restrictive colonial government. In fact, there was eventually a considerable transfer of ownership among the Africans, exactly in the same way, as the new owners sought to avoid the complications and uncertainties of relicensing.[86]

While conspiring in this way to evade regulation under the road service licences, the Asians and Africans also ignored the restrictions on the 'C' licences, which were the easiest to obtain and the cheapest to buy. Though restricted to carrying their own goods, many of those with 'C' licences illegally filled their lorries not only with the goods of others 'for hire or reward' but also with paying passengers. If stopped by the police, the drivers swore that all the goods were their own, and their passengers, coached beforehand by the drivers, all claimed that they were riding free of charge. In time the transporters made a mockery of the 'C' licences.[87]

The flaunting of the regulations and, in general, the rapid growth of road transport after the war posed new problems for the railways. Although beneficial to road transport in training drivers and mechanics and providing vehicles, the war was decidedly detrimental to the railways. After the war the railways suffered not only from wartime deferred maintenance and a severe shortage of locomotives and freight cars, but also from a shortage of coal from the customary source in Natal. In 1948 the Kenya, Uganda, and Tanganyika railways were merged under a single administration as East African Railways and Harbours, and the new organization promptly inaugurated a variety of road transport services of its own to carry goods and passengers to and from the rail stations. In Kenya a road service for goods traffic was established between Nairobi and Arusha (170 miles) connecting with rail and road services in Tanganyika. In Uganda a similar road transport service between Masindi Port and Butiaba and between Masindi Town and Kampala (217 miles) joined Lake Albert and the West Nile district to the main Kenya and Uganda rails. In Tanganyika the new road services connected the Mbeya and Iringa areas to Central Line depots at Morogoro, Kilosa, and Mikumi.[88]

These measures and co-ordination did not alleviate the problem. Imports piled up at the seaports faster than the railway could haul them. In 1951 ships arriving at Mombasa had to wait from thirty to forty days for a vacant berth and in 1952 up to fifty-one days. By the mid-1950s when the rolling stock was refurbished and diesel locomotives were imported to burn oil from the Persian Gulf, road transport had made great gains seemingly at the railways' expense. Transporters running parallel to the rails were carrying all sorts of goods formerly hauled by the railways. In 1961 fully 75 per cent of the imports landed at Mombasa went inland to Arusha by road although the rails ran parallel to the road for the entire 245 miles. Among the goods lost by the railways the most important were petrol and fuel oils, including paraffin (kerosene), which was rapidly replacing wood as the Africans' cooking fuel. In 1957 the railway administration estimated that its loss of revenue to road transport that year amounted to £598,000.[89]

The effect on the railway combined with the abuses of the licensing system and the increasing road traffic problem to spur the Kenya government to exert new controls over road transport. As early as February 1947 the chairman of the TLB confided, 'Personally I think the transport position has reached saturation point and very few of these new applications should be allowed'.[90] In July Nyanza's acting provincial commissioner agreed: 'We have erred on the liberal side in the granting of T.L.B. licences to the detriment of the routes and the financial loss of many'.[91] In November when a petrol shortage exacerbated the problem, the board's chairman was asked by officials in Nairobi to cancel half the licences in the colony. He avoided so drastic a step but promised to be 'very careful about increasing the number of lorries on the road'. At the next meeting of the board, January 1948, 'practically no new licences were approved'.[92] Such curtailment, however, could be only temporary. Because of the great public demand, the government could not effectively limit the number of licences.

In correcting the abuses of the vehicle regulations, the government also was ineffectual. In February 1948 while on a drive to Masseno, the Nyanza provincial commissioner interrupted his journey to stop and personally inspect an overcrowded lorry. He found that the vehicle, licensed to carry thirty passengers, had in addition to a heavy load of luggage forty-five persons in the passenger compartment, two more on the front seat beside the driver, and five others on the roof. The commissioner demanded that the police take action against the driver and the owner, in this instance, both Asians.[93] In July 1949 as vehicle violations continued, the commissioner asked the police to assign an officer to patrol the Nyanza roads for one month 'during which period he should be able to restore order'. Though unable to spare an officer for a month, the police arranged for intensive road patrols on two successive fortnights. The result was 102 arrests.[94] Such action, however, did not effect a permanent reform. Two years later, in April 1951, the TLB's chairman asked the district officer of Central Nyanza to undertake an 'enquiry into road service licence malpractices'. The report, two months later, described the many illegal operations of the Asian and African transporters but apparently led to no significant change.[95]

The only recourse was for the central government to revise the road transport legislation. During the 1950s as more and more Africans entered the industry and fretted over the many regulations, they came to regard the Transport Licensing Ordinance of 1937 not so much as a measure designed to protect railway interests as an ordinance specifically aimed at curtailing African enterprise. In 1956 the government amended the ordinance in minor particulars. Two years later partly because of the railway's decline and the long-standing inability to control road transport but also because of the growing African criticism, the government appointed a committee to examine the whole licensing structure. Composed of five members—three Europeans, an African, and an Asian—the committee was chaired by one of the most respected Asians, Chunilal Bhagwandas Madan, legislative councillor, Queen's Counsel, and president of the Law Society.[96]

The Madan committee confronted the rail problem but was unable to make any significant recommendations. In a dissenting minute to the committee report, the African member, Wanyutu Waweru, asserted, 'The African has never seen any advantage in goods vehicle licensing. Indeed he regards the present form of licensing as designed merely to prevent his entry into the goods transport industry'.[97] The committee concentrated on the competition with the railways. Declaring that the railways were more economical than road transport over long hauls, it supported the differential tariff and recommended that road transport along routes parallel to the rails be restricted by licence. A new 'X' licence for the 'controlled routes' parallel to the rails would impose a mileage limit for haulage of all goods except beer, soft drinks, and perishables such as vegetables that required frequent stops.[98]

The committee's recommendations proved ineffectual. In January and February 1960 new Transport Licensing Regulations imposed a limit of thirty miles for haulage on the controlled routes, but the 'X' licence was never instituted. In 1959 the railways narrowed the gap between its higher and lower rates. This attempt to become more competitive with road transport, however, 'did in fact little more', as the railway administration admitted, 'than halt the erosion of traffic'.[99] The annual profit, which had been £6.0 million in 1958, increased to only £6.2 million in 1962 and £7.1 million in 1963. The goods traffic, which in 1958 amounted to 1.53 billion ton-miles, grew to only 1.68 in 1962 and 1.77 in 1963.[100]

As these statistics and incidents illustrate, British efforts to control road transport in Kenya essentially failed. In Tanganyika and to a lesser degree in Uganda the situation was the same. In all three territories to the end of the colonial period the fierce competition, conspiracies against the law, neglect of mechanical maintenance, pirating of scheduled routes, and overloading of vehicles defied all attempts at regulation. Road transport continued to grow and thrive while the railways languished. The phenomenal growth through the two decades preceding independence is evident in Table 4.2.

The figures indicate a great advance in road transport in all three territories. Between 1939 and 1963 Kenya's motor vehicles increased nearly sixfold, Tanganyika's eightfold, and Uganda's sevenfold. Throughout the period Kenya retained a lead with more than twice the number in each of the other territories. Tanganyika, despite its supremacy in area and population, had until 1963 the lowest number.

Primarily because road and rail were more complementary in Uganda than in the other territories, Uganda did not impose licensing restrictions on the hauling of goods and passengers by motor vehicles. In 1958 the government commissioned Edward K. Hawkins to investigate the competition. In a memorandom on Hawkins's report the government stated an intention to protect the railway from competition from longhaul traffic extending beyond Uganda's borders but rejected the idea that a system of licensing was essential or could be effectively enforced.[101]

Tanganyika differed by following Kenya with a system of licensing. Although competition between rail and road had appeared insignificant between the wars, the Tanganyika government after 1945 began to consider competition as a reason for the country's sluggish economy. In 1956 with a Transport Licensing Ordinance it instituted two types of

TABLE 4.2   Expansion of Road Transport in East Africa, 1939-63

Kenya	1939	1945	1955	1963
Cars	8,832	8,251	25,901	42,738
Lorries, vans, pickups	3,225	5,160	24,845	31,123
Buses, taxis	363	584	648	1,547
Motorcycles	822	928	1,478	4,736
Totals	13,242	14,923	52,872	80,144

Tanganyika				
Cars	2,958	3,231	9,184	21,243
Lorries, heavy vans, busses, coaches	1,584	3,518	6,573	8,463
Pickups, light vans	10	117	5,756	8,038
Motorcycles	490	552	2,862	4,775
Totals	5,042	7,418	24,375	44,797

Uganda				
Cars	2,520	2,887	13,452	23,754
Commercial vehicles	1,929	2,276	9,136	10,109
Public service vehicles	150	221	369	680
Motorcycles	779	1,046	4,993	7,342
Totals	5,378	6,430	27,950	41,885

Sources: Uganda, 1957 Statistical Abstract (Entebbe: Government Printer, 1958), p. 41; 1964 (published 1965), p. 35; Tanganyika, Statistical Abstract 1938-51 (Dar es Salaam: Government Printer, 1953), p. 11; 1963 (published 1964), pp. 60-1.

road transport licence: a public carrier's licence permitting the haulage of goods and passengers for hire or reward and a private carrier's licence for conveyance of only the vehicle owner's goods. It also provided in the same ordinance for a Transport Licensing Authority to administer the new program with a view to preventing 'in the public interest' all 'uneconomic competition with other systems of transport'.[102] In its decisions the authority was very liberal in awarding the private licences but very conservative in granting the public licences. As a result the Tanganyika transporters, as in Kenya, circumvented the restrictions in all ways possible. In 1959 the authority reported that the private carrier's licence was being violated by 'operators of all races from all over the territory'.[103]

The government responded by imposing more restrictions. It first appointed an Advisory Committee, on the model of the Kenya Madan committee, to review the licensing system. Although the committee recommended several new forms of restrictions on road transport, the government accepted only one. It restricted each private carrier's licence to one of three areas: Dar es Salaam and its environs, Tanga and its environs, and the remainder of Tanganyika. The government thus chose a unique and subtle means of limiting competition with the railway. Like the Kenya plan of restricted routes, however, the Tanganyika scheme of restricted areas proved impossible to enforce.[104]

As in the interwar period Tanganyika and Uganda provided more opportunity than Kenya for the development of sizeable Asian transporting ventures. The Southern Highlands Roadways Ltd. and the Eastern Province Bus Co. Ltd. are two notable examples. In 1941 two families, the Manjis and the Bharmals, who had been operating separate transport businesses in southern Tanganyika, joined to form a large concern, the Southern Highlands Transport Co. Ltd., to serve European estates from a base in Mbeya. Within two years, to their chagrin, the government confiscated the company's assets and put the vehicles and the staff at the service of the railway. After the war the railway proved unable to meet the transporting needs, with the result that the government resumed the licensing of private transporters. R. K. Manji, the Bharmal brothers, and R. F. Jessa then revived the former company under a new name as the Southern Highlands Roadways Ltd. Accorded a monopoly by the government, the new company covered a large area of southern and central Tanganyika. From its Mbeya headquarters it established depots in Dar es Salaam, Dodoma, Moshi, Iringa, Tabora, Morogoro, and six other centres.[105]

The Uganda company acquired a similar monopoly. In 1928 Asians in Jinja formed the Eastern Province Bus Co. for service between Jinja, Mbale, and towns in eastern Uganda. Ten years later a crisis occurred as the government, to regularize service, began to grant exclusive licences.

A European concern, the Uganda Transport Co. Ltd., which had received an exclusive licence for Buganda Province, then sought to buy out the Asian firm with the intention of gaining an exclusive licence for the Eastern Province. The Asians refused to sell and sought financial backing from some of the wealthy Uganda Asians. The result was a considerable expansion of the resources of their firm and its conversion in 1954 to a public, limited company. The Eastern Province Bus Co. received the exclusive licence, and by the end of the colonial period it was operating 130 buses and employing 60 Asians and 340 Africans.[106]

The Contribution to Development

The statistics on the growth of motor vehicles and construction of roads illustrate the importance of road transport to East Africa's economic development. This growth, as shown in Table 4.3, closely paralleled the increase in foreign trade.

Although many other factors could be considered in measuring the overall development, these statistics provide an approximation in their revelation of the growth of the infrastructure, the production of cash crops, minerals, and other commodities for export, and the consumption of foreign products. There obviously was an extensive tranformation of the economy, and of this road transport was both a cause and a product. With the railway it provided the essential means for the movement of people and goods and the application of services. It was important to the collection as well as the distribution of commodities. It was also in itself a lucrative industry employing thousands of people. It was created by the need for trade and subsequently augmented by the increase in trade. Transport and commerce went hand in hand.

Because of the absence of statistics on the tonnage of goods and the number of passengers carried by motor vehicles, it is impossible, as most analysts have agreed, to distinguish with any precision the contribution of road transport as distinct from that of the railway. Certainly in the history of East Africa the two systems were complementary. Road transport carried goods and passengers between the rail stations and areas the rails could not reach, whereas the railway provided an efficient conveyance for most commodities between the inland stations and the ocean ports. Even in places where road and rail ran side by side, however, some commodities, such as beer, soft drinks, and petroleum, were carried more efficiently by motor vehicles because of the frequent stops along the routes. Of course, the two systems did compete for both passengers and commodities along the parallel routes. During a typical twenty-seven hours of daylight in 1958, for example, ninety commercial vehicles were counted as passing between Kenya and Uganda, and as-

TABLE 4.3   Growth Correlation of East African Trade, Motor
Vehicles, and Roads, 1920-60

| | Growth | | |
Subject	1920	1939	1960
External trade (£1,000)	13,000	19,000	266,000
Motor vehicles	6,000	24,000	170,000
Road mileage	8,000	29,000	55,000
Percentage of Growth			
External trade	–	46%	1,300%
Motor vehicles	–	300%	608%
Road mileage	–	363%	90%

Sources: *Colonial Reports* of the Colonial Office; *Statistical Abstracts* of the territories; and *East African Trade Indices* of the East African Common Services Organization.

suming that 250 tons of goods were carried daily, the annual volume during daylight hours alone must have been close to 30,000 tons. In 1960, to cite another example, the railway carried only 7,775 of the 30,000 tons exported from the southern Tanganyika ports of Mtwara and Lindi, and only 1,926 of the 33,847 tons imported.[107] Apparently all the rest, in both directions, was conveyed by road.

The competition resulted not only in legislation curtailing road transport but also in a lowering of the railway rates. The public interest seems to have been promoted by this competiton, and the government's restrictions on road transport appear more as a liability than an asset in the overall economic development. Occasionally a farsighted official in the colonial government, appreciative of road transport, protested against the licensing policy.[108] While fostering the growth of urbanization by making possible a rapid flow of people and commodities between towns and scattered rural areas, road transport promoted in ways that the railway could not the economic and social development of the hinterland. In Kenya it was ocean transport that created Mombasa, lake transport that led to Kisumu, and the railway that was the chief factor for Nairobi, Naivasha, Eldoret, and the several other centres that grew from the rail stops. It was road transport, however, that developed all the other towns—places such as Isiolo, Garissa, Wajir, Kericho, Kakamega, Kapenguria, Mandera, Lodwar, Moyale, Marsabit, Machakos, Narok, Embu, Meru, Kisii, Mumias, and Ngong—and it certainly contributed substantially to all those for which ocean, lake, and rail were primary. In 1979 after a comprehensive study of road transport in central Tanganyika, Frank M. Chiteji concluded, 'All important rural settlements of the region have received their first development impulses through roads'.[109]

Road transport was important to all communities. It provided an essential communication between the railways, on the one hand, and agricultural estates, mining operations, or forest industries, on the other, all of which were largely European enterprises. It afforded the Asians the vital linkage between the parent companies in the cities and the rural dukas. As Chiteji discovered in Tanzania, the completion of a road into a rural area was an immense benefit to the Africans. It led to the development of a dispensary and ensured the availability of both doctors and agricultural officers and the construction of modern buildings.[110] Road transport also opened the African reserves and made possible there not only the sale of outside manufactures, but also the collection of African produce. In the long run one of its main contributions was the promotion of an African cash-crop economy. African goods were transported mainly by lorry, but it was not unusual anywhere in East Africa to see the tops of buses crowded with baskets of farm produce.

In Kenya road transport was especially important to Africans in the Coast and Northern Provinces, the two areas neglected by the railway. The coconuts, cashews, mangrove poles, ivory, and other commodities produced in the fertile coastal belt were carried to Mombasa by lorry or dhow. In the vast northern desert the motor vehicle, as already explained, succeeded the camel as the conveyor of all the African produce, principally livestock and hides and skins taken to Nanyuki and Mombasa. Between 1953 and 1961 lorries carried some 55,000 cattle from Isiolo alone, and around Isiolo the double-decker goat lorries, speeding recklessly over the dusty roads, were notorious.[111]

In Uganda where most Africans, quite distinct from Kenya, were introduced to cash crops before World War I, road transport was even more important to the collection of raw materials. This is especially true for cotton, Uganda's chief export. In the early years African farmers carried the seed cotton by portage or bicycle to a local market where it was sold and then conveyed by Asian bullock cart to a ginnery. In the 1920s when too many ginneries were competing for too little cotton, some enterprising Asian ginners began to send lorries around the cotton fields to pick up the farmers and their cotton and, bypasssing the markets, proceed directly to the ginneries that paid the farmers directly. This increased the farmers' profits and stimulated production. Motor vehicles were also involved in carrying the cottonseed to oil mills and the lint to Port Bell and later to rail stations for export. As most of the ginneries were built before the railway and often were far removed from the lake and the rail stops, this road transport was essential. For the Africans' second largest export crop, coffee, Asian motor vehicles shared with the railway the haulage from the farming areas to the processing centres. With tobacco, the third such crop, road transport was all important. From Bunyoro and White Nile districts, where most of the tobacco was grown, Asian lorries had to carry the crop 440 miles to the cigarette factory at Jinja. Although steamer and rail transport were available, the leaves deteriorated rapidly in the heat and humidity and required the much faster motor vehicles.[112]

Though not so important as the railway in the haulage of the European and Asian estate crops, such as tea and sugar, road transport was vital to the movement in Uganda of African products that were consumed locally. Among these were such cash crops as bananas, groundnuts, and maize, and in lesser quantity, millet, cassava, sweet potatoes, sorghum, and beans. A large proportion of these foodstuffs were head-carried or bicycled to local markets, but lorries and buses, moving these perishables quickly, served for the longer distances. The fact that Uganda was the world's foremost producer of bananas but consumed them all indicates the extent of this trade. Instead of establishing a Maize Control, Uganda left the buying and distribution of maize to local marketing boards. Seeking the most economic means, these boards chose motor vehicles over rail. To the major centres of Uganda, road transport also brought cattle for slaughter, hides and skins for baling, lake fish for the markets, timber for milling, clay for brick making, and wolfram and beryl ores for smelting.[113]

In Tanganyika as in the other territories road transport, largely in Asian hands, supplied the necessary conveyance between the cash-crop areas and the railway, port, or urban centres. With perishables like fruits, vegetables, tobacco, and sesame, which required rapid transport, the motor vehicles were indispensable. Even with sisal, which until the disastrous fall of world prices beginning in 1952 was the country's main export, road transport usurped much of the haulage, and it surpassed the railway in the conveyance of minerals.[114] Because of the low density of roads and rail, however, there were many areas not served by modern transport. At the end of the British administration a large proportion of the agricultural population was still at a subsistence level. 'Tanganyika', in the words of the historian Cyril Ehrlich, 'remained at independence one of the poorest countries in tropical Africa'.[115]

As this study illustrates, road transport appears to have developed through three distinct periods in each of which the activities of a particular community became the focus. Before 1920 it was the Europeans who introduced motor vehicles, put them into government and private service in a number of ways, and employed them effectively during the

East Africa campaign. Between the wars the Asians adopted cars and lorries for business purposes by carrying commodities between urban centres and distributing merchandise and hauling cash crops in African areas. In successful competition with both the railway and the European transporters, they gained an ascendency in transporting passengers as well as goods. After World War II both Asians and Europeans were challenged by Africans. At independence, having combined with Asians successfully in the evasion of colonial restrictions and in the continuing expansion of road transport, the Africans were well established. For Africans as well as Asians road transport provided an economic and social mobility.

Despite the others' participation, road transport should be considered primarily an Asian contribution. As Arthur Hazlewood noted, road transport was 'a competitive industry of many relatively small firms'.[116] In this respect it was, like shopkeeping, an enterprise in which the Asians could excel, and they were mainly responsible for developing the new business, which, as distinct from the railway, was a product of private enterprise. The effect on the Africans was profound. Apart from opening the African areas to trade and making possible there a cash-crop economy, the Asians, by employing and training Africans as drivers and mechanics, made possible the Africans' eventual entrance into the ownership and management of road transport. Then, contrary to what is usually assumed, instead of constituting a barrier to the Africans' rise into a middle-class position, the Asians in this particular industry, in which the government was generally a retarding force, joined with Africans, assisted them financially, and merged with them in an expanded business.[117] Their history in this enterprise appears as a striking example of the Asians' providing in East Africa a transition, especially in the sphere of economics, from European colonialism to African independence.

The Asians' role in road transport rapidly diminished in the postcolonial years and by the late 1960s was insignificant. It paralleled the Asians' declining role in commerce. In Kenya the Asians were increasingly driven from positions of ownership and management in road transport by the regulatory and Africanization policies of the immediate post-war years. The Kenya legislation of 1966, which tied the renewal of licences to citizenship, and the subsequent discrimination against Asians in all forms of commerce and artisanry resulted in the displacement of the remaining Asian transporters. In Tanzania and Uganda the governments' transfer of private business to the government agencies, parastatals, and co-operatives gradually drove the Asians from all forms of commercial and transporting endeavour.

Notes

1. Vivienne De Watteville, *Speak to the Earth: Wanderings and Reflections Among Elephants and Mountains* (New York: Harrison Smith and Robert Hass, 1935), pp. 132–33.

2. Ronald Robinson and John Gallagher, *Africa and the Victorians: The Climax of Imperialism in the Dark Continent* (London: Macmillan, 1961), pp. 308ff. A. M. O'Connor, *Railways and Development in Uganda* (Nairobi: Oxford University Press, 1965), p. 147. Mervyn F. Hill, *Permanent Way:* vol. 2, *Story of the Tanganyika Railways* (Nairobi: East African Railways and Harbours, 1957).

3. East Africa Protectorate, *Blue Book for the Year Ended March 31st, 1915* (Nairobi: Government Printer, 1916), p. A21. *East Africa Protectorate, Report for 1912–13*, Cd. 7050 (London: HMSO, 1914), p. 35. W. W. Campbell, *East Africa by Motor Lorry: Recollections of an Ex-Motor Transport Driver* (London: John Murray, 1928).

4. See, for example, C. W. Hobley to Chief Secretary, Nairobi, 26 May 1917, doc. 17, file 191/2/3, 'Motor Transport, 1916–28', vol. 2, Coast Province daily correspondence, Syracuse University microfilm 1995, reel 87.

5. For the provincial and district use of cars, see Hobley to Secretary, Nairobi, 27 Dec. 1916, doc. 2, ibid. For the use of road transport in collecting night soil, see Hobley, Minute on Circular no. 3 to Superintendent of Conservancy, 24 Jan. 1917, doc. 5, ibid. For rickshaws, see *East African Standard*, 12 June 1909, pp. 9, 17.

6. *Uganda: Report for 1909–10*, Cd. 5467–6 (London: HMSO, 1911), p. 17; ibid., *1911–12*, Cd. 6007–43 (1916). p. 11; ibid., *1912–13*, Cd. 7050–28 (1914), p. 22.

7. *Uganda: Report for 1920 (Apr. to Dec.)*, Colonial Reports—Annual, no. 1112 (London: HMSO, 1922), p. 17.

8. Mehta, *Dream Half Expressed: An Autobiography* (Bombay: Vakils, Feffer and Simons, 1966), pp. 79, 81, 88, 90, 127–28, 134.

9. Hobley to Secretary, Nairobi, 27 Dec. 1916.

10. M. F. Hill, *Planters' Progress: The Story of Coffee in Kenya* (Nairobi: Coffee Board of Kenya, 1956), p. xi.

11. Shanti Pandit, ed., *Asians in East and Central Africa* (Nairobi: Panco, 1963), p. 355.

12. *East Africa Protectorate, Report for 1919–20*, Colonial Reports—Annual, no. 1089 (London: HMSO, 1920), p. 27.

13. Secretariat Circular no. 3, 'Disposal of Motor Vehicles by the Military on Cessation of Hostilities', 18 Jan. 1917, doc. 3, file 191/2/3, vol. 1. C. E. Spencer (for Acting Colonial Secretary), Circular no. 7, 31 Jan. 1921, doc. 97, ibid.

14. *Kenya Colony and Protectorate, Report for 1924*, Colonial Reports—Annual, no. 1282 (London: HMSO, 1925), pp. 12, 13. Ibid., *1928*, no. 2463 (1929), p. 42. *Colony and Protectorate of Kenya, Report for 1932: 1st April to 31st December*, Colonial Reports—Annual, no. 1659 (London: HMSO, 1933), p. 36. Kenya, *Blue Book . . . 1937* (Nairobi: Government Printer, 1938), pp. 237–38. Ibid., *1939* (1940), sec. 20, pp. 14, 43.

15. G.A.S. Northcote for Colonial Secretary, Circular no. 34, 'Abolition of the Mechanical Transport Branch', 25 Apr. 1922, doc. 150, file 191/2/3, vol. 1. W.

McGregor Ross (Director, Public Works Department) to All Heads of Departments, All Senior Commissioners et al., Circular no. 44, 15 May 1922, doc. 159, ibid. Ross, *Kenya from Within: A Short Political History* (London: Allen and Unwin, 1927), chap. 15.

16. H. H. Trafford (Acting District Commissioner, Kilifi) to Senior Coast Commissioner, 29 July 1922, doc. 165, file 191/2/3, vol. 1. Secretariat Circular no. 57, 'Motor Transport Regulations', 6 June 1924, doc. 191, ibid. Northcote for Colonial Secretary, Circular no. 9, 'Motor Transport', 18 Jan. 1924, doc. c. 182, ibid. Secretariat Circular no. 66, 'Motor Transport Regulations, 12 Oct. 1925, doc. c. 288, ibid.

17. *Annual Report . . . Kenya . . . 1935*, Colonial Reports—Annual, no. 1771 (London: HMSO, 1936), p. 32.

18. Ibid., *1937*, no. 1858, p. 39; *1938*, no. 1920, p. 44.

19. Acting Provincial Commissioner (Coast) to Acting District Commissioner (Nyika District), Rabai, 4 Dec. 1920, doc. 88, file 191/2/3, vol. 1. Acting Senior Agricultural Officer, Kisumu, to Provincial Commissioner, Nyanza Province, 15 July 1939, doc. 126, file ADM.3/3/8(2/557)–1934–45, 'Conferences, Committees, and Commissions: General Co-ordination of Transport', Nyanza Province daily correspondence, Syracuse University microfilm 1949, reel 3. Secretariat, Nairobi, 'Memo.: Transport Licensing Ordinance, 1937', 3 Feb. 1950, doc. l, file LEG. 14/7, 'Legislation: Transport Licensing Ordinance, 1937–61', Northern Province daily correspondence, Syracuse University microfilm 4753, reel 26.

20. Irene S. Van Dongen, *British East African Transport Complex* (Chicago: University of Chicago Department of Geography Research Paper no. 38, Dec. 1954), pp. 75–77, 134. Arthur Hazlewood, *Rail and Road in East Africa: Transport Co-Ordination in Under-Developed Countries* (Oxford: B. Blackwell, 1964), pp. 32–33.

21. Van Dongen, *British East African Transport Complex*, p. 121.

22. Hazlewood, *Rail and Road*, p. 34.

23. Ibid., pp. 42–43. Secretariat, Nairobi, 'Memo.: Transport Licensing Ordinance, 1937', 3 Feb. 1950.

24. Secretariat, Nairobi, 'Memo. . . . 1937', 3 Feb. 1950.

25. J. Edwin Holmstrom, *Railways and Roads in Pioneer Development Overseas* (London: P. S. King, 1934), p. 172.

26. Trafford to Senior Coast Commissioner, 29 July 1922, doc. 45; and District Commissioner, Nairobi, to Treasurer, Nairobi, 28 Feb. 1920, file 191/2/3, vol. 1.

27. Secretariat Circular no. 39, 'Hire of Motor Cars for the Conveyance of Government Passengers', 23 June 1926, doc. 11; Secretary, Central Tender Board, Treasury, Nairobi, to Senior Commissioner, Coast Province, 16 Aug. 1927, doc. 53, file 191/2/3, vol. 1. Major Patrick Gethin (interviewed by Gregory, 5 Sept. 1981, Syracuse, N.Y.) is the son of Captain Percy St. Lawrence Gethin who ran a taxi business in Nairobi between the wars.

28. Charles Udall, Nairobi, to Governor in Council, 27 Feb. 1920, with doc. 1; Udall to Governor in Council, 22 Apr. 1920, with doc. 5; Acting Provincial Commissioner (Coast) to Acting Secretary, Nairobi, 19 Mar. 1920, doc. 3; Udall to Governor in Council, 22 Apr. 1920, file 'Tramway: Motor Bus Service, Minute Paper no. 1365, 1920', Coast Province daily correspondence, Syracuse University mi-

crofilm 1995, reel 91. J. Y. Molley (Mombasa Agent, East African Agency Ltd.) to District Commissioner, Mombasa, 4 June 1920, with doc. 9, ibid.

29. Evident in proceedings of the Transport Licensing Board.

30. T. A. Denison (Secretary, Transport Licensing Board) to Provincial Commissioner, Nyanza, 24 Aug. 1944, c. doc. 217; Acting Provincial Commissioner, Nyanza, to Secretary, Co-ordination of Transport Committee, Nairobi, 10 Mar. 1936, doc. 29; and S. H. Fazan (Provincial Commissioner, Nyanza) to Chairman, Transport Licensing Board, Nairobi, 18 June 1942, with doc. 181, file ADM.3/3/9(2–823)–1946–50, 'Conferences, Committees, and Commissions: General: Co-ordination of Transport', Nyanza Province daily correspondence, Syracuse University microfilm 1949, reel 3. Also, Dhanwant Singh (Barrister), Kisumu, to Licensing Authority, Nairobi, 4 Dec. 1945, ibid.

31. T. Ainsworth Dickson (Chairman, District Committee, District Commissioner's Office), Mombasa, to Chief Secretary, Nairobi, 26 Aug. 1919, file 6/274, 'Motor Traffic Legislation, 1915–20', Coast Province daily correspondence, Syracuse University microfilm 1995, reel 36.

32. 'Extract from Mr. Trafford's Letter', Rabai, 23 Feb. 1923, file 191/2/3, vol. 1, ibid.

33. Trafford to Officer-in-Charge, Motor Transport, Nairobi, 15 Feb. 1922, ibid.

34. Messrs. Roadways (Kenya) Ltd., 'Memo. to Chairman and Executive Committee of the East African Chamber of Mines', 17 June 1939, file ADM.3/3/8(2/557)–1934–45.

35. Andrew Walter Stanley Hitch (Managing Director, Roadways) to Chairman, Transport Licensing Board, 10 Jan. 1939, ibid.

36. Ibid.
37. Ibid.
38. Ibid.
39. Hitch to Provincial Commissioner, Nyanza, 26 May 1939, ibid.

40. Acting Provincial Commissioner, Nyanza, Secretary, Co-ordination of Transport Committee, Nairobi, 10 Mar. 1936, ibid.

41. Provincial Commissioner, Nyanza, to Transport Licensing Board, Nairobi, 28 Dec. 1938, ibid.

42. Ibid. Hitch to Provincial Commissioner, Nyanza, 26 May 1939, ibid.

43. O'Connor, *Railways*, p. 124.

44. Ibid. Hazlewood, *Rail and Road*, p. 39.

45. Van Dongen, *British East African Transport Complex*, p. 61. Frank M. Chiteji, *Development and Socio-Economic Impact of Transportation in Tanzania, 1884–Present* (Washington, D.C.: University Press of America, 1980), pp. 33, 34. O'Connor, *Railways*, pp. 32, 138–39.

46. O'Connor, *Railways*, pp. 140, 143. Tanganyika, *Statistical Abstract 1938–51* (Dar es Salaam: Government Printer, 1953), p. 11. *Uganda Protectorate, 1938*, Colonial Reports—Annual, no. 1903 (London: HMSO, 1939), p. 28. Kenya, *Statistical Abstract, 1955* (Nairobi: Government Printer, 1957), p. 44.

47. J. A. Sachedina (son), interviewed by Honey, 29 June 1973, Njombe.

48. Company description, Pandit, *Asians*, p. 360.

49. *Uganda Protectorate, 1938*, p. 28.

50. F. Walter Odede, Masero, to Chairman, Transport Licensing Board, 18 May 1946, doc. 38, file ADM.3/3/9(2–823)–1946–50. Odede to Sgt. R. M. Obor, 16 May 1946, doc. 37, ibid. Dhanwant Singh (Barrister-at-Law), Kisumu, to Licensing Authority, Nairobi, 4 Dec. 1945, with doc. 7, ibid. David Ogega to District Commissioner, Kisii, 25 Feb. 1946, doc. 6, ibid. Budedu and six other Africans to Licensing Authority, Nairobi, 21 Dec. 1945, with doc. 7, ibid. For African purchase during the war, see W. Harragin (Chairman, Transport Licensing Board) to All Provincial Commissioners, District Commissioners and Officers in Charge of Districts, 19 Apr. 1940, doc. 160, file ADM.3/3/8(2/557)–1934–45.

51. Kenya, Government Notice no. 706, *Supplement to Official Gazette*, 30 July 1946. Registrar of Co-operative Societies to K. L. Hunter (Provincial Commissioner, Nyanza), 18 Apr. 1946, doc. 26; and H. R. Montgomery (Chairman, Transport Licensing Board) to Provincial Commissioners and Officers in Command Northern Frontier District and Masai, 1 Aug. 1946, doc. 65, file ADM.3/3/8(2/557)–1934–45. Registrar of Co-operative Societies to Hunter, 18 Apr. 1946, doc. 26. Provincial Commissioner, Nyanza, to Honourary Chief Secretary, Nairobi, 28 Mar. 1946, confidential, doc. 16; and Chairman, Transport Licensing Board, to Chief Secretary, Nairobi, 8 Apr. 1946, confidential, doc. 23, file ADM.3/3/9(2–823)–1946–50. E. H. Windley (Provincial Commissioner, Central Province) to All District Commissioners, Central Province, 12 July 1946, file District Commissioner/FH/25/2, 'Travelling and Transport Government Vehicles, 1944–53', Central Province daily correspondence, Syracuse University microfilm 4751, reel 39.

52. Odede to Chairman, Transport Licensing Board, 18 May 1946, doc. 38, file ADM.3/3/9(2–823)–1946–50.

53. Evident in documents describing subsequent events.

54. Harragin to All Provincial Commissioners et al., 19 Apr. 1940, doc. 160; and Secretary, Transport Licensing Board, to Provincial Commissioner, Kisumu, 29 July 1941, doc. 164, file ADM.3/3/8(2/557)–1934–45.

55. Secretariat, Nairobi, 'Memo.: Transport Licensing Ordinance', 3 Feb. 1950, doc. 1, file LEG.14/17, 'Legislation: Transport Licensing Ordinance, 1937–61', Northern Province daily correspondence, Syracuse University microfilm 4753, reel 26.

56. Odege (Ogega) to District Commissioner, Kisii, 25 Feb. 1946, doc. 6, file ADM.3/3/9(2–823)–1946–50. K. L. Hunter (Provincial Commissioner, Nyanza) to Chairman, Licensing Board, Nairobi, 21 Aug. 1944, with doc. 217, file ADM.3/3/8(2/557)–1934–45.

57. Opondo to Provincial Commissioner, Kisumu, 29 July 1946, doc. 60, file ADM.3/3/9(2–823)–1946–50.

58. Provincial Commissioner, Nyanza, to Opondo, 2 Aug. 1946, doc. 61; Provincial Commissioner to Martin, 3 Apr. 1946, doc. 19; W. A. Perreau (District Commissioner, Kisii) to Ogega, 27 Feb. 1946, with doc. 11; and W. A. Perreau to Ogega, 27 Feb. 1946, with doc. 11, ibid.

59. Described by Atkins's successor, T. A. Watts (District Commissioner, Central Nyanza), to Chairman, Transport Licensing Board, 12 June 1951, doc. 407, ibid.

60. K. G. Lindsay (Acting Chief Secretary), Nairobi, to All Provincial Commissioners et al., 9 Mar. 1946, circular letter no. 29, doc. 14, ibid.

61. District Commissioner, Kavirondo (Kakamega) to Provincial Commissioner, Nyanza, 29 Nov. 1946, doc. 148, ibid.

62. Letter, 28 Mar. 1946, confidential, doc. 17, ibid.

63. Letter, 16 Apr. 1946, confidential, doc. 25, ibid.

64. Obor to Provincial Commissioner, Nyanza, 19 Apr. 1946, doc. 30, ibid.

65. Provincial Commissioner, Nyanza, to Obor, 8 May 1946, doc. 33, ibid.

66. Letter, 16 May 1946, doc. 37, ibid.

67. Obor to Transport Licensing Board, n.d. (early June 1946), doc. 44, ibid.

68. The local District Commissioner strongly opposed the African monopoly: C. F. Atkins (District Commissioner, Central Kavirondo) to Licensing Authority, Nairobi, 10 June 1946, doc. 45; and 20 June 1946, doc. 52, ibid. See also an instance in which three Asian applicants were put below sixteen Africans in a list of priority: app. B, 17 July 1946, with doc. 58, file ADM.3/3/8(2/527)–1934–45. The individual applications and licences granted were regularly printed in the *Kenya Gazette*. There was no list of those rejected.

69. Pritam to Provincial Commissioner, Nyanza, 29 Jan. 1947, doc. 198; and Pritam to Hunter, 27 Feb. 1947, doc. 211, file ADM.3/3/9(2–823)–1946–50.

70. Encl. in District Commissioner, Kisii, to Chairman, Transport Licensing Board, Nairobi, 23 July 1946, doc. 58, file ADM.3/3/9(2–823)–1946–50, Nyanza Province daily correspondence. Chairman, Transport Licensing Board, to Provincial Commissioner, Nyanza, 30 Apr. 1946, doc. 28; and 'Minutes of a Meeting held at the office of the District Commissioner, Kisumu, on the 20th and 21st May, 1946', with doc. 68, file ADM.3/3/8(2/527)–1934–45. Secretariat, Nairobi, 'Memo.: Transport Licensing Ordinance, 1937', 3 Feb. 1950, doc. 1, file LEG.14/7, 'Legislation: Transport Licensing Ordinance, 1937–61', Northern Province daily correspondence, Syracuse University microfilm 4753, reel 26.

71. Division Engineer to Provincial Commissioner, Central Province, Nyeri, Provincial Commissioner, Northern Province, Isiolo, et al., 28 June 1961, doc. 86, file T&T.28/1/4, vol. 2, 'Transport, General, incl. Contracts, 1955–62', Northern Province daily correspondence, Syracuse University microfilm 4753, reel 34.

72. Proprietor, Ahamed Osman General Merchants, Isiolo, to Provincial Commissioner, Northern Province, 1 Jan. 1962, doc. 98; and G. P. Lloyd (Acting Secretary for African Officers, Ministry of Foreign Affairs) to Executive Officer, Transport Licensing Board, Nairobi, 26 Apr. 1956, doc. 12, ibid. K. G. Lindsay, Secretariat, Nairobi, to Gerald Reece (Officer in Charge, Northern Frontier District), Isiolo, 1 May 1946, doc. 25, file T&T.28/1/5, 'Transport of Stores and Food Stuff, 1929–63', Northern Province daily correspondence.

73. District Commissioner, Marsabit, to Provincial Commissioner, Northern Frontier Province, 31 Dec. 1959, doc. 67, file T&T.28/1/4, vol. 2. Bernard M. N. Brown (Supervisor, Government African School, Marsabit) to District Commissioner, Marsabit, 26 Apr. 1960, doc. 68, file T&T.l28/1/4, vol. 2. District Commissioner, Garissa, to Provincial Commissioner, Northern Frontier Province, 18 Sept. 1956, doc. 23, file T&T.128/1/4, vol. 2.

74. Secretary, Northern Province People's Progress Party, to Provincial Commissioner, 13 Feb. 1961, doc. 74; and District Commissioner, Isiolo, to Provincial

Commissioner, 21 Feb. 1961, doc. 77, ibid. P. E. Walters (Provincial Commissioner, Northern Province) to Division Engineer, Ministry of Works, Central Division (North), Nyeri, 23 Feb. 1961, doc. 78, ibid.

75. District Commissioner, Wajir, to Ismail Haji, 1 Aug. 1961, doc. 81/A; and J. Whitefield (for Director of Veterinary Services) to District Commissioner, Isiolo, 19 Sept. 1961, confidential, doc. 91, ibid. Khamisa's first name is spelled variously in the files as Kassam, Khassam, and Hassam.

76. Letter to Acting Province Engineer, Ministry of Works, Central Division (North), Nyeri, 4 Jan. 1962, doc. 99, ibid. Proprietor, Ahamed Osman General Merchants, Isiolo, to Provincial Commissioner, Northern Province, 1 Jan. 1962, doc. 98, ibid.

77. Letter (author illegible) for District Commissioner, Nanyuki, to N. K. Auto Stores, Nanyuki, 11 Jan. 1962, doc. 100, ibid.

78. Manager, N. K. Auto Stores, to Province Engineer, Ministry of Works, Nyeri, 12 Jan. 1961, doc. 101; and C. F. Atkins (Chairman, Transport Licensing Board), Nairobi, to Manager, N. K. Auto Stores, 22 Jan. 1962, doc. 103, ibid.

79. *Kenya Statistical Abstract, 1955* (Nairobi: Government Printer, 1957), p. 44. Ibid., *1964* (1965), p. 52. Kenya, *Annual Report: Transport Licensing Board, 1955* (Nairobi: Government Printer, 1956), p. 3. Hitch to Provincial Commissioner, Nyanza, 6 Mar. 1947, doc. 218, file ADM.3/3/9(2–823)–1946–50. N. C. Sige (Nyanza African Bus Service of Kisumu) to Provincial Commissioner, Nyanza, 10 Mar. 1947, doc. 217, file ADM.3/3/9(2–823)–1946–50.

80. P. Chrichton (District Officer) to Chairman, Transport Licensing Board, 'Enquiry into Road Service Licence Malpractices: Central Nyanza', 12 June 1951, doc. 407A, ibid.

81. Shadrack Lawi Ojuka, Kisumu, to (District Commissioner, Central Kavirondo?) with copy to Provincial Commissioner, Nyanza, 12 Oct. 1943, doc. 28, file 3/487(TT.4/3), 'Motor Traffic: Motor Transport and Traffic Census, 1953–58', Nyanza Province daily correspondence, Syracuse University microfilm 2800, reel 127.

82. Samson Okonb'o, Butere, to Provincial Commissioner, Nyanza, 12 Dec. 1949, doc. 375, file ADM.3/3/9(2–823)–1946–50.

83. Kenya, *Statistical Abstract, 1955* (Nairobi: Government Printer, 1957), p. 46; ibid., *1964*, p. 54.

84. T. A. Watts (District Commissioner, Central Nyanza) to Chairman, Transport Licensing Board, 12 June 1951, doc. 407, file ADM.3/3/9(2–283)–1946–50.

85. The best description of this is ibid.

86. N. G. Hardy (District Officer, Central Nyanza) to Chairman, Transport Licensing Board, 4 Aug. 1949, doc. 356, ibid. Chrichton, 'Enquiry'.

87. Hazlewood, *Rail and Road*, pp. 42–43.

88. Kenya, *Commerce and Industry in Kenya, 1961* (Nairobi: Ministry of Commerce and Industry, 1962), p. 5. O'Connor, *Railways*, p. 127.

89. Van Dongen, *British East African Transport Complex*, p. 77. Kenya, *East African Railways and Harbours, Annual Report, 1958* (Nairobi: Government Printer, 1959), p. 8. O'Connor, *Railways*, p. 146. Hazlewood, *Rail and Road*, pp. 44–45.

90. Letter to Provincial Commissioner, Nyanza, 11 Feb. 1947, doc. 204, file ADM.3/3/9(2–823)–1946–50.

91. E.R. St. A. Davis to Secretary, Transport Licensing Board, 31 July 1947, doc. 237, ibid.

92. Montgomery to Provincial Commissioner, Nyanza, 10 Jan. 1948, doc. 273, ibid.

93. Hunter to Superintendent of Police, Nyanza, Kisumu, 7 Feb. 1948, doc. 276, ibid.

94. Hunter to Superintendent of Police, 6 July 1949, doc. 352, ibid. N. Saudoshi (Senior Superintendent of Police, Nyanza) to Provincial Commissioner, Nyanza, 7 July 1949, doc. 353; H. F. Hertz-Smith (Acting Senior Superintendent of Police, Kisumu Division) to Senior Superintendent of Police, Nyanza, 31 Aug. 1949, doc. 360, ibid.

95. Chrichton, 'Enquiry'.

96. Madan was to become Chief Justice after Kenya's independence. Hazlewood, *Rail and Road,* p. 44. Transport Licensing (Amendment) Ordinance, no. 39 of 1956. *Kenya Gazette,* 25 Nov. 1958, p. 1371. A. B. Tannahill for Permanent Secretary, Ministry of African Affairs, to All Provincial Commissioners, 24 Nov. 1958, 'urgent', doc. 3, file LEG.14/17, 'Legislation: Transport Licensing Ordinance, 1937–61', Northern Province daily correspondence, reel 26.

97. Quoted, Hazlewood, *Rail and Road,* p. 79.

98. Kenya, *Report of the Committee of Enquiry Appointed to Examine the Transport Licensing Ordinance,* Sessional Paper no. 2 of 1959/60 (Nairobi: Government Printer, 1961), paragraphs 10, 12, 41. Hazlewood, *Rail and Road,* pp. 47–51.

99. Kenya, *East Africa Railways and Harbours, Annual Report, 1959* (Nairobi: Government Printer, 1960), p. 8. 'Transport Licensing (Amendment) Regulations', Legal Notice no. 23, 6 Jan. 1960, *Kenya Subsidiary Legislation, 1960,* vol. 39, New Series (Nairobi: Government Printer, 1961), pp. 70–71; 'Transport Licensing (Amendment) (No. 2) Regulations, 1960', Legal Notice no. 113, 18 Feb. 1960, ibid., p. 239.

100. Kenya, *East Africa Railways and Harbours, Annual Report, 1959,* p. 8; and *1963* (1964), pp. 7–11.

101. Hawkins's report was subsequently published as *Roads and Road Transport in an Under-developed Country: A Case Study of Uganda,* Colonial Research Studies no. 32 (London: HMSO, 1962). For the government's memo. on the report, see Uganda Sessional Paper no. 9 of 1960.

102. Transport Licensing (Amendment) Ordinance, no. 39 of 1956, clause 22.

103. Tanganyika, *Annual Report of the Transport Licensing Authority 1959,* (Dar es Salaam: Government Printer, 1960), para. 21.

104. Tanganyika, *Advisory Committee Report* (Dar es Salaam: Government Printer, c. 1961). The official policy was stated in Sessional Paper no. 2 of 1961 and enacted in the Transport Licensing (Amendment) Ordinance, no. 48 of 1962. Hazlewood, *Rail and Road,* p. 55.

105. Company description, Pandit, *Asians,* pp. 353–54.

106. Ibid., p. 301.

107. Hawkins, *Roads,* p. 55. O'Connor, *Railways,* pp. 125, 142–43.

108. Letter, 12 June 1951, doc. 47A, file ADM.3/3/9(2–823)–1946–50.

109. Chiteji, *Development,* p. 114.

110. Ibid., pp. 107–8.

111. O'Connor, *Railways,* p. 150.

112. District Commissioner, Isiolo, to Provincial Commissioner, 26 Aug. 1961, doc. 88/A, file T&T.28/1/4, vol. 2, 'Transport: General, including Contracts, 1955–62', Northern Province daily correspondence, Syracuse University microfilm 4753, reel 34. W.E.P. Kelly (Acting Provincial Commissioner, Northern Province), Isiolo, to Assistant Commissioner of Police, Northern Province, Isiolo, 15 Jan. 1958, doc. 8, file LEG.14/6, 'Legislation: Motor Traffic Ordinance 1928', ibid., reel 26.

113. O'Connor, *Railways,* pp. 8, 11–13.

114. Ibid., pp. 16–34 passim, 150.

115. C. Ehrlich, 'The Poor Country: The Tanganyika Economy from 1945 to Independence', chap. 7, *History of East Africa,* vol. 3, ed. D. A. Low and Alison Smith (Oxford: Clarendon, 1976), p. 330. O'Connor, *Railways,* p. 8. Chiteji, *Development,* pp. 82–107.

116. Hazlewood, *Rail and Road,* p. 28.

117. For a striking incident of an Asian's assisting an African to start a transport business, see H.K. Kaizzi Bulanja, 'A True Son of Uganda', chap. 34, *Jayant Muljibhai Madhvani: In Memorium,* ed. H. P. Joshi, Bhanumanti V. Kotecha, and J. V. Paun (Nairobi: Emco Glass Works, 1973), p. 56.

CHAPTER FIVE

■

Crafts and Construction

The actual daily apprenticeship of the African has been carried through to a successful issue by the Indian artisans and mechanics. They have trained more African workmen than all the industrial and technical schools put together.

—Charles F. Andrews, 1920[1]

In their work as artisans and contractors the Asians made a twofold contribution to economic development. They provided an essential service as skilled workers in masonry, carpentry, blacksmithing, and other crafts and as contractors in organizing both skilled and unskilled workers for various types of construction. In these endeavours they also provided a valuable training for Africans. The knowledge and skills that the Africans learned from the Asians in this informal, on-job experience proved in the long run far more useful and rewarding than the formal education they received in the governments' technical training schools.

Although description is lacking, Asian craftsmen, known in western India as fundis, were presumably among the immigrants who settled on the Zanzibar islands and East African coast centuries before the inception of British and German colonialism. It is known that beginning in 1593 the Portuguese imported stonemasons and dressers from India to build Mombasa's Fort Jesus.[2] Asians are known also to have constructed at least five of the seventeen mosques erected in Mombasa between 1837 and 1895.[3]

Makhan Singh, the Kenya trade unionist who became the principal scholar of East Africa's working class, has conjectured that the earliest craftsmen along the coast were Arabs and Asians whereas the unskilled workers were almost exclusively African slaves.[4] As has been pointed out in an earlier study, the Asians as well as the Arabs of East Africa owned slaves.[5] Although many of the slaves must have learned the skills of their masters, it would have been impossible for them in such an economy,

159

even if they obtained their freedom, to compete with the Arabs and Asians. These groups, therefore, must have enjoyed a monopoly of the skilled trades. Slavery was to be abolished by the British in their East African dependencies between 1897 and 1909 and in the German territory shortly after the British occupation in 1919, but by then neither the freed Africans nor the Arabs could compete significantly with the Asian craftsmen.[6]

Importation of Indentured Workers

The growth of the Asian artisan class was greatly stimulated by the Kenya-Uganda Railway. Faced with a need for large numbers of both skilled and unskilled workmen, the British imported indentured servants from India. Between 1896 and 1901 when the trunk line was completed from Mombasa to Kisumu, more than 34,000 Asians entered the East Africa Protectorate under three-year contracts. Subsequently they continued to be imported in lesser numbers, a few hundred each year, to construct the branch lines of the railway and to serve the Public Works Departments of the two British protectorates. By 1922 when an Indian Emigration Act terminated further indenture, a grand total of nearly 40,000 had entered East Africa. All these Asians were called 'coolies', but in a strict sense a coolie was an unskilled labourer, and many of the indentured were masons, carpenters, and other artisans as well as surveyors, clerks, and draughtsmen.[7]

With the exception of a brief period in 1897 when because of a plague in western India a few were recruited through Calcutta, the indentured Asians came from only two ports, Karachi and Bombay. Those who sailed from Karachi were largely from the Punjab and Sind, whereas those who left from Bombay were chiefly from the Punjab and the Bombay Presidency. Some who passed through the two ports came from Bengal, Assam, and Oudh. Through the period of importation the Punjabis were the predominant group, and overall there were more Sikhs than Muslims and more Muslims than Hindus. The skilled workers, a small minority of the whole, were recruited mainly from Bombay, and the unskilled came largely from Karachi.

In East Africa the indentured Asians had to work very hard under hazardous conditions. The unskilled were assigned to work gangs of 30 to 200 men under the supervision of the few with experience in railway construction, and they were employed mainly in the onerous tasks of clearing, grading, carrying, and laying ties and track. The main work of the carpenters was to erect the several stations at the various stops and the numerous temporary buildings essential for workers and equipment near the advancing railhead. The masons were involved with the foundations of more permanent buildings and the culverts and bridges. The blacksmiths fashioned the rail spikes and a variety of related items and repaired tools and machinery. Soon after beginning work in the humid coastal lowlands, the workers began to suffer from malaria, jiggers, dysentery, scurvy, ulcers, and various liver complaints. In the early years 50 per cent contracted malaria, and an average of 10 per cent and often half the labour force were on the sick list. At the end of the first seven years, 20.2 per cent had been invalided to India and 7.8 per cent had died.[8]

Among the minor hazards in East Africa were hostile Africans, maneating lions, and bubonic plague. Africans frequently stole goods from the 'coolie camps', and the Asians sometimes raided African shambas in retaliation. Asians in turn have been charged with stealing from the neighbouring peoples and inveigling African women into the camps. Through the heavily populated Kamba and Kikuyu areas there were many clashes. In the Nandi and Lumbwa districts the workers had to be protected by armed escorts and stockades around their camps. The story as to how for two weeks in 1898 at Tsavo, 136 miles from Mombasa, two voracious lions brought the construction to a complete stop is notorious in East African history. Each night Asians and Africans were dragged from their tents and eaten. Finally the panic-stricken Asians stopped work and demanded to be sent back to Mombasa. The more desperate halted a train by throwing themselves on the track, then piled their belongings into the cars and fled. Those who remained spent the nights on top of water tanks or in holes dug in the tent floors and covered with logs. Before the lions were shot, they had devoured twenty-eight Asians and scores of Africans.

As the danger from lions diminished, the hazard from plague increased. From Bombay where it was endemic, the plague spread to many of the rail stops where the Asians concentrated their dukas. Twice, in 1899 and 1902, the government ordered that the Nairobi bazaar be burned to the ground. It also began to quarantine and disinfect workers and their belongings on arrival. The problems of insanitation, however, continued, and outbreaks of plague were frequent before World War I.[9]

Despite these difficulties the Asian indentured servants employed on the railway and other public works are regarded as having made a significant contribution to the early economic development of British East Africa. Herbert Samuel, who visited the area as a member of Parliament (M.P.) in 1902, remarked that 'the progress of these portions of Africa would have been slow indeed, had it not been possible to draw upon our Asiatic possessions for unlimited supplies of subordinate labour with brain and hand'.[10] Sir John Kirk, former British consul and agent at Zanzibar, estimated in 1909 that 'the railway could not have been finished with native labour under twenty years'.[11] Mervyn F. Hill, official historian of the railway, observed years later that 'without the aid of Indian labour, artisans and subordinate staff, the railway would not have been built'.[12]

The skilled workers among the indentured were important not only in the various forms of construction but also in the training of the unskilled. Through the daily, on-job association with these artisans, many of the workers who had no useful skills at the time of their employment quickly learned the fundamentals of masonry, carpentry, and other crafts. At the expiration of their contracts, a large number apparently had acquired sufficient knowledge and skill to begin work as artisans in India or East Africa. The numerous Sikhs, who had left the Punjab in most instances with only a peasant background, soon acquired a reputation as handymen adept at any manual task.

The indentured who chose to remain in East Africa at the end of their contracts thus formed on the whole a pool of skilled labour useful to continuing work on the railway and other government projects and in the burgeoning private sector. In the early years only 10–15 per cent of the unskilled and a slightly higher proportion of the skilled renewed their contracts.[13] Although the percentages apparently increased as working conditions improved, most of the indentured preferred work in a free economy, and a large number decided to stay and become independent workers in East Africa. By 1903 when the Uganda Railway Committee submitted its final report, 6,724 of the 31,983 imported specifically for railway work had remained in East Africa, and about 2,000 of them were still working for the railway.[14] By 1922 when indenture ceased, a total of 7,278 among all the indentured (39,771)—more than 18 per cent—had not returned to India.[15]

Emergence of a Free Artisan Community

These skilled and semiskilled Asians were joined by other artisans, some of whom had been on Zanzibar or in the coastal settlements before the indentured system began, but most of whom had been attracted subsequently to East Africa by economic opportunity. 'A good deal of the Indian skilled class', as the historian Kenneth King has explained, 'came to East Africa with a long family tradition of working in tin, glass, wood, iron and other more specialised occupations'.[16]

Typical of those with a long history in East Africa were the Bohra tinsmiths who had settled on Zanzibar, Pemba, and Lamu and in Mombasa, Malindi, and other coastal towns. One of the pioneer Asians on Zanzibar was Adamjee Putwa, a tinsmith from Kutch who emigrated about 1850. Although many of these early metalworkers, like the Karimjee family, branched into business because of the greater economic reward, Putwa wanted to retain a mechanical emphasis, and he set up a soda-water factory.[17] As the focus of trade and administration shifted to the mainland and then into the interior, a number of Bohras moved to Mombasa and other coastal towns and thence westward into Thika, Machakos, Nairobi, and on into the new centres of Uganda. Among the early tinsmiths of Mombasa was Karimjee Walijee who specialized in making paraffin (kerosene) lamps. In Nairobi the Bohra tinsmiths soon included Esmail Abdulalli, Noorbhai Alibhai, Essajee Amijee, and Yusufali Ebramijee. Like Putwa on Zanzibar, many of these metalworkers advanced to a factory production. Some, as King has noted, diversified so rapidly that by 1970, for example, 'a grandson might be running a highly mechanized, modern factory in Nairobi's industrial area while the grandfather was still producing a series of lamps, funnels, and kerosene pumps entirely with hand-tools'.[18]

A similar community with a long residence in East Africa was the Bhadala Muslim sect. Traditionally its members had mended dhows. Early in the colonial period, one of their number, P. M. Aarup, acquired a reputation among the British in Mombasa as a yacht designer and builder. In 1908 he was commissioned by the government to build a boat for the upper Tana River.[19]

Throughout the colonial period Asian artisans continued to immigrate to East Africa. Most, at least in the early years, came from Bombay. There were over 600 immigrants from Bombay in 1898, some 2,000 in 1901, and many more in the succeeding years.[20] A large number among these free immigrants were recruited by private contractors such as Hussein Bux and A. M. Jeevanjee, both of whom also recruited initially for the railway.[21] Some of the skilled workers, including carpenters, hospital assistants, tailors, barbers, and cooks, came as camp followers of the Indian troops who were stationed in East Africa.[22] Most artisans, however, appear to have immigrated as individuals seeking financial advancement in self-employment. Shortly after arrival, they set up their dukas wherever prospects seemed most favourable. Once established, they were sometimes recruited by contractors for a construction project in another part of East Africa. Most of the Sikhs who settled in Arusha, for instance, are said to have been brought there as fundis by contracting firms from Nairobi.[23]

As this settlement of artisans developed in the British territories, a somewhat different pattern was emerging in German East Africa. In contrast to the British, the Germans relied almost exclusively on African labour to build their railways and imported only a small number of indentured workers from India. In 1902–03 they recruited about 100 agricultural labourers on three-year contracts from Ceylon and a number of artisans from Madras, and in 1904 a total of 9 Asians from western India, and in 1910–11 only 12 more.[24] Most of the artisans and other Asians thus went to German East Africa as free immigrants from India and Zanzibar. After arrival in Dar es Salaam they spread quickly into the other settlements as in the British territories. By 1913 nearly half the 9,000 Asians were associated with crafts or clerical work. After 1919 when the country became a British mandate, the artisans and other Asians were drawn to the area in greater numbers. As in Kenya and Uganda the Sikhs eventually became the most numerous artisan community and assumed a prominence in furniture making, metalworking, auto mechanics, and general construction.[25]

During the colonial and post-colonial years, statistics on Asian artisans in East Africa were issued infrequently and without co-ordination among the governments. As a result, both the changes occurring in any one area and any comparisons from one country to another are difficult to ascertain. The available statistics, however, do indicate the importance of Asians in the skilled labour section of the economy.

In 1948 at the beginning of a decade of unusual economic growth, the Asian artisans of Kenya were distributed by occupation as follows:[26]

Carpenters, sawyers	2,388
Bricklayers, masons	1,939
Tailors, dressmakers, textile workers	1,493
Mechanics, engineers, fitters	1,265
Shoemakers, repairers	666
Machine-shop drillers, erectors, fitters	502
Electricians	290
Goldsmiths, electroplaters	198
Blacksmiths	191
Painters, decorators	115
Compositors in printing	110
Stenographers, typists	100
Watch-makers	96
Plumbers	78
Stone quarriers	59
Printers, stereotypers	57
Drivers of road transport	33
Bakers, pastry cooks	33
Butchers, slaughterers	32
Grain-millers	25
Cabinet-makers, joiners	16
Gold miners	12
Dockworkers	12

The statistics for 1948 enable some comparisons within Kenya. Unfortunately, there is no information on the Africans, but the European and Arab skilled workers appear far less significant in the economy than do the Asians. The Europeans outnumbered the Asians only as gold miners (50 versus 12), textile workers (18 versus 16), butchers and slaughterers (33 versus 32), dockworkers (52 versus 12), and stenographers and typists (603 versus 100). The European bricklayers numbered only 7 (versus 1,939 Asian), the carpenters 15 (versus 2,388), electricians 58 (versus 290), shoemakers 12 (versus 666), tailors 32 (versus 1,477), and mechanics 392 (versus 1,265). There were no European blacksmiths or cabinetmakers.[27] Although such detail on the Arabs is lacking, the total of the Arab artisans was only 7,417 in contrast to 31,387 for the Asians. The Arab goldsmiths numbered only 13 (versus 198 Asian), the carpenters and sawyers 81 (versus 2,666), and the bricklayers and masons 70 (versus 1,939).[28]

The Goans were the only Asian community to receive separate consideration in 1948. Among the 3,102 Goan artisans in Kenya were 513 tailors and dressmakers, 80 mechanics, 33 stenographers and typists, 30 carpenters, 26 shoemakers, 19 electricians, 14 machine-shop workers, 13 bakers, 13 printing compositors, 4 dockworkers, 2 road-transport drivers, 2 stereotypers and printers, and 1 butcher. There were no Goan blacksmiths, plumbers, grain millers, cabinetmakers, masons, or painters.[29]

By 1962 when the next census was taken, the Asian artisans of Kenya appear far more important than the Europeans and Arabs. Though not including all the workers, Table 5.1 reveals a striking numerical difference.

For Tanganyika and Uganda detailed information like that for Kenya in 1948 is lacking, and there are no relevant statistics for Zanzibar.[30] Some comparisons can be made, however, for Tanganyika and Uganda. Statistics at the end of the colonial period reveal the importance of the Asian craftsmen. In 1961 the non-African employees in the two territories were distributed as shown in Tables 5.2 and 5.3.

Some additional information can be given on Tanganyika. The list in Table 5.4 of Tanganyika workers by some of the industries in 1960 indicates the Asians' role relative to the roles of the Africans and Europeans. No statistics were given on the Arabs.

Unfortunately the figures, like the preceding on Tanganyika and Uganda, are somewhat misleading. As they pertain only to employees, they do not show the self-employed, a large number of whom were Asians. Presumably, the self-employed also included a number of Europeans as in Kenya and also some Africans. Moreover, not all the workers in these lists were skilled, and probably the proportion of skilled Asians

TABLE 5.1   Asian, European, and Arab Employees in Kenya, 1962

	Numbers of Employees		
	Asian	European	Arab
Mechanics	2,833	563	224
Carpenters, cabinetmakers, joiners	1,634	19	76
Tailors, cutters	1,212	3	133
Masons	835	10	46
Electricians	496	115	24
Drivers (road, locomotive, crane)	439	75	426
Printers, compositors, lithographers	373	98	9
Blacksmiths	246	13	19
Totals	8,068	896	957

Source: Kenya Population Census, 1962: vol. 4, Non-African
Population (Nairobi: Government Printer, 1966), app. 8, p. 92.

was higher than that of the skilled Africans. The figures do illustrate, however, the numerical importance of the Asian workers.

Throughout East Africa the Asian artisans were indispensable to economic development. They provided the needed skills not only for construction of the railways and most of the public works but also for the erection and maintenance of the many buildings in the private sector, the assembly and repair of motor vehicles and farm equipment, and the variety of tasks associated with industrialization. During the early years of railway construction and for several years after completion of the main lines, nearly all the repair of farm equipment and other machinery in the private sector was performed by Asians in the railway workshops. In 1908 one of the main European importing firms, Gailey & Roberts Ltd., established the Nairobi Engineering Works to repair all kinds of machinery.[31] Asian blacksmiths and mechanics soon followed in the major centres with a number of smaller shops offering similar work. Among the first in Nairobi was Hirji Monji, who in 1916 was advertising himself as a motor expert with 'repairs to all cars at the cheapest rates'.[32] Meanwhile the Asian artisans had begun to move into the European agricultural areas, where they were forbidden to settle as farmers but were welcomed as craftsmen. During the 1940s, for instance, about fifty Asian heads of families were working on European farms around Nanyuki.[33] By

TABLE 5.2 Asian, European, and Arab Employees in Tanganyika, 1961

| | Numbers of Employees* | | |
	Asian	European	Arab
Commerce	3,143	759	356
Public Services	1,996	1,974	124
Manufacturing	1,746	431	94
Transport, communications	1,380	377	31
Agriculture, forestry, hunting, fishing	745	1,130	304
Electricity, gas, water	555	227	56
Construction	287	190	52
Mining, quarrying	193	521	5
Totals	10,045	5,609	1,022

*The table lists only Asians, Europeans, and 'Others'. On the assumption that nearly all the last would be Arabs, the author has substituted the word 'Arab' for 'Others'.

Source: Tanganyika, Statistical Abstract, 1962 (Dar es Salaam: Government Printer, 1962), table S.15, p. 151.

then there were also many Asians performing a similar service in the African reserves, and Asian craftsmen were employed not only by the railways and Public Works Departments but also by nearly every government agency.[34]

One of the main achievements of the Asian artisans during the colonial period was the construction of nearly all the buildings, public and private. A knowledgeable member of the community, Bachulal Gathani, has estimated that 99 per cent of the buildings in the towns, whether in the zones restricted to Europeans or in the Asian and African areas, were constructed with Asian skilled labour. These buildings were at first made with wooden walls and iron roofs but later replaced, again by Asians, with structures of stone and tile. 'An Indian gets wealth', Gathani explained, 'then he buys gold for his wife, and next he erects buildings'.[35] That, of course, is a simplification, but the Asian contribution in building was immense. The work was performed by Asian artisans but initiated and organized in most instances by Asian contractors. By 1960 there were about 350 major contractors in East Africa, and nearly all were Asian.[36]

TABLE 5.3   Asian, European, and Arab Employees in Uganda, 1961

	Numbers of Employees*	
	Asian and Arab	European
Commerce	3,166	616
Public services	1,950	2,121
Manufacturing (misc.)	1,548	415
Manufacturing (food products)	880	46
Cotton ginning	551	4
Construction	504	173
Agriculture	477	30
Educational and medical services	430	648
Misc. Services	425	313
Transport, communications	234	72
Mining, quarrying	176	193
Coffee curing	124	6
Forestry, fishing, hunting	6	0
Totals	10,471	4,637

*As in Table 5.2 the word 'Arab' has been substituted for 'Other'.

Source: Uganda, 1962 Statistical Abstract (Entebbe: Government Printer, 1962), table UP.11, p. 101.

Among the early contractors the most successful was A. M. Jeevanjee, whose commercial activities are described in Chapter 2. In addition to importing artisans for the Imperial British East Africa Company and the later protectorate, Jeevanjee contracted to erect buildings, cut stone, and prepare earthworks for construction of the railway. When the railhead reached Nairobi, he was asked by the sub-commissioner, John Ainsworth, to construct the government buildings of Nairobi, including the police lines, land and survey offices, and dispensary, and as partial payment for his services, he was granted a large parcel of land in the heart of the future city. In addition to erecting the government buildings, Jeevanjee laid out the bazaar street, lined it with shops of wood and corrugated iron, and then built the vegetable market. A large block of his land he donated to the government for use as a public park and there in 1906 erected the well-known statue of Queen Victoria.[37]

In 1910 during a visit to London, Jeevanjee told an incredulous press of his accomplishment. He had been in East Africa, he said, for twenty years:

> I may say almost I have made the country. All the best property in Nairobi belongs to me. I built all the Government buildings and leased them to the Administration. I built all the hospitals and post-offices between Mombasa and Port Florence [Kisumu]. I was the sole contractor on the Uganda Railway while it was building, and provided rations for the 25,000 coolies engaged in making the line.[38]

Despite denials from Europeans in East Africa, Jeevanjee's words were substantially true.

Among the hundreds of other contractors only a few can be mentioned here. In 1946 Bawa Singh Bharj established a small engineering works in Mbarara. Within two decades he transformed it into a major building and road-construction operation employing 40 Asians and 600 Africans.[39] Chanan and Pritam Singh, who began as building contractors in Mbale in 1936, ultimately added three branches and employed 80 Asians and 1,200 Africans. They also established a training centre at Mbale for 250 African masons and carpenters.[40] Arjan and Tara Singh, together with Abdul Rehman, formed in 1950 Coronation Builders Ltd. of Nairobi which erected many edifices, including the Kenya Ministry of Works and what for a time was the tallest building in East Africa, the twelve-story Standard Bank of Kampala.[41] Gurdial Singh in 1953 organized the Farmers' Construction Co. of Kampala. Among the more unusual projects he undertook was construction of sets for the famous 20th Century Fox film *The Lion*.[42] M. A. Latif in 1948 set up a building and civil engineering business in Kampala that rebuilt the kabaka's palace and constructed the Wamala Tomb of the kabaka's grandfather as well as the palace of the omukama of Toro.[43]

Informal Training of Africans

In the process of making a material contribution, the Asian contractors such as Jeevanjee and the many Asian craftsmen imparted to Africans a valuable training in artisanry. Side by side with the Asians on the Kenya-Uganda Railway were many unskilled Africans. In 1901 when the trunk line was completed, there were, for instance, 2,506 African workers together with 19,742 Asians.[44] Subsequently on the railway or other government projects and in the workshops public and private, wherever they might be, Asians and Africans both were employed, and in time through association and by example the Africans learned the Asians'

TABLE 5.4   Asian, European, and African Employees in Tanganyika, 1960

	Numbers of Employees		
	Asian	European	African
Jewelry and goldsmithing	80	0	24
Textile drying and bleaching	12	0	219
Cotton weaving	7	0	198
Bicycle assembly and repair	6	0	74
Printing (letter press)	6	0	18
Aluminiumware manufacture	5	0	20
Ice manufacture	4	0	44
Nail manufacture	3	0	20
Food manufacture	3	0	26
Vegetable oil extraction	3	0	9
Dry cleaning	2	0	10
Oil extraction	2	0	43
Salt manufacture	2	0	75
Scrap-metal processing	2	0	12
Tanning	2	0	36
Electroplating	1	0	4
Fez-cap manufacture	1	0	9
Honey processing	1	0	20
Paper manufacture	1	0	21
Totals	143	0	882

Source: Tanganyika, Annual Report of the Labour Division, 1960, pp. 70-2, C.O. 736/57.

skills. Although they were not to assume an important role in the economy until the 1930s, African artisans—carpenters, blacksmiths, and masons—were hired by the government, at least in Uganda, as early as 1910.[45]

Although some Europeans and Africans and even some Asians have charged that the Asian artisans were so fearful of competition that they jealously guarded their skills and refused to convey them to Africans, evidence indicates that the Africans during the colonial period learned their skills largely from the Asians. In a penetrating study of the African artisans in Kenya, King found that the training received from Asians in what he called the informal sector was much more important than that received from the government's technical training programs in the formal sector.[46] This does not mean that the Asians benevolently passed their skills to Africans with the aim of assisting them to establish independent, competitive businesses but rather that in seeking to complete tasks with maximum efficiency in a minimum time, they found it expedient to train their assistants. Nor does it mean that none of the Asian craftsmen sought to confine their skills to their families and ethnic communities. There was some of this among the Asians despite the fact that it was inexpedient.[47]

The training of the African workers began before the turn of the century with their first association with Asians in a common employment. Africans learned from the Asian skilled workers while, for instance, repairing shovels in a railway smithy, cutting stone blocks in a quarry, or constructing a veranda for a settler's home. Through observation and practice, the more diligent Africans eventually were able to perform these tasks. 'The result was', as King has explained, 'that from the whole range of Indian small enterprise (garages, blacksmithing, tinsmithing, tailoring, furniture and building, to mention only a few) there began to emerge Africans who had slowly acquired elements of Indian skill'.[48] In 1947, for instance, the River Road and Canal Road in Nairobi were described as areas in which Africans and Asians worked not only in close association but also in competition. Anyone walking along these roads, it was said, 'would notice that practically every Indian carpenter's or blacksmith's shop has a number of Africans learning or doing the work. Several African carpenters and smiths have started their workshops side by side with the Indians. No ill-feeling or lack of co-operation appears to have cropped up in these areas'.[49]

The informal training occurring between the two peoples eventually became widespread in many of the Asian and European industries. While hiring a few Asian fundis, these firms employed a number of unskilled Africans as casual labour. They let their African workers through the years 'sort themselves out into the more or less productive'. The better workers would work close to a fundi, learn skills, and then be taken on permanently while the others would remain as casual labourers.[50]

By the 1930s the Africans who had learned from the Asians were passing their skills to other Africans. As in the association with the Asians, the new workers acquired through observation the skills of the African craftsmen. In time this training was so valued that the novices began to offer payments for the opportunity to learn a trade. 'Often for a sheep or goat, amongst the Kikuyu', states King, 'a skilled man would agree to teach somebody else, and then as time went on a sum of money took the place of a gift'.[51] The system was flexible in that the learner could leave to begin work on his own as soon as he felt that he had sufficient skill. The training took place not only in the cities and towns where some African artisans set up shop, but also in the villages to which many of the skilled returned in search of better opportunity.

The Asians' predominance in skilled work was vigorously opposed by the Kenya Europeans who feared that it would stimulate further immigration from India. The European and African Trades Organization of 1923, which is described in Chapter 2, was aimed not only at displacing the Asian shopkeeper but also at substituting Europeans and Africans for the Asian artisans. Its boycott of the Asians failed and the organization collapsed, as explained previously, mainly because Europeans and Africans lacked the requisite skills and were unwilling to work in the rural areas. When the boycott began, the Europeans also attempted to dispense with Asian artisans in constructing the Nairobi Memorial Hall. The settlers' principal organization, the Convention of Associations, planned to use only African labour for this imposing building on Delamere Avenue that was to be leased to the government for the Legislative Council. Again, after several months of frustration the convention was forced to hire Asian craftsmen.[52]

The fact that they had to pay more for Asian than African skilled labour was especially disturbing to the Europeans. The Asian wages as late as 1951 were three times that of the Africans. Asian craftsmen in Uganda, for instance, were then receiving Shs 20–25 a day, and 'a good African artisan' only Shs 7–8.[53] In 1947, apparently as a result of Kenya settlers' prompting, a question was asked in the House of Commons whether the wages of the Kenya tailoring trade, 'largely a monopoly of Indian tailors', had recently quadrupled. This led to a further question as to why the wages of African tailors had remained comparatively low. On investigating, the Colonial Office found that the Asian tailors' wages had indeed increased by 300 to 350 per cent. The reasons offered by the Kenya government were that the Asian tailors were few in number, their skills were superior to those of Africans, and the wartime wage controls had been removed.[54] The Colonial Office later composed a 'Note of Indians in East

Africa' in which it explained that 'as artisans they are more reliable and continue to be employed in preference to Africans, and at a higher wage, until the latters' standard of reliability improves'.[55]

In 1949 while this issue of wage differences was being considered in Britain, a special committee on technical education in Kenya issued a report explaining why the Europeans as well as the Africans were then unable to compete with the Asians in becoming artisans:

> (1) The general opinion about the African youth is that he does not yet realize that he has an obligation not only to himself but also to his employer to complete his learnership or apprenticeship in any trade with one employer. As soon as he has been taught some little thing he takes advantage of that little additional knowledge to go elsewhere for higher wages.
> (2) Asian youths, on the other hand, study hard and are under considerable parental pressure to do so. Asian parents are also most willing to provide financial assistance for their children while studying.
> (3) European youths do not seem to appreciate that professional qualification can only be secured by hard work and study.[56]

Decline of Asian Influence

Like the European community of Kenya, the governments of the three mainland territories exhibited hostile attitudes towards the Asian artisans. The Tanganyika and Uganda governments, with the respective interests of administering a mandate and a protectorate, sought to emphasize African development to the detriment of the Asians. The Kenya government, reflecting the European-settler antagonism, sought to curb Asian enterprise of any kind. After 1923 when native paramountcy was the declared policy, the Kenya government had, in effect, authorization from Britain for such discrimination. A policy designed to replace Asian craftsmen with Africans would conceivably support native paramountcy without damaging settler interests. For all the governments the fact that Africans with the same skills as Asians' could be hired at much lower wages was an added inducement. Some prominent Kenya administrators, with Shirley V. Cooke foremost, were bitter in their denunciation of the Asian artisans. In 1944 in one of his many addresses on the subject, Cooke, a former district officer who represented the Coast Province in Legislative Council, called for controls on Asian immigration 'to protect the African from the unfair competiton of Indian mechanics and craftsmen'.[57]

Whenever possible the governments replaced Asian artisans with Africans. Uganda was the first to pursue this end. In 1910 the acting governor reported that 'all the masons and the larger population of carpenters and blacksmiths now employed by the public works are natives'.[58] At that time the Uganda administration was also beginning the training of Africans to supersede the Asian and European drivers of government lorries and cars. In 1920 it reported that 'practically all the driving of motor vehicles, Government and privately-owned, is done by natives, and the large increase in the mileage run points to the high standard of proficiency attained'. It stated, however, that Africans still remained deficient in mechanical knowledge.[59] At that time and later, none of the governments was able to dispense entirely with the Asian artisans. As late as 1948 the South Nyanza Local Native Council had to hire an Asian road supervisor and an Asian mechanic because no qualified Africans were available.[60]

During World War II what was described as an acute shortage of artisans and clerks in government service prompted the Kenya administration to conscript Asian skilled workers between the ages of eighteen and fifty-five for service as civilians.[61] Although Isher Dass, the Nairobi politician who became a government spokesman during the war, supported the move, most Asians opposed conscription of any kind, and Dass was stoned and barely escaped during one of his public speeches.[62] As part of its conscription program, the government in 1942 required all artisans to report within thirty days to the nearest labour officer for testing and classification as a first-, second-, or third-grade craftsman.[63] The government, however, remained antagonistic to the Asian artisans in the private sector. In 1942 without consulting the Asians it established minimum wages for labour hired by artisans. The new wage regulations were condemned by the Labour Trade Union of East Africa, the chairman of which asserted that they would result in 'curtailment of the rights of Indian artisans for all times to come'.[64]

After the war the Kenya administration continued to discriminate against Asian artisans. In 1946, for instance, the district commissisoner of South Kavirondo decided not to require the purchase of licences by African carpenters, bootmakers, and other craftsmen. 'They are so few', he explained, 'they need every encouragement'.[65]

Meanwhile the governments of all three territories sought to curb the informal apprentice system of the Asian artisans on the ground that it represented an exploitation of African labour. They issued regulations requiring the payment of at least the minimum wage. For a time the Asian craftsmen and African trainees, both of whom gained from the informal system, circumvented the official restrictions by signing legal letters to the effect that the Africans were receiving wage payments although in reality they were making payments. Many of these false contracts were soon perceived by diligent labour inspectors with the result that several Asian firms were prosecuted and forced to pay several thousand shillings of back pay to their apprentices. Soon only a few Asians dared to accept payment in return for training. After independence as the governments increasingly favoured the African businessmen, the Asian firms were forced to abandon this mode of training while many of the African employers, especially those operating on a small scale, were able to continue it.[66]

While suppressing the Asians' informal mode of imparting skills to Africans, the colonial governments had fostered the development of a formal system of training. In the early years they had entrusted the entire educational system to the missionaries who added training in manual skills, especially carpentry and masonry, to their instruction in Christianity, the 'three Rs', domestic arts, sanitation, and the basics of scientific agriculture. During the second decade of the century the British governments began to build their own schools, but it was not until the 1920s that they established the first trade schools. In Kenya the initiative was taken by the European community, which in the opening years of the decade pressed for the technical training of Africans as a means of diminishing the Asians' influence. The White Paper of 1923 and the Phelps-Stokes Commission of 1924 reinforced the settlers' arguments with the result that in 1924 the government opened a Native Industrial Training Depot at Kabete.[67]

Between 1924 and the early 1930s the Kenya government pursued, with only slight success, a five-year apprenticeship program. After four years of elementary education African boys with promise became apprentices in a program of technical training that included two years of primary school followed by three years at Kabete. As in the mission schools the emphasis was on carpentry and masonry. In the late 1920s Kabete graduates began to work for the settlers, railway, PWD, harbours, power and lighting, and some of the large European companies. Within a short time, however, it was evident that the system was not working. The graduates, who were highly privileged in their own communities, wanted to work only for the government or the large European firms. Among the approximately 1,000 who finished their training, comparatively few continued work as craftsmen, and the Asians certainly were not displaced. A large number of the Africans turned to retail trade and other business and invested their profits in land. The European settlers who hired the Kabete graduates found them not so skilled or knowledgeable as those who had been trained by the Asians, and the Asian employers were approached by very few of the government's trainees. For these reasons and also because the system was expensive, the government abandoned the program during the early years of the depression.[68]

Amritlal Raishi, who in 1929 founded the Kenya Builders & Timber Co. Ltd., was typical of the Asian employers. His firm developed quarries in Eastleigh in which between 200 and 400 Africans were employed and trained as stone cutters. He was surprised that none of the Kabete gradu-ates approached him or others in the Shah community for work. He con-cluded that the Kabete Africans 'never took artisan jobs'.[69]

At the outset of the economic depression the government abandoned the five-year program as expensive and unsuccessful and gradually evolved a new system in which training was emphasized at the post-primary level. Between 1935 and 1950 it added three technical training schools to the one at Kabete and devised a productive form of training in which the students produced saleable furniture or moved about the country to erect schools and other public buildings. In time the training became increasingly formal, the courses longer with more theory, and the examinations tied to those of the city and guilds in London. The suc-cessful students were ranked as Grade 1, 2, or 3 according to their skills.[70]

By 1960 Kenya had in addition to the Mombasa Institute and the Royal Technical College the following five technical training schools:

Kabete Technical and Trade School	309 Africans
Thika Technical and Trade School	271 Africans
Nyanza Technical and Trade School	267 Africans
Kwale Technical and Trade School	107 Africans
Machakos Technical and Trade School	9 Africans
Total	1,078 Africans

Most of the students were taking carpentry or masonry, and the rest, in descending numbers, were in painting and decorating, tailoring, sheet-metal working, plumbing, electrical wiring, fitting and turning, and farm and general mechanics.[71]

In Tanganyika a somewhat similar situation prevailed, though on a smaller scale. In 1960 there were two trade schools, one at Ifunda, the other at Moshi, and a technical institute under construction in Dar es Sa-laam. After three years in the schools the graduates were placed in 'suit-able firms' as apprentices and at the end of two years received certificates of apprenticeship. In 1960 a total of 441 boys graduated and 105 achieved certification.[72]

The formal training in Uganda followed a different pattern. In 1960 there were 60 rural trade schools at the primary level, 12 junior second-ary technical schools with a two-year course, and the Kampala Technical Institute giving two years of advanced training at the senior secondary level. The students totalled 267 in the trade schools, 177 in the technical schools, and 54 at the Institute.[73]

In all three territories the formal sector of technical education was served in the later colonial years primarily by these government schools but also by the Christian missions, YMCAs, private technical academies, and a number of other institutions. Both Makerere University and the University of Nairobi had begun as technical colleges. The principal institution established as a result of private initiative was the Mombasa Institute of Muslim Education. Opened in 1951 when the Kenya government matched gifts from the Aga Khan and the sultan of Zanzibar, the institute offered on the senior secondary level technical training in a wide range of subjects but served mainly Arab and Muslim-Asian students.[74] During the late 1950s in the belief that more training was needed, community development workers began to organize rudimentary courses in artisanry and homecrafts.[75]

Despite the experimentation and ever-increasing expenditure, the formal training of African artisans remained nearly as unsatisfactory as it had been before. In Kenya where the government's training was modelled on the highly structured, European system of masters and apprentices in which guilds and trade unions had a prominent role, the training proved most inadequate. Africans in the informal sector remained far superior to those emerging from the schools and institutes with the result that few of the graduates who sought employment as artisans were hired.[76] In Tanganyika and Uganda the situation was almost the same. The Tanganyika Ministry of Education understated its problem in 1960 with an admission that 'some difficulty was found in placing all the third year boys with suitable firms'.[77] Uganda's Department of Education revealed in 1960 that despite its expanding program of technical education, there had been over the past three years a 'decrease in number of openings for boys leaving technical training schools'.[78] The Department of Labour pointed out that in 1960 only 91 of the 177 graduates who applied to employers for apprenticeships were successful.[79]

These statistics combined with others reveal that the formal training of African artisans contributed comparatively little to the economic development of East Africa. Judging from the high percentage of failures in the testing for certification, the training was quite inadequate. In Uganda among the 121 graduates in 1960 who were trade tested, 55.3 per cent failed. In Kenya 734 out of 1,536 failed in the tests for Grade I, 271 out of 427 for Grade II, and 122 out of 241 for Grade III.[80] Moreover, the number of artisans produced by the governments' technical schools was insignificant with reference not only to the total population of East Africa but also to the total number of the African artisans. Although the Africans in East Africa totalled more than 21 million in 1960, only about 300 emerged from the five technical schools in Kenya each year. In 1960 there were 441 graduates in Tanganyika, but only 105 received Certificates of Apprenticeship, and in Uganda only 177 graduates applied for apprenticeship.[81]

Statistics on the number of African artisans were published infrequently by the colonial governments. For Kenya it is possible to show only how many Africans were employed in some of the key crafts that required skilled work. The following statistics are for 1960:[82]

Wood, cork manufacture	8,029
Stone quarrying	3,620
Textile manufacture	2,761
Apparel, made-up textile manufacture	1,617
Footwear manufacture	1,369
Printing, publishing, allied industries	1,366
Furniture, fixtures manufacture	1,293
Metal mining	870
Paper, paper products manufacture	564
Total	21,488

For Tanganyika statistics are available for all the African skilled workers in 1961:[83]

Drivers	8,986
Shop assistants, office messengers	7,797
Mechanics, fitters, electricians	5,551
Masons, bricklayers	4,757
Carpenters, joiners, cabinet makers	4,226
Other skilled workers	25,133
Total	56,450

Unfortunately, the published figures for Uganda are similar to those for Kenya in that they reveal only the number of African employees in the various industries and do not distinguish between skilled and unskilled workers. In 1960 Uganda Africans were employed in craft industries as follows:[84]

Construction	28,554
Miscellaneous manufacture	17,896
Transport, communications	9,631
Food product manufacture	7,768
Mining, quarrying	5,769
Forestry, fishing, hunting	3,742
Cotton ginning	3,319
Coffee curing	2,495
Total	79,174

Though inadequate, these figures are revealing of the extent of Asian influence on the training of African artisans. In combination with the statistics in Tables 5.1 through 5.4, they show not only a large number of both Asian and African skilled workers in the labour market but also far more skilled Africans than could possibly have been produced by the governments' technical schools and other institutions in the formal sector. By 1960–61 a considerable number of the Africans had learned their skills from other Africans, but obviously most, whether first or second generation among the skilled, had acquired their training in the informal sector, as King has explained, through association with the Asians.

After independence the new governments of East Africa, each in its own way, continued the unproductive policies of the colonial administrations by emphasizing the formal training of African artisans and discriminating against the Asian craftsmen. In Kenya, for instance, the African administrators soon realized that the graduates of the technical schools 'had no marketable skills at all'.[85] Instead of abolishing or curtailing the technical schools and emphasizing training in the informal sector, however, they continued the schools and added a more informal vocational training with boarding and certification for primary school leavers. During the early 1970s there was an unprecedented interest, planning, and fund-raising for institutes or colleges of technical education. Designed to take students after form four, these new institutions developed a full four-year secondary course. Administrators also initiated the self-help Harambee Schools, which were developed and funded by rural communities but stressed an academic, in-school system of education.[86]

Meanwhile the Kenya government introduced new programs of less formal training. One was the vocational education provided by the National Youth Service that offered two years of post-primary education in carpentry, masonry, motor vehicle repair, and electrical skills. Another, inspired by the National Christian Council of Kenya's publication—*After School What?*—was the vocational program of the village polytechnic. By 1974 there were more than sixty polytechnics, which designed training to the craft needs of each village. Midway between formal and informal apprenticeship, they were non-boarding, offered no standard certification, and trained particularly for rural employment.[87]

By the mid-1970s it was clear that the new system of vocational education was not working. The formal structure had continued. Even the polytechnics were becoming more formal. As in the colonial period the graduates were not finding employment. What surprised the administrators was that as Asian craftsmen left the country, displaced by the new regulations and practices on citizenship, licence fees, and trade permits, it was the African artisans from the informal sector, not the technical school graduates, who replaced the Asians.[88]

During the colonial years there were very few expressions of African opinion in support of the Asian artisans. A letter to the *East African Standard* in 1956 by Mwengi s/o (son of) Kimani portrays the prevailing sentiment. 'I have not yet', he stated, 'come across any Asian artisan willing—if capable—to teach us. . . . Some of us learned more from enemy artisans during the war, and the Europeans, than from any so-called Asian artisans'.[89]

Although the Asians' contribution in imparting to Africans the technical skills essential to economic development during the colonial period was not recognized by the Europeans or Africans, there was one notable exception. With remarkable perspicuity as early as 1949, Mbiyu (then Peter) Koinange realized what was happening. A son of the Kikuyu senior chief, educated in the United States and Britain, with a Ph.D. from the London School of Economics, he was widely travelled, highly educated, and beginning a teaching career that would culminate in his appointment as Kenya's minister of education. In August 1949 while sharing a platform in New Delhi with Jawaharlal Nehru, Koinange remarked that the fact was not publicized, but every craft the Africans had learned, like shoemaking or carpentry, had been taught to them by the Asians.[90] This was an exaggeration but essentially true.

Notes

1. Quoted, Shanti Pandit, ed., *Asians in East and Central Africa* (Nairobi: Panco, 1961), p. 7.

2. Justus Strandes, *The Portuguese Period in East Africa* (Nairobi: East African Literature Bureau, 1961), pp. 164–65.

3. F. J. Berg and B. J. Walter, 'Mosques, Population and Urban Development in Mombasa', chap. 4, *Hadith 1*, ed. Bethwell A. Ogot (Nairobi: East African Publishing House, 1968), pp. 62–64.

4. Makhan Singh, *Kenya's Trade Union Movement to 1952* (Nairobi: East African Publishing House, 1969), p. 1.

5. Robert G. Gregory, *India and East Africa: A History of Race Relations Within the British Empire, 1890–1939* (Oxford: Clarendon, 1971), pp. 19–25.

6. Ibid., p. 397. J. E. Flint, 'Zanzibar, 1890–1950', chap. 13, *History of East Africa*, vol. 2, ed. Vincent Harlow and E. M. Chilver (Oxford: Clarendon, 1965), pp. 648–50.

7. Only a summary is given here as detailed explanations of indentured importation can be seen in Gregory, *India and East Africa*, pp. 50–61, and J. S. Mangat, *History of the Asians in East Africa, c. 1886 to 1945* (Oxford: Clarendon, 1969), pp. 29–39.

8. Gregory, *India and East Africa*, p. 55.

9. Ibid., pp. 56–57.

10. Herbert Samuel, 'Uganda of Today', *Journal of the Society of the Arts* (London, 20 Mar. 1903), p. 395.

11. *Report of the Committee on Emigration from India to the Crown Colonies and Protectorates:* part 1, *Report,* Cd. 2164 (London: HMSO, 1910), p. 239.

12. Mervyn F. Hill, *Permanent Way:* vol. 1, *Story of the Kenya and Uganda Railway* (Nairobi: Government Printer, 1949), pp. 255–56.

13. F. O. O'Callaghan, 'Uganda Railway', *Professional Papers of the Corps of Royal Engineers (Occasional Papers Series),* 26 (London: HMSO, 1900), no. 18, p. 6. H.A.F. Currie (General Manager, Uganda Railway), witness, *Report of the Committee on Emigration:* part 2, *Evidence,* Cd. 5193, pp. 67–72.

14. *Final Report of the Uganda Railway Committee,* Cd. 2164 (London: HMSO, 1904), pp. 13ff.

15. Gregory, *India and East Africa,* p. 61.

16. Kenneth King, *African Artisan: Education and the Informal Sector in Kenya* (London: Heinemann, 1977), p. 26. Information on the Bohra tinsmiths was also provided by Y. Pirbhai, interviewed by Honey, 25 Feb. 1974, Dar es Salaam.

17. N. H. Putwa (great grandson), interviewed by Honey, 8 Feb. 1974, Dar es Salaam.

18. King, *African Artisan,* p. 144.

19. *East African Standard* (Nairobi), 11 Jan. 1908, p. 9. Yusufali Pirbhai, interviewed by Honey, 25 Feb. 1974, Dar es Salaam.

20. Mangat, *History of the Asians,* pp. 33–55, 72–73.

21. Gregory, *India and East Africa,* p. 54.

22. Mangat, *History of the Asians,* p. 44 n. 1.

23. G. Pirbhai, interviewed by Honey, 24 Dec. 1973, Arusha.

24. Gregory, *India and East Africa,* p. 103.

25. Mangat, *History of the Asians,* p. 77. A. Aloo, interviewed by Honey, 14 Oct. 1973, Dar es Salaam.

26. Kenya, *Report on the Census of the Non-Native Population of Kenya Colony and Protectorate Taken on the Night of the 25th Feb., 1948* (Nairobi: Government Printer, 1953), app. 12, pp. 114–18. Figures for Goans and 'Other Indians' were combined for these statistics.

27. Ibid.

28. Ibid., table 43, p. 73.

29. Ibid., app. 12, pp. 114–18.

30. The Zanzibar census taken in 1958 included information on employment, but the statistics were not included in the published report. See *Report of the Census of the Population of Zanzibar Protectorate Taken on the Night of the 19th and 20th March, 1958* (Zanzibar: Government Printer, 1960), p. 7.

31. *East African Standard,* 11 Apr. 1908, p. 6.

32. Advertisement, ibid.

33. A study of Asian artisans in African areas is being prepared for a separate publication. For Asian artisans employed by government agencies, see annual reports of Departments of Labour.

34. Gregory, *India and East Africa,* pp. 81–82.

35. B. T. Gathani, interviewed by Gregory, 9 Mar. 1973, Nairobi. Gathani was formerly general secretary of the Federation of Indian Chambers of Commerce and Industry in Eastern Africa.

36. *Kenya, Uganda, Tanganyika and Zanzibar Directory: Trade and Commercial Index*, 1959–60 ed. (Nairobi: East African Directory Co., 1960), pp. 10–11.

37. Mangat, *History of the Asians*, pp. 53–54. A. Raishi, interviewed by Gregory, 18 Aug. 1984, London. Raishi, as noted previously, worked for Jeevanjee in the 1920s.

38. Quoted, *Daily Chronicle* (London), 1 Sept. 1910, in A. M. Jeevanjee, *Appeal on Behalf of the Indians in East Africa* (Bombay, 1912), p. 13. The Public Record Office correspondence and the Ainsworth Papers contain convincing evidence of Jeevanjee's contribution to the early development of the protectorate. See Arthur Hardinge to Lord Salisbury, 8 Jan. 1900, F.O. 2/282; and 19 Mar. 1900, F.O. 2/285; James Hayes Sadler to Lord Elgin, 31 Jan. 1906, C.O. 533/11; and 20 Nov. 1906, C.O. 533/18. Also, John Ainsworth, entries 16 Nov. 1899, 6 Feb. 1900, 5 Feb. 1901, and 1 Jan. 1902, 'Diary', vol. 2, pp. 428, 435, 524, 583, Ainsworth Papers, Rhodes House, Oxford.

39. Bawa Singh Bharj Ltd., described in Pandit, *Asians*, p. 289.

40. Ibid., p. 294.

41. Ibid., p. 296.

42. Ibid., p. 304.

43. Ibid., p. 326.

44. *Final Report of the Uganda Railway Committee*, p. 13.

45. T. B. Kabwegyere, 'The Asian Question in Uganda, 1894–1972', p. 4, Historical Association of Kenya Annual Conference, 1973, University of Nairobi Library. See also King, *African Artisan*, p. 26.

46. King, *African Artisan*, pp. 44ff.

47. Ibid., p. 52.

48. Ibid., p. 26. King dates this process from the early 1930s, but the District Commissioners' reports and correspondence, combined with later trade union records and Local Native Council minutes, indicate that African artisans were emerging in the early years of the century.

49. General Secretary, East Africa Indian National Congress, to Henry S.L. Polak, 25 Mar. 1947, encl. Polak to Arthur Creech Jones, 1 Apr. 1947, file 'Indians in East Africa, 1947–48', C.O. 822/125/6.

50. King, *African Artisan*, p. 27.

51. Ibid.

52. Ibid.

53. Colonial Office, *Report on Uganda for the Year 1951* (London: HMSO, 1952), p. 20.

54. Secretary of State to Governor of Kenya, 14 Mar. 1947, teleg., file 'Indians in Africa, 1947–48', C.O. 822/125/6. Officer Administering Government of Kenya to Secretary of State, 8 May 1947, teleg., ibid.

55. Encl. H. S. Bates (Colonial Office) to Miss L.E.T. Storar (Commonwealth Relations Office), 9 Apr. 1951, confidential, file 'Indians in East Africa: Political, Social and Economic Position of Indians, 1951', C.O. 882/143/7.

56. Kenya, *Report of the Technical Institute Committee* (Nairobi: Government Printer, 1949), p. 6. The chairman was G. P. Willoughby.

57. *East African Standard*, 8 Sept. 1944, p. 10.

58. Quoted, Kabwegere, 'Asian Question in Uganda', p. 4.

59. *Uganda: Report for 1920 (Apr. to Dec.)*, Colonial Reports—Annual, no. 1112 (London: HMSO, 1922), p. 17.

60. 'Handing Over Report—South Nyanza', by A.A.M. Lawrence to P. W. Low [n.d., but 1948], p. 4, Syracuse University microfilm 2301, reel 8. Annual reports of the Labour Departments (Labour Division in Tanganyika) for 1960 show a large number of Asian labourers still in government service.

61. Governor to Secretary of State for the Colonies, 30 May 1942, teleg., file 'Compulsory Service: Conscription of Indians, 1942–43', C.O. 533/529/4.

62. *Colonial Times* (Nairobi), 9 May 1942, p. 3.

63. 'Defense (Employment of Artisans) Regulations, 1942', file 'Compulsory Service: Conscription of Indians, 1942–43', C.O. 533/529/4.

64. *Kenya Daily Mail* (Mombasa), 18 Nov. 1942, p. 6.

65. South Kavirondo District Annual Report—1946, p. 12, Syracuse University microfilm 2801, reel 38.

66. King, *African Artisan*, p. 53.

67. Ibid., p. 23. Huxley, *White Man's Country*, vol. 2, p. 28.

68. King, *African Artisan*, pp. 23–25, 27–28.

69. Interviewed 18 Aug. 1984, London.

70. Kenya, Education Department, *Annual Report, 1950* (Nairobi: Government Printer, 1951), pp. 24–25. *Labour Department Annual Report, 1960* (Nairobi: Government Printer, 1961), pp. 44–45. King, *African Artisan*, p. 28.

71. Kenya, *Labour Department Annual Report, 1960* (Nairobi: Government Printer, 1961), p. 43.

72. Tanganyika, *Annual Summary of the Ministry of Education, 1960: Statistics*, p. viii, C.O. 736/57.

73. Uganda, *Annual Report of the Education Department, 1960*, pp. 28–33, 79–80, C.O. 685/52.

74. Kenya, *Education Department Annual Report, 1953* (Nairobi: Government Printer, 1955), pp. 42–47.

75. King, *African Artisan*, p. 31.

76. Ibid., pp. 28–31.

77. Tanganyika, *Triennial Survey of Education in the Years 1958–60*, p. 9, C.O. 736/57.

78. Uganda, *Annual Report of the Education Department, 1960*, p. 28, C.O. 685/52.

79. Uganda, *Department of Labour Annual Report, 1960*, p. 9, C.O. 685/52.

80. Ibid., pp. 9–10. Kenya, *Labour Department Annual Report, 1960*, pp. 44–45.

81. Ibid., p. 43. Tanganyika, *Triennial Survey of Education in the Years 1958–60*, p. 9. Uganda, *Department of Labour Annual Report, 1960*, pp. 9–10.

82. Kenya, *Labour Department Annual Report, 1960*, pp. 29–30.

83. Tanganyika, *Statistical Abstract, 1962* (Dar es Salaam: Government Printer, 1962), table S.14, p. 151.

84. Uganda, *1962 Statistical Abstract* (Entebbe: Government Printer, 1962), table U.P.6(c), p. 98.

85. King, *African Artisan*, p. 32.

86. Ibid., pp. 32–33, 37.

87. Ibid.

88. Ibid., pp. 27, 34–39.

89. Clipping, 25 Apr. 1956, Zafrud-Deen Papers, Syracuse University microfilm 2174, reel 1.

90. Clipping, *Hindustan Times*, 5 Aug. 1949, file 'Indians in East Africa', C.O. 882/143/7.

CHAPTER SIX

—————— ■ ——————

Clerical Service

Wanted, a clerk. Preferably an Indian or Parsee. Good knowledge of accounts, able to typewrite well, trusted to file letters and do efficiently other routine work.
—Mombasa want ad, 1909[1]

Though difficult to assess in importance relative to other occupations, the Asians' clerical service in East Africa was essential to the functioning of government, commerce, and industry. Through nearly all the colonial period the Asians filled the middle ranks of the civil service, the railway and police administrations, and the office staff in business. Above them in these organizations was a privileged group, mostly European, of government officials and the managers of large private concerns. Although Asians increasingly shared management in the private sector, the Europeans virtually monopolized the higher ranks of government service until a few years before independence and enjoyed superior wage, pension, annual-leave, and housing provisions. Through most of the colonial period the Asians, as a matter of policy, were not appointed to the higher posts. Below them was the third group of office functionaries, those with less training and experience who received the lowest pay, shortest leaves, and were nonpensionable. Nearly all these functionaries were Africans. In this three-tiered system all three groups contributed significantly to the operation of government and business. It was the Asians, however, who performed most of the vital clerical service.

The work entailed a variety of tasks for which considerable training and experience and a knowledge of English were necessary. The Asians were scribes, typists, and stenographers; book keepers, accountants, and draftsmen; bank tellers, cashiers, and guards; customs officials and custodians. They were the rank and file of the police, the noncommissioned officers of the King's African Rifles, and the station masters, baggage masters, ticket sellers, and switchmen of the railway. They were also the principal assistants to the district and provincial officers and to the heads of departments and officials in the Secretariat. The Asian office workers were entrusted with many odd jobs, from brewing tea to arranging a *baraza* (a meeting with Africans). In supervising those with less training, these clerical workers were closely associated with the Africans.

There are many testimonials of the Asians' importance as clerical workers. Some Asians believe that their community's role in public service was perhaps the Asians' greatest contribution to development.[2] Sir Percy Girouard, governor of the East Africa Protectorate, expressed an almost similar view as early as 1909. The Asian's presence, he stated, 'makes government possible in that he provides the subordinate staff of nearly every department'.[3] The records of the provincial and district administrations contain many statements attesting to the value and service of the Asian clerks. In 1923, for instance, the acting government coast agent protested vigorously against the transfer of one of his Goan clerks, Francis F. de Souza. 'By transferring Mr. Souza from this office', he asserted, 'you have deprived me of the services of one of my most reliable clerks and, as already stated, the work of the office is seriously hampered'.[4]

Some scholars have also attested to the Asians' importance in public service. In his study of the Asians in Uganda, for example, the anthropologist H. S. Morris has described how those in the middle grade of the civil service acquired an exceptional knowledge of 'the plans and daily workings of the bureaucracy' that gave them 'an unofficial influence and a power and prestige' of unique value not only to the trading community but also to the higher administration. 'It was to these men', Morris wrote, 'that senior civil servants usually turned in the first instance for comment and advice on measures which affected the Indian population as a whole'.[5]

Despite such testimony by scholars and administrators, there has been very little study of the Asians' role or even of the public service generally. The only important publications are two brief descriptions of the civil service in Uganda by the Ismaili historian Nizar A. Motani—one a chapter on the Asians, the other a short monograph on the Africans.[6] Nothing of substance has been written about the Asian clerical workers or the service in the other territories.

The Asians' role in public service began on Zanzibar where, as explained in Chapter 2, the Omani sultans entrusted the collection of customs fees, the principal source of revenue throughout the empire, to their Asian associates. The successive collectors of customs in the last two-thirds of the century—Wat Bhima, Jairam Sewji, Tharia Topan, Nasser Lillani, and Peera Devji—acted in effect as high-level public servants while retaining their positions as heads of large trading and financial firms. Their agents in the coastal towns, such as Pisu on Pemba, Ramji in Bagamoyo, and Lakhmidas in Mombasa, in turn managed the local customs and assisted the sultan's *liwalis* (headmen), *mudirs* (district officers), and *khadis* (judges) as public servants of a lesser rank.[7]

After 1890 when Zanzibar became a British protectorate, a public service was established on the model of the renowned Indian Civil Service. Though described as multi-racial in that there were no differences in the conditions of employment among Arabs, Asians, and Africans, the new organization favoured the Arabs. The Arabs were accorded a monopoly of the higher administrative posts, whereas the Asians became the more numerous subordinates in all branches of the administration. In Zanzibar as in their other territories the British also prescribed and strictly enforced the rule that a civil servant could not engage in private business. Thus a professional class of servants developed that was quite different in its composition from the coterie of servants-businessmen who had served the sultans. The new Asian civil servants on Zanzibar numbered 566 in 1914 and 510 in 1925.[8]

Following the declarations of protectorates over Uganda and East Africa (later Kenya) in 1894 and 1895, the British increasingly employed Asians as clerical workers on the mainland. As noted in Chapter 5, not all the indentured servants were artisans or unskilled manual labourers. Some were clerks, draughtsmen, and other office workers. Most of the clerical workers needed in British East Africa, however, were recruited as free emigrants from India. In 1896 Uganda sent its first official to recruit in India, and he returned with five clerks as well as a number of artisans. By 1911 Uganda had 330 Asian clerks.[9] Meanwhile the East Africa Protectorate had been following a similar course. Both protectorates obtained from South Asia Goans, Brahmins, Patels, and other Asians as clerks for the various government departments and Punjabi Muslims and Sikhs for service in the police and King's African Rifles.[10]

Through most of the colonial period and even in some instances after independence, whenever their clerical needs could not be supplied locally, the governments and the larger private firms turned to India and Goa. They recruited through agents and advertisements in Indian and Goan newspapers.[11] As Motani has pointed out, it was less expensive to hire overseas than to train in East Africa.[12] As a result, the opportunities for employment with the East African governments became one of the main inducements to prospective immigrants.

Privilege and Racial Stratification

In administering their territories, the British developed a three-tiered civil service in which rank, salary, and responsibility were drawn on racial lines. Before World War I the East Africa and Uganda Protectorates evolved higher and lower echelons known respectively as the European Staff and the Non-European Sub-ordinate Staff. The first, as its name denotes, was exclusively European, and the second, despite its nomenclature, was almost entirely Asian. After the war in Kenya and Tanganyika, these became the Senior and Junior Services and then, beginning in 1935 in Kenya, the European Local Civil Service and the Local Asiatic Civil Service (later the Asian Local Civil Service). In Uganda the two echelons became the European Civil Service and the Asiatic Civil Service. In 1924 and 1927 Tanganyika and Uganda each grouped Africans separately in a Native Civil Service. Kenya followed a slightly different course in 1927 with an Arab and African Clerical Service (later the African Civil Service).[13] In 1940 Uganda combined Asians and Africans in a Local Civil Service, but the Asians soon occupied the upper division and the Africans the lower.[14]

In all three territories the racial basis of organization and the hierarchy of privilege were bitterly resented and criticized by Asians and Africans. In 1939 Shamsud-Deen, the leading Muslim politician of Kenya, bemoaned, 'An Indian, no matter how efficient, cannot rise above the rank of a wretched sub-inspector'.[15]

In 1947–48 the civil service throughout East Africa was investigated by a commission sent from Britain under the chairmanship of Sir Maurice Holmes, and it was then revised ostensibly along non-racial lines.[16] Although the nomenclature varied, the following five divisions of the civil service were established in each of the four British territories:

1. Subordinate Services. Almost entirely African. Largely unskilled workers with only a primary education. Salary in Kenya Shs 15–100 per month.

2. Clerical Services. African and Asian in the lower ranks, predominantly Asian in the higher. Field assistants in medicine, agriculture, veterinary work; laboratory assistants, field and office workers in the Public Works Department. Salary in Kenya £48–800 annually.

3. Executive and Technical Services. Mainly Asian, some Europeans. Office managers, accountants, draughtsmen, storekeepers, librarians, game rangers, foresters, agricultural and police officers. Salary in Kenya £500–1,000 annually.

4. Administrative and Professional Services. Mainly European, some Asians. District and provincial commissioners, doctors, laboratory officers. Salary in Kenya £550–1,320 annually.

5. Superscale Appointments. Almost entirely European. Governors and other high officials in the central governments. Salary in Kenya £1,108–3,150 annually.

Although terms such as European and Asiatic were no longer employed as division names, the civil service remained essentially racial in its selection of Europeans for the offices with the highest salaries and pensions and of Asians for those in the middle level. Asserting that the European officials, most of whom were recruited in Britain, had a higher cost of living in East Africa than the Asians and Africans, most of whom had local residences, the Holmes commission had recommended in 1948 that the Europeans receive, for similar work, a salary higher than that of the non-Europeans by a ratio of five to three.[17] For the succeeding six years this ratio was applied in the determination of salaries in all four territories. In 1953 continuing Asian and African dissatisfaction prompted the British government to appoint a second investigating commission under the chairmanship of Sir David Lidbury.

Reporting in 1954, the Lidbury commission strongly criticized the five-three rule and concluded that 'for the future there shall be no barrier in any part of the service which is in fact (even though not in name) one of race'. It justified, however, a continuing higher pay to Europeans as a necessary inducement to the recruitment of essential employees from areas outside East Africa.[18] As a result of the commission's recommendations, the inequalities in salaries and appointments were to continue to the end of the colonial administration.

The imperial government recognized and condoned this discrimination. In March 1951 when directed by Labour's Secretary of State Arthur Creech Jones, the Colonial Office apprised the Commonwealth Office of the long-standing policy on Asians in the East African civil service. It justified exclusion of Asians from the higher posts on the two grounds that only the British could transmit the tenets of western civilization to Africans and that Asian officers would not be accepted by the Africans:

It is inevitable that a British Administration, whose primary objective is to graft British culture and political and social conceptions, with appropriate modifications, on to the African traditional stem, should prefer to recruit candidates from Great Britain, Canada, Australia, and New Zealand for these posts. Further, the appointment of Indians in positions of authority and responsibility would undoubtedly be resented by the masses of the African population.[19]

Despite this discrimination, the Asians accepted public service employment in large numbers throughout the colonial period. Most of them were concentrated in Kenya. Unfortunately, although statistics were issued annually on the European service, there is very little information on the Asian employees.[20] In 1912 the government, apart from the railway, was employing 866 Asians, approximately twice the number in either Uganda or Zanzibar. By 1921 the number had increased to 1,447. In that year the railway staff serving Kenya and Uganda included an additional 2,022 Asians, and there were others in the private sector.[21] By 1946 the Kenya Asian Local Civil Service consisted of 1,750 'officers' and about 100 others in the Public Works Department, mainly artisans, who were classified as 'temporary' but had been employed in some cases as long as twenty years.[22]

By 1948 the Asian clerical workers of Kenya were distributed as follows:[23]

Clerical service	3,281
Railways and harbours	2,153
Military service, civilian	535
Bank clerks	316
Stenographers, typists	100
Total	6,286

In this total there were 2,665—42.4 per cent—who were not members of the civil service. The clerical workers as a whole comprised 20.0 per cent of all the Kenya Asians who were gainfully employed.[24]

In 1962 when the next Kenya census was taken, the Asians in clerical work were listed as follows:[25]

Clerks	11,836
Government executive officers	400
Bookkeepers	335
Draughtsmen	186
Stenographers, typists	67
Government administrators	12
Total	12,836

Among all these there were 3,867—30.1 per cent—who did not work for the government. Altogether the clerical workers constituted 31.6 per cent of the total Asian work force of 40,634.[26] The rise in the per centage of clerical workers relative to those in other occupations is probably explained by the fact that work in the private sector offered less security and remuneration with the approach of independence.

In the early years while the East Africa Protectorate had an abundance of Asian clerical staff composed of indentured and free immigrants, German East Africa suffered from a shortage. As shown in Chapter 1, a considerable number of Asians settled in the German protectorate—they numbered 8,784 in 1912 at the time of the first census—but apparently because of their unfamiliarity with the German language and administration, they were attracted more to trade than government service. Apart from the *akidas,* those Swahili-speaking Arabs and Africans who served as intermediaries between the government and the chiefs, the administration was composed entirely of Germans recruited mainly from the civil service at home and partly from the defunct German East Africa Company and the military.[27] At the turn of the century a German official confided to the commissioner of the British protectorate, 'We envy you your subordinate staff of Indian baboo clerks'.[28]

As a British mandate after World War I Tanganyika developed a civil service on the model of those in Kenya, Uganda, and Zanzibar. The Asians soon comprised most of the Junior Civil Service, which conducted most of the clerical work. By 1951 those in government service numbered 2,449.[29] In 1960 on the eve of Tanganyika's independence the Asian clerical workers were distributed as follows:[30]

Government service departments	1,186
East African Railways and Harbours	988
East African Posts and Telecommunications	285
Other high commission services	177
Municipal and town councils	107
Native authorities	7
Total	2,750
Nongovernment service	1,317
Grand total	4,067

Unlike the governments in Kenya and Tanganyika, the Uganda government began at an early date to Africanize its civil service with the result that the Asian clerical workers never rose to numbers comparable to those in the other territories. In 1911 when the first census was taken, there were 330 Asian clerks in a total Asian work force of 1,852.[31] By 1952 there were still only 441 Asians in the civil service. Although the total rose to 700 by 1958, it declined again because of increasing Africanization to 457 in 1960.[32] There were, of course, additional clerical workers in the private sector. In 1961, for instance, 425 Asians were described as performing 'miscellaneous services' in private industry as compared to a total of 1,950 in public services.[33]

Another comparison of the public service employees in the four territories was provided by the Lidbury commission. The following statistics for 1953 on employees who entered the civil service with at least the equivalent of the Cambridge School Certificate include some Africans in

Division 2 and some Europeans in Division 3, but the great majority in both divisions were Asians.[34]

	Kenya	Tanganyika	Uganda	Zanzibar
Division 2	2,875	3,000	1,700	530
Division 3	2,200	1,950	1,400	205
Totals	5,075	4,950	3,100	735

The Asians in public service varied from one territory to another not only in numbers but also by religious community. On Zanzibar the Ithnasheris who had been very successful in business occcupied the higher posts, and the Parsees filled the subordinate ranks.[35] In Kenya the first civil servants were mostly recruits from Goa and British India, largely Goans and Parsees who were relatively well educated and knew English. They were soon joined by others who had similar qualifications, especially the Brahmins and Patels, and in time by a number of Sikhs who acquired their training with the railway. The Goans, who initially had been predominant, were eventually a minority, but they remained very important in the higher positions in the central government, provinces, and districts.[36] In 1948 they constituted 20.2 per cent of all the Kenya Asians in public service.[37] In Tanganyika where the colonial service developed comparatively late, the Punjabis were the most numerous.[38] In Uganda the situation was similar to that in Kenya except that the Goans were relatively far more numerous. In 1952 the Asians in the Uganda civil service were enumerated as:[39]

Goans	235
Sikhs	51
Brahmins	36
Patidar (Patels)	28
Ismailis	7
Lohanas	5

The importance of clerical work to the Goans is illustrated by the following list of their occupations in Kenya in 1948:[40]

Government service	735
Clerical work, non–civil service	726
Textile manufacture (nearly all tailoring)	534
Railways and harbours administration	211
Personal service	209
Military employment	134

Metal working	100
Commerce, finance, insurance	94
Mechanics, engineering	80
Professional occupations	37

The Goans were prominent in the the provincial and district administrations. In 1911 the Nyanza Province of Kenya had sixteen clerks scattered through its various district offices. Of these clerks two were Europeans, ten were Goans, three were Sikhs, and one a Hindu.[41] In South Kavirondo District alone in 1920 there were two European administrators, two Goan clerks, and one Arab clerk.[42] In 1940 the district had six European administrators, two Goan clerks, and one Asian Muslim clerk.[43] By 1948 when a program of Africanization—initially called 'localization'—was in progress and the district had been renamed South Nyanza, the administrators included six Europeans and two Africans, and the clerks numbered four Goans, one Hindu, and seven Africans.[44] In 1960, three years before independence, South Nyanza had sixteen Europeans, six Asians, and five Africans who shared the administrative and clerical work. Three of the six Asians were Goans, the others Hindus.[45]

The experience of F. X. D'Mello may have been typical of that of most other Goans and perhaps of the Asian civil servants generally. D'Mello left Goa as a young man in 1941 to seek employment in Kenya. He worked at first for the army in a department that was soon absorbed by the government. He then obtained a position as a clerk in the Machakos district commissioner's office. Every few years he was shifted by the government to another location—to Kitui, Nakuru, Isiolo, Kapsabet, Eldama Ravine, and Meru. At each post he was frequently on safari to carry out various duties in the district or province. He retired in 1970 after twenty-nine years of service, took Kenya citizenship, and settled in Nakuru.[46]

After retirement D'Mello looked back on his long years of service with some reservation. The frequent change of location was not conducive to a close family life and was an impediment in his children's education. He had to work long hours often under trying circumstances, received a compensation that was very low compared to what might be earned in commerce or other private endeavour, and found promotions very difficult to obtain until the closing colonial years. The Asians performed almost all the executive work, he recalled, while the British merely signed the papers. He would write the letters, type them, and send them in for signatures. Moreover, despite his industry and dedication, he, like other Asian clerks, was generally not respected by either the British officials or the Africans. Soon after retiring, D'Mello joined a private firm, Nakuru Industries.[47]

Apparently most of those who initially acquired positions with the governments turned to private enterprise after accumulating some savings, making contacts, and perceiving the business opportunities. The most remarkable success story of an Asian who followed this course seems to be that of Indra Singh Gill, a Sikh from the Punjab who arrived in Kenya in 1922. He began in Nairobi as a telegraphist on the railway at a monthly salary of Shs 30 and after transfer to Uganda advanced to the position of station master at Shs 250. In Uganda he began to supplement his salary by loading cotton for ginners. By 1932 he had accumulated £600, and with it he purchased a farm of 600 acres that had a lot of timber. While continuing as station master, he employed Africans to cut the trees and shipped the timber to Nairobi. Sensing the opportunity, he purchased a used sawmill for Shs 800, brought it to his farm, and began to cut and transport lumber for much greater profit. It was then, in 1936, that he quit the railway to devote full time to his growing business.

After leaving the government, Gill demonstrated an extraordinary enterprise. In Uganda, as he cut trees, he replaced them with sugarcane. He purchased timber concessions and increased his sawmills to four. Borrowing money, he bought a ginnery, and then another, and set up a sugar factory. He expanded his timber business into Tanganyika, planted tea after felling the trees, and built a tea-processing factory. He also began a plywood factory. Eventually he moved into Kenya to purchase land, saw timber, and construct buildings such as Gill House in Nairobi. Meanwhile he brought many relatives from the extended Gill family into the business and hired more than 60 Asians and nearly 3,000 Africans. 'We people worked very hard, eighteen to twenty hours a day', Gill has recalled. 'We were never tired. The tiredness only comes when you work for someone else'.[48] Not surprisingly, Gill amassed a fortune.

For many others, though less spectacularly than for Gill, employment in government service proved a stepping stone to a more rewarding career. B. S. Varma of Kenya is a foremost example. Immigrating from the Gujarat in 1927, he went directly to Thika where his sister lived, and he obtained employment with the post office. During the fifteen years before his retirement in 1957, he was the postmaster of Thika. Meanwhile, however, he had joined his brother-in-law in establishing a general merchandise business in Machakos. Because government employees were not permitted to conduct a business, he founded the company in his mother's name. With the profits he bought land in Thika in his wife's name. He became the largest landowner in Thika. At retirement he founded the Prakesh Construction Co. Ltd. to build flats on the land. He also started a brick factory and a motor-car business, and as he prospered, he bought several coffee plantations. In 1973, joining with other Asians, he built the Amboseli Lodge. For many years Varma served as president of the local Indian Association, and he became a leading citizen of Thika.[49]

Two other leading Asians, V. R. Boal and Awtar Singh, are examples of civil servants who turned to other careers before retirement. Leaving Rajkot in 1911 at age twenty, Boal found a position in Nairobi with the military as a labour clerk recruiting African carriers. Though repatriated to India at the end of the war, he soon joined the judicial department in Tanganyika as a head clerk. After eighteen months he left for higher pay as a clerk in a Dar es Salaam law firm. In 1924 while retaining this job, he founded a newspaper, *Tanganyika Opinion*, and as it proved successful, he quit his clerical work to pursue what was to become a distinguished career in journalism.[50] Awtar Singh came from the Punjab in 1930 at age seventeen in search of a job. He was hired by the post office in Dar es Salaam, and for the next twenty-five years he continued this work. Meanwhile, blessed with an unusual flair for languages—learning to speak fourteen—he supplemented his income by teaching languages. Through correspondence he also studied law, and eventually he received leave to attend Lincoln's Inn in London. In 1955, having qualified as a barrister, he left the government to establish a law practice in Dar es Salaam. Success in law led to a political career. At independence he was vice-president of the local Asian Association and one of Tanganyika's leading Asian politicians.[51]

Some who left the government were unsuccessful in business but thrived on a challenge and excitement that would never have been possible in the civil service. Dahyabhai Chaturbhai Patel, for instance, was brought to Uganda in 1922 at age seventeen by an uncle who worked for the railway. After failing to be hired by the railway because he did not know English, Patel studied intensively on his own and soon was employed, like Gill and in the same year, as a telegraphist. Four years later when he was a station master in Naivasha, he resigned and, with savings, returned to India to marry and then opened a timber and hardware store in Thika. He became involved in social and political work, however, and as he said, never made a penny in the hardware business. In 1938 he joined a friend in establishing the Kisumu Motor Works. After an initial success, he decided to make a film depicting how the Asians came to East Africa. The resulting film, 'India in Africa', which he made in India, was never popular, and Patel lost all his money. He then founded in Nairobi a co-operative dealing in motor spares, Central Automobiles Ltd., and established branches throughout East Africa. Though never accumulating any significant capital, he was able to educate his chidren and live comfortably.[52]

A large number of the Asians remained in clerical service until retirement, which was compulsory at age fifty-five. Bhanubhai Acharya, emigrated to East Africa from Saurashtra in 1920. Though only sixteen years old and ignorant of English, he was hired in Nairobi for work as a postal clerk in Rumuruti, a remote outpost 140 miles to the north. The government offered to transport him there by bullock cart. Rather than spend twenty-one days in the cart, Acharya used his savings of Rs 80 to hire a motor-car and arrive in three or four days. For the next thirty-one years, serving in various locations, he worked for the post office and before retiring to India was the postmaster at Duke Street in Nairobi.[53] Another Asian, Francis Anthony de Souza, left Goa in 1927 at age eighteen to try his fortune in East Africa. He joined the Kenya civil service as an accountant and spent most of the ensuing three decades as a district clerk at a number of posts in the Northern Frontier District. Not until 1963 when he had served thirty-six years did he retire. He was designated a Member of the Order of the British Empire (M.B.E.) for meritorious service.[54]

For those who remained with the government, there were substantial rewards. About twenty Asians received the M.B.E., and many others received a gold medal. A comfortable pension after long service made retirement in India, where living expenses were comparatively low, especially attractive.[55] Acharya received a unique benefit. When the duke and duchess of Gloucester were on a tour of Kenya, Acharya rendered them a special service as assistant postmaster in Nakuru. The next day he was invited to accompany them to the Nakuru racecourse, and subsequently he and his family were their guests at Kensington Palace.[56]

The African Ascendency

In the long run it was not the Asian clerical workers' relationships with Europeans that were important but their relationships with Africans. From the beginning Africans were employed with Asians in the colonial service. As they gained experience and their training improved, Africans were hired in greater numbers and often for positions that had been occupied solely by the Asians. Africanization of the colonial service resulting in the displacement of Europeans as well as Asians proceeded rapidly during the last decade of colonialism.

The large number of Africans in public service compared to the numbers of Asians and Europeans is evident in the statistics for the three mainland territories shown in Table 6.1. Although the clerical workers are not distinguished from skilled and unskilled labourers, most of those employed were in clerical work. As the figures indicate, the Europeans and Asians in each territory remained almost equal in numbers as the public services grew in each territory, but the Africans increased considerably relative to the other two. Obviously during the last decade of colo-

TABLE 6.1   Public Service Employees by Racial Community in Kenya,
Tanganyika, and Uganda, 1950 and 1960

Community	Kenya	Tanganyika	Uganda
_1950_			
Asians	8,200	2,449	572
Europeans	4,800	2,074	310
Africans	96,500	56,447	46,481
_1960_			
Asians	11,800	2,750	1,950
Europeans	8,900	2,100	2,121
Africans	140,700	83,735	95,570

Sources: Compiled from the _Statistical Abstracts_ for each
territory.

nialism there was a growing Africanization of the government services.
This trend was to continue after independence when, as Motani has
wryly stated, 'the British masters had been replaced by African lords'.[57]
In 1967, for instance, the Kenya public service included only 5,300 Europeans and 8,500 Asians, but 194,800 Africans.[58]

The racial composition can be illustrated in more detail by the figures
in Table 6.2, which pertain to Tanganyika in 1960. Unfortunately, these
figures are like the preceding in that they do not differentiate between
clerks and manual workers.

Another view of racial differences in the public service is provided by
statistics relative to a single branch of government. Table 6.3 shows the
composition of the Kenya Police at ten-year intervals. The practice evident in these statistics, especially in the last decade, of moving Africans
in large numbers into positions with more responsibility and higher pay
was more disadvantageous to the Asians than to the Europeans. The personnel changes in the Kenya Police, which were typical of those in other
departments in all the territories, indicate that Europeans as well as Africans were employed at an increasingly higher rate than the Asians. Between 1950 and 1960 the Europeans increased by 187 per cent, Africans
by 98 per cent, and Asians by only 53 per cent. Moreover, the Asians' advance in numbers was not accompanied by an increase in position and
salary. Unlike the Europeans and Africans, the Asians remained in the
middle-level grades.

The governments' favouring Africans at the expense of Asians had begun long before the 1950s. Uganda may be cited as an example of what

TABLE 6.2 Categories of Public Service of Asians, Europeans, and
Africans in Tanganyika, 1960

| | Numbers of Employees | | |
	Asians	Europeans	Africans
Government Departments	1,186	1,523	50,660
East African Railways and Harbours	988	243	10,534
East African Posts and Telecommunications	285	79	1,315
Other High Commission services	177	152	1,029
Municipal and town councils	107	96	5,274
Native authorities	7	7	14,923
Totals	2,750	2,100	83,735

Source: R. R. Ramchandani, *Uganda Asians: The End of an Enterprise*
(Bombay: United Asia, 1976), p. 217.

occurred generally in the mainland territories. It was not only that the
Asians' presence was regarded by most administrators as an impediment to what they defined as the fundamentals of colonialism—
development and trusteeship—but also that the Asians were more expensive than the Africans. During the 1920s the cost of an Asian clerk in
Uganda was approximately eight times that of an African.[59] As early as
1912–13 the Uganda administration had begun to consider Africanization, and in 1929 the Secretariat issued a circular directing that 'as soon
as suitable native candidates become available, all vacancies occurring
in the present Asiatic Clerical and Non-clerical staff shall be filled by natives'. It also stated that in future the Asian contracts would be for only
three years and could be terminated with only seven days' notice.[60] After
1945 Uganda, in common with the other territories, intensified its efforts
towards Africanization.[61]

The Africanization policies were only partially successful. As the statistics denote, Asians continued to be employed in large numbers to the
end of the colonial period. As late as 1954 the African District Council of
South Nyanza, where employment of an all-African staff would most be
expected, still had a Goan cashier.[62] Even after independence the new
African governments, which intensified the efforts towards replacing
Asians, found it impossible, at least until Idi Amin's expulsion order, to
dispense with Asians entirely. Besides pursuing policies favouring Africans in hiring for public service, the African governments, beginning

TABLE 6.3   Kenya Police by Racial Community, 1940-60

Community	Officers	Inspectors	Sergeants, Constables	Totals
_1940_				
Europeans	28	137	0	165
Asians	0	32	4	38
Africans	0	6	2,798	2,804
_1950_				
Europeans	81	198	0	279
Asians	0	45	17	62
Africans	4	114	5,574	5,692
_1960_				
Europeans	210	591	0	801
Asians	0	95	0	95
Africans	683	303	10,264	11,250

Sources: Kenya Police Annual Report 1960 (Nairobi: Government Printer, 1981), p. 15; Police Department Annual Report, 1950, p. 2, C.O. 554/67. The latter includes statistics for 1940.

with Uganda in 1962, added local citizenship to the qualifications for employment. Because of continuing deficiencies in African education and training, however, they found that the Asians' skills and efficiency in many aspects of administration and especially in any matter concerning accounts were very difficult to replace. In 1967, four years after independence, Kenya, for instance, still had 8,500 Asians and 5,300 Europeans in public service together with 194,800 Africans.[63]

A reason for the continuing presence of the Asians in public service was that as Africanization proceeded certain communities considerably augmented the training of their young people for civil service positions. This was especially true of the Ismailis. Under the direction of the Aga Khan, as explained in Chapter 1, the community stressed westernization, practical education, and the education of women. Many Ismaili women were trained in English, shorthand, typing, and other secretarial skills as well as bookkeeping, and they were employed by the governments in increasing numbers. The Shahs soon followed the Ismailis in these ways and with similar results. It was the Goan community that was being displaced.[64]

Whether the training of Africans was an important aspect of the Asians' overall contribution in clerical work is a moot question. Motani, in his description of Africans in Uganda's civil service, believed that the Asian clerks were so heavily laden with duties that they had no time to train their African co-workers. Moreover, the supervision of African clerks, he stated, was officially assigned to the office superintendents, all of whom were Europeans.[65] Many Asians, in expressing a contrary opinion, have asserted that the association between the established Asian clerk and the African trainee was like that between the Asian artisan and his African employee. The performance of the work required that the skills and knowledge of the one be passed to the other. D'Mello, the Goan clerk who between 1941 and 1970 served in many district offices, maintained that in his work the training of his African associates was essential. He needed their competent assistance.[66]

As in other situations of colonial discrimination the Asians in the civil service advocated a system based on equality of opportunity and, failing that, sought to ally with Africans in opposition to the Europeans. In 1934 in Uganda, for instance, the Asian clerical workers petitioned the government for a non-racial civil service with competitive examinations and terms of service applicable to all. When that proved unacceptable, they agreed to the establishment of a Local Civil Service in which they would be grouped with Africans. Such a service was established in 1940.[67]

Despite the Asians' stand for policies that were beneficial to the Africans, there was considerable conflict between the two peoples. Just as the Asians bitterly protested the reservation of the higher posts and salaries for Europeans, the Africans deeply resented the continuing presence of the Asians in the middle levels of clerical service. As noted in the discussion of Uganda, the Africans in the early years were accorded far inferior salaries. Though modified, this situation continued through the colonial period. In 1952, for instance, the junior division of the Uganda civil service included 441 Asians and 1,856 Africans. All but seventeen of the Asians, some 96 per cent, received annually more than £200, but only 305 of the Africans, 16 per cent, earned that much. Many Asians earned close to £550.[68]

Contrary to African expectations, the discrepancy in wage levels between the two peoples continued after independence. To attract and retain the qualified clerical workers that they needed, the African governments not only had to employ Asians but also to offer them higher salaries. As shown in Table 6.4, the governments also continued to hire Europeans and at even higher salaries. It was the Asians, however, who occupied the positions immediately above the African employees, and so it was they who were the chief targets of African criticism.

TABLE 6.4 Average Salaries of Kenya Public Service Employees by Racial Community, 1960 and 1967

	Salaries (£)		
Year	Europeans	Asians	Africans
1960	1,270	559	102
1967	1,925	1,071	223

Sources: Compiled from Kenya, Statistical Abstracts, 1967, tables 171(a) and (b), pp. 150-1; 1968, tables 183(a) and (b), pp. 163-4.

The Africans' resentment against the Asians in the civil service was not based only on the differences in salary and position. Privilege breeds a pride and arrogance in any society. The Asians frequently criticized the European staff for its airs of superiority, but they themselves were often accused by their African co-workers of a similar insolent and imperious behaviour. In 1928 Kasimu Muwanika, a storekeeper in the Uganda Medical Department, complained to the director of racial insults and general victimization from the Asian clerk.[69] Similar complaints can be found throughout the colonial records.

The individuals exhibiting such behaviour, whether Asian or European, deserve censure, but to condemn either of the two peoples generally, as has often been done, is unfair. After independence when they were at the top, many Africans in the civil service were to show a similar arrogance. It was the colonial system that was at fault. To develop a civil service in three levels, with Europeans compartmentalized in one, Asians in another, and Africans in the third, to assign superior emoluments to one echelon, average to a second, and inferior to a third, and to prohibit movement from any one of the three levels to another—this was the root cause of the problem. It was inevitable that such a system would produce attitudes of racial superiority among those most favoured, deep resentment among the least privileged, and racial animosities among all that were bound to continue long after any reform was taken towards egalitarianism. When afforded opportunity, any people schooled in such a system would be inclined to take over and reserve the highest administrative posts exclusively for themselves.

Notes

1. *East African Standard*, 9 Jan. 1909, p. 9.

2. S. D. Kothari, interviewed by Gregory, 10 July 1973, Rajkot. M. J. Thakkar, interviewed by Gregory, 19 May 1973, Addis Ababa.

3. Girouard to Lord Crewe (Secretary of State for Colonies), 13 Nov. 1909, confidential, encl. interim report on the East Africa Protectorate and Uganda, C.O. 533/63.

4. Acting Government Coast Agent, Mombasa, to Director of Public Works, Nairobi, 1 Mar. 1923, item 47, file MP1487, 'Native Industries, Castor Seed Growing, Preparation of Hides, Skins, Bees Wax, etc., Coir Ropes, Karukal Rams, Ghee', Coast Province daily correspondence, Syracuse University microfilm 1995, reel 94.

5. H. S. Morris, *Indians in Uganda* (Chicago: University of Chicago Press, 1968), p. 141. See also J. S. Mangat, *History of the Asians in East Africa, c. 1886 to 1945* (Oxford: Clarendon, 1969), pp. 74–77.

6. Nizar A. Motani, 'The Ugandan Civil Service and the Asian Problem, 1894–1972', chap. 7, *Expulsion of a Minority: Essays on Ugandan Asians*, ed. Michael Twaddle (London: Athlone, 1975). Motani, *On His Majesty's Service in Uganda: The Origins of Uganda's African Civil Service, 1912–40* (Syracuse: Syracuse University Foreign and Comparative Studies Program, 1977). A number of other scholars have examined the subject briefly as a part of wider topics. See especially R. R. Ramchandani, *Uganda Asians: The End of an Enterprise* (Bombay: United Asia, 1976); Dharam P. Ghai and Yash P. Ghai, *Portrait of a Minority: Asians in East Africa* (Nairobi: Oxford University Press, 1970); and Mangat, *History of the Asians*.

7. Mangat, *History of the Asians*, pp. 16–25. 'Memo. regarding Banians or Natives of India in East Africa', in Sir Bartle Frere to Lord Granville (Foreign Office), 7 May 1873, F.O. 84/1391. Richard F. Burton, *Zanzibar: City, Island and Coast*, vol. 1, (London: Tinsley, 1872), pp. 328–29.

8. 'Asiatic Employees in Government Service', encl. British Resident, Zanzibar, to L. S. Amery (Secretary of State for Colonies), 4 Nov. 1927, file 'East Africa Asiatic Provident Fund, 1927', C.O. 822/3/1. *Report of the Commission on the Civil Services of the East African Territories and the East Africa High Commission, 1953–54*, vol. 1, (Margate, U.K.: Thanet, 1954), p. 23. Motani, 'Ugandan Civil Service', p. 99.

9. Uganda, *Census Returns, 1911* (Entebbe: Government Printer, 1911), table 13, p. 13.

10. Mangat, *History of the Asians*, p. 73 n. 1.

11. E. Shapurji Udwadia, a Parsee, is one of many Asians who have described their recruitment. In 1944, having just received a Bachelor of Commerce degree from Bombay University, he answered an advertisement for an accountant placed by Mehta, Patel and Co. of Nairobi, Mombasa, and Dar es Salaam. Interviewed by Honey, 28 July 1973, Dar es Salaam.

12. Motani, 'Ugandan Civil Service', p. 99.

13. Motani, *On His Majesty's Service*, pp. 6–36 passim. Kenya, *Interim Report of the Asian Civil Service Advisory Board* (Nairobi: Government Printer, 1946), pp. 3–4. Kenya, *Report of the Civil Service Commissioner (L. H. Hill, Esq., C.B.E., M.A., F.C.I.S.)* (Nairobi: Government Printer, 1945), p. 7. Tanganyika, *Provisional Regulations for the African Civil Service to Come into Force on 1st Aug., 1927* (Dar es Salaam: Government Printer, 1927). Uganda, *Regulations Setting forth Condi-*

tions, etc., of a Native Civil Service (Sanctioned by the Secretary of State) (Entebbe: Government Printer, 1927).

14. Motani, 'Ugandan Civil Service', pp. 104–5.

15. Kenya, *Legislative Council Debates*, 14 Feb. 1939, cols. 360–61.

16. *Report of the Commission on the Civil Services of Kenya, Tanganyika, Uganda and Zanzibar, 1947–48* (London: HMSO, 1948).

17. Ibid., para. 92.

18. *Report of the Commission on the Civil Services of the East African Territories and the East Africa High Commission, 1953–54*, vol. 1, pp. 27, 30–34.

19. 'Note on Indians in East Africa, Revised March 1951', encl. in H. S. Bates (Colonial Office) to Miss L.E.T. Storar (Commonwealth Relations Office), 9 Apr. 1951, confidential, file 'Indians in East Africa: Political, Social, and Economical Position of Indians, 1951', C.O. 322/143/7. See also 'Note for the Minister of State on the employment of Indians in higher posts of the public services in East Africa, Dec. 1951', file 'Employment of Indians in the higher posts of the public services in East Africa, 18 Dec. 1951', C.O. 822/726.

20. European employees were listed by name and position annually in the protectorate *Blue Books*.

21. Mangat, *History of the Asians*, pp. 74, 76.

22. Kenya, *Interim Report*, pp. 3–4.

23. Kenya, *Report on the Census of the Non-Native Population of Kenya Colony and Protectorate Taken on the Night of the 25th Feb., 1948* (Nairobi: Government Printer, 1953), app. 12, pp. 114–18.

24. Calculated from statistics ibid., table 43, p. 73, and app. 11, pp. 111–13.

25. *Kenya Population Census, 1962:* vol. 4, *Non-African Population* (Nairobi: Government Printer, March 1966), app. 8, p. 92. These statistics include adult males only.

26. Calculated from statistics ibid., app. 8, p. 92, and app. 9, p. 93.

27. John Iliffe, *Tanganyika Under German Rule, 1905–12* (Nairobi: East African Publishing House, 1969), pp. 143–45. Ralph Austin, *Northwest Tanzania under German and British Rule: Colonial Policy and Tribal Politics, 1889–1939* (New Haven: Yale University Press, 1968), pp. 63–65.

28. Quoted, Mangat, *History of the Asians*, p. 46, from Sir Arthur M. Hardinge, *A Diplomatist in the East* (London: J. Cape, 1928), p. 91.

29. Tanganyika, *Statistical Abstract, 1938–51* (Dar es Salaam: Government Printer, 1953), table 109, p. 45.

30. Tanganyika, *Annual Report of the Labour Division, 1960*, p. 25, C.O. 736/58.

31. Uganda, *Census Returns, 1911* (Entebbe: Government Printer, 1911), table 13, p. 13.

32. Civil service employees are enumerated for each of these years in Uganda's annual *Report of the Public Service Commission*. See also Morris, *Indians in Uganda*, p. 141; and Ramchandani, *Uganda Asians*, p. 222.

33. Uganda, *1962 Statistical Abstract* (Entebbe: Government Printer, 1962), tables U.P.1, 11, 12, pp. 94, 101, 102.

34. *Report of the Commission on the Civil Services of the East African Territories*, vol. 1, p. 23.

35. A. Vellani, interviewed by Honey, 13 and 14 Feb. 1974, Zanzibar. Mangat, *History of the Asians*, p. 74.

36. Dr. A. Ribeiro (interviewed by Gregory, 12 Nov. 1972, Nairobi) remarked that all the initial civil servants in Nairobi were Goans. M.M.R. Shah (interviewed by Bennett, 12 Apr. 1973, Nyeri) remembered the first civil servants in Nyeri as Punjabis, Goans, and a few Parsees. K. B. Dave (interviewed by Gregory, 10 June 1985, Nairobi) said Goans were trusted in the Secretariat because of their western orientation and Christianity.

37. Kenya, *Report of the Census . . . 1948*, table 37, p. 66.

38. M. Behal, interviewed by Honey, 12 Sept. 1973, Dar es Salaam.

39. Cited in Morris, *Indians in Uganda*, p. 142.

40. Kenya, *Report of the Census . . . 1948*, p. 72.

41. 'Nyanza Province, East Africa Protectorate: Report by the Provincial Commissioner for the Twelve Months Ending March 31st, 1911', p. 49, Kenya annual reports, Syracuse University microfilm 280l, reel 32.

42. 'South Kavirondo District Annual Report for the Year Ended 31st March 1920', p. 2, ibid., reel 37.

43. Ibid., 'for the Year Ended 31st Dec. 1940', p. l, reel 38.

44. 'Handing Over Report—S. Nyanza', by A.A.M. Lawrence to P. W. Low [n.d., but 1948], app., ibid., reel 38. For 'localization', see International Bank for Reconstruction and Development, *Economic Development of Kenya* (Baltimore: Johns Hopkins University Press, 1963), pp. 212–15.

45. 'South Nyanza District Annual Report 1960', app. A, ibid., reel 38.

46. F. X. D'Mello, interviewed by Bennett, 25 May 1973, Nakuru.

47. Ibid. For an explanation as to why Asians disliked transfers, see Motani, 'Ugandan Civil Service', p. 110.

48. Indra Singh Gill, interviewed by Bennett, 4 May 1973, Nairobi. Shanti Pandit, ed., *Asians in East and Central Africa* (Nairobi: Panco, 1963), p. 149.

49. B. S. Varma, interviewed by Bennett, 27 Apr. 1973, Thika.

50. V. R. Boal, interviewed by Gregory, 2 July 1973, Bombay.

51. Awtar Singh, interviewed by Honey, 25 July 1973, Dar es Salaam.

52. D. C. Patel, interviewed by Bennett, 28 Apr. 1973, Nairobi.

53. M. B. Acharya (son), interviewed by Gregory, 5 July 1973, Baroda.

54. F. A. de Souza, interviewed by Gregory, 28 June 1973, Porvorim, Bardez Goa.

55. J. P. de Souza and F. A. de Souza, interviewed by Gregory, 26 June 1973, Porvorim, Bardez Goa.

56. M. B. Acharya interview.

57. Motani, 'Ugandan Civil Service', p. 106.

58. Kenya, *Statistical Abstract, 1968* (Nairobi: Economic and Statistical Division, 1968), table 183(a), p. 163.

59. Ramchandani, *Uganda Asians*, p. 217.

60. Circular no. 12 of 5 June 1929, cited ibid., p. 216.

61. Morris, *Indians in Uganda*, p. 143.

62. 'South Nyanza District Annual Report, 1954', p. 12, Syracuse University microfilm 2801, reel 38.

63. Kenya, *Statistical Abstract, 1968,* table 183(a), p. 163. See also Ramchandani, *Uganda Asians,* pp. 217, 222–23, 226–27.

64. For the Ismaili and Goan changes, see Morris, *Indians in Uganda,* p. 143.

65. Motani, *On His Majesty's Service,* pp. 49–50.

66. F. X. D'Mello interview.

67. Motani, 'Ugandan Civil Service', pp. 104–5.

68. Uganda, Department of Commerce, *Annual Report* (Entebbe: Government Printer, 1952), p. 5, cited in Morris, *Indians in Uganda,* p. 141.

69. Cited in Ramchandani, *Uganda Asians,* p. 35 n. 2. Motani also describes Asian arrogant behavior: 'Ugandan Civil Service', p. 106.

PART TWO

The Secondary Occupations

CHAPTER SEVEN

Law, Medicine, and Teaching

The life of Asians in East Africa is something far more alive and complex than can be conveyed on paper, and this may account for the lack of published work about them.

—George Delf, 1963[1]

Because they were so conspicuous in their commercial, clerical, and construction activities, the fact that Asians were active in professions such as law, medicine, and teaching has scarcely been recognized. In these capacities the Asians were prominent, in some instances more numerous than the Europeans, and they helped to fill in each profession a vital need in colonial society. In law and medicine they served not only their own community but also the Europeans, Africans, and Arabs. On the basis of the economic security that these professions offered, the Asian advocates, physicians, and teachers undertook additional activities, many of which furthered the interests of the society as a whole.

Barristers and the Lure of Politics

As advocates, that is, as solicitors and barristers, the Asians conducted most of the legal work of East Africa. Unlike the practice of medicine, this work entailed a service not so much to Africans as to the Asian community, which was involved in considerable litigation because of its role in commerce. There were some Asian advocates, however, who took on the task, which the local European advocates studiously avoided, of defending African nationalists, including suspected Mau Mau, against government prosecution. There were other advocates who joined Africans in the poltical struggle for independence and assumed influential positions in the newly independent governments. In all but the early years, the Asians were predominant in the legal profession.

Unfortunately, very few records or even memories of the initial Asian advocates exist. Among the earliest was Kassum Jaffer, an Ismaili who in 1882, after qualification in India, emigrated to Zanzibar to begin his practice. Another Ismaili, Patalai Vellani, a fifth-generation resident of Zanzibar who studied in Europe, is said to have been the first Asian barrister in East Africa. The year was 1913. Not until after World War I did many Asian advocates appear on the mainland, and if not new immigrants from India, almost all were raised in the large urban centres. Madan Behal, a third-generation Punjabi Hindu who was the first to qualify from Arusha, did not receive his degree until 1959.[2]

During World War II when travel to Britain for the study of law was impossible, the examinations for law degrees were held in East Africa. Many young Asians seized the opportunity to study locally and receive qualification through these examinations. The result was a large increase in the number of Asian advocates.[3]

After the war the Asian barristers and solicitors increasingly surpassed the Europeans in numbers. In 1948 the Asian advocates in Kenya numbered 62, the Europeans 44. By 1961 the proportion was far different. The Asians then totalled 229, the Europeans only 124. In that year in Uganda the list of individuals and firms in legal practice included 59 Asians, only 8 Europeans, and 5 Africans.[4] After the mid-1960s the number of non-Africans rapidly diminished. In 1971 Tanzania is said to have had 70 Asian advocates, and two years later only 20.[5] The numerical importance of the Asians is illustrated in Table 7.1.[6]

On Zanzibar one of the most distinguished Asians in the legal profession was Hussein Alaiakhia Rahim. An Ithnasheri, he was unusual in that he was in government service. Born on Zanzibar in 1900, he started work at age fifteen as a clerk in the Police Department. He rose to the position of chief inspector, and after studying law, became public prosecutor and acting crown counsel. In 1952, appointed first class magistrate, he was the first Asian to preside in the High Court. Retiring in 1962, he left Zanzibar to act as secretary of the Tanzania Law Society in Dar es Salaam. Meanwhile he had received an M.B.E. as well as three medals for police and military service.[7]

In Kenya the outstanding Asian advocates included Achhroo Ram Kapila, V. V. Phadke, Ambalal Bhailalbhai Patel, Shivabhai Gordhanbhai Amin, J. M. Nazareth, Anant J. Pandya, F.R.S. de Souza, Chunilal Bhagwandas Madan, and Chanan Singh. All were barristers with degrees from the London Inns of Court. All but one had distinguished careers as politicians, at least three participated in journalism, and three became important magistrates. Kapila was the exclusive lawyer. A Punjabi Hindu and son of an early Nairobi advocate, Salig Ra Kapila, he studied at the London Lincoln's Inn and beginning in 1947 developed an extensive

TABLE 7.1   Advocates of East Africa by Racial Community, 1965*

Community	Kenya	Tanzania	Uganda	Total
Asians	170	2	4	176
Europeans	58	3	2	63
Africans	3	–	–	3
Arabs	5	–	–	5

*Includes only advocates who were currently in practice.

Source: East African Law Journal (Nairobi), vol. 1, no. 1 (March 1965), pp. 75-96.

practice in Nairobi with Asian and African clients. Phadke arrived in Kenya in 1917 already qualified at age thirty-two. After only three years of practice he was appointed to the Legislative Council and soon after became the first Asian on the Executive Council. In 1940 when nominated additional district magistrate and district judge, Phadke became the first Asian judge in the whole of East Africa.[8]

Patel, Amin, and Nazareth, like Phadke, were soon drawn into politics. A. B. Patel, who was born in Bombay State in 1898, studied at the London Inns of Court and moved directly to Mombasa to begin practice in 1923. He quickly rose to prominence in Mombasa in association with J. B. Pandya, and after Pandya's death in 1942 he became the foremost leader of the Indian community not only in Kenya but in East Africa as a whole. He was twice president of the East Africa Indian National Congress, a member of the Legislative Council and the Executive Council, and minister without portfolio. Before retiring in 1956 to an ashram in Pondicherry, he was awarded the Commander of the British Empire (C.B.E.) for distinguished service. S. G. Amin, five years younger, had a very similar career. Born in India and studying law in London, he established a practice in 1932 not in Mombasa but in Nairobi, where he soon became a communal leader. He was the first president of the Social Service League, twice president of the Congress, and a member of the Legislative Council. He eventually joined Patel in Pondicherry. Nazareth, a second-generation Goan born in Nairobi and ten years younger than Patel, attended the London Inner Temple, began his Nairobi law career in 1935, and entered politics in 1944. He was subsequently president of the Congress, the Law Society of Kenya, and the Gandhi Memorial Academy Society as well as a prominent legislative councillor. He also wrote for the militant Asian newspaper, the *Tribune*. He was honoured with appointment as Queen's Counsel.[9]

Two of the Kenya advocates, Pandya and de Souza, went directly into politics after receiving their law degrees. Anant Pandya, born in Mombasa in 1917 as the son of the eminent J. B. Pandya, never practised law. After qualifying as a barrister at Lincoln's Inn, he became president of the Mombasa Indian Association as well as a large number of social organizations. He also was vice-president of the Congress and of the Federation of Indian Chambers of Commerce and Industry. When Patel retired in 1956, it was Pandya who took his seat in the Legislative Council and in the view of most Asians succeeded him as the foremost political leader. F.R.S. de Souza, born in Bombay in 1929, accompanied his father to Zanzibar and then to Kenya at an early age. Before obtaining a Ph.D., he qualified for law at the Inns of Court. Returning in 1952 just before the emergency began, he threw himself into radical politics as well as journalism. It was the need to defend Kikuyu accused of involvement in Mau Mau that finally drew him into the practice of law.[10]

Although Nazareth was for a short time a puisne judge of the Supreme Court, Chunilal Madan and Chanan Singh were the only two appointed as permanent judges. A Punjabi Hindu, Madan was born in Kenya in 1912 and studied law at the London Middle Temple. Returning to Kenya in 1932, he had great difficulty in getting started in Nairobi at a time when there were only three other Asian advocates. He entered politics, becoming president of the Nairobi Indian Association and of the East African Indian National Congress, and in 1948 he was elected to the Legislative Council. In 1956 he replaced Patel as minister without portfolio, was soon after honoured, like Nazareth, as a Queen's Counsel, and in 1961 became the first Asian in Kenya appointed as a permanent puisne judge of the Supreme Court. After independence Madan became the chief justice of Kenya. Chanan Singh, though distinguished as a journalist, was primarily an advocate. Emigrating from the Punjab in 1923 when fifteen years old, he worked at first for the railway and, after qualification at Lincoln's Inn, did not begin his Nairobi law practice until 1945. He soon became a member of the Congress executive committee, president of the Indian Association, and subsequently president of the Law Society of Kenya. Representing with de Souza the radical wing of Asian politics, he was twice elected to the Legislative Council, and he became president of the Kenya Freedom Party. After independence, Chanan Singh served in the House of Representatives and as the parliamentary secretary. In 1964 he was appointed a puisne judge of the Supreme Court.[11]

In Tanganyika a list of distinguished advocates would include Iqbal Chand Chopra, Al Noor Kassum, Mahmud Nasser Rattansey, Kantilal Laxmichand Jhaveri, Awtar Singh, N. S. Patel, and N. Dharani. Unlike the advocates in Kenya, most of these men took their legal training in India. All but Chopra practised in Dar es Salaam. Born in the Punjab in 1896,

Chopra studied law in Ireland and England before 1930 when he moved to Mwanza to begin his legal career. Taking an active interest in public life, he soon became the leading politician not only in Mwanza but also in Tanganyika. In 1945 he entered the Legislative Council and soon afterward, the Railway and Executive Councils. Meanwhile, by befriending the founder of Williamson Diamonds Ltd., the country's principal mining company, Chopra had become the only other shareholder. Before retiring to Switzerland in 1958, he received honours as a Queen's Counsel, an O.B.E., and a C.B.E.[12]

Kassum, an Ismaili born in Dar es Salaam in 1924, attended Lincoln's Inn before returning to practise as a barrister. Like Chopra, he soon began a political career. He was a member of the Dar es Salaam Municipal Council before entering the Legislative Council. From 1959 to 1965 he served as chief whip of the Tanganyika African National Union (TANU) Parliamentary Party. He also became parliamentary secretary first to the Ministry of Education and then to the Ministry of Industries, Mineral Resources and Power. He was regarded as one of the most influential Asians in the newly independent government.[13]

Rattansey and Jhaveri were also attracted to politics. An Ithnasheri born in Dar es Salaam in 1916, M. N. Rattansey studied law in Bombay and at Lincoln's Inn. He began his practice in 1948 in Tabora and later moved to Dar es Salaam where he quickly became active in politics. While president of the Asian Association, he was nominated to the Legislative Council and then to the Central Legislative Assembly. Serving as Nyerere's counsellor in organizing TANU, he was at independence one of the country's most influential Asian politicians. K. L. Jhaveri, a Hindu from Kathiawar, came to Dar es Salaam in 1948 at age twenty-seven with a law degree from the Bombay Government Law College. In India he had been imprisoned for involvement in the nationalist movement, and in East Africa he joined Rattansey and other radicals in assisting Nyerere. He was nominated to the Legislative Council and subsequently, as a TANU candidate, elected to Parliament.[14]

Awtar Singh and N. S. Patel were closely associated with Rattansey and Jhaveri. Awtar Singh emigrated to Dar es Salaam from the Punjab in 1930 when seventeen years old. He obtained a job in the post office and, having a fluency in languages and learning fourteen, supplemented his income through language instruction. In 1955 on extended leave from the post office, he attained a law degree from Lincoln's Inn and then returned to set up his own law practice for mainly Asian and European clients. He soon became involved in the nationalist movement and served as vice-president and later president of the Asian Association. N. S. Patel, who was born near Ahmedabad and educated at Bombay University, established a law firm in Dar es Salaam in 1947, a year after his arrival at age twenty-eight. He entered politics 'to make good contacts'. He was a founding member of the Asian Association, its secretary, and later vice-president. With Jhaveri he helped start the multi-racial Shaban Roberts School.[15]

Dharani differed from these Tanganyika advocates by shunning politics. A Bhatia born in Dar es Salaam in 1912 when his father was a customs official in the German government, Dharani was late in studying law because of having to attend to family property in Kutch and because of volunteering for service in World War II. He did not begin his practice in Dar es Salaam until 1956 when he was forty-four. Catering to clients of all races, he developed an extensive legal practice, wrote for the press, and acquired agricultural property. He became the largest milk producer in Dar es Salaam.[16]

In Uganda the leading advocates included Sir Amar Nath Maini, Chunibhai Bhailalbhai Patel, Count B.K.S. Verjee, Jayant M. Madhvani, Chhotabhai Umedbhai Patel, Chandulal Kalidas Patel, Amratlal Girdhar Mehta, Gurdial Singh, and Anil Clerk. Maini, a Punjabi Hindu born in Nairobi, studied at the London Middle Temple before joining a Nairobi law firm in 1934 at age twenty-three. He was in the Legislative Council and the Nairobi Municipal Council before moving to Kampala in 1939. He then began an outstanding career of public service. He was the first mayor of Kampala, minister of commerce and industry, and from 1961, speaker of the East Africa Central Legislative Assembly. He received an O.B.E., C.B.E., and a knighthood. C. B. Patel, one of the earliest advocates in Uganda, was born in 1897 in India and after obtaining a law degree became public prosecutor in Petlad. He took further training at the Middle Temple and in 1927 set up practice in Kampala. While working as an advocate into the 1960s, he became the director of several businesses and president of the Law Society.[17]

Verjee, born in Mombasa in 1911, was the foremost leader of the Uganda Ismaili community. Like Patel, he attended the Middle Temple before beginning a practice in Uganda. Though a member of the Legislative Council and president of the Law Society, he is noted primarily for his service to the Aga Khan. He was the Aga Khan's private secretary during the Jubilee tour of 1937, chairman of the Supreme Tribunal, and member of the Supreme Council for all Africa. He was rewarded by the Aga Khan with the title of count and by the government with a C.B.E.[18]

Jayant Madhvani and C. U. Patel are noted primarily for their leadership in business. Madhvani, eldest son of the renowned Muljibhai who was one of the two founders of the Uganda sugar industry, was born in Jinja and studied law at the Inns of Court. In 1944 at the age of only twenty-two, he returned to Uganda not to open a practice but to assist his father in the management of an extensive agricultural and industrial group of companies. In 1958 when his father died, Jayant Madhvani assumed control of the family business empire, which eventually included sixty different organizations. Involved in many public services, he was a member of the Legislative Council, president of the Jinja Senior Secondary School, founder-president of the Jinja Lions Club, and a noted philanthropist. At the time of his early death in 1971 he was regarded by many as the foremost leader of the Uganda Asian community. C. U. Patel was born in India in 1909 and, after qualifying in law, emigrated to Uganda. Establishing a practice in Kampala in 1938, he quickly became involved in business as well as many Asian social activities. He was the director of nine companies.[19]

C. K. Patel, A. G. Mehta, Gurdial Singh, and Anil Clerk all assumed prominent roles in the Obote administration. Patel was born in India in 1904 and, after qualifying and practising as a pleader in Bombay, left for Mbale to work as a solicitor. He then went to England to become a barrister. In 1937 he began law practice in Jinja. Qualifying also as a chartered accountant and specializing in insurance, he became known for a wide range of interests and capabilities. He was appointed to the Legislative Council, received the awards of Queen's Counsel and a C.B.E., and became an honorary first class magistrate and Obote's minister of commerce. Mehta, born in Masaka in 1925, studied at Lincoln's Inn and in 1948 began to practice in Kampala. Entering politics, he sat in the City Council and supported African nationalists. He became legal adviser to Obote and as a leader of the Uganda People's Congress attended the Lancaster House conferences and was a member of the first Parliament. At the time of his death in 1969, at only age forty-four, he was mayor of Kampala and, according to his brother, 'at the right hand of Obote'.[20]

Gurdial Singh and Anil Clerk had very similar careers. Gurdial Singh, who was raised in Kenya, attended the London School of Economics and Lincoln's Inn before beginning practise in Kampala in 1957 at age twenty-four. Within a year, to establish a meaningful political association with Africans, he joined other Young Turks in forming the Uganda Action Group. After independence he became a member of the Kampala City Council, director of the Consultive Council and the Uganda Press Trust Ltd. and a member of several other government agencies. Like Gurdial Singh, Clerk became one of Obote's closest advisers. Though three years younger and born in Kampala, he, too, studied at the London School of Economics and the Inns of Court. He returned to Uganda in 1959 to become active in politics as well as law. He joined the Uganda Action Group, assisted Obote in organizing the Uganda People's Congress, and after independence sat in Parliament. In two famous court cases he defended first Obote and then Amin. During the Uganda exodus, Clerk was brutally murdered at the instigation of an ungrateful Amin.[21]

Clerk was not alone in the defense of African leaders. In Tanganyika Rattansey and Jhaveri combined with D. N. Pritt, the English barrister renowned for work on behalf of imperial subject peoples, in defending Nyerere against charges of sedition. After independence the young Ismaili barrister Noorali Velji incurred Nyerere's displeasure by defending Oscar S. Kambona and other Africans during the infamous Kambona treason trials. In Kenya S. G. Amin fought for the release of the Kamba leader Samuel Muindi Mbingu, and A. R. Kapila earned a reputation as a friend of Africans by representing individuals who had been physically abused by the government's paramount chiefs. Pranlal Sheth, the journalist who turned to law, was deported after independence because he had become the personal lawyer of Kenyatta's political rival Oginga Odinga.[22]

During the state of emergency in Kenya, several Asian advocates defended a large number of Africans charged with complicity in Mau Mau. In 1952 when Kenyatta and five other top officials of the Kenya African Union (KAU) were arrested, F.R.S. de Souza and the journalist Pio Pinto moved into a house with the acting KAU leaders Joseph Murumbi and W. W. Awori to organize a defense for the coming trial. At de Souza's suggestion, they invited Pritt to head the defense team. Pritt's legal assistants were to be, besides de Souza, the Nairobi barristers A. R. Kapila and Jaswant Singh, an eminent barrister from India, Chaman Lall, and two others, a Jamaican and a Nigerian. During the five-month trial at Kapenguria—the most important trial in the history of East Africa—de Souza, Kapila, and Singh, at considerable risk, travelled throughout the insurgent area to collect evidence and witnesses. Although the defense lost its case, the court's decision in the opinion of Pritt, de Souza, Kapila, and most non-Europeans was a travesty of justice.[23]

The Asians' subsequent efforts to secure Kenyatta's release from prison are to be described in another volume. Significant here is the fact that the the honorary legal adviser for the Release Jomo Kenyatta Campaign Committee was the young Asian barrister Vinubhai Vithalbhai Patel. Born in Nairobi in 1929, educated in India and at Lincoln's Inn, Patel had begun to practise law the year of Kenyatta's arrest. While rising to prominence in the Kenya Indian Congress, Nairobi Indian Association, and Patel Brotherhood, he associated with the radical Asian journalists and politicians who were actively supporting Africans in the drive for independence.[24]

As hundreds of other Africans were taken to court following the Kapenguria trial, the Asians assumed the responsiblity for their defense. In 1953 Kapila and J. M. Nazareth combined in defending Africans charged with the Lari massacre, and Kapila, working through Pritt, appealed approximately one hundred cases to the Privy Council. The next year Kapila served as the counsel for General China. De Souza, who was junior to Kapila in these trials, personally participated in the defense, as he recalled, of 116 Africans, of whom 65 were his personal clients. He won the release of many by proving that their confessions had been obtained through torture. Among the other Asian advocates who defended Africans in the Mau Mau trials were Shiek Mohamed Akram, Shaik Mohammad Amin, Maharaj Krishan Bhandari, Amritlal Ghadialy, S. P. Handa, Arvind Jamidar, Jaswant Singh, A. H. Malik, E. K. Nowrojee, Bhailal Patel, M. M. Patel, Sayeed Cockar, and K. D. Travadi. Bhailal Patel, who perhaps was typical of these advocates, moved to Nyeri, one of the trial centres, and during five months in 1955 participated in from forty to forty-five cases involving between 100 and 150 accused.[25]

Doctors, Dentists, and Pharmacists

The service rendered by the Asians in medicine is not unlike that in law. Asians were among the first medical doctors, dentists, and pharmacists in East Africa, and whether in private practice or employed by the government most of them administered to the needs of Africans, Arabs, and Europeans, as well as Asians. Like the advocates, they tended to use medicine as a spring-board into many other activities.

Though preceded in Mombasa by Dr. Luis Lobo, Rozendo Ayres Ribeiro was the first private medical practitioner in Nairobi. Like Lobo, he was a Goan. In 1898 at the age of twenty-eight he came to Mombasa from Goa and within a year followed the railhead to Nairobi where he at once set up his practice in a tent. After three years he built a house combined with an office on Victoria Street. Ribeiro administered to all patients who came to his door—Europeans, Asians, and Africans—and he soon had a reputation as a character as well as an able doctor. He rode a zebra while making his rounds. Missionaries sent him young Kikuyu for female circumcision, and it is said that he decorated his office walls with the hundreds of bits and pieces. Many patients came for cure of sore throats. Ribeiro would line them up, swab their throats with an anesthetic, and proceeding from one to another, snip off their tonsils with scissors. He sent each away with a piece of ginger to suck to reduce the pain. Ribeiro adorned the entrance to his building with a climbing red rose described as the most luxurious and beautiful in all East Africa. It was rumored that he fed it secretly with human blood.[26]

Ribeiro's eccentricities did not stand in the way of his attaining a distinguished medical and civic career. It was he who first identified the epidemic of 1900 as bubonic plague. At a time when medical supplies were scarce, he manufactured his own widely used anti-malarial pills. Assuming a leading position in the Goan community, he founded the Goan school that holds his name, and he was known for his philanthropy. Ribeiro became the Portuguese Vice-Consul in Nairobi and was awarded the British O.B.E. as well as the Grand Cross of the Portuguese Order of Merit. One of his sons, Craciano Gerald, was to follow his father as a physician in Nairobi. Another, Ayres Laurenco, was to become the police surgeon for Kenya and later the government pathologist.[27]

The second physician in Nairobi was A.C.L. de Souza, who came to Kenya in 1915 with a medical degree from Bombay. Beginning as a government medical officer, he served among the coastal Giriama during the rebellion and then in Kisumu. In 1919 he and his wife, Mary, who was also a physician, set up practice in Nairobi. Like Ribeiro, de Souza was a character, riding a British Douglas motor cycle on his rounds, ceaselessly smoking a long cheroot, and discoursing on almost any topic, but he was an able doctor and quickly developed a lucrative practice. As a devout Christian he charged very reasonable fees and donated large sums to charity. During the 1930s and 1940s he was the outstanding leader of the Goan community and one of the foremost Asians. He is noted not only as a physician but also as a journalist, politician, and public benefactor. In addition to serving many years in the Legislative Council, he was president of the East African Medical Association, the Desai Memorial Library, the Goan Overseas Association, and the Goan Institute.[28]

The de Souzas practised as a family. Mary, who was born in Bombay and graduated from Grant College of Medicine, winning two gold medals, married de Souza in 1919 and was the first woman physician in East Africa. Prominent in civic affairs, she was to be instrumental in founding the Lady Grigg Indian Maternity Home. In 1948 the de Souzas were joined in practice by their son Peter Antonius, who also received a medical degree from Bombay. Unlike his father, the younger de Souza never entered politics or journalism, but he, too, was noted for his reasonable fees. He set a limit to his personal income and donated all above that amount to charities. Respected and valued for his service, he continued to reside and practise in Kenya after independence.[29]

In Mombasa the most eminent physician seems to have been Shanker Dhondo Karve, who came to Kenya in 1922 at age twenty-eight after medical training and military service in India. He was the son of India's most honoured medical doctor, D. D. Karve, the pioneer in women's education who maintained his practice in Poona until his death at age 104. The younger Karve practised initially in Nairobi, then went to Edinburgh for further training, and on his return settled in Mombasa. There he was a principal founder and chief surgeon of the Pandya Memorial Clinic, which became the most important hospital in Mombasa and unlike the government institutions had a non-racial policy in admitting and accommodating its patients. Like Ribeiro, Karve acquired a reputation for philanthropy and public service. He initiated the Indian Girls' School of Mombasa and took a leading role in the Rotary Club and the East Africa Indian National Congress. He served on the Municipal Board for sixteen years and at various times sat in the Kenya Legislative and Executive Councils and the Council of State. He became one of the country's most respected Asians, and he too received the O.B.E.[30]

Another outstanding physician in Mombasa was the Punjabi Muslim, Mohamed Ali Rana. Two years younger than Karve, Rana was born in the Punjab and educated in Lahore and London. In 1924 after qualification, he began practice in Zanzibar where he was appointed physician to the household of the sultan. He soon moved to Mombasa and assumed a leading position in Muslim politics. While continuing to practise, he joined the Indian Association, helped found the Rotary Club, and became president of the Muslim Association. He was elected to the Mombasa Municipal Board and the Kenya Legislative Council. He also became the mayor of Mombasa. In 1944 for outstanding public service he was awarded the M.B.E. and in 1952 the O.B.E.[31]

In western Kenya there was an Asian doctor with a comparable reputation. Faqir Chand Sood, a Punjabi Hindu, emigrated to East Africa in 1929 when thirty years old after a medical education in Lahore. From that time he resided in Kisumu as the principal doctor in private practise. Like Ribeiro and Karve, Sood was highly respected not only as a medical practitioner but also as a social and political leader. He was chairman of the Kisumu Health Committee and a member of the Municipal Board since its inception. He was also president of the Nyanza Social Service League and the interracial Ambassador Club, secretary of the Kisumu Indian Association, and a prominent member of the Standing and Executive committees of the Kenya Congress.[32]

Amir Abdulkarim Alidina, an eminent physician in Tanganyika, differed from these three Kenya doctors by pursuing a career in the government's medical service. An Ismaili, born on Zanzibar in 1922, he studied medicine in Bombay and then obtained a Fellow of the Royal College of Surgeons (F.R.C.S.) degree in England. He was the first Ismaili in East Africa to receive this qualification, which enabled him to operate as well as dispense medicine. Hired by the Tanganyika government in 1954, he was sent to Lindi to serve as the surgeon for several government and mission hospitals. Although he administered to all peoples, his primary patients were Africans. In a Land Rover, leaving Lindi often for several days, Alidina visited remote villages and performed hundreds of operations in rooms without electricity or running water. As was the practice in government service, he was transferred every few years to a new post—from Lindi to Tabora, Mwanza, and Tanga—until 1961–62 when he undertook a year of special training in Britain for an ear, nose, and throat (ENT) specialization.

Alidina continued to work for the government until 1964 when he began a private practice with the new, non-racial Aga Khan Hospital and became head of the ENT department at the medical school of Dar es Salaam University. Meanwhile he donated his services to the government, which frequently flew him to hospitals throughout the country for special surgery. In 1970, assuming that his children would suffer discrimination in a country that, as President Nyerere said, would give priority to African development, Alidina moved with his family to the United States.[33]

A medical doctor with a somewhat similar career, in which an outstanding service was given to Africans, was Gunvantrai Jayantilal Bhatt, a Ugandan who in 1963 began private practice in Fort Portal. He had a medical degree from the University of Birmingham. After a few years Bhatt became, as he said, a 'bush doctor'. He set up dispensaries throughout the area and visited them regularly. He also worked at the local mission hospital. Before Amin's expulsion order forced his departure, Bhatt was ministering to approximately 20,000 African patients each year, and in his last year, as doctors hurriedly left Uganda, the number rose to 50,000. Like most other Asian physicians, Bhatt was prominent in social endeavours. He was chairman of a Lions Club committee that built a multi-racial school, and he was secretary of a multi-racial sports club. In 1973 he and his family were among the twelve Asian families offered sanctuary by Mauritius.[34]

One of the Uganda doctors, Muljibhai Motibhai Patel, became one of the Asian community's leading politicians. Born in Kaira District in 1897, Patel attended college in Poona and then received a medical training at Bombay University. Before his move to Kampala in 1925, he practised medicine in Bombay and Baroda. In Kampala he at once combined politics and medicine and quickly acquired a reputation as a champion of Asians suffering from discrimination or misfortune. He was a founder of the Social Service League and a member of the Advisory Council on Indian Education. He became president of the Central Council of Indian Associations as well as the Kampala Indian Association and the Arya Samaj. Twice nominated to the Legislative Council, he was in the two decades preceding independence the conservative leader of the majority of the Uganda Asians. In recognition of his public service the colonial government awarded him an O.B.E.[35]

A Kenya physician, Vithalbhai Raojibhai Patel, appears to have assumed a prominent role in African liberation. Patel came to Kenya in 1942 at age twenty-six after a medical training in Bombay. Both he and his wife had been in the Quit India movement and been imprisoned, and he emigrated before her release. He opened a private general practice in Nairobi and after a year became secretary of the East African Medical Association, then president, and after a few years a member of the British Medical Council. This was a rare accomplishment for an Asian. Specializing in jaundice, Patel read papers at professional meetings in England, the United States, and India. On three occasions he represented the Kenya Medical Association at annual meetings of the British Medical Association. Meanwhile, taking an interest in Asian politics, he became secretary, the youngest ever, of the East Africa Indian National Congress.[36]

During one year Patel joined F.R.S. de Souza, J. M. Desai, D. K. Sarda, and a few other young Asian radicals in a bold attempt to break the colour bar in the European-owned hotels. The group began with the notorious Staghead Hotel in Nakuru. Partly because some of the Comoro Islanders who served in these hotels were Patel's patients, the group was surprisingly successful.[37]

Two years after his arrival in Nairobi, Patel began to associate with African nationalists. 'I had been anti-British in India', he later recalled, 'so naturally I worked against the British in East Africa'.[38] To avoid attracting the attention of Europeans or the government, he opened an office in a run-down building on River Road. One of his three rooms had a dirt floor. There he administered to the poor, almost all of whom were Africans. On weekends he drove from 400 to 500 miles among his patients' villages to become acquainted with the people, country, and diseases. Recognized as a friend of Africans, he soon met Mbiyu Koinange and Jomo Kenyatta. In describing this relationship years later, Patel stated that he became very close to these men, attended their political meetings, and even collected funds from the Asians for a school started by Koinange. During the emergency, he recalled, he secretly gave money to African rebels and on a few occasions attended to them in his office at night. As a doctor he was able to travel and visit the rebels in remote areas. He was arrested three times, he said, when found outside Nairobi without his medical bag. After independence Patel, like Alidina of Tanzania, became increasingly concerned about his children's future, and in 1965 he retired to Baroda.[39]

Another physician noted for outstanding service to Africans during the emergency was Yusuf Ali Eraj, a Punjabi Muslim. Born in India, he received his medical training in Lahore and London. After moving to Nairobi in 1947, he began a private practice in which most of the patients were Africans. During the emergency, his office on Kimathi Street is said to have been swamped with the detainees' wives and children sent to him for medical care by the Goan journalist P. G. Pinto. For many years Eraj received no remuneration for this work.[40]

As these brief descriptions indicate, Asian doctors had a high prestige in their communities and were accorded positions of considerable responsibility. Unfortunately, very few records of their achievements are available, and only a few other important Asians can be cited. Gulamhussein Mohamedali Daya, the first Ismaili physician in Tanzania, was among the small group of Asians in Dar es Salaam who took an active part in the nationalist movement and assisted Nyerere in establishing TANU. Dr. Amritlal Ujamshi Sheth, beginning in the 1930s, became a leader in Mombasa politics, entered the Kenya Legislative Council, and was honoured with the Order of St. John and an M.B.E. Tiburcio D'Souza, who practised for three decades in Mbale and was chairman there of the Township Authority, became well known in Uganda and was Obote's friend. Kaiser Singh of the Second King's African Rifles Hospital of Mombasa was one of the first physicians in East Africa and an outstanding Sikh leader. In 1910 he laid the foundation stone of the first Sikh temple. Vishwanath Vithal Patwardhan, who practised four decades in Nairobi after 1931, became a member of the City Council, president of the Indian Association and the Hindu Union, and general secretary of the East Africa Indian National Congress.[41]

The Asian dentists of East Africa did not acquire positions of public leadership comparable to those of the physicians, and they began practice on the whole at least a generation later, but they were very important in their service to the Asian and African communities. The careers of three Asian dentists—Hassan Esmail Nathoo, Vijay Pal Vohra, and Bashir Ahmed Qureshi—well illustrate the Asian contribution.

Nathoo, brother of the Ismaili politician Ibrahim Nathoo, was the first Asian dentist in East Africa. With Licentiate in Dental Surgery (L.D.S.) and R.C.S. qualifications from the Royal Dental College in London, he began to practise in Nairobi in 1934 at age twenty-five. He soon became involved in a variety of social programs and was remarkably successful in raising funds for such projects as the Indian Maternity Home, the Suleman Verjee Indian Gymkhana, the Prince Aly Khan War Fund, and the United Kenya Club. He became the first Asian president of the East African Dental Association, president or chairman of a number of other organizations, an alderman of the City Council, and a *vazier* (an honorary title of merit) of the Aga Khan. In 1948 for outstanding social service, he was awarded an M.B.E.[42]

Vohra, the son of a Kenya civil servant, earned both medical and dental degrees in Edinburgh but decided to practise dentistry. In 1947 when he was twenty-seven, he began work in Nairobi as the second Asian dentist in Kenya. He trained his own technical staff of Africans, eventually five in number, and from the outset he took as his motto: 'If you want to make money, go into business, not medicine'. In 1973 while still practising in Nairobi, he claimed with pride that he had never charged an African more than Shs 5. He explained that he had invested his initial savings in local property that had appreciated to the degree that he did not have to earn a living from his practice. After independence he and his wife Anjana, a medical doctor, both of whom held British passports, applied for Kenya citizenship. To their great surprise, both were refused.[43]

Qureshi, a Punjabi Muslim who began his career a generation later, made a quite different contribution to East African dentistry. Born in Nairobi in 1933, he received degrees in the Punjab and Northern Ireland. In 1963, the year of Kenya's independence, he opened a well-equipped office in Nairobi and quickly assumed a foremost position among the country's dentists. Sponsored by the World Health Organization, he carried on epidemiological research, published papers, and organized international conferences. He became editor of three dental periodicals. Aware of the need for preventive care as Africans ate less of traditional foods, Qureshi trained an African woman to teach Africans about dental health and with government support sent her as part of a team to address audiences in Kisumu and the coast. He also initiated a government study of fluoride in Kenya water supplies.[44]

Like dentistry and medicine, pharmaceutical work attracted many Asians. Through most of the colonial period, however, only the European physicians wrote prescriptions for the pharmacists. Following the custom in India, the Asian physicians kept stocks of medicine in their dispensaries and employed compounders to prepare the mixtures or powders that they prescribed. They were thus able to augment their professional fees through the sale of medicine. The custom had its hazards. Unlike most Europeans, the Asian physicians extended credit to their patients, billing them monthly, and they sometimes lost both their fees and the costs of medicine. Despite the physicians' making and selling the medicines they prescribed, pharmacy became an important allied profession for Asians and Europeans and eventually for Africans. By 1960 East Africa had about ninety pharmacists, known usually as chemists, and about half of them were Asians.[45]

The foremost pharmacist among the Asians seems to have been John Shamsudin Karmali, an Ismaili who, like Vohra and Qureshi, was born in Nairobi and practised there. In 1936, after secondary school, Karmali attended a college of pharmacy in England and there married Joan Glenys, one of his classmates. He was then the third Asian in East Africa to marry an Englishwoman. While in England, Karmali experienced an intellectual awakening. 'I went mad on reading', he later recalled, and he discovered classical Indian music and then turned to European music. When he returned with his bride to Kenya in 1946, he was one of East Africa's most enlightened Asians. He and his wife, who had stayed in England an extra year to serve their apprenticeships, were also then the most qualified of all the pharmacists, European and Asian, in East Africa. There were then only seven other pharmacists: five Europeans and two Asians.[46]

Karmali, with his wife, opened a pharmacy in Nairobi in 1946 and then took on a number of other activities, not all of which were related to the pharmaceutical profession. He held diplomas in optics and chemistry, which led to an interest in lenses, photography, and laboratory equipment. Karmali devoted a section of the pharmacy to cameras and film and acquired the East Africa agency for Leica. Soon recognized as a specialist in both medical and photographic equipment, he helped design the related laboratories in the University of Nairobi and Makerere University. His knowledge of photography stimulated an interest in wildlife with the result that he became a trustee of the East African Wildlife Society, the World Wildlife Fund, and the National Parks of Kenya. He also served as chairman of the executive committee of the National Museum of Kenya. Applying his photographic knowledge, Karmali began to photograph wildlife, and he published two of the most coveted books on East African birds.[47] Meanwhile he had become one of the young radicals of the 1950s who chafed at the inequalities suffered by Asians and Africans. He eventually became involved in political reform and in establishing the first truly multi-racial school in Nairobi.

Although all the pharmacists and most of the physicians and dentists were in private practice, some Asians, as Dr. Kaiser Singh illustrates, were employed in government service from the beginning of the British administration. The numbers were small before World War II when Europeans predominated, but the Asians served in nearly all the district headquarters as well as the urban centres. In 1927, for instance, the South Kavirondo District headquarters had three Asians and one European as its medical staff and in 1930 five Asians and three Europeans.[48] Through the colonial period approximately two-thirds of the Asian physicians worked for the governments, but only a small proportion of the dentists, and apparently none of the pharmacists.

The physicians' work with the governments became increasingly important to the Africans. Before and during World War I, except in time of epidemic, the government physicians in the British territories attended almost exclusively the departmental officials and the troops. They ministered incidentally to only a few Africans at the administrative centres outside the reserves. During the war the medical examinations of thousands of Africans revealed a very poor state of health. As a result, the governments in 1919–20 began to establish medical centres within the African areas. The progress was initially very slow. By 1925 the 1 million people of Nyanza Province were served by only three medical officers, the 623,000 of Kikuyu Central Province by only two, the Coast Province outside Mombasa by none, and the 378,000 of the other areas by only one. There were then twenty-five medical officers in all Kenya. By 1936 the total had increased to only forty-eight, but after World II there was a rapid expansion. The Asians became increasingly involved after the war, and even in the early years most of the medical officers, who were all Europeans, were assisted by one or more Asians in the rank of subassistant surgeon or lower.[49]

Until the closing years of the colonial administration, the Asian medical personnel were considerably less numerous than the Europeans. In 1948, for instance, there were 96 Asians in Kenya as contrasted with 308 Europeans. The great difference arose mainly because the nursing profession was not entered by the traditional Asian woman. The Asian physicians numbered 66, the Europeans 89. The Asian dentists were 9 compared to 27 European. Asian nurses, sisters, and matrons, however, were outnumbered in the ratio of 21 to 192. In 1962 a list of adult males of Kenya in medical and health care revealed a preponderance of Asians.[50]

	Asians	Europeans
Doctors and dentists	266	204
Pharmacists	74	45
Nurses	2	8
Totals	342	257

By 1972, the year before the Uganda exodus, the Asians in private practice and government service in the three East African countries, as shown in Table 7.2, had become far more numerous and outnumbered both Europeans and Africans. Only in Tanzania were the Asian physicians less in number than the Europeans, and in all the countries the Asian dentists and pharmacists either equalled the Europeans or, in most cases, were predominant.[51]

Like those in other professions, Asian doctors suffered from hostility and discrimination on the part of the European community and the governments. In 1908 when a group of Asian doctors arrived from Bombay, the *East African Standard* carried an article stating, 'They work on the principle of no cure, no reward. They carry around with them badly printed books in Babu Language which set forth the various diseases man is heir to and add the amount of reward expected if a patient is cured of any or all'. The article concluded with a statement of apprehension that was to be heard frequently through the colonial period: 'This is possibly the beginning of a Policy of annexation by India'.[52] The *Stan-*

TABLE 7.2   Physicians, Dentists, and Pharmicists of East Africa, 1972

Professionals	Asians	Europeans	Africans	Others	Total
Kenya					
Physicians	514	301	98	5	918
Dentists	46	18	4	–	68
Pharmacists	102	28	14	–	144
Tanzania					
Physicians	167	257	19	–	443
Dentists	6	4	2	–	12
Pharmacists	?	?	?	?	27
Uganda					
Physicians	329	297	191	40	857
Dentists	18	18	3	–	39
Pharmacists	32	16	4	–	52
Totals	1,214+	939+	335+	45+	2,560

Source: Compiled from lists of names in the *East African Dental and Medical Directory, 1973.*

dard also printed articles ridiculing the Asians' method for reviving drowning victims and their ideas of sanitation. An Asian cook asked a housewife to buy some muslin for straining soup, related one writer, because 'he was finding it was spoiling his shirts'.[53]

On the whole the Asian medical practitioners who came to East Africa did not deserve such aspersion. Although some immigrants followed only the traditional, homeopathic arts, the vast majority were trained in western medicine at accredited medical schools. Such training was necessary for them to obtain licences and to practice. Most of the doctors who were first-generation immigrants came with at least one medical degree from the Grant College of Medicine in Bombay, and most of the second- or later-generation Asians attended British institutions, usually Edinburgh.

The discrimination Asians encountered was a barrier in the way of their performing the services for which they had been trained. The experience of Alidina, who, as explained, worked for the government in rural Tanganyika, well illustrates the problem. When he finished medical school in 1953, he had not only a Bachelor of Medicine (M.B.), Bachelor of Surgery (B.S.) qualification, the equivalent of the American M.D., but also an F.R.C.S., which enabled him to perform operations and to be classified in government service as a 'consultant', not just a 'medical officer'. He first applied to his home government at Zanzibar but was offered only the lower rank with inferior salary and no leave privileges to take refresher courses in Britain. Disillusioned, he moved to Tanganyika to begin private practice as a surgeon in Dar es Salaam, but he soon found that the operating facilities of the hospitals, all then European, would not be available to him. He was offered only the position of medical officer.

At length, through the intercession of a European friend, Alidina was assigned a position as consultant, and it was then that he was sent to Lindi, the most remote and least desirable of all the stations that employed a qualified surgeon. At Lindi, where a European surgeon had been expected, he was informed that a mistake had been made in assigning him the house reserved for the consultant and that he and his family would have to live in the Asian quarters with the other medical staff. Only by threatening to resign, knowing that no consultant would replace him, did Alidina obtain the housing that had been promised. A decade later, having become a citizen in independent Tanzania, Alidina encountered a new discrimination. On enquiry after being twice passed over for promotion, he was told by the African medical director, 'Sorry, that is our policy now'.[54]

Despite these difficulties, which were perhaps more onerous for those in professions than for those in commerce, the Asian medical practitioners were able to perform a very valuable service in East Africa. They shared with Europeans the introduction of modern medicine. In their positions of prestige they also provided many social services, which included the establishment of hospitals, nursing homes, and dispensaries. In these ways, as in many others, the Asians, with Europeans, provided a transition while Africans were in training.

Unfortunately the transition in medicine was incomplete when Asians were expelled from Uganda and because of discriminatory policies began an exodus also from Kenya and Tanzania. The loss to Africa, as shown in the following instance, was considerable. Dr. Prabhakar Ramchandra Puram, who was born in Dar es Salaam, became an opthamologist and for several years performed eye surgery in government service on Africans in Iringa and Kilwa. In 1966, worried over his children's future, he left Tanzania in the prime of his career to begin a private practice in Poona, and with him went his wife, a gynecologist. His sister (another gynecologist), his father (a pharmacist), and his uncle (a physician) also moved to Poona.[55]

The Asian Teachers

Although they did not become, like the advocates and physicians, important public figures in politics, business, or philanthropy, the Asian teachers rendered a valuable service within their own profession. The principal beneficiaries of this service were the Asians, who through the colonial period provided all the initiative and most of the financial support in establishing and maintaining their schools. Most of these schools reflected the segregation of British colonialism in that they were restricted to Asians, but through the colonial period, even in the early years of the century, there were a number of experiments with multiracialism. After independence all the Asian schools were opened to students irrespective of race.

As in the other professions, Asian teachers became increasingly more numerous during the colonial years. As the British administrations emphasized the development of an educational system for the European communities, a comparatively large number of Europeans were attracted to the teaching profession, and not until the closing years of the colonial period was there a marked difference between the two communities. In 1948 the Asian teachers in Kenya, for instance, were listed as 297, the European teachers as 200. By 1960 the Asians had increased sevenfold to 2,067, but the Europeans less than fourfold to 731.[56] The comparative numbers throughout East Africa in primary and secondary schools shortly before independence are shown in Table 7.3.

These statistics reveal that the Asian teachers were far more numerous throughout East Africa than were the European. Although the proportion of Asians to Europeans in the overall population was approximately three to one, the teacher ratio was five to one. During the later colonial years a considerable number of Asian teachers were employed in the African schools, especially in secondary education, and the number greatly increased after independence as the racial barriers were removed. Unfortunately there is no published information on the Asians who taught Africans.

Through the colonial period the Asians were generally less well qualified than Europeans as teachers, and both immigrant groups were much better qualified than the Africans. With the approach of independence, however, the differences became less pronounced. As shown in Table 7.4, the overall qualifications of the Asian teachers in Uganda by 1960 were probably superior to those of the Europeans. There was a far higher percentage of Asian teachers with a college education.

No one community among the Asians seems to have predominated in teaching. It has been said that in the early years the Goans, because of their superior education, supplied most of the Asian teaching needs. It

TABLE 7.3   Teachers in East Africa by Racial Community, 1960

Community	Kenya	Tanganyika	Uganda	Totals
Asians	2,067	861	1,794	4,722
Europeans	731	167	67	965
Arabs et al.	139	83	?	202+
Africans	16,875	9,362	18,578	44,785+

Sources: Compiled from *Statistical Abstracts* of the three territories, 1961.

TABLE 7.4   Teaching Qualifications by Racial Community in Uganda, 1960

	Asians		Europeans		Africans	
Qualifications	No.	%	No.	%	No.	%
Higher education						
Trained for teaching	256	29	4	6	205	1
Untrained	85	9	–	–	69	0.4
Secondary school completion						
Trained	152	17	61	91	251	1
Untrained	324	36	2	3	785	4
Some secondary school or none						
Some training	–	–	–	–	11,215	60
Untrained	80	9	–	–	6,053	33

Source: Uganda, *1961 Statistical Abstract* (Entebbe: Government Printer, 1961), table UR.4, p. 114.

has also been said that the Gujaratis, Punjabis, and Mahratis were most important. Complete statistics are not available on the Asian teachers' communal affiliations, but it is known that in 1948 the Goans numbered 45 in a Kenya Asian teaching population of 297.[57]

Because of the unusual opportunities for financial success in business and the comparatively modest income expected from teaching, East Africa never supplied all the teachers it needed. Both the Asians and the governments had to seek additional recruits in India. As indicated in

Table 7.5, most Asian teachers in Uganda in 1960 and all those with a higher education were expatriates.[58]

The attraction of a position in East Africa to teachers in India is well illustrated by the Gujarati, Hariprasad Poonamchandra Joshi. He was born near Baroda into a family so poor that as a boy he had no shoes. Eventually, however, he attained three degrees from Bombay University: a B.A. with honours, an M.A., and a Bachelor of Teaching. In 1954 when he was earning a monthly salary of Rs 250 as a headmaster in the Gujarat, Joshi read an advertisement in a local newspaper for teachers in East Africa. He applied, was interviewed in Baroda by two representatives from Uganda—a European and an Asian—and within a year was in Jinja with a monthly salary of Shs 900, more than eight times the amount of his salary in India. Eighteen years later when Amin forced his departure from Uganda, Joshi was deputy headmaster of the Jinja Senior Secondary School serving some 2,300 students.[59]

Although their salaries were on the whole well below those of men, Asian women were attracted to teaching more than to the other professions. Like European and African women, they suffered from discrimination in the colonial society. The British civil service commission, headed by Sir Maurice Holmes, that visited the four East African dependencies in 1947–48 condoned the salary differences. It recommended that the salaries of Asian women teachers in government employment be four-fifths those of Asian men.[60]

One of the foremost Asian women was Probahini Das Gupta of Kampala. Born at Gaya in 1900 and the recipient of a B.A. degree from Calcutta, she was a teacher before accompanying her husband to East Africa. She became successively principal of the Nairobi Shia Imami Ismailia Girls School, lady principal of the Kampala Aga Khan High School, and headmistress of the Kampala Government Indian Senior Secondary School. She was also a founding member of the Kampala Indian Women's Association, president of the Uganda Council of Women, and member of the Advisory Council on Indian Education.[61]

Two other Uganda women with important careers in education were Rasila Vaikunthlal and Sarla Markandeya. From Ahmedabad where she matriculated, Vaikunthlal moved to Kampala in 1926 at age nineteen and devoted herself to the education of preschool children. She helped found the Nursery School of the Kampala Indian Women's Association and later became its president. She also was the first honourary secretary and later president of the Women's Association. Markandeya, who was born at Campbelpur, received B.A. and M.A. degrees from Lahore University and was a lecturer in philosophy at Fateh Chand College before moving to East Africa in 1949 with her husband, a physician. Becoming interested in children's early education, she soon went to England for

TABLE 7.5   Origin of Asian Teachers in Uganda, 1960

Qualification	Expatriate	Local	Total	% Expatriate
Higher education	341	–	341	100
Secondary completion	363	113	476	76
Some secondary or none	–	80	80	–
Totals	704	193	897	78

Source: Uganda, 1961 Statistical Abstract, table UR.4, p. 114.

nursery training and on return was appointed headmistress of the Nursery School of the Kampala Women's Association.[62]

In Nairobi Kantaben Patel, wife of the noted physician V. R. Patel, made a somewhat unique contribution to African adult education. Born in Uganda, a graduate of Cheltenham College and the Royal School of Arts, she was accomplished in needlework and gave exhibitions of her embroidery. She helped found the multi-racial Kenya Women's Society, which performed a variety of social services. Joining her husband in a close association with African nationalist leaders, she perceived a need among the wives not only for improving their English but also for training in managing a modern home, serving as hostess, and attending to the many social tasks required of wives of prominent administrators. Patel then combined with several European women in organizing classes and teaching the much-needed subjects.[63]

Some teachers who participated in the founding of schools faced extraordinary problems. A foremost example is G. G. Desai, a poorly qualified but very clever and ambitious teacher-administrator who became principal of the Naivasha Indian School. The school was begun in 1919 as the Ismaili School but changed its name at the insistence of the government in 1921 when it began to receive financial aid. It was a mixed primary school serving many different sects within the Asian community. It was a combined day and boarding school that charged boys Shs 4 per month and admitted girls free. In 1923 because of low enrollment, the school closed and was unable to reopen until 1927. Between then and 1934 its enrollment grew from twenty-one to forty-six, and it was during this time apparently that Desai was hired. He was for a time the sole teacher as well as the principal. Despite the government subsidy and the enrollment increase, the school in 1934 had suffered a financial loss for three years, and Desai in vain petitioned the government to assume the full financial burden. A year later his application for a teaching certificate was rejected on the ground that he lacked the requisite qualifications.[64]

Desai then resigned and founded a rival school, the Shree Vishnu Vidyarthi Ashram, styled himself proprietor and later principal, hired three qualified teachers, and applied for government aid. Situated at first in the Naivasha Hindu Temple and then in a building on the Central Bazaar Road, the school offered instruction in Gujarati and English through Standard Five and opened with twenty students described as Hindu, Muslim, and Khoja. Though at first rejected in his application for aid, Desai had his pupils examined by qualified Nairobi teachers at the end of the year, and the government, apparently impressed by the fact that nineteen of the twenty passed, conferred a grant-in-aid. Meanwhile the Naivasha Indian School, still lacking qualified teachers, lost its grant and languished. In 1938 Desai combined the two schools in the new premises under the name the Indian School and declared himself principal.[65]

Just when his success seemed assured, Desai fell out of favour with the Naivasha Indian School Committee, which set policy and controlled expenditure and appointments. The Hindu committee members, who had surpassed the original Ismailis in number, had split into two factions, and the majority refused to confirm Desai as principal. When another Asian was appointed to the position, Desai tendered his resignation, quit the teaching profession, and opened a tailoring shop in Naivasha.[66] Though a failure as a teacher, Desai had been instrumental in founding a school that eventually was to serve Africans as well as Asians. There must have been many like him among the pioneer teachers in East Africa.

Late in the colonial period Asian teachers began to be employed in token numbers in higher education. Through most of its history, Makerere University, which had begun as a technical college in 1921, had restricted its student body to Africans and its administrative and teaching staff to Europeans. After 1949 when it became a university college within a projected University of East Africa, Makerere moved towards a multiracial policy. By 1962, however, it was still predominantly European in its administration and faculty. Among the twenty-two members of the College Council, there was only one Asian, Al Noor Kassum. The thirty-five members of the Academic Board and the five deans were all Europeans. The seven administrative committees included only one Asian, and the five faculty boards only three. Among more than one hundred faculty there were two Asians in arts, two in science, seven in medicine, two in agriculture, and two in education, a total of only fifteen.[67]

Contrary to what most Asians anticipated, this situation did not improve after independence. Although there was an increasing number of

well-qualified Asians, the policies of the new governments were to replace expatriate and local European staff as far as possible with Africans.
In 1973 the University of Dar es Salaam, which, like the other university
colleges, had acquired a national status in 1970 with the dissolution of
the University of East Africa, had only 31 Asians in a faculty of approximately 300. In the important Department of Political Science, there was
not one Asian. In 1984 the University of Nairobi employed 5 Asians in an
administrative staff of 78. Among the 29 composing the University
Council, only one, a representative of the Gandhi Memorial Academy,
was an Asian, and in the Senate of nearly 100 individuals, only 3 were
Asians. The faculty included 58 Asians, less than 8 per cent, in a total of
763.[68]
   In comparison to those in other professions, the Asian teachers were
not so visible in East African society. They were not, like many of the
journalists, the leaders of social reform or African nationalism. Nor with
the possible exception of women, were they so prominent in public affairs as the doctors and advocates. The great majority were caught in the
onerous and time-consuming work of preparing lectures and marking
papers, and their chief interest was the intellectual growth of their students. Typical of many was P. N. Joshi of Thika. Born in Thika, he was
hired as one of the first teachers in the town's new primary school. For
nearly forty years until he retired in 1957, he taught in the same school,
but 'Thika's Mr. Chips', as he was known, is not listed in any *Who's Who.*[69]
   In this description of the leading advocates, physicians, dentists,
pharmacists, and teachers, it is clear that the Asians in professions, not
only the more affluent Asians in business, rendered a significant service
to the peoples of East Africa. Their contribution was twofold. On the one
hand, as professionals they provided a much-needed service to all peoples. The assistance to African nationalists by the advocates and the
medical care extended to Africans by the physicians were very important. On the other hand, in many capacities other than those associated
with their professions the Asians provided a variety of services. Law,
medicine, and teaching were foundations for philanthropy.

Notes

   1. George Delf, *Asians in East Africa* (London: Oxford University Press, 1963),
p. ix.
   2. H. K. Jaffer (grandson), interviewed by Bennett, 9, 13 May 1973, Mombasa.
A. Vellani (nephew), interviewed by Honey, 13, 14 Feb. 1974, Zanzibar. M. Behal,
interviewed by Honey, 12 Sept. 1973, Dar es Salaam.
   3. Note by Amritlal Raishi, encl. Bachulal Gathani (Nairobi) to Gregory, 13 Feb.
1986. Kenya, *Report on the Census of the Non-Native Population of Kenya Colony
and Protectorate Taken on the Night of the 25th Feb., 1948,* app. 12, pp. 114–18.

4. *Saben's Commercial Directory: Handbook of Uganda, 1960–61* (Kampala: Saben's Directories, 1961), end section, p. 30.

5. P. Majithia, interviewed by Gregory, 19 Feb. 1973, Dar es Salaam.

6. The list apparently excludes advocates who were not practising, for example, Benedicto K.M. Kiwanuka, who practised as a barrister in Uganda 1956–59 but then went into politics and from 1961–62 was independent Uganda's first prime minister. In 1970 with a supplementary list of advocates practising outside Nairobi and Mombasa, the *East African Law Journal* (Nairobi) added thirty-four Asians, seven Europeans, and nine Africans: vol. 6, no. 1 (March 1970).

7. H. A. Rahim, interviewed by Honey, 10 July 1973, Dar es Salaam. A. R. Kapila, interviewed by Gregory, 19 Jan. 1973, Nairobi.

8. A. R. Kapila interview. *East African Standard*, 19 June 1940, p. 7. Shanti Pandit, ed., *Asians in East and Central Africa* (Nairobi: Panco, 1961), pp. 89, 159.

9. A. B. Patel, interviewed by Gregory, spring 1956, Nairobi. Pandit, *Asians*, pp. 106, 207–8. J. M. Nazareth was one of the few Asians who published autobiographies: *Brown Man Black Country: A Peep into Kenya's Freedom Struggle* (New Delhi: Tidings, 1981). Interviewed by Gregory on numerous occasions, 1972–73, Nairobi.

10. A. J. Pandya, interviewed by Gregory, 2 Dec. 1972, 27 Feb., 1, 4 Mar. 1973, Mombasa; 17 Nov., 16 Dec. 1972, Nairobi. F.R.S. de Souza, interviewed by Gregory, 6 Feb. 1973, Nairobi. Pandit, *Asians*, pp. 126, 203.

11. C. B. Madan, interviewed by Gregory, 30 Jan. 1973, Nairobi. Chanan Singh, interviewed by Gregory, 22 Jan. 1973, Nairobi. Pandit, *Asians*, pp. 115, 175.

12. B. G. Vaghela and J. M. Patel, eds., *East Africa Today (1958–59): Comprehensive Directory of British East Africa with Who's Who* (Bombay: Overseas Information, 1959), p. 671. Pandit, *Asians*, p. 118.

13. E. G. Wilson, ed., *Who's Who in East Africa, 1965–66* (Nairobi: Marco, 1966), Tanzania section, p. 35.

14. Ibid., pp. 29, 81. M. N. Rattansey, interviewed by Honey, 12 Feb. 1974, Dar es Salaam. K. L. Jhaveri, interviewed by Honey, 20 Feb., 16 Mar. 1973, 23 Apr., 22 Nov. 1974, Dar es Salaam.

15. Awtar Singh, interviewed by Honey, 25 July 1973, Dar es Salaam. N. S. Patel, interviewed by Honey, 5 Mar., 7 Sept. 1933, Dar es Salaam.

16. H. Dharani, interviewed by Honey, 19 Oct., 2 Nov. 1973, Dar es Salaam.

17. A. N. Maini, interviewed by Gregory, 22 Nov. 1984, London. Vaghela and Patel, *East Africa Today*, p. 577. Pandit, *Asians*, pp. 175–76.

18. B.R.S. (Jimmy) Verjee (nephew), interviewed by Seidenberg, 10 Apr. 1973, Nairobi. Wilson, *Who's Who*, Uganda section, p. 117.

19. N. J. Madhvani (son), interviewed by Gregory, 12 June 1985, Nairobi. Robert Becker and Nitin Jayant Madhvani, eds., *Jayant Madhvani* (London: privately printed, 1973). H. P. Joshi, Bhanumati V. Kotecha, and J. V. Paun, eds., *Jayant Muljibhai Madhvani* (Nairobi: Emco Glass Works, 1973). Vaghela and Patel, *East Africa Today*, p. 577.

20. A. K. Patel (brother of C. K.), interviewed by Gregory, 6 July 1973, Baroda. S. G. Mehta, interviewed by Gregory, 10 July 1973, Rajkot. Wilson, *Who's Who*, Uganda section, p. 67. Vaghela and Patel, *East Africa Today*, p. 617.

21. N. T. Karia (a founder of the Uganda Action Group), interviewed by Gregory, 13 July 1973, Porbandar. R. G. Suraiya (uncle of Clerk), interviewed by Gregory, 21 June 1973, Bombay. Wilson, *Who's Who*, Uganda section, pp. 18, 110.

22. S. Mhando (re. Rattansey, Jhaveri, and Pritt), interviewed by Honey, 15 Mar. 1973, Dar es Salaam. N. Velji, interviewed by Gregory, 24 Aug. 1974, Syracuse. P. P. Sheth, interviewed by Gregory, 29 Jan. 1977, 27 July 1989, London. A. R. Kapila interview. For Amin, see Ambu H. Patel, comp., *Struggle for Release Jomo and His Colleagues* (Nairobi: Pan African Press, 1966), p. 178.

23. Expressed by Pritt in a letter to me shortly after the trial. Also by F.R.S. de Souza (interviewed 30 Jan., 6 Feb. 1973, Nairboi) and A. R. Kapila (interview). For a summary of the Asians' role see Dana April Seidenberg, *Uhuru and the Kenya Asians: The Role of a Minority Community in Kenya Politics* (New Delhi: Vikas, 1983), p. 115.

24. 'Secretary's Report', *Struggle for Release Jomo*, by Patel, p. 33. A. R. Kapila and F.R.S. de Souza interviews. Seidenberg, *Uhuru*, p. 116.

25. M. M. Patel, interviewed by Gregory, 8 Mar. 1973, Nairobi. A. Ghadialy, interviewed by Bennett, 13 Apr. 1973, Nyeri. Bhailal Patel, interviewed by Bennett, 2 May 1973, Nairobi. Seidenberg, *Uhuru*, p. 116.

26. H. Ribeiro (grandson), interviewed by Gregory, 26, 27 June 1973, Porvorim, Goa.

27. Dr. A. Ribeiro (son), interviewed by Gregory, 12 Nov. 1973, Nairobi. Pandit, *Asians*, pp. 91–92.

28. Note by Amritlal Raishi.

29. Ibid. *East African Standard*, 10 July 1953, p. 9.

30. Dr. S. D. Karve, interviewed by Gregory, 26 Feb. 1973, Nairobi. Pandit, *Asians*, pp. 162–63.

31. Vaghela and Patel, *East Africa Today*, p. 529. Wilson, *Who's Who*, Kenya section, p. 127.

32. Dr. Sood was visited by me in 1955 in Kisumu. Pandit, *Asians*, pp. 262–63.

33. Dr. Amir A. Alidina, interviewed by Gregory, 25 June 1988, Syracuse. Also, Amir's personal memoir, typed, submitted by Dr. Arif A. Alidina (son), interviewed by Gregory, 18 Jan. 1986, Syracuse.

34. G. J. Bhatt, interviewed by Bennett, 22 Mar. 1973, Nairobi.

35. Wilson, *Who's Who*, Uganda section, p. 597. Pandit, *Asians*, p. 223.

36. A. K. Patel, interviewed by Gregory, 6 July 1973, Baroda.

37. Ibid.

38. Ibid.

39. Ibid. Pandit, *Asians*, pp. 231–32.

40. *Pio Gama Pinto, Independent Kenya's First Martyr: Socialist and Freedom Fighter* (Nairobi: Pan African Press, 1968), p. 7. *East African Dental and Medical Directory, 1973* (Nairobi: East African Dental Association, 1973), p. 63. Dr. G. M. Daya, interviewed by Honey, 25 Jan. 1974, Dar es Salaam. *Who's Who in East Africa*, Tanzania section, p. 17. Vaghela and Patel, *East Africa Today*, pp. 515–16, 635. Jose Pio de Souza (brother), interviewed by Gregory, 26 June 1973, Porvorim, Bardez Goa. *East African Standard*, 29 Jan. 1910, p. 9.

41. Wilson, *Who's Who*, Kenya section, p. 123. A. J. Pandya interview.

42. Pandit, *Asians*, p. 196.

43. V. P. Vohra, interviewed by Seidenberg, 9 Apr. 1973, Nairobi. Wilson, *Who's Who*, Kenya section, p. 148.

44. B. A. Qureshi, interviewed by Seidenberg, 4 Apr. 1973, Nairobi. His principal article is 'Dentistry in Kenya', *I.C.D., Science Education Bulletin*, 4/1 (1972), 74–78. Note by Amritlal Raishi.

45. East African Directory Co., *Kenya, Uganda, Tanganyika and Zanzibar Directory*, Trade Index section, pp. 22–23.

46. J. S. Karmali, interviewed by Gregory, 10, 13 June 1985, Nairobi. Wilson, *Who's Who*, Kenya section, p. 52.

47. J. S. Karmali, *Birds of Africa* (London: Collins, 1980); J. S. Karmali, *Beautiful Birds of Kenya* (Nairobi: Westlands Sundries, 1985).

48. 'South Kavirondo District: Annual Report for the Year Ending 31st Dec., 1927', p. 1, Syracuse University microfilm 2801, reel 37. Ibid., '1930', p. 1, reel 37.

49. For a short history of Kenya medicine to 1936, see *Report of the Commission Appointed to Enquire into and Report on the Financial Position and System of Taxation of Kenya*, Colonial no. 116 (London: HMSO, 1936), pp. 190–3.

50. Kenya, *Report on the Census . . . 1948*, app. 12, pp. 114–18. *Kenya Population Census, 1962*, vol. 4, app. 8, p. 92. The term physicians, as used in this paragraph, includes surgeons.

51. The numbers of each race are approximations. Also, the totals are slightly larger than shown because the pharmacists in Tanzania were not named.

52. *East African Standard*, 15 Feb. 1908, p. 9, and 25 Jan. 1908, p. 9.

53. Ibid., 22 Feb. 1908, p. 9.

54. Arif A. Alidina interview.

55. Dr. P. R. Puram, interviewed by Gregory, 24 June 1973, Poona.

56. Kenya, *Report on the Census . . . 1948*, app. 12, pp. 114–18. Kenya, *Statistical Abstract, 1961* (Nairobi: Government Printer, 1961), table 155, p. 124.

57. Kenya, *Report on the Census . . . 1948*, app. 12, pp. 114–18. A. Ribeiro interview.

58. Uganda was the only dependency to provide statistics on origin.

59. H. P. Joshi, interviewed by Gregory, 6 July 1973, Baroda.

60. *Report of the Commission on the Civil Services of Kenya, Tanganyika, Uganda and Zanzibar, 1947–48*, Colonial no. 223 (London: HMSO, 1948), pp. 32, 74, 87.

61. Vaghela and Patel, *East Africa Today*, p. 603. Ibid., p. 165.

62. Ibid., p. 609.

63. Mrs. Patel, interviewed with her husband Dr. V. R. Patel, by Gregory, 5 July 1973, Baroda.

64. Correspondence pertinent to Desai is in file 'Education Private Schools; Asian Schools (Naivasha School), 1933–39', Rift Valley Province daily correspondence, Syracuse University microfilm 4752, reel 35.

65. Ibid.

66. Ibid.

67. *Makerere University Calendar, 1962–63*, pp. 1–16. *University of Dar es Salaam Calendar, 1973–74*.

68. *University of Nairobi Calendar, 1984/85*.

69. *East African Standard*, 18 Jan. 1964, p. 6.

CHAPTER EIGHT

————————— ■ —————————

Agriculture

The agricultural Indian is ... almost unknown in Kenya.

—Duke of Devonshire, 1923[1]

Asian planters [in Uganda] planted more than 60 per cent of the area under cultivation; and they further accounted for around two-thirds of the total production.

—R. R. Ramchandani, 1976[2]

Although farming was not their principal activity, the Asians, contrary to what is often assumed, exercised a considerable influence on the agricultural development of East Africa. Part of this influence, as explained in Chapter 2, was in the marketing of African cash crops, the expansion of road transport, the provision of basic industries essential to agriculture, and the extension of credit useful to both European and African producers. The Asians also exerted an influence as farmers in their own right. Their influence on agricultural development was certainly not so important as that of the Europeans or Africans. The Asians were, however, primarily responsible for the introduction and cultivation of sugar; they took over from the Arabs much of the clove production; and, near the end of the colonial period, they began to compete with Europeans in the production of coffee, tea, and sisal. To many observers they appeared to have the potential for a far greater contribution, and the governments through most of the colonial years seriously considered plans for extensive Asian farming communities. Surprisingly, among all the scholars who have considered the agricultural history of East Africa, only one, the Indian historian R. R. Ramchandani, has recognized the Asians' agricultural importance.[3]

As illustrated in the description of their background in South Asia, most Asians who immigrated to the mainland territories in the early years were peasant farmers. Most of the Sikhs and Hindus imported to construct the Uganda Railway and serve in other public works came as unskilled labourers from the poorer agricultural areas of the Punjab. Most of the Shahs, Patels, Lohanas, and others—the Jains and Hindus of the Gujarat and Kutch—came from the agricultural villages. The Muslims also, the Bohras, Memons, and even the Ismailis and Ithnasheris, were largely of peasant background.

The fact that nearly all these Asians did not resume agricultural pursuits is explained chiefly by the new economic opportunities they found in East Africa. As noted in Chapter 1, their exclusion from the White Highlands of Kenya, though often cited by Asian politicians as the main reason, was relatively unimportant. The Sikhs and Punjabi Hindus who remained in East Africa at the end of their contractual obligations found it more rewarding to practise their new skills in carpentry, masonry, blacksmithing, and mechanics than to compete with Europeans, Arabs, and eventually Africans in cash-crop production. The early free immigrants—Muslims, Hindus, and Jains—readily fell into the pattern of the coastal traders who had preceded them by engaging in the importation and sale of foreign commodities and the purchase and exportation of local produce. Later immigrants, most of whom were also from peasant backgrounds, joined relatives or other village associates who had already established themselves in crafts or trade. For the great majority the course to economic improvement was initially business rather than agriculture. As early as 1902 J. L. Montgomery, who was to become the East Africa Protectorate's first commmissioner for land, had noted, 'If the agriculturists come, they generally turn into traders. We have very few people who seem to wish to take up agriculture'.[4]

Visions of an Extensive Asian Settlement

The attraction of trade to the early Asian immigrants was not appreciated by the administrators of the new dependencies in East Africa. During 1890–92 in establishing the Imperial British East Africa Co.'s claim to Uganda, Frederick D. Lugard repeatedly noted in his diary the unique opportunity for Asian agricultural settlements along the trade routes. In *The Rise of Our East African Empire*, published in 1893, he forecast that 'the simple implements of the Indian *ryot*, the use of the bullock, the sinking of wells, the system of irrigation and of manuring the soil, &c., would soon be imitated by the African, and the produce of his land would thus be vastly multiplied'.[5] Subsequently Lugard, J.R.L. Macdonald, and Sir Gerald Portal, the foremost authorities on the route to Uganda, all included the desirability of Asian agricultural settlement in their arguments for construction of a railway.[6] It was thus for Asian as well as European settlement that the rails were laid through the most fertile areas of the highlands.

The idea of an Asian agricultural settlement had many prominent supporters apart from Lugard, Macdonald, and Portal. In the early 1890s Jairam Sewji, the influential and wealthy Zanzibar Asian, proposed a mainland settlement financed by private capital. Attracted by the prospect, officials from German East Africa approached the British Foreign Office in 1894 with a view to obtaining Asian artisans as well as agriculturists. In 1899 and 1900 the Germans again pressed their case, this time with the support of the Aga Khan, for a scheme of Asian immigration. Among those urging an Asian settlement in the British territories were George Mackenzie, former director of the Imperial British East Africa Co., General W. H. Manning, former acting commissioner of the British Central Africa Protectorate, and George Whitehouse, chief engineer of the Uganda Railway.[7]

The British government eventually was persuaded. In 1900 the Foreign Office approached the India Office on the subject, and between 1900 and 1902 Lord Salisbury and his successor as secretary of state for foreign affairs, Lord Lansdowne, urged the protectorate governments to implement settlement schemes.[8] The Permanent Secretary Sir Clement L. Hill remarked, 'We are rather looking to India for our East African system and development'.[9] The initial response from Africa was favourable. In the East Africa Protectorate the Acting Commissioner C. H. Craufurd and then the successive commissioners Sir Arthur Hardinge and Sir Charles Eliot all were supportive. In Uganda Commissioner Sir Harry H. Johnston was enthusiastic.[10]

By 1902 opinion had changed in the British territories. The East Africa Protectorate had begun its policy of encouraging European settlement in the highlands. In January Eliot, having changed his view, recommended that Asians be excluded from the highlands, and by July he was openly remarking that 'the claims of the Europeans should be 'paramount'.[11] As early as January 1902 the European settlers had formed a committee to assert that 'the further immigration of Asiatics into this country is entirely detrimental to the European settler in particular and to the native inhabitant generally'.[12] So began the intense settler pressure that successfully precluded Asian settlement in the highlands. In 1908 the practice of excluding Asians was proclaimed as official policy by Lord Elgin, secretary of state for the colonies, and in 1915 the sale or lease of highlands property by Europeans to Asians or Africans was made subject to veto by a Crown Lands Ordinance.[13]

The alienated area, the White Highlands, was gradually expanded until its final delimitation in 1938–39, when it included nearly 7.5 million acres. About 4.1 million acres of the whole became plantations and cattle ranches with the remainder devoted to mixed farming. The land, however, was never to be fully utilized. A survey in 1942 showed that almost one million acres of the estate land was totally undeveloped and that much of the rest was 'very much under-developed'.[14]

In Uganda a policy designed to safeguard the interests of Africans rather than Europeans proved almost equally detrimental to Asian agriculture. By the Uganda Agreement of 1900, approximately 9,000 square miles of the best agricultural land were reserved for the kabaka of Buganda and his several chiefs. Under legislation in 1906 and 1908 the Ganda were prohibited from selling or leasing land to non-Africans without the consent of both their council of chiefs (*Lukiko*) and the governor. Outside Buganda similar restrictions made the acquisition of land very difficult for Asians. The Crown Lands Ordinance of 1903 required the secretary of state's permission for any grant by the government to non-Africans of freehold of more than 1,000 acres. In 1909 the secretary of state forbade Africans to transfer land of similar size to non-Africans without his prior consent. By 1915 only 20,000 acres had been planted by non-Europeans.[15]

As a result of the changing attitudes, the British government fostered only a small-scale settlement of Asian agriculturists in East Africa. The site was at Kibos, a railway stop in the lowlands of the Nyanza basin just north of Kisumu. In 1903 the East Africa Protectorate entrusted the task to a newly-appointed protector of immigrants, D. D. Waller, and he 'collected the waifs and strays who were willing to stay in the country', about thirty Asians, 'mostly people who were odds and ends left over from the Uganda Railway'.[16] He also directed the land survey, allotted the plots, gave financial assistance, and oversaw the planting of rice, cotton, sesame, and linseed on what he described as 'excellent black soil'.[17]

Encouraged by the experiment, the government explored the possibility of settling Asians in other areas that were unattractive to Europeans. In 1906 it appointed a Committee on Indian Immigration that, after a detailed study, recommended the settlement of Asian agriculturists in the lowlands between the coast and Kiu and between Fort Ternan and Lake Victoria. As a first step towards implementation, the governor sent Waller to India to recruit fifteen more families for Kibos. In a tour of Bihar, Madras, Bombay, and the Central Provinces Waller failed to attract any recruits. He found that suitable families were reluctant to leave India, and he met opposition from British officials who were unwilling to encourage emigration of the more successful farmers. Waller was convinced that the only recourse was to import more indentured labourers who at the end of their contracts might be induced to take up farming.[18] The government did nothing, however, to increase the number of indentured Asians.

For three decades despite lack of further government support, the Kibos settlement grew steadily and served as an example of the productiv-
ity of small-scale Asian agriculture. The residents steadily increased
from a low point in 1907 when they included only four Punjabi families
situated on 600 acres. In 1933 there were fifty-five landowners with
10,935 acres. They had 11 tractors, 150 ploughs, 1,512 work oxen, and
261 head of cattle. Although they had experimented with a variety of
crops, they had turned by 1933 exclusively to sugar-cane and maize.
Their production that year of 13,895 tons of cane and 725 tons of maize
represented a remarkably high yield. Their efficient use of the land, cultivating 7,645 acres, approximately 70 per cent of their total holding, differed markedly from that of the Europeans, who had only some 5 per
cent under cultivation, and afforded the Asian politicians reason to criti-
cize the Europeans' monopoly of the highlands. The fact that the Kibos
settlers resided in an area densely populated by Africans but never had
any trouble with their neighbours was also a source of pride to the
Asians.[19]

The Kibos settlement ceased to expand after 1933 and, like most of
the other Asian economic ventures, sharply declined shortly after independence. During the colonial period the Asian cultivators were prohibited from purchasing additional land from the surrounding Africans.
The farmers felt betrayed by the government. In 1933 through their organization, the Nyanza Farmers' Association, they complained to the
Carter Land Commission that the government had either ignored their
frequent requests for additional land or offered land at prohibitive
prices. By 1963 there were still fewer than sixty farms from 50 to 1,000
acres in size. Each then employed on the average about eight permanent
labourers and from twenty to thirty seasonal workers. After independence the Asians were gradually bought out by the large sugar firms, and
one by one they left the area.[20]

The initial success of the Kibos experiment and the Asians' intense resentment over their exclusion from the Kenya highlands prompted colonial authorities in Britain as well as East Africa after 1903 to consider the
establishment of sizeable Asian agricultural settlements in the lowlands
of Kenya and Uganda. Some Asian leaders responded with enthusiasm.
In 1905 the Aga Khan visited the East Africa and Uganda Protectorates
and offered, if given a suitable area of land, to introduce a large number
of Asian agriculturists. In 1908 following a tour of East Africa, Winston
Churchill, under secretary of state for the colonies, advocated opening
the lowlands for Asian settlement. Soon afterwards the Uganda governor, Sir H. Hesketh Bell, endorsed a request from the wealthy trader Allidina Visram for land in Busoga on which to settle Asians at his own
expense. The widespread interest in such a project prompted the secre-

tary of state for the colonies, Lord Crewe, to appoint in 1909 a parliamentary committee on emigration from India to the crown colonies. After examining eighty-three witnesses—nearly every knowledgeable person except Churchill—the Sanderson Committee recommended extensive settlement of Asians in the lowlands, especially in the area round Kibos, and accepted Waller's thesis that the immigrants would have to be indentured.[21]

Because of European opposition and diminishment of official interest following changes in personnel, the recommendations remained in abeyance until after World War I. During the war the possibility that German East Africa might be transferred to the government of India at the war's end and administered as an Indian colony added a new dimension to the issue of Asian immigration, and it became an important political concern in the early 1920s. Although it diverted attention from a special lowlands settlement, the colony issue also kept the lowlands consideration alive. The two proposals appeared as alternative solutions to the problem of Asian exclusion from the Kenya highlands.

The widespread interest in an Indian colony prompted a revival of the lowlands issue in 1919. In February the under secretary of state for the colonies, Leopold S. Amery, proposed to the India Office that certain areas of the former German territory and the adjacent British protectorate be reserved for Asian agriculture. He suggested beginning with a settlement of Indian ex-soldiers and their families after experts from India had examined the land. Though strongly endorsed by the India Office and received favourably by the Indian government, the proposal eventually was rejected for the same reasons as an Indian colony. Two investigators sent by the Indian government reported unfavourably. The climate, they claimed, was unhealthy and malarial, the land was too arid, and the prevalence of tsetse fly precluded use of the Indian bullock. The local Asian leaders, they found, preferred a policy of equal treatment to that of an exclusive Asian settlement, and Sir Horace Byatt, civil administrator of the former German territory, had allied with the Europeans in opposition. In India several provincial administrators opposed emigration of agriculturists, and Gandhi and his two lieutenants specially concerned with East Africa, Charles F. Andrews and Henry S.L. Polak, contended that any scheme for Asian or European privilege was inimical to African interests. In February 1921 after two years of intense controversy, a dispatch from the viceroy terminated further consideration of Amery's proposal.[22]

Although the movement for an Indian colony was at an end, the possibility of an Asian agricultural settlement in the lowlands continued to attract attention through the 1920s and into the 1930s. In his White Paper of July 1923 the Duke of Devonshire upheld the highlands reservation and stated that a lowlands area would be reserved temporarily for Asians to determine their agricultural demand.[23] Accordingly in March 1924 the Kenya governor, Sir Robert Coryndon, informed the East Africa Indian National Congress that he had 'earmarked provisionally' two lowland areas for Asian occupation: one of 100,000 acres south of the Tana River, the other of 1,000,000 acres between the Voi-Taveta Railway and the Tsavo River. Neither, he stated, would affect African interests.[24] Early in 1925 the East Africa Indian National Congress sent a party to look at the land and then asked for evaluation by an expert from India. Though urged by the Colonial Office and the India Office to comply, the Indian government, after a negative recommendation from its Standing Emigration Committee, refused.[25]

During the late 1920s an Asian agricultural settlement continued to attract attention in East Africa, Britain, and India, but the repeated requests by the Congress for examination by experts from India and for a survey by the Kenya government proved in vain. By 1933 when the Kenya land question in its entirety was examined by the Carter Commission, the Congress, because of humanitarian influences, had drastically changed its stance. To the commission it suggested that no more crown land be transferred either to Asians or Europeans and that all alienated land not under cultivation be returned to the Africans.[26]

The movement for a sizeable agricultural settlement involving new immigrants from India terminated in 1934 with the report of the Kenya Land Commission. Afterwards neither the Colonial Office nor the governments in East Africa were willing to contemplate any new stimulus to Asian immigration. In 1941 an Indian Land Settlement Board was appointed in India to prepare a settlement scheme for consideration by the government. In response the Kenya government in 1945 issued a sessional paper declaring that there could be no question of Asian immigration into Kenya for settlement purposes.[27]

After 1934 there were only two attempts in East Africa, one in Tanganyika and the other in Kenya, to establish Asian farming communities, but both involved settlement of Asians who were already in the territories. In 1950 to increase the exportation of cash crops, the Tanganyika government made available near Kilosa approximately sixty parcels averaging about 500 acres each to resident Asians who had a successful farming background. The government donated the land and through a Land Bank provided advances up to Shs 100,000 at a low 5 per cent interest. The Asians themselves had to clear the land, which was heavily forested, and to provide water for irrigation. They were free to select the crops but had to sell their produce to the government. The S. L. Patel family was probably typical of those who participated. The family, which had a flour mill business in Dar es Salaam and had previously raised vegetables, maize, and sugar-cane in Kilosa, obtained three of the parcels and later purchased a fourth. Employing on each farm from fifty to sixty Africans, the Patels grew sorghum, sunflower, and maize. Some others also grew cotton. Despite a shortage of water, the experiment in the early years was very successful.[28]

A different result occurred in Kenya. In 1952–53 the government tried to found a small settlement of Asians and Arabs on the coast, and it actually trained eight Asians, but the project failed for want of a single applicant.[29]

Early Farming Experiments

Apart from the organized settlements, a small number of the early Asian immigrants, apparently on their own initiatives, moved directly into agriculture either on arrival in East Africa or after serving their indentures. Most settled on farming plots close to the railway stops where they raised vegetables and fruit to sell in the new towns. Nairobi, Makindu, and Mazeras have been mentioned as having a number of these Asian market gardeners, and it is not coincidental that the Nairobi Public Market was conceived and built by A. M. Jeevanjee.[30] Some Asians moved into more rural areas, especially in Ukamba and Kavirondo, where they were encouraged by government officers to experiment with cash crops. 'As they do so', remarked a Kisumu official in 1906, 'they will be an object lesson for the different natives near them, and the influence will spread'.[31] Until 1905 when non-European settlement was definitely barred, a few Asians and Africans occupied land in the highlands. One of the pioneer Asian settlers, Mohammed Hanif, received a ten-acre farm there in 1900.[32]

For several reasons most of these settlements did not endure. In 1909 the Nairobi Asian growers—'shambawallas' as they were called—complained that they were being driven by European settlers from the banks of the Nairobi River. The following year there was a concerted attempt to exclude the Asians from the Nairobi marketplace.[33] After World War I the government officers began to discourage Asian activity in the reserves, and the 1915 prohibition of transfers of settler land to non-Africans gradually precluded the continuation of Asian farming in the highlands. There was also the lure of business that in East Africa was far more profitable than small-scale farming. African competitors, even at this early time, may also have been influential. After World War II they were to drive nearly all the Asian market gardeners out of business.

Most Asians who took up agriculture were primarily concerned with other endeavours. Among the early landowners on Zanzibar was Shapurji B. Sidhwa, who in the 1890s became engineer-in-charge of the

Sultan's Electric Works. He bought 2,000 acres on which he planted 43,800 clove trees, 40,400 coconut palms, and approximately 900 fruit trees. On the mainland one of the earliest was Mehta Pratap Singh, a Rajput from Kathiawar who arrived in the 1870s in the Omani sultan's mainland domain. After several years of trading with the Maasai near Arusha, he bought a large tract of land at Tanga and settled as a planter, businessman, and contractor. While adding to his holdings, he experimented with the importation of farm animals from India. Y. A. Khanbhai's life was similar. He settled on the coast opposite Zanzibar in 1836 and began to trade in local produce. He eventually developed an extensive business along the coast and bought many properties including a coconut plantation.[34]

Another pioneer, Allidina Visram, acquired plantations while developing his vast trading empire in the East Africa and Uganda Protectorates. By 1904 he had seven large plantations on which, in co-operation with the governments, he experimented with sugar, cotton, rubber, tea, grains, pulses, fruit, and flowers to find the most profitable crops. He employed about 3,000 African farm labourers who enjoyed, it is said, 'residential and social amenities' far superior to those obtaining on other plantations. At a Coast Products Exhibition held in Mombasa in 1907, Visram presented a large display not only of his own but also of Africans' produce. The following year a sample of the rubber he had developed was placed on exhibit in the Imperial Institute.[35]

Though less important to agricultural development than Visram, many other Asians acquired agricultural land in the early years of British rule. Successful businessmen invested in Arab coastal properties to the degree that the Europeans became alarmed. Most vocal was Ewart S. Grogan, one of the largest landowners, who strongly condemned the Asians' growing agricultural involvement.[36] In 1903 when an estate of nearly 140 acres within the Nairobi township was purchased at auction by a local Asian firm following bankruptcy by the previous settler-owner, there was an uproar from local Europeans. On Zanzibar as on the Kenya coast Asians increasingly invested in land. Typical perhaps was the Bohra Hassanali family that in 1910 after a generation of developing a hardware business in Zanzibar began to purchase Arab plantations on the island and along the coast adjacent to Mombasa.[37]

Much of the Arab and Swahili land was acquired by Asian merchants who, as explained in Chapter 2, extended credit in purchasing cash crops and in many instances when the owners were unable to pay, foreclosed and assumed title to the land. Having developed their plantations with slave labour, the Arabs were severely affected by abolition, and in the free economy of the early colonial years they were, as a whole, unable to compete with the other planters. Although European and African producers of cash crops also in times of hardship became indebted to the Asians, they were protected in retention of their land by legal prohibitions on interracial transfer in the highlands and the reserves. Thus with slight exception in the early decades, it was only the Arab and Swahili property that passed to the Asians.

Acquisition of Estates Between the Wars

On Zanzibar a crisis over the assumption of Arab land by Asians arose in the 1930s. By then the Asians had become the main producers of cloves, the mainstay of the Zanzibar economy, and virtually monopolized the clove-exporting market. European planters had also been acquiring Arab land, and together with European exporters they obtained the government's support in a move to oust the Asians and assume the dominant position. Between 1931 and 1934 five commissions investigated the problem of Arab indebtedness. Reporting that a large proportion of the clove property had been acquired by the Asians—estimates varied from 5 to more than 50 per cent—the commissioners impugned the Asians' system of credit and called for drastic reform.[38]

In June 1934 the protectorate issued six decrees aimed at improving the clove industry, alleviating the Arabs' financial burden, and restraining the Asians' economic activity. The decrees raised an existing European organization, the Clove Growers' Association, to a quasi-government agency and granted it exclusive authority to deal in agricultural produce, store cloves, manage estates, and lend money to growers. The decrees required the licensing of all exporters and the keeping of accounts in one of several specified languages, none of which was Gujarati. They also placed a one-year moratorium on Arab and African mortgage debts and permitted the courts to reopen any transaction involving credit to Arabs or Africans and to provide equitable relief.[39]

Viewing the decrees as primarily an attempt to transfer control of the clove industry to European growers and exporters, the Asians raised a storm of protest. Accusing the government of racial discrimination, the Indian National Association of Zanzibar stated that the decrees would compel most Asians to leave the country. The real reason for Arab indebtedness, it asserted, was, aside from the global depression, the high taxation and export duty on cloves. The association appealed to Asian organizations in Britain and India for aid. In India the Zanzibar problem assumed major political proportions and became for a time a focal point of nationalist demands. The Aga Khan, Sarojini Naidu, Jawaharlal Nehru, Valabhbhai Patel, Gandhi, Andrews, and many others roused a national concern. The Servants of India Society, National Liberal Federation, Imperial Indian Citizenship Association, Federation of Indian

Chambers of Commerce and Industry, and eventually the Indian National Congress all sought withdrawal of the decrees. In Britain the Indians Overseas Association, headed by Polak, echoed their demands.[40]

Although two commissions from India and one from Britain made further investigations, and the Indian government and the India Office recommended altering the decrees, the Zanzibar government, backed by the Colonial Office, remained adamant. It extended the moratorium on mortgage debts and issued further restrictive decrees. In desperation the Zanzibar Asians undertook a passive resistance campaign against compliance with the decrees, and the people of India, responding to a call from the Indian National Congress, imposed a nationwide embargo and boycott on the importation, sale, and use of cloves.[41]

By May 1938, ten months after the inception of passive resistance and the clove boycott, when the economy of Zanzibar was in ruins, the government entered into an agreement with the local Asians whereby it withdrew the Clove Growers' Association's monopoly and other discriminatory features of the decrees.[42] The two-year crisis, representing the greatest interest ever taken by India in East Africa, was at an end. After 1938 the Asian traders resumed the influential position they had previously held in Zanzibar, and the Asian planters continued to produce the major share of the island's cloves.

On the mainland Asian agricultural activity received a stimulus from the sale of German property at the end of World War I. At first Asians were barred from participation, and it was only through intervention by the Indian government that they were permitted equality with Europeans in bidding at the auctions. The scheduled sales were then widely publicized in East Africa and India. At the first sale in May 1921 Asians bought at least 15 of the 40 business lots auctioned in Dar es Salaam, and their purchases amounted to more than £50,000 in a total of £112,000. At the second sale in June the Asians obtained all but one or two of the twenty-three pieces of property that included plantations and *shambas* as well as business plots.[43]

At subsequent sales the Asians continued to buy a large proportion of the auctioned property. By June 1924 when only 96 township plots and 97 farms remained for sale, Europeans had purchased 301 parcels worth £494,000, Asians 239 parcels worth £332,000, and Asians in partnership with other nationals 11 parcels worth £72,000. Karimjee Jivanjee & Co., the largest Asian concern in Tanganyika, was the foremost buyer not only of business plots but also of coffee and sisal plantations. In 1925 when the Germans were permitted to return, some former owners repurchased their estates from Asians, but other Germans took posts as plantation managers under large Asian concerns. By 1936 British Indians had acquired 316,024 acres of agricultural and pastoral land in Tanganyika compared to 676,086 by British Europeans, 447,065 by Germans, 97,017 by Christian missions, 48,930 by South African Dutch, and 372,513 by others including Goans. The Asians thus had more than 16 per cent of the alienated land. Nearly all this was former German property as the British government before World War II transferred very little land to Europeans and Asians.[44]

Between the wars the Asians in Tanganyika competed mainly with British, Greeks, and Germans in estate production. The British were in coffee and sisal, the Greeks largely in sisal, and the Germans in coffee. The Asians were mainly in sisal and by 1939 are said to have owned 20 per cent of the sisal estates. The Karimjee family, the largest Asian landowner, had about twenty sisal properties in the vicinity of Tanga, which were managed principally by Abdulla Karimjee Jivanjee. Other pioneers in sisal were Taibali Essaji Sachak, who in 1920 bought sisal plantations at Ngombezi, Gombe, and Ngomeni, and Hassanali Nasser Virjee, who in 1922 purchased the only estate, some 450 acres, at Mwanza. Among Asians who came from outside to invest in Tanganyika agriculture were the Sachoo family from Mombasa, headed by Vilanali Sachoo, which bought and leased sisal estates, and the Kotecha family from Jinja, which through its parent company Damodar Jinabhai & Co. Ltd. also acquired sisal property. Another, as explained in the following paragraphs, was Nanji Kalidas Mehta. Among the few who grew crops other than sisal was S. L. Patel, who joined six other Asians about 1938 to establish a mechanized farm in Kilosa producing vegetables, maize, and sugarcane. There were also some Asians in Kilosa who grew cotton.[45]

During the same period the Asians were beginning an extensive agricultural development in Uganda primarily because of the initiatives of two individuals, Nanji Kalidas Mehta and Muljibhai Prabhudas Madhvani. Both were Lohanas of peasant stock from small villages—Mehta, as has been stated, from the area of Porbandar in Saurashtra, Madhvani from near Bileshwar in Saurashtra. Both were in the process of building fortunes in trade and the ginning of cotton when they became interested in agriculture and the sugar industry.

Mehta, whose trading activities are discussed in Chapter 2, became interested in agriculture shortly after joining his brother in a trade with Africans north of Jinja. As early as 1908 when the government was experimenting with Egyptian cotton, Mehta planted the India variety in back of his shop. It was the purchase and exportation of African cotton, however, that soon absorbed his interest, and from that, as explained in Chapter 9, he proceeded to ginning. In 1920 from an African chief he bought his first agricultural land, 2,000 acres between Kampala and Jinja, on which he did no more, apparently, than build a cottage. The next year, however, when German estates began to be auctioned in Tanganyika, Mehta purchased six sisal plantations, the first four totalling 22,000 acres, in Lindi, Mikindani, Tanga, and Dar es Salaam. In 1924 he transferred these to his brother in order to concentrate on the cultivation and manufacture of sugar. Two years earlier he had bought 4,000 acres at Lugazi, midway between Jinja and Kampala, and had begun to plant cane. The property was swamp land that the government had dismissed as worthless. Within two years Mehta opened at Lugazi the first sugar factory in Uganda.[46]

Subsequently Mehta established a reputation as a foremost agriculturist as well as industrialist. His sugar estate at Lugazi was to grow to 22,000 acres and remain the largest in Uganda. It employed, as he wrote in 1961, 'hundreds of tractors for mechanised farming, latest road transport system and modern machineries'.[47] While pioneering in sugar, Mehta moved to the cultivation of other crops. In 1934 he obtained permission to plant tea on 1,000 acres, eventually 2,000 acres, near Lugazi. Until then the cultivation of tea had been prohibited to all except Europeans. Mehta also began in 1934 to grow sisal on 4,000 acres on the banks of the Nile at Port Masindi. In beginning his plantations, he said, he brought from the Barada region of India two thousand Maher 'and other sturdy people' as 'a contingent of able-bodied loyal men who could work hard' and provide essential 'supervision' of the African labour he intended to train. At Lugazi he established a model agricultural and factory community with a hospital, sports grounds, clubs, and a school for 500 children.[48]

Mehta's career was closely paralleled by that of Muljibhai Madhvani. Born in 1894, five years younger than Mehta, Madhvani also sailed alone to East Africa when very young, age twelve, to join his brother who worked for Vithaldas Haridas & Co., one of the pioneering trading firms in Uganda. After three years he moved from Iganga to the head office in Jinja. Quickly rising in the firm and assuming the principal management, he expanded the company's trade into Kenya and Tanganyika and added ginning and agriculture to its activities. Through Vithaldas Haridas and other companies Madhvani planted coffee, then sugar and sisal, and gradually diversified into a wide range of farm-based industries in jaggery and refined sugar, oil and soap, maize flour, beer, cigarettes, and cattle feed. By 1946 when Vithaldas Haridas was dissolved, he was managing director of five companies. He then founded his own parent concern, Muljibhai Madhvani & Co. Ltd.[49]

Although he was to own sugar and sisal estates in Kenya and tea plantations in Uganda, Madhvani concentrated on cultivating and manufacturing sugar at Kakira, six miles from Jinja. Remarkably similar to Mehta's Lugazi, Kakira in 1936 consisted of 10,542 acres, Lugazi of 10,842. By 1958 when Madhvani died, Kakira had expanded to 22,400 acres, of which 19,000 were under sugar-cane. It was owned and managed by Madhvani's Uganda (Kakira) Sugar Works Ltd. and, like Lugazi, had its own factory together with health, educational, and recreational facilties. It even had its own railway with 100 miles of track and 17 diesel and 4 steam locomotives. Among it employees were 400 Asians and 12,000 Africans.[50]

Mehta and Madhvani were not the only Uganda Asians engaged in agriculture between the wars. By 1925 when Europeans had 160 estates and 24,414 acres under cultivation, the Asians owned 31 estates and had planted a total of 6,330 acres, of which 3,182 were in coffee, 2,696 in sugar-cane, 1,745 in rubber, and 552 in other crops. During the ensuing decade, especially in the depression years, an increasing number of Asians bought European estates that were producing mainly coffee or rubber. By 1933 there were 46 Asian agricultural properties comprising 42,512 acres in comparison to 219 European holdings of 101,949 acres. The Asians thus had 16.6 per cent of the estates and 29.4 per cent of the acreage. The actual land under cultivation—14,863 acres for the Asians compared to 22,986 for the Europeans—attests even more to the growing importance of Asian agriculture. By 1935 the Asians' total acreage under cultivation had risen to 21,306 and the Europeans' had fallen to 22,564. This trend continued with the result that by 1938 Asians owned 60 per cent of the total estate acreage under cultivation.[51]

A number of the new Asian agriculturists followed the Mehtas and Madhvanis in planting sugar. One of the foremost was Indra Singh Gill, the Sikh entrepreneur who, as described in Chapter 6, planted cane on the 600 acres cleared near Iganga in his lumber business. Although he continued his agricultural interests, it was in industry that he was to make his fortune.[52]

Among the Asians who cultivated crops other than sugar in Uganda were Mohamedali Rattansi, Vallabhdas Kalidas Radia, Rambhai Somabhai Patel, and Jamal Walji. After immigrating to East Africa in 1902, Rattansi worked for Allidina Visram and later Osman Allu. In 1927 he bought land near Masaka and planted it in tea. Patel founded the Central Cotton Trading Co. (Uganda) Ltd. in 1921, seven years after leaving India, and invested in two ginneries at Kikoma and Kiziba. He soon extended the business into the planting of coffee and cotton. Walji, who had come to Entebbe in 1904, founded a retail store, then moved to Hoima, branched into other centres, and like many others devoted his profits to the purchase of ginneries. In 1941, forming a subsidiary of his original firm, Jamal Walji & Co. Ltd., he bought plantations to cultivate coffee and rubber at Kalungu and establish a tea factory.[53]

Though not so important as in Uganda or the other territories between the wars, Asian agriculture was far more extensive in Kenya than has been assumed. The Asians continued to be active on the coast, where they were purchasing not only Arab land but also plantations that had been developed by Europeans. After the Europeans' exclusive right to the highlands was confirmed, many European companies and individuals sold their coastal lands to concentrate on estates 'up country'. In some years more of this land was transferred to Asians than Europeans. In 1935, for instance, the land acquired by Asians in the Coast Province was valued at £6,468 and that by Europeans at only £2,617. Among the coastal landowners during the interwar years was the Ismaili Kassim Lakha family which after 1870 had become prominent in business and agriculture on Zanzibar and then on Lamu and at Kisumu. Aziz R. Kassim Lakha was one of the first to cultivate cashews as a cash crop on the Kenya coast. Another Asian, S. L. Patel, who had entered East Africa in 1929, combined the farming of vegetables with managing a hotel in Mombasa before undertaking the previously described agricultural venture in Tanganyika. Though concentrating on Uganda, the Madhvani family between the wars purchased a European sugar-cane estate and factory on 1,000 acres at Ramisi, forty miles south of Mombasa. They managed the new estate through the Kenya Sugar Co., a subsidiary of Vithaldas Haridas.[54]

Asians also continued agricultural activity in other areas of Kenya. At the end of World War I some Indian soldiers were awarded land in Nyanza Province. A select list of Kenya estates in 1936 shows that coffee was raised by the Goans G. Perlo at Manira and J. H. and C. Sequeira at Makuyu. Among the sisal growers was Dwa Plantations Ltd. at Ndi, and among those planting tea was Jamji Estates at Kericho. One of the new landowners near Kisumu was Hasham Jamal, an Ismaili pioneer who had come to East Africa in 1900 to work for Allidina Visram. After the war, having established a chain of stores throughout East Africa selling produce and buying hides and skins, Jamal purchased 200 acres in Muhoroni, planted it in cane, and began to produce jaggery. Another sugar planter, Prahlad Singh Grewal, had started as a telegrapher on entering Kenya in 1929 and then developed a timber and transport business. In 1932 he bought a European sugar estate and factory, the Manoni Sugar Factory, at Kibwezi and began manufacturing jaggery. By the end of the colonial period Grewal was to have 'estates and sugar holdings' of 15,000 acres.[55]

Asian farming in South Kavirondo District was on a much smaller scale and seems to have been concentrated on raising fruits and vegetables and producing milk. In 1927 the shopkeepers at Kisii were described as raising fruit and vegetables, apparently for sale, on the plots in back of their shops. They were cultivating oranges, limes, pawpaws, loquats, guavas, almonds, and groundnuts as well as an assortment of African vegetables, and they had dug a trench to keep out the hippos.[56] In the early years of the British administration some Asians were permitted to establish dairies on land in the reserve. After establishing the local native councils, the Kenya government defined dairying as an industry and turned over its administration to the councils. The council at Kisii decided to let each African location determine its own policy on the establishment of dairies, with the result that the number of Asian dairies increased. By 1937 thirty Asian dairies were operating in Kisii alone. Among the owners was R. H. Patel, who that year received permission from the local native council to supply milk to Kisii township.[57]

The world depression and an African reaction against Asian activity in the reserves adversely affected Asian agriculture in the late 1930s. A hardware merchant in Thika who dealt with Asian farmers in the area had to extend them credit in 1938–39 because they were, as he recalled, near bankruptcy. During the same years Asians within African areas began to be excluded from agriculture as well as shopkeeping and artisanry. The government upheld the local native councils in decisions that the licensed Asian dairies, by reason of the Native Lands Trust Ordinance of 1930, possessed no tenure to the land that they occupied. On this basis the local council in Kisii, for instance, rejected all Asian applications for renewal of licences in 1937 with the result that all thirty Asian dairies had to close down.[58] Throughout Kenya dairy farming was increasingly reserved for Europeans and Africans.

During World War II the Kenya Asians expanded their vegetable production. With the rise of serious food shortages, the government began to urge European farmers to cultivate the essential food crops. Though not so encouraged, the Asians seized the opportunity by increasing their vegetable farms on the coast and round Nairobi. In the process, according to a knowledgeable Asian, they employed many Africans, and the Africans learned from the experience, with the result, as noted, that after the war they gradually took over the production of vegetables for local consumption.[59] There were, of course, other reasons for the Africans' success, but Asian influence was probably an important factor.

Post-war Expansion

In the post-war years the Kenya Asians increasingly invested their profits in estate production. After 1952 when the Supreme Court overthrew the legal provision restricting non-Europeans from coffee production and especially after 1955 when the interracial transfer of land was permitted in the highlands, the Asians began to purchase coffee estates. Among the new coffee planters were Khetshi N. Shah and Dr. Vithalbhai Raojibhai Patel. Shah directed Kenya Tanning Extract Co. Ltd., one of the industrial companies in the group founded by his illustrious brother-in-law, M. P. Shah, and with his brother he bought coffee and sisal estates. Patel, after developing a profitable medical practice in Nairobi, invested in agricultural as well as business properties and resided on one of his two coffee farms in Kiambu. Among those who invested in sugar was the prominent Ugandan Devjibhai Kamalshi Hindocha, who had been a partner with Madhvani in Vithaldas Haridas & Co. In 1946 when the firm was dissolved, Hindocha took over the Kenya interests and within a year purchased a European estate near Kisumu, the Miwani Sugar Mills Ltd., which included 4,500 acres of cane and a factory. In succeeding years Hindocha was to increase the acreage to 15,000, produce annually 20,000 tons of sugar, and employ 4,200 Africans.[60]

Dairy farming continued to be an important Asian agricultural activity in Kenya. A very successful newcomer to the business was Bharmal Kanji Shah, who had arrived in Kenya in 1929 and turned to agriculture after several commercial ventures. In 1951 he established the Highland Dairies Ltd. Soon amalgamating the business with the Nairobi Dairies Ltd. of Thika, he became one of the main milk suppliers to Nairobi. Shah also established two other agricultural companies—Shah Plantations Ltd. and Tinga Tinga Coffee Estates Ltd.—through which he cultivated coffee in Oldeani and engaged in mixed farming of maize, beans, wheat, and papaine (papaya juice).[61]

Not all those who invested in Kenya agriculture in the post-war period were successful. Kanji Naranji Lakhani, having accumulated a fortune through a wholesale trade in groceries, wines, and spirits, forsook business in 1949 to develop a large cashew estate at Kilifi. After three years, however, his land was confiscated for the Asian-Arab settlement scheme. He subsequently acquired a sisal estate in Tanganyika.[62] Bharmal Raishi Shah, a partner in Premchand Raichand & Co., and Mulchand S. Khimasia, the wealthy industrial and commercial businessman, also met misfortune through unforeseen circumstances. On dissolution of his firm, Shah acquired a 9,000-acre sugar estate. Because of continuing drought, the cane would not grow, so Shah in desperation planted sisal. The world fall in sisal prices during the late 1950s soon brought a heavy financial loss, and Shah was forced to sell most of the land to Khimasia who replanted the cane. After a few years, meeting no greater success, Khimasia sold the land to a Greek. A mistake, however, was made in drafting the sales agreement. Before making any payment, the Greek became the virtual owner and sold all the sugar machinery. The sellers lost everything, as has been said, 'lock, stock and barrel'.[63]

As in Kenya, World War II and the last years of colonialism opened new agricultural opportunities to the Asians in Tanganyika. When war began, the estates of the Germans who had reinvested in land were again confiscated and put up for auction. This time, however, the Asians, who were still suffering the effects of the depression, were not among the purchasers. After the war with the return of prosperity, Asians from all the territories invested in Tanganyika cash-crop production, especially in sisal as world prices rapidly advanced. During the 1950s when beginning their Kenya coffee plantation, the Uganda Kotechas purchased several sisal estates in Tanganyika. Lakhani, after losing his Kenya estate in 1952, bought two sisal estates in Tanganyika comprising 17,000 acres. Estate ownership by racial community in Tanganyika in 1960 is shown in Table 8.1.[64]

A number of Tanganyika Asians also invested in sisal after the war. Among the first were the Noorani brothers—Anverali, Badrudin, and Noordin—sons of one of the first industrialists, Hassanali Esmailjee Jivanjee of Zanzibar. They bought their first sisal plantation in 1945. With estates eventually totalling over 10,000 acres in Ngomemi, Muhesa, and Kisawini, they formed Noorani Plantations Ltd., built a factory, and became one of the main sisal producers. Ibrahim Mohamed Jivan and his brother Mohamed, whose parents since 1930 had been shopkeepers in Arusha, followed a similar course by purchasing two estates near their home. Other new sisal planters included Narshidas Mathuradas Mehta, M. S. Verji, A. K. Manji, and Amil Kaki, all of whom acquired estates near Lindi, and Hirji Nanji Ruparell, who purchased a plantation in Geita District. It was, however, the Karimjees, the planters of the interwar years, who were to retain the foremost position in sisal. Unfortunately the sisal planters old and new were to lose heavily with the sharp fall in world prices.[65]

Although sisal was most attractive in Tanganyika, a few Asians in these post-war years experimented with other crops. In 1957–58 Nasser M.H. Virjee uprooted the family's 450 acres of sisal to plant cashew nuts. A number of Asians came from the neighbouring territories to buy estates with various products. Jayantibhai Premchand Shah, with savings from an automobile workshop business near Thika, purchased a coffee and cattle plantation ten miles outside Arusha. Premchand Virpar Shah and his brother Gulabchand, who had been very successful in several businesses in the Nairobi area, bought a Greek coffee estate near Arusha and raised not only coffee but also maize, beans, and cattle. When Premchand died, the estate was sold, but his son Jayantilal joined Gulabchand and two other Shahs in purchasing an 'immaculate' 365-acre coffee plantation on the slope of Mt. Kilimanjaro, near Moshi, complete with formal gardens and a swimming pool. Employing 70 Africans permanently and from 300 to 600 seasonally, Jayantilal proudly maintained the estate, it is said, exactly as he found it. Ebrahim Sheriff and his nephew Yusuf, members of an ivory-exporting family from Zanzibar and

TABLE 8.1   Estate Ownership by Racial Community in Tanganyika, 1960

Community	Holdings	%	Acres (1000)	%
British Europeans	470	28.2	1,316	52.9
Other Europeans	494	29.7	683	27.4
Asians	298	17.9	262	10.5
Arabs	34	2.0	10	0.4
Africans	35	2.1	17	0.7
Missions	265	15.9	17	0.7
Totals	1,666	100.0	2,489	100.0

Source: Compiled from Annual Report of the Land Bank of Tanganyika, 1960, p. 10, C.O. 736/58.

Arusha, imported machinery to process beans grown by local Dutch farmers. They soon combined with these farmers in raising French beans. The Sheriffs' estate began with 300 acres in 1953, and by 1964 they were to serve 90,000 acres producing over ninety varieties of beans.[66]

In Uganda the Asians retained the predominant position that they had achieved before the war. In the post-war years the Uganda government adopted a policy of discouraging further development of non-African agriculture and sought to limit the size of new estates to a maximum of 10,000 acres, with the result that many Uganda businessmen, as noted, undertook agricultural ventures in the other territories. The Mehtas and Madhvanis, however, continued to expand and improve their Uganda sugar estates, which remained the largest and most productive plantations and served as models of agricultural and industrial accomplishment. In 1961 the two estates alone were employing 20,500 Africans as well as many Asians and Europeans. They included nearly all the 43,000 acres planted in sugar that year and produced almost all the 80,000 tons of sugar, which brought a return of £3,690,000. The Asians retained a monopoly of sugar production and apparently of sisal. In 1951 Uganda was described as having only one sisal plantation, an Asian enterprise. After the war the Asians had also become prominent in tea production. The acreage under tea grew from 3,000 in 1938 to 17,000 in 1960, and by 1960 approximately 35 per cent of it belonged to Asians. On a smaller scale a few members of the community cultivated coffee, rubber, and food crops.[67]

There were many new planters in Uganda, most of whom invested in agriculture after success in other forms of enterprise. Abdulla Pyralli, who had arrived in East Africa in 1912, at first sold piece-goods and fish-nets. Noting the profit from a petrol pump, which he had set up outside his Kampala shop, he expanded to establish a profitable petrol and auto-service business. In 1941 he began to buy coffee and tea plantations, the largest of which was the Buzira Sagama Estate comprising 635 acres of coffee near Fort Portal. Ramji Ladha Dalal, who had moved to Uganda in 1923 after eight years in Kenya, became Uganda's first cotton broker. In 1942 after purchasing four ginneries and an oil mill, Dalal formed the Uganda Sisal Estates Ltd. and bought a 10,000-acre sisal estate and fac-tory at Masindi Port. Another early immigrant, Aditbhai Punjabhai Patel, worked in motor and ginning firms from 1928 until 1944 when he estab-lished his own ginning company. Afterwards while incorporating more ginneries, he formed a subsidiary, Arvindbhai Coffee Estates, and bought coffee and rubber farms in Uganda and a coffee estate in Tan-ganyika. Jamnadas Gokaldas Thakrar, who had been an accountant and cotton buyer since his arrival in 1928, bought two rubber estates in 1945 and by 1960 had 1,000 acres of rubber, coffee, and cotton in Masindi.[68] Jamal Walji & Co. also continued to be important. Following the death of their father in 1946, Sheriff and Mawji Walji assumed control of the firm, and in 1952 they bought a large coffee and tea estate, 'some thousands of acres', from a European company at Jinja.[69]

Uganda continued to attract investment from India and Britain. Al-though most of the capital went into ginning, some was devoted to agri-cultural development. A prime example is offered by the Uganda Commercial Co., which had been purchased from previous owners in 1929 with £100,000 from India. The Uganda organizers—Ramakant Javerilal Mehta, Ravishanker Bhavanishanker Pandya, and Vishvanath Chhaganlal Trivedi—were Kampala businessmen who had interests in four Indian cotton mills. Although Mehta served as managing chairman, the Indian baronet, Chinubhai M. Ranchhodlal, was one of the four di-rectors. In 1949 after acquiring seven ginneries and serving as the local agency for an Indian insurance firm, the company purchased 400 acres on which it planted tea and erected a processing factory.[70]

On the Zanzibar islands there apparently was little change in the Asians' pre-war agricultural activity. The Asians continued their influ-ence in clove production and probably held more than half of all the clove estates. The full extent of their ownership is difficult to ascertain because much of the property had been transferred by 'fictitious sale', whereby the former Arab owners were allowed to remain on the land and retain the appearance of possession.[71]

Unfortunately, the official statistics for Britain's dependencies at the end of the colonial period vary considerably with each territory and re-veal only a partial picture of the Asians' agricultural contribution. The figures are the most informative for Tanganyika, where Asians in 1960 held 18 per cent of the plantations and nearly 11 per cent of the total estate acreage.[72] Although statistics on Asian agriculture in Kenya and Zanzibar have not been published, some information is available for Uganda. By 1960 the Asians accounted for more than 60 per cent of all the protectorate's estate cultivation.[73] In 1961 the non-Africans engaged primarily in Uganda agriculture included only 30 Europeans in comparison to 477 'Asians and others'.[74] Presumably, a large proportion of the Asians among the 477 were employees on the Mehta and Madhvani estates, but the figures do attest to the Asians' participation in agriculture. Another indication of the Asians' role is the fact that 14.7 per cent of the Asian wage earners in Uganda in 1958 were employed in agriculture and forestry as compared to 5.1 per cent of the Europeans.[75]

The agricultural exports from the four territories are also useful in assessing the Asians' contribution not only in Uganda but in all the territories. The leading exports for the East African dependencies in 1960 are shown in Table 8.2. Some generalizations can be made about the Asians' share in producing these exports. In Kenya where their contribution was apparently least important, the Asians were beginning to produce a small share of the important coffee, some of the sisal and tea, and perhaps, with a few remaining dairies, a portion of the butter and ghee. In Tanganyika the Asians contributed a significant proportion of the main export, sisal, and some of the coffee, tea, cashews, and cotton. Among the mainland territories, the agricultural involvement was clearly the greatest in Uganda, where Asians were responsible for nearly all the sugar and sisal, a third of the tea, a small portion of the coffee, and some of the cotton. On the Zanzibar islands they apparently accounted for more than half of the valuable export of cloves.

The Asians' production of sugar, which is not revealed in a list of exports, was another major contribution. In Kenya and Tanganyika all the sugar was consumed locally. In 1960 the sugar production in Kenya was 29,609 tons, in Tanganyika 28,730 tons, and in Uganda 92,978 tons. Nearly all this, representing a value on the world market of £4,312,535, was produced by Asians.[76]

For several years after 1960 extending into the period of independence, the Asians increased their participation in estate production. In Kenya the British government began in late 1960 a Million Acres Settlement Scheme to place Africans on land in the highlands. While Africans moved into the mixed-farming areas, many Asians bought sizeable holdings, especially coffee estates, from Europeans. In 1963 Harakhchand Meghji Shah and his father Shah Meghji Hirji, coffee millers in Thika and Nairobi, bought two coffee farms of 125 and 170 acres near Thika. In the

TABLE 8.2   Chief Agricultural Exports from East Africa, 1960

Commodity	Value £	Commodity	Value £
Kenya			
Coffee	10,277,852	Wattle bark, extract	962,709
Sisal	4,577,033	Cotton lint	841,827
Tea	4,410,922	Butter, ghee	734,512
Pyrethrum, extract	3,025,269	Maize	178,418
Tanganyika			
Sisal	15,441,631	Groundnuts	1,050,773
Cotton lint	8,827,131	Castor seed	874,320
Coffee	7,325,669	Beans, pulses	772,512
Cashews	2,125,788	Maize	757,957
Tea	1,150,671	Sesame	641,549
Uganda			
Coffee	16,987,063	Castor seed	90,558
Cotton lint, seed	16,591,744	Maize, maize flour	73,453
Sugar	4,397,117	Chillies	53,845
Tea	1,452,600	Sisal	51,585
Beans, pulses	113,093		
Zanzibar			
Cloves	3,535,221	Copra, coconuts, oil	721,334

Sources: Kenya, *Department of Agriculture Annual Report 1960, vol. 1*, pp. 16-17, C.O. 544/97; Tanganyika, *Annual Report of the Department of Agriculture, 1960, part 1*, p. 38, C.O. 736/57; Uganda, *Annual Report of the Department of Agriculture for the Year Ended 31st Dec., 1960*, p. 43, C.O. 685/52; for Zanzibar, see *Statesman's Year-Book, 1962* (London: Macmillan, 1962), p. 248.

same year Amritlal Raishi, leader of the Shah community in Nairobi, purchased a 46-acre coffee farm in the Marlborough area, and M. M. Patel and his wife Hansa, Nairobi advocates, bought their first coffee farm near Ruiru. By 1970 the Patels had three such estates. Others who acquired coffee farms in these years included Laxmichand Meghji Kanji, owner of Meka Plantations, T. S. Kotecha, proprietor of Acif Ltd., a jute-bag firm in Thika, B. S. Varma, the retired postmaster of Thika, and R. L. Shah, a businessman in Fort Hall.[77]

In the initial years the new coffee planters were very successful. Kanji is said to have been 'the biggest coffee exporter of his day'.[78] H. M. Shah, who like the Patels exported his own coffee, employed a European agent once each month to inspect his trees and suggest improvements. The Asians, he later remarked, proved to be the most productive planters. Kotecha agreed and claimed, apparently with some exaggeration, that the estates he shared with Kanji produced the best coffee in Kenya and yielded annually one ton per acre, twice that of any European estate.[79]

In Kenya a few Asians invested in crops other than coffee, especially sugar and wheat. After the dissolution of Vithaldas Haridas & Co., the Kenya Sugar Co.'s estate at Ramisi was managed by Nanjibhai Prabhudas Madhvani, Muljibhai's elder brother. Because of drought and mismanagement, however, the company was forced into bankruptcy. The estate was repurchased in 1962 by Jayant M. Madhvani, Nanjibhai's nephew, and thereafter managed successfuly through the Ramisi Sugar Co. (later the Associated Sugar Co.). Like the Madhvanis, the Mehta family extended its Uganda sugar interest into Kenya. At Muhoroni, just east of Kisumu, the Mehtas in 1968–69 combined with the Kenya government and West Germany in financing a sugar complex very similar to that at Lugazi. The project involved a settlement plan for African farmers as well as large estates, a factory, and social amenities. By 1969, in addition to Hindocha's Miwani estate, Kenya had three such complexes—Ramisi, Chemelil, and Muhoroni—which had raised the country's sugar production from 37,000 metric tons in 1963 to 81,000 in 1968.[80] Although the Mehtas contributed directly to only one of these, all were modelled on the Uganda Lugazi and Kakira estates.

The foremost Asian venture in wheat was undertaken by Chandubhai Kalidas Patel, a Jinja barrister who became one of the leading businessmen in Uganda. With his brother, A. Kalidas Patel, Chandubhai invested in a 9,000-acre wheat farm near Eldoret and soon raised the production to an impressive 25,000 bags of wheat each year.[81]

The Asian agricultural expansion in Tanganyika (Tanzania from October 1964) was similar to that in Kenya after 1960 as many Asian businessmen invested in estate production. It was in 1965 that the Shah group bought their 365-acre farm near Moshi. Another Kenya businessman, D. L. Patel of Nairobi, acquired a tea plantation, the Lupembe Estates, at Njombe in southwestern Tanzania. Three other Patels and an Ismaili purchased coffee estates in Karatu west of Ngorongoro Crater, and at least nine Asians bought coffee plantations nearby at Oldeani. Among others who invested in agriculture was an Ismaili who in 1963, after developing a piece-goods and road transport business in Njombe, bought a Greek's pyrethrum farm.[82]

During these years a unique agricultural enterprise was promoted by the Aga Khan. In 1963 after meeting with African political leaders in all three territories, Shah Karim decided to commit his community to the agricultural development of Tanganyika. He established the Industrial Promotion Services (Tanganyika), which entered into a co-operative agricultural project. The government set aside about 500,000 acres of virgin land for Asian settlement in two areas, one between Morogoro and Kilosa, the other near Moshi and Arusha. Both had been mainly pastoral land, but they were well watered and included a few scattered European and African farms. The government alienated the land as leasehold at a cost of about Sh 1 per acre. For his part, the Aga Khan encouraged his followers to settle and provided financial support. About 500 heads of families were attracted to the settlements, and most, but not all, were Ismailis. They settled on farms averaging about 1,000 acres. In some instances several families pooled their resources to buy and manage a farm as a co-operative. On the whole the Asians planted a variety of crops and in the initial years seemed to have excellent prospects for success.[83]

After Nyerere's Arusha Declaration of 1967, which portended an end to individual enterprise, it was with rare exception only Asians from outside with considerable financial security who invested in Tanzania. Though beginning a new phase in which industrial development was emphasized, the Aga Khan optimistically continued to promote the co-operative settlement. Meanwhile, just after the declaration the Madhvanis, led since 1958 by Muljibhai's dynamic eldest son, Jayant, bought a large plantation, the Mtibwa Sugar Estate, in central Tanzania and entered into a partnership with the government for its development. The ownership and profits were to be shared equally by the Madhvanis and a parastatal organization, the National Agricultural and Food Corp. (NAFCO), but the management was entrusted solely to the Madhvanis. Modelled after a new Madhvani sugar estate in Uganda, the Mtibwa factory was to take half its cane from African farmers, 'outgrowers', in the vicinity. Other major investors at this time included the two large firms, Indo-African Sisal Estates Ltd. and United Planters, which had financial backing from India as well as East Africa. The wealthy Jain grocery and sundries merchant of Dar es Salaam, Amritlal T.B. Sheth, was chairman of the two boards of directors.[84]

In Uganda after 1960 Asian agriculture continued to be dominated by the Mehtas and Madhvanis. In September 1969 when the Uganda government decided to initiate a third sugar complex similar to those at Lugazi and Kakira and opened bidding for contracts, the Mehtas won the construction and management. They also agreed to finance 7.5 per cent of the cost and arranged for a firm in India, Walchandnagar Industries

Ltd., to invest an equal amount. Construction on the £7,500,000 project, situated close to Murchison Falls and Masindi near the Congo border, began in September 1970. The work was half completed two years later when the Mehtas, together with the other Asians, were required to leave Uganda.[85]

The Madhvanis also expanded their investments in Uganda agriculture. After succeeding his father, Jayant introduced an African Outgrowers' Scheme to enable the peasants near Kakira to grow cane on their own farms for sale to the sugar factory. The Madhvanis donated their bulldozers and tractors to clearing and ploughing and provided planting, maintenance, and harvesting instruction. Jayant gave Shs 1,000 towards the formation of a Co-operative Growers' Society. By 1970 on the eve of Jayant's untimely death, 1,462 outgrowers were producing cane at a value that year of Shs 5,261,846. Meanwhile, at the request of the Ministry of Agriculture, Jayant had assisted the government in creating a citrus farm at Kasolwe, Busoga. He cleared the 200 acres free of charge. After his election to the Legislative Council, Jayant also had urged the establishment of an agricultural training school. Eventually he himself donated most of the money for the Muljibhai Madhvani School at Wairaika, a post-secondary school for training in crop production, animal husbandry, and poultry farming.[86]

The Eventual Exclusion

Despite their increasing involvement in the initial years of independence, almost all the Asian farmers were forced to abandon agriculture by the early 1970s. The process began on Zanzibar in January 1964 when the African coup d'etat brought a sudden end to the Arab regime. Asians and Arabs—the farmers as well as the shopkeepers—fled to the mainland, and their land and personal property were confiscated without compensation. In Uganda the Asian agriculturists suffered a similar fate following Idi Amin's expulsion orders of August 1972. Even the Mehtas and Madhvanis, who for a brief time were led to believe that they would be spared, were forced to leave. After sugar production at Lugazi and Kakira ground to a halt and work on the new complex in western Uganda terminated, these two families were invited to return, and after Amin's overthrow the invitation was extended to all Uganda's Asian exiles. Eventually the Mehtas and the Madhvanis were to return to Uganda in company with a relatively small number of other exiles, but the weakness in the central government and disorder in the rural areas were to preclude an effective resumption of Asian agriculture.[87]

In Kenya the exclusion of Asians was far more subtle. Even before it relinquished Kenya, the imperial government began to subsidize the purchase of European estates in the highlands. During 1962–64, apart from its sizeable contribution to the Million Acres Settlement Scheme, the United Kingdom provided funds for the purchase of 161 European estates. At the end of that time, as Kenya prepared a development plan for 1966–70, the United Kingdom agreed to continue its subsidy, estimated at £1 million, until 1970. In addition, the British government, the Commonwealth Development Corp., and the World Bank were to put up most of the money for the entire settlement project amounting to about £8,300,000. All this, including the British contribution and the Kenya expenditure, was designed solely for the Europeans and Africans. There were no inducements or aid for Asians to settle on the former European estates, and it was clear that they were not wanted. The Asians who purchased land in the highlands after 1960 had to rely entirely on their own resources and felt constrained to conceal the fact that they were among the new landowners.

In the late 1960s Asian agriculture in Kenya sharply diminished. Kenyatta began to take up the Asians' coffee estates in the highlands and their cashew plantations along the coast. Although he offered each owner a sum that invariably was a fraction of the market price, the Asians knew that they had no alternative but to sell. Some Asians, including H. M. Shah, wisely sold their coffee estates when Kenyatta was taking the land round them. Others, such as K. N. Shah, sold on the assumption that because of the government's attitude more profits were likely to be made in manufacturing than in agriculture. Following Kenyatta's lead, others in the Kenya government began to put pressure on the Asians to sell. They were mostly Kikuyu who easily obtained loans from banks, and the Asians, fearful of the consequences of resistance, felt that they had no alternative. At Kibos, as previously noted, the Asian settlement declined as the cane growers sold their farms to big sugar companies. In all these ways the trend at the end of the colonial period for the Kenya Asians to increase their investments in crop production was reversed in the late 1960s.

In Tanzania it was Nyerere's African socialism that drove the Asians from agriculture. Shortly after independence Nyerere began a policy of nationalizing the land, experimenting with village settlements, and mechanizing crop cultivation. In February 1967, disappointed with the results, he issued the Arusha Declaration outlining a considerable revision of the initial policy. Although emphasizing rural as distinct from urban development, and agriculture rather than industry, Nyerere turned from mechanization to hoe cultivation and from a toleration of individual or family farms to enforced settlement in *ujamaa* (self-help) village co-operatives. The new policy also entailed an increased centralization whereby the government would become the sole landowner, dictate the

types of crops to be planted, set prices, and through its agencies, parastatals, and co-operatives, manage both purchase and sale. In confiscat-
ing the European and Asian estates, Nyerere promised a full compensation to the owners.[88]

Nyerere's agricultural policies were as unfavourable for the Asians as
they were for the development of Tanzania. Those who retained their
land were forced to sell their crops through co-operatives at what one
Asian has estimated as 40 per cent of the market value. As nationalization proceeded, the European estate owners, like their counterparts in
Kenya, were well reimbursed, but the Asians, despite repeated assurances, received either insignificant offers or nothing at all. Those who
lost their farms were advised to join the ujamaa co-operatives. One of
the principal casualties was the extensive settlement of Asian food growers at Kilosa, where all the larger farms, one after another, were confiscated. The unique bean farm of the Sheriff family at Arusha met a similar
fate. So, too, did the Aga Khan's two Ismaili settlements, where nationalization provoked a rare criticism of his leadership: Some Asians were fortunate to sell before the full implications of Nyerere's policies were
realized, but the price of all farm land, especially in Tanzania, was de-
pressed in the wake of the Zanzibar coup. By 1973 a few estates, including the Shahs' 365 acres near Moshi, were still in private hands, but by
then there were no buyers, and most owners nervously awaited what
they foresaw as inevitable.[89] Only the Mehtas and Madhvanis, presumably because of their management skills and willingness to contribute
large sums to government projects, remained reasonably secure in their
agricultural investments.

The experience of Gulabchand Virpar Shah and his three partners is
probably not unique. Their 365-acre coffee estate at Moshi, which included five houses for the managers, five acres of gardens, and a factory
for cleaning, washing, pulping, and drying, was nationalized in 1973. It
was an estate of remarkable beauty, and it was producing a high yield of
a half ton of coffee per acre. The Shahs refused an offer of compensation
equivalent in their view to one-third the value, but the government expelled them, entrusted management of the estate to a co-operative, and
converted the houses to residences for officials on holiday. Twelve years
later when the Shahs were still negotiating for a fair compensation, they
were invited to resume the management. A visit disclosed, not much to
their surprise, that the houses were run-down and abandoned, the factory was in ruins, the garden grew only weeds, and nearly all the coffee
trees were dead.[90]

Despite the paucity of statistics on the magnitude of their estate ownership and production, it is obvious in view of the available information
that the Asians made a substantial contribution to the agricultural devel-

opment of East Africa. As with trade, clerical service, professional activity, and industry, they were active in agriculture through about seven decades overlapping the colonial period. At the end of that time they were responsible for about two-thirds of the estate production in Uganda, at least half of that in Zanzibar, and a considerable portion in Kenya as well as Tanzania.

Nearly all those involved, with the Kibos settlers the main exception, engaged in estate production as a secondary pursuit while carrying on their primary work in commerce, medicine, or another remunerative endeavour in which they had acquired capital for agricultural investment. In this way they differed from the European settlers and the African farmers. They also differed in that throughout the colonial period they were by far the least favoured people in the governments' agricultural policies and programs. A few Asians of exceptional vision and industry, notably Allidina Visram, N. K. Mehta, and the two Madhvanis, were able to overcome these obstacles and to rival, if not surpass, the leading Europeans in agriculture. Their accomplishment was extraordinary.

Whether the Asians' agricultural involvement should be regarded more as a contribution to the economic development of East Africa or as an instance of colonial exploitation will always be a debatable subject, but the evidence seems to fall heavily on the side of contribution. The magnitude of their investment in land and estate production certainly belies the assumption that the Asians exported to India or Britain all the profits from their commercial activities. In agriculture as in most of their other economic endeavours the Asians were motivated by the hope of monetary reward, and in this sense they were serving their own ends. Although it was not a part of their motivation, they were also serving the interests of international capital and industry by providing raw materials for the markets and factories of metropolitan centres outside Africa. Regardless of these considerations, the Asians were also serving the interests of the local dependencies, and subsequently the nation states, by contributing substantially to exports and a favourable balance of payments. The fact that the African governments since independence, even Tanzania in the long run, continued the estate production of the colonial period and sought to augment the exportation of cash crops indicates that this aspect of the Asians' economic activity was not without value.

Notes

1. *Indians in Kenya: Memo.*, Cmd. 1922 (London: HMSO, 1923), p. 1.
2. R. R. Ramchandani, *Uganda Asians: The End of an Enterprise* (Bombay: United Asia, 1976), p. 183.
3. Ibid., pp. 169–83.

4. Montgomery, witness, *Report of the Committee on Immigration from India to the Crown Colonies and Protectorates:* part 2, *Minutes of Evidence,* Cd. 5193 (London: HMSO, 1910), p. 210.

5. Margery Perham, ed., *Diaries of Lord Lugard,* vol. 1, (Evanston, Ill.: Northwestern University Press, 1959), pp. 75, 167, 169. Frederick Lugard, *The Rise of Our East African Empire,* vol. 1, (London: W. Blackwood, 1893), pp. 488–90.

6. S. Baker to A. M. Jeevanjee, 1920, quoted, *Indians Abroad: Kenya* (Bulletin no. 6, Imperial Indian Citizenship Association, Bombay, July 1923), pp. 17–18.

7. Kirk, witness, *Report of the Committee on Emigration,* part 2, p. 238. J. S. Mangat, *History of the Asians in East Africa, c. 1886 to 1945* (Oxford: Clarendon, 1969), p. 65. Baron von Waldhausen (German Consul, Calcutta) to T. W. Holderness, 20 Feb. 1900, and encl. 'Memo.', in Government of India, Department of Revenue and Agriculture, Emigration A, Sept. 1901, no. 12, Indian National Archives. Waldhausen's proposal was repeated in a letter from Baron Eckardstein, 14 Mar. 1901, encl. Foreign Office to Sir Charles Eliot (Commissioner, East Africa Protectorate), 14 May 1902, cited in F.O. 566/1659. Lord Lansdowne (Secretary of State for Foreign Affairs) to Eliot, 27 Aug. 1901, F.O. 2/433. Mackenzie's report is enclosed in Lansdowne to Eliot, 3 Aug. 1901, F.O. 2/571; Whitehouse's in Eliot to Lansdowne, 6 Sept. 1901, F.O. 2/450. See also M.P.K. Sorrenson, *Origins of European Settlement in Kenya* (London: Oxford University Press, 1968), chaps. 3, 4.

8. See, for example, Lord Salisbury to Sir Arthur Hardinge (Commissioner, East Africa Protectorate), 5 July 1900, F.O. 2/552; and Lansdowne to Eliot, 27 Aug. 1901, F.O. 2/443.

9. Note by Clement L. Hill (Foreign Office), 25 Feb. 1902, on Eliot to Lansdowne, 5 Jan. 1902, F.O. 2/443.

10. Craufurd to John Ainsworth, 2 Aug. 1899, file 'Ukamba Outward, 1899', Seyidie (Coast) Province daily correspondence, Syracuse University microfilm 1995, reel 117. Hardinge to Salisbury, 24 Aug. 1900, F.O. 2/552. Eliot to Lansdowne, 8 May 1902, F.O. 2/571. Johnston to Salisbury, 24 Aug. 1900, F.O. 2/671.

11. Eliot to Lansdowne, 5 Jan. 1902, F.O. 2/566. R. Meinertzhagen, *Kenya Diary, 1892–06* (London: Oliver and Boyd, 1957), p. 31.

12. Petition, 4 Jan. 1902, encl. Eliot to Lansdowne, 21 Jan. 1902, F.O. 2/805.

13. Elgin to James Hayes Sadler (Governor, East Africa Protectorate), 19 Mar. 1908, in *Correspondence Relating to the Tenure of Land in the East Africa Protectorate,* Cd. 4117 (London, 1908), pp. 29–34.

14. Kenya, *Development Plan, 1966–70* (Nairobi: Government Printer, 1966), p. 149. Roger van Zwanenberg, *Agricultural History of Kenya* (Nairobi: East African Publishing House, 1972), p. 9.

15. H. B. Thomas and Robert Scott, *Uganda* (London: Oxford University Press, 1935), pp. 105–7. Ramchandani, *Uganda Asians,* pp. 12, 173–74.

16. 'Narrative by Sir Edward Buck, K.C.S.I., of a Visit to the Protectorate in 1905', *Report of the Committee on Emigration:* part 3, *Notes of Evidence,* Cd. 5194, p. 58.

17. Waller to Acting Commissioner, 8 Feb. 1907, ibid., p. 43. See also Waller to Governor, 4 June 1908, ibid., pp. 49–50.

18. Montgomery, witness, ibid., part 2, pp. 206, 208, 210. Waller to Acting Commissioner, 8 Feb. 1907.

19. Waller to Acting Commissioner, 8 Feb. 1907. *Kenya-Uganda-Tanganyika and Zanzibar Directory: Trade and Commercial Index: Annual Issue of 1936* (Nairobi: East African Directory Co., 1936), Kenya section, pp. 135–36. A. B. Patel, reported in *Kenya Daily Mail* (Mombasa), 9 Dec. 1927, p. 12. Narain Singh, ed., *Kenya Independence-Day Souvenir: A Spotlight on the Asians of Kenya* (Nairobi: Kenya Indian Congress, 1963), p. 45.

20. 'Memo. from the Nyanza Farmers' Association, Feb. 1933', *Kenya Land Commission: Evidence and Memoranda*, Colonial no. 91, vol. 3, (London: HMSO, 1934), pp. 2174–75. A Kibos settler, W. Singh Ruprah, and a buyer of maize from the Kibos settlement, M. R. Shah, were interviewed by Bennett, 28 May 1973, Kisumu.

21. Winston Churchill, *My African Journey* (London: Hodder and Stoughton, 1908), pp. 49–50, 52, 54. Churchill's address to the National Liberal Club, *India* (London), 24 Jan. 1908, p. 43. *Report of the Committee on Emigration*, part 1, *Report*, pp. 23–24, 91–93. James Hayes Sadler, witness, *Report of the Committee on Emigration*, part 2, pp. 136–37, 318–20. Sir H. Hesketh Bell, witness, *Report of the Committee on Emigration*, part 2, p. 318. Bell to Secretary of State for the Colonies, teleg., 4 Apr. 1909, and dispatch, 15 Apr. 1909, *Report of the Committee on Emigration*, part 3, pp. 151–52.

22. Note by M. C. Seton, 13 Mar. 1919, encl. Edwin S. Montagu (Secretary of State for India) to Viceroy, 26 Mar. 1919, Government of India, Department of Commerce and Industry, Emigration A, Oct. 1919, nos. 1–8. Governor-General and Councillors to Secretary of State for India, 10 Feb. 1921, ibid., Mar. 1921, nos. 16–47. For more detail, see Robert G. Gregory, *India and East Africa: A History of Race Relations within the British Empire, 1890–1939* (Oxford: Clarendon, 1971), pp. 165–76.

23. *Indians in Kenya: Memo.*, Cd. 1922 (London: HMSO, 1923), p. 17.

24. Governor to Colonial Office, 29 Mar. 1924, Government of India, Department of Education, Health and Lands, Overseas A, Sept. 1925, nos. 1–92.

25. Secretary of State for India to Viceroy, telegs., 23 June 1925 and 28 Nov. 1925, ibid. 'Minutes, Standing Emigration Committee, 19 Aug. and 5 Sept. 1925', ibid., Overseas B, Oct. 1925, nos. 38–40. Viceroy to Secretary of State for India, teleg., 23 June 1925, ibid., Overseas A, Sept. 1925, nos. 93–102.

26. For more detail, see Gregory, *India and East Africa*, pp. 311–20, 339–43. *Kenya Land Commission: Evidence and Memoranda*, Colonial no. 91, vol. 3 (London: HMSO, 1934), pp. 2888–90.

27. 'Note on Indians in East Africa', Mar. 1951, confidential, encl. H. S. Bates (Colonial Office) to Miss L.E.T. Storar (Commonwealth Relations Office), 9 Apr. 1951, confidential, file 'Indians in East Africa: Political, Social, and Economical Position of Indians, 1951', C.O. 822/143/7.

28. N. S. Patel, interviewed by Honey, 5 Mar., 7 Sept. 1973, Dar es Salaam.

29. Kenya Press Office Handout no. 581, Nairobi, 10 Oct. 1953, file 'Agrarian Policy: Kenya, 1952–53', C.O. 822/192.

30. Ewart S. Grogan, witness, *Report of the Committee on Emigration*, part 2, p. 262. Hardinge to Salisbury, 24 Aug. 1900, F.O. 2/671. Bachulal T. Gathani, interviewed by Gregory, 20 Nov. 1972, Nairobi.

31. 'Report on the Progress and Condition of the Kisumu Province, East Africa Protectorate, for the Twelve Months Ending 31st March 1906', p. xxxii, Nyanza Province Annual Reports, Syracuse University microfilm 2801, reel 32.

32. W. McGregor Ross, *Kenya from Within: A Short Political History* (London: Allen and Unwin, 1927), pp. 301–2.

33. Allidina Vishram (President, Nairobi Indian Association) to Secretary of State for the Colonies, May 1909, C.O. 533/68. Note the spelling of Visram. A. M. Jeevanjee, *An Appeal on Behalf of the Indians in East Africa* (Bombay, 1912), pp. 101–3.

34. Shanti Pandit, ed., *Asians in East and Central Africa* (Nairobi: Panco, 1961), pp. 85–86, 95, 324–25.

35. Biography of A. Visram, ibid., pp. 66–68. *East African Standard* (Mombasa), 2 Nov. 1907, pp. 14–15; 15 Aug. 1908, p. 9.

36. Ibid., 25 Jan. 1908, p. 5.

37. Ross, *Kenya from Within*, pp. 300–301. S. Hassanali, interviewed by Honey, 15 Jan. 1974, Dar es Salaam.

38. C. F. Strickland, *Report on Co-operation and Certain Aspects of the Economic Condition of Agriculture in Zanzibar* (London: HMSO, 1932). R. S. Troup, *Report on Clove Cultivation in the Zanzibar Protectorate* (Zanzibar: Government Printer, 1932). Strickland and Sir Alan Pim, *Report of Sir Alan Pim . . . on the Financial Position and Policy of the Zanzibar Government in Relation to Its Economic Resources* (London: HMSO, 1932). C. A. Bartlett and J. S. Last, *Report on the Indebtedness of the Agricultural Classes* (Zanzibar: Government Printer, 1934). A. Vellani (interviewed by Honey, 13 Feb. 1974, Zanzibar) has described how his family bought clove plantations from Arabs, Africans, and Asians.

39. For the background of the decrees, see files 3801/6/33, 3886/33, 23806/34, and 23815/34, C.O. 618. For the introduction of the decrees, see *Official Gazette of the Zanzibar Protectorate: Proceedings of the Legislative Council,* Supplement no. 2, 43 (30 June 1934), pp. 20–25. For a summary of each decree, see Gregory, *India and East Africa,* pp. 461–62.

40. Memorial encl. Acting British Resident to Secretary of State for the Colonies, teleg., 23 June 1934, file 23815/34, C.O. 618/56. For detail, see Gregory, *India and East Africa,* pp. 463–72.

41. Gregory, *India and East Africa,* pp. 470–73. All India Congress Committee, *Indian National Congress, 1936–38: Being the Resolutions Passed by the Congress, the All India Congress Committee and the Working Committee During the Period Between April, 1936 to Jan., 1938* (Allahabad, c. 1939), pp. 68–69.

42. Zanzibar Sessional Paper no. 6 of 1938, cited in L. W. Hollingsworth, *Asians of East Africa* (London: Macmillan, 1960), pp. 118 n. 9. Gregory, *India and East Africa,* p. 473.

43. The Indian government received detailed accounts: Department of Revenue and Agriculture, Emigration, Sept. 1921, nos. 43–61, 73–74; Oct. 1921, nos. 8–9; Feb. 1922, nos. 17–17A.

44. R. B. Ewbank, 'Brief on Tanganyika History', 12 Mar. 1925, Government of India, Department of Education, Health and Lands, Overseas A, Sept. 1925, nos. 1–92. *Kenya-Uganda-Tanganyika and Zanzibar Directory . . . 1936,* Tanganyika section, p. 68. For 1933 figures when the Asians had 12 per cent, see *Report on the*

Liquidation, 1917–33, by the Custodian, Ernest Adams (Dar es Salaam: Government Printer, 1933), p. 12. Hans Ruthenberg, *Agricultural Development in Tanganyika* (Berlin: Springer-Verlag, 1964), p. 46.

45. K. J. Kotecha, interviewed by Gregory, 9 July 1973, Ahmedabad. A. Sachoo, interviewed by Honey, 29 Oct. 1973, Dar es Salaam. N.M.H. Virjee (grandson), interviewed by Honey, 5 Jan. 1974, Mombasa. N. S. Patel (son) interview.

46. Mehta's unique memoir reveals his pioneering spirit and accomplishments: *Dream Half Expressed: An Autobiography* (Bombay: Vakils, Feffer and Simons, 1966), especially pp. 98–99, 146, 154, 169, 172. D. N. Mehta (eldest son), interviewed by Gregory, 13 July 1973, Porbandar.

47. Mehta, *Dream Half Expressed*, p. 182.

48. Ibid., pp. 182, 198, 319.

49. Pandit, *Asians*, pp. 79–80. H. P. Joshi, Bhanumati V. Kotecha, and J. V. Paun, eds., *Jayant Muljibhai Madhvani* (Nairobi: Emco Glass Works, 1973), pp. 61, 89, 313, 314.

50. *Kenya-Uganda-Tanganyika and Zanzibar Directory . . . 1936*, Uganda section, p. 59. Pandit, *Asians*, pp. 79–80. Joshi et al., *Jayant*, p. 314.

51. Uganda, *Annual Report of the Department of Agriculture for the Year Ending 31st Dec., 1925*, app. 8; and *1935*, app. 9; both cited in Ramchandani, *Uganda Asians*, p. 176. Britain, *Annual Report on the Social and Economic Progress of the People of the Uganda Protectorate, 1933*, Colonial Reports—Annual, no. 1670 (London: HMSO, 1934), pp. 25–27. Also, Ramchandani, *Uganda Asians*, p. 181.

52. I. S. Gill, interviewed by Bennett, 4 May 1973, Nairobi.

53. H. Rattansi (son), interviewed by Bennett, 3 May 1973, Nairobi. Pandit, *Asians*, pp. 293, 313–14.

54. *Report of the Taxation Enquiry Committee, Kenya, 1947* (Nairobi: Government Printer, 1947), p. 10. A. R. Kassim Lakha, interviewed by Bennett, 9 May 1973, Mombasa. N. S. Patel interview. Acting Senior Commissioner, Coast, to Chief Native Commissioner, Nairobi, 17 July, 1926, file 'Alienation of Crown Lands, 1926–28', Seyidie (Coast) Province daily correspondence, Syracuse University microfilm 1995, reel 102.

55. V. H. Johanputra, interviewed by Bennett, 28 May 1973, Kisumu. *Kenya-Uganda-Tanganyika and Zanzibar Directory . . . 1936*, Kenya section, pp. 140–62. Pandit, *Asians*, pp. 139, 142–43, 317.

56. Lt. Col. E.L.B. Anderson, A.D.C., Kisii, 'Safari Diary', Oct. 1927, p. 1, file 'Nyanza Province Misc. Correspondence, 1925–27', Syracuse University microfilm 2802, reel 106. Also, 'Nyanza Provincial Diary—June, 1927', p. 2, ibid.

57. 'Minutes of a Meeting of the South Kavirondo Local Native Council Held in Kisii on 20th and 21st Jan., 1937', pp. 11–12, Local Authority Records, Syracuse University microfilm 2246, reel 24. 'Minutes . . . 21st Sep., 1937', p. 5, ibid.

58. D. C. Patel, interviewed by Bennett, 28 Apr. 1973, Nairobi. 'Minutes of a Meeting of the South Kavirondo Local Native Council Held in Kisii on 24th and 25th June 1937', p. 3, Local Authority Records, reel 24. 'South Kavirondo District Annual Report, 1937', p. 40, Nyanza Province Annual Reports, Syracuse University microfilm 2801, reel 38.

59. D. C. Patel interview.

60. A. C. Fernandes, 'The Coffee Industry', *Tribune* (Nairobi), 24 May 1952, p. 29. K. N. Shah, interviewed by Bennett, 27 Apr. 1973, Nairobi. Dr. V. R. Patel, interviewed by Gregory, 5, 6 July 1973, Baroda. D. K. Hindocha, interviewed by Bennett, 21 Apr. 1973, Miwani. Pandit, *Asians,* pp. 144–45.

61. Pandit, *Asians,* p. 294.

62. D. K. Naranji (son), interviewed by Bennett, 18 May 1973, Nairobi.

63. Note by Amritlal Raishi, encl. Bachulal Gathani to Gregory, 9 May 1987. M. S. Khimasia, interviewed by Bennett, 19 Apr. 1973, Nairobi.

64. A. Sachoo and K. J. Kotecha interviews. Pandit, *Asians,* p. 159.

65. Pandit, *Asians,* pp. 184–85, 333–35. I. M. Jivan, interviewed by Gregory, 16 Feb. 1973, Arusha. M. B. Versi, interviewed by Honey, 27 Feb. 1974, Dar es Salaam. According to K. J. Kotecha (interviewed), sisal, which had been £16 a ton in 1935–36, rose to £250 in 1952–53, then fell to £80 by 1973.

66. N.M.H. Virjee interview. J. P. Shah, interviewed by Honey, 11 July 1973, Moshi. A. G. Shah, interviewed by Gregory, 17 June 1985, Nairobi. Y. Sheriff, interviewed by Honey, 4 Jan. 1974, Malindi. Note by Amritlal Raishi.

67. Uganda, *1962 Statistical Abstract* (Entebbe: Government Printer, 1962), tables UF.11, 12, 13, p. 44. 'Note on Indians in East Africa', March 1951, C.O. 822/143/7. Ramchandani, *Uganda Asians,* p. 183.

68. Pandit, *Asians,* pp. 100, 207, 267, 337, 346, 359.

69. Ibid., pp. 313–14.

70. Ibid., p. 359.

71. Michael F. Lofchie, *Zanzibar: Background to Revolution* (Princeton: Princeton University Press, 1965), pp. 33, 110.

72. Ruthenberg, *Agricultural Development in Tanganyika,* p. 15.

73. Ramchandani, *Uganda Asians,* p. 183.

74. Uganda, *1962 Statistical Abstract,* table UP.11, p. 101.

75. United Nations, *Economic Survey of Africa since 1950* (New York: United Nations Department of Economic and Social Affairs, 1959), table 1-XXV, p. 48.

76. *Annual Report of the East African Common Services Organization for 1961* (Nairobi: Government Printer, 1962), p. 74. The world market price was taken from *Times* (London), 1 Jan. 1960, p. 16.

77. H. M. Shah, interviewed by Gregory, 14 June 1985, Nairobi. A. Raishi, interviewed by Gregory, 25 Jan. 1973, Nairobi. M. M. Patel, interviewed by Gregory, 8 Mar. 1973, Nairobi. T. S. Kotecha, interviewed by Bennett, 24 May 1973, Thika. B. S. Varma, interviewed by Bennett, 27 Apr. 1973, Thika. In his note Amrital Raishi added the names of other coffee buyers: Kalidas Virpal Shah, Popatlal Padamshi Shah, Dayalji Rajpal Shah, Motichand Ramji Shah, Devji Neghji Patel, Vershi Devshi, Salim Yakub, Bharmal Kanji Shah, Kanji Mepa Shah, Mepa Kanji, Padamshi Naya Shah, Premchand Lakhamshi Lalji Shah, Kanji Lalji Shah, and Chaturbhai K. Patel.

78. Note by Amritlal Raishi.

79. H. M. Shah and T. S. Kotecha interviews. Note by Amritlal Raishi.

80. Kenya, *Development Plan, 1966–70,* pp. 174–75; *1970–74* (Nairobi: Government Printer, 1970), p. 241. Nitan Jayant Madhvani to me, 19 Mar. 1987.

81. A. K. Patel, interviewed by Gregory, 6 July 1973, Baroda.

82. A. G. Shah interview. Information on D. L. Patel from D. G. Patel, interviewed by Honey, 9, 14 Oct. 1973, Dar es Salaam. R. G. Patel, interviewed by Honey, 10 Aug. 1973, Karatu. The Ismaili who purchased the Greek farm requested anonymity.

83. The Ismaili who provided this information requested anonymity.

84. Ibid. Philip C. Packard, 'Corporate Structure in Agriculture and Social Development in Tanzania: A Study of the National Agriculture and Food Corporation', chap. 16, *African Socialism in Practice: The Tanzanian Experience*, ed. Andrew Coulson (Nottingham: Spokesman, 1979), pp. 201, 206–7. A.T.B. Sheth, interviewed by Honey, 19 Feb. 1974, Dar es Salaam.

85. D. N. Mehta interview.

86. Joseph Mubiru, 'Economic Colossus', *Jayant Madhvani*, ed. Robert Becker and Nitin Jayant Madhvani (London: Muljibhai Madhvani, 1973), pp. 57–58. Mathias Ngobi, 'Nascent Uganda', ibid., pp. 66–67. Uganda, *Legislative Council Debates*, 16 Jan. 1958, p. 148.

87. S. Hassanali, 15 Jan. 1974; A.A.M. Lakha, 15 Jan. 1974; V. S. Patel, 8, 10 Jan. 1974; Y. Pirbhai, 25 Feb. 1974—all interviewed by Honey, Dar es Salaam. D. N. Mehta interview. N. J. Madhvani (Jayant's eldest son), interviewed by Gregory, 12 June 1985, Nairobi.

88. Kenya, *Development Plan, 1966–70*, pp. 154, 159. The results of the 1966–70 settlement schemes are described in *Development Plan, 1970–74*, pp. 199–210. H. M. Shah, K. N. Shah, and M. R. Shah interviews. Note by Amritlal Raishi. For a critical assessment as well as a full explanation of Nyerere's policies, see Goran Hyden, *Beyond Ujamaa in Tanzania: Underdevelopment and an Uncaptured Peasantry* (Berkeley: University of California Press, 1980). For the government's description, see Tanzania, *Second Five-Year Plan: Economic and Social Development, 1st July, 1969–30th June, 1974* (Dar es Salaam: Government Printer, 1969), Introduction and chaps. 2, 3.

89. A. Sachoo, A. G. Shah, N. S. Patel, Y. Sheriff, and J. P. Shah interviews.

90. A. G. Shah interview.

CHAPTER NINE

■

Industry

Had I willed it, I could have certainly set up ten or twelve other industries.

—Nanji Kalidas Mehta, 1961[1]

Madhvani expanded like hell after World War II. Why? To prove we had faith in East Africa's future.

—Madhusudn J. Thakkar, 1973[2]

The Asian contribution to the development of industrial manufacturing in East Africa has, like the Asians' role in agriculture, been very important. It too, however, has received slight recognition and in some aspects been seriously misinterpreted. Asians were responsible for much of the initial manufacturing, which consisted mainly of the processing of local agricultural produce. Between the wars while European settlers and foreign companies assumed the lead in Kenya, the Asians became the principal industrialists in the other territories. After World War II when manufacturing in the colonies for the first time received official encouragement, the Asians throughout East Africa expanded into many new types of industry. In the mainland territories this expansion continued beyond the colonial period to the late 1960s and early 1970s when it was cut short in Uganda by the expulsion order, suppressed in Tanzania by ujamaa, and stifled in Kenya by regulation and discrimination. Overall the Asians appear as the foremost industrialists of Tanganyika, Uganda, and Zanzibar. Even in Kenya, despite the fact that local Europeans and foreign firms introduced most of the large companies, the Asians initiated many of the key industries.

As in agriculture, the Asians' participation in manufacturing was curtailed through most of the colonial period by the imperial and colonial governments. There was no major racial restriction, such as the ban on non-European settlement in the Kenya highlands, but there was a sup-

271

pression of industrial development. Until World War II, in what has been called the classical period of imperialism, the British government suppressed all colonial industries that offered competition to those of the imperial centre. It encouraged only the processing of farm produce and minerals. The European settlers as well as the Asians were affected by the restrictive policy. As in other business endeavour, however, the Europeans were favoured in any competition with the Asians.[3]

The Initial Processing Industries

The nature of manufacturing in East Africa, as in other world areas, was determined essentially by the available natural resources. Through the first three decades of the European occupation, it appeared that East Africa's only mineral resource was the soda ash (calcium carbonate) of Lake Magadi. Although gold was subsequently discovered in Kenya and diamonds in Tanganyika, these minerals were never to provide much return and certainly not a foundation for manufacturing. The mainland territories were completely lacking in the two minerals most important for industrial development: oil for a petrochemical industry and iron for the manufacture of steel. Nor did the territories contain any mineral comparable to the gold of South Africa, copper of Northern Rhodesia, or varied mineral deposits of the Congo. Apart from ivory, rhino horn, other game products, an abundance of stone, and a moderate amount of timber and soda ash, East Africa's only wealth seemed to be its agricultural produce. The area's initial manufacturing thus involved the processing of its agricultural products together with the sawing of timber, quarrying of stone, refining of soda ash, and provision of such luxuries as ice, soda water (soft drinks), and electricity.

In manufacturing as in trade and agriculture the Asians preceded the Europeans. By 1860 Zanzibar had a number of Asian soda water factories, one of which belonged to the Bohra tinsmith, Adamjee Putwa. He had begun his factory in one room and reserved a corner for a bottling plant. About 1890, besides trading in perfumes and buying clove plantations, he built an ice factory. A similar concern, the Zanzibar Ice and Mineral Water Factory, which continued into the 1950s, was founded in 1907 by the Parsee engineer and plantation owner, Shapurji B. Sidhwa. A factory of another type was established in the early 1890s by a Memon named Abdulla, who came from Kutch to join others in his community who were milling oil from copra. He brought with him a wooden press, set up his own oil mill, and imported camels from the mainland for power. Not until 1908 was steam power first employed on Zanzibar. The factory owner who introduced it was the 'great pioneering industrialist' and Bohra, Hassanali Esmailjee Jivanjee.[4]

The Asians also created the first factories on the mainland. During 1893–94 the Ithnasheri Sachoo family, which had been trading in ivory and produce on the coast since 1851, established what is now remembered as the first industry in German East Africa. With camel-powered machinery crushing oil from copra, the Sachoos began to manufacture soap in Dar es Salaam. Five years later they built a soda water factory to compete with an established Bohra concern. About the same time the Bohra Abdulla Khalfan began what is thought to have been the first soap factory in Mombasa, and H. E. Jivanjee, extending his Zanzibar interests to the mainland, founded the Mombasa Electric Supply Co. Until his death many years later, when the East Africa Power and Lighting Co. purchased his plant, Jivanjee provided Mombasa's electrical needs.[5]

The opening of the interior at the turn of the century provided a stimulus to Asian manufacturing. As middlemen purchasing African produce, the Asians sensed the opportunity to grind maize into flour, gin raw cotton, extract the tannin from wattle bark, manufacture jaggery (crude sugar) from cane, and produce ghee (clarified butter) from milk. In supplying provisions and other commodities to the European settlers, the Asians also perceived the potential profit in processing the settlers' produce by milling wheat flour, hulling coffee beans, pulping and drying sisal, and, if Muslims, manufacturing meat products and bone meal.

East Africa's pre-eminent trader, Allidina Visram, was the most innovative and apparently the most important manufacturer in the early years of the new century. In 1907 while experimenting with a wide variety of imported plants on his plantations, Visram established a factory in Mombasa to produce coconut oil and soap. By 1908 he had a cotton-baling press and a factory to produce jaggery in Kampala as well as a hand-powered cotton ginnery in Entebbe. He next organized Fibre Uganda Ltd. for the manufacture of hardboard from papyrus in Kisumu. In 1910 he erected in Mombasa an industrial complex of four cotton gins and six mills for the manufacture of simsim (sesame) oil. By the time of his death in 1916 Visram had established several other factories and developed an industrial as well as a trading and plantation empire.[6]

During the same period many other Asians became active on the mainland. In 1902 a Goan, Augustino de Figueiredo, who five years earlier had been recruited in Bombay by the Imperial British East Africa Co., established in Entebbe his own store of provisions, wines, and spirits, with a tailoring section. Perceiving the Africans' demand for clothing, he imported a dozen tailors from Goa and began the manufacture of piece-goods. Soon increasing his tailors to forty, he expanded into Kampala and Jinja to become one of the two principal producers of African clothing. A similar industry was established in 1910 by Fazal Abdulla, a Bohra who had come to Zanzibar in 1899 at age six and eventually moved to

Uganda. In Kampala he set up his own sewing shop and began manufacturing safari tents, household upholstery, and for the new motor-cars, canvas cushions and tops. In 1907 an Ismaili family, forming Narsi Velji & Co., added a furniture factory to its Mombasa business of sign painting and metal engraving. During the same period Sheriff Dewji and Sheriff Jaffer, Ithnasheris, combined in Sheriff Jaffer & Co. to build a copra factory in Mombasa and produce 'blue mottled' soap. In many centres throughout the British territories, other Asians were beginning to manufacture maize meal, various types of oil, jaggery, and ghee. By 1911, for instance, there were six Asian 'corn grinding mills' and an Asian simsim oil factory in Nyanza Province alone. All were water powered. The huge grinding stones used in the mills were imported from India.[7] Asians in these prewar years also assumed a prominent role in the ginning of cotton.

Asians were not alone in such enterprise. As early as 1905 a company managed in Britain began manufacturing cigarettes in the East Africa Protectorate. By 1906 the Friends Africa Industrial Mission was operating a sawmill at Kaimosi and a brick factory at Maragoli. Two years later East Africa's leading settler, Lord Delamere, organized Unga to erect a flour mill, and in 1911 he started a factory for the 'disintegration of wattle bark'. That same year the Lumbwa settlers established the Lumbwa Creamery Ltd. to make butter, and they also started a bacon factory. Other Europeans in 1911 formed the Magadi Soda Co. to refine and market Lake Magadi's soda ash, and still others established East Africa Industries Ltd. in Nyanza to launch an oil-powered flour mill. Meanwhile the British East Africa Corp., which had been founded in 1906 largely with financing from the British Cotton Growing Association, was erecting cotton ginneries. In 1911 its ginnery at Kisumu was described as Nyanza Province's main industry.[8]

Ginning represented a combined Asian and European development and was centred in Uganda. Although Africans had been growing cotton before the beginning of colonial rule, ginning is said to have had its origin in 1909 when the first ginnery was erected by the Uganda Co. with shares subscribed by Europeans, Asians, and even some Africans. In that year the Uganda governor, Sir Hesketh Bell, distributed seeds of a superior variety and encouraged Africans in cotton cultivation. From the beginning the Asians, who were already trading in the interior in a variety of goods, served as middlemen in the purchase of cotton for the new ginnery. As African production increased, the BCGA built a number of ginneries. Unable to fill the need, it joined the government in encouraging the erection of ginneries by Asians and Germans. Visram, the leading cotton buyer, at once responded by forming the Allidina Cotton Buying & Ginning Co., which erected its first power ginnery in 1910. In 1916 his firm outbid the BCGA in buying Hansing's ginnery, the main German factory that because of the war had been confiscated and sold at auction. Other Asian traders also participated, with the result that by 1918 Asians owned nine of the thirty-one Uganda ginneries. Visram's firm had three, Narandas Rajaram & Co. two, and Bandali Jaffer & Co., Jaffer Allidina & Bros., and Hasham Jamal & Co. one each. Within a year the Asians were nearly to double their ginneries from nine to seventeen.[9]

Cotton, Sugar, and Other Interwar Manufacturing

During the interwar period partly as a result of the new ginning activity, Asian manufacturing greatly expanded and apparently in all territories except Kenya exceeded that of the local Europeans and foreign firms. As in the earlier years Asian manufacturing included an assortment of relatively small secondary industries but was concentrated in the processing of agricultural products and mineral resources. The factories thus continued to utilize local raw materials rather than imports. The area of greatest activity was Uganda, and the profits made there were to finance much of the new Asian manufacturing in Kenya and Tanganyika. Uganda cotton ginning was in the interwar years East Africa's principal industry. The dependency with the least activity was Zanzibar, which because of the decline in Omani political power and the migration of enterprising Asians to the mainland lost its industrial initiative and became relatively unimportant in everything except the production of cloves.

In Tanganyika where British rule attracted large numbers of European and Asian immigrants after the war, the Asians appear to have established most of the new industries. In the early years the Europeans owned the larger agricultural processing factories for cotton, sisal, sugar, tea, coffee, and tobacco as well as the salt mines, brick works, and the brewery. The Asians initially dominated the manufacture of rice and maize flour, soap, oil, soda water, and ice, and they acquired virtual monopolies in gold and silver work, tin-smithing, shoemaking, and tailoring. Aided by sizeable investment from Uganda and India, the Asians soon began to compete with the Europeans in ginning and the production of sisal and sugar. By 1939 despite severe hardship during the world depression and restrictions imposed by the colonial government, they seem to have controlled most of the industrial sector.[10]

In Kenya, although there was considerable Asian progress in manufacturing, industrial development was dominated between the wars by the settlers and foreign British companies. Forming state-sponsored cooperatives, notably the Kenya Farmers' Association, Kenya Co-operative Creameries, and the Kenya Planters' Union, the settlers arranged for the processing and exportation of most of their agricultural produce with large British firms. They also began a number of other types of industry, including the production of beer. Among the foreign firms Brooke Bond and James Finley gained a virtual monopoly of tea manufacture, Forestal Land & Timber controlled a large share of the wattle bark extraction industry, Liebigs managed the meat processing, the British Imperial Tobacco Co. manufactured cigarettes, and Gibson & Co. refined coffee and other produce. British firms were also engaged in other types of manufacturing—Ind coope in beer production, United Africa in servicing of machinery, Imperial Chemicals in soda ash processing, Balfour Beatty in power generation, and Associated Portland Cement Manufacturers in cement making.[11] As a result of the British involvement, the Kenya Asians retained a concentration on trade and established mainly peripheral industries, including the processing of African produce. There was, however, considerable Asian manufacture.

Most of the new Asian manufacturing occurred in Uganda where the Asians steadily increased their participation in the highly profitable buying, ginning, and exportation of cotton. By 1936 they owned 105 of Uganda's 137 ginneries, the Europeans only 21, and Japanese and Africans had respectively 10 and 1. Foremost among all those in the new industry, Asian or European, was the enterprising Lohana trader Nanji Kalidas Mehta. Beginning in 1908 while continuing to expand his duka trade, Mehta began to buy the new African cotton. In 1916, borrowing 100 ginning machines from the BCGA on the understanding that he would sell his lint to the company, Mehta built the first two of his ginneries. By 1925 when he turned from ginning to concentrate on the manufacture of sugar, he had accumulated twenty-nine ginneries. In the early 1920s when the Allidina Visram empire, lacking its founder's dynamic leadership, collapsed, other Asians bought the firm's ginneries. Typical was Nauharia Ram Maini, a Punjabi Hindu who since his arrival in 1901 had profited from selling furniture and dealing in Nairobi property. When Visram's Uganda properties were liquidated, Maini submitted bids and acquired four of the ginneries.[12]

As Maini's story illustrates, it was not only Asians engaged in the purchase of raw cotton or the exportation of lint but also those in other forms of trade who invested their profits in ginning. Norman Godinho, a Goan who came to Uganda in 1903, worked for a Goan trading firm for sixteen years, then founded his own business in Kampala, invested in urban land, and at the time of his death in 1946 had one of the largest holdings of real estate in Uganda. His firm, Norman Godinho & Sons Ltd., began to invest in ginneries shortly after its formation in 1920. Damodar Jinabhai Kotecha, a Lohana from Porbandar who also immigrated in 1903, formed his own trading company in 1910. Soon accompanied by his four brothers, Kotecha turned to ginning and quickly assumed a leading role in the industry. In 1911 another immigrant from Porbandar, Kakubhai Kalidas Radia, joined his brother Popat who had a general store in Kampala. Although he left the business to enlist in the army during World War I, he was able to finance the first of his two ginneries in 1920 and to begin a noted career as businessman, philanthropist, and civic leader.[13]

Three others in Uganda who began successful ginning enterprises between the wars were Jamal Walji, Ramjibhai Ladha Dalal, and A. Kalidas Patel. Walji, an Ismaili who after his arrival in 1904 expanded a shop-keeping business from Hoima to Masindi and Kampala, acquired the first of his several ginneries in 1924. Dalal, who in 1923, eight years after his arrival, became the first cotton broker in Uganda, began to invest in ginning as well as a number of other industries and plantations about 1930. A. K. Patel, who immigrated in 1929, ran a general store for Africans in Kakoro and became a cotton buyer before joining his brother Chandulal, the renowned barrister of Jinja, in acquiring eight ginneries.[14]

The financing of ginneries, a costly venture requiring an initial outlay of Rs 150,000 (£5,625) and seven or eight times that amount in the first eight months of operation, led in many instances to the sharing of capital through the formation of partnerships. Prominent among the new companies were Vithaldas Haridas & Co., which at the time of its dissolution in 1947 was to own nineteen ginneries, Damodar Jinabhai & Co., which was to acquire ten, the Uganda Commercial Co. Ltd. with seven, and the New India Cotton Co. Ltd. with two.[15] As these companies illustrate, most of the larger ginning companies at the time of their formation or soon afterwards incorporated to provide limited liability for the investors. After World War II, to gain additional capital, some were to advance from private to public status by offering shares to investors at large.

Although most were founded exclusively with local capital, a large number of ginning companies had financial backing from India. In 1915 Purshotamdas Thakurdas, president of the Imperial Indian Citizenship Association in Bombay and a pioneering industrialist, had visited East Africa and returned with a sample of Uganda cotton, which he showed to the Khatau Makhanji Mills. A favourable assessment prompted the parent company Narandas Rajaram & Co. (Private) Ltd. to form in 1920 an East African subsidiary, Narandas Rajaram (Africa) Ltd., to undertake ginning for the Indian mill. Subsequently the new firm acquired thirteen ginneries in Uganda and one in Tanganyika. A number of Indian industrial leaders, such as Sir Homi Mehta, Sheth Ambalal Sarabhai, and Sheth Mafatlal Gagalbhai, formed partnerships with Uganda Asians for the manufacture of cotton for Indian textile mills. In 1929 the Uganda Commercial Co., a ginning concern that had been founded by Europeans, was purchased with £100,000 brought from India mainly so that four textile mills in India could be ensured of a regular supply of lint. By 1938 India-based firms had invested in fifty-three of the eighty-two Asian ginneries.[16]

It was N. K. Mehta who, after an unsuccessful venture with an Indian firm, introduced the Japanese to the East African cotton industry. In 1919, concerned over the growing European opposition to the Asians' growing presence in ginning, Mehta went to India to find other buyers than the BCGA. With Sheth Mathurdas Gokhaldas, who owned six mills in Bombay, he formed a partnership, the Sheth Mathurdas Nanji & Co., whereby Gokhaldas advanced money for the exclusive purchase of Mehta's lint. Three years later after Gokhaldas failed to keep his end of the bargain, Mehta dissolved the partnership and persuaded the Toyo Menka Kaisha Cotton Co., a Japanese textile manufacturer, to buy Uganda cotton. In return for advances of money, he undertook to provide ginned cotton on a commission basis of 1 per cent.[17] Subsequently more Japanese companies invested in African cotton, and by 1936, as noted, the Japanese owned ten Uganda ginneries.

In Tanganyika and Kenya the cotton industry was never so important as in Uganda, but it was the Asians, especially the successful ginners from Uganda, who again took the lead. They focused on the Mwanza area of Tanganyika, which proved the most suitable for cotton cultivation. Although they had not participated during the German period when cotton plantations and ginning were reserved for Germans, the Asians joined the British in buying the German plantations and ginneries auctioned at the end of the war. In the early 1930s when Tanganyika had 20 ginneries compared to Uganda's 125, the Asians outnumbered the European owners by a ratio of three to one. The first to open a ginnery in Mwanza was the old trading family of Nasser Virjee. Others who followed included the Sachoo family, Bagwanji Sunaji, and, from Uganda, Vithaldas Haridas, N. K. Mehta, Indra Singh Gill, Chaturbhai Khushalbhai Patel, and Ishverbhai Vithalbhai Patel. There was also the Bombay firm of Narandas Rajaram.[18]

In Kenya, despite soil and climate factors suitable to cotton cultivation in Nyanza and along the coast, the Asians had less opportunity to develop a ginning industry. For a number of reasons, including a policy of official neglect through most of the colonial period, competing labour demands on the Africans, low profitability per acre in comparison to other crops, poor communications, and lack of research facilities in the reserves, conditions were not so favourable as in Uganda and Tanganyika. Thus there were comparatively few ginneries, only three during the colonial period, for instance, in Nyanza, the area of concentration. Among the Asian owners in Nyanza were Mehta, Hasham Jamal, and the

Kassim Lakha brothers. At Mazeras near the coast ginneries were constructed by Kanji Meghji Shah and the Ismaili Karmali Khimji Pradhan.
Kanji toured the area to persuade farmers, mostly Arabs with whom he
had great influence, to grow cotton. The Nairobi businessmen Premchand Vrajpal Shah and Meghji Pethraj Shah of Premchand Raichand &
Co. also began ginning at Sagana and Meru and, for the management,
formed a new firm, the Kenya Cotton & Produce Co.[19]

Though less consequential for the economies of East Africa than ginning, another major industry, the manufacture of sugar, was initiated
between the wars by Asians and remained predominantly an Asian enterprise. Like ginning, it was centred in Uganda, and as explained in
Chapter 8, it was dominated by N. K. Mehta and Vithaldas Haridas and
eventually by Muljibhai Madhvani. Erecting his Lugazi factory at a cost
of £100,000, Mehta began to manufacture sugar in 1924. During the first
year, however, he produced only 30,000 bags instead of the contemplated 50,000 and suffered a severe financial loss. After inspecting sugar
factories on Mauritius, he was able to improve production and quality so
that by 1929 on 6,000 acres he put out 70,000 bags and began to prosper.
Ultimately Mehta was to expand his acreage to 22,000 acres, reach a production capacity of 600,000 bags (60,000 tons), and employ 10,000 Africans. As shown in Chapter 8, Mehta's experiment was emulated by
Vithaldas Haridas & Co. at Kakira not many miles distant and on a much
smaller scale at Ramisi on the Kenya coast south of Mombasa.[20]

Although the factories at Lugazi and Kakira were by far the most important, sugar manufacturing was undertaken between the wars by Europeans and at least one other Asian. When Vithaldas Haridas
established Kakira, two European factories were begun in Kenya and one
in Tanganyika. During the early 1930s when sugar profits were drastically curtailed by the world depression, these three joined with Mehta in
a syndicate through which all pooled their sugar and received a return
proportional to their production. Despite this effort, the two ventures in
Kenya soon collapsed. The sugar manufacturers included Indra Singh
Gill who, as explained in Chapter 8, set up a factory near Iganga for sugar
production and with the profits began to buy ginneries.[21]

Meanwhile the manufacture of crude sugar in the form of jaggery had
greatly increased and had become an African as well as Asian and European enterprise. Although most of the Asians' production of jaggery was
on a very small scale, some establishments, such as Prahlad Singh
Grewal's Manoni factory at Kibwezi and Hasham Jamal's plant at
Muhoroni, served hundreds of acres of cane. Apparently learning from
both Europeans and Asians, numerous Africans were beginning to manufacture jaggery, which they used mostly for brewing *tembo* (African

beer). During 1926 in Kenya's Central Province alone, Africans built fifty-one new sugar mills.[22]

A third important Asian industry established between the wars was the manufacture of wattle extract for tanning. Although there had been some previous Asian experiments, all paled in comparison to that of seven Shahs who in 1930 formed at Thika the Kenya Tanning Extract Co. Ltd. Meghji Pethraj Shah, who had begun a remarkable career in business on his arrival in Kenya in 1919, together with his brothers Raichand and Vaghji and his brother-in-law Hemraj Nathoo Shah, joined Premchand Vrajpal Shah and his two brothers Kachra and Juthalal in pooling their resources to erect a factory. After starting production in 1934 the new company proved unusually profitable, employed 150 Africans, and exported finely powdered bark and dry extract to more than thirty countries. It continued to flourish despite the eventual competition from a factory owned by the large British firm Forestal.[23]

Asians introduced a number of other industries in the interwar years. By 1922 Asians had begun an industry of quarrying and carving the unique soapstone of South Kavirondo. The district commissioner reported that year that six or seven fundi working with soapstone had made a profit of about Shs 4,000.[24] About the same time Asian artisans or traders may have initiated the Kamba wood carving of game animals, which were valued by tourists. Though written evidence is lacking, the fact that the carved elephants well into the 1950s were representations of Indian rather than African species has led many to this assumption.[25] Another new industry was shoemaking. The presence of many Europeans, clad in the customary heavy footwear of the temperate regions, afforded opportunity for shoe repair. A number of the Asians who set up shops soon began to handcraft shoes and boots on individual order.[26] In 1930 the Premchand Raichand group erected an aluminium processing press in Mombasa for manufacturing pots and other kitchen utensils. In the late 1930s two Ismaili brothers, Kassamali and Umedali Abdulrasul Somji, formed in Mombasa a small food-manufacturing company, Pims Food Products, that was to continue into the 1970s. Another early manufacturer, Abdulhussein Adamjee, produced fireworks and also black powder for blasting work in stone quarries.[27]

One Asian initiated a new industry through an association with East Africa's most renowned author-settler, the Baroness Karen von Blixen. The Bohra Yusufali Mulla Alibhai was hired by the Blixens to fell trees for fuel on their farm near Ngong. Yusufali's brother, Gulamhussein, discovered that some of the felled trees were sandalwood. He proceeded to set up a factory, the first of its kind in East Africa, for the manufacture of sandalwood oil. Other Asians, including the Bohra Akberali Hassanali, soon followed Gulamhussein in producing this oil.[28]

In addition to these industries, of which ginning and sugar were by far the most important, Asians between the wars continued with their earlier industries, most of which involved the processing of agricultural produce and mineral resources. Although development of these secondary industries occurred in all four territories, the greatest progress was in Kenya, where the Asians had accumulated the most capital in trade and artisanry and were encouraged by the protective tariff of 1923.[29] Unfortunately, among the hundreds of Asians who undertook manufacturing projects between the wars, only a few can be mentioned here.

During the interwar years Meghji Pethraj Shah, who was to become one of Kenya's wealthiest Asians and its leading philanthropist, laid the basis of his fortune by investing his commercial profits in a wattle-extract industry. He had arrived in Kenya from Dabasang near Jamnagar in 1919 when fifteen years old. After two years working for a relative as a book-keeper, he opened a general store, Raichand Bros., in Nairobi with his two brothers. The firm soon established a branch in Mbale and expanded into road transport and the manufacture of hair oil. In 1929 M. P. and his brothers joined another trading family—Premchand Vrajpal Shah and his two brothers—and the businessman Hemraj Nathoo Shah in forming Premchand Raichand & Co. The seven partners, who were to remain together for fourteen years, continued the existing businesses and added the export of African produce and the quarrying of stone. In 1934 they formed the Kenya Tanning Extract Co. Ltd. in Thika for the manufacture of wattle extract. M. P. assumed a leading role in initiating and expanding the wattle industry, and in 1943 when Premchand's move to India led to dissolution of Premchand Raichand & Co., the tanning factory went to M. P. and his new brother-in-law Hemraj Nathoo. It became M. P.'s most profitable enterprise and the basis of his fortune. He was to retire in 1953 when only forty-nine years old with a capital worth of £2.5 million.[30]

Three other Shah families illustrate how enterprising Asians added manufacturing to existing businesses. In 1925 Somchand Manekchand Shah, who had arrived in Kenya in 1906 at age eight to work for his uncle, established his own store in Nairobi, Mulchand Bros., in the name of his brother and began to sell Indian spices and provisions. Shortly afterwards he added a mill for the grinding of the many Indian spices. In 1932 two brothers, Premchand and Gulabchand Virpar Shah, left their shop in Thika to move to Makuyu, sixteen miles distant, where they established a general store, the Makuyu Trading Co. The next step was to construct a mill to grind the local Africans' maize for sale to a nearby European sisal estate. In the early 1930s after running a Nairobi petrol station that fueled the cars of European coffee planters, Dharamshi Pancha Shah perceived the possibility of buying their coffee for export. Founding a company in his own name, he purchased a van and a warehouse and began to collect raw coffee from highland farms. The warehouse became a factory for grading, sorting, and bagging the coffee to sell overseas. Eventually about ten Asians were to compete with D. P. Shah in processing settler coffee for export and local consumption.[31]

Although the Shahs in the area of Nairobi were conspicuous, Asians from other communities throughout East Africa undertook similar ventures. Hasham Jamal, an Ismaili who in 1906 had begun an importing-exporting business in Kampala, expanded into ginning in 1916 and saw-milling in 1928. The Ithnasheris Sheriff Dewji & Sons added a maize mill to their Mombasa copra and soap factories in 1924. In 1926 after one year in East Africa, the Hindu Mulji Keshavji formed the Kampala firm Jagjiwan Mulji & Brothers Ltd., which eventually was to employ forty Africans and five Asians in the production of clothing. The Bohra S. V. Kotecha, the son of T. S. Kotecha who is described in Chapter 8, expanded in 1935 into oil and rice milling with Coastal Industries Ltd. S. L. Patel, following the collapse of his hotel business in Kenya, fled to Tanganyika to escape his creditors, changed his name, and, forming the Patel Flour Milling Company, set up in 1932 the first maize mill in Dar es Salaam. Kehar Singh Kalsi, in 1936 after sixteen years as an employee, founded his own construction and contracting firm in Nairobi and began an assortment of activities including the manufacture of furniture. Mistry Mangal Singh, who had been a cabinet-maker for twenty-two years in Kenya, established a Nairobi company in 1931 for coach and body building. The Kassim Lakha family and Jamal Ramji & Co. both began to process coffee in Uganda, and the Kassim Lakhas erected at Port Bell the country's largest coffee factory.[32]

In the late 1930s Mehta and Vithaldas Haridas & Co. devoted their profits in sugar to the establishment of other industries. While adding the distillation of spirits to his sugar factory at Lugazi, Mehta branched into the manufacture of tea and sisal. With a subsidiary, the Uganda Tea Estate Ltd., he erected a tea factory on his plantation near Lugazi, and to serve his estates in Tanganyika he constructed a sisal factory that was soon producing an annual 2,000 tons of fibre. Vithaldas Haridas founded the Nile Industries & Tobacco Co. Ltd. to begin the manufacture of cigarettes.[33]

The Asians' interwar industrial expansion provoked a hostile reaction from the British government, European settlers, and Africans. In Uganda the rapid increase in the Asian ginneries, combined with the Asians' virtual monopoly of buying the raw cotton and an increasing exportation of the ginned cotton to India, alarmed the BEAC and the British government. In 1916 the BEAC's general manager threatened to withdraw his company's support of the BCGA, which he accused of 'recklessness and shortsighted support of Indians'.[34] In 1917 the acting governor warned the Colonial Office that the Asian ginners were prepared to take the whole crop, and that Japanese agents were beginning to employ Asian buyers. 'It is cutthroat all round', he exclaimed.[35] The next year the Uganda manager of the BEAC wrote, 'A definite crisis has arisen, and we are faced with the prospect of the Cotton industry going almost entirely into Indian hands. . . . It appears to be only a question of time and evolution when the whole crop will be bought by Indians'.[36] Uganda's Governor Coryndon, confirming the seriousness of the situation, remarked that 'no responsible man, public or official, seemed to be alive to the hold on the trade of the country which the Indians have already obtained'. It was bad for Lancashire, he said, and 'the influence of this type of commercial morality upon the native African is not good'. Coryndon intimated that controls should be imposed on Asian immigration.[37]

Resentment against the Asian ginners and traders culminated in restrictive legislation. As early as 1913, to break the Asians' hold on the buying of cotton from African cultivators, the government had issued the Uganda Cotton Rules, which gave it control over the establishment of new ginneries and prohibited anyone other than a ginner from buying raw cotton. At the end of World War I when the rules began to be applied, the Asian traders formed an Association of Indian Cotton Merchants that solicited aid from the Indians Overseas Association in London in sending a deputation to the Colonial Office. Because of the protest, the rules were amended to permit anyone under licence to purchase cotton, but the government kept the annual licence fee at Rs 100 (£6 13s 4d), so high that most Asian traders were forced to become virtual agents of the main cotton dealers, Asian as well as European. It became increasingly difficult for traders to amass the capital essential for construction of a ginnery. In contrast, the existing Asian ginners such as Visram, Rajaram, Jaffer, Jamal, and Mehta could finance expansion with relative ease. In 1920 the government excluded merchants from buying cotton within a five-mile radius of existing or projected ginneries on the assumption that Africans within those areas could sell directly to the ginners. In 1930 a law applying to all territories restricted the buying by a ginnery to a single district.[38]

These measures not only curtailed the growth of the Asian cotton industry, but also created a division within the Asian community. After the war the Asian ginners tended to join with leading Europeans in the Uganda Chamber of Commerce and to ally with the government, whereas the smaller traders formed Indian Associations in the various urban centres and urged political, social, and economic reforms. The division became apparent in 1921 when the Uganda Chamber of Commerce and Uganda Development Commission, both with Asian membership, supported the government in a policy of municipal and residential segregation that the Kampala Indian Association bitterly opposed.[39]

As in Uganda, the rapid growth of Asian enterprise in the cotton industry of Tanganyika prompted the government to adopt a discriminatory policy. In 1932 the legislature enacted marketing ordinances that permitted monopoly, and in 1934 by government notice, ostensibly in the interest of African producers, the government inaugurated a policy of limiting the number of ginneries and regulating the cotton markets. Against vigorous protest from organizations such as the Middlemen Cotton Growers' Asociation of Morogoro, the government continued to bar the erection of new ginneries. Despite assurances that the policy was nondiscriminatory and in the interest of the country, guaranteeing the production of quality cotton, the excluded Asians believed that the policy was designed to promote vested European interests and gain revenue.[40]

In Zanzibar the Asians encountered stiff opposition in their attempts to establish facilities for the processing of cloves. In the early 1920s the cloves were shipped to Britain for processing by five British firms within the Association of British Chemical Manufacturers. In 1924 a group of Asian clove exporters applied for permission to set up a processing factory on Zanzibar. They were successfully opposed, however, by a local Agricultural Commission that reported in favour of maintaining the British monopoly.[41]

In Kenya, too, the essential British policy before World War II of discouraging the formation of industries in the colonies that would compete with the vested manufacturing interests at home adversely affected Asian initiatives. Under pressure from the powerful British textile manufacturers, several projects proposed by Asians to establish textile mills in Kenya were vetoed by the Colonial Office.[42]

During the 1930s in all the mainland territories, Asian industrial expansion was curtailed by marketing legislation, hostility from European settlers, rising competition from Africans, and a concerted move by the local native councils and district commissisoners to oust the Asians from all industry in the African areas. As noted in Chapter 2, the marketing legislation of 1932–35 confined Asian traders within African areas to a few designated trading centres. As ginners, millers, and other manufacturers involved in the processing of African produce usually bought directly from the African cultivators, they were severely restricted in their overall business. Meanwhile African competition, which had begun in many of the processing industries within the 1920s, steadily increased and was encouraged by the government, which offered training and other aid to Africans in industries such as brick-making, dairying, and wattle extraction. The local native councils, which were empowered to license almost all types of business in the African areas, began to withhold licences from Asian applicants for the operation of dairies, flour and oil mills, quarrying and brick-making, and similar industries and to aspire to an African monopoly of all manufacturing in their areas. They were assisted in this by the district officers. In the Kenya highlands there was a similar move by the settlers to deprive the Asians of any vested manufacturing interest.[43]

As a result of the growing restrictions, Asians found it difficult to recover from the effects of the Great Depression. The pace of their industrial development slowed during the 1930s, and the high numbers of business failures continued to the outbreak of war.[44] World War II, which not only severely limited foreign trade but also prompted the imposition of price controls, was a further hindrance to recovery. The demand for goods that could no longer be obtained from abroad, however, opened some opportunities for local manufacture.

A considerable number of Asians began new manufacturing ventures during the war. In Kenya Mohammed Manji and his son Madatally, who had opened a Nairobi bakery in 1938, greatly expanded to supply bread and biscuits for the British soldiers and macaroni for the Italian prisoners of war. The Kenya Overseas Co. Ltd. began in 1941 with wholesaling and soon added the manufacture of cosmetics, perfumes, creams, and hair oils. Quayum Dar established an important sawmill at Karatina in 1944. Dayalji Jeram Kharecha started to build bus and lorry bodies, Raman T. Thakore established a factory for brooms, brushes, and floor polish, and the brothers Mulchand, Ramniklal, and Keshavlal Bhagwanji moved into food canning and match manufacture. Gill increased his sawmills in Uganda to four and acquired two ginneries, and O. P. Bharadia opened a furniture factory in Tanga. In Uganda Abdulla Fazal, one of the leading coffee buyers, established two coffee factories.[45]

Post-war Growth and Increasing Regulation

World War II has been regarded as a turning point in the history of manufacturing in East Africa. A severe shortage of imported commodities during the war showed how dependent the territories were on foreign manufactures. Britain emerged from the war with a shattered economy and a huge foreign debt. In desperation it revised its traditional imperial policy to foster a greater economic production throughout the empire. The new policy, designed to increase colonial exports, had two points of emphasis: (1) the encouragement of manufacturing in the colonies, and (2) the development of African cash crops. Manufacturing was to be stimulated through financial aid, tariff protection against foreign manufactures, reduced duties on the importation of raw materials, tax concessions, and monopolies. Government was to assume a new role in industrial planning, financial assistance, regulation and control, and even the ownership of industry. The result was a redirection of capital from the support of estate agriculture to investment in manufacturing.[46]

During the two remaining decades of British colonialism, the manufacturing sector of all the economies on the mainland sharply advanced. In Kenya, which continued as the area of the greatest enterprise, the advance has been called 'spectacular'. Manufacturing contributed 13.8 per cent to Kenya's net domestic production in 1958 as compared to 8.5 per cent in 1947.[47] Nairobi's industrial area became the East African centre. The expansion in Kenya, as in the interwar years, was largely a result of outside initiative by foreign companies, most of which were British. Among the new subsidiaries of British firms were Kenya Canners Ltd. established by Pickering & West, Bamburi Portland Cement Co. Ltd. by Amalgamated Roadstone, Associated Packers Ltd. by Mitchell Cotts, E. A. Stationery Manufacturers Ltd. by Dickinson, Crown Cork Co. E.A. Ltd. by Crown Seals, East African Oil Refineries Ltd. by Shell-B.P., East African Tobacco Co. Ltd. by British American Tobacco, and Fitzgerald Baynes & Co. Ltd. by Canada Dry. Although the foreign firms were responsible for most of the new development, the Asians made a substantial contribution. Unlike the local Europeans, the Asians emerged from the war with sizeable savings from trade and artisanry, and they invested not only in the establishment of new factories, but also in the take-over of existing companies. With the foreign firms they rapidly absorbed the declining settler enterprise.[48]

Asian manufacturing in the post-war era underwent considerable change. Far more than before the war the new Asian industries were situated in the cities and towns. While continuing to expand in the processing of farm produce and other local goods, Asians took up a wide assortment of new manufacturing. They also began to import the essential raw materials and to produce products for export as well as local consumption. There are several reasons for these changes. Because of the difficulties of continuing in the rural areas, many of those who had undertaken some form of rural manufacturing moved to the cities and towns to begin a new business. They were joined by traders and artisans who were also increasingly constrained to leave the outlying regions. Some among these migrants, because of stiff competition from established urban businessmen and craftsmen, found more opportunity in a new form of manufacturing. The fact that many of the families who left the rural areas had become second- or third-generation residents of East Africa meant that one or more of the younger members had obtained a university degree in business administration, economics, engineering, or law. This enhanced the Asians' capacity for venturing into an enterprise that required a complex combination of capital formation, technology, management skills, and, in many instances, collaboration with foreign associates.

The wealthy Asians who had engaged extensively in manufacturing before the war continued to expand. The foremost in the first thirteen years of the post-war era was Muljibhai Prabhudas Madhvani. With the dissolution in 1946 of Vithaldas Haridas & Co., which he managed, the company's subsidiaries together with its nineteen ginneries, two oil mills, and two soap factories were divided (as previously noted) among its partners. While Muljibhai's elder brother Nanjibhai took over the Ramisi sugar factory on the Kenya coast, Muljibhai retained the sugar complex at Kakira. Within the next few years he established four new concerns: Muljibhai Madhvani & Co. Ltd., Uganda (Kakira) Sugar Works Ltd., Madhvani Industries Ltd., and Muljibhai Madhvani Investment Corp. Ltd. By 1958 when he died at age sixty-four, he had not only expanded the Kakira sugar works and cane plantations but also acquired two soap factories, three ginneries, a glass factory, a maize mill, a vegetable ghee factory, a jaggery plant, a sweets factory, and a tea plantation.[49]

Unlike Madhvani's, Mehta's industrial activity in East Africa, which had been spectacular between the wars, was less impressive in the post-war years because Mehta's interests and a sizeable portion of his capital were devoted to India. Entrusting the management of his sugar, tea, and sisal factories after the war to his sons and nephew, Mehta left East Africa to undertake building projects in India and eventually to retire to a life of religious contemplation in Porbandar.[50]

Despite Mehta's personal concern with affairs in India, the collective organization, known as the Mehta Group of Industries, continued to expand and improve its factory holdings in East Africa under the able direction of Mehta's son Mahendrabhai. In 1960 the group formed the Lugala Tea Estates Ltd. to develop a tea estate and factory. The next year it organized the East African Sugar Industries Ltd. to construct at Muhoroni, thirty-six miles from Kisumu, a sugar factory similar to but smaller than that at Lugazi. Designed for an annual production of 50,000 tons, this factory was a co-operative venture in which the Kenya government donated land for the plantation and the African workers were eventually to own 25 per cent of the company.[51]

Like the Madhvanis and Mehtas, the Shahs who had formed the Kenya Tanning Extract Co. joined the Chandaria firm of Premchand Bros. Ltd. in undertaking a rapid industrial expansion. By the end of the war the enlarged group had not only the parent companies, including Premchand Raichand & Co. and Premchand Bros. Ltd., but also flour mills in Mombasa, Meru, and Sagana; an aluminium stamping factory in Mombasa (Kenya Aluminium & Industrial Works Ltd.); a lumber mill in Limuru; a pasta-making factory in Nairobi (Pure Food Products Ltd.); a ginnery in Sagana; and a tanning factory in Limuru. Meanwhile some within the group, led by Premchand Vrajpal Shah, had moved to India to found textile mills, a stock brokerage, and a grain distribution business. It was differences over the expansion into India, as noted, that caused the group to split in 1943. While M. P. and H. N. Shah acquired Premchand Raichand and the Kenya Extract Tanning Co., Premchand continued with his Indian interests, B. R. Shah received Pure Food Products, and the Chandarias emerged with Premchand Bros. and Kenya Aluminium.[52]

After the division the members of the original group still in East Africa continued with further industrial ventures. In 1961 some of the Shahs, who had reorganized as the Premchandbhai Group Ltd., combined with Mulchand Somchand Khimasia, manager of Bhagwanji & Co. Ltd., in founding Sheets Manufacturers Ltd. The new company, situated in Mombasa, produced galvanized, corrugated iron sheeting from rolls of imported metal. In that same year a rival firm, Mabati Ltd., was founded in Dar es Salaam by the Chandaria family. For almost two years these two factories, the first to produce corrugated sheets in East Africa, engaged in a fierce competition. In 1962 they wisely amalagamated into Galsheet Sales Ltd. of Mombasa and proceeded, in co-operation with Kawasaki of Japan, to add the heavy machinery for rolling sheet metal from imported iron ingots. Galsheet was directed by Premchand Vrajpal's son, Kishor Premchand Shah.[53]

Most other Asians who had turned to manufacturing in the interwar period expanded their interests in the post-war years. The bread-maker Manji, sawmiller Gill, and oil-miller Kotecha are examples. As soon as foreign travel was permitted after the war, Manji visited bakeries in Europe, and he returned in 1949 to open in Nairobi the Whitehouse Bakery Ltd., the first automatic bread-making plant in East Africa. In 1953 after further expansion he established the House of Manji Ltd., the most modern biscuit factory in all tropical Africa. During the next five years he added equipment for the manufacture of vermicelli and noodles. Meanwhile Gill was extending his sawmilling operations from Uganda to Tanganyika. Entrusting management of his Uganda holdings to his son Balbinder, he founded Sikh Saw Mills (Tanganyika) Ltd. in 1949, set up a sawmill in Tanga, and began construction of a plywood factory. S. V. Kotecha's oil- and rice-milling business was augmented after the war by the addition of his son, T. S., who had obtained a university degree in industrial chemistry. The two expanded Coastal Industries Ltd. in Mombasa and in 1961 established a Nairobi factory, Sava Mills Ltd., which soon was milling 50 per cent of Kenya's rice crop. Meanwhile the Kotechas were acquiring ginneries in Uganda.[54]

There were also in the last two colonial decades a number of newcomers to manufacturing, some of whom were to become very prominent industrialists. Perhaps the foremost were the Chandarias. Jains, like the Shahs, the Chandarias began after the war a unique manufacturing development of international proportion. From a farming background near Jamnagar, Premchand Popat Chandaria had come to Nairobi in 1914 to work as a shop boy for an Asian importer. Three years later he had formed with three Khimasia brothers a provisions firm, Premchand Popat & Co. Joined by his brothers and nephews, he soon expanded to Mombasa. In 1928 Premchand separated from the Khimasias, who started their own retailing business under the name Bhagwanji & Co. He then combined with one of the Khimasia brothers, Raichand, in forming another retail trading firm, Premchand Raichand & Co. This was the situation in 1940 when he merged with the Shah group in the Kenya Tanning Extract Co. It was Premchand who later in the war had established Pure Food Products to produce pasta for the Italian prisoners of war.[55]

After the separation of 1943 the Chandaria interests were to be managed by Premchand's four able sons, Devchand (known as D. P.), Ratilal (R. P.), Keshavlal (K. P.), and Manu, together with their uncle, Maganlal (M. P.), and their cousins, Kanti, Kapur, and Anil. The university degrees in engineering and commerce-banking obtained by K. P., Manu, Kanti, and Kapur in 1950 and 1951 and later by Anil greatly enhanced the family's capability.[56]

During the 1950s the Chandarias began a rapid industrial expansion. Relocating and revising Kenya Aluminium in 1950, they increased production of stamped products two and one-half times and incorporated in the company's operation a maize grinding mill. In 1953 after R. P. had purchased machinery in Japan, they began in Dar es Salaam a similar factory, Aluminium Africa Ltd., to manufacture not only aluminium hollowware but also wire nails, galvanized iron pipe, and hurricane lamps. The next year in Mombasa, as a result of K. P.'s inspection of mills in Italy, the Chandarias established a rolling mill for sheet aluminium. It was the first such mill in tropical Africa. In Nairobi in 1957 after purchasing with Bhagwanji & Co. a factory from a failing European concern, they began to manufacture matches. That same year against intense opposition from the settler's Unga Ltd., they started wheat flour mills in Nairobi and Mombasa. Most of these ventures were not easily accomplished. The British government, in the words of K. P., 'gave us a hell of a time'. The East African Common Services Organization was anti-Asian and 'opposed much of what we did'.[57]

Partly because of the discrimination, the Chandarias had begun to expand outside East Africa. Unlike many other industrialists, they were not concerned with a long-range tie to India. After association with Premchand Vrajpal Shah in Indian stockbroking, speculating in commodities, distributing grain, and founding a small textile mill, they independently had run a dhow passenger service between Jamnagar and Mombasa, but after the war they withdrew from India to retain only a non-controlling interest in some Jamnagar salt beds. In 1950 to have a presence at the imperial centre, they formed a dummy company in London, and in 1960 R. P. moved there to open a permanent establishment, Comcraft Services Ltd., for management of their interests outside Africa. The Chandarias had decided, however, that Africa was the continent of greatest opportunity. In 1951 they sent Kanti to Burundi to set up an aluminium stamping plant in Bujumbura, and in 1960 R. P. established a similar factory at Bukavu in the Congo. Two years later while negotiating for industrial opportunity in Tanganyika, the family built an aluminium hollowware factory in Addis Ababa.[58]

Among other individuals who achieved prominence as manufacturers in the post-war years, Lakhamshi R. Shah deserves emphasis. After his arrival in East Africa at age fourteen, L. R. Shah, as he was known, began working in a Nairobi general store run by distant relatives. Three years later he pooled his savings with three others, including his father-in-law, Hemraj Bharmal Shah, to found Hemraj Bharmal & Co. In time this company, centred in Nairobi, developed an extensive trade in the sale of blankets and other imported textiles to Africans, and L. R. Shah took the major role in developing its business by personally scouting opportunities, as he later recalled, 'in every town and village in East Africa'.[59]

After World War II L. R. Shah decided to devote the profits of Hemraj Bharmal to the development of manufacturing. In 1955 he combined with other Asians in reorganizing and incorporating in Dar es Salaam the Chandarias' former company Pure Food Products for the production of canned fruit and juices. Three years later he persuaded Moses Chu, a Chinese man who had been supplying Hemraj Bharmal with textiles from Hong Kong, Taiwan, and Mauritius, to join him in forming a small manufacturing plant, Tanganyika Textile Industries Ltd., in Dar es Salaam. They shared the financing and profits on a fifty-fifty basis, and Chu managed the factory. It was the first textile mill in Tanganyika. In 1960 Shah persuaded his Japanese supplier of blankets, Maruki & Co. Ltd., to assist him in establishing Blanket Manufacturers (Tanganyika) Ltd. in Dar es Salaam. The Japanese were to provide the manufacturing technology and machinery and Shah the market research and sales, and both were to share equally the financing and profits. The new company was the second in East Africa—preceded by Nakuru Industries Ltd.—to manufacture blankets. Shah then undertook a similar venture in Kenya. In 1962 he negotiated in Japan with two of the largest textile firms, Shikishima Spinning Co. Ltd. and Nomura Trading Co. Ltd., to construct in Thika a weaving factory with a fifty-fifty shareholding. United Textiles Industries (Kenya) Ltd., the second mill of its type in Kenya, began production in 1963.[60]

Another important newcomer to industrial manufacturing in the post-war period was Mulchand Somchand Khimasia. Born in 1923 and sharing the Jain religion with the Shahs and Chandarias, he was the son of Somchand Meghji Khimasia, who had immigrated from Saurashtra to East Africa in 1917 and who, with his two brothers, had joined the Chandarias in founding Premchand Popat & Co. In 1936 Mulchand had joined the family business, which was then Bhagwanji & Co., and within two years had become the manager and enlarged the company's activities to include wholesaling, importing, and exporting. His first industrial venture occurred in 1955 when be combined with the Shah group in forming Pure Food Products Ltd. In 1958 when a failing European matchmaking factory on the Kinangop was offered for sale, Khimasia and other Asians were the only bidders. Because the factory was situated in the highlands, however, the government would not let the ownership be transferred to an Asian. After a year of fruitless negotiation, Khimasia purchased the machinery, moved it to Mombasa, and established the East African Match Co. (Kenya) Ltd. In 1959 he assumed control of Nath Brothers Ltd., an Asian spinning and knitting mill in Thika.[61]

Keshavji Jethabhai Chande also deserves mention among the post-war industrialists. A Lohana from the area of Junagadh in the Gujarat, he had come to Mombasa in 1922 to seek better opportunity to care for his widowed mother, three younger brothers, and two sisters. He worked for Asian firms in Mombasa and Bukene until 1927 when he established Keshavji Jethabhai & Brothers for trading in western Tanganyika. After ten years he invested the profits in a factory in Bukene for crushing oil and milling rice and maize. At the end of the war he sent his younger brother Ratansi to Dar es Salaam to found Chande Brothers Ltd. for the export of agricultural produce. Then in 1949 he established Chande Industries Ltd., which at a cost of £100,000 constructed a modern wheat and maize flour mill, an oil-crushing plant, a soap factory, and a honey refinery. By the time of his death in 1959 he had built another flour mill in Dar es Salaam and laid the foundation for an extensive industrial development by his son in independent Tanzania.[62]

Two other important Asians among the new industrialists were Devjibhai Karamshi Hindocha and Chhotabhai Motibhai Patel. Hindocha, who in 1906 at age eighteen had come to East Africa from Modpar, near

Jamnagar, became a partner in Vithaldas Haridas & Co. In 1946 when the company was dissolved, Hindocha obtained some of the Kenya interests, and within a year he purchased from an Australian family near Kisumu the Victoria Nyanza Sugar Co., which was producing about 3,000 tons per year. Renaming the company the Miwani Sugar Mills Ltd., expanding the acreage in cane, and modernizing the factory, Hindocha raised the annual production tenfold by 1960. In that year he added a distillery to produce industrial methylated and rectified alcohol. Chhotabhai Motibhai Patel, who arrived in Uganda as a boy in 1908 and worked successively for Allidina Visram and the BEAC, turned to manufacturing in 1940. In association with the well-known Kampala businessman Ishverbhai Vithalbhai Patel, he formed Pambani Ltd. for operating a ginnery at Mwanza. The two later acquired ginneries also at Kwimbaha and Nyayabiti. By 1960 C. M. Patel had added an oil mill at Mwanza as well as a steel factory in Baroda to what was known as the C. M. Group Ltd.[63]

Many other Asians who participated in the extensive post-war development of manufacturing could be mentioned, but space permits only a listing of their numerous ventures. Although few new ginneries were built, a number changed hands as traders with capital bought from pre-war owners. Flour milling, oil production, soap manufacture, sisal cording, coffee hulling, construction of motor-vehicle bodies, shoemaking, sawmilling, and furniture making also continued as attractive industries to those who took up manufacturing. A number of ironworking or vehicle repair businesses evolved into engineering works. The only industry of the pre-war years to decline was soda water manufacture, which suffered from the competition of Coca-Cola and other imports. The more unique Asian ventures included the manufacture of concrete pipe, fertilizer from seaweed, packaged tea, leather products, graphite, and confectionery. There was even a new factory for tinting sunglasses.[64]

By the end of the colonial period, manufacturing, as illustrated in Table 9.1, had become one of the main sectors of the East African economies. The greatest progress had occurred in Kenya, and Uganda had surpassed Tanganyika. In all the territories, however, manufacturing was still inferior to agriculture, commerce, and transport.

Because of a dearth of published information and the lack of parallel records in the territories, it is impossible to assess the Asians' contribution with precision and to make meaningful territorial comparisons. There are, however, some individual publications that afford an indication of the Asians' role. In Kenya in 1948, for instance, a census report revealed a surprising 7,351 Asians in manufacturing as compared to 10,265 in commerce, 4,674 in public services, 3,508 in construction, and 2,689 in transport and communication. In Uganda the Control of Indus-

TABLE 9.1 Manufacturing (£ million), in the GNP of the Mainland Territories, 1962

Economic Sector	Kenya	Tanganyika	Uganda	East Africa
Manufacturing	23.0 (13%)	8.5 (7%)	9.8 (9%)	41.3 (10%)
Agriculture	39.6 (22%)	48.5 (39%)	46.4 (43%)	134.5 (33%)
Trade and finance	42.4 (24%)	12.4 (10%)	18.1 (17%)	72.9 (18%)
Transportation, communication	25.2 (14%)	15.7 (13%)	8.3 (8%)	49.2 (12%)
Government services	28.0 (16%)	17.3 (14%)	7.3 (7%)	52.6 (13%)
Total GNP	180.0	123.2	107.9	411.1

Sources: Compiled from D. S. Pearson, *Industrial Development in East Africa* (Nairobi: Oxford University Press, 1969), table 4, p. 15.

tries Committee reported that from 1943 to 1948 a total of 123 licences for manufacturing had been issued to Asians in contrast to 29 to Europeans and 3 to Africans. Among the Asian licences 36 were for producing brake fluid, 21 for soap, 13 for vegetable oil, 9 for bricks and tiles, 8 for flour, 7 for brushes and brooms, 6 for buttons and combs, 4 for leather products, and 3 for starch.[65]

In all East Africa the Asians' potential for the development of manufacturing in the post-war years was curtailed by a sharp increase in government regulation, the co-operative movement, African competition, and the fostering of monopolies. The restrictions were most apparent in the cotton and coffee industries. As early as 1942 the Uganda government had begun to eliminate Asian middlemen in the cotton industry by buying and selling cotton. A Lint Marketing Board purchased the raw cotton from growers at a fixed price and then auctioned it to ginners. The government kept the difference, which before would have been shared by the growers and ginners. Although withholding licences for new ginneries from Asians, the government encouraged the establishment of ginneries by African co-operatives and, empowered by the Acquistion of Ginneries Ordinance of 1952, it began to take over ginneries for administration by Africans. By 1962 11 of Uganda's 134 ginneries were African co-operatives.[66]

In Tanganyika, where price-fixing and co-operatives were also favoured, the government during the war had begun a policy of zoning to save petrol. It allotted each ginnery a zone, the size of which was based on the ginnery's past performance, and required the ginnery to

confine its buying of cotton to its zone. Continued after the war, the zoning policy prevented innovation and expansion. In the post-war years
Tanganyika also restricted the licensing of ginners to about a dozen
Asians and Europeans who had large amounts of capital. Ostensibly designed to promote quality cotton and diminish the role of middleman,
the policy produced monopolies and in the view of the excluded Asians
was really intended to raise revenue.[67]

The coffee industry in Uganda was another instance of a government-
fostered monopoly. In the early 1930s the government had entrusted the
hulling and curing of African-grown coffee to three firms: A. Baumann &
Co., the Masaka Cotton Co., and Jamal Ramji & Co. A few other companies had been licensed before the war, but they were restricted to hulling
each year only a few hundred tons of coffee and were forced to pay a
high fee to the big three for curing and grading. No African coffee could
leave Uganda without going through these companies, and much of the
coffee had to be hauled long distances to reach them. During the ten
years preceding 1952, despite the fact that the African coffee crop doubled, no new hulling firms were licensed. The favoured companies had
no reason to upgrade their machinery; aspiring industrialists, whether
Asian, European, or African, were prevented from opening hulleries; and
the system was expensive for the smaller companies and the African
growers. The fact that the government's deputy coffee controller, H. A.
Frazer, was also the managing director of A. Baumann perhaps helps to
explain the continuance of the monopoly.[68]

In 1948 the governments of Kenya, Tanganyika, and Uganda introduced legislation for a common policy of industrial licensing. Administered by an East African Industrial Council, the legislation gave the
governments a control over manufacturing that they had not had previously. In the interest of protecting manufacturers in scheduled industries from competition, it permitted the governments to set monopolies
and waive customs duties on essential raw materials. In 1949 Nyanza
Textile Industries (NYTIL), which had been formed by the British firm
Calico Printers' Association in partnerhip with the Uganda government,
received a five-year exclusive licence for the production of cotton yarn
and piece-goods. Because of sharp criticism, the monopoly was withdrawn at the end of the five years with the result that Asian entrepreneurs like L. R. Shah were at last able to establish competing factories. By
1960 eleven industries—including cotton, woolen, and synthetic textiles; sheet glass, metal window and door frames; and enamel
hollowware—all had been scheduled. Despite recommendations by several investigating bodies that the legislation be abolished because of its
adverse effect on development, the licensing was retained.[69]

Within the two decades preceding independence the governments proceeded, as the NYTIL partnership illustrates, to assume a prominent role in manufacturing. In 1944 as a wartime measure Kenya created an Industrial Management Board to establish government factories for supplying the armed forces with essentials such as crockery, cooking oil, and sulphuric acid for batteries. After the war government intervention assumed new forms. Although Tanganyika went no further than to favour certain industries with monopolies and other concessions, Uganda and Kenya proceeded to government ownership. The primary function of the Uganda Development Corp. (UDC), formed in 1952, was to stimulate the growth of manufacturing through the government's lending money, granting favoured licences, and participating as a shareholder in new companies. With an initial capital of £5 million, the UDC was the largest such organization in East Africa, and by 1965 it was to hold a controlling interest in nine manufacturing subsidiaries and a substantial interest in seven 'associated' firms.[70]

The Kenya organization was created in 1954 when the Industrial Management Board was replaced with an Industrial Development Council (IDC). By 1960 the IDC had invested in two hotels, a soap factory, and a coastal fishing project. During the following year it participated in the establishment of factories for canning, cashew nut processing, and the manufacture of buttons and fluorescent lights. In such endeavour the IDC, like its counterpart in Uganda, promoted African industry often in co-operation with European firms and foreign governments. The various activities caused a great increase in expenditure. In Uganda, for instance, government expenditure from 1945 to 1960 increased by five times.[71]

Official encouragement of manufacturing is manifest in the drafting of development plans, creation of central lending agencies, promotion of African rural industries, and construction of the Owen Falls Dam. Uganda launched its first development plan in 1944, Tanganyika in 1946, and Kenya in 1954. Revised at three-year intervals, the plans increasingly emphasized the manufacturing sector and government intervention. In 1963 all three governments inaugurated development finance companies—for Kenya the DFCK, Tanganyika the TDFL, and Uganda the DFCU—each of which was financed initially at £1.5 million, comprising equal donations from the territorial government, the Commonwealth Development Corp., and the German Development Corp. These companies lent money for manufacturing but unlike the development corporations did not operate their own enterprises. In the rural areas the governments began to create their own dairies, brick works, and other secondary industries and to encourage Africans in similar manufacture, particularly through co-operatives, with loans from the central government and the African district councils. Joint boards, as noted in Chapter 2, became the agencies for providing training and loans to Africans through an International Co-operation Administration.[72]

The results of all these efforts were disappointing. Kenya's manufacturing output between 1955 and 1961 rose from £17.4 million to only £22.7 million, less than 5 per cent a year. Employment in 'manufactures and repairs' fell from an all-time high of 57,000 in 1957 to 42,500 in 1961. Expenditure on new machinery, equipment, and commercial motor vehicles by the private sector dropped during that time from £9 million to £7.5 million. The colonial government's principal agency for industrial development, the IDC, suffered from what has been described as 'loss of money followed by loss of nerve'.[73] Part of the explanation for the overall failure lies in the uncertainty accompanying the approach of independence. Part also must be ascribed to the growth of government restrictions, the emphasis on co-operatives and monopolies, and the increasing costs to the manufacturer. L. R. Shah confided that taxation alone began to kill incentive by 1960. 'In Kenya if we earned £10,000', he said, 'we were left with Shs 60,000 (£3,000)'.[74] At that time the tax on every pound of income over £9,000 earned by individuals was Shs 15 representing a rate of 75 per cent. In all three territories the income tax on public companies was 27.5 per cent, fairly low in comparison to that in most industrial countries, but for some private companies an added 'undistributed income tax' could raise the total to 75 per cent.[75] In addition to income taxes there were customs and excise duties, graduated personal taxes, licensing fees, transport taxes, and numerous other charges. The burden fell heavily on the Asians and Europeans and virtually excluded individual Africans from a role in manufacturing.

Adaptation to African Socialism

Despite the failings of the colonial administration's managed economy, the new governments of East Africa, as explained in Chapter 2, declared policies of African socialism, retained all the restrictive measures on individual enterprise, and proceeded to add others. It was in Tanzania and Uganda that the measures proved most onerous.

Tanzania undertook no significant alteration of its inherited industrial policies until promulgation of the Arusha Declaration in February 1967. It retained the colonial government's interest in promoting industry and encouraged foreign investment to reduce the country's reliance on overseas imports. With the Kampala Agreement of 1964 it also sought to diminish its dependency on imports from Kenya and to a lesser degree Uganda arising from the customs union of 1927. In 1964 the government replaced the development agencies that it had inherited from the colonial period with a parastatal National Development Corp. that, with far more money than its Kenya counterpart, emphasized the development of industry in the major urban centres. The Arusha Declaration, however, brought a drastic shift from industry to agriculture, from mechanized to 'hoe' cultivation, and from urban to rural development. Henceforth the ujamaa (self-help) village, rather than the commercial and industrial city or town, became the centre of Tanzanian enterprise.[76]

With these changes came a program of nationalization. All the private banks were brought into a National Banking Corp., the seven major flour mills were taken over by a National Milling Corp., all the Asian shops in rural areas were confiscated, and in 1971 under an Industrial Acquisition Act—what one Asian termed 'a black mark on Tanzanian history'—the government acquired the right to assume the major ownership in any industry. In Mwanza the government took all the ginneries, about seventeen, transferred them to a National Co-operatives Union, and, according to Asians, never honoured its promise of compensation.[77]

Although an alarming fall in both agricultural and industrial production prompted Nyerere in 1977 to revise his socialist experiment, the prospect for Asian initiatives in manufacturing remained far less than in Kenya. The Third Development Plan of 1977–81 switched the emphasis by devoting twice as much of the projected budget to the development of industry as to that for agriculture. Socialism in the form of government ownership and regulation, however, was retained as the essential policy. Industrial expansion was entrusted largely to seventy-one District Development Corporations, and a Small Industries Development Corp. Parastatals, which by 1981 numbered 380, continued to control more than half the economy. There was very little opportunity for private initiative in manufacturing in the mainland portion of Tanzania and even less on Zanzibar. During the revolution of January 1964 all thirteen factories on Zanzibar were confiscated in one day, and nearly all the Asians emigrated. During the subsequent administrations of Presidents Abeid Karume and Aboud Jumbe, they were not encouraged to return.[78]

Under Obote Uganda pursued a course very similar to that of Tanzania with a twofold policy of socialism and Africanization. Before 1967 when he introduced a new constitution, concentrating power in the office of president, Obote continued the British policy of encouraging the development of the industrial sector. At the outset of his administration he issued an Industrial Charter inviting both local and overseas investment in Uganda manufacturing. Under protective tariffs with joint investment by the UDC and local and foreign private capital, manufacturing grew at twice the pace of the economy. Nevertheless, Obote retained the British emphasis on government control and the transfer of ownership to co-operatives. By 1966 co-operatives controlled

42 of the country's 115 ginneries and were allocated 75 per cent of the crop. After the constitutional changes of 1967, Obote intensified the take-over of ginneries and began to regulate the economy through parastatals.[79] As explained in Chapter 2, however, he failed in his aim to raise farm prices by substituting parastatals for the Asian wholesalers, retailers, and artisans, with the result that there was widespread rural unrest and the assassination attempt of 1969.

Obote's subsequent 'move to the left' culminating in his Common Man's Charter was aimed at suppressing Asian industry as well as Asian trade and agriculture. It entailed an assumption by government of a 60 per cent ownership of all industry and offered no immediate compensation. The government's share was to be paid in succeeding years from the company profits. Obote appointed a Commission for Africanization of Commerce and Industry, and the commission introduced an immigration bill requiring all non-citizens to apply for entry permits. The aim, as expressed by his minister of commerce and industry, was to transfer the management of commercial and industrial companies to Africans.[80]

As explained in Chapter 2, Obote's policies proved less harmful to Asian interests in practice than in words. Although he nationalized 60 per cent of the industries, Obote negotiated individually with the leading Asian manufacturers with the result that none had to yield a 60 per cent share to the government. When it became apparent that many Asians were leaving Uganda, Obote announced that he was considering granting citizenship, and hence the right to continue their commerce and industrial development, to 30,000 Asians.[81] The contradictions between Obote's policies and actions created widespread unrest, increased African resentment against the Asians, and led to his overthrow. It was not Obote, but his successor, Amin, who effectively brought an end to Asian enterprise.

In Kenya the official policies towards manufacturing were far less oppressive. In 1958, replacing its long-standing system of granting preferential duties on an ad hoc basis, the government adopted a fully protective tariff for local industry. In its development plan for 1966–70 the government described its policy as 'basically positive and nonrestrictive'. It encouraged foreign investment by permitting repatriation of capital as well as earnings and promising full and prompt compensation in the event of a government take-over. It also promised incentives through import licensing and refunds of duties on imports of raw materials as well as tariff protection and financial assistance. By 1969 the government was permitting industrialists to write off against their corporate income tax over several years 120 per cent of the cost of their machinery, buildings, and fixed equipment.[82]

Despite these inducements that were beneficial to all the local entrepreneurs, Asian manufacturing in Kenya suffered from discriminatory
attitudes and regulations and could never realize its potential. In 1963
Kenya established the Development Finance Co. of Kenya, the main purpose of which was to attract industrial investment by foreign companies
through the provision of large loans. By 1967 the DFCK had invested approximately K£17 million in twenty-one projects, nearly all of which
were for European-sponsored industries. In 1964 to provide 'a spear-
head for Africanization of the industrial and commercial sectors of the
economy', Kenya replaced the IDC with an Industrial and Commercial
Development Corp. During the next two years the ICDC, which 'vastly
extended' the range of government operations, created two parastatal
bodies: the ICDC Investment Co. Ltd., to enable public investment in African industrial development; and the Kenya Industrial Estates Ltd., to
develop five industrial estates, first in Nairobi, then in Mombasa,
Nakuru, Kisumu, and Eldoret. The Nairobi estate, the largest, was to include twenty-five factories for lease to Africans. Obviously, none of the
new programs was designed to foster Asian industry. The increasing role
of government ownership is illustrated by the fact that by 1975 the government employed 42 per cent of all wage labour.[83]

Kenya's policy of Africanization evident in the ICDC was augmented
by measures requiring citizenship for enterprise, the employment of Africans in management, and increased participation by government. In
1967 the government passed legislation withholding trade licences and
work permits from all individuals who were not Kenya citizens. Greatly
increasing the Asians' insecurity, the laws prompted an exodus from Kenya beginning in December 1967. Subsequently as delays and other obstacles were put in the way of Asians who applied for citizenship, it
became evident that the government was discriminating against the
Asians. Although the citizenship laws applied to all businessmen, including manufacturers, they were directed primarily at the Asian shopkeepers and artisans whose businesses the Africans could more easily
take over. There were, however, pressures on the factory owners, Europeans as well as Asians, to admit Africans as partners or managers and to
share the ownership with the government.[84]

Industrial development in East Africa from 1954, when it was beginning to benefit from official encouragement, to 1969, when it began to
decline relative to other sectors of the economy, is revealed in Table 9.2.
It is apparent that the growth of manufacturing for all three countries occurred mainly in the post-colonial years and that the increases for Tanzania and Uganda in those years were remarkable. The effect of the
discriminations against non-Africans and the general restrictions on
private enterprise are illustrated in figures for Kenya after 1969. Al-

TABLE 9.2   Industrial Growth in East Africa, 1954-69: Manufacturing
(£ million) and Its Percentage of the GDP*

Year	Kenya	Tanzania	Uganda
1954	16.0 (12.6%)	3.7 (3.0%)	1.5 (1.2%)
1959	20.2 (9.5%)	7.1 (4.0%)	7.6 (5.1%)
1969	48.8 (15.8%)	25.3 (9.7%)	31.1 (13.9%)

*Zanzibar is included only in the statistics for 1969. The figures
for 1969 are adjusted for the decline of the Kenya shilling in
relation to sterling.

Sources: Compiled from East African Statistical Department,
Economic and Statistical Review and Quarterly Economic and
Statistical Bulletin; also from Uganda, Ministry of Economic
Affairs, Background to the Budget.

though manufacturing increased in Kenya in the four years after 1969 from £56.9 million to £98.9 million, its percentage in the GNP declined from 15.8 to 13.6. The percentage reached a low of 12.9 in 1977.[85]

Early in the post-colonial period before the restrictions became severe, Asian manufacturing reached its highest stage of development. As they were forced out of retailing-wholesaling, importing-exporting, construction, and artisanry to make room for Africans, the Asian businessmen either retired, emigrated, or turned to manufacturing. Under governmental policies that still left manufacturing largely to the private sector but offered tariff protection, Asians with capital had a very favourable opportunity at a time when Africans, lacking sufficient capital and management skills, could not offer significant competition.[86] Most of the new enterprise took place in Kenya where Asian and European capital was concentrated and where policies were most favourable. By 1972 about 15 per cent of the Asian assets there were in manufacturing.[87] Though not surpassing Kenya in output, Uganda had an even higher rate of increase. Considerable expansion also occurred in Tanzania, where Asians from Kenya and Uganda, attracted by Nyerere's promises of a non-racial society, invested in manufacturing. Foremost among the Asian investors in these years were the Madhvanis, Mehtas, Chandarias, L. R. Shah, and the Aga Khan.

The Madhvanis' industrial expansion under the management of Muljibhai's son Jayant has been described as 'phenomenal'.[88] In 1958 when only twenty-six years old, Jayant, as the eldest son, was entrusted with the administration of his father's extensive empire consolidated in five companies. Unlike many others in such a position, he proved more than equal to the task. He had degrees in science and law from India and a broad knowledge of industrial subjects. During a world tour in 1957 he had attended the great German Industrial Fair in Hanover and inspected factories in the United States, Britain, India, and Japan, as well as Germany.[89]

Between 1958 and 1971 Jayant developed the largest industrial, commercial, and agricultural complex in East Africa. He died in 1971, only forty-nine years old, but by then he controlled seventy-eight companies that employed 22,500 Africans. His invested capital had increased from £1.9 million to £16.7 million and his annual turnover from £2 million to £26 million. He is said to have controlled 40 per cent of Uganda's business and provided over one-tenth of its revenue. Apart from the sugar interests, his most important industry was the Steel Corporation of East Africa, the first steel-rolling mill in East Africa, which utilized scrap metal to produce rods, wire, and other items important to construction. The other main manufacturing concerns were the Emco Glass Works Ltd. and its counterpart Kenya Glass Works Ltd., the Nile Breweries Ltd. and Kilimanjaro Breweries Ltd., the Kolaba Textiles (Private) Ltd. and Mulco Textiles Ltd., the Chande Industries Ltd., and the Associated Match Co. Ltd. Through these and other companies Jayant manufactured not only sugar, steel, glassware, beer, textiles, and matches but also metal and paper boxes, soap, oil, tea, confectionery, and flour.[90]

Jayant's death cut short plans for additional manufacturing projects worth £10 million. The foremost was the erection of a smelting and rolling plant that would produce all East Africa's steel needs from local ores. He also was planning with the Tanzania government the construction of a major sugar factory that would involve a fifty-fifty investment and profit sharing but Madhvani management. In addition, Jayant had just completed negotiations with the United States government to include Uganda for the first time in the coveted sugar quota. Allotted an annual quota of 15,000 tons, Uganda was to receive in the first three years $7.5 million in U.S. currency.[91]

A key reason for Jayant's remarkable success during a time of diminishing opportunity is that he merged his interests with those of Africans. He was one of the first Asians to apply for Uganda citizenship. He continued his father's program of providing health, housing, educational, and recreational facilities for his African employees, and whenever feasible he employed handicapped Africans. His sweets factory at Thika, for instance, included blind workers. Unlike most Asian company owners, he employed Africans in top management. As discussed in Chapter 8, Jayant initiated an African 'outgrowers' scheme' providing loans, training, and encouragement for Africans to produce cane for the sugar factories. He also introduced a plan for African factory workers to purchase non-voting but high-interest-bearing shares in his companies. His dedication to Uganda and its people was one of the main reasons for his nomination in 1970 as the first chairman of Uganda's vital parastatal, the Export and Import Corp. He was then also president of the Uganda Federation of Industries.[92]

Although their expansion in East Africa was less significant than that of the Madhvanis in the independence years, the Mehtas continued to influence industrial development. While expanding the Lugazi and Muhoroni sugar estates, the Mehta Group, led by M. N. Mehta, undertook new ventures in Uganda and Tanzania. In 1963 it established at Lugazi the Ugma Steel and Engineering Corp. Ltd. for the manufacture of galvanized pipe and agricultural implements such as hoes, shovels, and ploughs. During the next two years it opened its sugar factory at Muhoroni and founded at Lugazi the Cable Corp. of Uganda Ltd. to manufacture steel rope and wire. In 1965 after organizing in Kampala an automobile and tractor dealership, Ecta Ltd., the Mehta Group set up in Jinja the Associated Paper Mills in partnership with the Madhvanis and the UDC.[93] At the time of Amin's coup, as explained in Chapter 8, the Mehtas were establishing a large sugar factory and plantation complex near Murchison Falls.

The Chandarias also continued the rapid industrial development they had begun before independence. During the early 1960s when the attitudes of the East African governments were uncertain, they expanded into other areas of Africa; but near the end of the decade as the Kenya government presented a favourable policy, they renewed their interest in East Africa. In planning their new ventures, they wisely employed within their top management Sir Ernest Vasey who through most of the last colonial decade had been Kenya's minister of economic planning and East Africa's preeminent financial authority. Between 1963 and 1975 with Vasey's aid, the Chandarias registered seven new companies in Kenya to manufacture PVC pipe and molding, metal window and door frames, stationery and other paper products, paints, wire, and a variety of steel and copper fasteners. They also established Johnson's Wax (E.A.) Ltd. in partnership with two other firms including Johnson's Wax International. They became, next to the Madhvanis and Mehtas, the third largest business establishment in East Africa.[94]

Although Kenya remained their headquarters and received most of their East African investment, the Chandarias continued to expand in Tanzania and Uganda after independence. In Tanzania, while retaining Aluminium Africa and Mabati, they added between 1962 and 1969 four new manufacturing firms in Dar es Salaam: Paper Products Ltd. for stationery, Shati Ltd. for shirts and other garments, Metal Products Ltd. for aluminium ware, and Wire Products Ltd. for drawn steel. They also began Primus East Africa Ltd. in Tanga to manufacture stoves. Beginning in

1969 they emphasized the production of aluminium and steel with the aim of developing an integrated manufacture including smelting, rolling, and finishing. In 1972 they introduced hot rolling and cold rerolling of iron and aluminium and the manufacture of galvanized pipe. They also created during 1971–73 two new companies: the Kibo Match Corp. Ltd. of Moshi, and Casements Africa Ltd. of Dar es Salaam. Meanwhile they had formed two new companies in Uganda, one for galvanized steel, the other for aluminium products.[95] By the mid-1970s, however, Nyerere's nationalization policies and Amin's expulsion order had discouraged further investment in Tanzania and Uganda. The Chandarias by then were putting most of their capital into other world areas where the official policies offered more opportunity.

Among the industrial entrepreneurs like the Chandarias, Mehtas, and Madhvanis, L. R. Shah was unique in attracting investment from Japan and India. He was unusual in his ability to establish close friendships with individuals in other cultures—Japanese and Chinese as well as Africans, Europeans, and South Asians of various communities. In the first decade of independence he expanded the textile mill that he had opened at Thika with Japanese aid in 1963 to include spinning, printing, and processing with the result that it became the second vertical mill in East Africa. In 1965, again combining with a Japanese firm, Chori & Co. Ltd., Shah established with a 60–40 per cent shareholding another textile factory, the African Garments and Textile Manufacturers Co., to make clothing at Mombasa from the cloth produced at Thika. Within the same year in a 40–60 per cent partnership with the largest cork manufacturer in India, the Indian Cork Mills, Shah established Kenya Industries and Agriculture Ltd. in Nairobi to produce blocks and sheets of cork. Unlike Japan, India would not permit the export of capital, but the Indian partner was allowed to supply the machinery and, by re-export, the raw Spanish cork. In 1967 Shah began construction of the Pan African Paper Mills in Broderick Falls in co-operation with the Birla Group of India. A huge project involving an investment of £15 million and employment of 4,000 Africans, the factory was to be financed jointly by Shah, Birla, and through the Kenya government, the World Bank. Birla was permitted by India to invest money that it had obtained from its sizeable exports.[96]

L. R. Shah's attempts to expand his textile interests into India were unsuccessful. In 1967 he conferred with the Indian minister for commerce and industry with the intention of starting a factory in Ahmedabad to manufacture metallic yarn. He was refused a licence, however, on the basis that India was planning to produce the essential polyester that Shah intended to import. In 1973 he sought to initiate a project for a metal crimping factory in India, but he was told that official permission could be obtained only by placing Shs 50,000 with a broker for 'key money' in the form of bribes.[97]

More than any of the major Asian industrialists, L. R. Shah endeavoured to further the industrial involvement of Africans. Like Madhvani and some others he placed Africans in top management. His factory at Thika, for instance, had only 3 non-Africans—two Japanese and one Asian—among 650 personnel. His main effort on behalf of Africans, however, was made in 1968 after visits to India and Japan. In India he noticed that 1,000 immigrants from East Africa, petty traders mainly from Kenya who had lost their businesses through quit notices, had settled near Bombay in Bhivandi, site of the largest hand-loom industry in the world. They had purchased their own looms and were prospering. Shah then went to Japan where during a visit to a Shishimi Textiles factory, he noticed a number of idle looms. Before leaving, he obtained a promise of 600 looms for a joint venture in East Africa. Back in Kenya he proposed to the government the erection of a large weaving factory in which each of the looms would be assigned to an African. Shah would provide the yarn, and the Africans, investing their profits, would soon become the owners of their looms.[98]

To Shah's surprise, the government rejected this highly innovative and pro-African proposal. The reason given was that the East African Industrial Council, which administered the Industrial Licensing Ordinances, had laid down a rule that if any textile organization manufactured more than 3 million yards per annum it had to be vertical, that is, spin as well as weave, ostensibly to protect the industry against a shortage of yarn. The proposed factory would have produced 17 million yards. Shah realized that the true reason was the opposition of Manchester's Calico Printers' Association, which had established NYTIL, the first vertical textile mill of East Africa. Calico had initiated the Industrial Council in 1943 and had assumed that no potential competitor would have the £2 million required for construction of a vertical mill. Although it had sold NYTIL to the Uganda government in 1957, Calico had kept the management and its interest in preventing competition.[99]

With L. R. Shah, the Chandarias, Mehtas, and Madhvanis, the Aga Khan ranks as one of the principal industrialists of the independence years. In 1963 he initiated the Industrial Promotion Services to foster the development of industry throughout East Africa. With contributions from the Ismaili community, the Aga Khan's Diamond Jubilee Investment Trust, Tanzania's NDC and Kenya's ICDC, Britain's Commonwealth Development Corp., West Germany's DEG, the National Bank of Pakistan, and the World Bank's Industrial Finance Corp. and International Development Agency, the IPS raised capital for numerous development projects in Tanzania and Kenya. To house its personnel and provide other office blocks, it constructed two of the most prominent buildings in East Africa: the fourteen-story IPS Building in Nairobi and its counterpart in Dar es Salaam.[100]

The Aga Khan concentrated on industrial projects in Tanzania and Kenya. In Tanzania, which attracted most of the investment, the main IPS project was the huge Kilimanjaro Textile Corp. Ltd. (Kiltex) of Arusha. Among others were the Dar es Salaam factories of Suitcases Manufactures of Tanzania Ltd. (SUMATA), Tanzania Wire Products Ltd., and KAMYN Industries (Tanzania) Ltd., a shirt factory. The projects in Kenya included Kenya Industries Ltd. for hosiery and shirts, Ocean Industries (Knitwear) Ltd. for women's apparel, Plastics and Rubber Industries Ltd. for footwear materials, Wire Products Ltd. for wood screws, and Embassy Industries Ltd. for travel goods. A number of other projects were in the planning stage when Tanzania's Industrial Acquisition and Building Acquistion acts of 1971, which resulted in confiscation of the I.P.S. Building in Dar es Salaam and a number of the industries, including the Kilimanjaro Textile Corp., caused the Aga Khan to halt all further IPS development.[101]

Among the major industrialists of Kenya who continued their expansion after independence were the Khimasia and Kotecha families. In 1963 while retaining their East African Match Co., Trufoods, and Nath Brothers, the Khimasias, operating through their parent organization, Bhagwanji & Co., purchased the Kabazi Canners Ltd., a major fruit and vegetable canning firm from the failing Gibson & Co. in Nakuru. They made it prosper and later invested in Mwanachi Ltd., a food-processing company in Dar es Salaam, and Pan Plastics Ltd., a Nairobi factory producing plastic bottles, tubes, and bags. M. S. Khimasia, who directed the family enterprise, believed that with 2,500 employees, he was, next to the breweries, the second largest employer in Kenya. The Kotechas, aided by their partnership with Laxmichand Meghji Kanji, employed profits from their oil- and rice-milling factories and their ginneries to undertake two new enterprises after 1963. Forming Acif Ltd. as a holding company, they built an edible-oil refinery in Nairobi and a large factory in Thika that employed 1,000 Africans in the manufacture of jute and sisal products. They also organized the Mesa Mining Co. Ltd. for production of soda ash.[102]

In Tanzania Gill and Jayantilal Keshavji Chande were able to carry on only a brief expansion of their family enterprises. Gill opened his plywood factory in 1963 and then built two more sawmills, at Bulwa and Kwamkoro, before 1970 when the government took over all his Tanzanian factories. Three years later he suffered a £2 million loss in Uganda when all his property was confiscated without compensation. He had been very proud of having been the very first Asian to take Ugandan citizenship, but like the other Asians, he lost that, too. He had employed 2,000 Africans in Uganda. Gill retained only his Kenya holdings—the Elgeyo Sawmill (Kenya) Ltd. and 318 acres of industrial land near Eldoret. Chande, who in 1959 succeeded his father as manager of Chande Industries Ltd., merged his family interests with those of the Madhvanis through his marriage to Muljibhai's daughter. He became the principal representative in Tanzania of the Madhvani as well as the Chande enterprises. Though not adding new companies, he considerably expanded those established earlier, especially the milling operations. Before nationalization terminated his industrial activities, Chande was apparently Tanzania's pre-eminent industrialist. In the 1960s he was the director of twenty-five companies as well as an outstanding political and social leader.[103]

An unusual success story among the Shahs is that of the five Dhanani brothers of Nairobi. Following the example of their father, Jethalal Namchand Dhanani, who in the 1920s had toured African farms in the area of Nairobi to buy and sell African produce, the brothers gradually developed a fruit and vegetable business under the company names of Dhanani Traders and Garden Fresh. In 1965 they formed Kenya Horticultural Exporters Ltd. to export African produce to London. They started an air shipment of 45 kg per day of fruit and vegetables and rapidly expanded. One of the brothers moved to England and there formed the Covent Garden Market Co. Ltd. to handle business 'at the other end'. In 1981, deciding to modernize, the Dhananis bought four and one-half acres in Nairobi's industrial area, built four warehouses, and equipped them with cold storage units and processing machinery. By 1985 they were shipping 6,000 tons per month, 40 per cent of all Kenya's fresh-produce export, and were employing 35 Asians in Britain and approximately 100 Africans in Kenya. They supplied the nearly 300 Africans who sold to them with seeds, fertilizer, and insecticides, even with petrol for their irrigation pumps, and employed two full-time horticultural experts to visit and advise them. Unlike the co-operatives and most others who bought from Africans, they paid the farmers in full when collecting their produce.[104]

Although not all were as successful as the Dhananis, many other Asians contributed to the industrial development of the independence years. Unfortunately, only a few can be mentioned as examples. Gulabchand Virpar Shah with Dhanani and three other Shahs began Stainless Steel Products Ltd. in Nairobi but sold it to the Khimasias when unable to compete with imports from India. Gulabchand and his son Ashwin then purchased a small Asian firm, the Kenya Threads Industry Ltd., that relied on imported yarn. Erecting a new factory at Athi River and importing German machinery, they began to spin their own cotton yarn as well as manufacture thread. Another entrepreneur, C. H. Somaia, established the Gossage Shirt Factory Ltd. in Tanga, which in 1973 had still escaped nationalization. Kanji Rupshi Shah, a textile trader, purchased Nakuru Blankets Inc., which had started as a European firm, renamed it Nakuru Industries Ltd., and became a principal blanket manufacturer. Kanjee Naranjee, one of the largest property owners in Nairobi, founded African Ropes and Twines Ltd.[105]

In addition to seeking their own profit, a few of the Asian manufacturers sought to encourage the development of African industry. Beginning in 1964 L. R. Shah and M. S. Khimasia began to consider with Pushkar U. Oza, the humanitarian journalist and insurance agent, and Prem Bhatia, the Indian high commissioner, how they might encourage Asians to shift from commerce into industry to make room for African traders and at the same time associate with Africans in the development of industry. Their aim, as Oza admitted, was to safeguard their own community's future as well as to assist the Africans. They decided to try to form a public development corporation with support from the Kenya and Indian governments as well as the Asian community. In 1965 after a favourable response from Tom Mboya, minister for economic planning and development, and Chege Kibachia, the veteran trade unionist, the group registered the Africindo Industrial Development Corp. Ltd. The directors included the prominent industrialists M. N. Mehta, D. P. Chandaria, M. R. Desai, M. K. Naranjee, C. M. and M. V. Patel, as well as Khimasia and L. R. Shah. Mehta was chairman.[106]

While soliciting subscriptions from the local commercial and industrial leaders, the group sent a deputation to seek assistance in India. Led by Oza, the members included Khimasia, L. R. and R. M. Shah, and Fitzval R.S. de Souza, who represented the Kenya government as a member of the House of Representatives. They conferred with Gandhi, the ministers of finance, commerce, and industry, and many leading industrialists and financiers. Before leaving, they obtained not only promises of investment in the corporation, but also a pledge from Gandhi to provide credit of Rs 10 million over ten years towards the purchase of Indian machinery and other exports, the training of 200 Africans, and the provision of Indian technical advisers. By June 1967 when the corporation was formally launched by Mboya, the subscriptions totalled K£750,000 of which K£160,000 had been contributed by the local Asians. About twenty of the subscribers were Africans.[107]

To the disappointment of its founders, the Africindo Industrial Corp. never achieved its aims. There was hope after the visit to India of attracting financial support from the World Bank, Britain, the United States, and Czechoslovakia as well as the Kenya government. Oza went to Uganda to persuade Jayant Madhvani to initiate a similar corporation there, and plans were made to do the same in Tanzania. There were many designs for industrial projects, such as the manufacture of grayboard (cardboard) from sugarcane, elephant grass, lime, and water. Not one of the projects, however, was ever implemented. The directors could not co-ordinate government personnel, Asian industrialists, and interested Africans in the formal start of any endeavour. The Asians were reluctant to accede to the government's insistence on a controlling interest, and the growing estrangement between Asians and Africans promoted by European settlers and businessmen and the African backbenchers in the legislature led to a climate of suspicion and mistrust. The timing was unfortunate. It was in 1967 that resentment against the Asians reached an all-time high and achieved expression in legislation that stimulated the 1968 exodus of traders, clerks, and artisans. The result was that the funds raised locally were invested in purchasing and selling Kenya buildings. The company continued to exist, but its primary aim of African-Asian joint enterprise was never realized.[108]

In all the countries the discriminatory and interventionist policies of the African administrations were harmful to almost all the Asian manufacturers other than the few with large amounts of capital. The move begun in the colonial period to oust the Asians from the processing of raw materials in the rural areas was completed, and in the urban centres the increasing governmental restrictions and control forced many of the new entrepreneurs out of manufacturing.

Before the expulsion order in Uganda, the situation was the worst in Tanzania. Ahmed Lakha, an Ithnasheri sixth-generation resident producing oil and soap from copra, was among the Zanzibar Asians whose factories were confiscated without payment. Azeez Lalani, chief officer of the Aga Khan's Industrial Promotion Services (Tanzania) Ltd., remarked that because of the Acquisition Act the Ismaili manufacturing projects had to be cut from ten to only one or two.[109] Naval Balvant Rajay, who until 1966 manufactured monthly in Tanga 216,000 shirts, reported in 1973 that high customs duty and sales tax had doubled the cost of imported cloth, with the result that his factory could run at only one-fourth its capacity and had reduced its work force from 800 to 200. Shiraj Pirbhai Haji, an Ismaili whose family after independence had established suitcase and furniture factories in Dar es Salaam, stated in 1974 that they were expanding both factories. 'Until the government takes over, we have to go on, but we are not putting up new factories. No one is'.[110] Among the factories confiscated were the Chandes' milling company, the Bhatias' razor-blade factory, the Alloos' match and plywood firms, and the Bhagwanjis' Manonga ginnery.[111]

Some industrialists accommodated rather well to Tanzania's nationalization policies, but they were mainly the wealthy few like the Madhvanis, Mehtas, and Gill. Gill, for instance, was forced to sell his plywood factory and sawmills to the NDC in 1970 for £500,000 to be paid over five years. Unlike some of the less important property owners, who never obtained compensation, he received monthly payments of the principal plus interest of 7 per cent. Moreover, the government retained him as manager of his former companies. Forming Gill Management Ltd. for the purpose, Gill and his brother each received annual salaries of £5,000, and Gill Management, 6 per cent of the profits. The government also employed the Gills in setting up a new sawmill in Moshi.[112]

At least one Asian achieved the 'impossible' in Tanzania by establishing an industry after the Arusha Declaration and continuing it as a private venture after the Acquistion Acts of 1971. In 1970 Priyavadan M. Majithia, a young Lohana advocate whose family had considerable money from commercial interests, decided to start a factory. A friend came in one day, he later recalled, and said that he knew how to make sweaters and requested: 'Let me have money for a factory'. Majithia was looking for something exciting. The next day the two formed a company, Majithia Bros. They bought several used knitting machines from Switzerland, situated them in a single room, hired twenty young African women through an employment agency, trained them in four weeks, and began to manufacture sweaters. Persuading salesmen from other concerns to sell their goods on the side, they sold at first to sports clubs in Moshi, Iringa, and other centres with cold climates. Soon the National Service was among their customers. Majithia and his partner toured Europe to find more machines. Within two years they were employing 200 women on fifty machines in a factory of 10,000 square feet, and they were exporting to Kenya, Uganda, Zambia, and Zaire. What 'started as a joke' had become a very successful enterprise.[113]

There were several reasons for the success. Majithia was not interested in making a profit. 'What kept me going', he explained, 'was a feeling that I was creating something and helping people'. He started his untrained workers at a monthly salary of Shs 240, a very generous figure for the time, and after their training he paid them on a piece-work basis with the opportuniity for considerably more money. He also kept his factory small, so as not to attract attention, and he refrained from introducing automated machinery. The first question from the government, he said, was 'How many people do you employ?'[114]

In Uganda the Asians' participation in manufacturing began to decline after Obote's reforms of 1967. Among the many whose ginneries were confiscated were L. R. Shah, K. J. Kotecha, and A. K. Patel. For his ginneries Shah was offered only 5 to 10 per cent of the cost of his machinery. He declined, hoping to move the machinery to Kenya, and lost everything after Amin's coup. Kotecha's ten ginneries were confiscated without compensation beginning in 1967. When Patel left Uganda in March 1972, all but two of his eight ginneries had been nationalized. He received compensation for the six, but for the other two, which soon met a similar fate, nothing. He also lost an oil mill without payment. His paper mill, in which government held at first a 25 per cent share, was taken over in annual increments of 5 per cent until the government had a controlling interest. He was paid for only the first 5 per cent.[115] As Patel's case illustrates, it was not only ginneries but industries of all kinds that were nationalized.

Jayant Madhvani, who among all industrialists was the closest to Obote, was in the end similarly affected. In 1967 he had offered the UDC a 25 per cent share in his companies and in 1969 a 50 per cent share. Both offers were rejected. It was clear that the government wanted a controlling interest. The take-over of the Madhvani companies, however, was still pending when the coup terminated Obote's administration. Before Jayant's death seven months later, Amin nationalized all the Madhvani holdings in Uganda except the sugar and steel complex at Kakira in which he assumed a 49 per cent interest. In 1973 even this enterprise fell to the government as all members of the Madhvani family, including Jayant's brother Manubhai, who had assumed the management, were included in the expulsion. It had been impossible even for the Madhvanis to avoid the disaster. Jayant had managed after 1967 to transfer only a small portion of the group's financial interests to other countries. He had founded two companies in Canada, one in Lebanon, and one in Britain.[116]

Because its discriminatory policies were less arduous, Kenya proved the most attractive to potential manufacturers in the independence years. During the 1960s as they met increasing difficulties in Tanzania and Uganda, a number of Asian manufacturers transferred their operations to Kenya. When Steel Africa Ltd. was nationalized in Tanzania, the Shahs who controlled it made Mombasa their company's new headquarters. Some Asians in other occupations also moved to Kenya to take up manufacturing, which, they realized, offered far more opportunity than trade or agriculture. Dwarkadas Kanji Naranji was typical. Recognizing the imminence of nationalization in Tanzania, he sold his two sisal estates and built a factory in Nairobi to manufacture rope and twine.[117] L. R. Shah, Gill, Bhagwanji, and the Chandarias were among the successful manufacturers who ultimately made Kenya the centre of their East African operations.

The Chandarias shrewdly safeguarded their investments in Kenya. After Tanzania locked in their capital and earnings, they established holding companies overseas to permit the exportation of earnings from Kenya and to take advantage of the other incentives offered to foreign industrialists. The holding companies for Eslon Plastics of Kenya Ltd., Kenya Aluminium and Industrial Works Ltd., Premchand Bros. Ltd., and E. A. Stationery Manufacturers Ltd., for instance, were in Jersey and Bermuda. Comcraft Services, situated in London, provided the overall management and was able to charge each of its associated companies in Kenya sizeable expenses for its services. To minimize the outlay of capital, the Chandarias combined with other investors and refrained from initiating new industries. Five of the nine Kenya companies they registered between 1959 and 1974 were take-overs, and three were partnerships.[118] During the first decade after independence, because of the discouraging prospects for further investment in East Africa, the Chandarias, as will be explained in Chapter 10, began to establish new industries in other areas of Africa and in Europe and Asia. By 1978 from a humble beginning in Nairobi, the family had become in a single generation a multi-national giant with assets of £40 million.[119]

None of the other industrialists matched the Chandarias in the ability to profit from adversity, and by the end of the 1980s it was difficult to find any Asian manufacturer, even in Kenya, who was optimistic about the future. Nearly all felt that their time was limited. Obviously, the last Asian enterprise in East Africa, that of industrial manufacturing, was approaching its end.

Asian and European Contributions

In this history of Asian manufacturing there is, especially for Asian interest, a crucial question of who contributed more to industrial development, the Asians with a modicum of support from India or the Europeans comprising settlers and foreign firms. A close analysis indicates that the Asians contributed most of the manufacturing development in Uganda, Zanzibar, and perhaps Tanganyika during the colonial period. During the first decade after independence the growth in Tanzania and Uganda was spectacular, and there is reason to believe that it occurred largely because of Asian investment and Asian initiative. In Kenya the answer is less clear. By 1961, according to Colin Leys, whose study on under-development is highly regarded, 'over 67 per cent of all the locally owned industrial enterprises with fifty or more employees were Asian-owned'.[120] This figure, however, does not take account of the foreign-owned concerns, most of which were a result of European initiative.

The Asian contribution in independent Kenya has not been recognized. Expressing a widely held view among scholars and politicians in 1969, the economist D. S. Pearson asserted that the Asians 'had neither the capital nor the skill' to move 'into more sophisticated types of commercial and technical activities as the African population advanced to the stage where it was able to take over the simpler types of business enterprises'. Pearson concluded that 'this failure on the part of a substantial section of the Asian business community to adjust itself to the rising economic competence of the African population . . . left the development of manufacturing industry almost exclusively in the hands of Europeans'.[121]

This interpretation is not supported by the numerous accounts of industrial enterprise and accomplishment in the biographies of the Asians nor by the available statistical information. It is evident that the Asians after World War II were steadily displaced by Africans in the processing and other basic secondary industries, and that many of these Asians, as they left these industries, moved into the more capital-intensive types of manufacturing. They were accompanied in this move by many other Asians, both traders and artisans, who had not previously been involved in manufacture. Certainly the Europeans were not alone in this endeavour. If the Asians had a shortcoming, it was perhaps, as the political scientist Nicola Swainson believes, a reluctance to admit outside capital into their family enterprises, with the result that many during the postwar years remained at the merchant level. Their failure to advance further in manufacturing, as Swainson has recognized, was also a result of political factors beyond their control.[122]

These considerations do not detract from the European contribution by the settler community and companies outside East Africa. Local and foreign European investment through the colonial period and after independence developed much of the manufacturing in Tanzania, Uganda, and especially in Kenya. A number of facts have been cited to illustrate the Europeans' importance. The twenty-six public companies in Kenya with a capitalization of over K£1 million in 1968 were all European except for one, the Chandaria's Steel Africa, which ranked twentieth. Among Kenya's top fifty directors—those directing the most companies—that year were only eight Asians, all but one of whom were clustered at the end of the list. The thirteen Kenya companies with more than one thousand employees in 1967 did not include one Asian concern.[123]

The European companies represented a combination mainly of Kenya settlers and Britons. Much of the European manufacturing, like that of the Asians, was in the processing or extractive industries. Ninety per cent of Kenya's wheat milling and half its maize milling were directed by the Kenya National Mills Ltd., which in turn was controlled by Unga Millers Ltd., a derivative of Delamere's 1908 company. The tea industry was dominated by the British companies of Brooke Bond Liebig and James Finlay through their subsidiaries Brooke Bond Equatoria Ltd., Brooke Bond Kenya Ltd., and the African Highlands Produce Co. Ltd. A large proportion of Kenya's sisal plantations and factories was controlled through Ralli Brothers (Kenya) Ltd. and the London firms General Guarantee Corp. Ltd. and Drages Ltd. A sizeable share of the canning industry was held by Kenya Canners Ltd., Kenya Orchards Ltd., and Pan African Foods Ltd., all local European concerns. Cement was manufactured mainly by the East African Portland Cement Co. Ltd. and the Bamburi Portland Cement Co. Ltd., both managed by the Associated Portland Cement Manufacturers Ltd. in London.[124]

The Europeans were also involved with other types of manufacture. East Africa's oil refinery at Mombasa was built by Shell and its ownership vested in a group of foreign oil companies including British Petroleum, Esso, and Caltex. Beer production was provided mainly by East African Breweries Ltd. representing a joint effort by local Europeans and British firms such as the Ind coope Group and H. & G. Simonds Ltd., and soft-drink bottling was a virtual monopoly of Coca-Cola, Canada Dry, and Schweppes. Most of Kenya's cigarettes were produced by the British American Tobacco Co. (Kenya) Ltd. and Rothmans of Pall Mall (Kenya) Ltd., both subsidiaries of foreign firms. Over half of the soap production came from East Africa Industries Ltd., a Unilever associated company, and most of the footwear from the East Africa Bata Shoe Co. Ltd., headquartered in Canada. Many of these firms were joined by interlocking directorates. One of the local Europeans, H. Travis, actually directed forty-three different companies.[125]

Additional evidence of the importance of the European contribution is provided in Table 9.3, which shows the percentage of capital held by foreign and local investors in Kenya companies at two important points in the post-colonial period. The foreign investment is clearly predominant in the three major categories of Kenya industry.

This impressive description of European accomplishment deserves some modification. A considerable number of the foreign companies represented in Table 9.3 were formed during the colonial period when foreign capital was clearly more important than that of the Asians. It is notable that the percentage of local investment increased considerably from 1967 to 1972. Moreover, some of the foreign capital was provided by Asians. The investments of the Madhvanis, Chandarias, and Aga Khan, for instance, would appear as foreign capital. According to a reliable estimate, approximately two-fifths of the shares in the public companies operating in Kenya in 1971 were owned by local Asians.[126] Another portion of the foreign investment came from firms in India, such as Raymond Textiles and Oriental Paper Mills.[127]

The list of Kenya's twenty-six largest public companies is also misleading in that it omits consideration of the private companies, which were far more numerous and in a few instances had more capital than

TABLE 9.3   Percentages of Foreign and Local Investment in Kenya
Industry, 1967 and 1972

Investment	Mining/ quarrying		Building/ construction		Manufacturing/ repairs	
	1967	1972	1967	1972	1967	1972
Foreign	93%	81%	87%	75%	71%	63%
Local	7%	19%	13%	25%	29%	37%

Source: Compiled from Nicola Swainson, *Development of Corporate Capitalism in Kenya, 1918-77* (London: Heinemann, 1980), table 40a, p. 220.

many of the twenty-six. The fact that such companies were not required to publish their accounts means that very little is known about them 'save what the proprietors tell'.[128] This legal exemption together with the Asians' extended family system of enterprise made the private company especially attractive to Asians. A very significant statistic, based on the inclusion of the private companies, is that in 1961 over 67 per cent of all the locally owned industrial enterprises with fifty or more employees in Kenya belonged to Asians. In 1966 the private companies registered in Kenya numbered 5,584—94 per cent—of the total of 5,910. As shown in Table 9.4, the Asians formed the greatest number of private companies during the first decade of independence.

Even the list of Kenya's top fifty directors needs qualification with reference to the description of products and companies. Despite the Europeans' concentration on Kenya, the Asians were predominant there in the manufacture of textiles, aluminium products, iron nails and wire, galvanized sheets, steel, and plastics, all of which were very important to the economy.[129]

Kenya's principal manufacturing development after independence was in textiles. Local Asians developed six of the main firms. The Thika Textile Mills Ltd., formerly Nath Brothers, was acquired and expanded by the Khimasias. The United Textile Industries Ltd. of Thika was L. R. Shah's company. Kenya Rayon Mills Ltd. of Nairobi belonged primarily to the Madhvanis. Kenya Textile Mills Ltd. of Nairobi had been organized by two brothers D. B. and P. B. Sharma. Nakuru Industries Ltd. and Kenwool Enterprises Ltd. of Kiambaa were owned by a Shah group. The other four leading textile organizations were created by outsiders. Midco Textiles (East Africa) Ltd. of Nairobi, Kisumu Cotton Mills Ltd., and Raymond Woolen Mills (Kenya) Ltd. were instigated respectively by India's Tanco, Khatau, and J. K. Groups. The remaining company, Kenya

TABLE 9.4   Private Companies Formed Annually in Kenya, 1963-73

	Number of Companies				Number of Companies		
Year	Asian	European	African	Year	Asian	European	African
1961	49	39	7	1968	30	20	33
1962	50	38	8	1969	38	14	28
1963	42	45	5	1970	37	13	30
1964	34	35	19	1971	39	15	33
1965	34	28	25	1972	30	17	37
1966	36	30	19	1973	24	15	46
1967	35	26	23		___	___	___
				Totals	478	335	313

Source: Compiled from Swainson, *Development of Corporate Capitalism in Kenya, 1918-77* (London: Heinemann, 1980), table 33, p. 195.

Toray Mills Ltd. of Thika, was a product of three Japanese firms. Thus all but one of the ten main textile companies belonged to local Asians or investors in India. Moreover, the Japanese had been attracted to Kenya by L. R. Shah. The only significant participation by Europeans was a partial ownership in Kenya Rayon Mills by Warner & Sons of Britain and in Kenwool Enterprises by Lanificio Bruno Parenti of Italy.[130]

Further evidence of the Asians' role in Kenya is provided by the statistics, shown in Table 9.5, on Asian and European companies. It is obvious from these statistics that both Europeans and Asians played a critical role in the economic development of Kenya during the transition years from 1955 to 1966. Although companies other than those engaged only in manufacturing are included, the figures probably afford a fair approximation of the two communities' initiative and investment in manufacturing. The Asians were a close second to the Europeans in the formation of new companies through the period, but in the years after independence they exceeded them. In overall investment they were surpassed by the Europeans in a ratio of three to two. It is significant, however, that during the four years immediately preceding independence—1959 through 1962—the Asians invested more capital than the Europeans in new companies. Only after the government made clear that a Foreign Investment Protection Act, permitting foreign companies to repatriate their profits overseas, would be introduced was significant European investment in Kenya resumed.

TABLE 9.5   Kenya Companies Incorporated by Racial Community:
Numbers and Capitalization (£1,000), 1955-66

	Asian		European		African	
Year	No.	Cap.	No.	Cap.	No.	Cap.
1955	99	(£ 3,559)	246	(£ 8,876)	1	(£ 1)
1956	108	(2,925)	204	(7,827)	3	(35)
1957	101	(2,539)	229	(8,306)	2	(6)
1958	85	(836)	133	(1,167)	2	(4)
1959	116	(1,126)	136	(1,101)	5	(14)
1960	126	(1,268)	151	(1,835)	11	(50)
1961	134	(1,073)	105	(814)	18	(113)
1962	116	(978)	89	(545)	18	(63)
1963	153	(1,199)	161	(3,085)	17	(52)
1964	147	(1,513)	151	(4,205)	18	(504)
1965	144	(1,206)	122	(918)	108	(804)
1966	165	(413)	138	(942)	87	(429)
Totals	1,494	(£19,635)	1,865	(£39,621)	272	(£2,070)

Source: Who Controls Industry in Kenya? (Nairobi: East African
Publishing House, 1968), p. 135.

The figures substantiate the claim of L. R. Shah, who was not only a
prominent industrialist, but also a member in 1972–73 of Kenya's National Chamber of Commerce and Industry and a former chairman of
the Kenya Indian Chamber of Commerce, that the Asians, far more than
the Europeans, invested local capital in manufacturing and devoted the
profits from their new industries to further development in East Africa.
Because Kenya's Foreign Investment Protection Act of 1964 permitted
exportation of profits derived only from investment that came from outside the country, most Asians were excluded from the purview of the act.
The subsequent Exchange Controls, prohibiting the exportation of locally earned money, thus prevented them from sending their profits out,
and they had no alternative other than smuggling out their currency to
re-invest in East Africa. There were only a few Asians, notably the Mehtas, Madhvanis, and Chandarias, who because of their extensive foreign
holdings and incorporation outside Africa were able to fall within the
protection of the act and thus export their capital. These few and the nu-

merous foreigners, mainly Europeans, who developed manufacturing in East Africa were able to export their annual dividends, estimated as usually 12 to 14 per cent and in some cases as high as 20 per cent; and also, on liquidation of an enterprise, they could repatriate an amount equal to their total investment.[131]

L. R. Shah, supported by other knowledgeable Asians, has also maintained that the Asian factories, unlike the European, were labour intensive. After independence the Asians refrained from automating their factories because of the consequent displacement of the African workers. In this they were motivated partly by the governments' interest in maintaining high employment, and partly by humanitarian concern.[132]

Another important consideration is that the Asians' mode of industrialization, unlike the Europeans', significantly fostered the rise of African industry. After World War II the colonial governments adopted educational and financial-aid programs for the training of Africans in small-scale industry as well as commerce and artisanry, but these programs, as explained in Chapter 5, were surprisingly unsuccessful. In the post-colonial period a number of the foreign European companies, as Swainson has noted, devised plans for training African personnel and brought a number of Africans into management.[133] The Europeans, however, were not alone in this. The larger Asian firms, such as those of the Madhvanis, Mehtas, Chandarias, and L. R. Shah, were providing similar African training and advancement. All the companies, European and Asian, whether large or small, had to do this to survive under policies of Africanization. These private efforts, however, affected relatively few Africans and were aimed at preparing them for administration of European and Asian firms rather than creating and managing their own industries.

The important training was taking place at a more elementary level as the more successful Africans in trade and artisanry invested their accumulated capital in manufacturing. They were, in effect, emulating the Asians—their former employers and others—with whom, in many instances, they were in close association. This logical progression occurred mainly in the years after independence, but as the following observation by a World Bank mission to Uganda in 1960 illustrates, it had begun in the colonial period:

There are also quite a number of small workshops in light industry—in the Kampala area there are some 600 registered under the Factories Ordinance—producing soap, furniture, retreaded tyres, window frames, doors, precast concrete blocks, soft drinks, etc. Most of these are run by Asians, who have moved into this backyard industry from trade and use little machinery and employ few workers. A small number of these enterprises are now owned and run by Africans.[134]

It is thus in three ways—the employment of African labour and the investment of earnings in local industry in the years since independence, and the stimulation of African manufacturing then and earlier—that the Asian industrial investment, even in Kenya, seems especially pertinent to African development.

Unfortunately, the advance of Asian manufacturing in East Africa—from the simple processing of raw materials to the fabrication of consumer products from these processed goods and on to the production of more sophisticated import-substitutes—was cut short before attaining its logical end, the development of a heavy or capital goods industry that would diminish the reliance on imports. The Madhvanis, Mehtas, and Chandarias were about to take this final step in one of the key industries, that of steel production. They had introduced rolling mills, and the Madhvanis were actually producing steel from local scrap. Both the Madhvanis and the Chandarias were planning the erection of smelters for the utilization of local ore. L. R. Shah had developed an integrated system of textile manufacture from the ginning of raw cotton to the spinning, weaving, and printing essential for production of blankets without any reliance on imports. Behind these men, only a few steps removed in the progression, and like them in most cases from humble beginnings as petty traders, were other key industrialists, such as the Khimasias, Kotechas, Gill, Chande, and the Aga Khan. Still further behind, but only by a few steps, was a host of Asians in a more rudimentary stage of manufacture. Primarily because of misguided government policies beginning in the late colonial years, the whole progression was stopped, and what affected the Asians also affected the Europeans and the Africans. As a result East Africa never proceeded to the manufacture of machinery and the other capital goods that would have allowed it, as the historian R.M.A. van Zwanenberg remarked, 'to break out of the inherited colonial economic pattern'.[135]

Notes

1. Mehta, *Dream Half Expressed: An Autobiography* (Bombay: Vakils, Feffer and Simons, 1966), p. 319.

2. M. J. Thakkar, interviewed by Gregory, 19 May 1973, Addis Ababa.

3. For an explanation of restrictions on colonial manufacturing, see E. A. Brett, *Colonialism and Underdevelopment in East Africa: The Politics of Economic Change, 1919–39* (New York: NOK, 1973), chap. 9. See also Nicola Swainson, *Development of Corporate Capitalism in Kenya, 1918–77* (London: Heinemann, 1980), pp. 26–31; Colin Leys, *Underdevelopment in Kenya: The Political Economy of Neo-Colonialism, 1964–71* (London: Heinemann, 1975), pp. 33, 41; and R.M.A. van Zwanenberg, 'Aspects of Kenya's Industrial History', *Kenya Historical Review*, 1/1 (1973), 46. For a striking instance of restriction, see

Uganda Governor Sir Hesketh Bell's alarm over Asians' competing with Lancashire mills in ginning: R. R. Ramchandani, *Uganda Asians: The End of an Enterprise* (Bombay: United Asia, 1976), p. 122.

4. N. H. Hassanali Putwa (great grandson), interviewed by Honey, 8 Feb. 1974, Dar es Salaam. Shanti Pandit, ed., *Asians in East and Central Africa* (Nairobi: Panco, 1963), pp. 95–96, 324, 334. Shapurji apparently was not the first to manufacture soda water as has been claimed. H.T.H. Abdulla (grandson), interviewed by Honey, 18 Jan. 1974, Dar es Salaam.

5. A. Sachoo, interviewed by Honey, 29 Oct. 1973, Dar es Salaam. A. M. Sheriff, interviewed by Honey, 22 Oct. 1973, Arusha. Pandit, *Asians*, p. 334.

6. Pandit, *Asians*, p. 67. *East African Standard*, 2 Nov. 1907, pp. 14–15; 1 Jan. 1910, p. 9. A. M. Sheriff interview. See also file 'Alidina Visram Soap Factory, 1907', Coast Province daily correspondence, Syracuse University microfilm 1995, reel 177.

7. H. S. Figueiredo (grandson), interviewed by Gregory, 27 June 1973, Saligao, Bardez Goa. For Fazal, see Pandit, *Asians*, p. 304. Ramchandani, *Uganda Asians*, p. 153. *East African Standard*, 7 Dec. 1907, p. 9. A. M. Sheriff (Dewji's grandson) interview. 'Nyanza Province, East Africa Protectorate. Report by the Province Commissioner for the Twelve Months Ending March 31st, 1911', p. 36, South Kavirondo Annual Reports, Syracuse University microfilm 2801, reel 32. Amritlal Raishi, 'Note on Industrial Manufacturing', encl. letter (Nairobi) to Gregory, 27 Nov. 1987.

8. International Bank for Reconstruction and Development, *Economic Development of Kenya* (Baltimore: Johns Hopkins University Press, 1963), pp. 150, 156. 'Report on the Trade of Kisumu and District During the Year Ending 31st Mar. 1907', Nyanza Province Annual Reports, Syracuse University microfilm 2801, reel 32. Elspeth Huxley, *White Man's Country: Lord Delamere and the Making of Kenya*, vol. 1 (London: Chatto and Windus, 1956), pp. 167, 177.

9. Mehta, *Dream*, p. 99. British East Africa Co. Ltd. to Colonial Office, 2 Jan. 1917; J. Arthur Hutton (Chairman, British Cotton Growing Association) to W. C. Bottomley (Colonial Office), 2 Jan. 1917; W. H. Leggett (Chairman, British East Africa Co.) to Bottomley, 2 Jan. 1916 [*sic*] (1917), C.O. 536/88. Ramchandani, *Uganda Asians*, p. 124. W. S. Garnham (Uganda Manager, British East Africa Co.) to General Manager, British East Africa Co., 6 June 1918, confidential, encl. Robert Coryndon (Governor, Uganda) to Colonial Office, 10 Nov. 1918, C.O. 536/91.

10. Martha Honey, foremost author on Asian manufacturing in Tanganyika, differs here in maintaining that Europeans retained the dominant position between the wars: 'Asian Industrial Activities in Tanganyika', *Tanzania Notes and Records*, no. 75 (Nov. 1974), pp. 59–61.

11. Swainson, *Development*, table 14a, pp. 64–65. Swainson is apparently the only scholar who has made extensive use of the records of the Registrar General of Companies in Kenya.

12. *Kenya-Uganda-Tanganyika and Zanzibar Directory: Trade and Commercial Index: Annual Issue of 1936* (Nairobi: East African Directory Co., 1936), Uganda section, p. 55. Mehta, *Dream*, pp. 136–73 passim. Sir Amar N. Maini (son), interviewed by Gregory, 22 Nov. 1984, London.

13. Pandit, *Asians*, pp. 74–75, 334. K. J. Kotecha (Damodar's brother), interviewed by Gregory, 9 July 1973, Ahmedabad. K. K. Radia, interviewed by Gregory, 12 July 1973, Porbandar.

14. Pandit, *Asians*, pp. 119–20, 313–14, 359. A. K. Patel, interviewed by Gregory, 6 July 1973, Baroda. The Patels formed three ginning companies.

15. Mehta, *Dream*, pp. 140–41. Pandit, *Asians*, pp. 356, 365. For Vithaldas Haridas & Co., see *Kenya Daily Mail* (Mombasa), 3 Feb. 1928, p. 30. Damodar Jinabhai & Co. was described by K. J. Kotecha (interview). Ramchandani, *Uganda Asians*, pp. 134–35.

16. R. G. Suraiya, interviewed by Gregory, 21 June 1973, Bombay. Mehta, *Dream*, p. 140. Pandit, *Asians*, p. 357. Ramchandani, *Uganda Asians*, p. 132.

17. Mehta, *Dream*, pp. 140–45, 163–67.

18. Ibid., pp. 147, 154. A. M. Samji, interviewed by Honey, 15 Aug. 1973, Mwanza. A. Sachoo, 29 Oct. 1973, and N.M.H. Virjee, 5 Jan. 1974, interviewed by Honey, Mombasa.

19. V. H. Johanputra, interviewed by Bennett, 28 May 1973, Kisumu. A.R. Kassim Lakha, interviewed by Bennett, 9 May 1973, Mombasa. 'Nyanza Province Provincial Diary for Sept. 1924', p. 1, and for 'Nov. 1927', p. 1, Kenya miscellaneous correspondence, Syracuse University microfilm 2804, reel 106. Raishi, 'Note on Industrial Manufacturing'. For explanation of Kenya's low production of cotton, see Brett, *Colonialism*, pp. 206-8; Gavin Kitching, *Class and Economic Change in Kenya: The Making of an African Petite Bourgeoisie, 1905-1970* (New Haven: Yale University Press), pp. 136–40; and Hugh Fearn, *An African Economy: A Study of the Economic Development of the Nyanza Province of Kenya, 1903-53* (London: Oxford University Press, 1961), pp. 76–77.

20. Mehta, *Dream*, pp. 156, 168–72, 179–82. K.N.K. Mehta (son), interviewed by Bennett, 30 Apr. 1973, Nairobi. Pandit, *Asians*, pp. 59, 79–80, 359–60. H. P. Joshi, Bhanumati V. Kotecha, and J. V. Paun, eds., *Jayant Muljibhai Madhvani* (Nairobi: Emco Glass Works, 1973), pp. 61, 89, 313, 314. *Kenya-Uganda-Tanganyika and Zanzibar Directory . . . 1936*, Uganda section, p. 59. Pandit, *Asians*, pp. 78–80. Surprisingly little has been written about Muljibhai Madhvani.

21. Mehta, *Dream*, p. 181. I. S. Gill, interviewed by Bennett, 4 May 1973, Nairobi.

22. Pandit, *Asians*, pp. 142–43, 139, 317. File 'History of Fort Hall from 1888–1944', pp. 33–34, Central Province daily correspondence, Syracuse University microfilm 4571, reel 24.

23. *East African Standard*, 25 Apr. 1963, p. 5; 18 Jan. 1964, pp. 5, 6. Pandit, *Asians*, p. 323. K. P. Chandaria, interviewed by Gregory, 9–12, 14 May 1973, Addis Ababa. G. D. Shah, interviewed by Gregory, 12 July 1973, Jamnagar. Raishi, 'Note on Industrial Manufacturing'. For Forestal's wattle involvement, see Swainson, *Development*, pp. 70–71.

24. 'South Kavirondo District Annual Report for the Year Ended 31st Mar. 1922', p. 23, Syracuse University microfilm 2801, reel 37.

25. It was extremely difficult to find a carving of an African elephant during my stay in Kenya in 1955–56. When questioned, local Europeans remarked that Asians had started the industry.

26. Ten shoemakers, at least three of whom were Asian, are listed in *Kenya-Uganda-Tanganyika and Zanzibar Directory. . . 1936*, Trade Index section., p. 65.

27. Pandit, *Asians*, pp. 352–53. Raishi, 'Note on Industrial Manufacturing'.

28. Raishi, 'Note on Industrial Manufacturing'. Gulamhussein is mentioned in *Out of Africa* and *Shadows on the Grass* (New York: Random House, 1985, 1937).

29. *Report of the Commission Appointed to Enquire into and Report on the Financial Position and System of Taxation of Kenya* [report by A. W. Pim], Colonial no. 116 (London: HMSO, 1936), pp. 30, 32, 269–72.

30. Paul Marett, *Meghji Pethraj Shah: His Life and Achievements* (London: Bharatiya Vidya Bhavan, 1988).

31. S. M. Shah, interviewed by Bennett, 6 July 1973, Nairobi. A. G. Shah (son of G. V. Shah), interviewed by Gregory, 17 June 1985, Nairobi. J. M. Shah (grandson of D. P. Shah), interviewed by Gregory, 19 Aug. 1985, Nairobi.

32. Pandit, *Asians*, pp. 312, 313, 321, 330. A. M. Sheriff interview. T. S. Kotecha (son), interviewed by Bennett, 24 May 1973, Thika. N. S. Patel (son), interviewed by Honey, 5 Mar., 7 Sept. 1973, Dar es Salaam. H. K. Jaffer, interviewed by Bennett, 9, 13 May 1973, Mombasa. Swainson, *Development*, p. 69.

33. Mehta, *Dream*, pp. 238–39. Pandit, *Asians*, pp. 79–80.

34. Leggett to Bottomley, 2 Jan. 1916 [*sic*] (1917), C.O. 536/88.

35. Henry R. Wallis (Acting Governor, Uganda) to Bottomley, 26 Mar. 1917, ibid.

36. Garnham to General Manager, British East Africa Co., 6 June 1918.

37. Coryndon to Colonial Office, 10 Nov. 1918.

38. Mehta, *Dream*, pp. 113–14. President, East Africa Indian Association (Kampala?) to Colonial Office, 14 Jan. 1914, C.O. 536/74. India Office to Colonial Office, 31 Jan. 1920, forwarding dispatch from Narandas Rajaram & Co., C.O. 536/105. A. Sachoo interview. The Sachoos lost a ginnery because of this law. They had sent Shs 40,000 to lobby Parliament.

39. 'Nyanza Province Provincial Diary for Dec., 1925', entry 3, Dec. 1925, p. 1, Syracuse University microfilm 2804, reel 106.

40. Government Notice no. 73 of 1934, explained in G. F. Sayers (Acting Secretary) to Secretary, Federated Chambers of Commerce Section, Indian Association, Dar es Salaam, 24 June 1935, items 62–65, Tanganyika Secretariat file 20614, 'Applications for Exclusive Licences Under Marketing Ordinance, 1932'. Tanganyika Secretariat file 18681, 'Policy for Controlling Competition', includes considerable correspondence on the subject.

41. Honey, 'Asian Industrial Activities', p. 63.

42. Swainson, *Development*, p. 27.

43. Introduction of the Kenya marketing legislation is explained in C.O. 533/3102. See also *Reports on Marketing Legislation by K.P.S. Menon, and Accompanying Correspondence, 1935* (New Delhi: Government Printer, 1935), pp. 2–6. For examples of African competition, see file 'History of Fort Hall from 1888–1944', p. 32. See also 'Handing-Over Report—South Nyanza by Mr. A.A.M. Lawrence to Mr. P. W. Low', (n.d., 1948), p. 47, South Kavirondo Annual Reports, reel 38. For government training, see 'South Kavirondo Annual Report, 1946:' part 3, chap. 2, 'An Outline of the History of the District of South Kavirondo—Kenya Colony, 1780–1946', p. 47, South Kavirondo Annual Reports, reel 38. For the Coun-

cil's actions, see 'Minutes of a Meeting of the South Kavirondo Local Native Council Held in Kisii on 19th and 20th June 1941', pp. 10–11, Local Authority Records, Syracuse University microfilm 2246, reel 24. Also, 'Nyanza Province Provincial Diary for Dec., 1925', entry 3 Dec. 1925, p. 1, Syracuse University microfilm 2804, reel 106.

44. Annual reports of the Registrar General, which record the number of bankruptcies, do not reveal the full extent of Asian business failures because many of those who failed received aid from members of their extended families in paying creditors.

45. M. Manji, interviewed by Seidenberg, 21 May 1973, Nairobi. Pandit, *Asians,* pp. 290–91, 292, 297, 321–22. Munawar-ud-Deen (cousin), interviewed by Gregory, 9 Jan. 1973, Karatina. R. T. Thakore, interviewed by Gregory, 7 Feb. 1973, Nairobi. I. S. Gill interview. A. Fazal, interviewed by Honey, 22 Nov. 1973, Upanga.

46. Swainson, *Development,* pp. 101, 105–7, 117. Van Zwanenberg, 'Aspects of Kenya's Industrial History', pp. 46–47.

47. *Kenya-Uganda-Tanganyika and Zanzibar Directory: Trade and Commercial Index, 1959–60* (Nairobi: East African Directory Co., 1960), Kenya section, p. 95.

48. Swainson, *Development,* pp. 55, 168, and table 27, pp. 131–32.

49. Pandit, *Asians,* pp. 79–80.

50. Mehta, *Dream,* pp. 204ff. D. N. Mehta (N. K'.s son), interviewed by Gregory, 13 July 1973, Porbandar.

51. Pandit, *Asians,* pp. 79–80.

52. 'Sheet Manufacturers Ltd. Supplement', *East African Standard,* 25 Apr. 1963. pp. 4ff. For K. P. Shah, see *Who's Who in East Africa, 1965–66* (Nairobi: Marco, 1966), p. 136.

53. G. D. Shah (son of P. V. Shah) and K. P. Chandaria interviews.

54. 'House of Manji Group', 6 Feb. 1967, typed history from M. Manji in interview, 21 May 1973. Pandit, *Asians,* p. 351. I. S. Gill and T. S. Kotecha interviews.

55. G. D. Shah amd K. P. Chandaria interviews.

56. K. P. Chandaria interview.

57. Ibid. Robin Murray, 'Chandarias: The Development of a Kenyan Multinational', *Readings on the Multinational Corporation in Kenya,* ed. Raphael Kaplinsky (Nairobi: Oxford University Press, 1978), p. 292.

58. Murray, 'Chandarias', p. 288.

59. Lakhamshi R. Shah, interviewed by Gregory, 27 Nov. 1972, 9 Mar. 1973, Nairobi; 30 June 1973, Bombay; 9 July 1973, Ahmedabad.

60. Ibid., 27 Nov. 1972, 30 June 1973.

61. M. S. Khimasia, interviewed by Bennett, 19 Apr. 1973, Nairobi.

62. 'Late Keshavji Jethabhai Chande', typed biography from J. K. Chande (son), interviewed by Honey, 1 Mar. 1973, Dar es Salaam. For biographies of Keshavji and Ratansi, see Pandit, *Asians,* p. 116.

63. D. K. Hindocha, interviewed by Bennett, 20 Apr. 1973, Miwani. Pandit, *Asians,* pp. 280–81, 296.

64. Pandit, *Asians,* pp. 287–361 passim.

65. Kenya, *Report on the Census of the Non-Native Population of Kenya Colony and Protectorate Taken on the Night of the 25th Feb., 1948* (Nairobi: Government Printer, 1953), table 37, p. 66. Control of Industries Committee, reported in the Register of Licenses, 1943–48, cited in Ramchandani, *Uganda Asians*, p. 158.

66. Kenya, Uganda, *Tanganyika and Zanzibar Directory: Trade and Commercial Index, 1961–62 Edition* (Nairobi: East African Directory Co., 1962), Uganda section, p. 3. K. J. Kotecha interview.

67. N.M.H. Virjee and A. M. Samji interviews. A. Jamal, interviewed by Honey, 15 Aug. 1973, Mwanza.

68. Gadfly, 'Black and White in Uganda's Coffee Industry', *Tribune* (Nairobi), 17 May 1952, p. 17.

69. International Bank for Reconstruction and Development, *Economic Development of Kenya*, pp. 165–66. International Bank for Reconstruction and Development, *Economic Development of Tanganyika* (Baltimore: Johns Hopkins University Press, 1961), p. 241.

70. Swainson, *Development*, pp. 55, 168. E. J. Stoutjesdijk, *Uganda's Manufacturing Sector: A Contribution to the Analysis of Industrialization in East Africa* (Nairobi: East African Publishing House, 1967), pp. 34–35, 61. D. S. Pearson, *Industrial Development in East Africa* (Nairobi: Oxford University Press, 1969), p. 183. International Bank for Reconstruction and Development, *Economic Development of Tanganyika*, pp. 23, 240. International Bank for Reconstruction and Development, *Economic Development of Uganda* (Baltimore: Johns Hopkins University Press, 1962), pp. 20–21. Van Zwanenberg, 'Aspects of Kenya's Industrial History', p. 50.

71. International Bank for Reconstruction and Development, *Economic Development of Kenya*, pp. 167–68. International Bank for Reconstruction and Development, *Economic Development of Uganda*, p. 31.

72. International Bank for Reconstruction and Development, *Economic Development of Uganda*, p. 45. Pearson, *Industrial Development*, pp. 288–89. Kenya, *Development Plan, 1966–70* (Nairobi: Government Printer, 1966), p. 241. See, for example, 'South Nyanza District Annual Report, 1950', p. 19, Syracuse University microfilm 2801, reel 38. Newsletter no. 1, 'International Co-operation Administration Scheme for Assistance to African Industrialists, Artisans and Businessmen', 12 July 1956; no. 2, 10 Nov. 1956; no. 3, 31 May 1957; G. D. Parkin (Ministry of Commerce and Industry) to All Provincial Commissioners, 22 Feb. 1961—all in file, 'Trade and Commerce: Credit Trade with Natives: Loans to African Traders (not Agriculture) & Traders' Courses, etc., 1951–61', Syracuse University microfilm 4750, reel 348. International Bank for Reconstruction and Development, *Economic Development of Kenya*, p. 168.

73. International Bank for Reconstruction and Development, *Economic Development of Kenya*, p. 151.

74. L. R. Shah interview.

75. Kenya, Uganda, *Tanganyika and Zanzibar Directory . . . 1961–62*, Kenya section, p. 119.

76. International Bank for Reconstruction and Development, *Economic Development of Tanganyika*, pp. 244–46. The most informative writing on the Tanzanian policies and organization appears to be A. Coulson, ed., *African Socialism*

in Practice: The Tanzanian Experience (Nottingham: Spokesman, 1979). See also Zaki Ergas, 'Tanzanian Economy: What Went Wrong? Who Is Responsible? What Can Be Done?' (paper, African Studies Association annual meeting, Nov. 1981, Bloomington, Ind.), p. 9; and Michael B.K. Darkoh, *Tanzania's Industrial Strategy*, Kenyatta University College History Pamphlet 1 (Kisumu: Anyange, 1984), pp. 5–13.

77. P. M. Majithia, interviewed by Gregory, 19 Feb. 1973, Dar es Salaam. M. J. Thakkar, interviewed by Gregory, 19 May 1973, Addis Ababa. N. Velji, interviewed by Gregory, 12–13 Apr. 1987, Washington, D.C.

78. Ergas, 'Tanzanian Economy', especially pp. 9, 23, 34. Darkoh, *Tanzania's Industrial Strategy*, pp. 20–28. Ahmed Lakha, a Zanzibar manufacturer, provided a vivid account of the revolution and the Asians' reaction. Interviewed by Honey, 15 Jan. 1974, Dar es Salaam.

79. Uganda, *Report of the Commission of Enquiry into the Cotton Industry* (Kampala: Government Printer, 1966), pp. 24–25. Mahmood Mamdani, *Politics and Class Formation in Uganda* (London: Monthly Review, 1976), pp. 260–62. Stoutjesdijk, *Uganda's Manufacturing Sector*, pp. 10–17.

80. Dr. A. Milton Obote, *Common Man's Charter* (Entebbe: Government Printer, 1970). Uganda, *Parliamentary Debates*, 23 July 1970, pp. 198–201. Yash Tandon, 'Pragmatic Industrialist', chap. 5, *Jayant Madhvani*, ed. Robert Becker and Nitin Jayant Madhvani (London: W. and J. Mackay, 1973), pp. 17–18.

81. Mamdani, *Politics*, pp. 270–81. S. H. Jaffer, interviewed by Bennett, 9 Apr. 1973, Nairobi.

82. Kenya, *Development Plan, 1966–70*, pp. 235, 238–9. *Development Plan, 1970–74* (Nairobi: Government Printer, 1969), p. 322. Swainson, *Development*, pp. 119–21.

83. Kenya, *Development Plan, 1966–70*, pp. 240–42. *Who Controls Industry in Kenya?* Report of Working Party, Department of Christian Education and Training, National Christian Council of Kenya (Nairobi: East African Publishing House, 1968), pp. 189–91. Kenya, *Development Plan, 1966–70*, pp. 242, 244. Frank C. Child, *Small-Scale Rural Industry in Kenya*, Occasional Paper no. 17, University of California at Los Angeles, African Studies Center, p. 19 n. 1. Swainson, *Development*, p. 219.

84. The Trades Licensing Act of 1967 set the guidelines for Africanization. Many Asians have testified to the nature of the policy.

85. Statistical Department, *Economic and Statistical Review* and *Quarterly Economic and Statistical Bulletin*; and Uganda, Ministry of Economic Affairs, *Background to the Budget*.

86. For examples of tariff benefits for specific Asian firms, see Swainson, *Development*, pp. 126–27.

87. Leys, *Underdevelopment*, p. 121 n. 5.

88. V. V. Radia, 'This Was a 'Man'', chap. 16, *Jayant Muljibhai Madhvani*, ed. Joshi et al., p. 28.

89. H. G. Ehrentraut, 'My Most Interesting and Impressive Meeting with Late Jayant M. Madhvani', chap. 98, ibid., pp. 195–96.

90. Paul Munyagwa-Nsibirwa, 'A Dynamic Industrialist', chap. 74, ibid., p. 103. Clipping from *Economic Times*, n.d. (Aug. 1971), ibid., p. 314. 'Speech of Mr.

Jayant Madhvani on Behalf of Steel Corporation of East Africa Ltd. . . . 21st of April, 1961', ibid., pp. 347–48. Joseph Mubiru, 'Economic Colossus', chap. 12, *Jayant Madhvani*, ed. Becker and Madhvani, pp. 55–56. A. T. Lal, interviewed by Gregory, 22 Feb. 1973, Dar es Salaam. H. P. Joshi, interviewed by Gregory, 6 July 1973, Baroda.

91. Tandon, 'Pragmatic Industrialist', pp. 12, 14–15. Robert Glynn, 'Tragedy and Triumph', chap. 9, *Jayant Madhvani*, ed. Becker and Madhvani, pp. 44–48.

92. Joshi et al., *Jayant Muljibhai Madhvani*, pp. 168–69. Tandon, 'Pragmatic Industrialist', caption, pp. 14–15. Munyagwa- Nsibirwa, 'Dynamic Industrialist', p. 103.

93. Mehta, *Dream*, p. 285. Pandit, *Asians*, pp. 359–60. D. N. Mehta interview.

94. K. P. Chandaria interview. Kashi Shah, interviewed by Gregory, 4 Mar. 1973, Mombasa. For a listing of the Chandaria companies and a very informative summary, see Murray, 'Chandarias', pp. 293–95.

95. K. P. Chandaria interview; and S. Das, interviewed by Honey, 18 Oct. 1973, Dar es Salaam..

96. L. R. Shah interview.

97. Ibid.

98. Ibid.

99. Ibid. Stoutjesdijk, *Uganda's Manufacturing Sector*, pp. 41–46.

100. N. Velji interview. *Who Controls*, p. 174.

101. N. Velji interview.

102. M. S. Khimasia and T. S. Kotecha interviews. *Who Controls*, pp. 40, 61, 125, 175.

103. I. S. Gill and J. K. Chande interviews. Pandit, *Asians*, p. 351.

104. N. J. Dhanani, interviewed by Gregory, 14 June 1985, Nairobi.

105. A. G. Shah interview. N. B. Rajay (Resident Director) and M. Y. Bhujwalla (Factory Manager), interviewed by Gregory, 24 Feb. 1973, Tanga. K. R. Shah, interviewed by Bennett, 25 May 1973, Nakuru. *Who Controls*, pp. 28, 75.

106. L. R. Shah interview. P. U. Oza, interviewed by Gregory, 2 July 1973, Bombay. *Who Controls*, pp. 174–75.

107. *Who Controls*, pp. 174–75. L. R. Shah interview.

108. P. U. Oza and L. R. Shah interviews. Raishi, 'Note on Industrial Manufacturing'.

109. L. R. Shah interview. Azeez Lalani, interviewed by Honey, 16 Oct. 1973, Dar es Salaam. *Who Controls*, pp. 123–26.

110. S. P. Haji, interviewed by Honey, 21 Feb. 1974, Dar es Salaam. N. B. Rajay interview.

111. J. K. Chande interview. A. J. Bhatia, interviewed by Honey, 15 Oct. 1973. A. Alloo, interviewed by Honey, 14 Oct. 1973, Dar es Salaam.

112. I. S. Gill interview.

113. P. M. Majithia, interviewed by Gregory, 19 Feb. 1973, Dar es Salaam.

114. Ibid.

115. L. R. Shah and K. J. Kotecha interviews. A. K. Patel interview.

116. N.J. Jayant Madhvani (Jayant's older son), interviewed by Gregory, 12 June 1985, Nairobi. Tandon, 'Pragmatic Industrialist', p. 17. Eugene Schreiber, 'A Legacy', chap. 17, *Jayant Madhvani*, ed. Becker and Madhvani, p. 75.

117. G. D. Shah interview. D. K. Naranji (son), interviewed by Bennett, 18 May 1973, Nairobi.

118. M. P. Chandaria, interviewed by Gregory, 31 Jan. 1973, Nairobi. K. P. Chandaria interview. Murray, 'Chandarias', pp. 298–300.

119. K. P. Chandaria interview. Murray, 'Chandarias', pp. 294–96.

120. Leys, *Underdevelopment*, p. 45.

121. Pearson, *Industrial Development*, p. 13.

122. Recognized by Swainson, *Development*, pp. 124–30.

123. *Who Controls*, pp. 133–34, 145–46.

124. Ibid., pp. 3–5, 20–21, 26, 39–40, 51–52. Van Zwanenberg, 'Aspects of Kenya's Industrial History', p. 52.

125. *Who Controls*, pp. 79, 102–3, 105–6, 121, 145, and back-cover insert depicting the interlocking structure of the Unga-Riziki Group. For a list of major foreign firms in Kenya and their countries of origin, see Swainson, *Development*, app. 1, pp. 236–37.

126. Leys, *Underdevelopment*, p. 120 n. 4.

127. Swainson, *Development*, app. 1, p. 238.

128. *Who Controls*, pp. 129–32. I. D. Chandaria, 'Development of Entrepreneurship in Kenya', B.A. thesis, Harvard College, 1963, p. 28, cited in Leys, *Underdevelopment*, p. 45.

129. *Who Controls*, pp. 61, 110–12, ll4, 124–26.

130. Ibid., pp. 123–26. L. R. Shah interview.

131. *Who Controls*, pp. 159–60. L. R. Shah interview.

132. L. R. Shah interview.

133. Swainson, *Development*, pp. 233–34, 269–71, 273.

134. International Bank for Reconstruction and Development, *Economic Development of Uganda*, p. 105.

135. Van Zwanenberg, 'Aspects of Kenya's Industrial History', pp. 49, 53.

PART THREE

The Exportation
of Savings and Profits

———————— ■ ————————

CHAPTER TEN

Foreign and Local Employment of Money

They have made enormous sums in trade . . . ; the great bulk of their total earnings go back to India.

—Sir Robert Coryndon, 1918[1]

You cannot blame anyone who safeguards his future by taking his money out. It is the fundamental right of a human being to do what he likes with his money.

—Dahyabhai Chaturbhai Patel, 1973[2]

Although they obviously invested the greater portion of their earnings in local enterprise, the Asians through their long history in East Africa sent considerable sums overseas. Through most of the period the exported money went almost entirely to India, but beginning in the mid-1950s, when the Asians began to have doubts about their future in East Africa, increasing amounts were directed to the United Kingdom, the United States, and eventually Canada and Switzerland. Why the Asians sent currency overseas, whether they were justified in this, how much was sent, where it went, and how the practice varied through time are difficult questions. Some involve moral issues for which there is no universal answer. Others cannot be answered with precision because the Asians did not keep systematic accounts of their remittances overseas; and after the mid-1960s when restrictions were imposed, the Asians naturally became reluctant to discuss the subject. Because of the existence of some relevant information in writing and the testimony of some Asians, however, it is possible to provide a fairly comprehensive description.

Exportation for Relatives, Education, and Retirement

During the nineteenth century most of the Hindus who settled on Zanzibar and traded in the coastal cities of East Africa retained very close ties to India. They usually left their wives in India, partly to safeguard them from the hazards and hardships of life in East Africa and partly to ensure a suitable education for their children in Indian schools. These Hindu businessmen thus made frequent trips to India, sent 'home' a relatively large proportion of their profits, and anticipated an eventual retirement in the vicinities of their places of birth. The same pattern is discernible in the lives of sons or other relatives who succeeded them in the family businesses.[3]

The Muslims more easily severed the ties to India. Their religious affiliation was to the Kaaba in Mecca rather than to temples in the Gujarat or Punjab. Although many Bohras retained a custom of returning to India to marry, nearly all the Ismailis and Ithnasheris selected wives from the local communities. Those who could afford to do so might educate their children in India simply because adequate facilties in East Africa were lacking, but they did not for long support relatives in India, make trips to India, nor so often plan retirement there. Instead, they assisted their relatives to join them overseas. The Ismailis were foremost in this. 'They left India', it is said, 'with the idea of making their homes in East Africa'.[4]

The indentured railway workers, who at the turn of the century were forerunners of a great wave of Asian immigrants, apparently remitted most of their earnings to India. As shown in Chapter 5, nearly 82 per cent (32,583) of the indentured Asians employed in East Africa between 1895 and 1922 returned to India.[5] In 1906 large numbers of the Punjabi workers were described as 'mailing away part of their monthly wages' at the Mombasa General Post Office. 'To judge from their half-starved appearance', reported the *East African Standard,* '99 per cent. of their wages were being disposed of in this way'.[6] Even the indentured Asians who opted to stay in Africa must have remitted a considerable amount of their wages to relatives in India. That the money earned by these workers should remain in East Africa, however, was never intended by the governments. Nor was there much money involved. The minimum monthly wage was only Rs 15 (£1 sterling).[7]

Although the free immigrants of the twentieth century obviously invested most of their money in East Africa, many retained close ties and sent a portion of their earnings to India. This is especially true of the first-generation immigrants who often had to reimburse relatives for passage costs and support wives, children, and others whom they had left behind. Kantilal Punamchand Shah, the Nairobi politician, like many others, had to borrow rupees for his steamship ticket to Mombasa in 1941, and he was expected to send Shs 15 of his monthly salary of Shs 100 until the amount was repaid. Abdulla Fazal, the Bukoba wholesaler and manufacturer, earned after he arrived in 1910 only Shs 25 per month, and of that he regularly sent Shs 10 to his mother in Kutch.

Hariprasad Bhatt, who in 1938 left Saurashtra to work in a Kampala motor-spares company, supported his wife in India for nearly four years and later supported three sons for several years during their education in India. Shankar Dass, who beginning in 1910 sold rations to the railway workers in Nairobi, saved his money to spend during repeated trips to the Punjab.[8]

For various reasons many Asians made frequent trips to South Asia. Shamsud-Deen, before settling in Kenya permanently and assuming leadership of the Muslim community, returned twice to Kashmir with the intention of settling there. Mepabhai Vershi Shah, a Fort Hall shopkeeper, moved temporarily to India during World War I to farm, and Dinshaw Byramjee, a Nairobi businessman, returned to Karachi with his wife and eleven children in 1921 because Standard Six was the highest level of education then offered to Asians in East Africa.[9]

For nearly all the Asians, whether first-, second-, or third-generation immigrants, the profits before 1945 were relatively small, and there was a pressing need for reinvestment in the local countries. Before 1930 most new immigrants were just beginning their business ventures, and during the depression years of the early 1930s they were lucky to survive.[10] On the whole, not much money could have been sent away. There were, of course, many exceptions. The Patel and Punjabi civil servants, it is said, went home on leave every three years, built additions to their homes, and looking forward to retirement on their pensions, 'poured money into India'.[11] The Shahs spent a lot of money in frequent trips to the Gujarat because, as one remarked, the social life of their community was there. Perhaps more than any other community, they also sent money regularly to families in India. Some individuals spent a considerable amount of money there. In 1913 after fifteen years in Africa, Dharamshi 'Bopa' Kala Kantaria, a shopkeeper at Escarpment, won Rs 5,500 in a lottery, went to India to spend it, and returned after a year with a wife.[12] In 1926 following a long association with the Kenya-Uganda Railway as contractors, two Punjabi brothers, Wazirchand and Gainchand Vohora, retired to India 'with a lot of money'.[13] Few in this period, however, could afford to follow the example of Shamsud-Deen who provided both secondary and higher education in India for his two sons, Zafrud and Yakub.[14]

For various reasons a large number of the Asians before World War II retained all their earnings in East Africa. Perceiving the unusual economic opportunity, many concentrated all their resources in local investment. Some of those who owned homes in South Asia sold them to obtain money for this purpose. Many, like the Eldoret shopkeeper Shah Somchand Keshavji who left the Gujarat in 1926, were quickly followed by their entire families with the result that they had no close relatives in

India. Others, of whom Shantibhai D. Kothari seems typical, were so financially strapped that they were unable to educate their children in India, support wives there, or send money for other reasons. Kothari, who had a varied career as teacher, police accountant, and wholesale merchant in Kenya, found the provision of his children's education, even in East Africa, a heavy burden. Even among the relatively few wealthy Asians there were some who retained no ties to the mother country. Kanji Naranji Lakhani, who made a fortune in wholesaling groceries and growing sisal after his arrival in 1908, became so involved in local business that he never left East Africa.[15]

World War II was a turning point in the relations with South Asia. Although some continued with difficulty to eke out a living in East Africa, the Asians as a whole were far more prosperous. They had the means not only to send their children to India or Pakistan but to the United Kingdom and even to the United States for secondary and higher education. Increasingly an education in Europe or America was recognized as more valuable and more prestigious. Moreover, as a greater proportion of the Asians were born locally, the retention of close ties to South Asia acquired less value. For many the motherland was no longer home. During the 1950s when Shamsud-Deen's son Zafrud returned to the ancestral home in Pampor, Kashmir, he was surprised to find that he could not converse in the language. He also discovered that he was not welcome. He was suspected by the village headman of wanting to acquire some of the land rich in saffron.[16]

Investment Overseas

Despite a growing cultural estrangement, the more affluent Asians looked first to South Asia when considering the investment of money overseas. During the late 1930s after his remarkable success in cotton ginning and sugar manufacture, Nanji Kalidas Mehta proposed to the Uganda government a co-operative venture in establishing a textile industry. When, to his disappointment, the government declined, he turned to his home area in Saurashtra. The maharana of Porbandar welcomed the project and offered full co-operation. In 1940, leaving family members in charge of his Uganda industries, Mehta moved to Porbandar to establish with Uganda money the Maharana Mills Ltd., a huge textile and weaving concern, together with a smaller ancillary enterprise, the Porbandar Ginning and Pressing Factory Ltd. He also began a vegetable glue factory. Although the last was soon discontinued, the other two were very successful. In 1961 from the profits of these factories, he introduced another large complex in Porbandar, the Saurashtra Cement and Chemical Industries Ltd. According to Mehta's sons, Uganda money was used only to initiate the Saurashtra industries, and until 1965 most of the profits made in Uganda were invested in East Africa.[17]

During the same period, though not so successful as Mehta in their initial foreign investments, a group of Shahs undertook several financial ventures in India. In 1940, as previously explained, Devchand Premchand Chandaria joined with Meghji Pethraj Shah, Premchand Vrajpal Shah, and several others to manage jointly a total of eight enterprises in different centres of Kenya. The next year they expanded into India. In Jamnagar they founded Premchand Popat & Co., which briefly preceded Mehta's textile factory as the first in Saurashtra. About the same time the organizers of this company, incorporating other Shahs, formed a large brokerage business in Jamnagar and dealt in futures of groundnuts, castor seed, cotton, and precious metals. They quickly acquired a monopoly of the delivery of silver to the entire area. As newcomers, however, they were resented by the establshed members of the Shah community in Jamnagar who dubbed them the *Mahjan* (untouchables). The group soon adopted the epithet with pride. In 1942 under the leadership of Devchand's brother Rupilal, some of the Mahjan undertook another venture—the building of four dhows in Mangalore and the inauguration of a passenger service between Bombay and Mombasa. During the war years when the Indian Ocean steamer traffic all but ceased, the dhows did a thriving business and made the voyage in as few as eight days.[18]

At the end of the war, for several reasons, the Shah experiment in India began to collapse. When steamship travel resumed, the dhow service was no longer profitable. Moreover, despite the success of the other businesses, most members of the group were beginning to realize that East Africa offered a much greater opportunity for investment. The independence of India in 1947 brought a sizeable increase in taxation with the result that income taxes became much higher than in East Africa. Also, after independence the government of India prohibited external banking accounts with the result that money sent to India could not be taken out. A crisis occurred in 1948 when the Mahjan overspeculated in silver futures and fell Rs 3,500,000 in debt. The Mahjan had anticipated a fall in the price of silver and had sold futures short. In September 1948, however, the British government without warning had devalued the pound. The price of silver rose steeply because the rupee was tied to the pound.[19]

Largely through subsidies from M. P. Shah and Hemraj Nathoo Shah, the group paid off its debts, but a sharp disagreement over continuing involvement in India produced an irreparable rift in the Mahjan. Premchand Popat & Co. was terminated, and all the Kenya members except P. V. Shah withdrew their investments and returned to East Africa. Terminating all forms of joint ownership, they even divided among themselves the original eight companies in Kenya. In India P. V. Shah began again in 1950 by forming a Jamnagar oil mill, Jam Oil Products, but all members of his family except a nephew, Gulabchand, left to renew their fortunes in East Africa. It was not profit from India but the proceeds of the family's new company in Kenya, Steel Africa Ltd., that within five years enabled P. V. and Gulabchand to become financially solvent.[20]

A number of other Asians invested in India during these post-war years. Though employing a greater percentage of his money in East Africa, Muljibhai Madhvani established a large factory in Bombay, the Mukesh Textile Mills (Private) Ltd., and with the proceeds expanded further in India. In 1942 Jagannath B. Pandya, the Mombasa business leader, set up in Bombay a branch of his hardware firm, East African Hardwares Ltd., and formed in Bhavnagar with his wife's brother a trading concern, Pandya & Trivedi Ltd. Later in the year when he was negotiating to purchase the Ahmedabad newspaper *Sandesh* (Message), all his investments were terminated by his early death. As Pandya and the others illustrate, it was the wealthier Asians who experimented in these years with investment in India. The Goan civil servants were a possible exception. Though their savings were meagre, the Goans were able to look forward to a comfortable retirement on government pensions, and many in anticipation built or purchased fine homes in Goa and Bombay. There were also some businessmen in this category. During four decades in Uganda A. Kalidas Patel acquired nine ginneries and then diversified into insurance, breweries, paper production, agriculture, and housing rental. In the years preceding exchange controls he transferred about 25 per cent of his profits to India for an eventual retirement in Baroda.[21]

Exportation for Security

During the late 1950s and early 1960s, as described in Chapter 2, a series of events in Africa created for Asians and Europeans alike a sense of insecurity and considerably augmented the move to transfer money to overseas countries. The 'winds of change' in the wake of Mau Mau culminated in the Lancaster House conferences of 1960 and 1962. Even before the second conference met, the transfer of power began as first Tanganyika, then Uganda, Zanzibar, and Kenya were to gain independence. After 1962 following Belgium's precipitous withdrawal, the Congo rapidly fell into turmoil. Two years later Zanzibar erupted in violent revolution, and armies mutinied in Tanganyika, Kenya, and Uganda. Perhaps even more ominous was the fact that many Africans in East Africa were declaiming against the Asians' presence.[22]

As a safeguard many Asians began to send money out of East Africa. A considerable number who hoped to remain opened bank accounts and

purchased securities in other countries, especially in the United Kingdom, Switzerland, and the United States. They turned to these countries
not only because of the countries' relative economic and political stabil-
ity, but also because most of the non-Western nations, including Pakistan as well as India, did not recognize external accounts. This does not
mean that these Asians ceased investing in East Africa on a permanent
basis. As the Chandarias illustrate, many of the wealthier Asians transferred their money into external accounts in foreign countries temporarily with the intention of reinvesting it in East Africa as opportunity
arose.[23] There was nevertheless a sizeable drain from the economy by
Europeans as well as Asians. After examining the records of savings with-
drawals in Kenya during 1959–60, Donald Rothchild concluded, 'Pan-
icky Europeans and Asians in all walks of life sent very considerable
sums of money to banks in Europe and Asia for safekeeping. Around
1959 some £4 million was withdrawn by non-Africans from building society deposits alone'.[24]

The uncertainty that produced a transfer of savings also prompted investment of profits in other countries. The Chandaria family perhaps
best illustrates this tendency to move outside East Africa. After withdrawing from the joint enterprise with the P. V. Shah family, the Chandarias retained in India a financial interest only in the Halar Salt Works
Co. of Jamnagar. During 1956–57, however, they opened in London a
branch office of their parent company, Premchand Brothers Ltd., and
acquired a controlling interest in a British holding company in steel,
Preet & Co. Ltd. In 1951 they built an aluminium stamping-press plant in
Bujumbura, Burundi, and in 1960 a similar factory in Bukavu, Congo. It
was in 1962 that they began to have serious apprehensions about their
African concentration. In that year Belgium abruptly abandoned the
Congo, and Patrice Lumumba in a much-publicized speech denounced
all foreign investment. The Chandarias contemplated leaving Africa entirely but on further reflection decided to spread their assets into more
African countries. In Kenya they terminated their manufacture of hurricane lamps and all organizations except two wire-producing plants,
which they amalgamated into East African Wire Industries Inc. Then
while retaining and expanding their operations in Burundi and Zaire,
they established industries in Ethiopia, Morocco, Malawi, Mozambique,
Nigeria, Rhodesia, and Zambia. For tax purposes they registered all the
new organizations in Bermuda.[25]

Further difficulties with their African holdings prompted the Chandarias to move into Europe and Asia. In 1966 after unfavourable experiences in Malawi, Mozambique, and Rhodesia, they decided to diversify
into western Europe, and within three years they had set up fifteen factories in seven countries. In these as in all the preceding, they built on their

East African experience by manufacturing aluminium ware, galvanized roofing, metal doors and windows, plastic pipes, paper packaging, and steel wire. Turning to Asia in 1974, they quickly erected similar plants in Malaysia, Indonesia, Singapore, Australia, the Philippines, and Papua New Guinea. By 1978, although 50 per cent of their holdings were still in Africa, they owned industries in at least twenty-two countries and, as mentioned, had acquired assets worth £40 million.[26]

Many other Asians were prompted by the uncertainties of the late 1950s and early 1960s to invest overseas. Beginning in 1965 with profits they had made from Steel Africa and its subsidiaries in East Africa and from Jam Oil Products in India, Gulabchand Devra Shah and his brothers Amichand and Hemraj established seven industries in the Gujarat, and in 1971, two months before nationalization of the companies in Tanzania, they sold out of Steel Africa. Because the purchaser of their shares was a foreign buyer, they were able to invest the proceeds in India. During the same years the family of Rahamtulla Kassim Lakha, which built the Oceanic Hotel in Mombasa and founded approximately fifty businesses, mostly in Uganda, set up jute mills in Bangladesh and began to invest in Canada and the United Kingdom.[27] In 1963 after founding a successful travel agency in Nairobi, Bhanubhai Acharya and his son Mahendra shifted the headquarters of their Acharya Travelling Agency to Baroda. There they developed, in Bhanubhai's words, 'a fantastic business' with Indians travelling not to East Africa but to North America. In 1971 with profits from the Baroda agency they bought three residential properties in London and opened an office to offer tourist visits to East Africa. Two years later they were in an ideal situation to provide about 150 charter flights for the Asians fleeing Uganda.[28]

Similar investments were undertaken by the industrialists Devjibhai Karamshi Hindocha, Chhotabhai Motibhai Patel, and Gordhendas Vasanji. Early in the 1950s after buying the Miwani Sugar Mills Ltd. in western Kenya, Hindocha founded and put his son Laljibhai in charge of the Horizon Sugar Mills in Pondicherry. In 1959 Patel, who had developed a widespread ginning, marketing, and industrial complex of companies in Uganda, took over the Khira Steel Works Ltd. in Bombay. The next year he established Chandan Metal Products Ltd. to produce steel furniture in Baroda. In 1964 Vasanji, owner of a very successful Mombasa hosiery and garment factory, the Kenya Rayon Mills Ltd., opened a factory in West Africa, the Sierra Leone Knitting Mills Ltd.[29]

Within this period the Shah community, fearing that their centre might have to be shifted from Nairobi, began to transfer money to the United Kingdom. Like many others, the Shahs also began to buy houses in South Asia and Europe, especially in England, not only for the purpose of future residence but also to obtain a rental income or hold for speculation. Much of the Asians' current rental property in the London environs was acquired in these years.[30]

Beginning in the mid-1960s the Asians' fears for a viable future in East Africa began to be realized. The Africanization of the civil service; the increasing application of the 'managed economy' with the growth of government agencies, parastatals, and co-operatives; the linkage of 'citizenship' to the issuance of work permits and trade licences; and the mounting popular agitation against the Asians—these factors generally were, as explained in Chapter 2, major causes of uncertainty in all the mainland countries. Moreover, even Kenya and Tanzania did not seem immune from the mass expulsions arising from the Zanzibar coup of 1964 and Amin's Uganda order of 1972.

In this situation most Asians sought to transfer as large a portion of their assets as possible outside East Africa. As Sir Ernest Vasey, Kenya's former minister for economic planning, observed in 1973, the Asians 'were desperate to get their money out'.[31] An Asian leader in Tanzania agreed. 'Even if a man could save only ten shillings per month', he remarked, 'he would try to get six shillings of it to England'.[32] Unfortunately for the Asians, the East African governments in 1965, acting apparently by common agreement, imposed exchange controls on the exportation of currency. Such controls in the non-Western world were not unusual. They were encouraged by the International Monetary Fund, World Bank, and other international lending organizations, and in East Africa it was not only the Asians who were exporting currency. The Asians, however, were the chief exporters, and it was primarily they at whom the controls were directed. Beginning with the 1965 legislation all Kenya residents were prohibited from removing curency except for personal travel, the education of children, or the support of dependents. The maximum travel allowance was £250 per year, permission for educational or dependent support required special application, and the amounts allowed were tightly constricted. Residents were forbidden to keep foreign currency or hold accounts in foreign banks. All Asians were placed in a special category, so that even those with British or Indian passports, quite unlike other foreigners, were denied permission to export their profits or assets. In time the initial controls were tightened with the result that the Asians were permitted a maximum of only £200 for travel every two years. Moreover, the delays in processing applications became increasingly a more serious impediment. To encourage Asian emigration, the government permitted departing heads of families to take out Shs 50,000 and to receive later installments of Shs 25,000.[33]

In Tanzania and Uganda the initial currency restrictions were essentially the same as in Kenya. In Tanzania they eventually became the most restrictive. In 1970, for instance, the Tanzania Asians were prohibited from exporting money even for educational purposes. In Uganda all the rules were changed during the exodus of 1973. The departing Asians were informed that they each could carry a maximum of Shs 200 through customs. At the Entebbe airport, however, the officials in most instances took the money from them with an assurance that an equivalent amount in British pounds would be refunded to them on arrival in England. Later, as expected, the Asians found no refund at Heathrow.[34]

Under these circumstances, in all three territories, the Asians were disillusioned, resentful, and in times of crisis, panic stricken. Despite initial assurances from the African governments of equal rights for all citizens, Kenya was openly discriminating against the Asians, Tanzania was moulding all society into a form highly unfavourable to Asian traditions, and Uganda, in its ultimate act, was expelling them. Clearly, the Asians were neither appreciated as Asians nor wanted as Asians in East African society. Although many met this situation with resignation, most felt a moral justification in transferring the money they had earned, despite all prohibiting laws or regulations, to other countries for safekeeping. The common sentiment was well expressed in 1973 by the Nairobi businessman and political leader, Dahyabhai Chaturbhai Patel. 'You cannot blame anyone who safeguards his future by taking his money out', Patel stated. 'It is the fundamental right of a human being to do what he likes with his money and it is an injustice to prevent him by law to do so'.[35] The restrictions on the exportation of currency applied to Africans and Europeans as well as Asians, and it has been for all a subject of great controversy.

Whether justified or not, the Asians managed through both open and devious means to send money overseas. A fortunate few, who at the invitation of the African governments had invested money from outside sources in the development of industry and other business, were permitted to withdraw a large percentage of the profits. In common with other expatriate investors the Chandarias, Madhvanis, and Mehtas were thus able to export legally from East Africa 30 per cent of their profits.[36] The East African governments, like those of developing countries everywhere, had to make such a concession to attract foreign investment. Most local Asians, however, had no option but some illegal means.

The Asians devised various means to get their money out. During the 1967–68 exodus from Kenya, a number of wealthy Asians spread considerable sums among the destitute whereby each, for some remuneration, carried out the maximum legal amount and later returned the 'money-on-loan' to its rightful owner. Others lent tourists and other visitors to East Africa local currency for spending during their stays with the understanding that equivalent sums would be deposited later in foreign banks. There were also attempts to carry currency illegally through customs in the false bottoms or linings of luggage and purses or sewn into clothing, and as a last resort there was always bribery. At more sophisticated levels there was the manipulation of bank records or the falsification of receipts for goods sold abroad so that a sizeable portion of the proceeds remained outside East Africa. Not all attempts at illegal exportation were successful. In 1973 in Tanzania alone nearly 100 Asians were in detention under charges of currency smuggling. Among those imprisoned in Kenya was the distinguished barrister Achhroo Ram Kapila who had defended Kenyatta at Kapenguria.[37]

On Zanzibar the politician Vaghjibhai Shankerbhai Patel and his son Babu devised a clever scheme to profit from the currency controls. After the revolution to retain as much of the Asian assets as possible, President Karume announced that departing Asians could no longer take out money. Instead, they each could take up to one ton of cloves. The purchase price of cloves on Zanzibar was then very low, approximately Shs 16,000 per ton, but not all Asians had that much money. The Patels offered to purchase the cloves with their own savings and to reimburse the Asians handsomely on their arrival in India. Many of the Asians agreed. True to the agreement, the Patels afterwards paid the emigrants, but in selling the cloves in the markets of India they received in rupees nearly ten times the purchase price. Although the father and son realized an immense profit, all those involved had benefitted without violation of Karume's order. The Patels' East African money had remained on Zanzibar.[38]

The amount of money taken overseas in these years or earlier for the purpose of savings or investment is a matter of conjecture. The Asians themselves disagree widely in their estimates. Some assert that the community began to export money only after the imposition of exchange controls. Most acknowledge, however, that the community regularly sent some money out during the entire period of its stay in East Africa, and they think that the total was sizeable. One knowledgeable individual has estimated that nearly 50 per cent of the Asians' profits left East Africa. Another has observed that billions of shillings went solely for the support of relatives in India. Still another has argued that only paltry sums went to Indian relatives. More, he maintains, was sent out for the education of Asian children. Others contend that the sums designated for education or family support were small compared to those that went for investment.[39]

Benevolence Overseas

Nearly all observers tend to overlook the considerable sums sent to India and other foreign countries for charitable purposes. Most of this philanthropic contribution went to India for relief occasioned by some natural disaster, but much was directed towards the construction of public buildings and the establishment of memorials. Some was given to support India's struggle for independence. Although India was the main recipient, South Africa, the Congo, and Saudi Arabia also were favoured.

Beginning apparently in the 1930s as they emerged from the economic depression, the Asians began to organize in aid of suffering caused by the natural disasters that periodically afflicted India and other parts of Asia. In 1936 when a severe drought produced a famine in western India, the Shah community of Nairobi held a series of meetings in which amounts as high as Shs 50,000 were subscribed and then sent to India. The following year as the famine continued, the community established a permanent Oshwal Education and Relief Board and appealed for new funds. By the end of 1937 the Shahs had forwarded a total of £20,000. In 1943 when a similar famine occurred in Bengal, the Nairobi Asians, despite the fact that scarcely any came from Bengal, organized a relief fund and appealed widely for donations. Local Asians responded by quickly raising £12,286. During the same year the Muslim Asians led by Shamsud-Deen initiated a Hejaz Famine Relief Fund for the aid of Arabs in the vicinity of Mecca.[40]

In the 1950s the Asians collected money for three new disasters in South Asia. In 1950 when Assam was devastated by an earthquake, the East Africa Indian National Congress established an Assam Relief Fund and called for donations from Europeans as well as Asians. Within a few weeks it was able to send Shs 86,291 to the government of India. Three years later the Asians launched a drive for famine relief in Maharashtra and in 1955 another for Indian flood victims. One Mombasa organization, the Shree Navnat Mahajan, which contributed Rs 2,501, received praise from the local Indian Association for its 'magnificent sum'.[41]

The Asians responded to a disaster of another kind in 1962 when the Chinese invaded India's mountain passes. The donations to an Aid-India Fund were described by the president of the Nairobi Indian Merchants' Chamber, which sponsored the drive, as 'overwhelming'. More than a million shillings had been subscribed, he explained. 'Money is pouring'.[42]

Three years later as rival political factions threw the newly independent Congo into chaos, the Asians eagerly supported the Kenya government's plea for aid to the Congo refugees. The honourary secretary of the Nairobi Central Chambers of Commerce at once appealed to all members for contributions. 'It is an imperative moral duty for us', he stated, 'to join the Government in providing whatever aid is possible to the unfortunate refugees of the Congo, who . . . have been compelled to leave their sweet homes helplessly'. In this instance the Asians donated food and clothing as well as money for shelter and medicine.[43]

While supporting such causes for disaster relief, the East Africa Asians also contributed to civil disobedience and passive resistance campaigns in India and South Africa. In 1923–24 and again in 1929 Mrs. Sarojini Naidu, Gandhi's associate in the Indian National Congress, visited East Africa and in co-operation with local Indian leaders established a Sarojini Congress Fund. Although a complete account of the drive is apparently no longer extant, there were at least 550 donors with contributions ranging from the Shs 1,272 given by the Patel Brotherhood to Shs 5 offered by several individuals. In 1932 and 1933 during Gandhi's two historic fasts, Indian organizations in East Africa called for mass meetings and presumably collected funds in support of the satyagraha movement. There were similar collections in subsequent years. As late as 1949, two years after India's independence, the Hindu Union of Arusha prepared to sell 1,000 flags for a 'Free India Day'. Meanwhile in times of crisis, the Asians had contributed to a South African Passive Resistance Fund that had been in existence in India since 1909. In 1948 the East Africa Indian National Congress was thanked by the Natal Indian Congress for its 'unstinted financial assistance', and in 1952 the Congress launched another appeal.[44]

The foremost fund raiser in East Africa on behalf of India in these years was the Nairobi businessman, Bachulal T. Gathani. Distinguished as the only individual who simultaneously was the president of both the East Africa Indian National Congress and the Federation of Indian Chambers of Commerce and Industry in Eastern Africa, he made use of his office in each to support philanthropic causes. For collecting more money for India than any Asian overseas, Gathani became known as the *Shere Hind* (Lion of India).[45]

Besides supporting disaster relief and resistance campaigns, the Asians contributed to the construction in India of schools, temples, hospitals, and public halls, and to the establishment of memorials. The principal memorial, that to Gandhi's wife, was provided by the Kasturba Gandhi Memorial Fund in 1949. Largely through the effort of the Bhagini Samaj of Nairobi, the Asians raised Rs 108,625. Public edifices were supported most generously, as might be expected, by the two Uganda industrialists N. K. Mehta and Muljibhai Madhvani and their Kenya counterpart, M. P. Shah. Mehta and Shah were exceptional in that they donated more to India than to Africa. Three-fourths of Mehta's total charitable contribution of more than Rs 24,000,000 is said to have gone to India, mostly to buildings in Porbandar, the city near his home village. Among the buildings he established in Porbandar are the Arya Samaj Girls' School and College, the Rokadia Hanuman Temple, the Arya Kanya

Gurukul, the N. K. Mehta Hospital, and the N. K. Mehta Science College. He also restored the Porbandar home in which Gandhi was born and raised.[46]

Mehta's main contribution outside Porbandar was the Shri Brihad Bharatiya Samaj in Bombay. The Samaj is a non-political society designed for the promotion of the economic, social, educational, and cultural interests of Indians abroad. It is situated in a spacious, six-story building, the N. K. Mehta International House, with a research wing, library, auditorium, hostel, and transit camp. Mehta was not the only donor for this building, which opened in 1963. There were literally thousands, and in fact the Asians of East Africa separately raised Rs 250,000 in a special fund drive. Mehta's donation of Rs 500,000, however, was by far the largest from any individual or organization and amounted to more than one-fourth of the total cost. Mehta also contributed to numerous other projects outside Porbandar, especially to those concerned with women's education. He subsidized, for example, a Gurukul in Baroda and another at Choki.[47]

The overseas donations of M. P. Shah nearly equalled those of Mehta. As described in Chapter 2, Shah retired to Jamnagar in 1963 when he was forty-nine years old and had a capital worth of £2.5 million. Through the Meghji Pethraj Shah Charitable Trust that he had established for philanthropy in India, he initiated a ten-year plan for social welfare projects in Kathiawar (later Saurashtra). He designed the projects, directed the construction, and provided one-third to one-half the cost in towns and one-fourth to one-third in villages. The government contributed the remaining cost and assumed the administration on completion of construction.[48]

The projects continued beyond the ten years to M. P. Shah's death in 1964. By then the Jamnagar trust had expended more than Rs 10 million, twice that of the Nairobi trust which had been supporting similar projects in East Africa. In western India Shah had provided facilities for 34,000 primary and secondary pupils and 4,000 college students, hostels for 1,200 children, hospitals with 1,200 beds, and 800 village libraries. The more costly edifices were the M. P. Shah All India Talking Book Centre for the blind in Bombay (Shah's contribution: Rs 1,800,000), the M. P. Shah Medical College in Jamnagar (Rs 1,500,000), the Shrimati Maniben M. P. Shah Women's College and the M. P. Shah Junior College for women in Bombay (Rs 700,000), and a glucose saline plant for the Gujarat Health Department (Rs 600,000). Other buildings included a leprosy sanatorium in Bhavnagar, a cancer hospital in Ahmedabad, a college of commerce and law in Jamnagar, and a technical training centre in Surendranagar. Shah spent the last seven years of his life in London, where he established two more trusts, for donations in England, and

bought a commodities brokerage and organized two companies—
Premchand Raichand London Ltd. and Oswal Investments Ltd.—to provide the capital. His subsequent donations in London, Leicester, and Jersey totalled $255,500.[49]

As the founding of the two British companies illustrates, a proportion
of the cost of Shah's overseas philanthropy, like that of Mehta, was financed by money-making projects outside East Africa. Some of Shah's
fortune had been acquired through Premchand Popat & Co. and the brokerage firm that he had established in Jamnagar with the Chandarias
and other Shahs in 1940. Four years later with his brothers and Chiman-
bhai U. Shah he had formed another Indian company, Raichand Brothers (India) Pvt. Ltd., which was soon purchasing from 80 to 90 per cent of
East Africa's wattle exports.[50]

Compared to those of Mehta and M. P. Shah, Madhvani's charitable
donations overseas appear insignificant. Madhvani, unlike the other
two, never stayed for long in India and concentrated his philanthropy on
the development of East Africa. He did, however, donate to numerous
charitable causes in India. He provided the library of the Shri Brihad
Bharatiya Samaj, which includes a valuable collection of literature on Indians overseas. He also built a school at Raval near his birthplace in Saurashtra and contributed Rs 30,000 to the Vallabh Kanya Vidyalaya.[51]
Madhvani was probably able to finance all these contributions with the
profits from his Mukesh Textile Mills and other business ventures in India.

The other Asians who as individuals endowed public edifices in India
are relatively few, and their donations have not been widely publicized.
Lakhamshi R. Shah, the Nairobi businessman, endowed a hall at the National High School in Jamnagar; and Pitamber A. Sachania, a Zanzibar
building contractor, during a ten-year stay in India, 1924–34, is described as having 'built rest houses, water fountains and donated generously at various places and to various causes in Saurashtra'.[52] The
members of the Shah community are said to have contributed to many
social welfare projects in their home villages round Jamnagar.[53]

Becoming increasingly sensitive to European charges that they were
exporting their profits, the Asians devised means to limit their donations
to India. In 1955 a resolution of the annual conference expressly prohibited the Kenya Indian Congress and its affiliated organizations from collecting funds for objects outside East Africa. Later in 1955 when a
delegation from India applied for Congress aid in collecting funds for the
Shri Brihad Bharatiya Samaj, the Congress agreed to extend the delegation 'all courtesy' but not to associate itself with the collection.[54] In subsequent years the Asian organizations differed in their enforcement of
the resolution. The Mombasa Indian Association refused to patronize

any appeal for a charitable fund for the people of India, and the Congress decided to make an exception for disaster relief.[55]

The Asians' charitable donations overseas present a pattern very similar to their exportations for investment, education, or support of relatives. Although they contributed generously in support of the needy overseas, their contributions were never sizeable during the seventy-year period in comparison to the amount invested in East Africa. Nor were they sizeable in comparison to their donations to charitable causes in Kenya, Tanganyika, Uganda, and Zanzibar. As with investments, a few key individuals, the wealthy, contributed a large proportion of the money devoted to charity, and much of what they gave came from the profits of the businesses that they had established in India.

Investment and Philanthropy in East Africa

Until the late 1950s when the Asians for the first time began to have serious doubts about their future in East Africa, the community appears to have reinvested by far the greater portion of its profits in local enterprise and charity.[56] There is truth in the Nairobi advocate Velji Devji Shah's vehement assertion, 'The accusation of taking all the money out is ridiculous. All one has to do is look at Nairobi'.[57] As another explained, the Asians believed in the future of East Africa, and so they invested in East Africa.[58] This statement means that the profits to be gained from the African environment during the first half of the twentieth century were much greater on the whole than any that could be realized in other areas with which the Asians were familiar.[59] Throughout the period before the mid-1960s only a relatively small proportion of the Asians' total income was devoted to the support of relatives and the education of children, mostly in India. Not until after World War II did many have sufficient wealth to invest money outside East Africa or to educate their children in the United Kingdom. It was during the six or seven years before the exchange controls of 1965 that a considerable amount of currency left East Africa for savings and investment. Local investment began to diminish during that time, and after 1965 it fell off rapidly. Moreover, despite all attempts at restriction, a large number of the Asians then managed to export most of their savings. After the Uganda exodus the amount that left East Africa apparently diminished steadily because of the dwindling of both savings and new investment.

There are some notable exceptions to these generalizations. Many of the Zanzibar and Uganda Asians lost all their investments in East Africa as their businesses, homes, personal property, and savings were confiscated without compensation, or, as in the case of the civil servants, their pensions were terminated. In Tanzania other Asians lost their business and rental properties through nationalization, and in Kenya those whose licences could not be renewed were often forced to sell at prices well below the value of their investments. Many Asians had no savings. Dahyabhai Chaturbhai Patel, who from Kisumu expanded an auto-spares business into a dealership throughout East Africa, was typical in that he ploughed all the profits back into his company, so that when he was forced to retire, he had almost no accumulated capital.[60] Anant J. Pandya, leader of the Kenya Asians during the 1960s, was unusual in that he refused for moral reasons to export capital. 'I kept my money tied up in Kenya', he explained in 1973. 'I said if you are going to have a country, then let it be your country—in all ways'.[61]

Although the statistical evidence is meagre, the magnitude of the Asians' African investment is manifest. East Africa's cities and towns were a result primarily of Asian enterprise. Most of the commercial edifices were established by Asians. Even the buildings belonging to Europeans were constructed largely by Asian contractors and artisans. Many of the non-commercial buildings, such as temples and mosques, schools, hospitals, and libraries, and most of the public parks and much of the impressive statuary were also created by Asians. Most of the ginneries and sugar mills that produced Uganda's main export commodities were additional contributions from Asians. Throughout East Africa the network of roads represents mainly the governments' response to the Asians' development of road transport.[62]

Despite the lack of comprehensive information there are some revealing statistics. Between 1935 and 1946 the Kenya Asians invested £32,709,000 in private companies, £2,379,000 in urban commercial property, and £223,000 in agricultural estates.[63] In 1946 they paid an estimated £860,000 in import and excise duties on commodities.[64] By 1936 a total of 6,680 Kenya Asians, as compared with 3,451 Europeans, held deposits in the Post Office Savings Bank.[65] In Tanganyika 349 Asians by 1936 held 316,000 acres, 16 per cent of the alienated agricultural and pastoral land.[66] In 1951 some 3,000 Tanganyika Asians were employing a total of 108,860 workers. A decade later 8,707 Tanganyika Asians were engaged in commerce, 1,999 in manufacturing, 1,953 in public services, 1,852 in transport, 898 in agriculture and forestry, 809 in construction, 540 in banking and insurance, 482 in teaching, and 149 in mining and quarrying.[67] In Uganda the Asians by 1933 had acquired 46 agricultural estates comprising 42,512 acres.[68] Three years later they were described as owning 105 of the 137 registered ginneries.[69] In Zanzibar 20 of the 22 licensed clove exporters in 1960 were Asians.[70] Other statistics such as these attest to the magnitude of the Asian investment.

Not all the Asians' local expenditure was intended for profit. A sizeable proportion was devoted to philanthropy. The Asians initiated and subsidized a large number of schools and libraries, hospitals and dispensaries, literary and artistic associations, and welfare organizations. Among the most notable of these were the University of Nairobi, the Allidina Visram High School, the Mombasa Institute of Muslim Education, the Aga Khan Hospitals, the Pandya Memorial Clinic, the Desai Memorial Library, the Jeevanjee Gardens of Nairobi, the Nairobi Municipal Market, the Dar es Salaam Town Hall, and the Zanzibar Sports Stadium. Despite the discriminatory colonial policies and practices, the Asians donated liberally to charities initiated and administered by the governments and European settlers. They also provided the principal support for numerous philanthropic causes that were non-racial in character, and they designed many projects specifically for Africans.

The Asians' emphasis on philanthropy can be explained partly by their religious mores and traditions in India and partly by the necessities of the new environment in Africa. The Asians came to East Africa with long-standing traditions of benevolence. The Hindu, Jain, and Muslim religions stressed the sharing of one's wealth with the needy, and in the Gujarat, Kutch, and the Punjab the fluctuations in agricultural production induced customs of sharing within the joint families and local communities. In East Africa where the colonial systems emphasized primarily the interests of the European settlers and secondarily those of the indigenous Africans, the Asians were left to provide nearly all their own social, cultural, and welfare organizations and services. Their charitable endeavour was thus mainly a response to the needs of the new environment. Unfortunately, it diminished markedly with the development of Asian insecurity in the early post-colonial years.

Notes

1. Dispatch to Colonial Office, 10 Nov. 1918, C.O. 536/91.

2. Untitled four-page typescript on the history of East Africa Asians submitted by D. C. Patel to Bennett during interview, 28 Apr. 1973, Nairobi.

3. Kashi Shah (interviewed by Gregory, 4 Mar. 1973, Mombasa) said this happened to her brother.

4. M. L. Shah, interviewed by Honey, 10 Jan. 1974, Dar es Salaam. S. Haji, interviewed by Honey, 27 June 1973, Iringa. In describing the tendency of Muslims to marry locally, Ali Mohamedjaffer, an Ithnasheri, made no distinction among Bohras, Ismailis, and Ithnasheris; interviewed by Honey, 22 Oct. 1973, Arusha. Yusufali Pirbhai, a Bohra, asserted that his community was an exception; interviewed by Honey, 25 Feb. 1974, Dar es Salaam.

5. Robert G. Gregory, *India and East Africa: A History of Race Relations Within the British Empire, 1890–1939* (Oxford: Clarendon, 1971), pp. 53, 55, 61.

6. *East African Standard*, 15 Sept. 1906, p. 7.

7. Gregory, *India and East Africa*, p. 55.

8. K. P. Shah, interviewed by Gregory, 7 Feb. 1973, Nairobi. A. Fazal, interviewed by Honey, 22 Nov. 1973, Bukoba. H. Bhatt, interviewed by Gregory, 9 July 1973, Ahmedabad. D. S. Dass (son), interviewed by Seidenberg, 5 May 1973, Nairobi.

9. Zafrud-Deen (son), interviewed by Gregory, 22 Nov. 1972, Nairobi. M. V. Shah, interviewed by Gregory, 22 July 1973, Jamnagar. J. D. Byramjee (son), interviewed by Gregory, 24 Jan. 1973, Nairobi.

10. Many knowledgeable Asians have testified to this, for example, M. K. Lalji, interviewed by Gregory, 28 Feb., 1, 2 Mar. 1973, Nairobi.

11. A. Raishi, interviewed by Gregory, 25 Jan. 1973, Nairobi.

12. V. K. Shah, interviewed by Gregory, 11 July 1973, Jamnagar. B. Kantaria (grandson), interviewed by Bennett, 19 May 1973, Nairobi.

13. K. L. Vohora (grandson), interviewed by Honey, 23 Dec. 1973, Arusha.

14. Zafrud-Deen interview.

15. Z. K. Shah, interviewed by Seidenberg, 26 July 1973, Nairobi. S. S. Keshavji, interviewed by Gregory, 22 July 1973, Jamnagar. S. D. Kothari, interviewed by Gregory, 10 July 1973, Rajkot. D. K. Naranji (Lakhani's son), interviewed by Bennett, 18 May 1973, Nairobi. Shanti Pandit, ed., *Asians in East and Central Africa* (Nairobi: Panco, 1963), p. 159.

16. Zafrud-Deen interview.

17. D. N. Mehta (eldest son of N. K.), interviewed by Gregory, 13, 14 July 1973, Porbandar. M. N. Mehta, interviewed by Bennett, 1 May 1973, Nairobi. Pandit, *Asians,* p. 184.

18. The eight firms were (1) Premchand Bros. & Co., Mombasa; (2) Premchand Raichand & Co., Nairobi; (3) Kenya Extract & Tanning Co., Thika; (4) Kenya Aluminium Co., Mombasa; (5) Limuru Tanning Co.; (6) Pure Food Products, Nairobi; (7) flour mills in Meru, Sangana, et al.; and (8) a lumber factory, Limuru. K. P. Chandaria (brother of D. P.), interviewed by Gregory, 9–12, 14 May 1973, Addis Ababa. G. D. Shah (P. V. Shah's nephew), interviewed by Gregory, 12 July 1973, Jamnagar. Dhiru P. Shah (P. V.'s son), interviewed by Gregory, 10 Mar. 1973, Nairobi.

19. M. K. Lalji and Dhiru P. Shah interviews. L. R. Shah, interviewed by Gregory, 27 Nov. 1972, 8, 9 Mar. 1973, Nairobi; 30 June 1973, Bombay; 9 July 1973, Ahmedabad.

20. K. P. Chandaria and G. D. Shah interviews.

21. J. P. de Sousa (interviewed by Gregory, 26 June 1973, Porvorim, Bardez Goa) has related how his brother, a physician, retired from Uganda to a large home he built in Bombay. Another brother, he said, retired to Britain to avoid the taxes he would have to pay in India on money he made in East Africa. C. P. Shah and L. V. Kakad, interviewed jointly by Gregory, 4 July 1973, Bombay. A. J. Pandya, interviewed by Gregory, 2 Dec. 1972, 28 Feb., 1, 4 Mar. 1973, Mombasa; 17 Nov., 16 Dec. 1972, Nairobi. F. A. de Souza, interviewed by Gregory, 18 June 1973, Porvorim, Bardez Goa. A. K. Patel, interviewed by Gregory, 6 July 1973, Baroda.

22. India, Ministry of External Affairs, *Annual Report, 1964–65* (New Delhi: Government Printer, 1965), p. 60.

23. A. J. Pandya interview.

24. Donald Rothchild, *Racial Bargaining in Independent Kenya* (New York: Oxford University Press, 1973), p. 134.

25. K. P. Chandaria interview.

26. Ibid. Robin Murray, 'Chandarias: The Development of a Kenyan Multinational', *Readings on the Multinational Corporation in Kenya*, ed. Raphael Kaplinsky (Nairobi: Oxford University Press, 1978), pp. 298–300.

27. G. D. Shah interview. A.R. Kassim Lakha (son), interviewed by Bennett, 9 May 1973, Mombasa.

28. M. B. Acharya, interviewed by Gregory, 5 July 1973, Baroda.

29. A. J. Pandya interview. Pandit, *Asians*, pp. 280–81, 296. G. Vasanji, interviewed by Bennett, 9 May 1973, Mombasa.

30. A. Raishi and A. J. Pandya interviews.

31. E. Vasey, interviewed by Gregory, 6 Feb. 1973, Nairobi.

32. F. Kapadia, interviewed by Gregory, 23 July 1973, New Delhi.

33. Kenya's Foreign Investment Protection Act is described in Colin Leys, *Underdevelopment in Kenya: The Political Economy of Neo-colonialism, 1964–71* (London: Heinemann, 1975), p. 120. V. B. Shah, interviewed by Gregory, 11 July 1973, Jamnagar.

34. K. L. Vohora interview. Usha Patel, interviewed by Gregory, 20 Oct. 1984, London.

35. Untitled four-page typescript by D. C. Patel.

36. K. P. Chandaria interview.

37. Dr. V. R. Patel, interviewed by Gregory, 5, 6 July 1973, Baroda. D. G. Patel, interviewed by Honey, 9, 14 Oct. 1973, Dar es Salaam. A. Nayar, interviewed by Honey, 18 Feb. 1973, Dar es Salaam. For a recent indictment of fourteen Asian bankers and businessmen, see *Daily Nation*, 13 Oct. 1987, p. 1; and *East African Standard*, 14 Oct. 1987, p. 1. Some Asian leaders contend that Kapila was framed by a hostile administrator.

38. A. Nayar interview. S. Hassanali, interviewed by Honey, 15 Jan. 1974, Zanzibar.

39. J. Mehta (High Commissioner for India to Tanzania), interviewed by Honey, 8 Sept. 1973, Dar es Salaam. M. J. Thakkar, interviewed by Gregory, 19 May 1973, Addis Ababa. D. S. Trivedi, interviewed by Gregory, 27, 28 Feb. 1973, Mombasa. S. D. Kothari and A. Raishi interviews.

40. L. R. Shah interview. See three letters of appeal, *East African Standard*, 28 Oct. 1943, p. 4; and the Asian response, 29 Oct. 1943, p. 10. For the collecting in Central Province, see 'History of Fort Hall from 1888–1944', file FH/43, DC/FH6/1, Central Province daily correspondence, Syracuse University microfilm 4751, reel 24. Letter by Shamsud-Deen, *East African Standard*, 6 Sept. 1943, p. 4.

41. Letters by Shamsud-Deen, *East African Standard*, 19 Sept. 1950, p. 5; 27 Sept. 1950, p. 4; 23 Oct. 1950, p. 5. P. N. Mehta (Honourary Secretary, Indian Association, Mombasa) to Honourary Secretary (Shree Navnat Vanik Mahajan), 26 Sept. 1955, Mombasa Indian Association records, Syracuse University microfilm 1926, reel 4; and S. C. Gautama (Honourary General Secretary, East Africa Indian National Congress) to Honourary Secretary (Indian Association, Mombasa), 6

July 1953, Mombasa Indian Association records, Syracuse University microfilm 1926, reel 4.

42. K. V. Shukla to Hon'ble Speaker (Lok Sabha, New Delhi), 4 Dec. 1962, Nairobi Central Chamber of Commerce records, Syracuse University microfilm 1924, reel 6.

43. V. R. Shah (Honourary Secretary, Central Chamber of Commerce, Nairobi) to All Members, 19 Jan. 1965, ibid.

44. Debi Singh (General Secretary, Natal Indian Congress, Durban) to Secretary, East Africa Indian National Congress, 3 June 1948, East Africa Indian National Congress records, Syracuse University microfilm 1929, reel 11. K. P. Shah (Organizer, East Africa Indian National Congress) to Honourary Secretary (Indian Association, Mombasa), 27 Sept. 1952, Mombasa Indian Association records, reel 4. 'List of Sarojini Congress Fund', n.d., and 'List of Donours of the Sarojini Congress Fund with the names of donours and the respective amounts donated', n.d., file 'General Correspondence [n.d.], File One', East Africa Indian National Congress records, reel 14. R. M. Shah (Honourary Secretary, Indian Association, Mombasa), 'Report of the Indian Association for 1932', 19 Dec. 1932, Mombasa Indian Association records, reel 11. Honourary Joint Secretary (Indian Association, Mombasa) to District Commissioner, Mombasa, 28 May 1933, reel 11. President (Hindu Union, Arusha) to President, East Africa Indian National Congress, 11 July 1949, East Africa Indian National Congress records, reel 11. Though supporting the resistance campaigns in India and South Africa with money, the Asian organizations refrained from assisting local Asians in attempts to join the movements. See the denial of a request in Honourary Joint Secretary (Indian Association, Mombasa) to Becharbhai G. Patel (Indian Affairs Committee, Mombasa), 13 Mar. 1932, Mombasa Indian Association records, reel 11.

45. B. T. Gathani, interviewed by Gregory, 8 Mar. 1973, Nairobi. Others confirmed this.

46. President (Bhagini Samaj, Nairobi) to Commissioner for Government of India in East Africa, Nairobi, 2 Aug. 1949, East Africa Indian National Congress records, reel 11. D. N. Mehta interview. Pandit, *Asians*, p. 184.

47. *Shri Brihad Bharatiya Samaj: Inaugural Souvenir, Oct. 1963* (Bombay: Jaya Art Printer, 1963), p. 170. Pandit, *Asians*, p. 184.

48. Paul Marett, *Meghji Pethraj Shah: His Life and Achievements* (London: Bharatiya Vidya Bhavan, 1988), pp. 57–58.

49. Ibid., pp. 57–79, 83–84, 104–5, 129–33.

50. Ibid., p. 45.

51. *Shri Brihad Bharatiya Samaj*, p. 171. Pandit, *Asians*, p. 80.

52. Pandit, *Asians*, p. 93. L. R. Shah interview.

53. The author looked for such evidence during a tour of the Gujarat and Goa during summer 1973. N. T. Karia, interviewed by Gregory, 13 July 1973, Porbandar.

54. President (Kenya Congress) to Honourary Secretary, Indian Association, Mombasa, 25 May 1955, Mombasa Indian Association records, reel 4. The Congress resolution was no. 12 of the 22d session.

55. Honourary Secretary (Indian Association, Mombasa) to Honourary Secretary, Surat District Association, 28 Sept. 1959, ibid.

56. This view has been supported by knowledgeable Asians, including D. N. Mehta and D. S. Trivedi.

57. V. D. Shah, interviewed by Bennett, 19 Apr. 1973, Nairobi.

58. M. J. Thakkar interview.

59. K. J. Kotecha (interviewed by Gregory, 9 July 1973, Ahmedabad) strongly supports this interpretation.

60. D. C. Patel, interviewed by Bennett, 28 Apr. 1973, Nairobi.

61. A. J. Pandya interview.

62. This is evident in the preceding chapters.

63. *Report of the Taxation Enquiry Committee, Kenya, 1947* (Nairobi: Government Printer, 1947), pp. 10–11.

64. Ibid., p. 79.

65. *Report of the Commission Appointed to Enquire into and Report on the Financial Position and System of Kenya*, Colonial no. 116 (London: HMSO, 1936), p. 15.

66. *Kenya, Uganda-Tanganyika and Zanzibar Directory: Trade and Commercial Index: Annual Issue of 1936* (Nairobi: East African Directory Co., 1936), Tanganyika section, p. 68.

67. Tanganyika, *Statistical Abstract, 1962* (Dar es Salaam: Government Printer, 1962), p. 151. Ibid., *1938–1951*, p. 45. The figure 3,000 for 1961 is estimated from a figure for 1957.

68. *Annual Report on the Social and Economic Progress of the People of the Uganda Protectorate, 1933*, Colonial Reports—Annual, no. 1670 (London: HMSO, 1934), p. 27.

69. *Kenya, Uganda-Tanganyika and Zanzibar Directory . . . 1936*, Uganda section, p. 55.

70. Ibid., *1959–60* (published 1960), Zanzibar section, p. 23.

CHAPTER ELEVEN

———————— ■ ————————

Conclusion

Even though they constituted around one per cent of the total population, there was no sector of the economy which did not feel their imprint and register their impact.

—R. R. Ramchandani, 1976[1]

A study of the Asians' economic and social evolution through the century beginning in 1890 appears very important to the history of East Africa. It reveals how and why these immigrants, most of whom left a situation of poverty in South Asia, responded to opportunities in their new environment, concentrated on business, branched into other forms of economic endeavour, and achieved on the whole a prosperity that seemed unattainable in their homeland. It indicates that some significant aspects of East Africa's economic and social history have not received adequate attention from scholars and that some of the prevailing concepts and theories of African history should be re-evaluated. It may also offer for the benefit of non-Western countries generally a useful study in economic development.

The period appears as a time of momentous change for all concerned—Europeans, Africans, Arabs, and Asians—and the change was mainly one of modernization, that is, bringing the pattern of life in East Africa into conformity with the pattern that had evolved in western Europe during the modern age. In this process that the colonialists labelled 'development', the Europeans assumed a variety of important functions. European administrators provided the overall planning, direction, and law and order as well as a certain education, training, and financial aid. European missionaries also imparted formal education as well as technical training, and the settlers and businessmen set examples in estate agriculture, commerce, and industry. The Africans, too, were important factors in the modernization process. Apart from their role in providing the essential labour for most of the European and Asian

351

economic endeavour, Africans demonstrated a resourcefulness in adapting to a transformation that affected nearly all aspects of their culture. Moreover, their initiatives in promoting economic and political change, like those of the Europeans, were important determinants in the overall history.

Although these considerations have received a general recognition from historians and scholars, and even by politicians, the Asians' role, as stated in the Introduction, has remained obscure and unappreciated. The Asians' contribution to the development of East Africa was quite different from that of the Europeans, Africans, and Arabs, and it is impossible to weigh the contributions one against the other with any precision or even to ascribe to any of them a chief importance. In view of their many economic and social activities detailed in the preceding pages, however, the Asians deserve far more recognition than they have received.

This does not mean that the Asian contribution should be treated, as has been attempted in the past, as a separate and distinct phenomenon, as an addendum to the main subjects in the narrative, and merely given a greater attention. It needs to be incorporated into the central narrative and integrated into the history as a whole. In view of the findings in this study, the subjects of commerce, transport, agriculture, and industry, which figure prominently in histories of East Africa, all need revision. Other general topics, such as clerical service, professional activity, and extension of credit, which have largely been ignored, deserve more description. There are also numerous more specific topics, such as the Seyidie famine of 1918, that should be brought into the wider narrative. In all these subjects the interaction of the various peoples, Asian and Arab as well as European and African, needs to be re-evaluated.

The Economic Contribution

The Asians' economic role merits special consideration because it seems to have been the most productive of constructive change. As labourers, both skilled and unskilled, Asians contributed significantly to construction of the Kenya-Uganda railway and many other public works. As the main importers, exporters, wholesalers, and retailers, they supplied settlers and Africans with most of the desired manufactures and exported a large portion of the agricultural produce. They financed and constructed many of the commercial buildings and private residences of the urban centres, and they were the principal skilled artisans. In developing road transport, they provided a cheaper and more efficient system of transportation than that of the railway and extended distribution into areas, including the African reserves, that the railways did not reach. The Asians also constituted the vital middle levels of the civil service. It has been estimated that in Kenya alone the Asians on the eve of independence 'probably owned nearly three-quarters of the private non-agricultural assets of the country'. As shown in Table 11.1, the Asians controlled about two-thirds of the industrial and commercial assets of Kenya as late as 1971.[2]

As doctors, dentists, pharmacists, advocates, accountants, and insurance agents, the Asians served the full spectrum of East African society in a professional capacity. It was exceptional for a European to seek treatment from an Asian doctor or dentist, but many sought the services of the pharmacists, lawyers, insurance agents, and accountants. For the Africans, who through most of the colonial years had few qualified specialists from their own community and who were rarely served by the Europeans, the Asian professional was indispensable. The many Asian doctors in government service ministered primarily to African needs and often provided the only medical care in rural areas. Asian lawyers, besides attending to the needs of their own community, represented Africans in both criminal and civil actions, and the Asian accountants and insurance agents served many of the new African businessmen.

The Asians contributed significantly to the more positive economic and social changes affecting Africans. They opened the more remote areas to the world of commerce by introducing foreign manufactures, stimulating the production of cash crops, and collecting and marketing the produce. Partly by setting an example and partly by employing Africans in their businesses, they promoted the rise of a competing class of African businessmen. The Africans' movement into commerce and basic industry, which served as alternatives to contract labour on European farms and public works, was mainly a result of African initiatives, but the Asians appear to have served as an important catalyst.[4] Through the extension of credit, Asians also aided African as well as European farmers in times of crop failure, alleviated famine, and subsidized African enterprise in trade, transport, and basic industry. The informal training of African artisans was so effective that the graduates of the government technical institutes could not compete in the search for employment.

The Asians' history indicates that the theories interpreting international capital as a principal determinant in East African history need some modification. Much of the capital involved in development was generated and expended locally. This was true of the capital arising from Asian and African enterprise, most of which was spent in the dependencies, and of the taxation revenue utilized by the government. It was this local capital, particularly the private capital, that produced the more positive economic and social changes for the Africans as well as the Asians. It deserves far more recognition that it has received from the

TABLE 11.1 Sectors of Wealth, Excluding Small Farms, 1971[3]

	Wealth (K£ million)	
Sector	Asian	Non-Asian
Industry or plantations	70	120
Shares in public companies	20	30
Real estate	200	15
Trade	100	25
Cash	35	35
Totals	425	225

Source: Colin Leys, Underdevelopment in Kenya: The Political Economy of Neo-Colonialism, 1964-71 (London: Heinemann, 1975), p. 120.

scholarly community. This is not to say that international capital was not sizeable or influential. The effects of international capital, however, seem to have been assessed correctly as on the whole detrimental to the indigenous peoples because it was devoted mainly to the support of the settlers' estate agriculture. The international capital thus furthered the system of wage labour while the local capital, at least a considerable portion of it, furthered the alternative systems of commerce, artisanry, industry, and cash-crop cultivation.[5]

Another concept in need of revision is that the Asians formed an impenetrable middle-class block. Instead of relegating the Africans permanently to a lower working-class and peasant stratum, the Asians appear to have encountered increasing competition from African traders, artisans, and building contractors during the later colonial years. Government restrictions on their commercial activity, such as the marketing legislation of the mid-1930s, and the government training and financial assistance programs for Africans were partly responsible for the Asians' displacement. The on-job training of Africans in association with their Asian employers, however, was apparently a far more important determinant. Instead of organizing in opposition to the Africans' progress in business and crafts, most Asians appear to have actively promoted it through the employment of Africans in positions of increasing responsibility and through the extension of credit.[6] By the end of the colonial period the Asians were still predominant only in importing and exporting where, because of their ties overseas, they retained a strong advantage. As the Africans advanced in commerce, transport, artisanry, and clerical service, the Asians moved into industry and agriculture.

The Asians' impact on the Arabs is more questionable. Certainly the Asians provided a valuable service to the sultan and contributed to the prosperity of Zanzibar and the Arab coastal domain before the establishment of the British protectorates. After the abolition of slavery, Asian money-lenders helped sustain many Arab planters in the period of transition to a free-labour system. Some Arabs, however, were unable to survive the transition, with the result that their estates were taken over by the Asians. The British deplored the Asian takeover and attributed it to unscrupulous financial manipulation. In retrospect, however, it appears that the transition was inevitable. Because of their changing economy, many Arabs were having to move from agriculture into trade and labour. In the absence of the Asians, it is probable that the Arab agriculturalists would have been displaced by the British and the Africans. The Asians merely hastened the transformation.

Until the closing years of the colonial administration, the Asians appear to have devoted most of their earnings and savings to support of business enterprise and charitable causes in East Africa. Only a minor portion of their money was sent overseas to support relatives and friends in the homeland, provide for the children's education, invest in foreign enterprise, and support political reform and philanthropic projects. In the mid-1960s as they were increasingly excluded from the various forms of economic endeavour and from politics, the Asians diminished their local investments and donations and sent most of their money overseas in preparation for a move to an environment offering more economic opportunity, personal security, and retention of ethnic identity. Even then, however, some of the remaining Asians, particularly those like the Chandarias whose commercial and industrial enterprise had attained an international dimension, continued to invest in East Africa, particularly in industry, and to support local charities.

The Asians' financial role was never understood by the colonial governments, which generally regarded the Asians not only as entrenched in their position, but also as exploitive and dishonest in many of their business activities. The critical assistance of the trading and financial community in food distribution and famine relief, and the appreciation by all communities of the Asians' system of credit, were largely ignored. To protect Africans as well as Arabs from the designing Asians thus became a principal aim of the paternally minded administrations. Unfortunately for all the non-European communities, that aim was soon translated into the goal of eliminating middle-class enterprise irrespective of the participating peoples.

By 1973 the Asians had been excluded from virtually all significant economic activity, with the possible exception of industry, because of two parallel policies. One was the colonial governments' application of a managed economy that after independence was continued and augmented as African socialism. This development began in the mid-1930s and entailed the formation of government agencies, parastatals, cooperatives, and monopolies as well as the imposition of burdensome regulation and taxation.[7] The other policy, defined by the governments themselves as 'Africanization', was applied before and after independence with the aim of excluding Asians from most areas of economic activity. It contributed to an Asian exodus from Kenya and Tanganyika and in the extreme led to the expulsion of nearly all Asians from Uganda and Zanzibar.

Social Considerations

One of the principal values of this study of Asian history is its contribution to a theory of African history. Although destructive of the concept that development was a product solely of the civilizing mission of European peoples, the study supports the colonialist school's concept of the importance of a vertical structure of society. There was indeed a compartmentalization of society into racial and ethnic categories. The Asians, Europeans, Africans, and Arabs were distinct peoples with strikingly different cultures before the advent of European colonialism, and they were reinforced in their separate identities during the colonial period. Racial segregation was a fundamental policy of the British administration in East Africa. The governments even attempted with considerable success to deepen and institutionalize the line in Asian society separating Muslims from non-Muslims.

The study provides little support for an interpretation of East African history in terms of class struggle. The Asians appear to have been divided not primarily along the horizontal lines of proletariat and bourgeoisie but according to the vertical divisions of Muslim and non-Muslim and more specifically of Ismaili, Ithnasheri, Bohra, Shah, Patel, Sikh, Goan, and other religious communities. Within each of these categories there were those who were rich and those who were relatively poor, with considerable gradation between. In most there were professional people, industrialists, landlords, traders, shopkeepers, craftsmen, servants, and labourers—a great conglomeration. Within these separate communities, however, there was no entrenched class cleavage such as that which developed in the industrial societies of Europe. Instead, there was a high degree of social and economic mobility. Caste restrictions on economic activity quickly disappeared. Asians at the bottom of the hierarchy of wealth and prestige within these communities were mostly the newer immigrants, and those at the top were generally members of the second and third, often the fourth or later, generation of residents. There was no evident class cleavage, partly because of the exceptional economic opportunity in the East African environment and partly because of the Asians' system of communal welfare. Economic opportunity and philanthropy were the important determinants of the pronounced upward mobility.[8]

What is true of the Asians also seems characteristic of the other peoples of East Africa. The Europeans were essentially planters, industrialists, and tradesmen. There was no European proletariat of significance. In the pre-colonial period the Africans were mainly small-scale subsistence farmers and, in lesser numbers, traders. Under colonialism, though some were able to remain on the land by converting, often initially with Asian assistance, to cash crops, and some others were able to enter a trading enterprise, most of the men were forced into work as wage labourers for the Europeans' plantations and the governments' public works, and it was these rural and urban labourers whom Makhan Singh sought to organize into trade unions.[9] With some modification of Marxist doctrine, these workers can be described as a proletariat. Makhan Singh's efforts, however, to join African and Asian labourers into common trade unions were never very successful. The vertical lines of racial separatism seem to have been stronger than the horizontal lines of workers' solidarity. Moreover, the employer against whom the union activity was directed was more often the socialist-oriented government than a capitalist bourgeoisie.

Although the vertical organization of society appears to have been predominant for all the peoples, the lines of separation were not impenetrable and became less pronounced with passage of time. Asian marriages across lines of caste and sect were never numerous, but they seem to have been more prevalent near the end of the colonial period, and intermarriage between Asians and Africans, Arabs, or Europeans sometimes occurred. The social barriers, however, remained largely intact. It was in politics and economics that intercultural association became common, especially among Asians, Africans, and Arabs. Asians combined particularly with Africans in the allied endeavours of politics, journalism, and, as far as leadership is concerned, in trade unionism. The same was true in economic endeavour as Asians and eventually Africans entered the European spheres of estate agriculture and industry and as Africans and, in lesser degree, Arabs displaced many of the Asians in commerce, transport, crafts, and construction. These political and economic topics, therefore, cannot be viewed as the province of one racial community alone. The development process involved all the peoples in a mutual association.

Association with Europeans and Africans

Europeans and Asians lived separately and associated for the most part only for business reasons. The Europeans had their separate residential and commercial areas, their own schools and libraries, and their exclusive sport and recreational facilities. Only the Goans and the Parsees were allowed occasionally to cross the boundaries, but even they rarely married into the local European community. In business, however, there was often an amicable relationship. Asian shopkeepers and artisans provided essential goods and services for the European farmers, and through the extension of credit the shopkeepers assisted many farmers in surviving the years of the Great Depression and other times of hardship.

On the whole there was a deep-seated resentment by both Asians and Europeans against the other's exclusiveness and behaviour. The Asians naturally resented the many privileges enjoyed by the European community and the sense of superiority exhibited by Europeans in the colonial situation. The Europeans' attitude requires more explanation.

European resentment appears to have arisen not so much from misconceptions of Asian origin and aspiration as from other factors. With few exceptions, the independent European traders who lacked the resources of sizeable companies were unable to compete, and both they and the planters, whose financial assets were vested in land, resented the wealth that accrued from the Asians' success. Most missionaries tended to regard all Asians as heathens, could not understand why so few were attracted to Christianity, and considered the Muslim Asians as rivals in the conversion of Africans. The colonial administrators viewed the Asians generally as immoral because of what they concluded was a lack of respect for law and authority.

Because of different experiences the two peoples varied markedly in their conceptions of law and morality. Britain's evolution of democracy in the nineteenth century had tied law to morality. Jeremy Bentham had provided the formula—the greatest good of the greatest number—whereby the people, by majority vote, could express morality in law. The twentieth-century colonial administrator, paternalistically applying the laws of democratic Britain, or laws enacted locally under imperial supervision, to the governance of Africa, considered any evasion of law as an infringement of morality. Quite to the contrary, the Asians, having suffered for centuries under laws imposed by successive invaders, including the British, saw little correlation between law and morality. Their codes of behaviour, far more than those of the British, were based on a combination of religious principle and self-interest. In business self-interest leading to agreements of mutual service seems to have been the prime determinant. Unlike Europeans in a colonial situation, most Asians had no qualms of conscience in violating colonial rules and regulations or evading colonial taxes that were not patently in their interest.

Much of the Asians' association with Africans has been misunderstood. As businessmen with a profit motive, the Asians dealt shrewdly with Africans as well as Europeans and fellow Asians, and in this situation some obviously took unfair advantage. Concrete evidences of Asian dishonesty, however, are surprisingly few in the historical records. It also appears that there was far more association between Asians and Africans in business than has been assumed. Despite their close communal and family ties, Asians merged their interests with Africans whenever it was profitable to do so.

The Asians avoided a close association with Africans socially not only because of a colour prejudice but also because of a traditional communal exclusiveness that separated them from Europeans as well as Africans and even from other Asians. As explained in Chapter 1, most Asians of all religions had inherited from India a tradition associating fair skin with superiority. This tradition in the African setting certainly contributed to the Asians' exclusiveness. It is a mistake, however, to attribute the Asians' attitudes, as is so often done, to this reason alone. The traditional communal separateness, strongly supported by religious mores, may have been more influential.

The Africans' resentment against the Asians, which became so pronounced after independence, should be viewed, it seems, partly as a result of the Asians' exclusive behaviour, partly as a continuation of the Europeans' criticism of the Asians during the colonial period, and partly as a product of the fact that the transfer of political power did not result in the anticipated economic progress. Apparently it was tempting for politicians to blame the lack of progress on the Asians' continuing presence and for the African farmers and aspiring businessmen to covet the Asians' place in commerce and service.[10]

During the 1980s Kenya, Tanzania, and Uganda were to modify their policies of the managed economy and encourage a greater Asian participation. The Asians who had left East Africa, however, had already established roots in Britain, Canada, and other countries offering a greater security, a better education for their children, and still more economic opportunity. The new immigrants to East Africa were to be mainly South Asians who had no previous experience in Africa, and few were to come because the environment had lost much of its former charm. The Asian population of East Africa was to remain about one-fourth what it had been in the early years of independence.

Despite the more favourable circumstances it was not possible for the Asians to regain their previous position in the economies of East Africa. From centres outside Africa, Asian enterprise such as that of the Chandarias, Mehtas, and Madhvanis in the form of international capital was still important to East Africa, like that of Europeans, particularly in industrial manufacturing. In Kenya, which remained the most attractive country economically, many local Asians had turned to industry. Asians also retained a principal involvement in importing, exporting, and wholesaling, but they were relatively unimportant in other sectors of the economy. With the exception of a few who had managed to survive in the larger urban centres, they had been excluded from retail business. They were no longer the artisans—the remaining Punjabis were mostly contractors—and they had no significant role in agriculture, clerical work, road transport, and the professions of law, medicine, and teaching. In all these activities they had been displaced by Africans.

The Wider Significance

The economic recession that afflicted Kenya and the other dependencies in the last years of colonialism indicates that the British policy of a managed economy was detrimental to development. The substitution of government agencies, parastatal companies, co-operatives, and monopolies for the relatively unrestrained forms of production, marketing, distribution, and consumption retarded not only Asian enterprise but also that of the independent African farmers and businessmen.[11] The cost of supporting the bureaucracy that the new system generated was an additional depressant. There is an obvious inference that the new African governments erred in continuing this colonial policy under the guise of African socialism. It also appears that the abrupt removal of Asians from an important role in the economy was damaging to African as well as Asian interests.

Why this situation occurred has been a subject of speculation by Africanist scholars. Jon M. Lonsdale and Bruce Berman, viewing colonial Kenya as 'a variant of the capitalist state', believe that it became 'the ultimate unit both of economic reproduction, or acccumulation, and of political reproduction, or social control'. The 'most salient feature' of the colonial state, they concluded, 'was its centrality in the political economy'.[12] Cyril Ehrlich has ascribed to the British administrators a 'moral or religious' criticism of materialism, an 'upper middle-class snobbery towards trade and manufacturers', that, he implies, led to a substitution of government ownership and management for free enterprise.[13] A. G. Hopkins has traced the cause to the early years of British rule:

> Right from the outset of the colonial period the governments found themselves more closely involved with the colonial economy than they had anticipated. The situation arose partly from the need to invest in projects (such as the creation of an infrastructure) that often failed to attract expatriate firms, partly from the wish to avoid the disruptive social and political consequences that frequently accompanied unfettered government enterprise, and partly from a paternalist ideology that justified internal intervention as the approved means of achieving orderly progress.[14]

Robert M. Maxon has stressed the role of the local officials who, he believes, were motivated by paternalist ideology and practical considerations of administration. 'The colonial experience in East Africa, as in other parts of the continent', he asserts, 'produced an increasingly comprehensive and powerful state apparatus'. Maxon, in common with some other scholars, maintains that after World War II, to counter the nationalist aspirations of African businessmen in the urban centres, the colonial administrations, particularly that of Kenya, sought to gain the favour of rural Africans, in effect, 'to capture the peasantry'. The result was a growing administrative apparatus with increasing controls and inducements, on the one hand, 'to hold capitalism in check' and, on the other, to foster the most rapid development of the African farming sector.[15]

David Throup, though evincing a similar interpretation, believes that 'it could equally be argued that . . . Fabian strategy swept through the Colonial Office between 1945 and 1959 and captured the official mind'.[16]

Throup's statement deserves elaboration. Socialist ideology, refined by the Fabian Society and adopted by the British Labour Party, certainly was an important influence. After World War II the British at home under Conservative as well as Labour leadership nationalized their major industries and took other major steps towards a socialistic economy. The dependencies, over which the administration exercised an almost absolute control, presented an almost virgin environment for the implementation of socialist principles with a minimum of opposition. A managed economy, designed and guided by teams of experts trained in the social sciences—economists, sociologists, political scientists, anthropologists, and the like—as a significant move toward socialism, would surely produce the most rapid development. It was not only the British administration but the scholarly community throughout the world that believed that development could best be achieved through centralized planning and management. There was very little dissent in either the Western or non-Western societies. To the subject peoples the concept appeared compatible with their traditions of communal ownership and with Marxist theories of liberation. Throughout Africa, indeed throughout the non-Western world, socialism became the ideal.

Whatever the reasons for its origin, there now is almost universal agreement that the managed economy failed to produce the anticipated development. During the three decades following the early 1960s, which for most non-Western peoples were years of political independence, the lack of promised progress from socialist economies in both the more developed and the less developed countries fostered a profound disillusionment in socialist ideology and a serious reconsideration of developmental theory. The non-Western countries, though avowing socialist principles, had varied in their application. In East Africa Tanzania had endeavoured to eliminate the private sector, and Kenya had aimed at a compromise. In West Africa a similar contrast appeared between Guinea and the Ivory Coast and in North Africa between Algeria and Tunisia. To the surprise of administrators and scholars alike, it quickly became apparent that economic growth as measured by the gross national product and other factors was occurring far more in Kenya, the Ivory Coast, and Tunisia than in Tanzania, Guinea, and Algeria. The contrast was startling. The more centralized and more controlled the economy— in fact, the greater the involvement of social scientists—the less the development. Stagnation in the British economy through the same period and in the great socialist countries, China and the Soviet Union, led to similar conclusions with the result that all these countries began to revise their economies towards an increased participation by the private sector. Even the United States reduced the government's role.

Within this context the Asians' history appears especially significant. It provides a unique insight into a colonial environment in which the two contrasting systems of development were applied. In the early decades when the colonial governments were unable to participate meaningfully in the economy, there was a maximum of opportunity for individual initiative. During that time the Asians made their greatest advance and the colonial economies achieved their highest annual growth. In the closing colonial decades with the expansion and consolidation of government and the imposition of a managed economy, the opportunity for individual achievement was markedly reduced. It was then, particularly in the decade of the 1950s, that the Asians were forced out of business, the Africans encountered great difficulty in assuming the Asians' role, and the economies no longer attained a spectacular growth. Much to the detriment of the new nations, Britain left East Africa in recession; and though the reason was obscure at the time, it now seems clear that the managed economy was a foremost cause of decline.

Discernible in Chapters 1 and 2 of this study is the premise that people and cultures are a product of their environment and that the response to an environment can be conditioned by mores developed in
preceding environments. Thus Asians coming to East Africa carried with
them their religions, castes, habits, prejudices, and ways of life generally.
Once in East Africa, they were confronted with a new environment that
offered far more opportunity for economic and social improvement
than the one they had experienced in South Asia. Most early Asian immigrants, as has been seen, were impoverished, poorly educated agriculturists, socially fragmented, and lacking in skills essential for business or
crafts. Contrary to what has been assumed, they had initially no significant ties to the major trading firms of western India. From humble beginnings the Asians responded to the opportunity in East Africa. Within
two or three generations they appeared as a dynamic, highly enterprising, successful, and prosperous people. Most were businessmen, some
were skilled craftsmen, and others, as has been shown, doctors, lawyers,
teachers, engineers, industrialists, and planters. There were also politicians, journalists, trade unionists, playwrights, and philanthropists.

Through the same period East Africa also underwent extensive
change. Cities and towns, railways, roads, airfields, schools, hospitals, libraries, office and residential buildings, imposing government and religious edifices, telephones, telegraphs, radios, airplanes, motor-cars,
buses, lorries, bicycles, water and sewage systems, and monetary and
postal systems—nearly all these were new in the African scene. Most
were initiated by the colonial administration, but it seems evident that
the Asians helped create the environment that made them essential and
participated significantly in their establishment.

What the Asians contributed in contrast to the Europeans and Africans is probably not so important as the change that took place among
the Asians themselves. The transformation experienced by the Asians is
essentially what all the less developed peoples in the world have sought
to achieve.[17] In view of the Asians' history, particularly their rapid progress in the early decades and their noticeable lack of appreciable
change in the later decades when the governments' increasing intervention seriously retarded their enterprise, it appears that the best means to
achieve a rapid transformation, where economic and social conditions
are similar to those that obtained in East Africa, is to provide a relatively
free environment.

Notes

1. R. R. Ramchandani, *Uganda Asians: The End of an Enterprise* (Bombay:
United Asia, 1976), p. vii.

2. The quotation is from Colin Leys, *Underdevelopment in Kenya: The Political Economy of Neo-Colonialism, 1964–71* (London: Heinemann, 1975), p. 45. I.R.G. Spencer, another scholar who is one of the few to recognize the Asian contribution, concluded that Asian traders 'were an important element in the early development of production and trade in the reserves': 'First Assault on Indian Ascendancy: Indian Traders in the Kenya Reserves, 1895–1929', *African Affairs*, 80/320 (July 1981), 341.

3. Table 11.1 was entitled 'Approximate Distribution of Private Non-Farm Assets (but including plantations), 1971' in Leys's book. In a footnote on the source for the table (p. 120 n. 4), Leys wrote, 'This estimate was made by a particularly well-informed business consultant in Nairobi. It is certainly very approximate, but various 'harder' figures do roughly correspond to it. For instance a study of the share registers of a sample of the major public companies in Kenya (see below [in Leys's book], p. 165) showed that Asians did own roughly two-fifths of the shares in these companies, and the total value of the quoted shares on the Stock Exchange in 1970 was £51 million; pre-tax company incomes for 1967 (the latest available figures in 1971) totalled £37.8 million, which at an average rate of return on net assets of, say, 20 per cent would yield a figure rather under the total company assets implied here, but perhaps would be closer to it if the basis of the income data were not income declared for tax purposes'.

4. Some other recent studies, contrary to much of the published literature, are indicating that merchant capital was not detrimental to African farmers. See, for example, Eric J. Arnold, 'Merchant Capital, Simple Reproduction, and Underdevelopment: Peasant Traders in Zinder, Niger Republic', *Canadian Journal of African Studies*, 20/3 (1986), 323–56.

5. A. G. Hopkins is one of few to have recognized that 'colonial capitalism ought not to be regarded simply as an extension abroad of the interests of metropolitan industry'. 'Big Business in African Studies', *Journal of African History*, 28 (1987), 133.

6. These findings are supported by Hugh Fearn who concluded that even before 1930 the African trader 'was an agent of the Asian buyer of produce'. *An African Economy: A Study of the Economic Development of the Nyanza Province of Kenya, 1903–53* (London: Oxford University Press, 1961), p. 117.

7. Cyril Ehrlich has described the 'crippling effects' of British policy 'upon the emergence and growth to maturity of an indigenous entrepreneurial class'. 'Building and Caretaking: Economic Policy in British Tropical Africa, 1890–1960', *African History Review*, 26 (1973), 651.

8. A similar mobility has been recognized among Africans. Gavin Kitching has explained how the categories of teacher, clerk, trader, and farmer were often combined in a single individual. *Class and Economic Change in Kenya* (New Haven: Yale University Press, 1980), p. 193.

9. Because trade unionism in East Africa was primarily a political movement, it is being reserved for description in a separate study of the Asians' political activities. Makhan Singh's two volumes remain the most detailed history: *Kenya's Trade Union Movement to 1952* (Nairobi: East African Publishing House, 1969); and *Kenya's Trade Unions, 1952–56* (Nairobi: Uzima, 1980).

10. Colin Leys noted how the post-colonial policies of socialism were fostered by the new African bourgeoisie: 'Development Strategy in Kenya since 1971', *Canadian Journal of African Studies*, 13/1, 2 (1979), especially p. 3.

11. Roger Van Zwanenberg has asserted that the governments' restrictive policies denied Africans 'access to a capitalist mode of production'. 'Neocolonialism and the Origin of the National Bourgeoisie in Kenya between 1940 and 1973', *Journal of East Africa Rural Development*, 4/2 (1974), 171.

12. John Lonsdale and Bruce Berman, 'Coping with the Contradictions: The Development of the Colonial State in Kenya, 1895–1914', *Journal of African History*, 20 (1979), 489; and 'Crises of Accumulation, Coercion and the Colonial State: The Development of the Labor Control System in Kenya, 1919–29', *Canadian Journal of African Studies*, 14/1 (1980), 56.

13. Ehrlich, 'Building and Caretaking', pp. 650–51.

14. Hopkins, 'Big Business', p. 132.

15. The quotations are from 'Comments on Economic and Social History of Asians', sent to me after reading the manuscript: encl. Robert M. Maxon to Gregory, 3 Dec. 1990. Maxon formed his interpretation initially during his pioneer study, *John Ainsworth and the Making of Kenya* (Lanham, Md: University Press of America, 1980).

16. David Throup, *Economic and Social Origins of Mau Mau, 1945–53* (London: J. Currey, 1988), p. 238.

17. Some recent studies, contrary to the findings here, indicate that internationalization of production and consumption is not always conducive to development. Abdi Samatar, 'Merchant Capital, International Livestock Trade and Pastoral Development in Somalia', *Canadian Journal of African Studies*, 21/3 (1987), 354–74; and S. Sanderson, *Transformation of Mexican Agriculture* (Princeton: Princeton University Press, 1986). Valji Jamal is one of many scholars who believe that the Asians' 'life-style was such that the Africans could reasonably aspire to it, and in this way they were effective carriers of the "demonstration effect" both in consumption and production'. 'Asians in Uganda, 1880–1972: Inequality and Expulsion', *Economic History Review*, 29 (1976), 603.

Bibliography

Because Asian economic and social history in the period since 1890 was so closely tied to the political and religious developments and the history of the other peoples in East Africa, it is difficult to compile a bibliography that differs appreciably from one devoted generally to the British colonial period and the initial years of African independence. The following reflects an attempt to compile a relatively brief bibliography of sources particularly valuable to this study.

Published Government Records: East Africa

Annual reports (Blue Books) (title varies). Initially published in Britain as Command Papers, they began to be issued in Kenya and Uganda in 1912–13. The first on Tanganyika, covering the period from the armistice to 1920, was published in 1921.

Annual reports of the various departments of the central governments.

Legislative Council Debates. Beginning in Kenya in 1906, Uganda in 1920, and Tanganyika and Zanzibar in 1926.

Official Gazettes. First published in Kenya in 1899, Uganda in 1908, and Tanganyika in 1919.

Reports of local commissions and legislative committees.

Published Government Records: Great Britain

Annual reports (Blue Books) for the East Africa and Uganda Protectorates through 1911–12.

Reports of royal commissions and parliamentary committees, published variously as Command Papers, Colonial Reports, or House of Commons or Lords Papers.

Statements of official British policy, published as Command Papers.

Statistical abstracts on Britain, India, and the British Empire 1890–, published as Command Papers.

Unpublished Government Records: Kenya

Annual, Quarterly, Handing-Over Reports. Syracuse University microfilm 2801.
Daily Correspondence of Provincial and District Officers: Central Province, Syracuse University microfilm 4751; Coast (Seyidie) Province, 1995, 4759; Northern Province, 4753; Nyanza Province, 1949, 2800; Rift Valley Province, 4752. Southern Province, 2804.
Intelligence Reports, 2805.
Local Authority Records, 2246.
Miscellaneous Correspondence, 2802.
Registry of Trade Unions, 2081.
Secretariat Circulars, 2807

Unpublished British Government Records: Tanganyika

Secretariat Files, 1916–53.
Provincial Files: Central Province (Dodoma), Eastern Province (Morogoro), Lake Province (Mwanza), Northern Province (Arusha), Tanga Province (Tanga), Western Province (Tabora).
District, Area, and Regional Files: Bagamoyo, Bukoba, Iringa, Karagwe, Lindi, Lushoto, Mbeya, Pangani.

Unpublished Government Records in Britain

General: C.O. 822 (East Africa), original correspondence, 1927–; F.O. 2 (Africa), original correspondence, 1895–1905; F.O. 84 (Africa), slave trade, 1880–92; F.O. 367 (Africa: New Series), original correspondence, 1906–13.
Kenya: C.O. 533, original correspondence, 1905–; C.O. 630, sessional papers, 1903–.
Tanganyika: C.O. 691, original correspondence, 1916–; C.O. 736, sessional papers, 1918–.
Uganda: C.O. 536, original correspondence, 1905–; C.O. 537, railway original correspondence, 1895–1905; C.O. 685, sessional papers, 1918–.
Zanzibar: C.O. 618, original correspondence, 1913–; C.O. 688, sessional papers, 1909–.

Asian Records

East Africa Indian National Congress, Syracuse University microfilm 1929; Congress Supplemental Records, 2085.
Federation of Indian Chambers of Commerce and Industry of Eastern Africa, 1923.
Kisumu Indian Association, 2232.
Mombasa Indian Association, 1926.
Mombasa Indian Merchants' Chamber, 1922.
Nairobi Central Chamber of Commerce, 1924.

Nairobi Indian Association, 1929.
Nakuru Indian Association, 2081.
Zafrud-Deen Papers, 2174.

Newspapers

Colonial Times (Nairobi)
Dar es Salaam Times
Democrat (Mombasa)
East Africa and Rhodesia (London)
East African Standard (Nairobi)
Kenya Daily Mail (Mombasa)
Kenya Weekly News (Nakuru)
Leader of East Africa (Nairobi)
Samachar (Zanzibar)
Tanganyika Standard (Dar es Salaam)
Tanganyika Times (Dar es Salaam)
Tribune (Nairobi)

Writings by Asians

Aga Khan. *India in Transition: A Study in Political Evolution.* London: P. L. Warner, 1918.
Aga Khan III. *Memoirs of the Aga Khan.* London: Cassell, 1954.
Amiji, Hatim. 'The Bohras of East Africa'. *Journal of Religion in Africa.* 7 (1975), 27–61.
_____ . 'Some Notes on Religious Dissent in Nineteenth-century East Africa'. *International Journal of African Historical Studies.* 4 (1971), 603–16.
Desai, R. H. 'The Family and Business Enterprise Among the Asians in East Africa'. *East African Institute of Social Research Conference Papers—Jan. 1965.* Kampala: Makerere University. *Gandhi Memorial Academy Society, Souvenir Vol. 1;* and *Vol. 2.* Nairobi: Gandhi Memorial Academy Society, 1956.
Ghai, Dharam, and Yash P. Ghai, eds. *Portrait of a Minority.* Nairobi: Oxford University Press, 1970.
Ghai, Yash P. 'Amin and the Asians'. *Times Literary Supplement.* 4 July 1975. Pp. 738–9.
_____ . *Taxation for Development: A Case Study of Uganda.* Nairobi: East African Publishing House, 1966.
_____ . and Dharam Ghai. *The Asian Minorities of East and Central Africa (up to 1971).* London: Minority Rights Group, 1971.
Jamal, Vali. 'Asians in Uganda, 1880–1972: Inequality and Expulsion'. *Economic History Review.* 29 (1976), 602–16.
Jeevanjee, A. M. *An Appeal on Behalf of the Indians in East Africa.* Bombay, 1912.
Maini, Sir Amar Nath. 'Asians and Politics in Late Colonial Uganda: Some Personal Recollections'. Chap. 8 in *Expulsion of a Minority: Essays on Uganda Asians,* edited by Michael Twaddle. London: Athlone, 1975.

Makhan Singh. *Kenya's Trade Union Movement to 1952.* Nairobi: East African
    Publishing House, 1969.
_____ . *Kenya's Trade Unions, 1952–56.* Nairobi: Uzima, 1980.
Mamdani, Mahmood. *From Citizen to Refugee.* London: F. Pinter, 1973.
_____ . *Imperialism and Fascism in Uganda.* Trenton, N.J.: Africa World Press,
    1984.
_____ . *Politics and Class Formation in Uganda.* London: Monthly Review
    Press, 1976.
Mangat, J. S. *History of the Asians in East Africa, c. 1886 to 1945.* Oxford: Claren-
    don, 1969.
_____ . 'The Immigrant Communities (2): The Asians'. Chap. 12 in *History of
    East Africa,* edited by D. A. Low and Alison Smith. Oxford: Clarendon, 1976.
Mehta, Nanji Kalidas. *Dream Half Expressed: An Autobiography.* Bombay: Vakils,
    Feffer and Simons, 1966.
Mohamed, H. E. *The Asian Legacy in Africa and the White Man's Colour Culture.*
    New York: Vantage, 1979.
Motani, Nizar A. *On His Majesty's Service in Uganda: The Origins of Uganda's Afri-
    can Civil Service, 1912–40.* Syracuse University Foreign and Comparative
    Studies Program, 1977.
Mustafa, Sophia. *Tanganyika Way: A Personal Story of Tanganyika's Growth to In-
    dependence.* London: Oxford University Press, 1962.
Narain Singh, ed. *Kenya Independence-Day Souvenir: A Spotlight on the Asians of
    Kenya.* Nairobi: Kenya Indian Congress, 1963.
Nazareth, J. M. *Brown Man Black Country: A Peep into Kenya's Freedom Struggle.*
    New Delhi: Tidings, 1981.
Pandit, Shanti, ed. *Asians in East and Central Africa.* Nairobi: Panco, 1961.
Rizvi, Seyyid Saeed Akhtar, and Noel Q. King. 'Some East African Ithna-Asheri
    Jamaats (1840–1967)'. *Journal of Religion in Africa.* 5 (1973), 12–22.
Sheriff, Abdul. *Slaves, Spices and Ivory in Zanzibar: Integration of an East African
    Commercial Empire into the World Economy, 1770–1873.* London: J. Currey,
    1987.
Shivji, Issa G. *Class Struggles in Tanzania.* New York: Monthly Review Press, 1976.
_____ . *Law, State and the Working Class in Tanzania, c. 1920–64.* London: J.
    Currey, 1986.
_____ . *Silent Class Struggle.* Dar es Salaam: Tanzania Publishing House, 1973.
_____ , ed. *The State and the Working People in Tanzania.* Trenton, N.J.: Africa
    World Press, 1989.
_____ . *Tourism and Social Development.* Dar es Salaam: Tanzania Publishing
    House, 1973.
Tandon, Yashpal. *Problems of a Displaced Minority: The New Position of East Af-
    rica's Asians.* London: Minority Rights Group, 1973.
_____ , ed. *Technical Assistance Administration in East Africa.* Stockholm: Al-
    mqvist Wiksell, 1973.
_____ , and Dilshad Chandarana, eds. *Horizons of African Diplomacy.* Nairobi:
    East African Literature Bureau, 1974.
Varghese, Mary I. Noozhumurry. 'The East African Indian National Congress,
    1914 to 1939: A Study of Indian Political Activity in Kenya'. Ph.D. diss., Dal-
    housie University, Halifax, NS, 1976.

Walji, Shirin Remtulla. 'Ismailis on Mainland Tanzania, 1850–1948'. Ph.D. diss., University of Wisconsin, 1969.

Other Pertinent Writings

Alpers, Edward A. *Ivory and Slaves in East Central Africa.* London: Heinemann, 1975.

Anderson, David, and David Throup. 'Africans and Agricultural Production in Colonial Kenya: The Myth of the War as a Watershed'. *Journal of African History.* 26 (1985), 327–45.

Aranow, Philip Thompson. 'Alien Entrepreneurs: The Indians in Uganda'. B.A. honors thesis, Harvard College, 1969.

Atieno-Odhiambo. 'The Rise and Decline of the Kenya Peasant, 1888–1922'. In *African Social Studies: A Radical Reader,* edited by Peter Gutkind and Peter Waterman. Pp. 233–40. London: Heinemann, 1977.

Austin, Ralph. *Northwest Tanzania Under German and British Rule: Colonial Policy and Tribal Politics, 1889–1939.* New Haven: Yale University Press, 1968.

Bager, Torben. *Marketing Cooperatives and Peasants in Kenya.* Uppsala: Scandinavian Institute of African Studies, 1980.

Bahadur Singh, I. J., ed. *The Other India: The Overseas Indians and Their Relationship with India: Proceedings of a Seminar.* New Delhi: Gulab Vazirani for Arnold-Heinemann, 1979.

Bairoch, Paul. *The Economic Development of the Third World Since 1900.* Trans., Cynthia Postan. Berkeley: University of California Press, 1975.

Balachandran, P. K. 'An Embattled Community: Asians in East Africa Today'. *African Affairs.* 80 (1981), 317–25.

Becker, Robert, and Nitin Jayant Madhvani, eds. *Jayant Madhvani.* London: W. and J. Mackay, 1973.

Bennett, Charles. 'Persistence amid Adversity: The Growth and Spatial Distribution of the Asian Population of Kenya, 1903–63'. Ph.D. diss., Syracuse University, 1976.

Bennett, Norman R. *Mirambo of Tanzania, c. 1840–84.* New York: Oxford University Press, 1971.

Berman, B. J., and J. M. Lonsdale. 'Crises of Accumulation, Coercion and the Colonial State: The Development of the Labor Control System in Kenya, 1919–29'. *Canadian Journal of African Studies.* 14/1 (1980), 55–81.

Bharati, Agehananda. *Asians in East Africa: Jaihind and Uhuru.* Chicago: Nelson-Hall, 1972.

Bienefeld, M. A. 'Socialist Development and the Workers in Tanzania'. In *Development of an African Working Class: Studies in Class Formation and Action,* edited by Richard Sandbrook and Robin Cohen. Pp. 239–60. Toronto: University of Toronto Press, 1975.

_____ . *Trade Unions and Peripheral Capitalism: The Case of Tanzania.* Brighton: University of Sussex Institute of Development Studies, Discussion Paper 112, June 1977.

Bolton, Dianne. 'Unionization and Employer Strategy: The Tanganyika Sisal Industry, 1958–64'. In *African Labor History,* edited by Peter C.W. Gutkind, Robin Cohen, and Jean Copans. Pp. 175–204. Beverly Hills: Sage, 1978.

Boyes, John. *John Boyes, King of the Wa-Kikuyu: A True Story of Travel and Adventure in Africa.* London: Methuen, 1911.

Brett, E. A. *Colonialism and Underdevelopment in East Africa: The Politics of Economic Change, 1919–39.* New York: NOK, 1973.

Bunker, Stephen. *Peasants against the State: The Politics of Market Control in Bugisu, Uganda, 1900–83.* Urbana: University of Illinois Press, 1987.

Burton, Richard F. *Zanzibar: City, Island and Coast.* 2 vols. London: Tinsley, 1872.

Campbell, W. W. *East Africa by Motor Lorry: Recollections of an Ex–Motor Transport Driver.* London: J. Murray, 1928.

Chattopadhyaya, Haraprasad. *Indians in Africa: A Socio-Economic Study.* Calcutta: Bookland, 1970.

Christie, James. *Cholera Epidemics in East Africa: An Account of the Several Epidemics of the Disease in That Country from 1821 till 1872, with an Outline of the Geography, Ethnology, and Trade Connections of the Regions Through Which the Epidemics Passed.* London: Macmillan, 1876.

Churchill, Winston S. *My African Journey.* London: Hodder and Stoughton, 1908.

Clark, W. E. *Socialist Development and Public Investment in Tanzania, 1964–73.* Toronto: University of Toronto Press, 1978.

Clayton, Anthony. *The 1948 Zanzibar General Strike.* Uppsala: Scandinavian Institute of African Studies, Research Report No. 12, 1976.

———, and Donald C. Savage. *Government and Labour in Kenya, 1895–1963.* London: F. Cass, 1974.

Cliffe, L., and J. S. Sayl, eds. *Socialism in Tanzania.* Dar es Salaam: East African Publishing House, 1973.

Cobbold, Lady Evelyn. *Kenya, the Land of Illusion.* London: John Murray, 1935.

Cohen, Michael. 'Commodity Production in Kenya's Central Province'. In *Rural Development in Tropical Africa,* edited by Judith Heyer et al. Nairobi: Oxford University Press, 1976.

Cooper, Frederick. *From Slaves to Squatters: Plantation Labor and Agriculture in Zanzibar and Coastal Kenya, 1890–1925.* New Haven: Yale University Press, 1981.

Coulson, Andrew, ed. *African Socialism in Practice: The Tanzanian Experience.* Nottingham: Spokesman, 1979.

Darkoh, Michael B. K. *Tanzania's Industrial Strategy.* Kenyatta University College History Pamphlet 1. Kisumu: Anyange, 1984.

Delf, George. *Asians in East Africa.* London: Oxford University Press, 1963.

Dinesen, Isaak. *Out of Africa and Shadows on the Grass.* New York: Random House, 1985, first published 1937.

Don Nanjira, Daniel D. C. *Status of Aliens in East Africa: Asians and Europeans in Tanzania, Uganda, and Kenya.* New York: Praeger, 1976.

Ehrlich, Cyril. 'Building and Caretaking: Economic Policy in British Tropical Africa, 1890–1960'. *African Historical Review.* 26 (1973), 649–67.

———. 'The Marketing of Cotton in Uganda, 1900–50'. Ph.D. diss., University of London, 1958.

_____. 'The Uganda Economy, 1903–1945'. Chap. 8 in *History of East Africa*, vol. 2, edited by Vincent Harlow and E. M. Chilver. Oxford: Clarendon, 1965.

Fearn, Hugh. *An African Economy: A Study of the Economic Development of the Nyanza Province of Kenya, 1903–53*. London: Oxford University Press, 1961.

Fieldhouse, D. K. *Black Africa, 1945–80: Economic Decolonization and Arrested Development*. London: Allen and Unwin, 1986.

Frankel, S. Herbert. *Capital Investment in Africa: Its Course and Effects*. London: Oxford University Press, 1938.

Fransman, Martin, ed. *Industry and Accumulation in Africa*. London: Heinemann, 1982. Includes chapter by Leys.

Freund, Bill. 'The Modes of Production Debate in African Studies'. *Canadian Journal of African Studies*. 19/1 (1985), 23–29.

Friedland, William H. *Vutu Kamba: The Development of Trade Unions in Tanganyika*. Stanford: Hoover Institute, 1984.

Furedi, Frank. 'The Development of Anti-Asian Opinion among Africans in Nakuru Dist'. *African Affairs*. 73 (1974), 347–53.

Gray, Richard, and David Birmingham, eds. *Pre-Colonial African Trade*. London: Oxford University Press, 1971.

Gregory, Robert G. *India and East Africa: A History of Race Relations Within the British Empire, 1890–1939*. Oxford: Clarendon, 1971.

_____. *Quest for Equality: Asian Politics in East Africa, 1900–80*. New Delhi: Orient Longman, forthcoming 1992.

_____. *The Rise and Fall of Philanthropy in East Africa: The Asian Contribution*. New Brunswick, N.J.: Transaction, 1992.

Gundara, Jagdish. 'Fragment of Indian Society in Zanzibar: Conflict and Change in the Nineteenth Century'. *Africa Quarterly*. 21 (1981), 23–40.

Gupta, Anirudha, ed. *Indians Abroad: Asia and Africa: Report of an International Seminar*. New Delhi: Orient Longman, 1971.

_____. *Reporting Africa*. Bombay: People's Publishing House, 1969.

Gutkind, Peter C. W., and Peter Waterman. *African Social Studies: A Radical Reader*. London: Heinemann, 1977. Includes chapter by Atieno-Odhiambo.

_____, Robin Cohen, and Jean Copans, eds. *African Labor History*. Beverly Hills: Sage, 1978. Includes chapters by Bolton and Stichter.

Hansen, Holger Bernt, and Michael Twaddle, eds. *Uganda Now: Between Decay and Development*. London: J. Currey, 1988.

Hardinge, Sir Arthur. *A Diplomatist in the East*. London: J. Cape, 1928.

Harlow, Vincent, and E. M. Chilver, eds. *History of East Africa*, vol. 2. Oxford: Clarendon, 1965. Includes chapters by Ehrlich and Wrigley.

Harper, Malcolm. *The African Trader: How to Run a Business*. Nairobi: East African Publishing House, 1973.

Hawkins, Anthony. *Roads and Road Transport in an Under-developed Country: A Case Study of Uganda*. Colonial Research Studies No. 32. London: HMSO, 1962.

Hawkins, H.C.G. *Wholesale and Retail Trade in Tanganyika: A Study of Distribution in East Africa*. New York: Praeger, 1965.

Hazlewood, Arthur. *Rail and Road in East Africa: Transport Co-ordination in Under-developed Countries*. Oxford: B. Blackwell, 1964.

Heyer, Judith, Pepe Roberts, and Gavin Williams, eds. *Rural Development in Tropical Africa.* Nairobi: Oxford University Press, 1976. Includes chapter by Cohen.

Hill, Mervyn F. *Permanent Way.* Vol. 1, *The Story of the Uganda Railway;* vol. 2, *The Story of the Tanganyika Railways.* Nairobi: East Africa Railways and Harbours, 1949, 1957.

————. *Planters' Progress: The Story of Coffee in Kenya.* Nairobi: Coffee Board of Kenya, 1956.

Hobley, Charles W. *Kenya from Chartered Company to Crown Colony.* London: Witherby, 1929.

Hofmeier, Rolf. *Transportation and Economic Development in Tanzania with Particular Reference to Roads and Road Transport.* Munich: Veltforum Verlag, 1973.

Hollingsworth, L. W. *Asians of East Africa.* London: Macmillan, 1960.

Holmstrom, J. Edwin. *Railways and Roads in Pioneer Development Overseas.* London: P. S. King and Son, 1934.

Honey, Martha. 'History of Indian Merchant Capital and Class Formation in Tanganyika, c. 1840–1940'. Ph.D. diss., University of Dar es Salaam, 1982.

Hopkins, A. G. 'Big Business in African Studies'. *Journal of African History.* 28 (1987), 119–40.

————. 'Imperial Business in Africa', Part 1: 'Sources', and Part 2: 'Interpretations'. *Journal of African History.* 18 (1976), 29–48, 167–90.

Huxley, Elspeth. *No Easy Way: A History of the Kenya Farmers' Association and Unga Ltd.* Nairobi: East African Standard, 1957.

————. *White Man's Country: Lord Delamere and the Making of Kenya.* 2 vols. London: Macmillan, 1935.

Hyden, Goran. *Beyond Ujamaa in Tanzania: Underdevelopment and an Uncaptured Peasantry.* Berkeley: University of California Press, 1980.

Ibingira, Grace. *The Forging of an African Nation.* New York: Viking, 1973.

Iliffe, John. *Tanganyika Under German Rule, 1905–12.* Cambridge: Cambridge University Press, 1969.

————. 'History of the Dockworkers of Dar es Salaam'. *Tanzania Notes and Records.* 71 (1970), 119–48.

————. 'The Creation of Group Consciousness: A History of the Dockworkers of Dar Es Salaam'. In *Development of an African Working Class,* edited by Richard Sandbrook and Robin Cohen. Pp. 49–72. Toronto: University of Toronto Press, 1975.

Ingrams, W. H. *Zanzibar: Its History and Its People.* London: Witherby, 1921.

International Bank for Reconstruction and Development. *Economic Development of Kenya.* Baltimore: Johns Hopkins Press, 1963.

————. *Economic Development of Tanganyika.* Baltimore: Johns Hopkins Press, 1961.

————. *Economic Development of Uganda.* Baltimore: Johns Hopkins Press, 1962.

Jackson, Sir Frederick J. *Early Days in East Africa.* London: E. Arnold, 1930.

Jorgensen, Jan Jelmert. *Uganda, a Modern History.* New York: St. Martin's, 1981.

Joshi, H. P., Bhanumanti V. Kotecha, and J. V. Paun, eds. *Jayant Muljibhai Madhvani: In Memorium.* Nairobi: Emco Glass Works, 1973.

Kabwegyere, T. B. 'The Asian Question in Uganda, 1894–1972'. *East Africa Journal*. 9/6 (June 1972), 10–3.

Kaplinsky, Raphael, ed. *Readings on the Multinational Corporation in Kenya*. Nairobi: Oxford University Press, 1978. Includes chapter by Murray.

Kenya, Uganda, Tanganyika and Zanzibar Directory: Trade and Commercial Index, 1959–60. Nairobi: East African Directory, 1960.

Killingray, David, and Richard Rathbone, eds. *Africa and the Second World War*. New York: St. Martin's, 1986. Includes chapter by Lonsdale.

King, Kenneth, *African Artisan: Education and the Informal Sector in Kenya*. London: Heinemann, 1977.

King, Kenneth, and Ahmed Salim, eds. *Kenya Historical Biographies*. Nairobi: East African Publishing House, 1971.

Kirkpatrick, Colin, and Frederick Nixson. 'Transnational Corporations and Economic Development'. *Journal of Modern African Studies*. 11 (1981), 367–99.

Kitching, Gavin. *Class and Economic Change in Kenya: The Making of an African Petite-Bourgeoisie, 1905–70*. New Haven: Yale University Press, 1980.

_____. 'Suggestions for a Fresh Start on an Exhausted Debate'. *Canadian Journal of African Studies*. 19/1 (1985), 116–26.

_____. 'The Role of a National Bourgeoisie in the Current Phase of Capitalist Development: Some Reflections'. Chap. 2 in *The African Bourgeoisie*, edited by Paul M. Lubeck. Boulder: Lynne Rienner, 1987.

Kiwanuka, Semakula. 'The Uganda National Movement and the Trade Boycott of 1959–60: A Study of Politics and Economics in Uganda on the Eve of Independence'. Typescript. Kampala: Makerere University Department of History, 1973.

Kuczynski, Robert R. *Demographic Survey of the British Colonial Empire*. 3 vols. London: Oxford University Press, 1948.

Langdon, Steven. 'Industry and Capitalism in Kenya: Contributions to a Debate'. Chap. 11 in *The African Bourgeoisie: Capitalist Development in Nigeria, Kenya and the Ivory Coast*, edited by Paul M. Lubeck. Boulder: Lynne Rienner, 1987.

Leys, Colin. *Underdevelopment in Kenya: The Political Economy of Neo-Colonialism, 1964–71*. London: Heinemann, 1975.

_____. 'Accumulation, Class Formation and Dependency: Kenya'. Chap. 8 in *Industry and Accumulation in Africa*, edited by Martin Fransman. London: Heinemann, 1982.

_____. 'Development Strategy in Kenya since 1971'. *Canadian Journal of African Studies*. 13/1, 2 (1979), 299–311.

Leys, Colin, with Jane Borges and Hyam Gold. 'State Capital in Kenya: a Research Note'. *Canadian Journal of African Studies*. 14/2 (1980), 307–17.

Lonsdale, Jon M. 'The Depression and the Second World War in the Transformation of Kenya'. Chap. 4 in *Africa and the Second World War*, edited by David Killingray and Richard Rathbone. New York: St Martin's, 1986.

_____, and Bruce Berman. 'Coping with the Contradictions: The Development of the Colonial State in Kenya, 1895–1914'. *Journal of African History*. 20 (1979), 487–505.

Low, D. A., and Alison Smith, eds. *History of East Africa*, vol. 3. Oxford: Clarendon, 1976. Includes chapters by Mangat and Wrigley.

Lubeck, Paul M., ed. *The African Bourgeoisie: Capitalist Development in Nigeria, Kenya and the Ivory Coast.* Boulder: Lynne Rienner, 1987. Includes chapters by Kitching, Langdon, and Swainson.

Lugard, Frederick D. *Rise of Our East African Empire: Early Efforts in Nyasaland and Uganda.* 2 vols. London: Frank Cass, 1968, first published 1893.

Maddox, Gregory H. "NJAA: Food Shortages and Famines in Tanzania Between the Wars." *International Journal of African Historical Studies.* 19/1 (1986), 17–34.

Marett, Paul. *Meghji Pethraj Shah: His Life and Achievements.* Bombay: Bharatiya Vidya, 1988.

Marris, Peter, and Anthony Somerset. *African Businessmen: A Study of Entrepreneurship and Development in Kenya.* London: Routledge and Kegan Paul, 1971.

Maxon, Robert M. *Conflict and Accommodation in Western Kenya: The Gusii and the British, 1907–63.* Rutherford, N.J.: Farleigh Dickinson University Press, 1989.

———. *John Ainsworth and the Making of Kenya.* Lanham, Md.: University Press of America, 1980.

Mbithi, P. M., and B. Wisner. 'Drought and Famine in Kenya: Magnitude and Attempted Solutions'. *Journal of East African Rural Development.* 4/2 (1974), 161–88.

McCormack, Richard T. *Asians in Kenya.* Brooklyn: T. Gaus' Sons, 1971.

Mehta, Surendra, and G. M. Wilson. 'The Asian Communities of Mombasa'. Chap. 6 in 'Mombasa Social Survey, Part 1', edited by G. M. Wilson. Unpublished typescript, Nairobi, n.d., 1950s. Syracuse University microfilm 2081, reel 12.

Meinertzhagen, R. *Kenya Diary, 1892–1906.* London: Oliver and Boyd, 1957.

Morris, H. Stephen. *Indians in Uganda.* Chicago: University of Chicago Press, 1968.

———. 'Indians in East Africa: A Study in a Plural Society'. *British Journal of Sociology.* Sept. 1956, pp. 194–211.

Mungeam, G. H. *British Rule in Kenya, 1895–1912: The Establishment of Administration in the East Africa Protectorate.* Oxford: Clarendon, 1966.

Munro, J. Forbes. *Britain in Tropical Africa, 1880–1960: Economic Relationships and Impact.* London: Macmillan, 1984.

Murray, Robin. 'The Chandarias: The Development of a Kenyan Multinational'. Chap. 7 in *Readings on the Multinational Corporation in Kenya*, edited by Raphael Kaplinsky. Nairobi: Oxford University Press, 1978.

Mutaha, A. Z. *Co-operatives in Tanzania: Problems of Organization Building.* Dar es Salaam: Tanzania Publishing House, 1976.

Mwangi, Jacob Ngucie Asaph. 'The Development of Small-Scale African Retailers in Kenya'. M.B.A. thesis, University of Nairobi, 1975.

Naseem, Abdul Waheed. 'Nature and Extent of the Indian Enterprise Along the East African Coast and Subsequent Role in the Development of Kenya, 1840–1905'. Ph.D. diss., St. John's University, 1975.

Njonjo, Apollo L. 'The Kenya Peasantry: A Re-assessment'. *Review of African Political Economy.* 20 (1981), 27–40.

Nyerere, Julius K. *Freedom and Development: A Selection from Writings and Speeches, 1968–73*. Dar es Salaam: Oxford University Press, 1973.

O'Connor, A. M. *Railways and Development in Uganda*. Nairobi: Oxford University Press, 1965.

Patel, Hasu H. *Indians in Uganda and Rhodesia: Some Comparative Perspectives on Minority in Africa*. Vol. 5, no. 1, *Studies in Race and Nations*. Denver: Center on International Relations, University of Denver, 1973.

Pearce, Major F. B. *Zanzibar: The Island Metropolis of Eastern Africa*. New York: Dutton, 1920.

Pearson, D. S. *Industrial Development in East Africa*. Nairobi: Oxford University Press, 1969.

Pratt, Cranford. *The Critical Phase in Tanzania, 1945–68: Nyerere and the Emergence of a Socialist Strategy*. Cambridge: Cambridge University Press, 1976.

Rai, Kauleshwar. *Indians and British Colonialism in East Africa, 1983–1939*. Patna, India: Associated Book Agency, 1979.

Ramchandani, R. R., ed. *India and Africa*. Atlantic Highlands, N.J.: Humanities Press, 1980.

———. *Uganda Asians: The End of an Enterprise*. Bombay: United Asia, 1976.

Roberts, Andrew D., ed. *Tanzania before 1900*. Nairobi: East African Publishing House, 1968.

Rothchild, Donald. *Racial Bargaining in Independent Kenya*. New York: Oxford University Press, 1973.

Ruthenberg, Hans. *Agricultural Development in Tanganyika*. Berlin: Springer-Verlag, 1964.

Rweyemamu, J. F. *Underdevelopment and Industrialization in Tanzania*. Nairobi: Oxford University Press, 1973.

Saben's Commercial Directory and Handbook of Uganda, 1960–61. Kampala: Saben's Directories, 1961.

Sandbrook, Richard, and Robin Cohen, eds. *Development of an African Working Class: Studies in Class Formation and Action*. Toronto: University of Toronto Press, 1975. Includes chapters by Bienefield, Iliffe, and Stichter.

Skarstein, Rune, and Samuel M. Wangwe. *Industrial Development in Tanzania: Some Critical Issues*. Uppsala: Scandinavian Institute of African Studies, 1986.

Smith, Hadley E., ed. *Readings on Economic Development and Administration in Tanzania*. London: Oxford University Press, 1966.

Sorrenson, M.P.K. *Origins of European Settlement in Kenya*. Nairobi: Oxford University Press, 1968.

Spencer, I.R.G. 'The First Assault on Indian Ascendency: Indian Traders in the Kenya Reserves, 1895–1929'. *African Affairs*. 80/320 (July 1981), 327–43.

Stichter, Sharon. 'Formation of a Working Class in Kenya'. *Development of an African Working Class*, edited by Richard Sandbrook and Robin Cohen. Pp. 21–48. Toronto: University of Toronto Press, 1975.

———. *Migrant Labour in Kenya: Capitalism and the African Response*. London: Oxford University Press, 1982.

———. 'Trade Unionism in Kenya, 1947–52: The Militant Phase'. Chap. 6 in *African Labor History*, edited by Peter C.W. Gutkind, Robin Cohen, and Jean Copans. Beverly Hills: Sage, 1978.

Stirling, Leander. *Bush Doctor: Being Letters from Dr. Leander Stirling, Tanganyika Territory.* Westminster: Parrett and Neves, 1947.

Stonehouse, John. *Prohibited Immigrant.* London: Bodley Head, 1960.

Stoutjesdijk, E. J. *Uganda's Manufacturing Sector: A Contribution to an Analysis of Industrialization in East Africa.* Nairobi: East African Publishing House, 1967.

Stroebel, Margaret. *Muslim Women in Mombasa, 1890–1975.* New Haven: Yale University Press, 1979.

Swainson, Nicola. *Development of Corporate Capitalism in Kenya, 1918–77.* London: Heinemann, 1980.

_____. 'Indigenous Capitalism in Postcolonial Kenya'. Chap. 2 in *African Bourgeoisie,* edited by Paul M. Lubeck. Boulder: Lynne Rienner, 1987.

Tamarkin, M. 'Changing Social and Economic Role of Nakuru Africans, 1929–52'. *Kenya Historical Review.* 6/1, 2 (1978), 104–25.

Thomas, H. B., and Robert Scott. *Uganda.* London: Oxford University Press, 1935.

Throup, David. *Economic and Social Origins of Mau Mau, 1945–53.* London: J. Currey, 1981.

Tignor, Robert L. *Colonial Transformation of Kenya: The Kamba, Kikuyu, and Maasai from 1900 to 1939.* Princeton: Princeton University Press, 1976.

Tilbe, Douglas. *East Africa Asians.* London: Race Relations Committee, Friends House, 1970.

Twaddle, Michael, ed. *Expulsion of a Minority: Essays on Ugandan Asians.* London: Athlone, 1975. Includes chapter by Maini.

United Nations. *Economic Survey of Africa since 1950.* New York: United Nations Department of Economic and Social Affairs, 1959.

Vaghela, B. G., and J. M. Patel, eds. *East Africa To-Day (1958–1959): Comprehensive Directory of British East Africa with Who's Who.* Bombay: Overseas Information Publishers, 1959.

Van Dongen, Irene S. *The British East African Transport Complex.* Chicago: University of Chicago Department of Geography Research Paper No. 38, Dec. 1954.

Van Zwanenberg, Roger. *The Agricultural History of Kenya.* Nairobi: East Africa Publishing House, 1972.

_____. 'Aspects of Kenya's Industrial History'. *Kenya Historical Review.* 1/1 (1973), 45–61.

_____. 'Neocolonialism and the Origin of the National Bourgeoisie in Kenya between 1940 and 1973'. *Journal of East African Rural Development.* 4/2 (1974), 161–88.

Westcott, Nicholas. 'The East African Sisal Industry, 1929–49: The Marketing of a Colonial Commodity During Depression and War'. *Journal of African History.* 25 (1984), 445–61.

White, Paul. *Doctor of Tanganyika.* Sydney: George M. Dash, 1942.

_____. *Jungle Doctor.* London: Paternoster, 1942.

Who Controls Industry in Kenya. Report of Working Party, National Christian Council of Kenya. Nairobi: East African Publishing House, 1968.

Wilson, G. M. 'Mombasa Social Survey'. Unpublished typescript, Nairobi, n.d., 1950s. Syracuse University microfilm 2081, reel 12.

Wrigley, Christopher C. 'Changes in East African Society'. Chap. 14 in *History of East Africa*, vol. 1, edited by D. A. Low and Alison Smith. Oxford: Clarendon, 1976.

_____. 'Kenya: The Patterns of Economic Life, 1902–45'. Chap. 5 in *History of East Africa*, vol. 2, edited by Vincent Harlow and E. M. Chilver. Oxford: Clarendon, 1965.

Yoshida, Masao. *Agricultural Marketing Intervention in East Africa: A Study in the Colonial Origins of Marketing Policies, 1900–65*. Tokyo: Institute of Development Economics, 1984.

Youe, Christopher P. 'Peasants, Planters and Cotton Capitalists: the "Dual Economy" in Colonial Uganda'. *Canadian Journal of African Studies*. 12/2 (1978), 163–84.

Young, Crawford. *Cooperatives and Development: Agricultural Politics in Ghana and Uganda*. Madison: University of Wisconsin Press, 1981.

Zarwan, John Irving. 'Indian Businessmen in Kenya during the Twentieth Century: A Case Study'. Ph.D. diss., Yale University, 1977.

Asians Interviewed

Abdulla, Haji T. H. Zanzibar, Dar es Salaam businessman. 18 Jan. 1974, Dar es Salaam.

Acharya, Mahendra Bhanubhai. Nairobi, Baroda, London travel agent. 5 July 1973, Baroda.

Adhia, B. V. Morogoro. Insurance agent, accountant, sisal planter. 25 Apr. 1974, Dar es Salaam.

Ahmed, Haroon. Nairobi journalist. 3, 4, 5 July 1973, Nairobi.

Akbar Singh. Mwanza businessman. 15 Aug. 1973, Mwanza.

Alidina, Dr. Amir Abdulkarim. Tanzanian surgeon. 25 June 1988, Syracuse.

Alidina, Dr. Arif Amir. U.S. medical doctor, son of Dr. Amir Abdulkarim Alidina. 18 Jan. 1986, Syracuse.

Aloo, Abbas. Dar es Salaam merchant, industrialist. 14 Oct. 1973, Dar es Salaam.

Amin, M. V. Nairobi civil engineer, city councillor, civic leader. 2 May 1973, Nairobi.

Awtar Singh. Dar es Salaam advocate, communal leader. 25 July 1973, Dar es Salaam.

Bagchi, Ganesh. Kampala teacher, playwright. 22 July 1973, New Delhi.

Barve, P. G. Dar es Salaam company director. 19 June 1973, Bombay.

Basheer-ud-Deen. Kisumu sawmiller, politician. 28 May 1973, Kisumu.

Behal, Madan. Arusha advocate. 12 Sep. 1973, Dar es Salaam.

Bharmal, Fakru. Zanzibar, mainland industrialist. 13 Sep. 1974, Dar es Salaam.

Bharwani, P. J. Dar es Salaam hotelier, businessman, Ismaili leader. 22 Feb. 1973, Dar es Salaam.

Bhasin, K. L. Nairobi businessman, politician. 4 May 1973, Nairobi.

Bhatia, Alibhai J. Tanzanian import-exporter, manufacturer. 19 Sept. 1973, Dar es Salaam.

Bhatia, Lutof Ali. Sawmiller, industrialist, son of Alibhai. 17 Sept. 1973, Dar es Salaam.

Bhatt, Bachubhai H. Ahmedabad industrialist. 9 July 1973, Ahmedabad.

Bhatt, Gunvantrai Jayantilal. Fort Portal medical doctor. 22 Mar. 1973, Nairobi.

Bhatt, Hariprasad. Kampala motor spares dealer. 9 July 1973, Ahmedabad.

Bhatt, S. M. Nairobi businessman, publisher. 18 Jan. 1973, Nairobi. Bhatty, Jagpal Singh. Mwanza teacher. 15 Aug. 1973, Mwanza.

Bhojak, Pravin. Dar es Salaam store clerk, Zanzibar background. 14 Mar. 1974, Dar es Salaam.

Bhowan, Lalji. Mwanza shopkeeper, Lohana leader. 14 Aug. 1973, Mwanza.

Boal, V. R. Dar es Salaam journalist. 2 July 1973, Bombay.

Bodalbhai, Taherali Hassanali. Pemba clove merchant, Kunduchi poultry farmer. 6 Dec. 1974, Kunduchi.

Byramjee, Jamshed Dinshaw. Company director, social worker, civic leader. 24 Jan., 5, 13, 22 Feb. 1973, Nairobi.

Capila, Bal Raj. Nairobi businessman, property owner, Hindu leader, politician. 30 Apr. 1973, Nairobi.

Cassum, Anar. Dar es Salaam economist, adviser to Nyerere. 20 Sept. 1973, Dar es Salaam.

Chakravarty, R. D. Deputy secretary, ministry of external affairs, government of India. 19 July 1973, New Delhi.

Chanan Singh. Nairobi advocate, journalist, politician, communal leader. 22 Jan., 13 Feb. 1973, Nairobi.

Chandaria, Devchand Premchand. Nairobi industrialist. 27 Apr. 1973, Nairobi.

Chandaria, Keshav Premchand. East African industrialist. 9, 10, 11, 14 May 1973, Addis Ababa.

Chandaria, Manu Premchand. East African industrialist. 31 Jan. 1973, Nairobi.

Chandaria, Ratilal Premchand. East African industrialist. 6 Oct. 1985, 18 June 1988, London.

Chande, Girish K. Tanzania mechanical engineer, industrialist. 16 Mar. 1974, Dar es Salaam.

Chande, Jayantilal Keshavji. Dar es Salaam industrialist; business, civic, and political leader. 7 Aug. 1973, Dar es Salaam.

Chauhan, Dr. P. S. Nairobi medical doctor. 1 Mar. 1973, Nairobi.

Chinchankar, P. Y. Bombay commercial leader. 4 July 1973, Bombay.

Dar, Qayyum. Karatina sawmiller. 9 Jan. 1973, Karatina.

Das, S. Manager, Chandaria company in Dar es Salaam. 18 Oct. 1973, Dar es Salaam.

Dass, Dharm Shankar. Businessman based in Nairobi. 5 May 1973, Nairobi.

Dastur, Nergis. Dar es Salaam councillor. 18 Sept. 1973, Dar es Salaam.

Datoo, Gulamali Gulamhussein. Mombasa accountant. 27 Feb. 1973, Mombasa.

Datoo, Hassanali Gulamhussein. Mombasa auctioneer. 27 Feb. 1973, Mombasa.

Datoo, Rajabali Gulamhussein. Nairobi glassware merchant, property owner, civic and Ithnasheri leader. 22 Nov. 1972, Nairobi.

Dave, J. M. Tanga advocate. 23 Feb. 1973, Tanga.

Dave, Kanaulal Bhavanishankar. Kenya civil servant. 10 June 1985, Nairobi.

Dawoodbhai, Hatim. Dar es Salaam advocate, sisal planter. 20 Mar. 1974, Dar es Salaam.

Daya, Dr. Gulamhussein Mohamedali. Dar es Salaam medical doctor, industrialist, businessman. 25 Jan. 1974, Dar es Salaam.

Desai, Jashbhai Motibhai. Nairobi insurance agent, property owner, publisher, civic leader. 31 Jan., 5 Feb. 1973, Nairobi.

Desai, M. R. Nairobi businessman, Patel leader. 24 May 1973, Nairobi.

Desai, Narendra N. Nairobi insurance agent, politician. 7 May 1973, Nairobi.

Desai, Ramesh Manilal. Nairobi businessman, Hindu civic leader. 14 June 1985, Nairobi.

Devani, Manilal Mathurdas. Dar es Salaam mayor, banker, merchant. 19 Jan. 1973, Nairobi; 17 Feb. 1973, 9 Mar. 1974, Dar es Salaam.

Dhalla, Fatehali. Mombasa grocer, Ismaili leader. 11 May 1973, Mombasa.

Dhanani, Nemchand Jethalal. Nairobi produce buyer, exporter. 14 June 1985, Nairobi.

Dharani, H. Dar es Salaam advocate. 19 Oct. 1973, Dar es Salaam.

Dhupelia, C. D. Bombay company director. 20 June 1973, Bombay.

Din, Shamsu. Nanyuki hotelier. 12 April 1973, Nanyuki.

D'Mello, F. X. Kenya civil servant, Nakuru industrialist. 25 May 1973, Nakuru.

Doshi, Dhirajlal Devchand. Mombasa advocate, civic leader, politican. 14 Apr. 1973, Mombasa.

Doshi, Vikamshi. Dar es Salaam textile merchant. 18 Feb. 1974, Dar es Salaam.

D'Souza, Father Aloysyus. Mwanza headmaster. 15 Aug. 1973, Mwanza.

D'Souza, Jose Pio. Nairobi accountant. 26 June 1973, Porvorim, Bardez Goa.

Fazal, Abdulla. Bukoba merchant, manufacturer. 22 Nov. 1973, Upanga.

Fernandes, Linette. Daughter of Dar es Salaam accountant, civil servant. 27 June 1973, Porvorim, Bardez Goa.

Fernandes, Silvestre Loyola. Nairobi civil servant. 27 June 1973, Mapuca, Bardez Goa.

Figueiredo, Henry Souza. Kampala businessman, politician, Portuguese Consul. 27 June 1973, Saligao, Bardez Goa.

Gathani, Bachulal Tribhovan. Nairobi businessman, politician, business and communal leader. 20 Nov. 1972, 8, 9 Mar. 1973, 6 June 1985, Nairobi.

Gathani, Batuk Bachulal. Nairobi, London journalist. 12 Jan. 1973, Nairobi.

Gautama, Satish Chandra. Eldoret and Nairobi barrister, Congress leader. 2 May 1973, Nairobi.

Ghadialy, Amritlal. Nyeri advocate, civic leader. 13 Apr. 1973, Nyeri.

Gheevala, C. L. Bombay commercial leader. 20 June 1973, Bombay.

Gill, Indra Singh. East African industrialist, planter. 4 May 1973, Nairobi.

Haji, Saleh. Iringa general merchant, political leader. 27 June 1973, Iringa.

Haji, Shiraz Pirbhai. Dar es Salaam suitcase manufacturer, restaurant owner. 21 Feb. 1974, Dar es Salaam.

Hassanali, Shirin. Zanzibar and Dar es Salaam ministerial secretary. 15 Jan. 1974, Dar es Salaam.

Hemani, G. H. Dar es Salaam bookstore proprietor. 11 Jan. 1974, Dar es Salaam.

Hindocha, Devjibhai Karamshi. Kisumu industrialist, planter. 20 Apr. 1973, Miwani.

Hirjee, Abdulla Rahimtulla Waljee. Nairobi businessman, property owner. 18 Apr. 1973, Nairobi.

Hooda, Nizar. Dar es Salaam footwear manufacturer, property owner. 27 Mar. 1974, Dar es Salaam.

Hudani, Abdul Karim. Nairobi journalist. 5 Sept. 1973, Nairobi.

Inamdar, Vinay P. Nairobi insurance agent, arts leader. 31 Jan. 1972, 21 May 1973, Nairobi.

Ishar, Mohamed. Nairobi petrol station owner. 6 Sept. 1973, Nairobi.

Jaffer, Habib Kassumali. Kampala insurance agent, businessman, legislator, C.B.E. 9, 13 May 1973, Mombasa.

Jaffer, R. R. Dar es Salaam deputy mayor, shopkeeper, politician. 20 Apr. 1974, Dar es Salaam.

Jaffer, Sultan Habib. Kampala insurance agent, civic leader. 9 Apr. 1973, Nairobi.

Jamal, Abdul. Mwanza merchant, furniture manufacturer. 15 Aug. 1973, Mwanza.

Jamal, Mohamed. Tanzanian industrialist, builder. 27 Jan. 1974, Dar es Salaam.

Janmohamed, Mussa. Arusha grocer. 22 Dec. 1973, Arusha.

Jasmer Singh. Nairobi publisher, sports organizer. 24 May 1973, Nairobi.

Jetha, Hassanally Mussa. Mombasa businessman, Ismaili and Muslim leader. 18 Apr. 1973, Mombasa.

Jhaveri, Kantilal Laximichand. Dar es Salaam advocate, political leader. 20 Feb., 16 Mar. 1973, 23 Apr., 22 Nov. 1974, Dar es Salaam.

Jhaveri, Mrs. Urmila. Dar es Salaam women's leader. 24 Jan. 1974, Dar es Salaam.

Jivan, Ibrahim Mohamed. Arusha merchant, sisal planter. 16 Feb. 1973, Arusha.

Johanputra, Vithalji Harji. Kisumu printer, civic leader. 28 May 1973, Kisumu.

Joshi, Hariprasad Poonamchandra. Jinja teacher. 6 July 1973, Baroda.

Kaba, Kassamali Gulamhusein. Iringa businessman, hotelier. 26 June 1973, Iringa.

Kakad, L. V. East African manager, Madhvani branch operations. 4 July 1973, Bombay.

Kanji, Walji. Father of Mzibozi textile merchant. 21 Sept. 1974, Dar es Salaam.

Kantaria, Batuk. Nairobi auto spares dealer, sawmiller. 19 May 1973, Nairobi.

Kapadia, Farrokh. Under Secretary, Ministry of Commerce, India. 23 July 1973, New Delhi.

Kapila, Achhroo Ram. Nairobi advocate, civic leader. 19 Jan. 1973, Nairobi.

Kara, Ramnik Bhowan. Tanga businessman. 23 Feb. 1973, Tanga.

Karia, Natoo T. Kampala politician, businessman. 13 July 1973, Porbandar.

Karimjee, Abdulkarim Yusufali Alibhai. Tanzanian planter, businessman, political and civic leader. 20 Feb., 20 Mar. 1973, 19 Sept. 1974, Dar es Salaam.

Karmali, John Shamsudin. Nairobi pharmacist, photographer, educator. 10, 13 June 1985, Nairobi.

Karve, Dr. Shankar Dhondo. Mombasa medical doctor, civic leader, politician, O.B.E. 26 Feb. 1973, Mombasa.

Kazi, Subodh B. East Africa manager, Bank of India. 4 July 1973, Bombay.

Keshavji, S. S. Mombasa businessman. 22 July 1973, Mombasa.

Keshavji, Shah Somchand. Eldoret wholesaler. 11 July 1973, Jamnagar.

Khimasia, Mulchand Somchand. Kenya businessman, industrialist, planter. 19 Apr. 1973, Nairobi.

Khimji, Mohamed Adoula. Dar es Salaam merchant, miller, printer, politician. 30 Mar. 1973, Dar es Salaam.

Kitabwalla, S.M.A. Dar es Salaam Bohra leader. 24 Mar. 1973, Dar es Salaam.

Kotak, H. M. Dar es Salaam accountant, civic leader. 18 Jan. 1974, Dar es Salaam.

Kotecha, Mrs. Dogar. Kampala civic leader, educator. 13 July 1973, Porbandar.

Kotecha, G. O. Kampala car dealer, politician, civic leader. 30 Apr. 1974, Nairobi.

Kotecha, Kalidas Jinabhai. Uganda ginner, industrialist, exporter, planter. 9 July 1973, Ahmedabad.

Kotecha, T. S. Kenya industrialist, planter. 24 May 1973, Thika.

Kothari, Shantibhai D. Kenya teacher, accountant, wholesaler. 10 July 1973, Rajkot.

Krishna, Baldev. Tanga medical doctor, politician. 19 Apr. 1974, Dar es Salaam.

Kurji, Feroz. Dar es Salaam graduate student. 28 Feb. 1974, Dar es Salaam.

Ladak, Gulamhusein Rajpar. Kigoma merchant, industrialist, civic leader. 14, 18 Jan. 1974, Dar es Salaam.

Ladha, Kassamali Mohamed. Iringa manager of motor agency. 26 June 1973, Iringa.

Lakha, Ahmed A. M. Zanzibar merchant, political leader. 15 Jan. 1974, Dar es Salaam.

Lakha, Aziz R. Kassim. Mombasa hotelier, planter, industrialist. 9 May 1973, Mombasa.

Lalani, Azeez. Tanzania businessman, Ismaili leader. 16 Oct., 1 Nov. 1973, Dar es Salaam.

Lalji, Manubhai K. Mombasa journalist. 28 Feb., 1, 2 Mar., 27 Dec. 1973, Mombasa.

Lalji, Shanshu. Mafia merchant, transporter. 28 July 1974, Mafia.

Lal, A. T. First secretary, Indian High Commission, Tanzania. 22 Feb., 7 Sept. 1973, Dar es Salaam.

Lashker Singh. Dar es Salaam building contractor. 24 Apr. 1974, Dar es Salaam.

Madan, Chunilal Bhagwandas. Kenya chief justice, Nairobi barrister, politician, Q.C. 22 Nov. 1972, 30 Jan. 1973, Nairobi.

Madhvani, Nitin Jayant. East Africa industrialist, planter. 12 June 1985, Nairobi.

Maini, Sir Amar Nath. Uganda advocate, politician, civic leader, O.B.E., C.B.E. 22 Nov. 1984, London.

Majithia, Priyavadan M. Dar es Salaam sweater manufacturer. 19 Feb. 1973, Dar es Salaam.

Makhan Singh. Nairobi trade unionist, printer. 10 Jan. 1973, Nairobi.

Malde, Lakhamshi Jethabhai. Moshi shopkeeper. 11 July 1973, Jamnagar.

Mamujee, Akbarali Adamjee. Nairobi hardware dealer, Bohra leader. 19 July 1973, Nairobi.

Manji, Gulamhusein Karim. Iringa businessman, property owner. 26 June 1973, Iringa.

Manji, Madatally. Nairobi bakery owner, builder, Ismaili leader. 21 May 1973, Nairobi.

Manji, Rhemtulla G. Nairobi car rebuilder, safari leader. 6 Feb. 1973, Nairobi.

Master, Roshanani Hassanali. Zanzibar editor. 11 July 1973, Dar es Salaam.

Mawji, Shule. Tanzanian lumberman, sisal planter, miller, businessman. 18 Mar. 1974, Dar es Salaam.

Mehta, Dhirendra Nanji. Lugazi industrialist, eldest son of N. K. Mehta. 13, 14 July 1973, Porbandar.

Mehta, Dichand. Zanzibar merchant. 4 Apr. 1974, Zanzibar.

Mehta, Jagnet. High commissioner for India, Tanzania. 8 Sept. 1973, Dar es Salaam.

Mehta, Khimjibhai Nanji Kalidas. Uganda industrialist, planter, son of N. K. Mehta. 30 Apr. 1973, Nairobi.

Mehta, Mahendra Nanji. Uganda industrialist, planter, parliamentarian, son of N. K. Mehta. 1 May 1973, Nairobi.

Mehta, Mrs. Medha Dhirendra. Kampala civic leader, educator, wife of D. N. Mehta. 13 July 1973, Porbandar.

Mehta, R. J. Kampala political, civic leader. 19 June 1973, Bombay.

Mehta, Surendra Girdhar. Rajkot businessman, son of G. P. Mehta of Kampala. 10 July 1973, Rajkot.

Mehta, Umedlal. Zanzibar shopkeeper, Hindu leader. 4 Apr. 1974, Zanzibar.

Mehta, V. D. Bombay company director. 30 June 1973, Bombay.

Menezes, Pius. Kampala curator, civil servant, Goan leader. 23 May 1973, Nairobi.

Merali, Firoz. Tanga printer, stationer. 15 Mar. 1974, Dar es Salaam.

Modi, B. T. Nairobi advocate, civic leader. 21 May 1973, Nairobi.

Mohamedjaffer, Ali. Arusha businessman. 22 Oct. 1973, Arusha.

Moledina, Fidahusein Rashid. Mombasa coffee exporter, Ithnasheri leader. 18 Apr. 1973, Mombasa.

Molu, Abdul Hussein. Mombasa company manager, civic leader. 10 May 1973, Mombasa.

Moraji, Ranchod (Tapoo). Nakuru property owner, businessman. 25, 26 May 1973, Nakuru.

Munawar-ud-Deen. Karatina sawmiller, son of Zafrud-Deen. 9 Jan. 1973, Karatina.

Mustafa, Mrs. Sophia. Arusha politician, civic leader. 31 Apr. 1947, Nairobi.

Nadiadi, Batul Jeevanjee. Nairobi artist, art instructor. 19 July 1973, Nairobi.

Namjoshi, Dr. M. V. Professor, Mehta National Institute of Co-operative Management, Poona. 24 June 1973, Poona.

Nandra, Tarlok Singh. Nairobi architect, city councillor, civic leader. 17 Apr. 1973, 9 Nov. 1978, Nairobi.

Naranji, Dwarkadas Kanji. East Africa industrialist, planter, civic leader. 18 May 1973, Nairobi.

Natu, Hirji. Nanyuki draper, communal leader. 13 Apr. 1973, Nanyuki.

Nayar, Adarsh. Dar es Salaam photographer, journalist. 18 Feb. 1973, Dar es Salaam.

Nazareth, John Maximian. Nairobi advocate, politician, communal leader, Q.C. 12 Nov., 17, 20 Dec. 1972, 1, 14 Feb., 10 Mar. 1973, Nairobi.

Neogy, Rajat. Kampala journalist. 8 Feb. 1974, Syracuse.

Noorani, N. A. Zanzibar shopkeeper. 28 Aug. 1974, Zanzibar.

Oza, Pushkar U. Dar es Salaam journalist, politician. 2 July 1973, Bombay; 8 May 1981, Syracuse.

Palray, Mohinder Singh. Dar es Salaam furniture manufacturer. 23 Sept. 1974, Dar es Salaam.

Pandit, Dr. Ramu. Teacher, School of Business Administration, Bajaj Institute, Bombay. 22 June 1937, Bombay.

Pandya, Anant Jagannath. Mombasa politician, businessman, civic leader. 17 Nov., 16 Dec. 1972, Nairobi; 2 Dec. 1972, 27 Feb., 1, 4 Mar. 1973, Mombasa; 18 Sep. 1973, Syracuse.

Pandya, Hansa. Mombasa social worker, wife of A. J. Pandya. 7 July 1977, 10 Aug. 1980, Syracuse; 13, 14 Oct. 1984, 1 Aug. 1985, London.

Pant, Apa Bala. Indian high commissioner to East and Central Africa. 2, 3 Oct. 1985, Syracuse.

Parkar, Bahuddin Tajuddin. Mombasa advocate, politician. 16 Apr. 1973, Mombasa.

Paroo, Kassamali Rajabali. Nairobi businessman, politician, Ismaili leader (Count). 1 Mar. 1973, Nairobi.

Paroo, Mrs. Kassamali Rajabali. Associated with the Waljee Hirjee and Rahimtullah families. 10 May 1973, Mombasa.

Patel, A. Kalidas. Uganda ginner, insurance agent, planter. 6 July 1973, Baroda.

Patel, Ambu H. Nairobi pro-African printer, journalist. 3 Aug. 1977, Nairobi.

Patel, Ambulal Bhailalbhai. Mombasa barrister, politican, civic leader. Spring 1957, Nairobi.

Patel, B. K. Mbale textile worker. 9 July 1973, Ahmedabad.

Patel, Bhailal. Nairobi advocate. 2 May 1973, Nairobi.

Patel, C. K. Mwanza cotton buyer, ginner. 10 Sept. 1973, Dar es Salaam.

Patel, Dr. Chandrakant Becharbhai. Mombasa medical doctor. 2 Dec. 1972, Mombasa.

Patel, D. G. Dar es Salaam accountant, insurance agent, Hindu leader. 9, 14 Oct. 1973, Dar es Salaam.

Patel, Dahyabhai Chaturbhai. Nairobi automobile dealer, Congress leader. 28 Apr. 1973, Nairobi.

Patel, Hansa. Nairobi advocate, actress, daughter of B. T. Gathani, wife of M. M. Patel. 8 Mar. 1973, Nairobi.

Patel, I. S. Nairobi headmaster. 29 Jan. 1973, Nairobi.

Patel, J. V. Zanzibar, Dar es Salaam building contractor. 25 Mar. 1974, Dar es Salaam.

Patel, Jethabhai Patel. Kisumu hardware dealer, Congress and civic leader. 30 May 1973, Kisumu.

Patel, Dr. Kanti H. Tanzania medical doctor. 21 Apr. 1974, Dar es Salaam.

Patel, Kantibhai Vashjibhai. East Africa motor parts and car dealer, planter, industrialist. 27 Apr. 1973, Nairobi.

Patel, M. M. Nairobi advocate, playwright, actor. 8 Mar. 1973, Nairobi.

Patel, Mahendra Ranchhodi. Nairobi automobile dealer. 7 July 1973, Ahmedabad.

Patel, N. S. Dar es Salaam advocate, planter, industrialist, communal leader. 5 March, 7 Sept. 1973, Dar es Salaam.

Patel, Nagin. Mombasa advocate, communal political leader. 11 May 1973, Mombasa.

Patel, Ramanbhai Becharbhai. Mombasa company director, legislator, civic leader. 12 May 1973, Mombasa.

Patel, Ramanbhai Muljibhai. Uganda farm overseer. 6 July 1973, Baroda.

Patel, Ratilla Gordhanbhai. Karatu produce buyer, property owner, planter. 10 Aug. 1973, Karatu.

Patel, Umedbhai T. Nairobi timber and hardware dealer. 3 May 1973, Nairobi.

Patel, Usha. Kampala resident. 20 Oct. 1984, London.

Patel, Vaghjibhai Shankerbhai. Zanzibar teacher, editor, politician. 8, 10 Jan. 1974, Dar es Salaam.

Patel, Dr. Vithalbhai Raojibhai. Nairobi medical doctor. 5, 6 July 1973, Baroda.

Patel, Zarina. Mombasa, Nairobi social worker. 22 Jan. 1973, Nairobi.

Patel, Zinabhai Valji. Kampala textile merchant. 11 July 1973, Jamnagar.

Patil, A. K. Bombay politician. 22 June 1973, Bombay.

Pawa, Harpal Singh. Kampala architect, communal leader. 16 Mar. 1973, Nairobi.

Pereire, Ann. Daughter of Dar es Salaam factory storekeeper. 27 June 1973, Porvorim, Bardez Goa.

Pirbhai, Sir Eboo. Kenya Ismaili politician, civic and Muslim leader. 6 Apr. 1973, Mombasa.

Pirbhai, Gulamabbas. Arusha furniture dealer. 24 Dec. 1973, Arusha.

Pirbhai, Yusufali. Dar es Salaam hardware dealer, brush manufacturer. 25 Feb. 1974, Dar es Salaam.

Puram, Dr. Prabhakar Ramchandra. Tanzania medical doctor. 24 June 1973, Poona.

Puri, D. P. Deputy secretary, Ministry of Education, India. 19 July 1973, New Delhi.

Putwa, Nuruddin Hassanali. Dar es Salaam soap and oil manufacturer. 8 Feb. 1974, Dar es Salaam.

Qureshi, Bashir Ahmed. Nairobi dentist. 4 Apr. 1973, Nairobi.

Radia, Kakubhai K. Kampala ginner, builder, civic leader, O.B.E. 12 July 1973, Porbandar.

Rahim, Hussein Alaiakhia. Dar es Salaam advocate, magistrate. 10 July 1973, Dar es Salaam.

Raishi, Amritlal. Nairobi businessman, Shah leader. 25 Jan. 1973, 7, 10 June 1985, Nairobi; 18 Aug. 1984, 18 June 1989, London.

Rajay, N. B. Tanga journalist, politician, manufacturer. 24 Feb. 1973, Tanga.

Rajguru, Vinayak (and wife). Kampala auditor (wife, medical doctor). 24 June 1973, Poona.

Ramdas, Dr. Ravindranath Vaman. Librarian, Shri Brihad Bharatiya Samaj, Bombay. 19 June 1973, Bombay.

Rao, K. S. Deputy secretary, Ministry of Commerce, India. 21, 23 July 1973, New Delhi.

Rattansey, Mahmud Nasser. Dar es Salaam advocate, businessman, politician. 12 Feb. 1974, Dar es Salaam.

Rattansi, Hassan. Kenya businessman, planter. 3 May 1973, Nairobi.

Ribeiro, Dr. Ayres Lourenco. Kenya government pathologist, civic leader. 12 Nov. 1972, Nairobi.

Ribeiro, Hubert. Nairobi poet. 26, 27 June 1973, Porvorim, Bardez Goa.

Rizvi, Seyyid Saeed Ashtar. Dar es Salaam Ithnasheri priest, scholar. 18 Feb. 1974, Dar es Salaam.

Ruparalia, Bharat K. East Africa industrialist, planter. 21 Mar. 1974, Dar es Salaam.

Ruprah, Waltan Singh. Kisumu businessman, planter, councillor, communal leader. 28 May 1973, Kisumu.

Sachak, Sultan Abdulhusein. Bukoba, Dar es Salaam town clerk. 8 Apr. 1974, Dar es Salaam.

Sachedina, Janmohamed Asar. Njombe textile merchant, transporter, planter. 29 June 1973, Njombe.

Sachoo, Abdulrasul. Tanzania industrialist, planter. 29 Oct. 1973, Dar es Salaam.

Saleh, Akbarali G. Mafia coconut planter, politician. 21 Sept. 1974, Upanga.

Saleh, Madatali G. Mafia planter, transporter, merchant. 28 July 1974, Mafia.

Samji, Akbar M. Mwanza general merchant, car salesman. 15 Aug. 1973, Mwanza.

Shah, Arun Amritlal. Kenya civil servant. 20 Nov. 1984, London.

Shah, Ashwin Gulabchand. Nairobi industrialist. 9, 17 June 1985, Nairobi.

Shah, Bhimji Ghela. Kisii shopkeeper. 12 July 1973, Jamnagar.

Shah, C. P. East Africa manager, Bank of Baroda. 4 July 1973, Bombay.

Shah, Devchand Kimchand (Sahib). Kisumu, Nairobi general merchant. 11 July 1973, Jamnagar.

Shah, Devshi Lalji. Saba Saba shopkeeper. 12 July 1973, Jamnagar.

Shah, Dhiru Premchand. Nairobi industrialist. 10 Mar. 1973, Nairobi.

Shah, Gulabchand Devra. Nairobi industrialist, businessman. 12 July 1973, Jamnagar.

Shah, H. D. Zanzibar, Dar es Salaam merchant, politician. 24 July 1973, Dar es Salaam.

Shah, Harakhchand Meghji. Nairobi, Thika coffee miller, planter. 14 June 1985, Nairobi.

Shah, Jagdish Manilal. Nairobi coffee processor, exporter. 19 Aug. 1985, Nairobi.

Shah, Jamtibhai Premchand. Mkuyu businessman, Moshi coffee planter, Mkuyu businessman. 11 Feb. 1973, Moshi.

Shah, Jeshand Punja. Kitale shopkeeper. 11 July 1973, Jamnagar.

Shah, Jivraj Devshi. Nairobi shopkeeper. 12 July 1973, Jamnagar.

Shah, Kanji Hemraj. Muranga (Fort Hall) shopkeeper. 16 June 1985, Muranga.

Shah, Kantilal Punamchand. Nairobi shopkeeper, industrialist, property owner, politician. 7 Feb., 16 Apr. 1973, Nairobi.

Shah, Kashi. Mombasa social worker. 4 Mar. 1973, Mombasa.

Shah, Mrs. Kauchan J. Nairobi teacher. 29 Jan. 1973, Nairobi.

Shah, Khanji Rupshi. Nakuru businessman, industrialist, Congress leader. 25 May 1973, Nakuru.

Shah, Khetshi N. Thika. Industrialist, communal leader. 27 Apr. 1973, Thika.

Shah, Lakhamshi R. Nairobi. Textile merchant, East Africa industrialist, business and civic leader. 27 Nov. 1972, 8, 9 Mar. 1973, Nairobi; 30 June 1973, Bombay; 9 July 1973, Ahmedabad.

Shah, Lalji Ladha. Mombasa shopkeeper. 12 July 1973, Jamnagar.

Shah, Liladhar Nevya. Nairobi shopkeeper. 12 July 1973, Jamnagar.

Shah, M. L. Dar es Salaam textile merchant, business leader. 10 Jan. 1974, Dar es Salaam.

Shah, Maganlal Meghji Rupshi. Nyeri dealer in building materials. 12 Apr. 1973, Nyeri.

Shah, Mepabhai Vershi. Fort Hall (Muranga) shopkeeper. 11 July 1973, Jamnagar.

Shah, Mohanlal Nathu. Nairobi businessman. 11 July 1973, Jamnagar.

Shah, Motichand Ramji. Kisumu hardware merchant, produce buyer, councillor. 28 May 1973, Kisumu.

Shah, Pethraj Raishi. Kisumu shopkeeper. 12 July 1973, Jamnagar.

Shah, R. L. Fort Hall (Muranga) shopkeeper. 11 Apr. 1973, Muranga.

Shah, R. M. Nairobi textile manufacturer. 21 May 1973, Nairobi.

Shah, Rashmi Amritlal. Nairobi businessman. 13 Feb. 1973, Nairobi.

Shah, Shobag P. Dar es Salaam footwear, furniture manufacturer. 16 Oct. 1973, Dar es Salaam.

Shah, Somchand Karamshi. Mombasa shopkeeper. 12 July 1973, Jamnagar.

Shah, Somchand Manek Chand. Nairobi provisions dealer. 6 Apr. 1973, Nairobi.

Shah, Somchand Manichand. Mabeni shopkeeper. 6 July 1973, Jamnagar.

Shah, Veljee Devji. Nairobi advocate. 19 Apr. 1973, Nairobi.

Shah, Velji Khimji. Tanga shopkeeper. 12 July 1973, Jamnagar.

Shah, Velji Tejshi. Nyeri general merchant. 12 Apr. 1973, Nyeri.

Shah, Vemchand Khimchand. Nairobi shopkeeper. 11 July 1973, Jamnagar.

Shah, Vinodchand Raishi. Nyeri dealer in building materials, business leader. 21 May 1973, Nyeri.

Shah, Vinodchandra. President, Brihad Vishwa Gujarati Samaj, Ahmedabad. 9 July 1973, Ahmedabad.

Shah, Vinodrai Bhimji. Kisii hardware merchant. 11 July 1973, Jamnagar.

Shah, Zaverchand K. Kenya retailer, wholesaler, exporter. 26 July 1973, Nairobi.

Sheriff, Ali Mohamedjaffer. Mombasa, Kisumu, Arusha merchant, industrialist. 22 Oct. 1973, Arusha.

Sheriff, Yusuf. Arusha, Moshi merchant, industrialist. 4 Jan. 1974, Malindi.

Sheshadri, A. N. Under Secretary, Economics Division, Ministry of External Affairs, India. 21 July 1973, New Delhi.

Sheth, Amritlal T. B. Dar es Salaam merchant. 19 Feb. 1974, Dar es Salaam.

Sheth, Pranlal Purashotam. Nairobi journalist and trade unionist. 29 Jan. 1977, 27 July 1989, London.

Shivshanker, Kalyanji Kotedia. Zanzibar jeweler, civic leader. 3 Mar. 1974, Zanzibar.

Shukla, Mayashanker Maganlal. Dar es Salaam furniture manufacturer. 23 Sept. 1974, Dar es Salaam.

Singh, Dr. Sarab Bhatia. Nairobi medical doctor. 26 Jan. 1973, Nairobi.

Sondhi, Jagdish R. Mombasa builder, civic leader. 2, 3 Mar. 1973, Mombasa.

Soochak, Satish. Dar es Salaam textile manufacturer, sisal and cashew planter. 26 June 1974, Dar es Salaam.

Souza, Christie de. Dar es Salaam businessman, Goan leader. 5 Aug. 1973, Dar es Salaam.

Souza, Fitzval R. S. de. Nairobi advocate, politician, civic leader. 30 Jan., 6 Feb. 1973, Nairobi.

Souza, Francis Anthony de. Kenya civil servant, M.B.E. 28 June 1973, Porvorim, Bardez Goa.

Suraiya, Jayantilal Chimanlal. Uganda director, Narandas Rajaram and Co. 21 June 1973, Bombay.

Suraiya, Ramanlal Gokaldas. Chairman, Narandas Rajaram and Co. 21 June 1973, Bombay.

Tapya, Abdulrahim Karimbhai. Dar es Salaam furniture and brush manufacturer, sisal planter. 9 Apr. 1974, Dar es Salaam.

Tara Singh. Dar es Salaam building contractor. 30 Apr. 1974, Dar es Salaam.

Tejpal, Abdulla Hassam Kassam. Dar es Salaam supermarket owner, Ismaili leader. 27 Mar. 1973, Dar es Salaam.

Thakar, Surendra Banushanker. Dar es Salaam publisher. 16 Mar. 1971, Syracuse; 8 Mar. 1973, Dar es Salaam.

Thakkar, Madhusudn Jethalal. Madhvani company manager. 19 May 1973, Addis Ababa.

Thakkar, Sureshchandra Jethalal. Mwanza ginner, Dar es Salaam merchant, printer. 5 Sept. 1973, Dar es Salaam.

Thakore, Ramanlal Trimbaklal. Nairobi arhitect, estate agent, dramatist. 7 Feb. 1973, Nairobi.

Thakore, Sharad. Nairobi businessman, arts leader. 8 Feb. 1973, Nairobi.

Thanki, Shyam T. Lindi, Dar es Salaam insurance agent, planter, businessman, politician. 9 Sept. 1973, 24 Oct. 1973, Dar es Salaam.

Thawer, A.A.J. Dar es Salaam Ismaili leader. 24 Oct. 1973, Dar es Salaam.

Trivedi, D. S. Mombasa accountant, communal leader. 28 Feb. 1973, Mombasa.

Udwadia, E. Shapurji. Dar es Salaam hardware merchant. 28 July 1973, Dar es Salaam.

Vadgama, Lalji Naran. Nairobi carpenter, buiding contractor. 23 May 1973, Nairobi.

Varma, B. S. Thika property owner, builder, planter, industrialist. 27 Apr. 1973, Thika.

Vasanji, Gordhendas. East Africa sundries merchant, textile manufacturer. 9 May 1973, Mombasa.

Velji, Juthalal. Dar es Salaam textile merchant, produce exporter, oil miller. 16 Mar. 1974, Dar es Salaam.

Velji, Noorali. Dar es Salaam advocate. 24 Aug. 1974, Syracuse; 12, 13 Apr. 1987, Washington, D.C.

Velji, Shirin Kassam. Dar es Salaam airlines employee, wife of Noorali. 4, 5 Jan. 1980, Honolulu.

Vellani, Akbar. Zanzibar clove grower, exporter, Ismaili leader. 13, 14 Feb. 1974, Zanzibar.

Verjee, Badrudeen Rajabali Sukman (Jimmy). Nairobi advocate, businessman, Ismaili leader. 10 Apr. 1973, Nairobi.

Versi, Bashir A.S. Dar es Salaam advocate. 4 Mar. 1974, Dar es Salaam.

Versi, Mohamedhusein Bandali. Lindi sisal planter, exporter, politician. 27 Feb. 1974, Dar es Salaam.

Vidyarthi, Bhushan. East Africa printer. 23 Mar. 1973, Nairobi.
Vidyarthi, Girdhari Lal. Nairobi printer, newspaper owner. 14 Feb., 26 April 1973, Nairobi.
Vidyarthi, Sudhir. East Africa printer. 16 Mar. 1973, Nairobi.
Virjee, Nasser M.H. Mwanza ginner, sisal planter, communal leader. 5 Jan. 1974, Mombasa.
Visram, Varas Allidina. Wife of Allidina Visram's grandson. 1 May 1988, London.
Vohora, Krishan Lal. Arusha banker, coffee planter. 23 Dec. 1973, Arusha.
Vohra, Vijay Pal. Nairobi dentist. 9 Apr. 1973, Nairobi.
Vyas, Dr. M. R. Member of Parliament (India), economist, Ph.D., son of Kenya accountant. 3 July 1974, Bombay.
Wadhwani, Baldev D. Mombasa textile importer, wholesaler, civic leader. 16 Apr. 1973, Nairobi.
Yacub, Salim. Nairobi teacher, insurance agent, city councillor. 19 July 1973, Nairobi.
Zafrud-Deen. Nairobi politician, Muslim and civic leader, sawmiller. 19, 22 Nov. 1972, 6 Jan. 1973, Nairobi.

Africans and Arabs Interviewed

Abuor, C. Ojwando. Nairobi journalist, Luo. 18 Mar., 26 Apr. 1973, Nairobi.
Gachau, O. G. Thika director of Asian company subsidiary, Kikuyu. 7 Nov. 1973, Thika.
Gakunju, Zackariah Kimemia. Nairobi businessman, Kikuyu. 7 Sept. 1973, Nairobi.
Gichimo, Bernard. Nairobi journalist, Kikuyu. 20 Sept. 1973, Nairobi.
Gichina, Rosemary. Thika shopkeeper, Kikuyu. 27 Oct. 1973, Thika.
Kamau, Peter. Thika shopkeeper, electrician, Kikuyu. 7 Nov. 1973, Thika.
Kamau, Samuel. Thika restaurant owner, Kikuyu. 27 Oct. 1973, Thika.
Kariuki, Lawrence N. Nairobi owner of liquor stores, Kikuyu. 20 Sept. 1973, Nairobi.
Karu, Douglas. Thika hardware dealer, Kikuyu. 8 Nov. 1973, Thika.
Kenyanjui, James. Nairobi hardware dealer, Kikuyu. 8 Nov. 1973, Nairobi.
Kibe, John. Nairobi art and curio dealer, Kikuyu. 15 Sept. 1973, Nairobi.
Kietti, Charles. Machakos clothier, Kamba. 12 Nov. 1973, Machakos.
Kimani, Charles. Thika hotelier, Kikuyu. 27 Oct. 1973, Thika.
Kimani, Stephen N. Nairobi textile dealer, Kikuyu. 13 Sept. 1973, Nairobi.
Kinothya, Mutisya. Machakos textile dealer, Kamba. 13 Nov. 1973, Machakos.
Kinyanjui, James Samuel. Nairobi textile dealer, Kikuyu. 12 Sept. 1973, Nairobi.
Kirundi, John. Thika clothier, Kikuyu. 27 Oct. 1973, Thika.
Kisalo, Mutua. Machakos cook, Kamba. 15 Nov. 1973, Machakos.
Macao, Simon. Machakos butcher, Kamba. 14 Nov. 1973, Machakos.
Mbindyo, Mawia. Machakos dry cleaner, Kamba. 17 Nov. 1973, Machakos.
Mbugua, Joel M. Nairobi clothier, Kikuyu. 17 June 1973, Nairobi.
Mhando, Steven. Dar es Salaam journalist, politician, teacher. 15 Mar. 1973.
Millinga, John. Dar es Salaam TANU official. 2 Aug. 1974, Dar es Salaam.
Miyesa, Martin. Thika agricultural engineer, Kikuyu. 27 Oct. 1973, Thika.

Mohammed, Mrs. Abdul Rahman. Zanzibar women's rights leader, wife of A. M. Babu. 16 Jan. 1974, Dar es Salaam.

Mualuko, Jeremiah. Machakos hotelier, Kamba. 15 Nov. 1973, Machakos.

Muema, Peter Mutiso. Machakos shopkeeper, Kamba. 13 Nov. 1973, Machakos.

Muema, Raphael. Machakos general merchant, Kamba. 12 Nov. 1973, Machakos.

Muhoho, Anne. Thika grocer, Kikuyu. 7 Nov. 1973, Thika.

Mully, Peter. Machakos tailor, Kamba. 14 Nov. 1973, Machakos.

Mumo, Frederick. Machakos mechanic, Kamba. 17 Nov. 1973, Machakos.

Munyao, Steven. Machakos tailor, Kamba. 16 Nov. 1973, Machakos.

Musau, Benson. Son of prominent Machakos dry goods dealer, Kamba. 13 Nov. 1973, Machakos.

Mutiso, Francis M. Machakos road transporter, Kamba. 14 Nov. 1973, Machakos.

Mwenda, John. Thika dry goods dealer, Kikuyu. 7 Nov. 1973, Thika.

Ndavikata, Bernard. Machakos employee in wholesale business, Kamba. 14 Nov. 1973, Machakos.

Ndirangu, John Bacha. Nairobi textile dealer, Kikuyu. 13 Sept. 1973, Nairobi.

Ndolo, Peter Kioko. Employee of Asian shopkeeper in Machakos, Kamba. 12 Nov. 1973, Machakos.

Ndunda, Jotham. Machakos clothier and textile dealer, Kamba. 14 Nov. 1973, Machakos.

Njoroge, Patrick. Thika tailor, Kikuyu. 8 Nov. 1973, Thika.

Nzezi, William. Employee in Sikh sawmill in Machakos, Kamba. 13 Nov. 1973, Machakos.

Opande, Philip. Nairobi salesman in Asian general store, Luo. 17 July 1973, Nairobi.

Salim, Sharrif Abdulla. Mombasa Arab leader. 8 May 1973, Mombasa.

Suleiman, Abudlla Amour. Zanzibar journalist. 31 Jan. 1974, Dar es Salaam.

Tangia, A. A. Ujamaa ya Ushirika officer, Mufindi. 28 June 1973, Dar es Salaam.

Willy, Musila. Machakos salesman in Asian general store, Kamba. 17 Nov. 1973, Machakos.

Europeans Interviewed

Allinson, Anthony. Kenya district officer. 20 Aug. 1972, London.

Gethin, Major Patrick. Namanga hotelier, Karen planter. 5 Sept. 1981, Syracuse.

Mortimer, Sir Charles. Kenya colonial administrator. 15 June 1973, Nairobi.

Ratcliff, Arthur. Mombasa town clerk. 18 Apr. 1973, Mombasa.

Slade, Sir Humphrey. Kenya settler leader, politician. 9 Feb. 1973, Nairobi.

Vasey, Sir Ernest. Kenya European financial leader, politician. 6 Feb. 1973, Nairobi.

Wilson, Peter Edward Day. Nairobi banker from old settler family. 15 July 1973, Nairobi.

About the Book
and Author

The South Asians who sought a new home in colonial East Africa underwent a remarkable transformation. However, despite the Asians' range of activity, the value of their presence has not been widely recognized. Many political leaders, both European and African, have vilified the Asians as exploiters.

Whether free immigrants or indentured servants, most Asians arrived as impoverished petty farmers. In Africa, sensing the opportunity to serve as middlemen in a trade with European settlers and Africans, nearly all the Asians turned from farming to business. They became importers and exporters, retailers and wholesalers, skilled artisans, and building contractors. Asians also filled the middle level of the civil service; some became doctors, lawyers, teachers, and other professionals. In time, many invested their savings in manufacturing and estate agriculture. Stressing industry, thrift, and education, the community prospered.

Based on numerous archival sources and extensive interviews, this book is the first comprehensive study of the Asians' social and economic experience in the region. Dr. Gregory provides evidence of a substantial Asian economic and social contribution and indicates that the history of East Africa needs considerable revision to adequately acknowledge the Asians' true role.

Robert G. Gregory is professor of history at the Maxwell School of Citizenship and Public Affairs, Syracuse University.

Index